www.wadsworth.com

wadsworth.com is the World Wide Web site for Wadsworth and is your direct source to dozens of online resources.

At *wadsworth.com* you can find out about supplements, demonstration software, and student resources. You can also send e-mail to many of our authors and preview new publications and exciting new technologies.

wadsworth.com
Changing the way the world learns®

ANALYTIC PHILOSOPHY
Classic Readings

Steven D. Hales

Bloomsburg University

WADSWORTH

THOMSON LEARNING

Australia • Canada • Mexico • Singapore • Spain • United Kingdom • United States

Philosophy Editor: Peter Adams
Assistant Editor: Kara Kindstrom
Editorial Assistant: Chalida Anusasananan
Executive Marketing Manager: Dave Garrison
Print Buyer: Tandra Jorgensen
Permissions Editor: Bob Kauser
Production Service: Matrix Productions

Copy Editor: Vicki Nelson
Cover Designer: Laurie Anderson
Cover Printer: Webcom
Compositor: Omegatype Typography, Inc.
Printer: Webcom

Printed in Canada
1 2 3 4 5 6 7   04 03 02 01

For permission to use material from this text,
contact us by Web: http://www.thomsonrights.com
Fax: 1-800-730-2215
Phone: 1-800-730-2214

For more information about our products, contact us:
Thomson Learning Academic Resource Center
1-800-423-0563
http://www.wadsworth.com

International Headquarters
Thomson Learning
International Division
290 Harbor Drive, 2nd Floor
Stamford, CT 06902-7477
USA

UK/Europe/Middle East/South Africa
Thomson Learning
Berkshire House
168-173 High Holborn
London WC1V 7AA
United Kingdom

For more information contact:
Wadsworth/Thomson Learning
10 Davis Drive
Belmont, CA 94002-3098
USA

Asia
Thomson Learning
60 Albert Street, #15-01
Albert Complex
Singapore 189969

Canada
Nelson Thomson Learning
1120 Birchmount Road
Toronto, Ontario M1K 5G4
Canada

Library of Congress Cataloging-in-Publication Data

Analytic philosophy : classic readings / [edited by] Steven D. Hales.—1st ed.
     p.   cm.
   Includes bibliographical references.
   ISBN 0-534-51277-1
   1. Analysis (Philosophy)   I. Hales, Steven D.

B808.5 .A5315 2001
146'.4—dc21

00-053443

 This book is printed on acid-free recycled paper.

Contents

Part IV: *Philosophy of Mind*   221

A History of Early Analytic Philosophy of Mind by John Heil

Part V: *Ethics*   305

A History of Early Analytic Ethics by Michael J. Zimmerman

Preface

ANALYTIC PHILOSOPHY was the most successful and influential philosophical movement of the twentieth century. Now, at the dawn of the new millennium, analytic philosophy is far and away the most prominent approach to philosophy in the English-speaking world. The best universities in Britain, Canada, and Australia have overwhelmingly analytic philosophy departments, as do all the Ivy League universities, all the leading state research universities, the majority of the main campuses of the second-tier state research universities, and most of the top liberal arts colleges in America. Moreover, analytic philosophy is on the rise in continental Europe, a fact partly spurred by the fall of communism in central and eastern Europe. Countries like Poland, with a glorious history of great logicians, are now beginning to recover from the twin blows of Nazism and communism.

To understand contemporary philosophy, one must understand analytic philosophy. And to understand that, one must first grasp what the currently debated issues are and how they are approached. Current debates do not appear in an historical vacuum, and to see why philosophers stake out the positions they do, or what kinds of potential criticisms they fear, one must realize that these are the legacy of moves and countermoves made by early analytic philosophers. This anthology is devoted to chronicling the statement and development of some of the major themes in early analytic philosophy. It is essential to recognize that the selections that follow, written between 1874 and 1963, are now *historical*. That is, contemporary philosophers no longer fly the flags of logical positivism, phenomenalism, behaviorism, or ordinary language philosophy. Yet current defenses of, say, epistemological naturalism owe much to the links forged between philosophy and modern science by the early analytics. Practically no one defends "good" as an unanalyzable primitive anymore, or thinks that the naturalistic fallacy is a clearly recognizable mistake. Yet these views were formative predecessors to contemporary debates of realism and anti-realism in metaethics. The purpose of this anthology is to give students the background of recent philosophical history that they need in order to become fully engaged with current issues before the profession.

There are three things that make this book distinctive. The first is organization. The essays have been topically divided into the areas of the greatest investigation: philosophy of language, metaphysics, epistemology, philosophy of mind, and ethics. Organization by topics is preferable to telling the story of analytic philosophy via the "great heroes," or to recounting movements like ordinary language philosophy or logical positivism because it makes perspicuous to students the theoretical background they need to have mastered before proceeding to more advanced systematic courses in topical areas like philosophy of mind, ethics, and the like. Furthermore, the present volume's approach is less arbitrary and idiosyncratic than either selecting one's personal idols and trumping them up to world-historical figures that drive the entire field or trying to parse overlapping or coincident movements.

The second thing that makes this book distinctive is its focus on those papers that are seminal contributions to analytic philosophy and still keep the jargon to a minimum. Students without any knowledge of symbolic logic will be able to understand the selections.

A third key advantage of this book is the introductory essays commissioned from leading philosophers that introduce each of the five topical divisions of the book. These have been written by Dale Jacquette (philosophy of language), Kevin Mulligan (metaphysics), Richard Fumerton (epistemology), John Heil (philosophy of mind), and Michael J. Zimmerman (ethics). These new introductions offer an overview of the topic and set the issues discussed in each part in historical context. Written specifically with undergraduates in mind, the introductions provide easy-to-read entrées to the main selections. In addition to the commissioned introductions to each part, a general editor's introduction to the volume explains the nature of analytic philosophy and presents a synopsis of its historical origins.

I wish to thank my colleagues in the philosophy department at Bloomsburg University for their support of this project and the university for granting me reassigned time to pursue it. Peter Adams, my editor at Wadsworth, has been encouraging and positive about this project the entire way, for which I am grateful. I would also like to thank the authors who wrote original contributions to this anthology for their generosity, timeliness, and philosophical acumen. And finally, I am grateful to the reviewers of the book for their helpful suggestions: James Baillie, University of Portland; Jan Boxill, University of North Carolina; James Campbell, Washington State University; Richard Feldman, University of Rochester; Heimir Geirsson, Iowa State University; David Haugen, Western Illinois University; Lynn Pasquerella, University of Rhode Island; Cindy Stern, California State University, Northridge; Kerry Walters, Gettysburg College; Kent Wilson, University of Illinois, Chicago; and Dean Zimmerman, University of Notre Dame.

A Brief Introduction to the Nature and Origins of Analytic Philosophy

STEVEN D. HALES

What Is Analytic Philosophy?

Science is defined by a methodology—the scientific method. While it is difficult to give an exact specification of this method, it clearly includes proposing hypotheses, testing these hypotheses through experimentation or observation, and developing theories that retrodict prior data and predict future experience. All fields within science employ this methodology. What separates scientific fields is their subject matter—biology is the study of living things and organic systems, chemistry is the study of the composition and properties of molecules, and so on.

In philosophy, it is just the reverse. Philosophy is defined by its subject matter and treats questions such as "What is a person, and what makes me different from you?" "What is justice?" "How should we live?" "What can we know, and how?" "What is the mind?" "Do we have free will, and in what sense?" "How can we reason well?" and "What is truth?" Within philosophy there are different methodologies. Some have argued that these methodologies are so ill defined, and overlap to such an extent, that carving out what is properly called "analytic philosophy" is next to impossible. Dagfinn Føllesdal has broached the view that "the flaws of the classification of contemporary philosophical trends are not unlike the flaws of the following classification in a 'certain Chinese encyclopedia' which has been reported by Jorge Luis Borges" (Føllesdal 1996, 194):

> Animals are divided into: (a) animals belonging to the Emperor, (b) embalmed, (c) tame, (d) sucking pigs, (e) sirens, (f) fabulous, (g) stray dogs, (h) included in the present classification, (i) frenzied, (j) innumerable, (k) drawn with a very fine camel hair brush, (l) *et cetera*, (m) having just broken the water pitcher, (n) that from a long way off look like flies.

Such a wild cross-categorization is unlikely to be of much help. While a full accounting of the nature of analytic versus other types of philosophy is beyond the scope of this introduction, nevertheless we may attempt to make some kind of distinctions in philosophical method,[1] keeping in mind that there are not hard-and-fast boundaries between the kinds. At the risk of some oversimplification, three methodologies are most prominent in contemporary philosophy. In roughly reverse order by number of proponents, they are phenomenology, ideological philosophy, and analytic philosophy.

Phenomenology assumes that philosophical questions will be answered by careful attention to the felt quality of human experience. According to phenomenologists, how it feels to live in the world is both the root of philosophical puzzlement and the source of its resolution. There is a sharp divide between phenomenology and science, with the former emphasizing the role of intuition and the meaning of human experience in understanding reality. Science, on the other hand, stresses experimentation and strives for an objective characterization of reality that does not give pride of place to humanity. Phenomenology is in part a reaction to Immanuel Kant (1724–1804). Kant believed that the unity of consciousness could only be explained by appeal to a "transcendental" reality independent of our categories or conditions of experience. Phenomenologists hold that debate over a transcendental reality can be bracketed off and that the unity of consciousness can be explained as the result of a purely descriptive psychology.

At this juncture it is worth noting that phenomenology and analytic philosophy arose at approximately the same time: the late nineteenth and early twentieth centuries. Interestingly, the same figures stand at the headwaters of both rivers of thought, particularly Edmund Husserl (1859–1938) and Alexius Meinong (1853–1920). Husserl maintained that philosophy should precisely describe the nature of our experiences, offering both a *noematic analysis,* or objective description of the experience, and a *noetic analysis,* or description of the subjective conscious activity that we bring to bear on the experience. Through a kind of intuition we are then able to uncover the essential natures of both the objects of our experiences and mental events like perception and judging. Meinong was likewise interested in the essential nature of objects (their *Sosein*) which things might possess even if they did not exist. So a unicorn may have an essential nature even if there are no unicorns. And we can think about unicorns—Meinong defended the view that our thoughts can be directed upon nonexistent, even impossible objects. These views influenced both subsequent phenomenological and analytic approaches to epistemology, ontology, and the philosophy of mind.[2]

Another methodology is ideological. This approach assumes that some political ideology is correct and then addresses philosophical issues with a view to advancing its agenda. One example of the ideological methodology is Marxism. One may study Karl Marx, publish scholarly work on Marx, and think that Marx is an important philosopher, but if one also believes that capitalism is the best form of political economy, one cannot be a Marxist. Being a Marxist philosopher requires a commitment to the promotion of some version of Marxism, to some degree.

While Marxism is waning in popularity, another form of ideological philosophy is waxing: feminist philosophy. One can be a philosopher (= interested in philosophical questions like those just listed), and one can also be a feminist (= believe that women and men have equal moral worth), but still not be a feminist philosopher. Feminist philosophers address philosophical questions with a view towards the political and economic advancement of women. Precisely what this advancement consists in, or how it may be achieved, is not settled in advance. Yet if one does not accept some sort of political agenda devoted to promoting women, one cannot be a feminist philosopher.

The third methodology is that of analytic philosophy.

As a specific school or approach, analytic philosophy is primarily a twentieth-century phenomenon, although one that recognizes Bolzano, Berkeley, Descartes, Hume, Kant, Leibniz, and Locke (among others) as forebears. In fact, the method of analysis traces its roots back to the ancient Greek sage Socrates (469–399 B.C.E.). Socrates went about questioning those who considered themselves to be wise, testing their purported wisdom by asking his interlocutors "What is justice?" or "What is knowledge?" He would then challenge their answers. For example, in the dialogue *Euthyphro* Socrates asks the eponymous hero to define "piety." Euthyphro, on his way to court to prosecute his father for murdering a serf, replies that piety is doing as he is doing, namely, prosecuting murderers. Socrates rejoins that this is an unsatisfactory reply, as he is looking for a general definition of "piety" that would allow him to evaluate various different acts as pious or impious. Euthyphro tries again, this time defining "piety" as those acts which the gods love. Socrates notes an ambiguity here: Are the pious things those which only *some* of the gods love, or those which *all* the gods love? If the former, then Hera might consider an act to be pious, whereas Hephaestus might regard the same act as impious. This would make obeying the gods a difficult matter indeed. Euthyphro replies that pious acts are those that all the gods love. Socrates proceeds to examine difficulties with this definition also.

This vignette illustrates a classic analytic-style exchange. It begins with one person offering a definition, or analysis, of a concept. As the German iconoclast Friedrich Nietzsche (1844–1900) commented in *The Gay Science* (§355), what we want from knowledge is the reduction of the strange to the familiar. This is what Euthyphro tried to do: explain the problematic concept "piety" in more familiar terms. This proposal is then tested to see if it is genuinely explanatory (Euthyphro's first definition of "piety" was not), unambiguous, and immune to counterexamples (Euthyphro's second definition was not), and if it has acceptable implications (an issue they pursue with the third definition).

There are difficulties with this approach. One is that common words like "piety" are vague, and a rigorous analysis of such concepts may demand more of them than they can provide. British polymath Bertrand Russell (1872–1970) puts this problem beautifully:

> A certain difficulty as regards the use of words is unavoidable here, as in all philosophical inquiries. The meanings of common words are vague, fluctuating, and ambiguous, like the shadow thrown by a flickering street-lamp on a windy night; yet in the nucleus of this uncertain patch of meaning, we may find some precise concept for which philosophy requires a name. If we choose a new technical term, the connexion with ordinary thought is retarded; but if we use the common word with a new precise significance, we may seem to run counter to usage, and we may confuse the reader's thoughts by irrelevant associations. It is impossible to lay down a rule for the avoidance of these opposite dangers; sometimes it will be well to introduce a new technical term, sometimes it will be better to polish the common word until it becomes suitable for technical purposes. (Russell 1914, 128–129)

Many have thought that Russell's polish-or-replace approach to ordinary language merely scratches the surface of the importance language and meaning have for philosophy. At the extreme is the view of the distinguished Oxford philosopher Michael Dummett, who wrote in his book *Origins of Analytical Philosophy,* "What distinguishes analytical philosophy, in its diverse manifestations, from other schools is the belief, first, that a philosophical account of thought can be attained only through a philosophical account of language, and, secondly, that a comprehensive account can only be so attained" (Dummett 1993, 4). Thus for Dummett the philosophy of language is foundational for all other enterprises of analytic philosophy.

While most scholars think he overstates matters a bit, there is an element of truth in Dummett's proposal. It is undeniable that analytic philosophers have spilled much ink over issues pertaining to language and meaning. It was the German philosopher Gottlob Frege (1848–1925) who first focused contemporary attention on the nature of meaning. Paragraph 62 of his 1884 book *Die Grundlagen der Arithmetik* (*The Foundations of Arithmetic*) begins by asking about the nature of numbers, a familiar metaphysical question about what there is. By the end of the paragraph, Frege had segued into a discussion of the meanings of sentences containing number words. Dummett identifies this "linguistic turn," by which an apparently ontological problem about the nature of numbers is converted into an issue of sentence meaning, as the precise moment when analytic philosophy was born.[3]

Frege was responsible for another crucial step in the development of analytic philosophy as well: the invention in the *Begriffsschrift* (*Concept-Writing*), (1879) of quantified predicate logic. The power of this new logic, the first real innovation in logic since Aristotle,[4] has inspired generations of philosophers. In the preface to their epochal *Principia Mathematica*, Alfred North Whitehead and Bertrand Russell write, "In all questions of logical analysis, our chief debt is to Frege." (Whitehead and Russell 1913, vii). Ludwig Wittgenstein also acknowledges his indebtedness to "Frege's great works." (Wittgenstein 1961, preface). Rudolf Carnap concurs, "Above all I am indebted to the writings and lectures of Frege" (Carnap 1937, xvi.)

Frege rejected the view that logic represented psychological laws of thought. Instead, he considered logical laws to be the laws of truth and logic an abstract formal language the complete development of which would be able to capture all that was respectable in natural languages. In this way the early analytic philosophers became interested in the possibility of a "perfect language," one free from ambiguity, vagueness, and the intensional idioms that posed certain logical difficulties for ordinary natural languages.

This quest took two paths. One was in the direction of mathematics, the language of science and thus, as Galileo claimed, the "language of nature." In the three hefty volumes of *Principia Mathematica,* Whitehead and Russell attempted to prove that arithmetic can be derived from set theory and pure logic alone. Thus they tried to show that mathematics is, in a fundamental way, connected with formal logic. Famously, it took the authors halfway into the second volume before they were able to prove that $1 + 1 = 2$. The perfect language was to be the formal language of *Principia:* rigorously and painstakingly precise.[5]

Ludwig Wittgenstein (1889–1951) took the study of logic along a different avenue: that of natural language. In *Tractatus Logico-Philosophicus* (1921) Wittgenstein maintained that the structure of language reveals the structure of reality (§4.121). Since logic is the abstract structure of language, it "is not a body of doctrine, but a mirror-image of the world" (§6.13), and its study will reveal to us the limits of any reality we can understand. Wittgenstein had been a pupil of Russell's and was well aware of the results in *Principia.* Wittgenstein thought that insofar as mathematics was the consequence of logic, and logic was the backbone of language, then mathematics was no more than a system of tautologies. This was a view that depressed Russell, but one he eventually came to believe (Russell 1959, 211–112). The real purpose of philosophy, Wittgenstein argued, was the logical clarification of thoughts (§4.112); that is, philosophy is simply an activity that elucidates the propositions of the natural sciences and makes clear the boundaries of what can be thought, what is meaningful, and what is not (§6.53).

Wittgenstein's book greatly impressed a group of scholars in Vienna who gathered together to discuss philosophy and called themselves the Vienna Circle. The members were Moritz Schlick, Rudolf Carnap, Otto Neurath, Herbert Feigl, Friedrich Waismann, Edgar Zilsel, Victor Kraft, Philipp Frank, Karl Menger, Kurt Gödel, and Hans Hahn. The Vienna Circle promoted a logical, scientific approach to philosophical problems and had a profound influence on leading philosophers outside their group. Their evangelism concerning methodology led to the widespread development of the school known as logical positivism.

Carnap (1891–1970), a logical positivist, embraced the quest for a perfect language, one in which the traditional conundrums of philosophy could not even be expressed and would thus be exposed as pseudoproblems. This task, he wrote, is of "great philosophical importance" and "at present occupies the logicians" ("The Elimination of Metaphysics through the Logical Analysis of Language," this volume, 105). Ordinary language, the *material mode* of speech contains sentences like (A): "the sense-qualities, such as colors, smells, etc. belong to the primitive data" (Carnap 1937, 306). Such sentences are apparently about objects: colors, smells, and sensory data. Carnap thought that material mode sentences "mislead us into thinking that we are dealing with extra-linguistic objects such as numbers, things, properties, experiences, states of affairs, space, time, and so on . . . in reality it is a case of language and its connections" (Carnap 1937, 298). To make this clear, we need to translate sentences in the material mode into ones in the *formal mode,* that is, into sentences that highlight the linguistic aspects of the sentence. So, for example, (A) above becomes in the formal mode (B): "symbols of sense-qualities, such as color-symbols, smell-symbols, etc. belong to the descriptive primitive symbols." Sentences that cannot be given meaningful formal mode translations drop out as pseudosentences. Carnap thought that most metaphysical sentences fell into this category; it was only because of the logical defects of language that passages such as this one from Martin Heidegger seem sensible at all.

> What is to be investigated is being only and—*nothing* else; being alone and further—*nothing;* solely being, and beyond being—*nothing. What about this Nothing? . . . Does the Nothing exist only because the Not, i.e., the Negation, exists?* Or is it the other way around? *Does Negation and the Not exist only because the Nothing exists? . . .* We assert: *the Nothing is prior to the Not and the Negation. . . .* Where do we seek the Nothing? How do we find the Nothing? We know the Nothing. . . . *Anxiety reveals the Nothing. . . .* That for which and because of which we were anxious, was "really"—nothing. Indeed: the Nothing itself—as such—was present. . . . *What about this Nothing?—The Nothing itself Nothings.*[6]

Carnap argued that language in the material mode allows us to treat "Nothing" as a noun that refers to something, and hence something subject to metaphysical investigation. But in fact it is all nonsense, which is evident when we attempt to translate such passages into the formal mode. Such translation, Carnap argues, is impossible. According to Carnap, philosophy itself is the uncovering and elimination of pseudoproblems caused by the material mode of language. He writes: "There is no such thing as speculative philosophy, a system of sentences with a special subject matter on a par with those of the sciences. To pursue philosophy can only be to clarify the concepts and sentences of science by logical analysis. The instrument for this is the new logic" (Carnap 1959, 145).

The pursuit of an ideal language reached its apotheosis with the advent of phenomenalism and Carnap's book *Der Logische Aufbau der Welt* (1928, translated in 1967 as *The Logical Structure of the World*). Carnap and the other phenomenalists (e.g. Ayer, in "The Constitution of Material Things," this volume, 118–32) argued that all sentences that made reference to material objects could be translated into sentences that referred only to sensory experience or sense data. All that is immediately present to us is the testimony of our senses, thought the phenomenalists, and restricting our talk to possible sensations and relations among our sensations avoids an unwarranted commitment to a world of mind-independent objects. Such a translation or reduction has the desired consequence of retaining a sort of pure empiricism untainted by metaphysical projection. The language of phenomenalism was the final entry in the sweepstakes for a "perfect" language.

Many philosophers, persuaded by the critical arguments of Roderick Chisholm[7] (1916–1999) and others, rejected phenomenalism, and with its demise came the abandonment of the project to construct a perfect language. By the 1950s the study of *ordinary* language came to dominate British analytic philosophy. Just as Wittgenstein had anticipated the development of logical positivism back in 1921, he was again at the fore with his posthumously published *Philosophical Investigations* of 1953. Behind *Investigations* was the idea that philosophical problems arose not because our language is imperfect, but because we are bewitched by language and fail to pay close attention to how it is employed.[8] Wittgenstein eschewed the idea of understanding as involving an inner process of interpretation and instead treated it as an ability to engage in a public practice of using symbols and signs in certain ways. Attention to the details of the ways in which ordinary language is used is the hallmark of the members of this school such as J. L. Austin and P. F. Strawson. Others, like Russell, criticized the ordinary language approach as abandoning philosophy and taking up lexicography.

It is undeniable, then, that deep interest in logic and language has been crucially important in analytic philosophy. However, contra Dummett, concerns about language are not the whole, or even the root, story. Many analytic philosophers have denied that a philosophical assessment of language has any sort of foundational priority. Russell, in *An Inquiry into Meaning and Truth,* rejected the idea that we must have a philosophical assessment of language before we can give an account of thought. He argued that it is only by first understanding psychology that we will be able to understand the nature of language; philosophy of mind has priority over the philosophy of language.[9] Franz Brentano (in "The Distinction between Mental and Physical Phenomena" this volume, 231–43), H. P. Grice (in "Meaning," this volume, 76–81) and more recently Chisholm[10] have defended the primacy of the intentional, the thesis that the reference of language is to be explicated in terms of the intentionality of thought. Recently Michael Devitt, a contemporary analytic philosopher, has made it clear that his slogan is "metaphysics first," and that an adequate semantic theory will follow the prior development of a solid ontology.[11] Whatever the merits of these claims, Russell, Chisholm, Devitt, Grice, and to some extent Brentano are paradigmatic analytic philosophers and any adequate explanation of the analytic movement must accommodate their views.

Part of the development of analytic philosophy resulted not from an assessment of language, but a rejection of metaphysical idealism. Idealists like G. W. F. Hegel and F. H. Bradley held that everything believed via common sense is mere appearance and that what makes a thing real is its being in some way an aspect of a sentient experience. J. M. E. McTaggart is famous for his view that time itself is unreal; only selves and their interactions are ontologically genuine. These were prominent, mainstream views at the end of the nineteenth century. G. E. Moore (1873–1958) led the revolt against idealism, and his celebrated 1903 essay "The Refutation of Idealism" was the shot across the bow. Russell followed quickly, embracing common-sense realism with "a sense of emancipation" (Russell 1944, 12).

Correlative to the rejection of idealism was an increasing sense that philosophy is in some manner continuous with science. This too is a hallmark of analytic philosophy. At the beginning of the twentieth century fundamental changes in scientific knowledge occurred, including the development of general relativity. Relativity theory led to philosophical criticism of the power of a priori reason. For a long time, philosophers believed that Euclidean geometry was self-evident and that pure reason had revealed it to be the geometric structure of nature. With Einstein came the realization that the universe is non-Euclidean, an empirical refutation of what many had thought to be true a priori.[12] Analytic philosophers turned their attention away from the a priori and purported "analytic" truths to a study of the nature of a posteriori knowledge, induction, perception and "synthetic" truths. W. V. Quine (1908–2000) went so far as to deny any salient difference between analytic and synthetic truths ("Two Dogmas of Empiricism," this volume, 193–206). For Quine, everything knowable is so by the methods of science.

A separate connection of analytic philosophy to science is the role of reductionism. Many analytic philosophers hold that philosophers do well to study and apply the methods of science to solving philosophical problems,[13] and one of these methods is holding reductionism as an ideal. According to Nobel Prize–winning physicist Steven Weinberg, reductionism is the view that "scientific principles are the way they are because of deeper scientific principles . . . and that all these principles can be traced to one simple connected set of laws" (Weinberg 1992, 52). Biologist E. O. Wilson has stated that "reductionism is the primary and essential activity of science" (Wilson 1998, 54). These scientists assume that there are few brute, inexplicable, facts about reality and that interactions in nature from the behavior of ants to the behavior of electrons are explainable in terms of more basic laws of nature.

Reductionism among the early analytic philosophers initially took the form of conceptual analysis. As Socrates and Euthyphro did with piety, Moore and others argued that concepts become intelligible when they are analyzed into their constituent concepts (Moore 1899, 182). Once we understand these simple components, then more complicated ideas can be grasped. Inspired by Wittgenstein, Russell developed this approach into a full-blown program of *logical atomism*. The world is a world of facts, and these facts make propositions true or false. Propositions themselves were types of complex symbols, the meaning of which can be broken down into the meanings of their component symbols and their logical interrelations.

Other forms of reductionism were of the sort practiced by the phenomenalists— "reducing" sentences ostensibly about material objects into sentences that made reference only to sense data or sensory states. This particular reductionist project has been criticized by Quine ("Two Dogmas of Empiricism"). Nevertheless, the general scientific notion of reductionism has proven to be quite influential even in fields like ethics, typically thought to be far removed from science. Moore writes: "Just as physics cannot rest content with the discovery that light is propagated by waves of ether [sic], but must go on to discover the particular nature of the ether-waves corresponding to each several color; so Casuistry, not content with the general law that charity is a virtue must attempt to discover the relative merits of every different form of charity" ("On Defining 'Good,'" this volume, 314). In other words, ethicists do not rest content with an indefinite series of unconnected moral maxims like "Charity is a virtue," but try to find the deeper, more general principles that give rise to the maxims and show the connections among them.

Is Analytic Philosophy a Good Methodology?

The early analytic philosophers thought that their new method was superior to previous approaches for several reasons. One was that they saw and embraced the philosophical relevance of advances in logic, mathematics, and the natural sciences. They believed in the unity of knowledge and viewed hermetic attempts to carve out a special place for philosophical initiates with great skepticism. The early analytics also thought that earlier philosophy was marred by obscure, woolly language and ill-defined neologisms. They believed that close attention to the logical structure of language would avoid many pitfalls that had snared other philosophers. We saw an instance of this focus earlier with Carnap's distinction between the material and formal modes of language and his concomitant dismissal of Heidegger's metaphysics. Another example is Russell's treatment of definite descriptions. He writes:

> Everyone agrees that "the golden mountain does not exist" is a true proposition. But it has, apparently, a subject, "the golden mountain," and if this subject did not designate some object,

the proposition would seem to be meaningless. [Alexius] Meinong inferred that there is a golden mountain, which is golden and a mountain, but does not exist. He even thought that the existent golden mountain is existent, but does not exist. This did not satisfy me, and the desire to avoid Meinong's unduly populous realm of being led me to the theory of descriptions. (1944: 13)

In his 1905 paper "On Denoting" (this volume, 33–40), Russell argues that definite descriptions like "the golden mountain" are meaningless in isolation. They are "incomplete symbols" that acquire sense only in complete sentences. He offers a logical analysis of such descriptions that allows "the golden mountain does not exist" to be a true proposition, and yet makes rigorously clear that no ontological commitment to existing golden mountains is required. The technique of logical/linguistic analysis allowed Russell to resolve the puzzle of "the golden mountain does not exist" without becoming mired in a bizarre Meinongian metaphysics. The apparent success of Russell's theory of descriptions provoked the Cambridge prodigy F. P. Ramsey (1903–1930) to remark that the theory was "a paradigm of philosophy."[14]

Some have objected to the analytic approach on the grounds that it downgrades philosophy from its lofty historical role as a set of meditations on the grand questions of human existence and turns it into a crabbed, narrow series of nit-picking exchanges over picayune topics. Some think analytic philosophy degrades existence for us in the way Nietzsche once spoke of reason, reducing philosophy "to a mere exercise for a calculator and an indoor diversion for mathematicians" (*The Gay Science*, §373).

Nothing could be further from the truth. In the first place, analytic philosophy is intensely concerned with issues of substantial personal interest to ordinary folks. Russell, for example, bent his formidable intellect to the careful analysis of many popular issues of great practicality. One of his most notorious books was *Marriage and Morals* (1929), which advocated premarital sex and cohabitation forty years ahead of its time. In this book Russell maintained that "the total amount of undesired sex endured by women is probably greater in marriage than in prostitution" (Russell 1929, 103) and suggested that polygamy is instinctual. In 1940 Russell quit his job to take up a teaching post at the City College of New York, when the furor over *Marriage and Morals* caused the blue-nosed trustees of CCNY to brand him a dangerous immoral heretic and rescind his job offer, leaving him unemployed. Ten years later, the very same book secured Russell a Nobel Prize for Literature.[15] Such public attention rebuts the notion that what analytic philosophers do is of interest only within the ivory tower.

Well, a skeptic might rejoin, even if analytic philosophy does occasionally deal with ethics and how we are to live, *most* of it is splitting hairs over trivial topics. What relevance could the philosophy of *language* have, for God's sake? Or *logic*? The answer may be surprising; seemingly technical, obscure issues have unforeseen consequences for the "larger" issues of human existence. For example, Ayer and his fellow logical positivists argued that only statements that were, in principle, empirically verifiable were meaningful. Unverifiable statements might be poetic, express emotion, or serve some other function, but they can't convey information. Since "God exists" is empirically unverifiable, it too is meaningless. So not only does God fail to exist, but even the assertion of his existence is nonsense. Indeed, all supernatural and religious claims have no cognitive content, according to the positivists. This religious skepticism came directly out of technical investigations into the nature of meaning and the philosophy of language, esoteric matters that proved to have far-reaching implications.

Even purely formal logic, the most highly abstract and precise area of philosophy, has had striking successes on topics of general interest. In the early part of the twentieth century, Leopold Löwenheim and Thoralf Skolem proved that if a sentence has a model, then it has a model over the natural numbers. In other words, take any string of symbols and suppose we can come up with an interpretation of these symbols so that they actually mean something and the sentence is saying something either true or false. What would the string of symbols be about? They could be musical notations, or a recipe, or the periodic table of elements. The Löwenheim-Skolem theorem states that if we can come up with a consistent interpretation of the symbols at all, then we can devise an interpretation according to which the string of symbols is about the natural numbers.

What is the practical upshot of this technical result? Here's one. Suppose the Search for Extraterrestrial Intelligence (SETI) project is successful, and we receive electromagnetic radiation from space that we are convinced came from intelligent extraterrestrials. We could be persuaded of this on purely syntactic grounds—the waveforms exhibit patterns and regularities otherwise not found in nature. But what are the extraterrestrials saying to us? How could we figure it out? According to the Löwenheim-Skolem theorem, it is logically impossible for us to know; we can't know just from the symbols (in this case electromagnetic waves) alone. For all we can tell, the aliens are beaming truths about the numbers at us. Of course it could be the alien version of *The Jerry Springer Show*, but we have no way of deciding what the correct interpretation is.

To be sure, analytic philosophy is careful and slow, and some may feel that philosophy should dance across the great issues with fine pronouncements and maxims. The method of analysis is like that of basic science. It is only by proceeding in incremental steps, each meticulously argued and defended, that we can advance with confidence towards the truth. Fine declamations accompanied by vague and sweeping statements about the World Spirit may be psychologically satisfying but are to the analytic approach as herbal remedies are to modern medicine. Analytic philosophers maintain that precision, clarity, and argumentation are *the* cardinal virtues of good philosophy and assiduously seek to cultivate them.[16]

NOTES

1. As does Føllesdal, who stresses argument and justification as essential to the analytic approach. See Føllesdal 1996, 201.

2. For more on this influence, see Philipse 1994, Smith 1989, and Dummett 1993.

3. See Monk 1996, 3.

4. Some scholars dispute this, arguing that many important logical innovations were made in the medieval period. However, the medieval discoveries were like Leif Erikson's "discovery" of America, whereas Frege is like Christopher Columbus. It is Columbus, not Erikson, who has had the real impact on world history. So too with Frege.

5. Russell (1956, p. 198) explicitly says this. For more on Russell's interest in a logically perfect language, see Sainsbury 1979, chap. 5.

6. From Heidegger's "What Is Metaphysics?" quoted in Carnap, "The Elimination of Metaphysics through the Logical Analysis of Language," this volume, 105.

7. See Chisholm 1948.

8. See Wittgenstein 1953, §109.

9. Cf. Monk 1996, 8.

10. Chisholm 1989, chap. 14.

11. See Devitt 1999.

12. For discussion, see Coffa 1991, chap. 10.

13. For example, Russell 1917, 98.

14. Ramsey 1931, 263.

15. See Ryan 1988, 105.

16. Thanks to Richard Brook, Kurt Smith, Dale Jacquette, Scott Lowe, and Wendy Lee-Lampshire for helpful comments on an earlier version.

REFERENCES

Carnap, Rudolf. 1937. *Logical Syntax of Language.* Trans. Amethe Smeaton. London: Routledge and Kegan Paul.

———. 1959. "The Old and the New Logic." In *Logical Positivism,* edited by A. J. Ayer. New York: Free Press.

Chisholm, Roderick M. 1948. "The Problem of Empiricism." *The Journal of Philosophy* 45: 512–517.

———. 1989. *On Metaphysics.* Minneapolis: University of Minnesota Press.

Coffa, J. Alberto. 1991. *The Semantic Tradition from Kant to Carnap to the Vienna Station.* Cambridge: Cambridge University Press.

Devitt, Michael. 1999. "A Naturalistic Defense of Realism." In *Metaphysics: Contemporary Readings,* edited by S. D. Hales. Belmont, CA: Wadsworth.

Dummett, Michael. 1993. *Origins of Analytical Philosophy.* Cambridge: Harvard University Press.

Føllesdal, Dagfinn. 1996. "Analytic Philosophy: What Is It and Why Should One Engage in It?" *Ratio* 9 (3):193–208.

Monk, Ray. 1996. "What Is Analytical Philosophy?" In *Bertrand Russell and the Origins of Analytical Philosophy,* edited by R. Monk and A. Palmer. Bristol, UK: Thoemmes Press.

Moore, G. E. 1899. "The Nature of Judgement." *Mind* 5 (8):176–93.

Philipse, Herman. 1994. Husserl and the Origins of Analytical Philosophy. *European Journal of Philosophy* 2 (2):165–84.

Ramsey, Frank Plumpton. 1931. *The Foundations of Mathematics.* London: Routledge and Kegan Paul.

Russell, Bertrand. 1914. "On the Nature of Acquaintance." In *Logic and Knowledge*, edited by R. C. Marsh. London: Unwin Hyman.

———. 1917. *Mysticism and Logic.* London: Longmans, Green.

———. 1929. *Marriage and Morals.* London: Horace Liveright.

———. 1944. "My Mental Development." In *The Philosophy of Bertrand Russell,* edited by P. A. Schilpp. La Salle, IL: Open Court.

———. 1956. "The Philosophy of Logical Atomism." In *Logic and Knowledge.* London: Unwin Hyman.

———. 1959. *My Philosophical Development.* London: Allen and Unwin.

Ryan, Alan. 1988. *Bertrand Russell: A Political Life.* New York: Hill and Wang.

Sainsbury, Mark. 1979. *Russell.* In *The Arguments of the Philosophers,* edited by T. Honderich. London: Routledge and Kegan Paul.

Smith, Barry. 1989. "On the Origins of Analytic Philosophy." *Grazer Philosophische Studien* 35: 153–73.

Weinberg, Steven. 1992. *Dreams of a Final Theory.* New York: Pantheon Books.

Whitehead, Alfred North, and Bertrand Russell. 1913. *Principia Mathematica.* Cambridge: Cambridge University Press.

Wilson, E. O. 1998. *Consilience.* New York: Knopf.

Wittgenstein, Ludwig. 1953. *Philosophical Investigations.* Trans. G. E. M. Anscombe. Oxford: Blackwell.

———. 1961. *Tractatus Logico-Philosophicus.* Trans. D. F. Pears and B. F. McGuinness. London: Routledge and Kegan Paul.

Part I

Philosophy of Language

DALE JACQUETTE

Dale Jacquette is professor of philosophy at the Pennsylvania State University. He has published extensively in many areas of philosophy; his recent work in the philosophy of language includes *Wittgenstein's Thought in Transition* (1998) and *Meinongian Logic: The Semantics of Existence and Nonexistence* (1996). He is also the author of *Philosophy of Mind* (1994). Recently Professor Jacquette was the William J. Fulbright Distinguished Professor of the Philosophy of Language at the University of Venice, Italy.

A History of Early Analytic Philosophy of Language

Analytic Philosophy

T HE TERM *ANALYTIC PHILOSOPHY* refers to a family of related approaches to philosophical method. A narrow interpretation of philosophical analysis assumes that it is possible at least in principle to break down the meaning of language or the structures of the world into increasingly simpler units built out of ultimately simple components. Analytic philosophy in this sense is analogous to analytic chemistry, as a method of logical, conceptual, metaphysical or ontological analysis by which complex linguistic and corresponding truth-making entities or states of affairs are decomposed into basic elements.

There are not many philosophers who have preached or practiced modern analytic philosophy in this limited sense. We should think especially of Bertrand Russell's 1917–1918 lectures on *The Philosophy of Logical Atomism* (1985) and Ludwig Wittgenstein's (1922) *Tractatus Logico-Philosophicus*. Wittgenstein's *Tractatus* and Russell's work during this period, as forays into *logical atomism,* for this reason are virtually the only examples recognized as genuinely analytic by P. M. S. Hacker in his (1996) commentary, *Wittgenstein's Place in Twentieth-Century Analytic Philosophy*. Yet the category is too exclusive to do justice to the ways in which most philosophers have spoken of analytic philosophy. Russell, Wittgenstein, and a handful of others are certainly paradigm pioneering analytic philosophers. But analytic philosophy existed less self-consciously before its brief incarnation as logical atomism, and it has continued to evolve in new directions ever since. The possibilities of analytic philosophy are not exhausted by logical atomism, and analytic philosophers do not disqualify themselves as such by disagreeing with the principles of logical atomism.

This essay was commissioned especially for this volume and appears here for the first time.

Nor is analytic philosophy essentially committed to the *logical positivist verification criterion of meaning.* The verification criterion states that a sentence is meaningful either because it expresses a proposition that is necessarily true or necessarily false by virtue of the definitions of terms it contains, or because it is possible at least in principle to determine by observation or experiment that the sentence is contingently true or false. The sentence, "There is uranium on Mars," is meaningful, according to the verification criterion, because, although we do not yet know the answer, it is conceivable that we might verify or refute what the sentence asserts by an appropriate empirical investigation. Although analytic philosophy was once strongly identified with logical positivism, it too has survived the rise and fall of the verification criterion of meaning. How, then, should analytic philosophy be described?

Analytic philosophy is often understood to mean any effort to address philosophical problems by means of the rigorous clarification of concepts and consideration of arguments. The word *analysis,* even in nontechnical parlance, often denotes an evaluation that sheds light on a presumed problem, without necessarily being atomistic in its conclusions. This is roughly the same sense of analysis in which we speak of a medical, economic, military, or political analysis, or, say, a news analysis of current events. An analysis in the generic sense is expected to clarify a situation, help us understand its meaning and implications, and possibly help to solve or resolve a difficulty. Analytic philosophy by this conception is any inquiry that proceeds by means of definitions of concepts and critical evaluation of arguments as an adjunct to the advancement of mathematics, science, value inquiry and decision making, and in general our philosophical understanding of these subjects and activities. By contrast, nonanalytic philosophy in the relevant sense is often characterized by adherents and detractors alike as a literary rather than broadly scientific project, in which truth is not always the goal, and clear definitions and arguments are not obligatory.

If we interpret the subdiscipline in this way, then it is clear why analytic philosophy is sometimes thought to be closely allied to philosophy of language. If analytic philosophy involves the clarification of concepts or advancement of theses by arguments, then it is inherently at least partially, often primarily, a semantic project, devoted to the discovery, interpretation, and elaboration of meanings. Analytic philosophers of language have intrinsic and instrumental motivations. They are interested in how language works, how meaning is encoded and conveyed by language, for its own sake, as a subject that stands in need of philosophical explanation and as a means to an end, in solving or avoiding philosophical problems and for practical guidance in ethical, political, and aesthetic judgment and action.

Meaning, Sense, and Reference

Analytic philosophy of language begins with Gottlob Frege's landmark (1892) essay, "Über Sinn und Bedeutung" ("On Sense and Reference," this volume, 21–32). Frege distinguishes among *idea, sense,* and *reference.* By *idea* (*Bild, Vorstellung*), Frege means the associated mental imagery that sometimes accompanies language use. When I utter the name "Aristotle," I might call to mind a picture of Aristotle as I imagine him to be or as I remember seeing him represented in sculpture or in later artistic interpretations.

Frege mentions idea only to set it aside as irrelevant to a scientific semantics, on the grounds that idea is subjective and mental associations are inessential. He concentrates instead on the presumably more objective concepts of sense (*Sinn*) and reference (*Bedeutung*). He offers a parallel analysis of the meaning of proper names or singular referring expressions and sentences, whereby both proper names and sentences have sense and reference. The sense of a proper name, which Frege also speaks of as its *intension,* determines its reference, or *extension*. The reference of the proper name "Aristotle" is a certain person, an ancient Greek philosopher. The sense of the name is the complete set of Aristotle's properties, including the properties of being Greek, being born in Stagira in Macedonia, having such and such parents, living at such and such a time, being the student of Plato, the teacher of Alexander the Great, the author of the *Physics, Nicomachean Ethics,* and so on. Frege admits that opinions about the sense of a name can differ, because language users are not omniscient and lack the cognitive capacity to entertain the infinite set of properties associated with any existent object referred to by any proper name. But in the abstract, the sense of a name like "Aristotle" is an indefinitely large set of properties that collectively belong only to Aristotle. Sense determines reference, or intension determines extension, in Frege's philosophy of language, because the properties specified by the sense of a proper name single out a unique existent object to which the name refers.

Sentences, according to Frege, have a comparable division of sense and reference. The sense of a sentence is a function of the senses of the meaningful terms it contains. This is sometimes known as Frege's *compositionality* thesis. The reference of a sentence, its extension, is likewise determined by its sense or intension, which Frege stipulates somewhat artificially by maintaining that the reference of a true sentence is *the True* and the reference of a false sentence is *the False,* reified as special semantic objects.

Frege applies the sense-reference distinction to solve a puzzle about identity. To say that the evening star = the morning star appears to express an astronomical discovery, something that is not automatically known merely by virtue of understanding the meanings of the words. The identity in this case seems to have what Frege calls *cognitive significance,* expressing an advance in knowledge. Yet because no two distinct things can ever be identical, identity is best understood as a relation holding between names rather than things, since the same thing can sometimes be designated by different proper names. To maintain that the evening star = the morning star, in that case, does not seem to say anything more or less than that the evening star = the evening star, or that the morning star = the evening star. Indeed, the evening star, the first and brightest star seen in the evening, is identical to what is also called the morning star, the last brightest star seen in the morning; these are two names for the planet Venus, also known to the ancient Greeks as Hesperus and Phosphorus.

The proper name "the evening star" refers to the same object as the proper name "the morning star," as do "Venus," "Hesperus," and "Phosphorus." The truth of an identity statement depends on the fact that the same existent objects are referred to by both of its terms. The term, "the morning star," nevertheless has a different sense than the term, "the evening star." One term mentions the morning, and so has the property of appearing in the morning as part of its sense, while the other term, unlike the first, mentions the evening, and thereby has the property of appearing in the evening as part of its sense. Yet by virtue of relating terms with different senses, "the evening star = the morning star" is cognitively significant. Frege accounts for the fact that an identity statement like "the evening star = the morning star" can be true (thanks to both terms having the same reference, i.e., referring to the same object), and cognitively significant (thanks to the two terms having different sense).

Frege's study sets the stage for all subsequent developments in analytic philosophy of language, even for philosophers who disagree with his conclusions. His emphasis on the extensionality of meaning and his distinction among idea, sense, and reference and elimination of subjective psychology in the associated ideas of language use from scientific semantics provide a framework within which analytic philosophy of language has flourished and a standard position against which dissenting voices have defined their opposition.

Ideal, Transcendent, and Ordinary Language

Ordinary language, and its technical refinements in specialized fields like science, is logically problematic. To mention just two frequently remarked difficulties, ordinary language (1) is riddled with ambiguities that stymie efforts at systematic interpretation and lead to philosophical confusions and logical fallacies of equivocation; and (2) includes terms that fail to denote existent objects, thus complicating semantics logically and metaphysically. Analytic philosophy of language responds to these limitations in a variety of ways.

Frege is so disparaging of ordinary language, with all of its logical infelicities, that he recommends abandoning it altogether for scientific purposes. He proposes to replace it with a more exacting tool for the precise expression of meaning, in the form of an ideal language. In his (1879) *Begriffsschrift: Eine der arithmetischen nachgebildete Formelsprache des reinen Denkens* (literally, "Concept Writing: An Arithmetically Modeled Formula Language of Pure Thought"), Frege develops a logical symbolism for the perspicuous expression of ideas, to take the place of colloquial discourse. Frege's *Begriffsschrift* is intended to be a perfect, ideal language, in which there can be no equivocation, because no term refers to more than one object, and in which all terms of the language refer only to existent objects. Russell agrees with Frege that ordinary language is hopeless, and, in his monumental (1910–13) three-volume work, *Principia Mathematica,* coauthored with Alfred North Whitehead, presents what is supposed to be a more perfect ideal language, that, like Frege's *Begriffsschrift* which inspired it, is dedicated to the task of reducing mathematics to the principles of logic.

Another approach to colloquial language is represented by Wittgenstein's *Tractatus.* Wittgenstein, in passage 5.5563, maintains that "All propositions of our colloquial language are actually, just as they are, logically completely in order." Unlike his mentors Frege and Russell, Wittgenstein does not renounce ordinary discourse but believes that an adequate semantic philosophy must explain the meaningfulness of any logically possible language capable of expressing determinate meaning. From an anthropological point of view, Wittgenstein is on solid ground in insisting on understanding how ordinary language works rather than abandoning it in preference for a logically unproblematic ideal language. Artificial languages are invented only as an improvement of natural languages that are already functioning for the meaningful expression of ideas. If we cannot understand how meaning is conveyed by ordinary language, then we cannot hope to understand how meaning is conveyed in extraordinary ideal languages like symbolic logic. If ordinary language is not meaningful, or if its meaning cannot be explained by a general philosophical semantics, then there is no prospect of avoiding its admitted limitations by replacing colloquial expression with a logically more circumspect ideal language.

Wittgenstein, nevertheless, is well aware of the obscurities of colloquial language. He remarks in *Tractatus* 4.002:

> Colloquial language is a part of the human organism and is not less complicated than it.
> From it it is humanly impossible to gather immediately the logic of language.
> Language disguises the thought; so that from the external form of the clothes one cannot infer the form of the thought they clothe, because the external form of the clothes is constructed with quite another object than to let the form of the body be recognized.
> The silent adjustments to understand colloquial language are enormously complicated.

To understand the expression of meaning in any possible language, without ignoring the logical defects of the vernacular, Wittgenstein, in his early philosophy of language, distinguishes between *sign* and *symbol.* By *sign,* Wittgenstein means the perceptible aspect of language, different in English, German, Japanese, and other natural languages, as well as ideal languages such as symbolic logic. Because of the cultural evolution of each sign system, signs exhibit all the logical disadvantages of which Frege and Russell despair.

Symbol, by contrast, is imperceptible and transcendent. The symbolic aspect of language is what all languages beneath the superficial appearance of their multiple sign systems have in common, by virtue of which they are capable of true or false representations of any logically possible state of affairs. As such, symbol is the essence of language, the reality of language as it exists independently of its accidental formulation in ordinary or specialized artificial languages. The symbolic aspect of language is similar to the ideal language to which Frege and Russell aspire, although Wittgenstein's distinction between sign and symbol also applies to Frege's *Begriffsschrift* and Russell's *Principia*. By invoking the sign-symbol distinction, Wittgenstein in his early semantic philosophy avails himself of the advantages of an ideal language, without turning his back on colloquial forms of expression and without denying the obvious, even if only superficial, failings of ordinary language. In *Tractatus* 5.5563, Wittgenstein significantly does not maintain that colloquial language per se is logically completely in order, but only that the *propositions* of colloquial language are logically completely in order. By this careful wording, he leaves himself plenty of room to argue that much of colloquial language is not genuinely propositional but consists of *Scheinsätze* or pseudopropositions.

Finally, without trying to exclude other possibilities, there is an approach to analytic philosophy of language that takes ordinary language at face value. What is sometimes called ordinary language philosophy sees the richness and diversity of ordinary language as a semantic asset in clarifying and dissolving philosophical problems that arise through abuses of language, rather than as an insurmountable obstacle to a correct theory of meaning. There are several main types of ordinary language philosophy, associated with the work of the later Wittgenstein in *The Blue and Brown Books* (1958), *Philosophical Investigations* (1957), and posthumously published writings from his later period, as well as important studies by, among others, Gilbert Ryle, John Wisdom, J. L. Austin, and H. P. Grice.

We can appreciate how ordinary language philosophy compares with ideal and transcendental theories by discussing a famous illustration in detail. An ordinary language philosopher like Austin in his posthumously edited (1962) lectures, *How to Do Things with Words*, closely observes the grammatical nuances of different uses of language in accomplishing specific purposes. Austin distinguishes what he calls a "total speech act" in a "total speech act situation" into *constatives* and *performatives* and describes these in turn as having *locutionary meaning*, *illocutionary force*, and *perlocutionary effect*. Constatives are not limited to, but exemplified by, true or false descriptions of states of affairs. Locutionary meaning for Austin is the interpretation of a speech act in terms of the reference of its terms. If I say, "The cat is on the mat," then the locutionary meaning of my speech act is that the cat is on the mat, meaning by "the cat" a certain feline, and by "the mat" a certain floor covering, by "on" a certain spatial relation, and by "is" a predication of the on relation to the cat and the mat. Illocutionary force usually involves the expression of a judgment or rendering of a verdict about a state of affairs, in this case, by declaring that the cat is on the mat. The perlocutionary effect of a speech act is the causal impact it can have on others, such as producing in them also the belief or at least the belief that I believe that the cat is on the mat, or the desire to shoo the cat away or bring it a dish of milk.

Austin finds the illocutionary force and perlocutionary effect of performatives more philosophically interesting than the locutionary meaning of constatives. An example of what he means by doing things with words is seen in the total speech act situation of saying "I do" in the context of a marriage ceremony. This does not merely communicate information, although that is also something we can do, but accomplishes a much larger purpose. Austin distinguishes five types of performatives, including verdictives, exercitives, commissives, behavitives, and expositives. A verdictive is a speech act that renders judgment or pronounces a verdict, as when the foreperson of a jury with potentially enormous perlocutionary effect utters the words, "Guilty" or "Not guilty." A commissive commits a speaker to doing something, as in making a promise. A behavitive, such as the expression of an apology or condolence, relates a language user's behavior to social circumstances. And so on.

One of the dominant themes of ordinary language philosophy is its method of resolving philosophical problems by investigating key terms that can give rise to conceptual puzzles and paradoxes and then showing how such problems disappear when we clarify the ways in which these terms are actually used in everyday discourse. Thus, Wittgenstein, who would probably have rejected the label of ordinary language philosopher, argues in *Philosophical Investigations* §§246, 288, and 303 that, contrary to egocentric epistemologies, I cannot know, let alone know with privileged access to a special order of facts, that I am in pain, whereas others can know this about me only indirectly through observation and inference. The reason, according to Wittgenstein, is that the philosophical grammar of the word "know," as it is used in everyday linguistic practice, or in what Wittgenstein refers to as its nonphilosophical "language games," entails that I cannot know something unless I can also doubt it, where, presumably, I can never intelligibly doubt that or wonder whether I am in pain.

Naming, Reference, and Predication

The concepts of naming, reference, and predication are central to the philosophy of language, regardless of whether linguistic expression is understood from the standpoint of ideal, transcendent, or ordinary language. These are among the most fundamental problems for any semantic theory.

Analytic philosophy of language has among its labors trying to understand exactly how names name things, how it is possible to refer to objects, and how properties are predicated of objects in describing states of affairs. The proper linguistic analysis of naming and predication offers as a further dividend the prospect that by clarifying the meaning of language it may be possible simultaneously to settle metaphysical questions about what kinds of things must exist in order to be represented in language; the ontological or existence status of what can be referred to; and the entities, if any, corresponding to grammatical parts of speech other than nouns and pronouns, such as adjectives, adverbs, and the like, and the logical relations by which they may be connected.

How does a name refer to an object? What do we do when we name something? Naming is a familiar practice, which any child choosing a name for a goldfish knows how to accomplish. But it is often the most basic kinds of activities that we are inclined to take for granted that provide an opportunity for philosophical reflection.

When we consider a child naming the goldfish, there is not much drama to behold. The child might mentally decide that the fish from now on is to be called "Goldie" and may but need not actually say the name aloud, perhaps while pointing at the creature in its fishbowl. The pointing by itself, whether mental or involving the movement of a finger, does not seem necessary or sufficient for naming to take place. Certainly, there is nothing essential about extending a finger that guarantees the attachment of the name to the object. Wittgenstein, in *Philosophical Investigations,* emphasizes that trying to define, or to teach or learn, the name of an object ostensively by pointing at the object that is supposed to be named, underdetermines reference to a specific object. How do we know whether the child in pointing at the goldfish and uttering the name "Goldie" is naming the fish, as opposed to the color of the fish, a part of the fish such as its eyes or scales, the fishbowl, the space occupied by the fish in the water, or anything else in the vicinity, or, for that matter, anywhere else in the world?

Wittgenstein further tries to refute the idea that reference can be achieved by means of internal or mental ostension in what has come to be known as the *private language argument* (this volume, 64–76). There Wittgenstein argues that there can be no semantically private psychological naming of objects because naming requires *criteria of correctness* by which it is possible to know in practice whether the same object is being named by the same name on different occasions. The naming of publicly observable objects admits of such criteria, but where private mental objects are concerned, Wittgenstein holds that in the nature of the case there is no way to distinguish between actually following a rule to use the same name for the same object and merely believing that one is following the rule. He compares the problem of trying to break outside the circle of beliefs that the same object is being named by the same object, in the absence of more objective criteria of correctness, to reading several copies of the same morning newspaper to verify that the information it reports is true.

The difficulty of understanding naming in terms of physical or mental ostension, if the objection is correct, leaves only a few options for semantic theory. Wittgenstein, in later sections of *Philosophical Investigations,* explains naming in pragmatic terms as something we do as part of the *form of life* in which we are engaged, in *language games* that integrate linguistic and nonlinguistic activities, by which we live our lives. Yet it is compatible with, and even suggested by some of Wittgenstein's discussion of these topics, that the *intentionality* or "aboutness" of thought and language is a primitive, conceptually irreducible relation that obtains intrinsically between thought and its intended objects, and derivatively between language use and the objects to which language refers.

Russell, in his influential (1905) paper, "On Denoting" (this volume, 33–40) presents a Fregean theory of reference for *definite descriptions.* Unlike Frege, Russell distinguishes between proper names, such as "Aristotle," and definite descriptions, such as "the first person to walk on the moon." The meaning of a proper name on this account follows Frege's thesis that sense determines reference. A name names an object, according to the *description theory of reference,* by abbreviating the long list of properties that collectively describe and thereby distinguish it from other objects, by virtue of being uniquely true of the object named. The properties constitute the sense of the name, which determine the object designated as the name's reference. Russell's theory regards proper names as disguised definite descriptions and reduces the meaning of definite descriptions to three conditions. The sentence, "The first person to walk on the moon was an American," is interpreted by Russell as involving (1) an *existence* condition, here that there exists at least one person who was first to walk on the moon; (2) a *uniqueness* condition, in this case that there exists exactly one or no more than one person who was first to walk on the moon; and (3) the *predication* of a property to the existent object uniquely determined by conditions (1) and (2); in this case, that the object in question has the property of being an American. The uniqueness condition in Russell's analysis specifies enough of the sense of a definite description to distinguish it from every other object, so that the individual reference of a proper name to a particular object is explained if proper names abbreviate definite descriptions.

The description theory of reference has been criticized on several grounds. It was unchallenged until the publication of P. F. Strawson's (1950) essay, "On Referring" (this volume, 41–54). Strawson offers minor technical objections, and the central complaint that Russell's existence condition in analyzing definite descriptions appears more reasonably understood as *presupposed* by the use of a sentence to make a statement, rather than *implied* by a sentence considered only as a form of words independently of its use. Strawson's critique, answered by Russell in a later (1959) essay, "Mr. Strawson on Referring," calls attention to the uses of language as opposed to static linguistic structures in the abstract. Russell's theory of definite descriptions is also clearly unsatisfactory if it is supposed to require language users to be in a position to substitute definite descriptions for names when an object is named. A speaker might not know enough of an object's properties to distinguish it from other objects, or might have mistaken beliefs about the object, falsely attributing properties to one object that actually belong to another.

An alternative to the description theory that has seemed attractive to many analytic philosophers of language is known as the *causal* or *historical theory of reference*. Dispensing altogether with descriptions as the meanings of names, the causal theory of reference shifts the attention in philosophy of language to the external circumstances surrounding linguistic practice. When a name is used for the first time, a causal network of uses of the name to refer to an object is initiated, as one language user sees or hears the name used and passes it along to others in the network. The meaning of a name can then be understood, not as a matter of being able to substitute a description of an object's properties in specifying a name's sense, but of tracing the right sort of causal connections from link to link in the network back to the particular object referred to by the name. The causal or historical theory of reference has enjoyed a wide and enthusiastic following, in part because it seems to hold out what some philosophers like Frege regard as the welcome promise of eliminating mental concepts from philosophical semantics. Yet Saul A. Kripke, in his lectures on *Naming and Necessity* (1980), in which the causal "picture" of naming is presented as an alternative to description theory, explicitly requires that all uses of a name be made with the *intention* to refer to the object named, which seems to make psychological states indispensable in the theory of reference.

Controversies in Linguistic Analysis

A fundamental debate persists in contemporary philosophy of language concerning the choice between *intensional* and *extensional* linguistic theory. An *intensional semantics* defines meaning in terms of properties, as the Fregean sense of a proper name or sentence. *Extensional semantics* defines meaning in terms of existent entities that stand as the reference of a proper name or sentence.

An important implication of intensional semantics is that it suggests the possibility of referring to and truly predicating properties of nonexistent objects. Frege's semantics rejects this type of theory in holding that in ordinary language some names and sentences can have sense but lack reference. An obvious source is fictional discourse, in which we seem to speak of objects like Shakespeare's "Othello" or Philip Roth's "Portnoy," which for Frege have sense, by virtue of being associated with sets of properties described by the authors, but lack reference, because no existent entity is named. The history of science contains numerous nonexistent-object-denoting terms and phrases, such as "phlogiston," "vortices," and "philosopher's stone." In some intensional semantics, by contrast with mainstream extensional theories, it is possible to refer and truly predicate properties to existent and nonexistent objects. Analytic philosophers of language today tend to fall on one side of the intensional-extensional dispute or the other, and while most are probably extensionalist in outlook, there is a growing interest in intensionalist semantics.

Analytic philosophy of language recognizes a difference between intensional and extensional linguistic contexts. An *extensional context* is one that supports the intersubstitution of coreferential terms without changing its truth value. Truth-preserving intersubstitutability in an extensional context is in turn interpreted as a criterion of coreferentiality. For example, the context, "_____ kicked a cat," is extensional. If we complete the context by inserting a proper name like "Mark Twain," and then exchanging it for the coreferential proper name, "Samuel Clemens," referring to the same person, then we do not change the completed sentence's truth value. By contrast, the context, "Mary believes that _____ kicked a cat," is intensional. We can change a true completed sentence involving this context to a false sentence, depending on what Mary happens to believe. If Mary believes that Mark Twain kicked a cat, it will not necessarily follow that she believes that Samuel Clemens kicked a cat, if she does not also believe that Mark Twain is the same person as Samuel Clemens. The logically more complicated behavior of intensional linguistic contexts has led some philosophers of language to reject them altogether, and to propose ingenious if not always successful methods of doing away with intensional contexts or reducing them to purely extensional contexts. An important example is W. V. Quine in his invaluable (1960) book, *Word and Object,* in which he proposes to explain meaning in philosophically behavioristic terms via the concept of *stimulus meanings* and advocates a "flight from intension." But other philosophers of language have seen intensional contexts and an intensional approach to linguistic analysis as essential in understanding psychology. In this topic area, there is a fruitful intersection of interests in philosophy of language and philosophy of mind.

   Another problem at the crossroads of philosophical semantics and psychology is the question: Which comes first, thought or language? Is language required or presupposed by thought, or is language only a vehicle for the expression of thought? Philosophers who emphasize the intentionality of thought usually argue that thought precedes and is sometimes conveyed by language, while a new wave of theorists impressed by the mechanical model of mind as a living information-processing computer are inclined to hold that thought cannot exist without at least some sort of innate neurophysiological language. The view is typified by Jerry A. Fodor's (1975) book, *The Language of Thought.* Noam Chomsky's conclusion that impressively rapid language learning in children can best be explained by appeal to the existence of an innate *transformational grammar* hardwired into the brain as part of the human genetic endowment, similarly gives language logical precedence over thought in his (1966) *Syntactic Structures* and (1972) *Studies on Semantics in Generative Grammar.* The issue is by no means decided, however, and represents a focus of continuing philosophical dispute.

   There are also philosophical difficulties about the correct analysis of *indexical* or *demonstrative terms* like "this," "that," "here," "now," and "I," that shift reference depending on context of use and speaker. Because of its connection with personal identity and the philosophy of mind, the meaning of the personal pronoun "I" is especially important and controversial. The pragmatic determination of *anaphoric reference,* of the antecedents of pronouns holistically in contexts of language, invites similar inquiry. The program to develop a philosophy of language that tries to explain indexicals among other linguistic phenomena by distinguishing among *utterer's meaning, word meaning,* and *sentence meaning* is generally associated with the philosophical position outlined in the essays collected in Grice's (1989) *Studies in the Way of Words.* The interpretation of simile, metaphor, analogy, irony, and the aesthetics, music, and poetry of language; the requirements of translation from one language into another; the relation of logic to language; and the ontology of sentences and propositions are among the longstanding problems of contemporary linguistic theory.

   Philosophers have similarly been interested in semantic paradoxes, such as the *liar sentence,* which says of itself that it is false and seems as a result to be true if and only if it is false.

Analytic linguistic theorists have considered semantic paradoxes as pointing toward the need to articulate provisions in the concept of meaning to avoid contradiction by establishing truth conventions for meaning, and prohibiting any sentence from expressing its own truth value. A notable contributor to this discussion is Donald Davidson, in his essay "Truth and Meaning" and other writings published in his (1984) *Inquiries into Truth and Interpretation.* Here the controversy about whether meaning depends on truth, or truth on meaning, like the precedence of thought over language versus language over thought, is a conceptual watershed that is likely to divide analytic philosophy of language far into its future.

REFERENCES

Austin, J. L. 1962. *How to Do Things with Words.* Ed. by J. O. Urmson. New York: Oxford University Press.
Chomsky, Noam. 1966. *Syntactic Structures.* The Hague: Mouton.
———. 1972. *Studies on Semantics in Generative Grammar.* The Hague: Mouton.
Davidson, Donald. 1984. *Inquiries into Truth and Interpretation.* Oxford: Clarendon Press.
Fodor, Jerry A. 1975. *The Language of Thought.* Cambridge: Harvard University Press.
Frege, Gottlob. 1879. *Begriffsschrift: Eine der arithmetischen nachgebildete Formelsprache des reinen Denkens.* Halle Germany: L. Nebert. Translated by Terrell Ward Bynum under the title *Conceptual Notation and Related Articles.* Oxford: Clarendon Press, 1972.
———. 1892. "Über Sinn und Bedeutung," *Zeitschrift für Philosophie und philosophische Kritik* 100. Translated by Max Black under the title "On Sense and Reference." In *Translations from the Philosophical Writings of Gottlob Frege,* edited by P. T. Geach and Max Black. Oxford: Blackwell, 1970, 56–78.
Grice, H. P. 1989. *Studies in the Way of Words.* Cambridge: Harvard University Press.
Hacker, P. M. S. 1996. *Wittgenstein's Place in Twentieth-Century Analytic Philosophy.* Oxford: Basil Blackwell.
Kripke, Saul A. 1980. *Naming and Necessity.* Cambridge: Harvard University Press.
Quine, W. V. 1960. *Word and Object.* Cambridge: MIT Press.
Russell, Bertrand. 1905. "On Denoting." *Mind* 14: 479–93.
———. 1959. "Mr. Strawson on Referring." In *My Philosophical Development.* London: Allen and Unwin, 238–45.
———. 1985. *The Philosophy of Logical Atomism.* Edited by David Pears. LaSalle, IL: Open Court.
Whitehead, A. N., and Russell, Bertrand. 1925–27. *Principia Mathematica,* 2d ed. [first edition 1910–13]. Cambridge: Cambridge University Press.
Wittgenstein, Ludwig. 1922. *Tractatus Logico-Philosophicus.* Edited by C. K. Ogden. London: Routledge and Kegan Paul.
———. 1957. *Philosophical Investigations.* Edited and translated by G. E. M. Anscombe, 3d ed. Oxford: Blackwell.
———. 1958. *The Blue and Brown Books.* Oxford: Blackwell.

On Sense and Reference 1

GOTTLOB FREGE

EQUALITY[1] GIVES RISE to challenging questions which are not altogether easy to answer. Is it a relation? A relation between objects, or between names or signs of objects? In my *Begriffsschrift*[2] I assumed the latter. The reasons which seem to favour this are the following: $a = a$ and $a = b$ are obviously statements of differing cognitive value; $a = a$ holds *a priori* and, according to Kant, is to be labelled analytic, while statements of the form $a = b$ often contain very valuable extensions of our knowledge and cannot always be established *a priori*. The discovery that the rising sun is not new every morning, but always the same, was one of the most fertile astronomical discoveries. Even to-day the identification of a small planet or a comet is not always a matter of course. Now if we were to regard equality as a relation between that which the names 'a' and 'b' designate, it would seem that $a = b$ could not differ from $a = a$ (i.e., provided $a = b$ is true). A relation would thereby be expressed of a thing to itself, and indeed one in which each thing stands to itself but to no other thing. What is intended to be said by $a = b$ seems to be that the signs or names 'a' and 'b' designate the same thing, so that those signs themselves would be under discussion; a relation between them would be asserted. But this relation would hold between the names or signs only in so far as they named or designated something. It would be mediated by the connexion of each of the two signs with the same designated thing. But this is arbitrary. Nobody can be forbidden to use any arbitrarily producible event or object as a sign for something. In that case the sentence $a = b$ would no longer refer to the subject matter, but only to its mode of designation; we would express no proper knowledge by its means. But in many cases this is just what we want to do. If the sign 'a' is distinguished from the sign 'b' only as object (here, by means of its shape), not as sign (i.e., not by the manner in which it designates something), the cognitive value of $a = a$ becomes essentially equal to that of $a = b$, provided $a = b$ is true. A difference can arise only if the difference between the signs corresponds to a difference in the mode of presentation of that which is designated. Let a, b, c be the lines connecting the vertices of a triangle with the midpoints of the opposite sides. The point of intersection of a and b is then the same as the point of intersection of b and c. So we have different designations for the same point, and these names ('point of intersection of a and b,' 'point of intersection of b and c') likewise indicate the mode of presentation; and hence the statement contains actual knowledge.

It is natural, now, to think of there being connected with a sign (name, combination of words, letter), besides that to which the sign refers, which may be called the reference of the sign, also what I should like to call the *sense* of the sign, wherein the mode of presentation is contained. In our example, accordingly, the reference of the expressions 'the point of intersection of a and b' and 'the point of intersection of b and c' would be the same, but not their senses. The reference of 'evening star' would be the same as that of 'morning star,' but not the sense.

It is clear from the context that by 'sign' and 'name' I have here understood any designation representing a proper name, which thus has as its reference a definite object (this word taken in the widest range), but not a concept or a relation, which shall be discussed further in another article.[3] The designation of a single object can also consist of several words or other signs. For brevity, let every such designation be called a proper name.

Translations from the Philosophical Writings of Gottlob Frege, ed. and trans. P. Geach and M. Black (New York: Philosophical Library, 1952), 56–78. Originally published as "Über Sinn und Bedeutung" in *Zeitschrift für Philosophie und philosophische Kritik* 100 (1892): 25–50. Reprinted by permission of the Philosophical Library.

The sense of a proper name is grasped by everybody who is sufficiently familiar with the language or totality of designations to which it belongs;[4] but this serves to illuminate only a single aspect of the reference, supposing it to have one. Comprehensive knowledge of the reference would require us to be able to say immediately whether any given sense belongs to it. To such knowledge we never attain.

The regular connexion between a sign, its sense, and its reference is of such a kind that to the sign there corresponds a definite sense and to that in turn a definite reference, while to a given reference (an object) there does not belong only a single sign. The same sense has different expressions in different languages or even in the same language. To be sure, exceptions to this regular behaviour occur. To every expression belonging to a complete totality of signs, there should certainly correspond a definite sense; but natural languages often do not satisfy this condition, and one must be content if the same word has the same sense in the same context. It may perhaps be granted that every grammatically well-formed expression representing a proper name always has a sense. But this is not to say that to the sense there also corresponds a reference. The words 'the celestial body most distant from the Earth' have a sense, but it is very doubtful if they also have a reference. The expression 'the least rapidly convergent series' has a sense; but it is known to have no reference, since for every given convergent series, another convergent, but less rapidly convergent, series can be found. In grasping a sense, one is not certainly assured of a reference.

If words are used in the ordinary way, what one intends to speak of is their reference. It can also happen, however, that one wishes to talk about the words themselves or their sense. This happens, for instance, when the words of another are quoted. One's own words then first designate words of the other speaker, and only the latter have their usual reference. We then have signs of signs. In writing, the words are in this case enclosed in quotation marks. Accordingly, a word standing between quotation marks must not be taken as having its ordinary reference.

In order to speak of the sense of an expression 'A' one may simply use the phrase 'the sense of the expression "A"'. In reported speech one talks about the sense, e.g., of another person's remarks. It is quite clear that in this way of speaking words do not have their customary reference but designate what is usually their sense. In order to have a short expression, we will say: In reported speech, words are used *indirectly* or have their *indirect* reference. We distinguish accordingly the *customary* from the *indirect* reference of a word; and its *customary* sense from its *indirect* sense. The indirect reference of a word is accordingly its customary sense. Such exceptions must always be borne in mind if the mode of connexion between sign, sense, and reference in particular cases is to be correctly understood.

The reference and sense of a sign are to be distinguished from the associated idea. If the reference of a sign is an object perceivable by the senses, my idea of it is an internal image,[5] arising from memories of sense impressions which I have had and acts, both internal and external, which I have performed. Such an idea is often saturated with feeling; the clarity of its separate parts varies and oscillates. The same sense is not always connected, even in the same man, with the same idea. The idea is subjective: one man's idea is not that of another. There result, as a matter of course, a variety of differences in the ideas associated with the same sense. A painter, a horseman, and a zoologist will probably connect different ideas with the name 'Bucephalus.' This constitutes an essential distinction between the idea and the sign's sense, which may be the common property of many and therefore is not a part of a mode of the individual mind. For one can hardly deny that mankind has a common store of thoughts which is transmitted from one generation to another.[6]

In the light of this, one need have no scruples in speaking simply of *the* sense, whereas in the case of an idea one must, strictly speaking, add to whom it belongs and at what time. It might perhaps be said: Just as one man connects this idea, and another that idea, with the same word, so also one man can associate this sense and another that sense. But there still remains a difference in the mode of connexion. They are not prevented from grasping the same sense; but they cannot have the same idea. *Si duo idem faciunt, non est idem.* If two persons picture the same thing, each still has his own idea. It is indeed sometimes possible to establish differences in the ideas, or even in the sensations, of different men; but an exact comparison is not possible, because we cannot have both ideas together in the same consciousness.

The reference of a proper name is the object itself which we designate by its means; the idea, which we have in that case, is wholly subjective; in between lies the sense, which is indeed no longer subjective like the idea, but is yet not the object itself. The following analogy will perhaps clarify these relationships. Somebody observes the Moon through a telescope. I compare the Moon itself to the reference; it is the object of the observation, mediated by the real image projected by the object glass in the interior of the telescope, and by the retinal image of the observer. The former I compare to the sense, the latter is like the idea or experience. The optical image in the telescope is indeed one-sided and dependent upon the standpoint of observation; but it is still objective, inasmuch as it can be used by several observers. At any rate it could be arranged for several to use it simultaneously. But each one would have his own retinal image. On account of the diverse shapes of the observers' eyes, even a geometrical congruence could hardly be achieved, and an actual coincidence would be out of the question. This analogy might be developed still further, by assuming A's retinal image made visible to B; or A might also see his own retinal image in a mirror. In this way we might perhaps show how an idea can itself be taken as an object, but as such is not for the observer what it directly is for the person having the idea. But to pursue this would take us too far afield.

We can now recognize three levels of difference between words, expressions, or whole sentences. The difference may concern at most the ideas, or the sense but not the reference, or, finally, the reference as well. With respect to the first level, it is to be noted that, on account of the uncertain connexion of ideas with words, a difference may hold for one person, which another does not find. The difference between a translation and the original text should properly not overstep the first level. To the possible differences here belong also the colouring and shading which poetic eloquence seeks to give to the sense. Such colouring and shading are not objective, and must be evoked by each hearer or reader according to the hints of the poet or the speaker. Without some affinity in human ideas art would certainly be impossible; but it can never be exactly determined how far the intentions of the poet are realized.

In what follows there will be no further discussion of ideas and experiences; they have been mentioned here only to ensure that the idea aroused in the hearer by a word shall not be confused with its sense or its reference.

To make short and exact expressions possible, let the following phraseology be established:

A proper name (word, sign, sign combination, expression) *expresses* its sense, *stands for* or *designates* its reference. By means of a sign we express its sense and designate its reference.

Idealists or sceptics will perhaps long since have objected: 'You talk, without further ado, of the Moon as an object; but how do you know that the name 'the Moon' has any reference? How do you know that anything whatsoever has a reference?' I reply that when we say 'the Moon,' we do not intend to speak of our idea of the Moon, nor are we satisfied with the sense alone, but we presuppose a reference. To assume that in the sentence 'The Moon is smaller than the Earth' the idea of the Moon is in question, would be flatly to misunderstand the sense. If this is what the speaker wanted, he would use the phrase 'my idea of the Moon.' Now we can of course be mistaken in the presupposition, and such mistakes have indeed occurred. But the question whether the presupposition is perhaps always mistaken need not be answered here; in order to justify mention of the reference of a sign it is enough, at first, to point out our intention in speaking or thinking. (We must then add the reservation: provided such reference exists.)

So far we have considered the sense and reference only of such expressions, words, or signs as we have called proper names. We now inquire concerning the sense and reference for an entire declarative sentence. Such a sentence contains a thought.[7] Is this thought, now, to be regarded as its sense or its reference? Let us assume for the time being that the sentence has reference. If we now replace one word of the sentence by another having the same reference, but a different sense, this can have no bearing upon the reference of the sentence. Yet we can see that in such a case the thought changes; since, e.g., the thought in the sentence 'The morning star is a body illuminated by the Sun' differs from that in the sentence 'The evening star is a body illuminated by the Sun.' Anybody who did not know that the evening star is the morning star might hold the one thought to be true, the other false. The thought, accordingly, cannot be the reference of the sentence, but must rather be considered as the sense. What is the position now with regard to the reference? Have we a right even to inquire about it? Is it possible that a sentence as a whole has only a sense, but no reference? At any rate, one might expect that such sentences occur, just as there are parts of sentences having sense but no reference. And sentences which contain proper names without reference will be of this kind. The sentence 'Odysseus was set ashore at Ithaca while sound asleep' obviously has a sense. But since it is doubtful whether the name 'Odysseus,' occurring therein, has reference, it is also doubtful whether the whole sentence has one. Yet it is certain, nevertheless, that anyone who seriously took the sentence to be true or false would ascribe to the name 'Odysseus' a reference, not merely a sense; for it is of the reference of the name that the predicate is affirmed or denied. Whoever does not admit the name has reference can neither apply nor withhold the predicate. But in that case it would be superfluous to advance to the reference of the name; one could be satisfied with the sense, if one wanted to go no further than the thought. If it were a question only of the sense of the sentence, the thought, it would be unnecessary to bother with the reference of a part of the sentence; only the sense, not the reference, of the part is relevant to the sense of the whole sentence. The thought remains the same whether 'Odysseus' has reference or not. The fact that we concern ourselves at all about the reference of a part of the sentence indicates that we generally recognize and expect a reference for the sentence itself. The thought loses value for us as soon as we recognize that the reference of one of its parts is missing. We are therefore justified in not being satisfied with the sense of a sentence, and in inquiring also as to its reference. But now why do we want every proper name to have not only a sense, but also a reference? Why is the thought not enough for us? Because, and to the extent that, we are concerned with its truth value. This is not always the case. In hearing an epic poem, for instance, apart from the euphony of the language we are interested only in

the sense of the sentences and the images and feelings thereby aroused. The question of truth would cause us to abandon aesthetic delight for an attitude of scientific investigation. Hence it is a matter of no concern to us whether the name 'Odysseus,' for instance, has reference, so long as we accept the poem as a work of art.[8] It is the striving for truth that drives us always to advance from the sense to the reference.

We have seen that the reference of a sentence may always be sought, whenever the reference of its components is involved; and that this is the case when and only when we are inquiring after the truth value.

We are therefore driven into accepting the *truth value* of a sentence as constituting its reference. By the truth value of a sentence I understand the circumstance that it is true or false. There are no further truth values. For brevity I call the one the True, the other the False. Every declarative sentence concerned with the reference of its words is therefore to be regarded as a proper name, and its reference, if it has one, is either the True or the False. These two objects are recognized, if only implicitly, by everybody who judges something to be true—and so even by a sceptic. The designation of the truth values as objects may appear to be an arbitrary fancy or perhaps a mere play upon words, from which no profound consequences could be drawn. What I mean by an object can be more exactly discussed only in connexion with concept and relation. I will reserve this for another article.[9] But so much should already be clear, that in every judgment,[10] no matter how trivial, the step from the level of thoughts to the level of reference (the objective) has already been taken.

One might be tempted to regard the relation of the thought to the True not as that of sense to reference, but rather as that of subject to predicate. One can, indeed, say: 'The thought, that 5 is a prime number, is true.' But closer examination shows that nothing more has been said than in the simple sentence '5 is a prime number.' The truth claim arises in each case from the form of the declarative sentence, and when the latter lacks its usual force, e.g., in the mouth of an actor upon the stage, even the sentence 'The thought that 5 is a prime number is true' contains only a thought, and indeed the same thought as the simple '5 is a prime number.' It follows that the relation of the thought to the True may not be compared with that of subject to predicate. Subject and predicate (understood in the logical sense) are indeed elements of thought; they stand on the same level for knowledge. By combining subject and predicate, one reaches only a thought, never passes from sense to reference, never from a thought to its truth value. One moves at the same level but never advances from one level to the next. A truth value cannot be a part of a thought, any more than, say, the Sun can, for it is not a sense but an object.

If our supposition that the reference of a sentence is its truth value is correct, the latter must remain unchanged when a part of the sentence is replaced by an expression having the same reference. And this is in fact the case. Leibniz gives the definition: '*Eadem sunt, quae sibi mutuo substitui possunt, salva veritate.*' What else but truth value could be found, that belongs quite generally to every sentence if the reference of its components is relevant, and remains unchanged by substitutions of the kind in question?

If now the truth value of a sentence is its reference, then on the one hand all true sentences have the same reference and so, on the other hand, do all false sentences. From this we see that in the reference of the sentence all that is specific is obliterated. We can never be concerned only with the reference of a sentence; but again the mere thought alone yields no knowledge, but only the thought together with its reference, i.e., its truth value. Judgments can be regarded as advances from a thought to a truth value. Naturally this cannot be a definition. Judgment is something quite peculiar and incomparable. One might also say that judgments are distinctions of parts within truth values. Such distinction occurs by a return to the thought. To every sense belonging to a truth value there would correspond its own manner of analysis. However, I have here used the word 'part' in a special sense. I have in fact transferred the relation between the parts and the whole of the sentence to its reference, by calling the reference of a word part of the reference of the sentence, if the word itself is a part of the sentence. This way of speaking can certainly be attacked, because the whole reference and one part of it do not suffice to determine the remainder, and because the word 'part' is already used in another sense of bodies. A special term would need to be invented.

The supposition that the truth value of a sentence is its reference shall now be put to further test. We have found that the truth value of a sentence remains unchanged when an expression is replaced by another having the same reference: but we have not yet considered the case in which the expression to be replaced is itself a sentence. Now if our view is correct, the truth value of a sentence containing another as part must remain unchanged when the part is replaced by another sentence having the same truth value. Exceptions are to be expected when the whole sentence or its part is direct or indirect quotation; for in such cases, as we have seen, the words do not have their customary reference. In direct quotation, a sentence designates another sentence, and in indirect quotation a thought.

We are thus led to consider subordinate sentences or clauses. These occur as parts of a sentence complex, which is, from the logical standpoint, likewise a sentence—a main sentence. But here we meet the question whether it is also true of the subordinate sentence that its reference is a truth value. Of indirect quotation we already know the opposite. Grammarians view subordinate clauses as representatives of parts of sentences and divide them accordingly into noun clauses, adjective clauses, adverbial clauses. This might generate the supposition that the reference of a subordinate clause was not a truth value but rather of the same kind as the reference of a noun or adjective or adverb—in short, of a part of a sentence, whose sense was not a thought but only a part of a thought. Only a more thorough investigation can clarify the issue. In so doing, we shall not follow the grammatical categories strictly, but rather group together what is logically of the same kind. Let us first search for cases in which the sense of the subordinate clause, as we have just supposed, is not an independent thought.

The case of an abstract[11] noun clause, introduced by 'that,' includes the case of indirect quotation, in which we have seen the words to have their indirect reference coinciding with what is customarily their sense. In this case, then, the subordinate clause has for its reference a thought, not a truth value; as sense not a thought, but the sense of the words 'the thought, that . . . ,' which is only a part of the thought in the entire complex sentence. This happens after 'say,' 'hear,' 'be of the opinion,' 'be convinced,' 'conclude,' and similar words.[12] There is a different, and indeed somewhat complicated, situation after words like 'perceive,' 'know,' 'fancy,' which are to be considered later.

That in the cases of the first kind the reference of the subordinate clause is in fact the thought can also be recognized by seeing that it is indifferent to the truth of the whole whether the subordinate clause is true or false. Let us compare, for instance, the two sentences 'Copernicus believed that the planetary orbits are circles' and 'Copernicus believed that the apparent motion of the sun is produced by the real motion of the Earth.' One subordinate clause can be substituted for the other without harm to the truth. The main clause and the subordinate clause together have as their sense only a single thought, and the truth of the whole includes neither the truth nor the untruth of the subordinate clause. In such cases it is not permissible to replace one expression in the subordinate clause by another having the same customary reference, but only by one having the same indirect reference, i.e., the same customary sense. If somebody were to conclude: The reference of a sentence is not its truth value, for in that case it could always be replaced by another sentence of the same truth value; he would prove too much; one might just as well claim that the reference of 'morning star' is not Venus, since one may not always say 'Venus' in place of 'morning star.' One has the right to conclude only that the reference of a sentence is not *always* its truth value, and that 'morning star' does not always stand for the planet Venus, viz. when the word has its indirect reference. An exception of such a kind occurs in the subordinate clause just considered which has a thought as its reference.

If one says 'It seems that . . . ' one means 'It seems to me that . . .' or 'I think that . . .'. We therefore have the same case again. The situation is similar in the case of expressions such as 'to be pleased,' 'to regret,' 'to approve,' 'to blame,' 'to hope,' 'to fear.' If, toward the end of the battle of Waterloo,[13] Wellington was glad that the Prussians were coming, the basis for his joy was a conviction. Had he been deceived, he would have been no less pleased so long as his illusion lasted; and before he became so convinced he could not have been pleased that the Prussians were coming—even though in fact they might have been already approaching.

Just as a conviction or a belief is the ground of a feeling, it can, as in inference, also be the ground of a conviction. In the sentence: 'Columbus inferred from the roundness of the Earth that he could reach India by travelling towards the west,' we have as the reference of the parts two thoughts, that the Earth is round, and that Columbus by travelling to the west could reach India. All that is relevant here is that Columbus was convinced of both, and that the one conviction was a ground for the other. Whether the Earth is really round, and whether Columbus could really reach India by travelling to the west, are immaterial to the truth of our sentence; but it is not immaterial whether we replace 'the Earth' by 'the planet which is accompanied by a moon whose diameter is greater than the fourth part of its own.' Here also we have the indirect reference of the words.

Adverbial final beginning 'in order that' also belong here; for obviously the purpose is a thought; therefore: indirect reference for the words, subjunctive mood.

A subordinate clause with 'that' after 'command,' 'ask,' 'forbid,' would appear in direct speech as an imperative. Such a clause has no reference but only a sense. A command, a request, are indeed not thoughts, yet they stand on the same level as thoughts. Hence in subordinate clauses depending upon 'command,' 'ask,' etc., words have their indirect reference. The reference of such a clause is therefore not a truth value but a command, a request, and so forth.

The case is similar for the dependent question in phrases such as 'doubt whether,' 'not to know what.' It is easy to see that here also the words are to be taken to have their indirect reference. Dependent clauses expressing questions and beginning with 'who,' 'what,' 'where,' 'when,' 'how,' 'by what means,' etc., seem at times to approximate very closely to adverbial clauses in which words have their customary references. These cases are distinguished linguistically [in German] by the mood of the verb. With the subjunctive, we have a dependent question and indirect reference of the words, so that a proper name cannot in general be replaced by another name of the same object.

In the cases so far considered the words of the subordinate clauses had their indirect reference, and this made it clear that the reference of the subordinate clause itself was indirect, i.e., not a truth value but a thought, a command, a request, a question. The subordinate clause could be regarded as a noun, indeed one could say: as a proper name of that thought, that command, etc., which it represented in the context of the sentence structure.

We now come to other subordinate clauses, in which the words do have their customary reference without however a thought occurring as sense and a truth value as reference. How this is possible is best made clear by examples.

Whoever discovered the elliptic form of the planetary orbits died in misery.

If the sense of the subordinate clause were here a thought, it would have to be possible to express it also in a separate sentence. But this does not work, because the grammatical subject 'whoever' has no independent sense and only mediates the relation with the consequent clause 'died in misery.' For this reason the sense of the subordinate clause is not a complete thought, and its reference is Kepler, not a truth value. One might object that the sense of the whole does contain a thought as part, viz. that there was somebody who first discovered the elliptic form of the planetary orbits; for whoever takes the whole to be true cannot deny this part. This is undoubtedly so; but only because otherwise the dependent clause 'whoever discovered the elliptic form of the planetary orbits' would have no reference. If anything is asserted there is always an obvious presupposition that the simple or compound proper names used have reference. If one therefore asserts 'Kepler died in misery,' there is a presupposition that the name 'Kepler' designates something; but it does not follow that the sense of the sentence 'Kepler died in misery' contains the thought that the name 'Kepler' designates something. If this were the case the negation would have to run not

Kepler did not die in misery

but

Kepler did not die in misery, or the name 'Kepler' has no reference.

That the name 'Kepler' designates something is just as much a presupposition for the assertion

Kepler died in misery

as for the contrary assertion. Now languages have the fault of containing expressions which fail to designate an object (although their grammatical form seems to qualify them for that purpose) because the truth of some sentences is a prerequisite. Thus it depends on the truth of the sentence:

There was someone who discovered the elliptic form of the planetary orbits

whether the subordinate clause

Whoever discovered the elliptic form of the planetary orbits

really designates an object or only seems to do so while having in fact no reference. And thus it may appear as if our subordinate clause contained as a part of its sense the thought that there was somebody who discovered the elliptic form of the planetary orbits. If this were right the negation would run:

Either whoever discovered the elliptic form of the planetary orbits did not die in misery or there was nobody who discovered the elliptic form of the planetary orbits.

This arises from an imperfection of language, from which even the symbolic language of mathematical analysis is not altogether free; even there combinations of symbols can occur that seem to stand for something but have (at least so far) no reference, e.g., divergent infinite series. This can be avoided, e.g., by means of the special stipulation that divergent infinite series shall stand for the number 0. A logically perfect language (*Begriffsschrift*) should satisfy the conditions, that every expression grammatically well constructed as a proper name out of signs already introduced shall in fact designate an object, and that no new sign shall be introduced as a proper name without being secured a reference. The logic books contain warnings against logical mistakes arising from the ambiguity of expressions. I regard as no less pertinent a warning against apparent proper names having no reference. The history of mathematics supplies errors which have arisen in this way. This lends itself to demagogic abuse as easily as ambiguity—perhaps more easily.

'The will of the people' can serve as an example; for it is easy to establish that there is at any rate no generally accepted reference for this expression. It is therefore by no means unimportant to eliminate the source of these mistakes, at least in science, once and for all. Then such objections as the one discussed above would become impossible, because it could never depend upon the truth of a thought whether a proper name had a reference.

With the consideration of these noun clauses may be coupled that of types of adjective and adverbial clauses which are logically in close relation to them.

Adjective clauses also serve to construct compound proper names, though, unlike noun clauses, they are not sufficient by themselves for this purpose. These adjective clauses are to be regarded as equivalent to adjectives. Instead of 'the square root of 4 which is smaller than 0,' one can also say 'the negative square root of 4.' We have here the case of a compound proper name constructed from the expression for a concept with the help of the singular definite article. This is at any rate permissible if the concept applies to one and only one single object.[14]

Expressions for concepts can be so constructed that marks of a concept are given by adjective clauses as, in our example, by the clause 'which is smaller than 0.' It is evident that such an adjective clause cannot have a thought as sense or a truth value as reference, any more than the noun clause could. Its sense, which can also be expressed in many cases by a single adjective, is only a part of a thought. Here, as in the case of the noun clause, there is no independent subject and therefore no possibility of reproducing the sense of the subordinate clause in an independent sentence.

Places, instants, stretches of time, are, logically considered, objects; hence the linguistic designation of a definite place, a definite instant, or a stretch of time is to be regarded as a proper name. Now adverbial clauses of place and time can be used for the construction of such a proper name in a manner similar to that which we have seen in the case of noun and adjective clauses. In the same way, expressions for concepts bringing in places, etc., can be constructed. It is to be noted here also that the sense of these subordinate clauses cannot be reproduced in an independent sentence, since an essential component, viz. the determination of place

or time, is missing and is only indicated by a relative pronoun or a conjunction.[15]

In conditional clauses, also, there may usually be recognized to occur an indefinite indicator, having a similar correlate in the dependent clause. (We have already seen this occur in noun, adjective, and adverbial clauses.) In so far as each indicator refers to the other, both clauses together form a connected whole, which as a rule expresses only a single thought. In the sentence

If a number is less than 1 and greater than 0, its square is less than 1 and greater than 0

the component in question is 'a number' in the conditional clause and 'its' in the dependent clause. It is by means of this very indefiniteness that the sense acquires the generality expected of a law. It is this which is responsible for the fact that the antecedent clause alone has no complete thought as its sense and in combination with the consequent clause expresses one and only one thought, whose parts are no longer thoughts. It is, in general, incorrect to say that in the hypothetical judgment two judgments are put in reciprocal relationship. If this or something similar is said, the word 'judgment' is used in the same sense as I have connected with the word 'thought,' so that I would use the formulation: 'A hypothetical thought establishes a reciprocal relationship between two thoughts.' This could be true only if an indefinite indicator is absent;[16] but in such a case there would also be no generality.

If an instant of time is to be indefinitely indicated in both conditional and dependent clauses, this is often achieved merely by using the present tense of the verb, which in such a case however does not indicate the temporal present. This grammatical form is then the indefinite indicator in the main and subordinate clauses. An example of this is: 'When the Sun is in the tropic of Cancer, the longest day in the northern hemisphere occurs.' Here also, it is impossible to express the sense of the subordinate clause in a full sentence, because this sense is not a complete thought. If we say: 'The Sun is in the tropic of Cancer,' this would refer to our present time and thereby change the sense. Just as little is the sense of the main clause a thought; only the whole, composed of main and subordinate clauses, has such a sense. It may be added that several common components in the antecedent and consequent clauses may be indefinitely indicated.

It is clear that noun clauses with 'who' or 'what' and adverbial clauses with 'where,' 'when,' 'wherever,' 'whenever' are often to be interpreted as having the sense of conditional clauses, e.g., 'who touches pitch, defiles himself.'

Adjective clauses can also take the place of conditional clauses. Thus the sense of the sentence previously used can be given in the form 'The square of a number which is less than 1 and greater than 0 is less than 1 and greater than 0.'

The situation is quite different if the common component of the two clauses is designated by a proper name. In the sentence:

Napoleon, who recognized the danger to his right flank, himself led his guards against the enemy position

two thoughts are expressed:

1. Napoleon recognized the danger to his right flank
2. Napoleon himself led his guards against the enemy position.

When and where this happened is to be fixed only by the context, but is nevertheless to be taken as definitely determined thereby. If the entire sentence is uttered as an assertion, we thereby simultaneously assert both component sentences. If one of the parts is false, the whole is false. Here we have the case that the subordinate clause by itself has a complete thought as sense (if we complete it by indication of place and time). The reference of the subordinate clause is accordingly a truth value. We can therefore expect that it may be replaced, without harm to the truth value of the whole, by a sentence having the same truth value. This is indeed the case; but it is to be noticed that for purely grammatical reasons, its subject must be 'Napoleon,' for only then can it be brought into the form of an adjective clause belonging to 'Napoleon.' But if the demand that it be expressed in this form be waived, and the connexion be shown by 'and,' this restriction disappears.

Subsidiary clauses beginning with 'although' also express complete thoughts. This conjunction actu-

ally has no sense and does not change the sense of the clause but only illuminates it in a peculiar fashion.[17] We could indeed replace the conditional clause without harm to the truth of the whole by another of the same truth value; but the light in which the clause is placed by the conjunction might then easily appear unsuitable, as if a song with a sad subject were to be sung in a lively fashion.

In the last cases the truth of the whole included the truth of the component clauses. The case is different if a conditional clause expresses a complete thought by containing, in place of an indefinite indicator, a proper name or something which is to be regarded as equivalent. In the sentence

If the Sun has already risen, the sky is very cloudy

the time is the present, that is to say, definite. And the place is also to be thought of as definite. Here it can be said that a relation between the truth values of conditional and dependent clauses has been asserted, viz. such that the case does not occur in which the antecedent stands for the True and the consequent for the False. Accordingly, our sentence is true if the Sun has not yet risen, whether the sky is very cloudy or not, and also if the Sun has risen and the sky is very cloudy. Since only truth values are here in question, each component clause can be replaced by another of the same truth value without changing the truth value of the whole. To be sure, the light in which the subject then appears would usually be unsuitable; the thought might easily seem distorted; but this has nothing to do with its truth value. One must always take care not to clash with the subsidiary thoughts, which are however not explicitly expressed and therefore should not be reckoned in the sense. Hence, also, no account need be taken of their truth values.[18]

The simple cases have now been discussed. Let us review what we have learned.

The subordinate clause usually has for its sense not a thought, but only a part of one, and consequently no truth value as reference. The reason for this is either that the words in the subordinate clause have indirect reference, so that the reference, not the sense, of the subordinate clause is a thought; or else that, on account of the presence of an indefinite indicator, the subordinate clause is incomplete and expresses a thought only when combined with the main clause. It may happen, however, that the sense of the subsidiary clause is a complete thought, in which case it can be replaced by another of the same truth value without harm to the truth of the whole—provided there are no grammatical obstacles.

An examination of all the subordinate clauses which one may encounter will soon provide some which do not fit well into these categories. The reason, so far as I can see, is that these subordinate clauses have no such simple sense. Almost always, it seems, we connect with the main thoughts expressed by us subsidiary thoughts which, although not expressed, are associated with our words, in accordance with psychological laws, by the hearer. And since the subsidiary thought appears to be connected with our words of its own accord, almost like the main thought itself, we want it also to be expressed. The sense of the sentence is thereby enriched, and it may well happen that we have more simple thoughts than clauses. In many cases the sentence must be understood in this way, in others it may be doubtful whether the subsidiary thought belongs to the sense of the sentence or only accompanies it.[19] One might perhaps find that the sentence

Napoleon, who recognized the danger to his right flank, himself led his guards against the enemy position

expresses not only the two thoughts shown above, but also the thought that the knowledge of the danger was the reason why he led the guards against the enemy position. One may in fact doubt whether this thought is merely slightly suggested or really expressed. Let the question be considered whether our sentence be false if Napoleon's decision had already been made before he recognized the danger. If our sentence could be true in spite of this, the subsidiary thought should not be understood as part of the sense. One would probably decide in favour of this. The alternative would make for a quite complicated situation: We would have more simple thoughts than clauses. If the sentence

Napoleon recognized the danger to his right flank

were now to be replaced by another having the same truth value, e.g.,

Napoleon was already more than 45 years old

not only would our first thought be changed, but also our third one. Hence the truth value of the latter might change—viz. if his age was not the reason for the decision to lead the guards against the enemy. This shows why clauses of equal truth value cannot always be substituted for one another in such cases. The clause expresses more through its connexion with another than it does in isolation.

Let us now consider cases where this regularly happens. In the sentence:

Bebel mistakenly supposes that the return of Alsace-Lorraine would appease France's desire for revenge

two thoughts are expressed, which are not however shown by means of antecedent and consequent clauses, viz.:

1. Bebel believes that the return of Alsace-Lorraine would appease France's desire for revenge
2. the return of Alsace-Lorraine would not appease France's desire for revenge.

In the expression of the first thought, the words of the subordinate clause have their indirect reference, while the same words have their customary reference in the expression of the second thought. This shows that the subordinate clause in our original complex sentence is to be taken twice over, with different reference, standing once for a thought, once for a truth value. Since the truth value is not the whole reference of the subordinate clause, we cannot simply replace the latter by another of equal truth value. Similar considerations apply to expressions such as 'know,' 'discover,' 'it is known that.'

By means of a subordinate causal clause and the associated main clause we express several thoughts, which however do not correspond separately to the original clauses. In the sentence: 'Because ice is less dense than water, it floats on water' we have

1. Ice is less dense than water;
2. If anything is less dense than water, it floats on water;
3. Ice floats on water.

The third thought, however, need not be explicitly introduced, since it is contained in the remaining two. On the other hand, neither the first and third nor the second and third combined would furnish the sense of our sentence. It can now be seen that our subordinate clause

because ice is less dense than water

expresses our first thought, as well as a part of our second. This is how it comes to pass that our subsidiary clause cannot be simply replaced by another of equal truth value; for this would alter our second thought and thereby might well alter its truth value.

The situation is similar in the sentence

If iron were less dense than water, it would float on water.

Here we have the two thoughts that iron is not less dense than water, and that something floats on water if it is less dense than water. The subsidiary clause again expresses one thought and a part of the other.

If we interpret the sentence already considered

After Schleswig-Holstein was separated from Denmark, Prussia and Austria quarrelled

in such a way that it expresses the thought that Schleswig-Holstein was once separated from Denmark, we have first this thought, and secondly the thought that at a time, more closely determined by the subordinate clause, Prussia and Austria quarrelled. Here also the subordinate clause expresses not only one thought but also a part of another. Therefore it may not in general be replaced by another of the same truth value.

It is hard to exhaust all the possibilities given by language; but I hope to have brought to light at least the essential reasons why a subordinate clause may not always be replaced by another of equal truth value without harm to the truth of the whole sentence structure. These reasons arise:

1. when the subordinate clause does not stand for a truth value, inasmuch as it expresses only a part of a thought;

2. when the subordinate clause does stand for a truth value but is not restricted to so doing,

inasmuch as its sense includes one thought and part of another.

The first case arises:

a. in indirect reference of words

b. if a part of the sentence is only an indefinite indicator instead of a proper name.

In the second case, the subsidiary clause may have to be taken twice over, viz. once in its customary reference, and the other time in indirect reference; or the sense of a part of the subordinate clause may likewise be a component of another thought, which, taken together with the thought directly expressed by the subordinate clause, makes up the sense of the whole sentence.

It follows with sufficient probability from the foregoing that the cases where a subordinate clause is not replaceable by another of the same value cannot be brought in disproof of our view that a truth value is the reference of a sentence having a thought as its sense.

Let us return to our starting point.

When we found '$a = a$' and '$a = b$' to have different cognitive values, the explanation is that for the purpose of knowledge, the sense of the sentence, viz. the thought expressed by it, is no less relevant than its reference, i.e., its truth value. If now $a = b$, then indeed the reference of 'b' is the same as that of 'a,' and hence the truth value of '$a = b$' is the same as that of '$a = a$.' In spite of this, the sense of 'b' may differ from that of 'a,' and thereby the sense expressed in '$a = b$' differs from that of '$a = a$.' In that case the two sentences do not have the same cognitive value. If we understand by 'judgment' the advance from the thought to its truth value, as in the above paper, we can also say that the judgments are different.

NOTES

1. I use this word strictly and understand '$a = b$' to have the sense of 'a is the same as b' or 'a and b coincide.'

2. [The reference is to Frege's *Begriffsschrift, eine der arithmetischen nachgebildete Formelsprache des reinen Denkens* (Halle, 1879).]

3. [See his 'Über Begriff und Gegenstand' (*Vierteljahrsschrift für wissenschaftliche Philosophie* XVI [1892], 192–205).]

4. In the case of an actual proper name such as 'Aristotle' opinions as to the sense may differ. It might,

for instance, be taken to be the following: the pupil of Plato and teacher of Alexander the Great. Anybody who does this will attach another sense to the sentence 'Aristotle was born in Stagira' than will a man who takes as the sense of the name: the teacher of Alexander the Great who was born in Stagira. So long as the reference remains the same, such variations of sense may be tolerated, although they are to be avoided in the theoretical structure of a demonstrative science and ought not to occur in a perfect language.

5.   We can include with ideas the direct experiences in which sense-impressions and acts themselves take the place of the traces which they have left in the mind. The distinction is unimportant for our purpose, especially since memories of sense-impressions and acts always help to complete the perceptual image. One can also understand direct experience as including any object, in so far as it is sensibly perceptible or spatial.

6.   Hence it is inadvisable to use the word 'idea' to designate something so basically different.

7.   By a thought I understand not the subjective performance of thinking but its objective content, which is capable of being the common property of several thinkers.

8.   It would be desirable to have a special term for signs having only sense. If we name them, say, representations, the words of the actors on the stage would be representations; indeed the actor himself would be a representation.

9.   [See his 'Über Begriff und Gegenstand' (*Vierteljahrsschrift für wissenschaftliche Philosophie* XVI [1892], 192–205).]

10.   A judgment, for me, is not the mere comprehension of a thought, but the admission of its truth.

11.   [A literal translation of Frege's 'abstracten Nennsätzen' whose meaning eludes me.]

12.   In 'A lied in saying he had seen B,' the subordinate clause designates a thought which is said (1) to have been asserted by A (2) while A was convinced of its falsity.

13.   [Frege uses the Prussian name for the battle— 'Belle Alliance.']

14.   In accordance with what was said above, an expression of the kind in question must actually always be assured of reference, by means of a special stipulation, e.g., by the convention that 0 shall count as its reference, when the concept applies to no object or to more than one.

15.   In the case of these sentences, various interpretations are easily possible. The sense of the sentence, 'After Schleswig-Holstein was separated from Denmark, Prussia and Austria quarrelled' can also be rendered in the form 'After the separation of Schleswig-Holstein from Denmark, Prussia and Austria quarrelled.' In this version, it is surely sufficiently clear that the sense is not to be taken as having as a part the thought that Schleswig-Holstein was once separated from Denmark, but that this is the necessary presupposition in order for the expression 'after the separation of Schleswig-Holstein from Denmark' to have any reference at all. To be sure, our sentence can also be interpreted as saying that Schleswig-Holstein was once separated from Denmark. We then have a case which is to be considered later. In order to understand the difference more clearly, let us project ourselves into the mind of a Chinese who, having little knowledge of European history, believes it to be false that Schleswig-Holstein was ever separated from Denmark. He will take our sentence, in the first version, to be neither true nor false but will deny it to have any reference, on the ground of absence of reference for its subordinate clause. This clause would only apparently determine a time. If he interpreted our sentence in the second way, however, he would find a thought expressed in it which he would take to be false, beside a part which would be without reference for him.

16.   At times an explicit linguistic indication is missing and must be read off from the entire context.

17.   Similarly in the case of 'but,' 'yet.'

18.   The thought of our sentence might also be expressed thus: 'Either the Sun has not risen yet or the sky is very cloudy'—which shows how this kind of sentence connexion is to be understood.

19.   This may be important for the question whether an assertion is a lie, or an oath a perjury.

On Denoting

2

BERTRAND RUSSELL

BY A 'DENOTING PHRASE' I mean a phrase such as any one of the following: a man, some man, any man, every man, all men, the present King of England, the present King of France, the centre of mass of the solar system at the first instant of the twentieth century, the revolution of the earth round the sun, the revolution of the sun round the earth. Thus a phrase is denoting solely in virtue of its *form*. We may distinguish three cases: (1) A phrase may be denoting, and yet not denote anything; e.g., 'the present King of France'. (2) A phrase may denote one definite object; e.g., 'the present King of England' denotes a certain man. (3) A phrase may denote ambiguously; e.g., 'a man' denotes not many men, but an ambiguous man. The interpretation of such phrases is a matter of considerable difficulty; indeed, it is very hard to frame any theory not susceptible of formal refutation. All the difficulties with which I am acquainted are met, so far as I can discover, by the theory which I am about to explain.

The subject of denoting is of very great importance, not only in logic and mathematics, but also in theory of knowledge. For example, we know that the centre of mass of the solar system at a definite instant is some definite point, and we can affirm a number of propositions about it; but we have no immediate *acquaintance* with this point, which is only known to us by description. The distinction between *acquaintance* and *knowledge about* is the distinction between the things we have presentations of, and the things we only reach by means of denoting phrases. It often happens that we know that a certain phrase denotes unambiguously, although we have no acquaintance with what it denotes; this occurs in the above case of the centre of mass. In perception we have acquaintance with objects of perception, and in thought we have acquaintance with objects of a more abstract logical character; but we do not necessarily have acquaintance with the ob-

jects denoted by phrases composed of words with whose meanings we are acquainted. To take a very important instance: there seems no reason to believe that we are ever acquainted with other people's minds, seeing that these are not directly perceived; hence what we know about them is obtained through denoting. All thinking has to start from acquaintance; but it succeeds in thinking *about* many things with which we have no acquaintance.

The course of my argument will be as follows. I shall begin by stating the theory I intend to advocate;[1] I shall then discuss the theories of Frege and Meinong, showing why neither of them satisfies me; then I shall give the grounds in favor of my theory; and finally I shall briefly indicate the philosophical consequences of my theory.

My theory, briefly, is as follows. I take the notion of the *variable* as fundamental; I use '$C(x)$' to mean a proposition[2] in which x is a constituent, where x, the variable, is essentially and wholly undetermined. Then we can consider the two notions '$C(x)$ is always true' and '$C(x)$ is sometimes true'.[3] Then *everything* and *nothing* and *something* (which are the most primitive of denoting phrases) are to be interpreted as follows:

C(everything) means '$C(x)$ is always true';
C(nothing) means ' "$C(x)$ is false" is always true';
C(something) means 'It is false that "$C(x)$ is false" is always true'.[4]

Here the notion '$C(x)$ is always true' is taken as ultimate and indefinable, and the others are defined by means of it. *Everything, nothing,* and *something* are not assumed to have any meaning in isolation, but a meaning is assigned to *every* proposition in which they occur. This is the principle of the theory of denoting I wish to advocate: that denoting phrases never have any meaning in themselves, but

Mind 14 (1905): 479–93. Reprinted by permission of *Mind*.

that every proposition in whose verbal expression they occur has a meaning. The difficulties concerning denoting are, I believe, all the result of a wrong analysis of propositions whose verbal expressions contain denoting phrases. The proper analysis, if I am not mistaken, may be further set forth as follows.

Suppose now we wish to interpret the proposition, 'I met a man'. If this is true, I met some definite man; but that is not what I affirm. What I affirm is, according to the theory I advocate:

'"I met x, and x is human" is not always false'.

Generally, defining the class of men as the class of objects having the predicate *human*, we say that:

'C(a man)' means '"$C(x)$ and x is human" is not always false'.

This leaves 'a man', by itself, wholly destitute of meaning, but gives a meaning to every proposition in whose verbal expression 'a man' occurs.

Consider next the proposition 'all men are mortal'. This proposition[5] is really hypothetical and states that *if* anything is a man, it is mortal. That is, it states that if x is a man, x is mortal, whatever x may be. Hence, substituting 'x is human' for 'x is a man', we find:

'All men are mortal' means '"If x is human, x is mortal" is always true.'

This is what is expressed in symbolic logic by saying that 'all men are mortal' means '"x is human" implies "x is mortal" for all values of x'. More generally, we say:

'C(all men)' means '"If x is human, then $C(x)$ is true" is always true'.
Similarly
'C(no men)' means '"If x is human, then $C(x)$ is false" is always true'.
'C(some men)' will mean the same as 'C(a man)',[6] and
'C(a man)' means 'It is false that "$C(x)$ and x is human" is always false'.
'C(every man)' will mean the same as 'C(all men)'.

It remains to interpret phrases containing *the*. These are by far the most interesting and difficult of denoting phrases. Take as an instance 'the father of Charles II was executed'. This asserts that there was an x who was the father of Charles II and was executed. Now *the,* when it is strictly used, involves uniqueness; we do, it is true, speak of '*the* son of So-and-so' even when So-and-so has several sons, but it would be more correct to say '*a* son of So-and-so'. Thus for our purposes we take *the* as involving uniqueness. Thus when we say 'x was *the* father of Charles II' we not only assert that x had a certain relation to Charles II, but also that nothing else had this relation. The relation in question, without the assumption of uniqueness, and without any denoting phrases, is expressed by 'x begat Charles II'. To get an equivalent of 'x was the father of Charles II', we must add 'If y is other than x, y did not beget Charles II', or, what is equivalent, 'If y begat Charles II, y is identical with x'. Hence 'x is the father of Charles II' becomes: 'x begat Charles II; and "if y begat Charles II, y is identical with x" is always true of y'.

Thus 'the father of Charles II was executed' becomes:

'It is not always false of x that x begat Charles II and that x was executed and that "if y begat Charles II, y is identical with x" is always true of y'.

This may seem a somewhat incredible interpretation; but I am not at present giving reasons, I am merely *stating* the theory.

To interpret 'C(the father of Charles II)', where C stands for any statement about him, we have only to substitute $C(x)$ for 'x was executed' in the above. Observe that, according to the above interpretation, whatever statement C may be, 'C(the father of Charles II)' implies:

'It is not always false of x that "if y begat Charles II, y is identical with x" is always true of y',

which is what is expressed in common language by 'Charles II had one father and no more'. Consequently if this condition fails, *every* proposition of the form 'C(the father of Charles II)' is false. Thus e.g., every proposition of the form 'C(the present King of France)' is false. This is a great advantage in the present theory. I shall show later that it is not contrary to the law of contradiction, as might be at first supposed.

The above gives a reduction of all propositions in which denoting phrases occur to forms in which no such phrases occur. Why it is imperative to effect such a reduction, the subsequent discussion will endeavour to show.

The evidence for the above theory is derived from the difficulties which seem unavoidable if we regard denoting phrases as standing for genuine constituents of the propositions in whose verbal expressions they occur. Of the possible theories which admit such constituents the simplest is that of Meinong.[7] This theory regards any grammatically correct denoting phrase as standing for an *object*. Thus 'the present King of France', 'the round square', etc., are supposed to be genuine objects. It is admitted that such objects do not *subsist*, but nevertheless they are supposed to be objects. This is in itself a difficult view; but the chief objection is that such objects, admittedly, are apt to infringe the law of contradiction. It is contended, for example, that the existent present King of France exists, and also does not exist; that the round square is round, and also not round, etc. But this is intolerable; and if any theory can be found to avoid this result, it is surely to be preferred.

The above breach of the law of contradiction is avoided by Frege's theory. He distinguishes, in a denoting phrase, two elements, which we may call the *meaning* and the *denotation*.[8] Thus 'the centre of mass of the solar system at the beginning of the twentieth century' is highly complex in *meaning*, but its *denotation* is a certain point, which is simple. The solar system, the twentieth century, etc., are constituents of the *meaning*; but the *denotation* has no constituents at all.[9] One advantage of this distinction is that it shows why it is often worth while to assert identity. If we say 'Scott is the author of *Waverley*', we assert an identity of denotation with a difference of meaning. I shall, however, not repeat the grounds in favor of this theory, as I have urged its claims elsewhere (loc. cit.), and am now concerned to dispute those claims.

One of the first difficulties that confront us, when we adopt the view that denoting phrases *express* a meaning and *denote* a denotation,[10] concerns the cases in which the denotation appears to be absent. If we say 'the King of England is bald', that is, it would seem, not a statement about the complex

meaning 'the King of England', but about the actual man denoted by the meaning. But now consider 'the king of France is bald'. By parity of form, this also ought to be about the denotation of the phrase 'the King of France'. But this phrase, though it has a *meaning* provided 'the King of England' has a meaning, has certainly no denotation, at least in any obvious sense. Hence one would suppose that 'the King of France is bald' ought to be nonsense; but it is not nonsense, since it is plainly false. Or again consider such a proposition as the following: 'If *u* is a class which has only one member, then that one member is a member of *u*', or as we may state it, 'If *u* is a unit class, *the u* is a *u*'. This proposition ought to be *always* true, since the conclusion is true whenever the hypothesis is true. But 'the *u*' is a denoting phrase, and it is the denotation, not the meaning, that is said to be a *u*. Now is *u* is *not* a unit class, 'the *u*' seems to denote nothing; hence our proposition would seem to become nonsense as soon as *u* is not a unit class.

Now it is plain that such propositions do *not* become nonsense merely because their hypotheses are false. The King in *The Tempest* might say, 'If Ferdinand is not drowned, Ferdinand is my only son'. Now 'my only son' is a denoting phrase, which, on the face of it, has a denotation when, and only when, I have exactly one son. But the above statement would nevertheless have remained true if Ferdinand had been in fact drowned. Thus we must either provide a denotation in cases in which it is at first sight absent, or we must abandon the view that the denotation is what is concerned in propositions which contain denoting phrases. The latter is the course that I advocate. The former course may be taken, as by Meinong, by admitting objects which do not subsist, and denying that they obey the law of contradiction; this, however, is to be avoided if possible. Another way of taking the same course (so far as our present alternative is concerned) is adopted by Frege, who provides by definition some purely conventional denotation for the cases in which otherwise there would be none. Thus 'the King of France', is to denote the null-class; 'the only son of Mr. So-and-so' (who has a fine family of ten), is to denote the class of all his sons; and so on. But this procedure, though it may not lead to actual logical error, is plainly artificial, and does not give an exact analysis of the matter. Thus if we allow that denoting phrases, in general, have the two sides of meaning and denotation, the cases where there seems to be no denotation cause difficulties both on the assumption that there really is a denotation and on the assumption that there really is none.

A logical theory may be tested by its capacity for dealing with puzzles, and it is a wholesome plan, in thinking about logic, to stock the mind with as many puzzles as possible, since these serve much the same purpose as is served by experiments in physical science. I shall therefore state three puzzles which a theory as to denoting ought to be able to solve; and I shall show later that my theory solves them.

(1) If *a* is identical with *b*, whatever is true of the one is true of the other, and either may be substituted for the other in any proposition without altering the truth or falsehood of that proposition. Now George IV wished to know whether Scott was the author of *Waverley;* and in fact Scott *was* the author of *Waverley.* Hence we may substitute *Scott* for *the author of 'Waverley',* and thereby prove that George IV wished to know whether Scott was Scott. Yet an interest in the law of identity can hardly be attributed to the first gentleman of Europe.

(2) By the law of the excluded middle, either '*A* is *B*' or '*A* is not *B*' must be true. Hence either 'the present King of France is bald' or 'the present King of France is not bald' must be true. Yet if we enumerated the things that are bald, and then the things that are not bald, we should not find the present King of France in either list. Hegelians, who love a synthesis, will probably conclude that he wears a wig.

(3) Consider the proposition '*A* differs from *B*'. If this is true, there is a difference between *A* and *B,* which fact may be expressed in the form 'the difference between *A* and *B* subsists'. But if it is false that *A* differs from *B*, then there is no difference between *A* and *B,* which fact may be expressed in the form 'the difference between *A* and *B* does not subsist'. But how can a non-entity be the subject of a proposition? 'I think, therefore I am' is no more evident than 'I am the subject of a proposition, therefore I am'; provided 'I am' is taken to assert subsistence or being,[11] not existence. Hence, it would appear, it must always be self-contradictory to deny the being of anything; but we have seen, in connexion with Meinong, that to admit being also sometimes leads to contradictions. Thus if *A* and *B* do not differ, to suppose either that there is, or that there is not, such an object as 'the difference between *A* and *B*' seems equally impossible.

The relation of the meaning to the denotation involves certain rather curious difficulties, which seem in themselves sufficient to prove that the theory which leads to such difficulties must be wrong.

When we wish to speak about the *meaning* of a denoting phrase, as opposed to its *denotation,* the natural mode of doing so is by inverted commas. Thus we say:

The centre of mass of the solar system is a point, not a denoting complex;
'The centre of mass of the solar system' is a denoting complex, not a point.
Or again,
The first line of Gray's Elegy states a proposition.

'The first line of Gray's Elegy' does not state a proposition. Thus taking any denoting phrase, say *C,* we wish to consider the relation between *C* and '*C*', where the difference of the two is of the kind exemplified in the above two instances.

We say, to begin with, that when *C* occurs it is the *denotation* that we are speaking about; but when '*C*' occurs, it is the *meaning.* Now the relation of meaning and denotation is not merely linguistic through the phrase: there must be a logical relation involved, which we express by saying that the meaning denotes the denotation. But the difficulty which confronts us is that we cannot succeed in *both* preserving the connexion of meaning and denotation *and* preventing them from being one and the same; also that the meaning cannot be got at except by means of denoting phrases. This happens as follows.

The one phrase *C* was to have both meaning and denotation. But if we speak of 'the meaning of *C*', that gives us the meaning (if any) of the denotation. 'The meaning of the first line of Gray's Elegy' is the same as 'The meaning of "The curfew tolls the knell of parting day",' and is not the same as 'The meaning of "the first line of Gray's Elegy".' Thus in order to get the meaning we want, we must speak not of 'the meaning of *C*', but 'the meaning of "*C*",' which is the same as '*C*' by itself. Similarly 'the denotation of *C*' does not mean the denotation we want, but means something which, if it denotes at all, denotes what is denoted by the denotation we want. For example, let '*C*' be 'the denoting complex occurring in the second of the above instances'. Then

C = 'the first line of Gray's Elegy', and

the denotation of *C* = The curfew tolls the knell of parting day. But what we *meant* to have as the denotation was 'the first line of Gray's Elegy'. Thus we have failed to get what we wanted.

The difficulty in speaking of the meaning of a denoting complex may be stated thus: The moment we put the complex in a proposition, the proposition is about the denotation; and if we make a proposition in which the subject is 'the meaning of *C*', then the subject is the meaning (if any) of the denotation, which was not intended. This leads us to say that, when we distinguish meaning and denotation, we must be dealing with the meaning: the meaning has denotation and is a complex, and there is not something other than the meaning, which can be called the complex, and be said to *have* both meaning and denotation. The right phrase, on the view in question, is that some meanings have denotations.

But this only makes our difficulty in speaking of meanings more evident. For suppose that *C* is our complex; then we are to say that *C is* the meaning of the complex. Nevertheless, whenever *C* occurs without inverted commas, what is said is not true of the meaning, but only of the denotation, as when we say: The centre of mass of the solar system is a point. Thus to speak of *C* itself, i.e., to make a proposition about the meaning, our subject must not be *C*, but something which denotes *C*. Thus '*C*', which is what we use when we want to speak of the meaning, must not be the meaning, but must be something which denotes the meaning. And *C* must not be a constituent of this complex (as it is of 'the meaning of *C*'); for if *C* occurs in the complex, it will be its denotation, not its meaning, that will occur, and there is no backward road from denotations to meaning, because every object can be denoted by an infinite number of different denoting phrases.

Thus it would seem that '*C*' and *C* are different entities, such that '*C*' denotes *C;* but this cannot be an explanation, because the relation of '*C*' to *C* remains wholly mysterious; and where are we to find the denoting complex '*C*' which is to denote *C*?

Moreover, when *C* occurs in a proposition, it is not *only* the denotation that occurs (as we shall see in the next paragraph); yet, on the view in question, *C* is only the denotation, the meaning being wholly relegated to '*C*'. This is an inextricable tangle, and seems to prove that the whole distinction between meaning and denotation has been wrongly conceived.

That the meaning is relevant when a denoting phrase occurs in a proposition is formally proved by the puzzle about the author of *Waverley*. The proposition 'Scott was the author of *Waverley*' has a property not possessed by 'Scott was Scott', namely the property that George IV wished to know whether it was true. Thus the two are not identical propositions; hence the meaning of 'the author of *Waverley*' must be relevant as well as the denotation, if we adhere to the point of view to which this distinction belongs. Yet, as we have just seen, so long as we adhere to this point of view, we are compelled to hold that only the denotation can be relevant. Thus the point of view in question must be abandoned.

It remains to show how all the puzzles we have been considering are solved by the theory explained at the beginning of this article.

According to the view which I advocate, a denoting phrase is essentially *part* of a sentence, and does not, like most single words, have any significance on its own account. If I say 'Scott was a man', that is a statement of the form '*x* was a man', and it has 'Scott' for its subject. But if I say 'the author of *Waverley* was a man', that is not a statement of the form '*x* was a man', and does not have 'the author of *Waverley*' for its subject. Abbreviating the statement made at the beginning of this article, we may put, in place of 'the author of *Waverley* was a man', the following: 'One and only one entity wrote *Waverley,* and that one was a man'. (This is not so strictly what is meant as what was said earlier; but it is easier to follow.) And speaking generally, suppose we wish to say that the author of *Waverley* had property ϕ, what we wish to say is equivalent to 'One and only one entity wrote *Waverley,* and that one had the property ϕ'.

The explanation of *denotation* is now as follows. Every proposition in which 'the author of *Waverley*' occurs being explained as above, the proposition 'Scott was the author of *Waverley*' (i.e., 'Scott was identical with the author of *Waverley*') becomes 'One and only one entity wrote *Waverley,* and Scott was identical with that one'; or, reverting to the wholly explicit form: 'It is not always false of *x* that *x* wrote *Waverley,* that it is always true of *y* that if *y* wrote *Waverley y* is identical with *x,* and that Scott is identical with *x.*' Thus if '*C*' is a denoting phrase, it may happen that there is one entity *x* (there cannot be more than one) for which the proposition '*x* is identical with *C*' is true, this proposition being interpreted as above. We may then say that the entity *x* is the denotation of the phrase '*C*'. Thus Scott is the denotation of 'the author of *Waverley*'. The '*C*' in inverted commas will be merely the *phrase,* not anything that can be called the *meaning.* The phrase *per se* has no meaning, because in any proposition in which it occurs the proposition, fully expressed, does not contain the phrase, which has been broken up.

The puzzle about George IV's curiosity is now seen to have a very simple solution. The proposition 'Scott was the author of *Waverley*', which was written out in its unabbreviated form in the preceding paragraph, does not contain any constituent 'the author of *Waverley*' for which we could substitute 'Scott'. This does not interfere with the truth of inferences resulting from making what is *verbally* the substitution of 'Scott' for 'the author of *Waverley*', so long as 'the author of *Waverley*' has what I call a *primary* occurrence in the proposition considered. The difference of primary and secondary occurrences of denoting phrases is as follows:

When we say: 'George IV wished to know whether so-and-so', or when we say 'So-and-so is surprising' or 'So-and-so is true', etc., the 'so-and-so' must be a proposition. Suppose now that 'so-and-so' contains a denoting phrase. We may either eliminate this denoting phrase from the subordinate proposition 'so-and-so', or from the whole proposition in which 'so-and-so' is a mere constituent. Different propositions result according to which we do. I have heard of a touchy owner of a yacht to whom a guest, on first seeing it, remarked, 'I thought your yacht was larger than it is'; and the owner replied, 'No, my yacht is not larger than it is'. What the guest meant was, 'The size that I thought your yacht was is greater than the size your yacht is'; the meaning attributed to him is, 'I thought the size of your yacht was greater than the size of your yacht'. To return to

George IV and *Waverley,* when we say 'George IV wished to know whether Scott was the author of *Waverley*' we normally mean 'George IV wished to know whether one and only one man wrote *Waverley* and Scott was that man'; but we *may* also mean: 'One and only one man wrote *Waverley,* and George IV wished to know whether Scott was that man'. In the latter, 'the author of *Waverley*' has a *primary* occurrence; in the former, a *secondary.* The latter might be expressed by 'George IV wished to know, concerning the man who in fact wrote *Waverley,* whether he was Scott'. This would be true, for example, if George IV had seen Scott at a distance, and had asked 'Is that Scott?' A *secondary* occurrence of a denoting phrase may be defined as one in which the phrase occurs in a proposition *p* which is a mere constituent of the proposition we are considering, and the substitution for the denoting phrase is to be effected in *p,* and not in the whole proposition concerned. The ambiguity as between primary and secondary occurrences is hard to avoid in language; but it does no harm if we are on our guard against it. In symbolic logic it is of course easily avoided.

The distinction of primary and secondary occurrences also enables us to deal with the question whether the present King of France is bald or not bald, and generally with the logical status of denoting phrases that denote nothing. If '*C*' is a denoting phrase, say 'the term having the property *F*', then

'*C* has the property ϕ' means 'one and only one term has the property *F,* and that one has the property ϕ'.[12]

If now the property *F* belongs to no terms, or to several, it follows that '*C* has the property ϕ' is false for *all* values of ϕ. Thus 'the present King of France is bald' is certainly false; and 'the present King of France is not bald' is false if it means

'There is an entity which is now King of France and is not bald', but is true if it means
'It is false that there is an entity which is now King of France and is bald'.

That is, 'the King of France is not bald' is false if the occurrence of 'the King of France' is *primary,* and true if it is *secondary.* Thus all propositions in which 'the King of France' has a primary occurrence are false; the denials of such propositions are true, but in them 'the King of France' has a secondary occurrence. Thus we escape the conclusion that the King of France has a wig.

We can now see also how to deny that there is such an object as the difference between *A* and *B* in the case when *A* and *B* do not differ. If *A* and *B* do differ, there is only and only one entity *x* such that '*x* is the difference between *A* and *B*' is a true proposition; if *A* and *B* do not differ, there is no such entity *x*. Thus according to the meaning of denotation lately explained, 'the difference between *A* and *B*' has a denotation when *A* and *B* differ, but not otherwise. This difference applies to true and false propositions generally. If '*a R b*' stands for '*a* has the relation *R* to *b*', then when *a R b* is true, there is such an entity as the relation *R* between *a* and *b*; when *a R b* is false, there is no such entity. Thus out of any proposition we can make a denoting phrase, which denotes an entity if the proposition is true, but does not denote an entity if the proposition is false. E.g., it is true (at least we will suppose so) that the earth revolves round the sun, and false that the sun revolves round the earth; hence 'the revolution of the earth round the sun' denotes an entity, while 'the revolution of the sun round the earth' does not denote an entity.[13]

The whole realm of non-entities, such as 'the round square', 'the even prime other than 2', 'Apollo', 'Hamlet', etc., can now be satisfactorily dealt with. All these are denoting phrases which do not denote anything. A proposition about Apollo means what we get by substituting what the classical dictionary tells us is meant by Apollo, say 'the sun-god'. All propositions in which Apollo occurs are to be interpreted by the above rules for denoting phrases. If 'Apollo' has a primary occurrence, the proposition containing the occurrence is false; if the occurrence is secondary, the proposition may be true. So again 'the round square is round' means 'there is one and only one entity *x* which is round and square, and that entity is round', which is a false proposition, not, as Meinong maintains, a true one. 'The most perfect Being has all perfections; existence is a perfection; therefore the most perfect Being exists' becomes:

'There is one and only one entity *x* which is most perfect; that one has all perfections; existence is a perfection; therefore that one exists.' As a proof, this

fails for want of a proof of the premiss 'there is one and only one entity *x* which is most perfect'.[14]

Mr. MacColl (*Mind*, N.S., No. 54, and again No. 55, page 401) regards individuals as of two sorts, real and unreal; hence he defines the null-class as the class consisting of all unreal individuals. This assumes that such phrases as 'the present King of France', which do not denote a real individual, do, nevertheless, denote an individual, but an unreal one. This is essentially Meinong's theory, which we have seen reason to reject because it conflicts with the law of contradiction. With our theory of denoting, we are able to hold that there are no unreal individuals; so that the null-class is the class containing no members, not the class containing as members all unreal individuals.

It is important to observe the effect of our theory on the interpretation of definitions which proceed by means of denoting phrases. Most mathematical definitions are of this sort; for example '$m - n$ means the number which, added to n, gives m'. Thus $m - n$ is defined as meaning the same as a certain denoting phrase; but we agreed that denoting phrases have no meaning in isolation. Thus what the definition really ought to be is: 'Any proposition containing $m - n$ is to mean the proposition which results from substituting for "$m - n$" "the number which, added to n, gives m".' The resulting proposition is interpreted according to the rules already given for interpreting propositions whose verbal expression contains a denoting phrase. In the case where m and n are such that there is one and only one number x which, added to n, gives m, there is a number x which can be substituted for $m - n$ in any proposition containing $m - n$ without altering the truth or falsehood of the proposition. But in other cases, all propositions in which '$m - n$' has a primary occurrence are false.

The usefulness of *identity* is explained by the above theory. No one outside of a logic-book ever wishes to say '*x* is *x*', and yet assertions of identity are often made in such forms as 'Scott was the author of *Waverley*' or 'thou are the man'. The meaning of such propositions cannot be stated without the notion of identity, although they are not simply statements that Scott is identical with another term, the author of *Waverley*, or that thou art identical with another term, the man. The shortest statement of 'Scott is the author of *Waverley*' seems to be 'Scott wrote *Waverley*;

and it is always true of y that if y wrote *Waverley*, y is identical with Scott'. It is in this way that identity enters into 'Scott is the author of *Waverley*'; and it is owing to such uses that identity is worth affirming.

One interesting result of the above theory of denoting is this: when there is an anything with which we do not have immediate acquaintance, but only definition by denoting phrases, then the propositions in which this thing is introduced by means of a denoting phrase do not really contain this thing as a constituent, but contain instead the constituents expressed by the several words of the denoting phrase. Thus in every proposition that we can apprehend (i.e., not only in those whose truth or falsehood we can judge of, but in all that we can think about), all the constituents are really entities with which we have immediate acquaintance. Now such things as matter (in the sense in which matter occurs in physics) and the minds of other people are known to us only by denoting phrases, i.e., we are not *acquainted* with them, but we know them as what has such and such properties. Hence, although we can form propositional functions $C(x)$ which must hold of such and such a material particle, or of So-and-so's mind, yet we are not acquainted with the propositions which affirm these things that we know must be true, because we cannot apprehend the actual entities concerned. What we know is 'So-and-so has a mind which has such and such properties' but we do not know 'A has such and such properties', where A is the mind in question. In such a case, we know the properties of a thing without having acquaintance with the thing itself, and without, consequently, knowing any single proposition of which the thing itself is a constituent.

Of the many other consequences of the view I have been advocating, I will say nothing. I will only beg the reader not to make up his mind against the view—as he might be tempted to do, on account of its apparently excessive complication—until he has attempted to construct a theory of his own on the subject of denotation. This attempt, I believe, will convince him that, whatever the true theory may be, it cannot have such a simplicity as one might have expected beforehand.

NOTES

1. I have discussed this subject in *Principles of Mathematics,* Chap. V, and §476. The theory there advocated is very nearly the same as Frege's, and is quite different from the theory to be advocated in what follows.

2. More exactly, a propositional function.

3. The second of these can be defined by means of the first, if we take it to mean, 'It is not true that "$C(x)$ is false" is always true'.

4. I shall sometimes use, instead of this complicated phrase, the phrase '$C(x)$ is not always false', or '$C(x)$ is sometimes true', supposed *defined* to mean the same as the complicated phrase.

5. As has been ably argued in Mr. Bradley's *Logic,* Book I, Chap. II.

6. Psychologically 'C (a man)' has a suggestion of *only one,* and 'C (some men)' has a suggestion of *more than one*; but we may neglect these suggestions in a preliminary sketch.

7. See *Untersuchungen zur Gegenstandstheorie und Psychologie* (Leipzig, 1904) the first three articles (by Meinong, Ameseder and Mally respectively).

8. See his 'Über Sinn und Bedeutung', *Zeitschrift für Phil. und Phil. Kritik,* Vol. 100. ["On Sense and Reference," in this volume 21–32.]

9. Frege distinguishes the two elements of meaning and denotation everywhere, and not only in complex denoting phrases, Thus it is the *meanings* of the constituents of a denoting complex that enter into its *meaning,* not their *denotation.* In the proposition 'Mont Blanc is over 1,000 metres high', it is, according to him, the *meaning* of 'Mont Blanc', not the actual mountain, that is a constituent of the *meaning* of the proposition.

10. In this theory, we shall say that the denoting phrase *expresses* a meaning; and we shall say both of the phrase and of the meaning that they *denote* a denotation. In the other theory, which I advocate, there is no *meaning,* and only sometimes a *denotation.*

11. I use these as synonyms.

12. This is the abbreviated, not the stricter, interpretation.

13. The propositions from which such entities are derived are not identical either with these entities or with the propositions that these entities have being.

14. The argument can be made to prove validly that all members of the class of most perfect Beings exist; it can also be proved formally that this class cannot have *more* than one member; but, taking the definition of perfection as possession of all positive predicates, it can be proved almost equally formally that the class does not have even one member.

On Referring   3

P. F. STRAWSON

I

WE VERY COMMONLY use expressions of certain kinds to mention or refer to some individual person or single object or particular event or place or process, in the course of doing what we should normally describe as making a statement about that person, object, place, event, or process. I shall call this way of using expressions the 'uniquely referring use'. The classes of expressions which are most commonly used in this way are: singular demonstrative pronouns ("this" and "that"); proper names e.g., "Venice," "Napoleon," "John"); singular personal and impersonal pronouns ("he," "she," "I," "you," "it"); and phrases beginning with the definite article followed by a noun, qualified or unqualified, in the singular (e.g., "the table," "the old man," "the king of France"). Any expression of any of these classes can occur as the subject of what would traditionally be regarded as a singular subject-predicate sentence; and would, so occurring, exemplify the use I wish to discuss.

I do not want to say that expressions belonging to these classes never have any other use than the one I want to discuss. On the contrary, it is obvious that they do. It is obvious that anyone who uttered the sentence, "The whale is a mammal," would be using the expression "the whale" in a way quite different from the way it would be used by anyone who had occasion seriously to utter the sentence, "The whale struck the ship." In the first sentence one is obviously *not* mentioning, and in the second sentence one obviously *is* mentioning, a particular whale. Again if I said, "Napoleon was the greatest French soldier," I should be using the word "Napoleon" to mention a certain individual, but I should not be using the phrase, "the greatest French soldier," to mention an individual, but to say something about an individual I had already mentioned. It would be natural to say

that in using this sentence I was talking *about* Napoleon and that what I was *saying* about him was that he was the greatest French soldier. But of course I *could* use the expression, "the greatest French soldier," to mention an individual; for example, by saying: "The greatest French soldier died in exile." So it is obvious that at least some expressions belonging to the classes I mentioned *can* have uses other than the use I am anxious to discuss. Another thing I do not want to say is that in any given sentence there is never more than one expression used in the way I propose to discuss. On the contrary, it is obvious that there may be more than one. For example, it would be natural to say that, in seriously using the sentence, "The whale struck the ship," I was saying something about both a certain whale and a certain ship, that I was using each of the expressions "the whale" and "the ship" to mention a particular object; or, in other words, that I was using each of these expressions in the uniquely referring way. In general, however, I shall confine my attention to cases where an expression used in this way occurs as the grammatical subject of a sentence.

I think it is true to say that Russell's theory of descriptions, which is concerned with the last of the four classes of expressions I mentioned above (i.e., with expressions of the form "the so-and-so"), is still widely accepted among logicians as giving a correct account of the use of such expressions in ordinary language. I want to show in the first place, that this theory, so regarded, embodies some fundamental mistakes.

What question or questions about phrases of the form "the so-and-so" was the theory of descriptions designed to answer? I think that at least one of the questions may be illustrated as follows. Suppose someone were now to utter the sentence, "The king of France is wise." No one would say that the sentence which had been uttered was meaningless.

Mind 59 (1950): 320–44. Reprinted by permission of *Mind*.

Everyone would agree that it was significant. But everyone knows that there is not at present a king of France. One of the questions the theory of descriptions was designed to answer was the question: How can such a sentence as "The king of France is wise" be significant even when there is nothing which answers to the description it contains, i.e., in this case, nothing which answers to the description "The king of France"? And one of the reasons why Russell thought it important to give a correct answer to this question was that he thought it important to show that another answer which might be given was wrong. The answer that he thought was wrong and to which he was anxious to supply an alternative, might be exhibited as the conclusion of either of the following two fallacious arguments. Let us call the sentence "The king of France is wise" the sentence S. Then the first argument is as follows:

(1) The phrase, "the king of France," is the subject of the sentence S.
Therefore (2) if S is a significant sentence, S is a sentence *about* the king of France.
But (3) if there in no sense exists a king of France, the sentence is not about anything, and hence not about the king of France.
Therefore (4) since S is significant, there must in some sense (in some world) exist (or subsist) the king of France.

And the second argument is as follows:

(1) If S is significant, it is either true or false.
(2) S is true if the king of France is wise and false if the king of France is not wise.
(3) But the statement that the king of France is wise and the statement that the king of France is not wise are alike true only if there is (in some sense, in some world) something which is the king of France.
Hence (4) since S is significant, there follows the same conclusion as before.

These are fairly obviously bad arguments, and, as we should expect, Russell rejects them. The postulation of a world of strange entities, to which the king of France belongs, offends, he says, against "that feeling for reality which ought to be preserved even in the most abstract studies." The fact that Russell rejects these arguments is, however, less interesting than the extent to which, in rejecting their conclusion, he concedes the more important of their principles. Let me refer to the phrase, "the king of France," as the phrase D. Then I think Russell's reasons for rejecting these two arguments can be summarized as follows. The mistake arises, he says, from thinking that D, which is certainly the *grammatical* subject of S, is also the *logical* subject of S. But D is not the logical subject of S. In fact S, although grammatically it has a singular subject and a predicate, is not logically a subject-predicate sentence at all. The proposition it expresses is a complex kind of *existential* proposition, part of which might be described as a "uniquely existential" proposition. To exhibit the logical form of the proposition, we should rewrite the sentence in a logically appropriate grammatical form, in such a way that the deceptive similarity of S to a sentence expressing a subject-predicate proposition would disappear, and we should be safeguarded against arguments such as the bad ones I outlined above. Before recalling the details of Russell's analysis of S, let us notice what his answer, as I have so far given it, seems to imply. His answer seems to imply that in the case of a sentence which is similar to S in that (1) it is grammatically of the subject-predicate form and (2) its grammatical subject does not refer to anything, then the only alternative to its being meaningless is that it should not really (i.e., logically) be of the subject-predicate form at all, but of some quite different form. And this in its turn seems to imply that if there are any sentences which are genuinely of the subject-predicate form, then the very fact of their being significant, having a meaning, guarantees that there *is* something referred to by the logical (and grammatical) subject. Moreover, Russell's answer seems to imply that there are such sentences. For if it is true that one may be misled by the grammatical similarity of S to other sentences into thinking that it is logically of the subject-predicate form, then surely there must be other sentences grammatically similar to S, which *are* of the subject-predicate form. To show not only that Russell's answer seems to imply these conclusions, but that he accepted at least the first two of them, it is enough to consider what he says about a class of expressions which he calls "logically proper names" and contrasts with expressions, like D, which he calls "definite descriptions." Of logically proper names Russell says or implies the following things:

1. That they and they alone can occur as subjects of sentences which are genuinely of the subject-predicate form.

2. That an expression intended to be a logically proper name is *meaningless* unless there is some single object for which it stands: for the *meaning* of such an expression just is the individual object which the expression designates. To be a name at all, therefore, it *must* designate something.

It is easy to see that if anyone believes these two propositions, then the only way for him to save the significance of the sentence S is to deny that it is a logically subject-predicate sentence. Generally, we may say that Russell recognizes only two ways in which sentences which seem, from their grammatical structure, to be about some particular person or individual object or event, can be significant:

1. The first is that their grammatical form should be misleading as to their logical form, and that they should be analyzable, like S, as a special kind of existential sentence.

2. The second is that their grammatical subject should be a logically proper name, of which the meaning is the individual thing it designates.

I think that Russell is unquestionably wrong in this, and that sentences which are significant, and which begin with an expression used in the uniquely referring way, fall into neither of these two classes. Expressions used in the uniquely referring way are never either logically proper names or descriptions, if what is meant by calling them "descriptions" is that they are to be analyzed in accordance with the model provided by Russell's theory of descriptions.

There are no logically proper names and there are no descriptions (in this sense).

Let us now consider the details of Russell's analysis. According to Russell, anyone who asserted S would be asserting that:

1. There is a king of France

2. There is not more than one king of France

3. There is nothing which is king of France and is not wise

It is easy to see both how Russell arrived at this analysis, and how it enables him to answer the question with which we began, viz. the question: How can the sentence S be significant when there is no king of France? The way in which he arrived at the analysis was clearly by asking himself what would be the circumstances in which we would say that anyone who uttered the sentence S had made a true assertion. And it does seem pretty clear, and I have no wish to dispute, that the sentences (1)–(3) above do describe circumstances which are at least *necessary* conditions of anyone making a true assertion by uttering the sentence S. But, as I hope to show, to say this is not at all the same thing as to say that Russell has given a correct account of the use of the sentence S or even that he has given an account which, though incomplete, is correct as far as it goes; and is certainly not at all the same thing as to say that the model translation provided is a correct model for all (or for any) singular sentences beginning with a phrase of the form "the so-and-so."

It is also easy to see how this analysis enables Russell to answer the question of how the sentence S can be significant, even when there is no king of France. For, if this analysis is correct, anyone who utters the sentence S today would be jointly asserting three propositions, one of which (viz. that there is a king of France) would be false; and since the conjunction of three propositions, of which one is false, is itself false, the assertion as a whole would be significant, but false. So neither of the bad arguments for subsistent entities would apply to such an assertion.

II

As a step towards showing that Russell's solution of his problem is mistaken, and towards providing the correct solution, I want now to draw certain distinctions. For this purpose I shall, for the remainder of this section, refer to an expression which has a uniquely referring use as "an expression" for short; and to a sentence beginning with such an expression as "a sentence" for short. The distinctions I shall draw are rather rough and ready, and, no doubt, difficult cases could be produced which would call for their refinement. But I think they will serve my purpose. The distinctions are between:

A1. a sentence

A2. a use of a sentence

A3. an utterance of a sentence

and, correspondingly, between:

B1. an expression

B2. a use of an expression

B3. an utterance of an expression

Consider again the sentence, "The king of France is wise." It is easy to imagine that this sentence was uttered at various times from, say, the beginning of the seventeenth century onwards, during the reigns of each successive French monarch; and easy to imagine that it was also uttered during the subsequent periods in which France was not a monarchy. Notice that it was natural for me to speak of "the sentence" or "this sentence" being uttered at various times during this period; or, in other words, that it would be natural and correct to speak of *one and the same* sentence being uttered on all these various occasions. It is in the sense in which it would be correct to speak of one and the same sentence being uttered on all these various occasions that I want to use the expression (A1) "a sentence." There are, however, obvious differences between different *occasions of the use* of this sentence. For instance, if one man uttered it in the reign of Louis XIV and another man uttered it in the reign of Louis XV, it would be natural to say (to assume) that they were respectively talking about different people; and it might be held that the first man, in using the sentence, made a true assertion, while the second man, in using the same sentence, made a false assertion. If on the other hand two different men simultaneously uttered the sentence (e.g., if one wrote it and the other spoke it) during the reign of Louis XIV, it would be natural to say (assume) that they were both talking about the same person, and, in that case, in using the sentence, they *must* either both have made a true assertion or both have made a false assertion. And this illustrates what I mean by *a use* of a sentence. The two men who uttered the sentence, one in the reign of Louis XV and one in the reign of Louis XIV, each made a different use of the same sentence; whereas

the two men who uttered the sentence simultaneously in the reign of Louis XIV, made the same use[1] of the same sentence. Obviously in the case of this sentence, and equally obviously in the case of many others, we cannot talk of *the sentence* being true or false, but only of its being used to make a true or false assertion or (if this is preferred) to express a true or a false proposition. And equally obviously we cannot talk of *the sentence* being *about* a particular person, for the same sentence may be used at different times to talk about quite different particular persons, but only of *a use* of the sentence to talk about a particular person. Finally it will make sufficiently clear what I mean by an utterance of a sentence if I say that the two men who simultaneously uttered the sentence in the reign of Louis XIV made two different utterances of the same sentence, though they made the same *use* of the sentence.

If we now consider not the whole sentence, "The king of France is wise," but that part of it which is the expression, "the king of France," it is obvious that we can make analogous, though not identical distinctions between (1) the expression, (2) a use of the expression, and (3) an utterance of the expression. The distinctions will not be identical; we obviously cannot correctly talk of the expression "the king of France" being used to express a true or false proposition, since in general only sentences can be used truly or falsely; and similarly it is only by using a sentence and not by using an expression alone, that you can talk about a particular person. Instead, we shall say in this case that you *use* the expression to *mention* or *refer to* a particular person in the course of using the sentence to talk about him. But obviously in this case, and a great many others, the *expression* (B1) cannot be said to mention, or refer to, anything, any more than the *sentence* can be said to be true or false. The same expression can have different mentioning-uses, as the same sentence can be used to make statements with different truth-values. 'Mentioning', or 'referring', is not something an expression does; it is something that someone can use an expression to do. Mentioning, or referring to, something is a characteristic of *a use* of an expression, just as 'being about' something, and truth-or-falsity, are characteristics of *a use* of a sentence.

A very different example may help to make these distinctions clearer. Consider another case of an expression which has a uniquely referring use, viz. the expression "I"; and consider the sentence, "I am hot." Countless people may use this same sentence; but it is logically impossible for two different people to make *the same use* of this sentence: or, if this is preferred, to use it to express the same proposition. The expression "I" may correctly be used by (and only by) any one of innumerable people to refer to himself. To say this is to say something about the expression "I": it is, in a sense, to give its meaning. This is the sort of thing that can be said about *expressions*. But it makes no sense to say of the *expression* "I" that it refers to a particular person. This is the sort of thing that can be said only of a particular use of the expression.

Let me use "type" as an abbreviation for "sentence or expression." Then I am not saying that there are sentences and expressions (types), *and* uses of them, *and* utterances of them, as there are ships *and* shoes *and* sealing-wax. I am saying that we cannot say *the same things* about types, uses of types, and utterances of types. And the fact is that we do talk about types; and that confusion is apt to result from the failure to notice the differences between what we can say about these and what we can say only about the *uses* of types. We are apt to fancy we are talking about sentences and expressions when we are talking about the uses of sentences and expressions.

This is what Russell does. Generally, as against Russell, I shall say this. Meaning (in at least one important sense) is a function of the sentence or expression; mentioning and referring and truth or falsity, are functions of the use of the sentence or expression. To give the meaning of an expression (in the sense in which I am using the word) is to give *general directions* for its use to refer to or mention particular objects or persons; to give the meaning of a sentence is to give *general directions* for its use in making true or false assertions. It is not to talk about any particular occasion of the use of the sentence or expression. The meaning of an expression cannot be identified with the object it is used, on a particular occasion, to refer to. The meaning of a sentence cannot be identified with the assertion it is used, on a particular occasion, to make. For to talk about the meaning of an expression or sentence is not to talk about its use on a particular occasion, but about the rules, habits, conventions governing its correct use,

on all occasions, to refer or to assert. So the question of whether a sentence or expression *is significant* or *not* has nothing whatever to do with the question of whether the sentence, *uttered on a particular occasion,* is, on that occasion, being used to make a true-or-false assertion or not, or of whether the expression is, on that occasion, being used to refer to, or mention, anything at all.

The source of Russell's mistake was that he thought that referring or mentioning, if it occurred at all, must be meaning. He did not distinguish (B1) from (B2); he confused expressions with their use in a particular context; and so confused meaning with mentioning, with referring. If I talk about my handkerchief, I can, perhaps, produce the object I am referring to out of my pocket. I cannot produce the meaning of the expression, "my handkerchief," out of my pocket. Because Russell confused meaning with mentioning, he thought that if there were any expressions having a uniquely referring use, which were what they seemed (i.e., logical subjects) and not something else in disguise, their meaning must *be* the particular object which they were used to refer to. Hence the troublesome mythology of the logically proper name. But if someone asks me the meaning of the expression "this"—once Russell's favorite candidate for this status—I do not hand him the object I have just used the expression to refer to, adding at the same time that the meaning of the word changes every time it is used. Nor do I hand him all the objects it ever has been, or might be, used to refer to. I explain and illustrate the conventions governing the use of the expression. This *is* giving the meaning of the expression. It is quite different from giving (in any sense of giving) the object to which it refers; for the expression itself does not refer to anything; though it can be used, on different occasions, to refer to innumerable things. Now as a matter of fact there is, in English, a sense of the word "mean" in which this word does approximate to "indicate, mention or refer to"; e.g., when somebody (unpleasantly) says, "I mean you"; or when I point and say, "That's the one I mean." But *the one I meant* is quite different from *the meaning of the expression* I used to talk of it. In this special sense of "mean," it is people who mean, not expressions. People use expressions to refer to particular things. But the meaning of an expression is not the set of things or the single thing it may correctly be used to refer to: the meaning is the set of rules, habits, conventions for its use in referring.

It is the same with sentences: even more obviously so. Everyone knows that the sentence, "The table is covered with books," is significant, and everyone knows what it means. But if I ask, "What object is that sentence about?" I am asking an absurd question—a question which cannot be asked about the sentence, but only about some use of the sentence: and in this case the sentence has not been used to talk about something, it has only been taken as an example. In knowing what it means, you are knowing how it could correctly be used to talk about things: so knowing the meaning has nothing to do with knowing about any particular use of the sentence to talk about anything. Similarly, if I ask: "Is the sentence true or false?" I am asking an absurd question, which becomes no less absurd if I add, "It must be one or the other since it is significant." The question is absurd, because the *sentence* is neither true nor false any more than it is *about* some object. Of course the fact that it is significant is the same as the fact that it *can* correctly be used to talk about something and that, in so using it, someone will be making a true or false assertion. And I will add that it will be used to make a true or false assertion *only* if the person using it *is* talking about something. If, when he utters it, he is not talking about anything, then his use is not a genuine one, but a spurious or pseudo-use: he is not making either a true or a false assertion, though he may think he is. And this points the way to the correct answer to the puzzle to which the theory of descriptions gives a fatally incorrect answer. The important point is that the question of whether the sentence is significant or not is quite independent of the question that can be raised about a particular use of it, viz. the question whether it is a genuine or a spurious use, whether it is being used to talk about something, or in make-believe, or as an example in philosophy. The question whether the sentence is significant or not is the question whether there exist such language habits, conventions or rules that the sentence logically could be used to talk about something; and is hence quite independent of the question whether it is being so used on a particular occasion.

III

Consider again the sentence, "The king of France is wise," and the true and false things Russell says about it.

There are at least two true things which Russell would say about the sentence:

1. The first is that it is significant; that if anyone were now to utter it, he would be uttering a significant sentence.

2. The second is that anyone now uttering the sentence would be making a true assertion only if there in fact at present existed one and only one king of France, and if he were wise.

What are the false things which Russell would say about the sentence? They are:

1. That anyone now uttering it would be making a true assertion or a false assertion.

2. That part of what he would be asserting would be that there at present existed one and only one king of France.

I have already given some reasons for thinking that these two statements are incorrect. Now suppose someone were in fact to say to you with a perfectly serious air: "The king of France is wise." Would you say, "That's untrue"? I think it is quite certain that you would not. But suppose he went on to *ask* you whether you thought that what he had just said was true, or was false; whether you agreed or disagreed with what he had just said. I think you would be inclined, with some hesitation, to say that you did not do either; that the question of whether his statement was true or false simply *did not arise,* because there was no such person as the king of France. You might, if he were obviously serious (had a dazed astray-in-the-centuries look), say something like: "I'm afraid you must be under a misapprehension. France is not a monarchy. There is no king of France." And this brings out the point that if a man seriously uttered the sentence, his uttering it would in some sense be *evidence* that he *believed* that there was a king of France. It would not be evidence for his believing this simply in the way in which a man's reaching for his raincoat is evidence for his believing that it is raining. But nor would it be evidence for his believing this in the way in which a man's saying, "It's raining," is evidence for his believing that it is raining. We might put it as follows. To say "The king of France is wise" is, in some sense of 'imply', to *imply* that there is a king of France. But this is a very special and odd sense of 'imply'. 'Implies' in this sense is certainly not equivalent to 'entails' (or 'logically implies'). And this comes out from the fact that when, in response to his statement, we say (as we should) "There is no king of France," we should certainly *not* say we were *contradicting* the statement that the king of France is wise. We are certainly not saying that it is false. We are, rather, giving a reason for saying that the question of whether it is true or false simply does not arise.

And this is where the distinction I drew earlier can help us. The sentence, "The king of France is wise," is certainly significant; but this does not mean that any particular use of it is true or false. We use it truly or falsely when we use it to talk about someone; when, in using the expression, "The king of France," we are in fact mentioning someone. The fact that the sentence and the expression, respectively, are significant just is the fact that the sentence *could* be used, in certain circumstances, to say something true or false, that the expression *could* be used, in certain circumstances, to mention a particular person: and to know their meaning is to know what sort of circumstances these are. So when we utter the sentence without in fact mentioning anybody by the use of the phrase, "The king of France," the sentence does not cease to be significant: We simply *fail* to say anything true or false because we simply fail to mention anybody by this particular use of that perfectly significant phrase. It is, if you like, a spurious use of the sentence, and a spurious use of the expression; though we may (or may not) mistakenly think it a genuine use.

And such spurious uses[2] are very familiar. Sophisticated romancing, sophisticated fiction,[3] depend upon them. If I began, "The king of France is wise," and went on, "and he lives in a golden castle and has a hundred wives" and so on, a hearer would understand me perfectly well, without supposing *either* that I was talking about a particular person, *or* that I was making a false statement to the effect that there existed such a person as my words described. (It is worth adding that where the use of sentences and expressions is overtly fictional, the sense of the word "about" may change. As Moore said, it is perfectly natural and correct to say that some of the statements in *Pickwick Papers* are *about* Mr. Pickwick. But where the use of sentences and expressions is not overtly fictional, this use of "about" seems less correct; i.e., it would not *in general* be correct to say that a statement was about Mr. X or the so-and-so, unless there were such a person or thing. So it is where the romancing is in danger of being taken seriously that we might answer the question, "Who is he talking about?" with "He's not talking about anybody"; but, in saying this, we are not saying that what he is saying is either false or nonsense.)

Overtly fictional uses apart, however, I said just now that to use such an expression as "The king of France" at the beginning of a sentence was, in some sense of 'imply', to imply that there was a king of France. When a man uses such an expression, he does not *assert*, nor does what he says *entail*, a uniquely existential proposition. But one of the conventional functions of the definite article is to act as a *signal* that a unique reference is being made—a signal, not a disguised assertion. When we begin a sentence with "the such-and-such" the use of "the" shows, but does not state, that we are, or intended to be, referring to one particular individual of the species "such-and-such." *Which* particular individual is a matter to be determined from context, time, place, and any other features of this situation of utterance. Now, whenever a man uses any expression, the presumption is that he thinks he is using it correctly: so when he uses the expression, "the such-and-such," in a uniquely referring way, the presumption is that he thinks both that there is *some* individual of that species, and that the context of use will sufficiently determine which one he has in mind. To use the word "the" in this way is then to imply (in the relevant sense of 'imply') that the existential conditions described by Russell are fulfilled. But to use "the" in this way is not to *state* that those conditions are fulfilled. If I begin a sentence with an expression of the form, "the so-and-so," and then am prevented from saying more, I have made no statement of any kind; but I may have succeeded in mentioning someone or something.

The uniquely existential assertion supposed by Russell to be part of any assertion in which a uniquely referring use is made of an expression of the form "the so-and-so" is, he observes, a compound of two assertions. To say that there is a ϕ is to say something compatible with there being several ϕs; to say there is not more than one ϕ is to say something compatible with there being none. To say there is one ϕ and one only is to compound these two assertions. I have so far been concerned mostly with the alleged assertion of existence and less with the alleged assertion of uniqueness. An example which throws the emphasis on the latter will serve to bring out more clearly the sense of 'implied' in which a uniquely existential assertion is implied, but not entailed, by the use of expressions in the uniquely referring way. Consider the sentence, "The table is covered with books." It is quite certain that in any normal use of this sentence, the expression "the table" would be used to make a unique reference, i.e., to refer to some one table. It is a quite strict use of the definite article, in the sense in which Russell talks on p. 30 of *Principia Mathematica,* of using the article "*strictly, so as to imply uniqueness.*" On the same page Russell says that a phrase of the form "the so-and-so," used strictly, "will only have an application in the event of there being one so-and-so and no more." Now it is obviously quite false that the phrase "the table" in the sentence "the table is covered with books," used normally, will "only have an application in the event of there being one table and no more." It is indeed tautologically true that, in such a use, the phrase will have an application only in the event of there being one table and no more *which is being referred to,* and that it will be understood to have an application only in the event of there being one table and no more which it is understood as being used to refer to. To use the sentence is not to assert, but it is (in the special sense discussed) to imply, that there is only one thing which is *both* of the kind specified (i.e., a table) *and is being referred to* by the speaker. It is obviously not to assert this. To refer is not to say you are referring. To say there is *some table or other* to which you are referring is not the same as referring to a particular table. We should have no use for such phrases as "the individual I referred to" unless there were something which counted as referring. (It would make no sense to say you had pointed if there were nothing which counted as pointing.) So once more I draw the con-

clusion that referring to or mentioning a particular thing cannot be dissolved into any kind of assertion. To refer is not to assert, though you refer in order to go on to assert.

Let me now take an example of the uniquely referring use of an expression not of the form, "the so-and-so." Suppose I advance my hands, cautiously cupped, towards someone, saying, as I do so, "This is a fine red one." He, looking into my hands and seeing nothing there, may say: "What is? What are you talking about?" Or perhaps, "But there's nothing in your hands." Of course it would be absurd to say that, in saying "But you've got nothing in your hands," he was *denying* or *contradicting* what I said. So "this" is not a disguised description in Russell's sense. Nor is it a logically proper name. For one must know what the sentence means in order to react in that way to the utterance of it. It is precisely because the significance of the word "this" is independent of any particular reference it may be used to make, though not independent of the way it may be used to refer, that I can, as in this example, use it to *pretend* to be referring to something.

The general moral of all this is that communication is much less a matter of explicit or disguised assertion than logicians used to suppose. The particular application of this general moral in which I am interested is its application to the case of making a unique reference. It is a part of the significance of expressions of the kind I am discussing that they can be used, in an immense variety of contexts, to make unique references. It is no part of their significance to assert that they are being used or that the conditions of their being so used are fulfilled. So the wholly important distinction we are required to draw is between

1. using an expression to make a unique reference; and

2. asserting that there is one and only one individual which has certain characteristics (e.g., is of a certain kind, or stands in a certain relation to the speaker, or both).

This is, in other words, the distinction between

1. sentences containing an expression used to indicate or mention or refer to a particular person or thing; and

2. uniquely existential sentences.

What Russell does is progressively to assimilate more and more sentences of class (1) to sentences of class (2), and consequently to involve himself in insuperable difficulties about logical subjects, and about values for individual variables generally: difficulties which have led him finally to the logically disastrous theory of names developed in the *Enquiry into Meaning and Truth* and in *Human Knowledge*. That view of the meaning of logical-subject-expressions which provides the whole incentive to the Theory of Descriptions at the same time precludes the possibility of Russell's ever finding any satisfactory substitutes for those expressions which, beginning with substantival phrases, he progressively degrades from the status of logical subjects.[4] It is not simply, as is sometimes said, the fascination of the relation between a name and its bearer, that is the root of the trouble. Not even names come up to the impossible standard set. It is rather the combination of two more radical misconceptions: first, the failure to grasp the importance of the distinction (section II above) between what may be said of an expression and what may be said of a particular use of it; second, a failure to recognize the uniquely referring use of expressions for the harmless, necessary thing it is, distinct from, but complementary to, the predicative or ascriptive use of expressions. The expressions which can in fact occur as singular logical subjects are expressions of the class I listed at the outset (demonstratives, substantival phrases, proper names, pronouns): to say this is to say that these expressions, together with context (in the widest sense), are what one uses to make unique references. The point of the conventions governing the uses of such expressions is, along with the situation of utterance, to secure uniqueness of reference. But to do this, enough is enough. We do not, and we cannot, while referring, attain the point of complete explicitness at which the referring function is no longer performed. The actual unique reference made, if any, is a matter of the particular use in the particular context; the significance of the expression used is the set of rules or conventions which permit such references to be made. Hence we can, using significant expressions, pretend to refer, in make-believe or in fiction, or mistakenly think we are referring when we are not referring to anything.[5]

This shows the need for distinguishing two kinds (among many others) of linguistic conventions or rules: rules for referring, and rules for attributing and ascribing; and for an investigation of the former. If we recognize this distinction of use for what it is, we are on the way to solving a number of ancient logical and metaphysical puzzles.

My last two sections are concerned, but only in the barest outline, with these questions.

IV

One of the main purposes for which we use language is the purpose of stating facts about things and persons and events. If we want to fulfill this purpose we must have some way of forestalling the question, "What (who, which one) are you talking about?" as well as the question, "What are you saying about it (him, her)?" The task of forestalling the first question is the referring (or identifying) task. The task of forestalling the second is the attributive (or descriptive or classificatory or ascriptive) task. In the conventional English sentence which is used to state, or to claim to state, a fact about an individual thing or person or event, the performance of these two tasks can be roughly and approximately assigned to separable expressions.[6] And in such a sentence, this assigning of expressions to their separate roles corresponds to the conventional grammatical classification of subject and predicate. There is nothing sacrosanct about the employment of separable expressions for these two tasks. Other methods could be, and are, employed. There is, for instance, the method of uttering a single word or attributive phrase in the conspicuous presence of the object referred to; or that analogous method exemplified by, e.g., the painting of the words "unsafe for lorries" on a bridge, or the tying of a label reading "first prize" on a vegetable marrow. Or one can imagine an elaborate game in which one never used an expression in the uniquely referring way at all, but uttered only uniquely existential sentences, trying to enable the hearer to identify what was being talked of by means of an accumulation of relative clauses. (This description of the purposes of the game shows in what sense it would be a game: this is not the normal use we make of existential sentences.) Two points require emphasis. The first is that the necessity of performing these two tasks in order to state particular facts requires no transcendental explanation: To call attention to it is partly to elucidate the meaning of the phrase, "stating a fact." The second is that even this elucidation is made in terms derivative from the grammar of the conventional singular sentence; that even the overtly functional, linguistic distinction between the identifying and attributive roles that words may play in language is prompted by the fact that ordinary speech offers us separable expressions to which the different functions may be plausibly and approximately assigned. And this functional distinction has cast long philosophical shadows. The distinctions between particular and universal, between substance and quality, are such pseudo-material shadows, cast by the grammar. of the conventional sentence, in which separable expressions play distinguishable roles.[7]

To use a separate expression to perform the first of these tasks is to use an expression in the uniquely referring way. I want now to say something in general about the conventions of use for expressions used in this way, and to contrast them with conventions of ascriptive use. I then proceed to the brief illustration of these general remarks and to some further applications of them.

What in general is required for making a unique reference is, obviously, some device, or devices, for showing both *that* a unique reference is intended and *what* unique reference it is; some device requiring and enabling the hearer or reader to identify what is being talked about. In securing this result, the context of utterance is of an importance which it is almost impossible to exaggerate; and by "context" I mean, at least, the time, the place, the situation, the identity of the speaker, the subjects which form the immediate focus of interest, and the personal histories of both the speaker and those he is addressing. Besides context, there is, of course, convention—linguistic convention. But, except in the case of genuine proper names, of which I shall have more to say later, the fulfillment of more or less precisely stateable contextual conditions is *conventionally* (or, in a wide sense of the word, *logically*) required for the correct referring use of expressions in a sense in which this is not true of correct ascriptive uses. The requirement for the correct application of an expression in its ascriptive use to a certain thing is simply that the thing should be of a certain kind,

have certain characteristics. The requirement for the correct application of an expression in its referring use to a certain thing is something over and above any requirement derived from such ascriptive meaning as the expression may have; it is, namely, the requirement that the thing should be in a certain relation to the speaker and to the context of utterance. Let me call this the contextual requirement. Thus, for example, in the limiting case of the word "I" the contextual requirement is that the thing should be identical with the speaker; but in the case of most expressions which have a referring use this requirement cannot be so precisely specified. A further, and perfectly general, difference between conventions for referring and conventions for describing is one we have already encountered, viz. that the fulfillment of the conditions for a correct ascriptive use of an expression is a part of what is stated by such a use; but the fulfillment of the conditions for a correct referring use of an expression is never part of what is stated, though it is (in the relevant sense of 'implied') implied by such a use.

Conventions for referring have been neglected or misinterpreted by logicians. The reasons for this neglect are not hard to see, though they are hard to state briefly. Two of them are, roughly: (1) the preoccupation of most logicians with definitions; (2) the preoccupation of some logicians with formal systems.

(1) A definition, in the most familiar sense, is a specification of the conditions of the correct ascriptive or classificatory use of an expression. Definitions take no account of contextual requirements. So that in so far as the search for the meaning or the search for the analysis of an expression is conceived as the search for a definition, the neglect or misinterpretation of conventions other than ascriptive is inevitable. Perhaps it would be better to say (for I do not wish to legislate about "meaning" or "analysis") that logicians have failed to notice that problems of use are wider than problems of analysis and meaning.

(2) The influence of the preoccupation with mathematics and formal logic is most clearly seen (to take no more recent examples) in the cases of Leibniz and Russell. The constructor of calculuses, not concerned or required to make factual statements, approaches applied logic with a prejudice. It is natural that he should assume that the types of convention with whose adequacy in one field he is

familiar should be really adequate, if only one could see how, in a quite different field—that of statements of fact. Thus we have Leibniz striving desperately to make the uniqueness of unique references a matter of logic in the narrow sense, and Russell striving desperately to do the same thing, in a different way, both for the implication of uniqueness and for that of existence.

It should be clear that the distinction I am trying to draw is primarily one between different roles or parts that expressions may play in language, and not primarily one between different groups of expressions; for some expressions may appear in either role. Some of the kinds of words I shall speak of have predominantly, if not exclusively, a referring role. This is most obviously true of pronouns and ordinary proper names. Some can occur as wholes or parts of expressions which have a predominantly referring use, and as wholes or parts of expressions which have a predominantly ascriptive or classificatory use. The obvious cases are common nouns; or common nouns preceded by adjectives, including participial adjectives; or, less obviously adjectives or participial adjectives alone. Expressions capable of having a referring use also differ from one another in at least the three following, not mutually independent, ways.

(1) They differ in the extent to which the reference they are used to make is dependent on the context of their utterance. Words like "I" and "it" stand at one end of this scale—the end of maximum dependence—and phrases like "the author of *Waverley*" and "the eighteenth king of France" at the other.

(2) They differ in the degree of 'descriptive meaning' they possess: by 'descriptive meaning' I intend 'conventional limitation, in application, to things of a certain general kind, or possessing certain general characteristics'. At one end of this scale stand the proper names we most commonly use in ordinary discourse; men, dogs, and motor-bicycles may be called "Horace." The pure name has no descriptive meaning (except such as it may acquire *as a result of* some one of its use as a name). A word like "he" has minimal descriptive meaning, but has some. Substantival phrases like "the round table" have the maximum descriptive meaning. An interesting intermediate position is occupied by 'impure' proper names like "The Round Table"—substantival phrases which have grown capital letters.

(3) Finally, they may be divided into the following two classes: (i) those of which the correct referring use is regulated by some *general* referring-cum-ascriptive conventions; (ii) those of which the correct referring use is regulated by no general conventions, either of the contextual or the ascriptive kind, but by conventions which are ad hoc for each particular use (though not for each particular utterance). To the first class belong both pronouns (which have the least descriptive meaning) and substantival phrases (which have the most). To the second class belong, roughly speaking, the most familiar kind of proper names. Ignorance of a man's name is not ignorance of the language. This is why we do not speak of the meaning of proper names. (But it won't do to say they are meaningless.) Again an intermediate position is occupied by such phrases as "The Old Pretender." Only an old pretender may be so referred to; but to know which old pretender is not to know a general, but an ad hoc, convention.

In the case of phrases of the form "the so-and-so" used referringly, the use of "the" together with the position of the phrase in the sentence (i.e., at the beginning, or following a transitive verb or preposition) acts as a signal *that* a unique reference is being made; and the following noun, or noun and adjective, together with the context of utterance, shows *what* unique reference is being made. In general the functional difference between common nouns and adjective is that the former are naturally and commonly used referringly, while the latter are not commonly, or so naturally, used in this way, except as qualifying nouns; though they can be, and are, so used alone. And of course this functional difference is not independent of the descriptive force peculiar to each word. In general we should expect the descriptive force of nouns to be such that they are more efficient tools for the job of showing what unique reference is intended when such a reference is signalized; and we should also expect the descriptive force of the words we naturally and commonly use to make unique references to mirror our interest in the salient, relatively permanent and behavioral characteristics of things. These two expectations are not independent of one another; and, if we look at the differences between the commoner sort of common nouns and the commoner sort of adjectives, we find them both fulfilled. These are differences of the kind that Locke quaintly reports, when he speaks of our ideas of substances being *collections* of simple ideas; when he says that "powers make up a great part of our ideas of substances"; and when he goes on to contrast the identity of real and nominal essence in the case of simple ideas with their lack of identity and the shiftingness of the nominal essence in the case of substances. 'Substance' itself is the troublesome tribute Locke pays to his dim awareness of the difference in predominant linguistic function that lingered even when the noun had been expanded into a more or less indefinite string of adjectives. Russell repeats Locke's mistake with a difference when, admitting the inference from syntax to reality to the extent of feeling that he can get rid of this metaphysical unknown only if he can purify language of the referring function altogether, he draws up his program for "abolishing particulars"; a programme, in fact, for abolishing the distinction of logical use which I am here at pains to emphasize.

The contextual requirement for the referring use of pronouns may be stated with the greatest precision in some cases (e.g., "I" and "you") and only with the greatest vagueness in others ("it" and "this"). I propose to say nothing further about pronouns, except to point to an additional symptom of the failure to recognize the uniquely referring use for what it is; the fact, namely, that certain logicians have actually sought to elucidate the nature of a variable by offering such *sentences* as "he is sick," "it is green," as examples of something in ordinary speech like a *sentential function*. Now of course it is true that the word "he" may be used on different occasions to refer to different people or different animals: so may the word "John" and the phrase "the cat." What deters such logicians from treating these two expressions as quasi-variables is, in the first case, the lingering superstition that a name is logically tied to a single individual, and, in the second case, the descriptive meaning of the word "cat." But "he," which has a wide range of applications and minimal descriptive force, only acquires a use as a referring word. It is this fact, together with the failure to accord to expressions, used referringly, the place in logic which belongs to them (the place held open for the mythical logically proper name), that ac-

counts for the misleading attempt to elucidate the nature of the variable by reference to such words as "he," "she," "it."

Of ordinary proper names it is sometimes said that they are essentially words each of which is used to refer to just one individual. This is obviously false. Many ordinary personal names—names *par excellence*—are correctly used to refer to numbers of people. An ordinary personal name is, roughly, a word, used referringly, of which the use is *not* dictated by any descriptive meaning the word may have, and is *not* prescribed by any such general rule for use as a referring expression (or a part of a referring expression) as we find in the case of such words as "I," "this" and "the," but is governed by ad hoc conventions for each particular set of applications of the word to a given person. The important point is that the correctness of such applications does not follow from any *general* rule or convention for the use of the word as such. (The limit of absurdity and obvious circularity is reached in the attempt to treat names as disguised description in Russell's sense; for what is in the special sense implied, but not entailed, by my now referring to someone by name is simply the existence of someone, *now being referred to,* who is *conventionally referred to* by that name.) Even this feature of names, however, is only a symptom of the purpose for which they are employed. At present our choice of names is partly arbitrary, partly dependent on legal and social observances. It would be perfectly possible to have a thorough-going *system* of names, based e.g., on dates of birth, or on a minute classification of physiological and anatomical differences. But the success of any such system would depend entirely on the convenience of the resulting name-allotments for the purpose of making unique references; and this would depend on the multiplicity of the classifications used and the degree to which they cut haphazardly across normal social groupings. Given a sufficient degree of both, the selectivity supplied by context would do the rest; just as in the case with our present naming habits. Had we such a system, we could use name-words descriptively (as we do at present, to a limited extent and in a different way, with some famous names) as well as referringly. But it is by criteria derived from consideration of the requirements of the referring task that we should assess the adequacy of any system of naming. From the naming point of view, no kind of classification would be better or worse than any other simply because of the kind of classification—natal or anatomical—that it was.

I have already mentioned the class of quasi-names, of substantival phrases which grow capital letters, and of which such phrases as "the Glorious Revolution," "the Great War," the Annunciation," "the Round Table" are examples. While the descriptive meaning of the words which follow the definite article is still relevant to their referring role, the capital letters are a sign of that extralogical selectivity in their referring use, which is characteristic of pure names. Such phrases are found in print or in writing when one member of some class of events or things is of quite outstanding interest in a certain society. These phrases are embryonic names. A phrase may, for obvious reasons, pass into, and out of, this class (e.g., "the Great War").

V

I want to conclude by considering, all too briefly, three further problems about referring uses.

(a) *Indefinite references:* Not all referring uses of singular expressions forestall the question "What (who, which one) are you talking about?" There are some which either invite this question, or disclaim the intention or ability to answer it. Examples are such sentence-beginnings as "A man told me that . . . ," "Someone told me that . . .". The orthodox (Russellian) doctrine is that such sentences are existential, but not uniquely existential. This seems wrong in several ways. It is ludicrous to suggest that part of what is asserted is that the class of men or persons is not empty. Certainly this is *implied* in the by now familiar sense of implication; but the implication is also as much an implication of the *uniqueness* of the particular object of reference as when I begin a sentence with such a phrase as "the table." The difference between the use of the definite and indefinite articles is, very roughly, as follows. We use "the" either when a previous reference has been made, and when "the" signalizes that the same reference is being made; or when, in the absence of a previous indefinite reference, the context (including the hearer's assumed knowledge) is expected to enable the hearer to tell

what reference is being made. We use "a" either when these conditions are not fulfilled, or when, although a definite reference *could* be made, we wish to keep dark the identity of the individual to whom, or to which, we are referring. This is the *arch* use of such a phrase as "a certain person" or "someone"; where it could be expanded, not into "someone, but you wouldn't (or I don't) know who" but into "someone, but I'm not telling you who."

(b) *Identification statements:* By this label I intend statements like the following:

(i*a*) That is the man who swam the channel twice on one day.

(ii*a*) Napoleon was the man who ordered the execution of the Duc d'Enghien.

The puzzle about these statements is that their grammatical predicates do not seem to be used in a straightforwardly ascriptive way as are the grammatical predicates of the statements:

(i*b*) That man swam the channel twice in one day.

(ii*b*) Napoleon ordered the execution of the Duc d'Enghien.

But if, in order to avoid blurring the difference between (i*a*) and (i*b*) and (ii*a*) and (ii*b*), one says that the phrases which form the grammatical complements of (i*a*) and (ii*a*) are being used referringly, one becomes puzzled about what is being said in these sentences. We seem then to be referring to the same person twice over and either saying nothing about him and thus making no statement, or identifying him with himself and thus producing a trivial identity.

The bogy of triviality can be dismissed. This only arises for those who think of the object referred to by the use of an expression as its meaning, and thus think of the subject and complement of these sentences as meaning the same because they could be used to refer to the same person.

I think the differences between sentences in the (*a*) group and sentences in the (*b*) group can best be understood by considering the differences between the circumstances in which you would say (i*a*) and the circumstances in which you would say (i*b*). You would say (i*a*) instead of (i*b*) if you knew or believed that your hearer knew or believed that *someone* had swum the channel twice in one day. You say (i*a*) when you take your hearer to be in the position of one who can ask: "Who swam the channel twice in one day?" (And in asking this, he is not saying that anyone did, though his asking it implies—in the relevant sense—that someone did.) Such sentences are like answers to such questions. They are better called 'identification-statements' than 'identities'. Sentence (i*a*) does not assert more or less than sentence (i*b*). It is just that you say (i*a*) to a man whom you take to know certain things that you take to be unknown to the man to whom you say (i*b*).

This is, in the barest essentials, the solution to Russell's puzzle about 'denoting phrases' joined by "is"; one of the puzzles which he claims for the theory of descriptions the merit of solving.

(3) *The logic of subjects and predicates:* Much of what I have said of the uniquely referring use of expressions can be extended, with suitable modifications, to the non-uniquely referring use of expressions; i.e., to some uses of expressions consisting of "the," "all the," "all," "some," "some of the," etc. followed by a noun, qualified or unqualified, in the *plural;* to some uses of "they," "them," "those," "these"; and to conjunctions of names. Expressions of the first kind have a special interest. Roughly speaking, orthodox modern criticism, inspired by mathematical logic, of such traditional doctrines as that of the Square of Opposition and of some of the forms of the syllogism traditionally recognized as valid, rests on the familiar failure to recognize the special sense in which existential assertions may be implied by the referring use of expressions. The universal propositions of the fourfold schedule, it is said, must *either* be given a negatively existential interpretation (e.g., for A, "there are no Xs which are not Ys") *or* they must be interpreted as conjunctions of negatively and positively existential statements of, e.g., the form (for A) "there are no Xs which are not Ys, and there are Xs." The I and O forms are normally given a positively existential interpretation. It is then seen that, whichever of the above alternatives is selected, some of the traditional laws have to be abandoned. The dilemma, however, is a bogus one. If we interpret the propositions of the schedule as neither positively, nor negatively, nor positively *and* negatively, existential, but as sentences such that *the question of whether they are being used to make true or*

false assertions does not arise except when the existential condition is fulfilled for the subject term, then all the traditional laws hold good together. And this interpretation is far closer to the most common uses of expressions beginning with "all" and "some" than is any Russellian alternative. For these expressions are most commonly used in the referring way. A literal-minded and childless man asked whether all his children are asleep will certainly not answer "Yes" on the ground that he has none; but nor will he answer "No" on this ground. Since he has no children, the question does not arise. To say this is not to say that I may not use the sentence, "All my children are asleep," with the intention of letting someone know that I have children, or of deceiving him into thinking that I have. Nor is it any weakening of my thesis to concede that singular phrases of the form "the so-and-so" may sometimes be used with a similar purpose. Neither Aristotelian nor Russellian rules give the exact logic of any expression of ordinary language; for ordinary language has no exact logic.

NOTES

1. This usage of "use" is, of course, different from (a) the current usage in which 'use' (of a particular word, phrase, sentence) = (roughly) 'rules for using' = (roughly) 'meaning'; and from (*b*) my own usage in the phrase "uniquely referring use of expressions" in which "use" = (roughly) 'way of using'.

2. The choice of the word "spurious" now seems to me unfortunate, at least for some nonstandard uses. I should now prefer to call some of these "secondary" uses.

3. The unsophisticated kind begins: "Once upon time there was . . ."

4. And this in spite of the danger-signal of that phrase, "*misleading* grammatical form."

5. This sentence now seems to me objectionable in a number of ways, notably because of an unexplicitly restrictive use of the word 'refer'. It could be more exactly phrased as follows: 'Hence we can, using significant expressions, refer in secondary ways, as in make-believe or in fiction, or mistakenly think we are referring to something in the primary way when we are not, in that way, referring to anything'.

6. I neglect relational sentences; for these require, not a modification in the principle of what I say, but a complication of the detail.

7. What is said or implied in the last two sentences of this paragraph no longer seems to me true, unless considerably qualified.

The Meaning of a Word   4

J. L. AUSTIN

Specimens of Sense

1.1.	What-is-the-meaning-of (the word) 'rat'?
1.11.	What-is-the-meaning-of (the word) 'word'?
1.21.	What is a 'rat'?
1.211.	What is a 'word'?
1.22.	What is the 'muzzle' of a rat?
2.1.	What-is-the-meaning-of (the phrase) 'What-is-the-meaning-of'?
2.11.	What-is-the-meaning-of (the sentence) 'What-is-the-meaning-of (the word) "*x*"?'?

Specimens of Nonsense

1.1.	What-is-the-meaning-of a word?
1.11.	What-is-the-meaning-of any word?
1.12.	What-is-the-meaning-of a word in general?
1.21.	What is the-meaning-of-a-word?
1.211.	What is the-meaning-of-(the-word)-'rat'?
1.22.	What is the 'meaning' of a word?
1.221.	What is the 'meaning' of (the word) 'rat'?
2.1.	What-is-the-meaning-of (the phrase) 'the-meaning-of-a work'?
2.11.	What-is-the-meaning-of (the sentence) 'What is the-meaning-of-(the-word)-"*x*"?'?
2.12.	What-is-the-meaning-of (the sentence) 'What is the "meaning" of "the word" "*x*"?'?

THIS PAPER IS ABOUT the phrase 'the meaning of a word'. It is divided into three parts, of which the first is the most trite and the second the most muddled: all are too long. In the first, I try to make it clear that the phrase 'the meaning of a word' is, in general, if not always, a dangerous nonsense-phrase. In the other two parts I consider in turn two questions, often asked in philosophy, which clearly need new and careful scrutiny if that facile phrase 'the meaning of a word' is no longer to be permitted to impose upon us.

I

I begin, then, with some remarks about 'the meaning of a word'. I think many persons now see all or part of what I shall say: but not all do, and there is a tendency to forget it, or to get it slightly wrong. In so far as I am merely flogging the converted, I apologize to them.

A preliminary remark. It may justly be urged that, properly speaking, what alone has meaning is a *sentence*. Of course, we can speak quite properly of, for example, 'looking up the meaning of a word' in a dictionary. Nevertheless, it appears that the sense in which a word or a phrase 'has a meaning' is derivative from the sense in which a sentence 'has a meaning': to say a word or a phrase 'has a meaning' is to say that there are sentences in which it occurs which 'have meanings': and to know the meaning which the word or phrase has, is to know the meanings of sentences in which it occurs. All the dictionary can do when we 'look up the meaning of a word' is to suggest aids to the understanding of sentences in which it occurs. Hence it appears correct to say that what 'has meaning' in the primary sense is the sentence. And older philosophers who discussed the problem of 'the meaning of words' tend to fall into *special* errors, avoided by more recent philosophers, who discuss rather the parallel problem of 'the meaning of

J. L. Austin, *Philosophical Papers*, ed. J. O. Urmson and G. J. Warnock. © Oxford University Press, 1961, 1970, 1979. Originally written in 1940. Reprinted by permission of Oxford University Press.

sentences'. Nevertheless, if we are on our guard, we perhaps need not fall into these special errors, and I propose to overlook them at present.

There are many sorts of sentence in which the words 'the meaning of the word so-and-so' are found, e.g., 'He does not know, or understand, the meaning of the word *handsaw*': 'I shall have to explain to her the meaning of the word *pikestaff*': and so on. I intend to consider primarily the common question, 'What is the meaning of *so-and-so?*' or 'What is the meaning of *the word so-and-so?*'

Suppose that in ordinary life I am asked: 'What is the meaning of the word *racy?*' There are two sorts of thing I may do in response: I may reply *in words*, trying to describe what raciness is and what it is not, to give examples of sentences in which one might use the word *racy*, and of others in which one should not. Let us call this *sort* of thing 'explaining the syntactics' of the word 'racy' in the English language. On the other hand, I might do what we may call 'demonstrating the semantics' of the word, by getting the questioner to *imagine*, or even actually to *experience*, situations which we should describe correctly by means of sentences containing the words 'racy' 'raciness', etc., and again other situations where we should *not* use these words. This is, of course, a simple case: but perhaps the same two *sorts* of procedure would be gone through in the case of at least most ordinary words. And in the same way, if I wished to find out 'whether he understands the meaning of the word *racy*', I should test him at some length in these two ways (which perhaps could not be entirely divorced from each other).

Having asked in this way, and answered, 'What is the meaning of (the word) "rat"?', 'What is the meaning of (the word) "cat"?', 'What is the meaning of (the word) "mat"?' and so on, we then try, being philosophers, to ask the further *general* question, 'What is the meaning of a word?' But there is something spurious about this question. We do not intend to mean by it a certain question which would be perfectly all right, namely, 'What is the meaning of (the word) "word"?': *that* would be no more general than is asking the meaning of the word 'rat', and would be answered in a precisely similar way. No: we want to ask rather, 'What is the meaning of a-word-in-general?' or 'of *any* word'—not meaning 'any' word *you like to choose*, but rather *no particular* word

at all, just 'any word'. Now if we pause even for a moment to reflect, this is a perfectly absurd question to be trying to ask. I can only answer a question of the form 'What is the meaning of "*x*"?' if "*x*" is some *particular* word you are asking about. This supposed *general* question is really just a spurious question of a type which commonly arises in philosophy. We may call it the fallacy of asking about 'Nothing-in-particular' which is a practice decried by the plain man, but by the philosopher called 'generalizing' and regarded with some complacency. Many other examples of the fallacy can be found: take, for example, the case of 'reality'—we try to pass from such questions as 'How would you distinguish a real rat from an imaginary rat?' to 'What is a real thing?', a question which merely gives rise to nonsense.

We may expose the error in our present case thus. Instead of asking 'What is the meaning of (the word) "rat"?' we might clearly have asked 'What is a "rat"?' and so on. But if our questions have been put in *that* form, it becomes very difficult to formulate any *general* question which could impose on us for a moment. Perhaps 'What is anything?'? Few philosophers, if perhaps not none, have been foolhardy enough to pose such a question. In the same way, we should not perhaps be tempted to generalize such a question as 'Does he know the meaning of (the word) "rat"?' 'Does he know the meaning of a word?' would be silly.

Faced with the nonsense question 'What is the meaning of a word?', and perhaps dimly recognizing it to be nonsense, we are nevertheless not inclined to give it up. Instead, we transform it in a curious and noteworthy manner. Up to now, we had been asking '*What-is-the-meaning-of* (the word) "rat"?', etc.; and ultimately '*What-is-the-meaning-of* a word?' But now, being baffled, we change so to speak, the hyphenation, and ask 'What is *the-meaning-of-a-word?*' or sometimes, 'What is the "meaning" of a word?' (1.22): I shall refer, for brevity's sake, only to the other (1.21). It is easy to see how very different this question is from the other. At once a crowd of traditional and reassuring answers present themselves: 'a concept', 'an idea', 'an image', 'a class of similar sensa', etc. All of which are equally spurious answers to a pseudo-question. Plunging ahead, however, or rather retracing our steps, we now proceed to ask such questions as

'What is the-meaning-of-(the-word) "rat"?' which is as spurious as 'What-is-the-meaning-of (the word) "rat"?' was genuine. And again we answer 'the idea of a rat' and so forth. How quaint this procedure is, may be seen in the following way. Supposing, a plain man puzzled, were to ask me 'What is the meaning of (the word) "muggy"?', and I were to answer, 'The idea or concept of "mugginess"' or 'The class of sensa of which it is correct to say "This is muggy"': the man would stare at me as at an imbecile. And that is sufficiently unusual for me to conclude that that was not at all the sort of answer he expected: nor, in plain English, *can* that question *ever* require that sort of answer.

To show up this pseudo-question, let us take a parallel case, where perhaps no one has yet been deluded, though they well might be. Suppose that I ask 'What is the point of doing so-and-so?' For example, I ask Old Father William 'What is the point of standing on one's head?' He replies in the way we know. Then I follow this up with 'What is the point of balancing an eel on the end of one's nose?' And he explains. Now suppose I ask as my third question 'What is the point of doing *anything*—not anything *in particular,* but just *anything*?' Old Father William would no doubt kick me downstairs without the option. But lesser men, raising this same question and finding no answer, would very likely commit suicide or join the Church. (Luckily, in the case of 'What is the meaning of a word?' the effects are less serious, amounting only to the writing of books.) On the other hand, more adventurous intellects would no doubt take to asking 'What is the-point-of-doing-a-thing?' or 'What is the "point" of doing a thing?': and then later 'What is the-point-of-eating-suet?' and so on. Thus we should discover a whole new universe of a kind of entity called 'points', not previously suspected of existence.

To make the matter clearer, let us consider another case which is precisely *unlike* the case of 'What is the meaning of?' I can ask not only the question, 'What is the square root of 4?', of 8, and so on, but also 'What is the square root of a number?': which is either nonsense or equivalent to 'What is the "square root" of a number?' I then give a definition of the 'square root' of a number, such that, for any given number $x,$ 'the square root of x' is a definite description of another number y. This differs from

our case in that 'the meaning of p' is not a definite description of any entity.

The general questions which we want to ask about 'meaning' are best phrased as, 'What-is-the-meaning-of (the phrase) "what-is-the-meaning-of (the word) 'x'?"?' The *sort* of answer we should get to these quite sensible questions is that with which I began this discussion: viz. that when I am asked 'What-is-the-meaning-of (the word) "x"?', I naturally reply by explaining its syntactics and demonstrating its semantics.

All this must seem very obvious, but I wish to point out that it is fatally easy to forget it: no doubt I shall do so myself many times in the course of this paper. Even those who see pretty clearly that 'concepts', 'abstract ideas', and so on are fictitious entities, which we owe in part to asking questions about 'the meaning of a word', nevertheless themselves think that there *is something* which is 'the meaning of a word'. Thus Mr. Hampshire[1] attacks to some purpose the theory that there is such a thing as '*the* meaning of a word': what *he* thinks is wrong is the belief that there is a *single* thing called *the* meaning: 'concepts' are nonsense, and no single particular 'image' can be *the* meaning of a general word. So, he goes on to say, the meaning of a word must really be 'a *class* of similar particular ideas'. 'If we are asked "What does this mean?" we point to (!) a class of particular ideas.' But a 'class of particular ideas' is every bit as fictitious an entity as a 'concept' or 'abstract idea'. In the same way Mr. C. W. Morris (in the *Encyclopaedia of Unified Science*) attacks, to some purpose, those who think of 'a meaning' as a definite something which is 'simply located' somewhere: what *he* thinks is wrong is that people think of 'a meaning' as a kind of entity which can be described wholly without reference to the total activity of 'semiosis'. Well and good. Yet he himself makes some of the crudest possible remarks about 'the designatum' of a word: every sign has a designatum, which is not a particular thing but a *kind* of object or *class* of object. Now this is quite as fictitious an entity as any 'Platonic idea': and is due to precisely the same fallacy of looking for 'the meaning (or designatum) of a word'.

Why are we tempted to slip back in this way? Perhaps there are two main reasons. First, there is the curious belief that all words are *names,* i.e., in effect *proper* names, and therefore stand for something or designate it in the way that a proper name does. But this view that general names 'have denotation' in the same way that proper names do, is quite as odd as the view that proper names 'have connotation' in the same way that general names do, which is commonly recognized to lead to error. Secondly, we are afflicted by a more common malady, which is this. When we have given an analysis of a certain sentence, containing a word or phrase '*x*', we often feel inclined to ask, of our analysis, 'What *in it, is* "*x*"?' For example, we give an analysis of 'The State owns this land', in sentences about individual men, their relations and transactions: and then at last we feel inclined to ask: well now, *what*, in all that, *is* the State? And we might answer: the State *is* a collection of individual men united in a certain manner. Or again, when we have analysed the statement 'trees can exist unperceived' into statements about sensing sensa, we still tend to feel uneasy unless we can say *something 'really does'* 'exist unperceived': hence theories about 'sensibilia' and what not. So in our present case, having given all that is required, viz. an account of 'What-is-the-meaning-of "What is-the-meaning-of (the word) '*x*'?" ' we *still* feel tempted, wrongly supposing our original sentence to contain a constituent 'the-meaning-of (the-word)-"*x*" ', to ask 'Well now, as it turns out, what *is* the meaning of the word "*x*", after all?' And we answer, 'a class of similar particular ideas' and what not.

Of course, all my account of our motives in this matter may be only a convenient didactic schema: I do not think it is—but I recognize that one should not impute motives, least of all rational motives. Anyhow, what I claim is clear, is that there is *no* simple and handy appendage of a word called 'the meaning of (the word) "*x*" '.

II

I now pass on to the first of the two points which need now a careful scrutiny if we are no longer to be imposed upon by that convenient phrase 'the meaning of a word'. What I shall say here is, I know, not as clear as it should be.

Constantly we ask the question, 'Is *y* the meaning, or *part* of the meaning, or *contained* in the meaning, of *x*?—or is it *not*?' A favourite way of putting the question is to ask, 'Is the judgement "*x* is *y*" analytic or synthetic?' Clearly, we suppose, *y must* be *either* a part of the meaning of *x*, *or* not any part of it. And, if *y is* a part of the meaning of *x*, to say '*x* is not *y*' will be self-contradictory: while if it is *not* a part of the meaning of *x*, to say '*x* is not *y*' will present no difficulty—such a state of affairs will be readily 'conceivable'. This seems to be the merest common sense. And no doubt it *would* be the merest common sense *if* 'meanings' were things in some ordinary sense which contained parts in some ordinary sense. But they are *not*. Unfortunately, many philosophers who know they are not, still speak as though *y* must either be or not be 'part of the meaning' of *x*. But this is the point: *if* 'explaining the meaning of a word' is really the complicated sort of affair that we have seen it to be, and *if* there is really nothing to call 'the meaning of a word'—*then* phrases like 'part of the meaning of the word *x* are completely undefined; it is left hanging in the air, we do not know what it means at all. *We are using a working-model which fails to fit the facts that we really wish to talk about.* When we consider what we really do want to talk about, and not the working-model, what would really be meant at all by a judgement being 'analytic or synthetic'? We simply do not know. Of course, we feel inclined to say 'I can easily produce examples of analytic and synthetic judgements; for instance, I should confidently say "Being a professor is *not* part of the meaning of being a man" and so forth.' 'A is A is analytic.' Yes, but it is when we are required to give a *general definition* of what we mean by 'analytic' or 'synthetic', and when we are required to justify our dogma that *every* judgement is either analytic or synthetic, that we find we have, in fact, nothing to fall back upon *except our working-model.* From the start, it is clear that our working-model fails to do justice, for example, to the distinction between syntactics and semantics: for instance, talking about the contradictory of every sentence having to be either self-contradictory or not so, is to talk as though all sentences which we are prohibited from saying were sentences which offended against *syntactical* rules, and could be formally reduced to verbal self-contradictions. But this overlooks all semantical considerations, which philosophers are sadly prone to do. Let us consider two cases of some things which we simply *cannot say:* although they are *not* 'self-contradictory' and although—and this of course is where many will have axes to grind—we cannot possibly be tempted to say that we have 'synthetic *a priori*' knowledge of their contradictions.

Let us begin with a case which, being about *sentences* rather than *words,* is not quite in point, but which may encourage us. Take the well-known sentence 'The cat is on the mat, and I do not believe it'. That seems absurd. On the other hand 'The cat is on the mat, and I believe it' seems trivial. If we were to adopt a customary dichotomy, and to say *either* a proposition *p* implies another proposition *r,* or *p* is perfectly compatible with not-*r*, we should at once in our present case be tempted to say that 'The cat is on the mat' *implies* 'I believe it': hence both the triviality of adding 'and I believe it' and the absurdity of adding 'and I do not believe it'. But of course 'the cat is on the mat' does *not* imply 'Austin believes the cat is on the mat': nor even 'the speaker believes the cat is on the mat'—for the speaker may be lying. The doctrine which is produced in this case is, that not *p* indeed, but *asserting p* implies 'I (who assert *p*) believe *p*'. And here 'implies' must be given a special sense: for of course it is not that 'I assert *p*' implies (in the ordinary sense) 'I believe *p*', for I may be lying. It is the sort of sense in which by asking a question I 'imply' that I do not know the answer to it. By asserting *p* I *give it to be understood* that I believe *p*.

Now the reason why I cannot say 'The cat is on the mat and I do not believe it' is not that it offends against syntactics in the sense of being in some way 'self-contradictory'. What prevents my saying it, is rather some semantic convention (implicit, of course), about the way we use words *in situations.* What precisely is the account to be given in this case we need not ask. Let us rather notice one significant feature of it. Whereas '*p* and I believe it' is somehow trivial, and '*p* and I do not believe it' is somehow nonsense, a third sentence '*p* and *I might not have* believed it' makes perfectly good sense. Let us call these three sentences Q, not Q, and 'might not Q'. Now what prohibits us from saying '*p*' implies 'I believe *p*' in the ordinary sense of 'implies', is precisely shown by this fact: that although not-Q is (*somehow*) absurd, 'might not Q' is not at all absurd. For in ordinary cases of implications, not merely is not Q absurd, but 'might not Q' is *also* absurd: e.g., 'triangles are

figures and triangles have no shape' is no more absurd than 'triangles are figures and triangles might have had no shape'. Consideration of the sentence 'might not Q' will afford a rough test as to whether *p* 'implies' *r* in the *ordinary* sense, or in the special sense, of 'implies'.

Bearing this in mind, let us now consider a sentence which, as I claim, cannot possibly be classified as *either* 'analytic' *or* 'synthetic'. I refer to the sentence, 'This *x* exists', where *x* is a sensum, e.g., 'This noise exists'. In endeavouring to classify it, one party would point to the triviality of 'This noise exists', and to the absurdity of 'This noise does not exist'. They would say, therefore, that *existence* is 'part of the meaning of' *this.* But another party would point out, that 'This noise might not have existed' makes perfectly good sense. *They* would say, therefore, that *existence* cannot be 'part of the meaning of' *this.*

Both parties, as we are now in a position to see, would be correct in their *arguments,* but incorrect in their *conclusions.* What seems to be true is that *using the word 'this'* (not: the word 'this') *gives it to be understood that* the sensum referred to 'exists'.

Perhaps, historically, this fact about the sentence-trio, 'This noise exists', 'This noise does not exist', and 'This noise might not have existed', was pointed out before any philosopher had had time to pronounce that 'This noise exists' is analytic, or is synthetic. But such a pronouncement might well have been made: and *to this day,* even when the fact has been pointed out, many philosophers *worry* about the case, supposing the sentence *must* be one or the other but painfully aware of the difficulties in choosing either. I wish to point out that consideration of the analogy between this case and the other, should cure us once and for all of this bogy, and of insisting on classifying sentences as *either* analytic *or* synthetic. It may encourage us to consider again what the facts in their actual complexity really are. (One thing it suggests is a reconsideration of 'Caesar is bald' and similar propositions: but I cannot go into that.)

So far, however, we have scarcely begun in earnest: we have merely felt that initial trepidation, experienced when the firm ground of prejudice begins to slip away beneath the feet. Perhaps there are other cases, or other sorts of cases, where it will not be possible to say either that *y* is a 'part of the meaning' of *x* or that it is not, without being misleading.

Suppose we take the case of 'being thought good by me' and 'being approved of by me'. Are we to rush at this with the dichotomy: *either* 'being approved of by me' *is* part of the meaning of 'being thought good by me' *or* it is *not*? Is it *obvious* that 'I think *x* good but I do not approve of it' is self-contradictory? Of course it is not *verbally* self-contradictory. That it either is or is not 'really' self-contradictory would seem to be difficult to establish. Of course, we think, it must be one or the other—only 'it's difficult to decide *which*': or 'it depends on how you use the words'. But are those really the difficulties which baffle us? Of course, *if* it were certain that every sentence *must* be either analytic or synthetic, those *must* be the difficulties. But then, it is not certain: no account even of what the distinction means, is given except by reference to our shabby working-model. I suggest that 'I think *x* good but I do not approve of it' may very well be neither self-contradictory nor yet 'perfectly good sense' in the way in which 'I think *x* exciting but I do not approve of it' *is* 'perfectly good sense'.

Perhaps this example does not strike you as awkward. It cannot be expected that all examples will appeal equally to all hearers. Let us take some others. Is 'What is good ought to exist' analytic or synthetic? According to Moore's theory, this must be 'synthetic': yet he constantly in *Principia Ethica* takes its truth for granted. And that illustrates one of the main drawbacks of insisting on saying that a sentence *must* be either analytic or synthetic: you are almost certain to have left on your hands some general sentences which are certainly not analytic but which you find it difficult to conceive being false: i.e., you are landed with 'synthetic *a priori* knowledge'. Take that sentence of ill fame 'Pink is more like red than black'. It is rash to pronounce this 'synthetic *a priori* knowledge' on the ground that 'being more like red than black' is not 'part of the meaning' or 'part of the definition' of 'pink' and that it is not 'conceivable' that pink should be more like black than red: I dare say, so far as those phrases have any clear meaning, that it is *not*: but the question is: *is* the thing therefore 'synthetic' *a priori* knowledge?

Or, again, take some examples from Berkeley: is *extended* 'part of the meaning' of *coloured* or of *shaped*, or *shaped* 'part of the meaning' of *extended*? Is 'est sed non percipitur' self-contradictory (when said of a sensum), or is it not? When we worry thus, is it not worth considering the possibility that we are oversimplifying?

What we are to say in these cases, what even the possibilities are, I do not at present clearly see. (1) Evidently, we must throw away the old working-model as soon as we take account even of the existence of a distinction between syntactics and semantics. (2) But evidently also, our *new* working-model, the supposed 'ideal' language, is in many ways a most inadequate model of any *actual* language: its careful separation of syntactics from semantics, its lists of explicitly formulated rules and conventions, and its careful delimitation of their spheres of operation—all are misleading. An *actual* language has few, if any, explicit conventions, no sharp limits to the spheres of operation of rules, no rigid separation of what is syntactical and what semantical. (3) Finally, I think I can see that there are difficulties about our powers of imagination, and about the curious way in which it is enslaved by words.

To encourage ourselves in the belief that this sort of consideration may play havoc with the distinction 'analytic or synthetic', let us consider a similar and more familiar case. It seems, does it not, perfectly obvious that every proposition must have a contradictory? Yet it does not turn out so. Suppose that I live in harmony and friendship for four years with a cat: and then it delivers a philippic. We ask ourselves, perhaps, 'Is it a real cat? or is it *not* a real cat?' 'Either it *is*, or it *is not*, but we cannot be sure which.' Now actually, that is not so: *neither* 'It is a real cat' *nor* 'it is not a real cat' fits the facts semantically: each is designed for other situations than this one: you could not say the former of something which delivers philippics, nor yet the latter of something which has behaved as this has for four years. There are similar difficulties about choosing between 'This *is* a hallucination' and 'This is *not* a hallucination'. With sound instinct, the plain man turns in such cases to Watson and says 'Well now, *what would you* say?' 'How would you *describe* it? The difficulty is just that: there is *no* short description which is not misleading: the only thing to do, and that can easily be done, is to set out the description of the facts at length. Ordinary language breaks down in extraordinary cases. (In such cases, the cause of the breakdown is semantical.) Now no doubt an *ideal* language would *not* break down, whatever happened. In doing physics, for example, where our language is tightened up in order precisely to describe complicated and unusual cases concisely, we *prepare linguistically for the worst*. In ordinary language we do not: *words fail us*. If we talk as though an ordinary must be like an ideal language, we shall misrepresent the facts.

Consider now 'being extended' and 'being shaped'. In ordinary life we never get into a situation where we learn to say that anything is extended but not shaped nor conversely. We have all learned to use, and have used, the words only in cases where it is correct to use both. Supposing now someone says '*x* is extended but has no shape'. Somehow we cannot see what this 'could mean'—there are no semantic conventions, explicit or implicit, to cover this case: yet it is not prohibited in any way—there are no limiting rules about what we might or might not say *in extraordinary cases*. It is not *merely* the difficulty of imagining or experiencing extraordinary cases, either, which causes worry. There is this too: we can only describe what it is we are trying to imagine, by means of words which precisely describe and evoke the *ordinary* case, which we are trying to think away. Ordinary language *blinkers* the already feeble imagination. It would be difficult, in this way, if I were to say 'Can I think of a case where a man would be neither at home nor not at home?' This is inhibiting, because I think of the *ordinary* case where I ask 'Is he at home?' and get the answer, 'No': when certainly he is not at home. But supposing I happen *first* to think of the situation when I call on him just after he has died: then I see at once it would be wrong to say either. So in our case, the only thing to do is to imagine or experience all kinds of odd situations, and then suddenly round on oneself and ask: there, *now* would I say that, being extended it must be shaped? A new idiom might in odd cases be demanded.

I should like to say, in concluding this section, that in the course of stressing that we must pay attention to the facts of *actual* language, what we can and cannot say, and *precisely* why, another and converse point takes shape. Although it will not do to force actual language to accord with some preconceived model: it *equally* will not do, having discovered the facts about 'ordinary usage' *to rest content* with that, as though there were nothing more to be discussed and discovered. There may be plenty that might happen and does happen which would need new and better language to describe it in. Very often philosophers are only engaged on this task, when they seem to be perversely using words in a way which makes no sense according to 'ordinary usage'. There may be extraordinary facts, even about our everyday experience, which plain men and plain language overlook.

III

The last, and perhaps least unimportant point I have to make is the following: it seems to me that far more *detailed* attention ought to be given to that celebrated question, the posing of which has given birth to, and still keeps alive, so many erroneous theories, namely: why do we call different things by the same name? In reply to this, the philoprogenitive invent theories of 'universals' and what not: some entity or other to be that of which the 'name' is the name. And in reply to *them*, the more cautious (the 'nominalists') have usually been content to reply simply that: the reason why we call different things by the same name is simply that the things are *similar*: there is nothing *identical* present in them. This reply is inadequate in many respects: it does not, for example, attack the misleading form in which the question is posed, nor sufficiently go into the peculiarities of the word 'similar'. But what I wish to object to in it tonight is rather this: that *it is not in the least true* that all the things which I 'call by the same (general) name' *are* in general 'similar', in any ordinary sense of that much abused word.

It is a most strange thing that 'nominalists' should rest content with this answer. Not merely is it untrue to the facts; but further, if they had examined the facts, which are, in themselves, interesting enough, they could have produced with little trouble a far more formidable case against their opponents. So long as they say the things *are similar,* it will always be open to someone to say: 'Ah yes, similar *in a certain respect*: and that can only be explained by means of universals' (or whatever the name may be that they prefer for that well-tried nostrum): or again to maintain that similarity is only 'intelligible' as partial *identity*: and so on. And even those who are not persuaded entirely, may yet go so far as to allow that the 'similarity' and 'identity' languages are *alternatives,* the choice between which is indifferent. But surely, if it were made evident that we often 'call different things by the same name', and for perfectly 'good reasons',[2] when the things are not even in any ordinary sense 'similar', it will become excessively difficult to maintain that there is something 'identical' present in each—and after all, it is in *refuting* that position that the nominalist is really interested. Not, of course, that we can really *refute* it, or hope to cure those incurables who have long since reached the tertiary stage of universals.

Leaving historical disputes aside, it is a matter of urgency that a doctrine should be developed about the various kinds of good reasons for which we 'call different things[3] by the same name'. This is an absorbing question, but habitually neglected, so far as I know, by philologists as well as by philosophers. Lying in the no man's land between them, it falls between two schools, to develop such a doctrine fully would be very complicated and perhaps tedious: but also very useful in many ways. It demands the study of *actual* languages, *not* ideal ones. That the Polish semanticists have discussed such questions I neither know nor believe. Aristotle did to a quite considerable extent, but scrappily and inexactly.

I shall proceed forthwith simply to give some of the more obvious cases where the reasons for 'calling different sorts of things by the same name' are not to be dismissed lightly as 'similarity'. And show how consideration of these facts may warn us against errors which are constant in philosophy.

1. A very simple case indeed is one often mentioned by Aristotle: the adjective 'healthy': when I talk of a healthy body and again of a healthy complexion, of healthy exercise: the word is *not* just being used *equivocally.* Aristotle would say it is being used 'paronymously'.[4] In this case there is what we may call a *primary nuclear* sense of 'healthy': the sense in which 'healthy' is used of a healthy body: I call this *nuclear* because it is 'contained as a part' in the other two senses which may be set out as 'productive of healthy bodies' and 'resulting from a healthy body'.

This is a simple case, easily understood. Yet constantly it is forgotten when we start disputing as to whether a certain word *has* 'two senses' or has *not* two senses. I remember myself disputing as to whether 'exist' has two senses (as used of material objects and again of sensa), or only one: actually we were agreed that 'exist' is used paronymously, only he called that 'having two senses', and I did not. Prichard's paper[5] on ἀγαθόν (in Aristotle) contains a classic instance of misunderstanding about paronymity, and so worrying about whether a word really 'has always the same meaning' or 'has several different meanings'.

Now are we to be content to say that the exercise, the complexion, and the body are all called 'healthy' 'because they are similar'? Such a remark cannot fail to be misleading. Why make it? And why not direct attention to the important and actual facts?

2. The next case I shall take is what Aristotle calls 'analogous' terms. When A : B :: X : Y then A and X are often called by the same name, e.g., the foot of a mountain and the foot of a list. Here there is a good reason for calling the things both 'feet' but are we to say they are 'similar'? Not in any ordinary sense. We may say that the relations in which they stand to B and Y respectively are similar relations. Well and good: but A and X are not the relations in which they stand: and anyone simply told that, in calling A and X both 'feet' I was calling attention to a 'similarity' in them, would probably be misled. Anyhow, it is most necessary to remember that 'similarity' covers such possibilities if it is to do so. (An especially severe case of 'analogy' arises when a term is used, as Aristotle says 'in different categories': e.g., when I talk about 'change' as qualitative change, change of position, place, etc., how far is it true to say these 'changes' are 'similar'?)

3. Another case is where I call B by the same name as A, because it resembles A, C by the same name because it resembles B, D, . . .

and so on. But ultimately A and, say, D do not resemble each other in any recognizable sense at all. This is a very common case: and the dangers are obvious, when we search for something 'identical' in all of them!

4. Another case which is commonly found is this. Take a word like 'fascist': this originally connotes, say, a great many characteristics at once: say *x, y,* and *z.* Now we will use 'fascist' subsequently of things which possess only *one* of these striking characteristics. So that things called 'fascist' in these senses, which we may call 'incomplete' senses, need not be similar at all to each other. This often puzzles us most of all when the original 'complete' sense has been forgotten: compare the various meanings of 'cynicism': we should be puzzled to find the 'similarity' there! Sometimes the 'incompleteness' of the resemblance is coupled with a positive lack of resemblance, so that we invent a phrase to mark it as a warning, e.g., 'cupboard love'.

5. Another better-known case is that of a so-called determinable and its determinates: colour and red, green, blue, etc., or rather 'absolutely specific' reds, greens, blues, etc. Because this is better known, I shall not discuss it, though I am as a matter of fact rather sceptical about the accounts usually given. Instead, it should be pointed out how common this sort of relationship is and that it should be suspected in cases where we are prone to overlook it. A striking example is the case of 'pleasure': pleasures we may say not merely resemble each other in being pleasant, but also *differ* precisely in the way in which they are pleasant.[6] No greater mistake could be made than the hedonistic mistake (copied by non-hedonists) of thinking that pleasure is always a single similar feeling, somehow isolable from the various activities which 'give rise' to it.

6. Another case which often provides puzzles, is that of words like 'youth' and 'love': which sometimes mean the object loved, or the thing which is youthful, sometimes the passion 'Love' or the quality (?) 'youth'. These cases are of course easy (rather *like* 'healthy'?). But suppose we take the noun 'truth': here is a case where the disagreements between different theorists have largely turned on whether they interpreted this as a name of a substance, of a quality, or of a relation.

7. Lastly, I want to take a specially interesting sort of case, which is perhaps commoner and at the bottom of more muddles than we are aware of. Take the sense in which I talk of a cricket bat and a cricket ball and a cricket umpire. The reason that all are called by the same name is perhaps that each has its part—its *own special* part—to play in the activity called cricketing: it is no good to say that cricket *simply* means 'used in cricket': for we cannot explain what we mean by 'cricket' *except* by explaining the special parts played in cricketing by the bat, ball, etc. Aristotle's suggestion was that the word 'good' might be used in such a way: in which case it is obvious how far astray we should go if we look for a 'definition' of the word 'good' in any ordinary simple sense: or look for the way in which 'good' things are 'similar' to each other, in any ordinary sense. If we tried to find out by such methods what 'cricket' meant, we should very likely conclude that it too was a simple unanalysable supersensible quality.

Another thing that becomes plain from such examples is that the apparently common-sense distinction between 'What is the meaning of the word *x*' and 'What particular things *are x* and to what degrees?' is not of universal application by any means. The questions cannot be distinguished in such cases. Or a similar case would be some word like 'golfing': it is not sense to ask 'What is the meaning of golfing?' 'What things are golfing?' Though it *is* sense to ask what component activities go to constitute golfing, what implements are used in golfing ('golf' clubs, etc.) and in what ways. Aristotle suggests 'happiness' is a word of this kind: in which case it is evident how far astray we shall go if we treat it as though it were a word like 'whiteness'.

These summarily treated examples are enough to show how essential it is to have a thorough knowledge of the different reasons for which we call different things by the same name, before we can embark confidently on an inquiry. If we rush up with a demand for a definition in the simple manner of Plato or many other philosophers, if we use the rigid dichotomy 'same meaning, different meaning', or 'What *x* means', as distinguished from 'the things which are *x*', we shall simply make hashes of things. Perhaps some people are now discussing such questions seriously. All that is to be found in traditional Logics is the mention that there are, besides univocal and equivocal words, 'also analogous words': which, without further explanation, is used to lump together all cases where a word has not always absolutely the same meaning, nor several absolutely different meanings. All that 'similarity' theorists manage is to say that all things called by some one name are similar to some one pattern, or are all more similar to each other than any of them is to anything else; which is *obviously* untrue. Anyone who wishes to see the complexity of the problem, has only got to look in a (good) dictionary under such a word as

'head': the different meanings of the word 'head' will be related to each other in all sorts of different ways at once.

To summarize the contentions of this paper then. Firstly, the phrase 'the meaning of a word' is a spurious phrase. Secondly and consequently, a re-examination is needed of phrases like the two which I discuss, 'being a part of the meaning of' and 'having the same meaning'. On these matters, dogmatists require prodding: although history indeed suggests that it may sometimes be better to let sleeping dogmatists lie.

NOTES

1. 'Ideas, Propositions and Signs', in the *Proceedings of the Aristotelian Society*. 1939–40.
2. We are not interested in mere equivocation, of course.
3. Strictly, *sorts* of things rather than *particular* things.
4. But there are other varieties of paronymity of course.
5. 'The Meaning of *ΑΓΑΘΟΝ* in the *Ethics* of Aristotle', by H. A. Prichard. Reprinted in his *Moral Obligation,* Oxford, 1949.
6. If we say that they are all called 'pleasures' 'because they are similar', we shall overlook this fact.

5   Rules and Private Language

LUDWIG WITTGENSTEIN

199. IS WHAT WE CALL "obeying a rule" something that it would be possible for only *one* man to do, and to do only *once* in his life?—This is of course a note on the grammar of the expression "to obey a rule".

It is not possible that there should have been only one occasion on which someone obeyed a rule. It is not possible that there should have been only one occasion on which a report was made, an order given or understood; and so on.—To obey a rule, to make a report, to give an order, to play a game of chess, are *customs* (uses, institutions).

To understand a sentence means to understand a language. To understand a language means to be master of a technique.

200. It is, of course, imaginable that two people belonging to a tribe unacquainted with games should sit at a chess-board and go through the moves of a game of chess; and even with all the appropriate mental accompaniments. And if *we* were to see it we should say they were playing chess. But now imagine a game of chess translated according to certain

Philosophical Investigations, trans. G. E. M. Anscombe (Oxford: Basil Blackwell, 1953). Originally written in 1945. Reprinted by permission of Blackwell Publishers.

rules into a series of actions which we do not ordinarily associate with a *game*—say into yells and stamping of feet. And now suppose those two people to yell and stamp instead of playing the form of chess that we are used to; and this in such a way that their procedure is translatable by suitable rules into a game of chess. Should we still be inclined to say they were playing a game? What right would one have to say so?

201. This was our paradox: no course of action could be determined by a rule, because every course of action can be made out to accord with the rule. The answer was: if everything can be made out to accord with the rule, then it can also be made out to conflict with it. And so there would be neither accord nor conflict here.

It can be seen that there is a misunderstanding here from the mere fact that in the course of our argument we give one interpretation after another; as if each one contented us at least for a moment, until we thought of yet another standing behind it. What this shews is that there is a way of grasping a rule which is *not* an *interpretation*, but which is exhibited in what we call "obeying the rule" and "going against it" in actual cases.

Hence there is an inclination to say: every action according to the rule is an interpretation. But we ought to restrict the term "interpretation" to the substitution of one expression of the rule for another.

202. And hence also 'obeying a rule' is a practice. And to *think* one is obeying a rule is not to obey a rule. Hence it is not possible to obey a rule 'privately': otherwise thinking one was obeying a rule would be the same thing as obeying it.

203. Language is a labyrinth of paths. You approach from *one* side and know your way about; you approach the same place from another side and no longer know your way about.

204. As things are I can, for example, invent a game that is never played by anyone.—But would the following be possible too: mankind has never played any games; once, however, someone invented a game—which no one ever played?

205. "But it is just the queer thing about *intention*, about the mental process, that the existence of a custom, of a technique, is not necessary to it. That, for example, it is imaginable that two people should play chess in a world in which otherwise no games existed; and even that they should begin a game of chess—and then be interrupted."

But isn't chess defined by its rules? And how are these rules present in the mind of the person who is intending to play chess?

206. Following a rule is analogous to obeying an order. We are trained to do so; we react to an order in a particular way. But what if one person reacts in one way and another in another to the order and the training? Which one is right?

Suppose you came as an explorer into an unknown country with a language quite strange to you. In what circumstances would you say that the people there gave orders, understood them, obeyed them, rebelled against them, and so on?

The common behaviour of mankind is the system of reference by means of which we interpret an unknown language.

207. Let us imagine that the people in that country carried on the usual human activities and in the course of them employed, apparently, an articulate language. If we watch their behaviour we find it intelligible, it seems 'logical'. But when we try to learn their language we find it impossible to do so. For there is no regular connexion between what they say, the sounds they make, and their actions; but still these sounds are not superfluous, for if we gag one of the people, it has the same consequences as with us; without the sounds their actions fall into confusion—as I feel like putting it.

Are we to say that these people have a language: orders, reports, and the rest?

There is not enough regularity for us to call it "language".

208. Then am I defining "order" and "rule" by means of "regularity"?—How do I explain the meaning of "regular", "uniform", "same" to anyone?—I shall explain these words to someone who, say, only speaks French by means of the corresponding French words. But if a person has not yet got the

concepts, I shall teach him to use the words by means of *examples* and by *practice*.—And when I do this I do not communicate less to him than I know myself.

In the course of this teaching I shall shew him the same colours, the same lengths, the same shapes, I shall make him find them and produce them, and so on. I shall, for instance, get him to continue an ornamental pattern uniformly when told to do so.—And also to continue progressions. And so, for example, when given: . .. ... to go on: ....

I do it, he does it after me; and I influence him by expressions of agreement, rejection, expectation, encouragement. I let him go his way, or hold him back; and so on.

Imagine witnessing such teaching. None of the words would be explained by means of itself; there would be no logical circle.

The expressions "and so on", "and so on ad infinitum" are also explained in this teaching. A gesture, among other things, might serve this purpose. The gesture that means "go on like this", or "and so on" has a function comparable to that of pointing to an object or a place.

We should distinguish between the "and so on" which is, and the "and so on" which is not, an abbreviated notation. "And so on ad inf." is *not* such an abbreviation. The fact that we cannot write down all the digits of π is not a human shortcoming, as mathematicians sometimes think.

Teaching which is not meant to apply to anything but the examples given is different from that which '*points beyond*' them.

209. "But then doesn't our understanding reach beyond all the examples?"—A very queer expression, and a quite natural one!—

But is that *all*? Isn't there a deeper explanation; or mustn't at least the *understanding* of the explanation be deeper?—Well, have I myself a deeper understanding? Have I *got* more than I give in the explanation?—But then, whence the feeling that I have got more?

Is it like the case where I interpret what is not limited as a length that reaches beyond every length?

210. "But do you really explain to the other person what you yourself understand? Don't you get him to *guess* the essential thing? You give him examples—but he has to guess their drift, to guess your intention."—Every explanation which I can give myself I give to him too.—"He guesses what I intend" would mean: various interpretations of my explanation come to his mind, and he lights on one of them. So in this case he could ask; and I could and should answer him.

211. How can he *know* how he is to continue a pattern by himself— whatever instruction you give him?—Well, how do I know?—If that means "Have I reasons?" the answer is: my reasons will soon give out. And then I shall act, without reasons.

212. When someone whom I am afraid of orders me to continue the series, I act quickly, with perfect certainty, and the lack of reasons does not trouble me.

213. "But this initial segment of a series obviously admitted of various interpretations (e.g., by means of algebraic expressions) and so you must first have chosen *one* such interpretation."—Not at all. A doubt was possible in certain circumstances. But that is not to say that I did doubt, or even could doubt. (There is something to be said, which is connected with this, about the psychological 'atmosphere' of a process.)

So it must have been intuition that removed this doubt.—If intuition is an inner voice—how do I know *how* I am to obey it? And how do I know that it doesn't mislead me? For if it can guide me right, it can also guide me wrong.

((Intuition an unnecessary shuffle.))

214. If you have to have an intuition in order to develop the series 1 2 3 4 . . . , you must also have one in order to develop the series 2 2 2 2 . . . .

215. But isn't *the same* at least the same?

We seem to have an infallible paradigm of identity in the identity of a thing with itself. I feel like saying: "Here at any rate there can't be a variety of interpretations. If you are seeing a thing you are seeing identity too."

Then are two things the same when they are what *one* thing is? And how am I to apply what the *one* thing shews me to the case of two things?

216. "A thing is identical with itself."—There is no finer example of a useless proposition, which yet is connected with a certain play of the imagination. It is as if in imagination we put a thing into its own shape and saw that it fitted.

We might also say: "Every thing fits into itself." Or again: "Every thing fits into its own shape." At the same time we look at a thing and imagine that there was a blank left for it, and that now it fits into it exactly.

Does this spot ▷ '*fit*' into its white surrounding?— *But that is just how it would look* if there had at first been a hole in its place and it then fitted into the hole. But when we say "it fits" we are not simply describing this appearance; not simply this *situation*.

"Every coloured patch fits exactly into its surrounding" is a rather specialized form of the law of identity.

217. "How am I able to obey a rule?"—if this is not a question about causes, then it is about the justification for my following the rule in the way I do.

If I have exhausted the justifications I have reached bedrock, and my spade is turned. Then I am inclined to say: "This is simply what I do."

(Remember that we sometimes demand definitions for the sake not of their content, but of their form. Our requirement is an architectural one; the definition a kind of ornamental coping that supports nothing.)

218. Whence comes the idea that the beginning of a series is a visible section of rails invisibly laid to infinity? Well, we might imagine rails instead of a rule. And infinitely long rails correspond to the unlimited application of a rule.

219. "All the steps are really already taken" means: I no longer have any choice. The rule, once stamped with a particular meaning, traces the lines along which it is to be followed through the whole of space.——But if something of this sort really were the case, how would it help?

No; my description only made sense if it was to be understood symbolically.—I should have said: *This is how it strikes me.*

When I obey a rule, I do not choose.

I obey the rule *blindly*. . . .

243. A human being can encourage himself, give himself orders, obey, blame and punish himself; he can ask himself a question and answer it. We could even imagine human beings who spoke only in monologue; who accompanied their activities by talking to themselves.—An explorer who watched them and listened to their talk might succeed in translating their language into ours. (This would enable him to predict these people's actions correctly, for he also hears them making resolutions and decisions.)

But could we also imagine a language in which a person could write down or give vocal expression to his inner experiences—his feelings, moods, and the rest—for his private use?——Well, can't we do so in our ordinary language?—But that is not what I mean. The individual words of this language are to refer to what can only be known to the person speaking; to his immediate private sensations. So another person cannot understand the language.

244. How do words *refer* to sensations?—There doesn't seem to be any problem here; don't we talk about sensations every day, and give them names? But how is the connexion between the name and the thing named set up? This question is the same as: how does a human being learn the meaning of the names of sensations?—of the word "pain" for example. Here is one possibility: words are connected with the primitive, the natural, expressions of the sensation and used in their place. A child has hurt himself and he cries; and then adults talk to him and teach him exclamations and, later, sentences. They teach the child new pain-behaviour.

"So you are saying that the word 'pain' really means crying?"—On the contrary: the verbal expression of pain replaces crying and does not describe it.

245. For how can I go so far as to try to use language to get between pain and its expression?

246. In what sense are my sensations *private*?— Well, only I can know whether I am really in pain; another person can only surmise it.—In one way this is wrong, and in another nonsense. If we are using the word "to know" as it is normally used (and how else are we to use it?), then other people very often

know when I am in pain.—Yes, but all the same not with the certainty with which I know it myself!—It can't be said of me at all (except perhaps as a joke) that I *know* I am in pain. What is it supposed to mean—except perhaps that I *am* in pain?

Other people cannot be said to learn of my sensations *only* from my behaviour—for *I* cannot be said to learn of them. I *have* them.

The truth is: it makes sense to say about other people that they doubt whether I am in pain; but not to say it about myself.

247.   "Only you can know if you had that intention." One might tell someone this when one was explaining the meaning of the word "intention" to him. For then it means: *that* is how we use it.

(And here "know" means that the expression of uncertainty is senseless.)

248.   The proposition "Sensations are private" is comparable to: "One plays patience by oneself".

249.   Are we perhaps over-hasty in our assumption that the smile of an unweaned infant is not a pretence?—And on what experience is our assumption based?

(Lying is a language-game that needs to be learned like any other one.)

250.   Why can't a dog simulate pain? Is he too honest? Could one teach a dog to simulate pain? Perhaps it is possible to teach him to howl on particular occasions as if he were in pain, even when he is not. But the surroundings which are necessary for this behaviour to be real simulation are missing.

251.   What does it mean when we say: "I can't imagine the opposite of this" or "What would it be like, if it were otherwise?"—For example, when someone has said that my images are private, or that only I myself can know whether I am feeling pain, and similar things.

Of course here "I can't imagine the opposite" doesn't mean: my powers of imagination are unequal to the task. These words are a defence against something whose form makes it look like an empirical proposition, but which is really a grammatical one.

But why do we say: "I can't imagine the opposite"? Why not: "I can't imagine the thing itself"?

Example: "Every rod has a length." That means something like: we call something (or *this*) "the length of a rod"—but nothing "the length of a sphere." Now can I imagine 'every rod having a length'? Well, I simply imagine a rod. Only this picture, in connexion with this proposition, has a quite different role from one used in connexion with the proposition "This table has the same length as the one over there". For here I understand what it means to have a picture of the opposite (nor need it be a mental picture).

But the picture attaching to the grammatical proposition could only shew, say, what is called "the length of a rod'. And what should the opposite picture be?

((Remark about the negation of an a priori proposition.))

252.   "This body has extension." To this we might reply: "Nonsense!"—but are inclined to reply "Of course!"—Why is this?

253.   "Another person can't have my pains."—Which are *my* pains? What counts as a criterion of identity here? Consider what makes it possible in the case of physical objects to speak of "two exactly the same", for example, to say "This chair is not the one you saw here yesterday, but is exactly the same as it".

In so far as it makes *sense* to say that my pain is the same as his, it is also possible for us both to have the same pain. (And it would also be imaginable for two people to feel pain in the same—not just the corresponding—place. That might be the case with Siamese twins, for instance.)

I have seen a person in a discussion on this subject strike himself on the breast and say: "But surely another person can't have THIS pain!"—The answer to this is that one does not define a criterion of identity by emphatic stressing of the word "this". Rather, what the emphasis does is to suggest the case in which we are conversant with such a criterion of identity, but have to be reminded of it.

254.   The substitution of "identical" for "the same" (for instance) is another typical expedient in philosophy. As if we were talking about shades of meaning and all that were in question were to find words to hit on the correct nuance. That is in question in philosophy only where we have to give a psy-

chologically exact account of the temptation to use a particular kind of expression. What we 'are tempted to say' in such a case is, of course, not philosophy; but it is its raw material. Thus, for example, what a mathematician is inclined to say about the objectivity and reality of mathematical facts, is not a philosophy of mathematics, but something for philosophical *treatment*.

255. The philosopher's treatment of a question is like the treatment of an illness.

256. Now, what about the language which describes my inner experiences and which only I myself can understand? *How* do I use words to stand for my sensations?—As we ordinarily do? Then are my words for sensations tied up with my natural expressions of sensation? In that case my language is not a 'private' one. Someone else might understand it as well as I.—But suppose I didn't have any natural expression for the sensation, but only had the sensation? And now I simply *associate* names with sensations and use these names in descriptions.—

257. "What would it be like if human beings shewed no outward signs of pain (did not groan, grimace, etc.)? Then it would be impossible to teach a child the use of the word 'tooth-ache'."—Well, let's assume the child is a genius and itself invents a name for the sensation! —But then, of course, he couldn't make himself understood when he used the word.—So does he understand the name, without being able to explain its meaning to anyone?—But what does it mean to say that he has 'named his pain'?—How has he done this naming of pain?! And whatever he did, what was its purpose?—When one says "He gave a name to his sensation" one forgets that a great deal of stage-setting in the language is presupposed if the mere act of naming is to make sense. And when we speak of someone's having given a name to pain, what is presupposed is the existence of the grammar of the word "pain"; it shews the post where the new word is stationed.

258. Let us imagine the following case. I want to keep a diary about the recurrence of a certain sensation. To this end I associate it with the sign "S" and write this sign in a calendar for every day on which I have the sensation.——I will remark first of all that a definition of the sign cannot be formulated.—But still I can give myself a kind of ostensive definition.— How? Can I point to the sensation? Not in the ordinary sense. But I speak, or write the sign down, and at the same time I concentrate my attention on the sensation—and so, as it were, point to it inwardly.— But what is this ceremony for? for that is all it seems to be! A definition surely serves to establish the meaning of a sign.—Well, that is done precisely by the concentrating of my attention; for in this way I impress on myself the connexion between the sign and the sensation.—But "I impress it on myself" can only mean: this process brings it about that I remember the connexion *right* in the future. But in the present case I have no criterion of correctness. One would like to say: whatever is going to seem right to me is right. And that only means that here we can't talk about 'right'.

259. Are the rules of the private language *impressions* of rules?—The balance on which impressions are weighed is not the *impression* of a balance.

260. "Well, I *believe* that this is the sensation S again."—Perhaps you *believe* that you believe it!

Then did the man who made the entry in the calendar make a note of *nothing whatever*?—Don't consider it a matter of course that a person is making a note of something when he makes a mark— say in a calendar. For a note has a function, and this "S" so far has none.

(One can talk to oneself.—If a person speaks when no one else is present, does that mean he is speaking to himself?)

261. What reason have we for calling "S" the sign for a *sensation*? For "sensation" is a word of our common language, not of one intelligible to me alone. So the use of this word stands in need of a justification which everybody understands.—And it would not help either to say that it need not be a *sensation*; that when he writes "S", he has *something*—and that is all that can be said. "Has" and "something" also belong to our common language.—So in the end when one is doing philosophy one gets to the point where one would like just to emit an inarticulate sound.—But such a sound is an expression only as it occurs in a particular language-game, which should now be described.

262. It might be said: if you have given yourself a private definition of a word, then you must inwardly *undertake* to use the word in such-and-such a way. And how do you undertake that? Is it to be assumed that you invent the technique of using the word; or that you found it ready-made?

263. "But I can (inwardly) undertake to call THIS 'pain' in the future."—"But is it certain that you have undertaken it? Are you sure that it was enough for this purpose to concentrate your attention on your feeling?"—A queer question.—

264. "Once you know *what* the word stands for, you understand it, you know its whole use."

265. Let us imagine a table (something like a dictionary) that exists only in our imagination. A dictionary can be used to justify the translation of a word X by a word Y. But are we also to call it a justification if such a table is to be looked up only in the imagination? —"Well, yes; then it is a subjective justification."—But justification consists in appealing to something independent.—"But surely I can appeal from one memory to another. For example, I don't know if I have remembered the time of departure of a train right and to check it I call to mind how a page of the time-table looked. Isn't it the same here?"—No; for this process has got to produce a memory which is actually *correct*. If the mental image of the time-table could not itself be *tested* for correctness, how could it confirm the correctness of the first memory? (As if someone were to buy several copies of the morning paper to assure himself that what it said was true.)

Looking up a table in the imagination is no more looking up a table than the image of the result of an imagined experiment is the result of an experiment.

266. I can look at the clock to see what time it is: but I can also look at the dial of a clock in order to *guess* what time it is; or for the same purpose move the hand of a clock till its position strikes me as right. So the look of a clock may serve to determine the time in more than one way. (Looking at the clock in imagination.)

267. Suppose I wanted to justify the choice of dimensions for a bridge which I imagine to be building, by making loading tests on the material of the bridge in my imagination. This would, of course, be to imagine what is called justifying the choice of dimensions for a bridge. But should we also call it justifying an imagined choice of dimensions?

268. Why can't my right hand give my left hand money?—My right hand can put it into my left hand. My right hand can write a deed of gift and my left hand a receipt.—But the further practical consequences would not be those of a gift. When the left hand has taken the money from the right, etc., we shall ask: "Well, and what of it?" And the same could be asked if a person had given himself a private definition of a word; I mean, if he has said the word to himself and at the same time has directed his attention to a sensation.

269. Let us remember that there are certain criteria in a man's behaviour for the fact that he does not understand a word: that it means nothing to him, that he can do nothing with it. And criteria for his 'thinking he understands', attaching some meaning to the word, but not the right one. And, lastly, criteria for his understanding the word right. In the second case one might speak of a subjective understanding. And sounds which no one else understands but which I '*appear to understand*' might be called a "private language".

270. Let us now imagine a use for the entry of the sign "S" in my diary. I discover that whenever I have a particular sensation a manometer shews that my blood-pressure rises. So I shall be able to say that my blood-pressure is rising without using any apparatus. This is a useful result. And now it seems quite indifferent whether I have recognized the sensation *right* or not. Let us suppose I regularly identify it wrong, it does not matter in the least. And that alone shews that the hypothesis that I make a mistake is mere show. (We as it were turned a knob which looked as if it could be used to turn on some part of the machine; but it was a mere ornament, not connected with the mechanism at all.)

And what is our reason for calling "S" the name of a sensation here? Perhaps the kind of way this sign is employed in this language-game.—And why a "particular sensation," that is, the same one every time? Well, aren't we supposing that we write "S" every time?

271. "Imagine a person whose memory could not retain *what* the word 'pain' meant—so that he constantly called different things by that name—but nevertheless used the word in a way fitting in with the usual symptoms and presuppositions of pain"—in short he uses it as we all do. Here I should like to say: a wheel that can be turned though nothing else moves with it, is not part of the mechanism.

272. The essential thing about private experience is really not that each person possesses his own exemplar, but that nobody knows whether other people also have *this* or something else. The assumption would thus be possible—though unverifiable—that one section of mankind had one sensation of red and another section another.

273. What am I to say about the word "red"?—that it means something 'confronting us all' and that everyone should really have another word, besides this one, to mean his *own* sensation of red? Or is it like this: the word "red" means something known to everyone; and in addition, for each person, it means something known only to him? (Or perhaps rather: it *refers* to something known only to him.)

274. Of course, saying that the word "red" "refers to" instead of "means," something private does not help us in the least to grasp its function; but it is the more psychologically apt expression for a particular experience in doing philosophy. It is as if when I uttered the word I cast a sidelong glance at the private sensation, as it were in order to say to myself: I know all right what I mean by it.

275. Look at the blue of the sky and say to yourself "How blue the sky is!"—When you do it spontaneously—without philosophical intentions—the idea never crosses your mind that this impression of colour belongs only to *you*. And you have no hesitation in exclaiming that to someone else. And if you point at anything as you say the words you point at the sky. I am saying: you have not the feeling of pointing-into-yourself, which often ac-

companies 'naming the sensation' when one is thinking about 'private language'. Nor do you think that really you ought not to point to the colour with your hand, but with your attention. (Consider what it means "to point to something with the attention".)

276. But don't we at least *mean* something quite definite when we look at a colour and name our colour-impression? It is as if we detached the colour-*impression* from the object, like a membrane. (This ought to arouse our suspicions.)

277. But how is even possible for us to be tempted to think that we use a word to *mean* at one time the colour known to everyone—and at another the 'visual impression' which *I* am getting *now*? How can there be so much as a temptation here?——I don't turn the same kind of attention on the colour in the two cases. When I mean the colour impression that (as I should like to say) belongs to me alone I immerse myself in the colour—rather like when I 'cannot get my fill of a colour'. Hence it is easier to produce this experience when one is looking at a bright colour, or at an impressive colour-scheme.

278. "I know how the colour green looks to *me*"—surely that makes sense!—Certainly: what use of the proposition are you thinking of?

279. Imagine someone saying: "But I know how tall I am!" and laying his hand on top of his head to prove it.

280. Someone paints a picture in order to shew how he imagines a theatre scene. And now I say: "This picture has a double function: it informs others, as pictures or words inform——but for the one who gives the information it is a representation (or piece of information?) of another kind: for him it is the picture of his image, as it can't be for anyone else. To him his private impression of the picture means what he has imagined, in a sense in which the picture cannot mean this to others."— And what right have I to speak in this second case of a representation or piece of information—if these words were rightly used in the *first* case?

281. "But doesn't what you say come to this: that there is no pain, for example, without *pain-behaviour*?"—It comes to this: only of a living human being and what resembles (behaves like) a living human being can one say: it has sensations; it sees; is blind; hears; is deaf; is conscious or unconscious.

282. "But in a fairy tale the pot too can see and hear!" (Certainly; but it *can* also talk.)

"But the fairy tale only invents what is not the case: it does not talk *nonsense*."—It is not as simple as that. Is it false or nonsensical to say that a pot talks? Have we a clear picture of the circumstances in which we should say of a pot that it talked? (Even a nonsense-poem is not nonsense in the same way as the babbling of a child.)

We do indeed say of an inanimate thing that it is in pain: when playing with dolls for example. But this use of the concept of pain is a secondary one. Imagine a case in which people ascribed pain *only* to inanimate things; pitied *only* dolls! (When children play at trains their game is connected with their knowledge of trains. It would nevertheless be possible for the children of a tribe unacquainted with trains to learn this game from others, and to play it without knowing that it was copied from anything. One might say that the game did not make the same *sense* to them as to us.)

283. What gives us *so much as the idea* that living beings, things, can feel?

Is it that my education has led me to it by drawing my attention to feelings in myself, and now I transfer the idea to objects outside myself? That I recognize that there is something there (in me) which I can call "pain" without getting into conflict with the way other people use this word?—I do not transfer my idea to stones, plants, etc.

Couldn't I imagine having frightful pains and turning to stone while they lasted? Well, how do I know, if I shut my eyes, whether I have not turned into a stone? And if that has happened, in what sense will *the stone* have the pains? In what sense will they be ascribable to the stone? And why need the pain have a bearer at all here?!

And can one say of the stone that it has a soul and *that* is what has the pain? What has a soul, or pain, to do with a stone?

Only of what behaves like a human being can one say that it *has* pains.

For one has to say it of a body, or, if you like of a soul which some body *has*. And how can a body *have* a soul?

284. Look at a stone and imagine it having sensations.—One says to oneself: How could one so much as get the idea of ascribing a *sensation* to a *thing*? One might as well ascribe it to a number!—And now look at a wriggling fly and at once these difficulties vanish and pain seems able to get a foothold here, where before everything was, so to speak, too smooth for it.

And so, too, a corpse seems to us quite inaccessible to pain.—Our attitude to what is alive and to what is dead, is not the same. All our reactions are different.—If anyone says: "That cannot simply come from the fact that a living thing moves about in such-and-such a way and a dead one not", then I want to imitate to him that this is a case of the transition 'from quantity to quality'.

285. Think of the recognition of *facial expressions*. Or of the description of facial expressions—which does not consist in giving the measurements of the face! Think, too, how one can imitate a man's face without seeing one's own in a mirror.

286. But isn't it absurd to say of a *body* that it has pain?——And why does one feel an absurdity in that? In what sense is it true that my hand does not feel pain, but I in my hand?

What sort of issue is: Is it the *body* that feels pain?—How is it to be decided? What makes it plausible to say that it is *not* the body?—Well, something like this: if someone has a pain in his hand, then the hand does not say so (unless it writes it) and one does not comfort the hand, but the sufferer: one looks into his face.

287. How am I filled with pity *for this man*? How does it come out what the object of my pity is? (Pity, one may say, is a form or conviction that someone else is in pain.)

288. I turn to stone and my pain goes on.—Suppose I were in error and it was no longer *pain*?

——But I can't be in error here: it means nothing to doubt whether I am in pain!—That means: if anyone said "I do not know if what I have got is a pain or something else", we should think something like, he does not know what the English word "pain" means; and we should explain it to him.—How? Perhaps by means of gestures, or by pricking him with a pin and saying: "See, that's what pain is!" This explanation, like any other, he might understand right, wrong, or not at all. And he will shew which he does by his use of the word, in this as in other cases.

If he now said, for example: "Oh, I know what 'pain' means; what I don't know is whether *this*, that I have now, is pain"—we should merely shake our heads and be forced to regard his words as a queer reaction which we have no idea what to do with. (It would be rather as if we heard someone say seriously: "I distinctly remember that some time before I was born I believed . . .".)

That expression of doubt has no place in the language-game; but if we cut out human behaviour, which is the expression of sensation, it looks as if I might *legitimately* begin to doubt afresh. My temptation to say that one might take a sensation for something other than what it is arises from this: if I assume the abrogation of the normal language-game with the expression of a sensation, I need a criterion of identity for the sensation; and then the possibility of error also exists.

289. "When I say 'I am in pain' I am at any rate justified *before myself*."—What does that mean? Does it mean: "If someone else could know what I am calling 'pain', he would admit that I was using the word correctly"?

To use a word without a justification does not mean to use it without right.

290. What I do is not, of course, to identify my sensation by criteria: but to repeat an expression. But this is not the *end* of the language-game: it is the beginning.

But isn't the beginning the sensation—which I describe?—Perhaps this word "describe" tricks us here. I say "I describe my state of mind" and "I describe my room". You need to call to mind the differences between the language-games.

291. What we call "*descriptions*" are instruments for particular uses. Think of a machine-drawing, a cross-section, an elevation with measurements, which an engineer has before him. Thinking of a description as a word-picture of the facts has something misleading about it: one tends to think only of such pictures as hang on our walls: which seem simply to portray how a thing looks, what it is like. (These pictures are as it were idle.)

292. Don't always think that you read off what you say from the facts; that you portray these in words according to rules. For even so you would have to apply the rule in the particular case without guidance.

293. If I say of myself that it is only from my own case that I know what the word "pain" means—must I not say the same of other people too? And how can I generalize the *one* case so irresponsibly?

Now someone tells me that *he* knows what pain is only from his own case!——Suppose everyone had a box with something in it: we call it a "beetle". No one can look into anyone else's box, and everyone says he knows what a beetle is only by looking at *his* beetle.—Here it would be quite possible for everyone to have something different in his box. One might even imagine such a thing constantly changing.—But suppose the word "beetle" had a use in these people's language?—If so it would not be used as the name of a thing. The thing in the box has no place in the language-game at all; not even as a *something*: for the box might even be empty.—No, one can 'divide through' by the thing in the box; it cancels out, whatever it is.

That is to say: if we construe the grammar of the expression of sensation on the model of 'object and designation' the object drops out of consideration as irrelevant.

294. If you say he sees a private picture before him, which he is describing, you have still made an assumption about what he has before him. And that means that you can describe it or do describe it more closely. If you admit that you haven't any notion what kind of thing it might be that he has before him—then what leads you into saying, in spite of that, that he has something before him? Isn't it as if I were to say of someone: "He *has* something. But

I don't know whether it is money, or debts, or in empty till."

295. "I know . . . only from my *own* case"—what kind of proposition is this meant to be at all? An experiential one? No.—A grammatical one?

Suppose everyone does say about himself that he knows what pain is only from his own pain.—Not that people really say that, or are even prepared to say it. But *if* everybody said it——it might be a kind of exclamation. And even if it gives no information, still it is a picture, and why should we not want to call up such a picture? Imagine an allegorical painting taking the place of those words.

When we look into ourselves as we do philosophy, we often get to see just such a picture. A full-blown pictorial representation of our grammar. Not facts; but as if it were illustrated turns of speech.

296. "Yes, but there is *something* there all the same accompanying my cry of pain. And it is on account of that that I utter it. And this something is what is important—and frightful."—Only whom are we informing of this? And on what occasion?

297. Of course, if water boils in a pot, steam comes out of the pot and also pictured steam comes out of the pictured pot. But what if one insisted on saying that there must also be something boiling in the picture of the pot?

298. The very fact that we should so much like to say: "*This* is the important thing"—while we point privately to the sensation—is enough to shew how much we are inclined to say something which gives no information.

299. Being unable—when we surrender ourselves to philosophical thought—to help saying such-and-such; being irresistibly inclined to say it—does not mean being forced into an *assumption*, or having an immediate perception or knowledge of a state of affairs.

300. It is—we should like to say—not merely the picture of the behaviour that plays a part in the language-game with the words "he is in pain", but also the picture of the pain. Or, not merely the par-adigm of the behaviour, but also that of the pain.—It is a misunderstanding to say "The picture of pain enters into the language-game with the word 'pain'." The image of pain is not a picture and *this* image is not replaceable in the language-game by anything that we should call a picture.—The image of pain certainly enters into the language game in a sense; only not as a picture.

301. An image is not a picture, but a picture can correspond to it.

302. If one has to imagine someone else's pain on the model of one's own, this is none too easy a thing to do: for I have to imagine pain which I *do not feel* on the model of the pain which I *do feel*. That is, what I have to do is not simply to make a transition in imagination from one place of pain to another. As, from pain in the hand to pain in the arm. For I am not to imagine that I feel pain in some region of his body. (Which would also be possible.)

Pain-behaviour can point to a painful place—but the subject of pain is the person who gives it expression.

303. "I can only *believe* that someone else is in pain, but I *know* it if I am."—Yes: one can make the decision to say "I believe he is in pain" instead of "He is in pain". But that is all.——What looks like an explanation here, or like a statement about a mental process, is in truth an exchange of one expression for another which, while we are doing philosophy, seems the more appropriate one.

Just try—in a real case—to doubt someone else's fear or pain.

304. "But you will surely admit that there is a difference between pain-behaviour accompanied by pain and pain-behaviour without any pain?—Admit it? What greater difference could there be?—"And yet you again and again reach the conclusion that the sensation itself is a *nothing*."—Not at all. It is not a *something*, but not a *nothing* either! The conclusion was only that a nothing would serve just as well as a something about which nothing could be said. We have only rejected the grammar which tries to force itself on us here.

The paradox disappears only if we make a radical break with the idea that language always functions in one way, always serves the same purpose: to convey thoughts—which may be about houses, pains, good and evil, or anything else you please.

305. "But you surely cannot deny that, for example, in remembering, an inner process takes place."—What gives the impression that we want to deny anything? When one says "Still, an inner process does take place here"—one wants to go on: "After all, you *see* it." And it is this inner process that one means by the word "remembering".—The impression that we wanted to deny something arises from our setting our faces against the picture of the 'inner process'. What we deny is that the picture of the inner process gives us the correct idea of the use of the word "to remember". We say that this picture with its ramifications stands in the way of our seeing the use of the word as it is.

306. Why should I deny that there is a mental process? But "There has just taken place in me the mental process of remembering . . ." means nothing more than: "I have just remembered . . .". To deny the mental process would mean to deny the remembering; to deny that anyone ever remembers anything.

307. "Are you not really a behaviourist in disguise? Aren't you at bottom really saying that everything except human behaviour is a fiction?"—If I do speak of a fiction, then it is of a *grammatical* fiction.

308. How does the philosophical problem about mental processes and states and about behaviourism arise?——The first step is the one that altogether escapes notice. We talk of processes and states and leave their nature undecided. Sometime perhaps we shall know more about them—we think. But that is just what commits us to a particular way of looking at the matter. For we have a definite concept of what it means to learn to know a process better. (The decisive movement in the conjuring trick has been made, and it was the very one that we thought quite innocent.)—And now the analogy which was to make us understand our thoughts falls

to pieces. So we have to deny the yet uncomprehended process in the yet unexplored medium. And now it looks as if we had denied mental processes. And naturally we don't want to deny them.

309. What is your aim in philosophy?—To shew the fly the way out of the fly-bottle.

310. I tell someone I am in pain. His attitude to me will then be that of belief; disbelief; suspicion; and so on.

Let us assume he says: "It's not so bad."—Doesn't that prove that he believes in something behind the outward expression of pain?——His attitude is a proof of his attitude. Imagine not merely the words "I am in pain" but also the answer "It's not so bad" replaced by instinctive noises and gestures.

311. "What difference could be greater?"—In the case of pain I believe that I can give myself a private exhibition of the difference. But I can give anyone an exhibition of the difference between a broken and an unbroken tooth.—But for the private exhibition you don't have to give yourself actual pain; it is enough to *imagine* it—for instance, you screw up your face a bit. And do you know that what you are giving yourself this exhibition of is pain and not, for example, a facial expression? And how do you know what you are to give yourself an exhibition of before you do it? This *private* exhibition is an illusion.

312. But again, *aren't* the cases of the tooth and the pain similar? For the visual sensation in the one corresponds to the sensation of pain in the other. I can exhibit the visual sensation to myself as little or as well as the sensation of pain.

Let us imagine the following: The surfaces of the things around us (stones, plants, etc.) have patches and regions which produce pain in our skin when we touch them. (Perhaps through the chemical composition of these surfaces. But we need not know that.) In this case we should speak of pain-patches on the leaf of a particular plant just as at present we speak of red patches. I am supposing that it is useful to us to notice these patches and their shapes; that we can infer important properties of the objects from them.

313. I can exhibit pain, as I exhibit red, and as I exhibit straight, and crooked and trees and stones.—*That* is what we *call* "exhibiting".

314. It shews a fundamental misunderstanding, if I am inclined to study the headache I have now in order to get clear about the philosophical problem of sensation.

315. Could someone understand the word "pain", who had *never* felt pain?—Is experience to teach me whether this is so or not?—And if we say "A man could not imagine pain without having sometime felt it"—how do we know? How can it be decided whether it is true?

6   Meaning

H. P. GRICE

CONSIDER the following sentences:

> "Those spots mean (meant) measles."
> "Those spots didn't mean anything to me, but to the doctor they meant measles."
> "The recent budget means that we shall have a hard year."

(1) I cannot say, "Those spots meant measles, but he hadn't got measles,' and I cannot say, "The recent budget means that we shall have a hard year, but we shan't have." That is to say, in cases like the above, *x meant that p* and *x means that p* entail *p*.

(2) I cannot argue from "Those spots mean (meant) measles" to any conclusion about "what is (was) meant by those spots"; for example, I am not entitled to say, "What was meant by those spots was that he had measles." Equally I cannot draw from the statement about the recent budget the conclusion "What is meant by the recent budget is that we shall have a hard year."

(3) I cannot argue from "Those spots meant measles" to any conclusion to the effect that somebody or other meant by those spots so-and-so. *Mutatis mutandis,* the same is true of the sentence about the recent budget.

(4) For none of the above examples can a restatement be found in which the verb "mean" is followed by sentence or phrase in inverted commas.

Thus "Those spots meant measles" cannot be reformulated as "Those spots meant 'measles' " or as "Those spots meant 'he has measles'."

(5) On the other hand, for all these examples an approximate restatement can be found beginning with the phrase "The fact that . . ."; for example, "The fact that he had those spots meant that he had measles" and "The fact that the recent budget was as it was means that we shall have a hard year."

Now contrast the above sentences with the following:

> "Those three rings on the bell (of the bus) mean that the 'bus is full'."
> "That remark, 'Smith couldn't get on without his trouble and strife', meant that Smith found his wife indispensable."

(1) I can use the first of these and go on to say, "But it isn't in fact full—the conductor has made a mistake"; and I can use the second and go on, "But in fact Smith deserted her seven years ago." That is to say, here *x means that p* and *x meant that p* do not entail *p*.

(2) I can argue from the first to some statement about "what is (was) meant" by the rings on the bell and from the second to some statement about "what is (was) meant" by the quoted remark.

The Philosophical Review 66, no. 3 (1957): 377–88. Reprinted by permission of *The Philosophical Review*.

(3) I can argue from the first sentence to the conclusion that somebody (viz., the conductor) meant, or at any rate should have meant, by the rings that the bus is full, and I can argue analogously for the second sentence.

(4) The first sentence can be restated in a form in which the verb "mean" is followed by a phrase in inverted commas, that is, "Those three rings on the bell mean 'the bus is full'." So also can the second sentence.

(5) Such a sentence as "The fact that the bell has been rung three times means that the bus is full" is not a restatement of the meaning of the first sentence. Both may be true, but they do not have, even approximately, the same meaning.

When the expressions "means," "means something," "means that" are used in the kind of way in which they are used in the first set of sentences, I shall speak of the sense, or senses, in which they are used, as the *natural* sense, or senses, of the expressions in question. When the expressions are used in the kind of way in which they are used in the second set of sentences, I shall speak of the sense, or senses, in which they are used, as the *nonnatural* sense, or senses, of the expressions in question. I shall use the abbreviation "means$_{NN}$" to distinguish the nonnatural sense or senses.

I propose, for convenience, also to include under the head of natural senses of "mean" such senses of "mean" as may be exemplified in sentences of the pattern "*A* means (meant) *to do* so-and-so (by *x*)," where *A* is a human agent. By contrast, as the previous examples show, I include under the head of nonnatural senses of "mean" any senses of "mean" found in sentences of the patterns "*A* means (meant) something by *x*" or "*A* means (meant) by *x* that. . . ." (This is overrigid; but it will serve as an indication.)

I do not want to maintain that *all* our uses of "mean" fall easily, obviously, and tidily into one of the two groups I have distinguished; but I think that in most cases we should be at least fairly strongly inclined to assimilate a use of "mean" to one group rather than to the other. The question which now arises is this: "What more can be said about the distinction between the cases where we should say that the word is applied in a natural sense and the cases where we should say that the word is applied in an nonnatural sense?" Asking this question will not of course prohibit us from trying to give an explanation of "meaning$_{NN}$" in terms of one or another natural sense of "mean."

This question about the distinction between natural and nonnatural meaning is, I think, what people are getting at when they display an interest in a distinction between "natural" and "conventional" signs. But I think my formulation is better. For some things which can mean$_{NN}$ something are not signs (e.g., words are not), and some are not conventional in any ordinary sense (e.g., certain gestures); while some things which mean naturally are not signs of what they mean (*cf.* the recent budget example).

I want first to consider briefly, and reject, what I might term a causal type of answer to the question, "What is meaning$_{NN}$?" We might try to say, for instance, more or less with C. L. Stevenson,[1] that for *x* to mean$_{NN}$ something, *x* must have (roughly) a tendency to produce in an audience some attitude (cognitive or otherwise) and a tendency, in the case of a speaker, to *be* produced *by* that attitude, these tendencies being dependent on "an elaborate process of conditioning attending the use of the sign in communication."[2] This clearly will not do.

(1) Let us consider a case where an utterance, if it qualifies at all as meaning$_{NN}$ something, will be of a descriptive or informative kind and the relevant attitude, therefore, will be a cognitive one, for example, a belief. (I use "utterance" as a neutral word to apply to any candidate for meaning$_{NN}$; it has a convenient act-object ambiguity.) It is no doubt the case that many people have a tendency to put on a tail coat when they think they are about to go to a dance, and it is no doubt also the case that many people, on seeing someone put on a tail coat, would conclude that the person in question was about to go to a dance. Does this satisfy us that putting on a tail coat means$_{NN}$ that one is about to go to a dance (or indeed means$_{NN}$ anything at all)? Obviously not. It is no help to refer to the qualifying phrase "dependent on an elaborate process of conditioning. . . ." For if all this means is that the response to the sight of a tail coat being put on is in some way learned or acquired, it will not exclude the present case from being one of meaning$_{NN}$. But if we have to take seriously the second part of the qualifying phrase ("attending the use of the sign in communication"), then the account of meaning$_{NN}$ is obviously circular.

We might just as well say, "X has meaning$_{NN}$ if it is used in communication," which, though true, is not helpful.

(2) If this is not enough, there is a difficulty—really the same difficulty, I think—which Stevenson recognizes: how we are to avoid saying, for example, that "Jones is tall" is part of what is meant by "Jones is an athlete," since to tell someone that Jones is an athlete would tend to make him believe that Jones is tall. Stevenson here resorts to invoking linguistic rules, namely, a permissive rule of language that "athletes may be nontall." This amounts to saying that we are not prohibited by rule from speaking of "nontall athletes." But why are we not prohibited? Not because it is not bad grammar, or is not impolite, and so on, but presumably because it is not meaningless (or, if this is too strong, does not in any way violate the rules of meaning for the expressions concerned). But this seems to involve us in another circle. Moreover, one wants to ask why, if it is legitimate to appeal here to rules to distinguish what is meant from what is suggested, this appeal was not made earlier, in the case of groans, for example, to deal with which Stevenson originally introduced the qualifying phrase about dependence on conditioning.

A further deficiency in a causal theory of the type just expounded seems to be that, even if we accept it as it stands, we are furnished with an analysis only of statements about the *standard* meaning, or the meaning in general, of a "sign." No provision is made for dealing with statements about what a particular speaker or writer means by a sign on a particular occasion (which may well diverge from the standard meaning of the sign); nor is it obvious how the theory could be adapted to make such provision. One might even go further in criticism and maintain that the causal theory ignores the fact that the meaning (in general) of a sign needs to be explained in terms of what users of the sign do (or should) mean by it on particular occasions; and so the latter notion, which is unexplained by the causal theory, is in fact the fundamental one. I am sympathetic to this more radical criticism, though I am aware that the point is controversial.

I do not propose to consider any further theories of the "causal-tendency" type. I suspect no such theory could avoid difficulties analogous to those I have outlined without utterly losing its claim to rank as a theory of this type.

I will now try a different and, I hope, more promising line. If we can elucidate the meaning of

"x meant$_{NN}$ something (on a particular occasion)" and
"x meant$_{NN}$ that so-and-so (on a particular occasion)"

and of

"A meant$_{NN}$ something by x (on a particular occasion)" and
"A meant$_{NN}$ by x that so-and-so (on a particular occasion),"

this might reasonably be expected to help us with

"x means$_{NN}$ (timeless) something (that so-and-so),"
"A means$_{NN}$ (timeless) by x something (that so-and-so),"

and with the explication of "means the same as," "understands," "entails," and so on. Let us for the moment pretend that we have to deal only with utterances which might be informative or descriptive.

A first shot would be to suggest that "x meant$_{NN}$ something" would be true if x was intended by its utterer to induce a belief in some "audience" and that to say what the belief was would be to say what x meant$_{NN}$. This will not do. I might leave B's handkerchief near the scene of a murder in order to induce the detective to believe that B was the murderer; but we should not want to say that the handkerchief (or my leaving it there) meant$_{NN}$ anything or that I had meant$_{NN}$ by leaving it that B was the murderer. Clearly we must at least add that for x to have meant$_{NN}$ anything, not merely must it have been "uttered" with the intention of inducing a certain belief but also the utterer must have intended an "audience" to recognize the intention behind the utterance.

This, though perhaps better, is not good enough. Consider the following cases:

1. Herod presents Salome with the head of St. John the Baptist on a charger.

2. Feeling faint, a child lets its mother see how pale it is (hoping that she may draw her own conclusions and help).

3. I leave the china my daughter has broken lying around for my wife to see.

Here we seem to have cases which satisfy the conditions so far given for meaning$_{NN}$. For example, Herod intended to make Salome believe that St. John the Baptist was dead and no doubt also intended Salome to recognize that he intended her to believe that St. John the Baptist was dead. Similarly for the other cases. Yet I certainly do not think that we should want to say that we have here cases of meaning$_{NN}$.

What we want to find is the difference between, for example, "deliberately and openly letting someone know" and "telling" and between "getting someone to think" and "telling."

The way out is perhaps as follows. Compare the following two cases:

1. I show Mr. X a photograph of Mr. Y displaying undue familiarity to Mrs. X.

2. I draw a picture of Mr. Y behaving in this manner and show it to Mr. X.

I find that I want to deny that in (1) the photograph (or my showing it to Mr. X) meant$_{NN}$ anything at all; while I want to assert that in (2) the picture (or my drawing and showing it) meant$_{NN}$ something (that Mr. Y had been unduly unfamiliar), or at least that I had meant$_{NN}$ by it that Mr. Y had been unduly familiar. What is the difference between the two cases? Surely that in case (1) Mr. X's recognition of my intention to make him believe that there is something between Mr. Y and Mrs. X is (more or less) irrelevant to the production of this effect by the photograph. Mr. X would be led by the photograph at least to suspect Mrs. X even if instead of showing it to him I had left it in his room by accident; and I (the photograph shower) would not be unaware of this. But it will make a difference to the effect of my picture on Mr. X whether or not he takes me to be intending to inform him (make him believe something) about Mrs. X, and not to be just doodling or trying to produce a work of art.

But now we seem to be landed in a further difficulty if we accept this account. For consider now, say, frowning. If I frown spontaneously, in the ordinary course of events, someone looking at me may well treat the frown as a natural sign of displeasure. But if I frown deliberately (to convey my displeasure), an onlooker may be expected, provided he

recognizes my intention, *still* to conclude that I am displeased. Ought we not then to say, since it could not be expected to make any difference to the onlooker's reaction whether he regards my frown as spontaneous or as intended to be informative, that my frown (deliberate) does *not* mean$_{NN}$ anything? I think this difficulty can be met; for though in general a deliberate frown may have the same effect (as regards inducing belief in my displeasure) as a spontaneous frown, it can be expected to have the same effect only *provided* the audience takes it as intended to convey displeasure. That is, if we take away the recognition of intention, leaving the other circumstances (including the recognition of the frown as deliberate), the belief-producing tendency of the frown must be regarded as being impaired or destroyed.

Perhaps we may sum up what is necessary for A to mean something by x as follows. A must intend to induce by x a belief in an audience, and he must also intend his utterance to be recognized as so intended. But these intentions are not independent; the recognition is intended by A to play its part in inducing the belief, and if it does not do so something will have gone wrong with the fulfillment of A's intentions. Moreover, A's intending that the recognition should play this part implies, I think, that he assumes that there is some chance that it will in fact play this part, that he does not regard it as a foregone conclusion that the belief will be induced in the audience whether or not the intention behind the utterance is recognized. Shortly, perhaps, we may say that "A meant$_{NN}$ something by x" is roughly equivalent to "A uttered x with the intention of inducing a belief by means of the recognition of this intention." (This seems to involve a reflexive paradox, but it does not really do so.)

Now perhaps it is time to drop the pretense that we have to deal only with "informative" cases. Let us start with some examples of imperatives or quasi-imperatives. I have a very avaricious man in my room, and I want him to go; so I throw a pound note out of the window. Is there here any utterance with a meaning$_{NN}$? No, because in behaving as I did, I did not intend his recognition of my purpose to be in any way effective in getting him to go. This is parallel to the photograph case. If on the other hand I had pointed to the door or given him a little push, then my behavior might well be held to constitute a meaningful$_{NN}$ utterance, just because the recognition of my intention would be intended by me to be effective in speeding his departure. Another pair of cases would be (1) a policeman who stops a car by standing in its way and (2) a policeman who stops a car by waving.

Or, to turn briefly to another type of case, if as an examiner I fail a man, I may well cause him distress or indignation or humiliation; and if I am vindictive, I may intend this effect and even intend him to recognize my intention. But I should not be inclined to say that my failing him meant$_{NN}$ anything. On the other hand, if I cut someone in the street I do feel inclined to assimilate this to the cases of meaning$_{NN}$, and this inclination seems to me dependent on the fact that I could not reasonably expect him to be distressed (indignant, humiliated) unless he recognized my intention to affect him in this way. (Cf., if my college stopped my salary altogether I should accuse them of ruining me; if they cut it by 2/6^d I might accuse them of insulting me; with some intermediate amounts I might not know quite what to say.)

Perhaps then we may make the following generalizations.

(1) "A meant$_{NN}$ something by x" is (roughly) equivalent to "A intended the utterance of x to produce some effect in an audience by means of the recognition of this intention"; and we may add that to ask what A meant is to ask for a specification of the intended effect (though, of course, it may not always be possible to get a straight answer involving a "that" clause, for example, "a belief that . . .").

(2) "x meant something" is (roughly) equivalent to "Somebody meant$_{NN}$ something by x." Here again there will be cases where this will not quite work. I feel inclined to say that (as regards traffic lights) the change to red meant$_{NN}$ that the traffic was to stop; but it would be very unnatural to say, "Somebody (e.g., the Corporation) meant$_{NN}$ by the red-light change that the traffic was to stop." Nevertheless, there seems to be *some* sort of reference to somebody's intentions.

(3) "x means$_{NN}$ (timeless) that so-and-so" might as a first shot be equated with some statement or disjunction of statements about what "people" (vague) intend (with qualifications about "recognition") to effect by x. I shall have a word to say about this.

Will any kind of intended effect do, or may there be cases where an effect is intended (with the required qualifications) and yet we should not want to talk of meaning$_{NN}$? Suppose I discovered some person so constituted that, when I told him that whenever I grunted in a special way I wanted him to blush or to incur some physical malady, thereafter whenever he recognized the grunt (and with it my intention), he did blush or incur the malady. Should we then want to say that the grunt meant$_{NN}$ something? I do not think so. This points to the fact that for x to have meaning$_{NN}$, the intended effect must be something which in some sense is within the control of the audience, or that in some sense of "reason" the recognition of the intention behind x is for the audience a reason and not merely a cause. It might look as if there is a sort of pun here ("reason for believing" and "reason for doing"), but I do not think this is serious. For though no doubt from one point of view questions about reasons for believing are questions about evidence and so quite different from questions about reasons for doing, nevertheless to recognize an utterer's intention in uttering x (descriptive utterance), to have a reason for believing that so-and-so, is at least quite like "having a motive for" accepting so-and-so. Decisions "that" seem to involve decisions "to" (and this is why we can "refuse to believe" and also be "compelled to believe").

(The "cutting" case needs slightly different treatment, for one cannot in any straightforward sense "decide" to be offended; but one can refuse to be offended.) It looks then as if the intended effect must be something within the control of the audience, or at least the *sort* of thing which is within its control.

One point before passing to an objection or two. I think it follows that from what I have said about the connection between meaning$_{NN}$ and recognition of intention that (insofar as I am right) only what I may call the primary intention of an utterer is relevant to the meaning$_{NN}$ of an utterance. For if I utter x, intending (with the aid of the recognition of this intention) to induce an effect E, and intend this effect E to lead to a further effect F, then insofar as the occurrence of F is thought to be dependent solely on E, I cannot regard F as in the least dependent on recognition of my intention to induce E. That is, if (say) I intend to get a man to do something by giving him some information, it cannot be regarded as relevant to the meaning$_{NN}$ of my utterance to describe what I intend him to do.

Now some question may be raised about my use, fairly free, of such words as "intention" and "recognition." I must disclaim any intention of peopling all our talking life with armies of complicated psychological occurrences. I do not hope to solve any philosophical puzzles about intending, but I do want briefly to argue that no special difficulties are raised by my use of the word "intention" in connection with meaning. First, there will be cases where an utterance is accompanied or preceded by a conscious "plan," or explicit formulation of intention (e.g., I declare how I am going to use *x,* or ask myself how to "get something across"). The presence of such an explicit "plan" obviously counts fairly heavily in favor of the utterer's intention (meaning) being as "planned"; though it is not, I think, conclusive; for example, a speaker who has declared an intention to use a familiar expression in an unfamiliar way may slip into the familiar use. Similarly in nonlinguistic cases: if we are asking about an agent's intention, a previous expression counts heavily; nevertheless, a man might plan to throw a letter in the dustbin and yet take it to the post; when lifting his hand he might "come to" and say *either* "I didn't intend to do this at all" *or* "I suppose I must have been intending to put it in."

Explicitly formulated linguistic (or quasi-linguistic) intentions are no doubt comparatively rare. In their absence we would seem to rely on very much the same kinds of criteria as we do in the case of nonlinguistic intentions where there is a general usage. An utterer is held to intend to convey what is normally conveyed (or normally intended to be conveyed), and we require a good reason for accepting that a particular use diverges from the general usage (e.g., he never knew or had forgotten the general usage). Similarly in nonlinguistic cases: we are presumed to intend the normal consequences of our actions.

Again, in cases where there is doubt, say, about which of two or more things an utterer intends to convey, we tend to refer to the context (linguistic or otherwise) of the utterance and ask which of the alternatives would be relevant to other things he is saying or doing, or which intention in a particular situation would fit in with some purpose he obviously has (e.g., a man who calls for a "pump" at a fire would not want a bicycle pump). Nonlinguistic parallels are obvious: context is a criterion in settling the question of why a man who has just put a cigarette in his mouth has put his hand in his pocket; relevance to an obvious end is a criterion in settling why a man is running away from a bull.

In certain linguistic cases we ask the utterer afterward about his intention, and in a few of these cases (the very difficult ones, like a philosopher asked to explain the meaning of an unclear passage in one of his works), the answer is not based on what he remembers but is more like a decision, a decision about how what he said is to be taken. I cannot find a nonlinguistic parallel here; but the case is so special as not to seem to contribute a vital difference.

All this is very obvious; but surely to show that the criteria for judging linguistic intentions are very like the criteria for judging nonlinguistic intentions is to show that linguistic intentions are very like nonlinguistic intentions.

NOTES

1. *Ethics and Language* (New Haven, 1944), Ch. 3.
2. *Ibid.,* p. 57.

Part II

Metaphysics

KEVIN MULLIGAN

Kevin Mulligan is professor of philosophy at Université de Genève, Switzerland. He has published widely on early analytic philosophy, the emotions, and the theory of perception. His books include *Language, Truth, and Ontology* (1992) and *Mind, Meaning, and Metaphysics* (1990).

A History of Early Analytic Metaphysics

Introduction

WHAT IS THERE? Answers to this short, strange question have the form "There is/are. . . ." Some possible, more or less plausible answers to the question are:

> There are tables, Frenchmen, lollipops, atoms, genes, marriages, games, plays by Shakespeare, numbers, wars; there is inflation, liberalism, poverty, globalization and Continental philosophy

Answers such as these tend not to be of interest to philosophers. Some of them, indeed, are of little interest to anyone, although scientists and others are or have been interested in whether or not there are atoms or genes. And only slight modifications of our answers turn them into bits of information of interest to some: there are lollipops in the drawer; there is inflation in the Belgian Empire and Continental philosophy in the United States.

But once we notice that tables might be thought to be things or substances, that a Frenchman might be said to be a person, a play by Shakespeare a mere fiction, and a game a process, we see that there are also answers to our question of the following sort:

> There are substances
> There are persons
> There are fictions
> There are processes
> There is matter

This essay was commissioned especially for this volume and appears here for the first time.

Such claims and their negations—for example, there are no substances—form the diet of metaphysics. Metaphysics, indeed, is often described as the discipline that studies what there is, and much metaphysics has been concerned with whether there are objects falling under such very general categories as substance, process, person. It is obvious that no philosophical investigation of metaphysical questions is likely to get very far without giving an account of what *is* and *are* mean, an account of existence (cf. W. V. Quine, this volume, 133–141) And no account of existence is complete without an account of identity (cf. Max Black, this volume, 142–147). Another task is to explain what it is for something to be a substance, a person, or a process. And, finally, in the course of arguing for or denying the existence of, say, substances, a metaphysician is likely to find herself giving arguments for or against the view that what look like substances are actually processes.

Unfortunately, the claims here said to form the diet of "metaphysics" are often also said to belong to "ontology." Use of the the two terms varies considerably (cf. Donald C. Williams's label *analytic ontology* in his contribution to this volume, 147–156). One way of regimenting their use in accordance with the usage of some philosophers is to reserve "ontology" for matters that are either more basic than metaphysics or that make up the most fundamental part of metaphysics. Ontology, then, we may say, deals with such questions as the nature of existence and identity; the most general claims about what there is; and the nature of negation, necessity, and dependence. Other less basic metaphysical questions concern, for example, the nature of mind, whether there are mind-independent objects, the existence of a God, and so on. Such questions can only be answered with the help of ontology. Thus the epistemological realist who claims that science tells us about a mind-independent reality and the idealist or postmodernist who denies this claim must both provide an account of dependence. The theist and the atheist must rely on an account of the nature of necessity if they are to argue about whether there is something that exists necessarily. The materialist who claims that mental states are identical with brain states must rely on an account of identity.

In what follows we look briefly at what early analytic metaphysics and ontology had to say about a handful of very general categories.

Universals: Properties and Relations

Suppose that Sam is sad and that Mary is sad. According to a long tradition, in such a situation, we have two substances or persons and one property, or universal. One and the same property of being sad is exemplified by Sam and by Mary. They are in space and in time, but the property enjoys no spatial or temporal location; it is an ideal entity, a denizen of what Gottlob Frege (this volume, 93–105) calls the Third Realm. Bertrand Russell accepts this traditional view but extends and defends it. In addition to properties (qualities, attributes) there are relations, which are ideal like properties but connect two or more objects. If Sam loves Mary, then the relation of loving connects Sam and Mary in that order:

> Even among philosophers, we may say, broadly, that only those universals which are named by adjectives or substantives have been much or often recognized, while those named by verbs and prepositions have been usually overlooked. This omission has had a very great effect upon philosophy. . . . The way this has occurred is, in outline, as follows: Speaking generally, adjectives and common nouns express qualities or properties of single things, whereas prepositions and verbs tend to express relations between two or more things. Thus the neglect of prepositions and verbs led to the belief that every proposition can be regarded as attributing a property to a single thing, rather than as expressing a relation between two or more things. (Russell [1912] 1986, 54).

Russell argues that at least one relation must be a universal and suggests that if this is the case, then nothing stands in the way of allowing for both universal properties and relations:

> If we wish to avoid the universals whiteness and triangularity, we shall choose some particular patch of white or some particular triangle, and say that anything is white or a triangle if it has the right sort of resemblance to our chosen particular. But then the resemblance required will have to be a universal. Since there are many white things, the resemblance must hold between many pairs of particular white things; and this is the characteristic of a universal. It will be useless to say that there is a different resemblance for each pair, for then we shall have to say that these resemblances resemble each other, and thus at last we shall be forced to admit resemblance as a universal. The relation of resemblance, therefore, must be a true universal. And having been forced to admit this universal, we find that it is no longer worth while to invent difficult and unplausible theories to avoid the admission of such universals as whiteness and triangularity. (Russell [1912] 1986, 55).

The view rejected by Russell to the effect that for a piece of paper to be white is just for it to resemble in the right way other white objects is sometimes called "resemblance nominalism". It is defended by H. H. Price (1953). *Nominalism* is the bad but traditional name for views that reject ideal entities in favour of concrete or temporal entities. The view that countenances ideal entities is sometimes called *Platonic realism;* the adjective serves to allude to Plato and his Ideas but also to distinguish metaphysical or ontological realism from epistemological realism about the external world, the view that many objects are mind independent.

One assumption made by Russell is that the distinction between properties and things or other objects marks a genuine metaphysical difference. This assumption was criticized by F. Ramsey (1990).

Tropes

If Sam is sad and Mary is sad, then, says the friend of universals, the property of being sad is exemplified by both Sam and Mary. But an equally powerful intuition has it that Sam's sadness is numerically distinct from Mary's sadness, as Sam is numerically distinct from Mary. Objects such as Sam's sadness were called *tropes* by Williams, for the bizarre reason given on page 149. Friends of tropes often claim that these entities are particulars with a position in time or in space-time, a claim also made about substances such as Sam and tables. Obviously, a philosopher may hold that there are both tropes and universals or properties. Or he may hold that universals or properties are superfluous or can be constructed out of tropes and that all of the roles that have been assigned to universals can be played by tropes, a positum known as *trope nominalism*. Similarly, a philosopher may hold that tropes depend on substances or that substances can be constructed out of tropes. Finally, friends of tropes disagree about the different types of trope that should be admitted. It is one thing to say that someone's sadness or headache—an example that Williams gives—is a trope. But suppose Mary embraces Sam. Is her embrace a trope? A philosopher who thinks that all tropes are parts of substances will find it difficult to specify the substance of which the embrace is a part. More generally, are all states, events, and processes tropes?

Under other names (*instances, particular characteristics*), tropes enjoyed a peculiar history within early analytic philosophy. Russell and C. E. Moore initially accepted certain types of tropes in addition to universals. Thus, in his 1901 paper "Identity," Moore asks of his black coat and of his black waistcoat, "Why should the blackness of both be one and the same, and not that of each a single blackness exactly like the other?" (Moore 1901, 106).

His discussion brings out clearly a possible connection between ontological commitment to a certain type of object and Leibniz's metaphysical principle of identity, "The Identity of Indiscernibles." According to this principle, if two objects are numerically different, then there is some nonrelational property that one of the objects has and the other lacks or some kind to which one but not the other object belongs. Moore thinks that the blacknesses of his coat and of his waistcoat show the falsity of this claim. The two blacknesses differ from one another only numerically. It might be thought that they differ in that one blackness belongs to the coat and the other to the waistcoat, or that each blackness stands in the same spatio-temporal relation as its bearer. But these are claims about the relations in which the two blacknesses stand not any difference in the kinds to which they belong. In his paper "Qualities" (Moore 1902, 406), Moore asserts that only particular instances of a relation such as difference can relate. In *Principia Ethica* (Moore [1903] 1954, 41), one contrast Moore makes between natural properties such as yellowness and nonnatural value properties such as goodness is that the former are particulars that make up natural objects whereas the latter are ideal properties.

In early manuscripts, Russell, too, accepts both particular properties and relations:

> Thus redness in this place is one existent, and redness in that place is another. These two are materially diverse, each is an existent and each may be a logical subject. (Russell 1897, quoted in Foster 1983–84, 130)

> [I]t would appear that there is one important type of relations, to wit those of causation, which are existent relations between things, or at least between their attributes. When one temporal or spatio-temporal particular has caused another, it would seem that the particular case of causation must exist. There may be other relations which, like qualities, have a spatial or temporal distribution, and in such cases the particulars, presumably, are existents. (Russell 1897, quoted in Foster 1983–84, 132)

But Russell and Moore quickly tired of tropes. Russell rejects both particular relations and particular qualities in the *Principles of Mathematics* (cf., e.g., §55) although his appeal to events in such later passages as

> When we hear the sentence, "Charles I's head was cut off", we may naturally enough think of Charles I, of Charles I's head, and of the operation of cutting off his head, which are all particulars; but we do not naturally dwell on what is meant by the word "head" or the word "cut", which is a universal. (Russell [1912] 1986, 54)

may suggest that his infidelity to tropes was not constant.

In his 1923 paper "Are the Characteristics of Particular Things Universal or Particular?" Moore finds the claim of G. F. Stout, who had been one of the teachers in Cambridge of both Moore and Russell, that

> every character which characterizes a particular thing or a concrete individual is particular and not universal. . . . [E]ach [of two billiard balls] has its own particular roundness, separate and distinct from that of the other . . . the particular happiness of Jones is separate and distinct from that of Robinson (Stout 1921, 158; cf. Stout 1923)

almost completely incomprehensible. One good criticism that Moore makes of Stout is that sneezes and headaches and such objects as the happiness of Jones are not predicable and do not characterize. This is quite true. To predicate is to apply a predicate (says the nominalist) or the sense of a predicate, a concept (says the conceptualist), to one or more objects, or to attribute a property or relation to one or more objects (says the Platonic realist).

But to predicate is not to predicate a particular of anything. On the other hand, no claim about the nature of predication is likely to settle the question about whether there are tropes.

One common move in metaphysics, as noted, is to try to show that a certain ontological category can be reduced to another. A trope nominalist can provide just such an alternative to universals. For Sam to be sad is just for him to be the bearer of, or partly constituted by, a sadness trope that belongs to the class of sadness tropes. Variants of this approach are defended by Stout and Williams. Of course, it is essential for such a view that a class or collection of tropes is a temporal entity, unlike properties and sets.

Modality and Relations—External and Internal

Suppose Mary embraces Sam. She need not have done so. The relation is external to its terms. Suppose Sam, like Mary, is sad. Sam, like Mary, need not be sad or even exist. It is a contingent matter of fact that they exist, as also that they are sad. But consider their two states of sadness and assume they are tropes. Must those two states not stand in the relation of being greater than or equal to one another? To give an affirmative question to this question is to admit internal relations into one's ontology.

To say that the two sadnesses must be similar to one another or greater than one another or equal to one another, to say that Mary need not have embraced Sam, is to talk of necessities and possibilities. Modal talk, it is often said, is not taken seriously in early analytic metaphysics. It is true that Russell, for example, adopts a reductive or deflationary attitude toward modality. In his 1918 paper "The Philosophy of Logical Atomism," he reduces modality to time: for a propositional function, such as "If x is a man, x is mortal," to be necessary is for it to be true always (Russell 1989, 231; see also Quine, this volume, 133).

Moore, however, takes modality at face value. Throughout his writings we find claims to the effect that certain properties—not tropes—are necessarily coexemplified or cannot be coexemplified. Thus in his discussion of ethical and aesthetic value properties he claims: "A kind of value is intrinsic if and only if, it is impossible that x and y should have different values of the kind, unless they differ in intrinsic nature . . ." (Moore 1922, 265). He goes on to claim that when he talks of necessity and possibility, he means something stronger than the modalities of scientific laws. Like Russell, however, Moore rejects the view that all relations are internal.

Wittgenstein, in the *Tractatus,* adopts a position that takes into account views like those of both Russell and Moore. The language of science, properly understood, contains no modal expressions. But in his metaphysical glosses on this language and its necessary formal features, Wittgenstein endorses the view that certain entities depend one-sidedly on other entities, could not exist without them: a state of affairs, for example, cannot obtain unless its components exist.

Of the two fundamental relations in which D. C. Williams's (this volume, 149) tropes can stand, similarity and location, location is external and similarity is internal.

Facts and States of Affairs

Suppose Sam judges that Mary is sad. What is his judgment about? Suppose it is agreed that Sam's judgment is about Mary and about the property of being sad. Sam's judgment may be true or false. Suppose it is true. Is there something that makes it true? One candidate would be the existence of the complex object that is Mary's sadness. This, we have seen, might be understood to consist of a trope and a person or of a person and a universal. But if Sam's judgment is assumed to be about the property rather than the trope, then it may seem plausible to say that the complex object that is Mary's sadness belongs to a new ontological category distinct from the categories of its parts, a person and a universal.

Perhaps there is a difference between the complex object that is Mary's sadness, which exists if Sam's judgment is true and does not exist if it is false, and the state of affairs that Mary is sad, which obtains if Sam's judgment is true and does not obtain if it is false. For consider Sam's judgment that Mary is not sad. What is this judgment about? It is not clear what it might mean to say that it is about Mary's nonsadness. But it is slightly more plausible to say that it is about the state of affairs that Mary is not sad, a state of affairs that obtains if Sam's judgment is true and does not obtain if it is false. Similarly, a judgment by Sam to the effect that all wars are evil, a judgment the content of which is general, could be said to be true if the general state of affairs that all wars are evil obtains. Whether Sam's judgments are said to be about complexes or states of affairs, the existence of a complex containing a universal, like the obtaining of a state of affairs, might be called a "fact."

To say that Sam's judgment that Mary is sad is about Mary, her sadness and a complex object or state of affairs, is not to say very much until some account is given of the way in which all these relations of aboutness hang together. Is Sam's judgment a simple unanalysable binary relation between Sam and a complex object or state of affairs? Or is it a complex relation built up out of Sam's thinking of Mary and his predicating sadness of her?

All these questions and options are explored in some detail by Russell (1989) and Wittgenstein during the first two decades of the twentieth century. Unlike the venerable ontological or metaphysical categories of substance and universals, the categories of states of affairs and facts are relative newcomers to the philosophical stage. One sympathetic account of their rise to prominence has it that the discovery by Frege and Russell of the category of relations made it apparent that substances and relations hang together in wholes that are neither relations nor substances. A more cynical view has it that the spread of journalism at the end of the nineteenth century, and the consequent popularity of the idioms of indirect speech ("Sam judged/claimed/said that Mary is sad") and of nominalizations such as "the fact that" and "the claim that," led philosophers to introduce into ontology such entities as states of affairs and facts. For, the view goes, to accept such entities as obtaining general, negative states of affairs or complexes—for example, that which makes true Sam's judgment that not all German philosophers are obscure— is to succumb to the worst sort of scholasticism. Further, the very idea that relations such as "making true," "correspondence," "agreement," and "representation" might link up judgments or propositions, on one hand, and anything else at all on the other, is riddled with confusions (cf. Frege's second contribution to this volume, 93–105). Russell himself at one point was tempted by this deflationary point of view. In 1904 he wrote that

> true propositions express *fact,* while false ones do not. This at once raises the problem: What is a fact? And the difficulty of this problem lies in this, that a fact appears to be merely a true proposition . . . (Russell 1904, 75).

Similarly, Frege in 1918 (cf. his contribution to this volume, 102) wrote that "A fact is a thought that is true."

Substance and Sense-Data

We have seen that the sadnesses of Sam and Mary, as well as their embrace, admit of a variety of different metaphysical construings. But who—or better—what are Sam and Mary?

According to both common sense and much traditional metaphysics, they are substances—that is, entities that endure through time; have spatial but no temporal parts; undergo and produce changes (tropes) or acquire and lose properties; and exemplify necessarily a property often called an *essential property,* the property of being a person. If necessity is not taken seriously, then this view will need to be modified. We should then no longer say that Mary is necessarily a person. And so we cannot say that she is essentially a person. One more substantive modification of the view, popular with friends of tropes, is that such substances are built up out of tropes. This modification is most far reaching if tropes can stand only in external relations to each other, less far reaching if tropes are allowed to be necessarily connected to each other. Similarly, if a philosopher denies the existence of temporal entities that have no temporal parts, then she may well want to say that Mary is a process, albeit a rather long one. All these alternatives to the traditional view are purely metaphysical alternatives. A series of even more substantive modifications of the traditional view appears to be dictated by certain epistemological views.

Two traditional epistemologies for substances are naive or direct realism and critical realism or representationalism. On the first view, Sam may directly see Mary, in person. On the second view, Sam is always only directly aware of his sensory experiences and typically infers from these experiences to Mary's existence. On both views, epistemic contact with substances that are normally independent of such contact is possible—direct contact in the first case, indirect in the second case.

A third view, *phenomenalism* or *neutral monism* claims—incredibly—that Mary is just a suitably coherent sequence of actual or possible sensory experiences. Clearly, phenomenalism may easily lead to some form of epistemological idealism.

Whitehead and Russell launched an enormously influential philosophical project that oscillates between critical realism and a phenomenalism that strives to avoid idealism. An essential feature of the project is the extensive use of a new version of the idea already encountered, that a certain type or category of entity can be reduced to a more basic type or category and, since economy is a good thing, should be so reduced if possible. The new version of this idea is the logico-metaphysical method of logical construction: apparent references to entities of a certain type are to be analysed into sentences which refer, if at all, to entities of some different kind. The method's slogan is:

> Wherever possible, substitute constructions out of known entities for inference to unknown entities. (Russell 1989, 326)

Although Russell was quite aware of the importance of distinguishing the epistemological order and the logico-metaphysical order (cf. Russell 1989, 326), the following passage illustrates how epistemological considerations can influence metaphysical considerations:

> What makes you say on successive occasions, I am seeing the same desk? The first thing to notice is this, that it does not matter what is the answer, so long as you have recognised that the answer consists in something empirical and not in a recognized metaphysical identity of substance. There is something given in experience which makes you call it the same desk, it is that something (whatever it is) that makes you call it the same desk which shall be *defined* as *constituting* it the same desk, and there shall be no assumption of a metaphysical substance which is identical throughout. (Russell 1989, 273; emphases are Russell's)

One important formulation of the presuppositions of Russell's project is to be found in a paper of his published in French in 1911, "Le réalisme analytique" (Russell 1992). The paper also enjoys a certain claim to fame because Russell there baptizes his philosophy as "logical atomism," almost christens analytical philosophy ("The philosophy of which I am in favour is analytic"), and seems to refer to himself as an "analyst" ("contradictions are merely errors, and in order to resolve them one needs only the patience and genius of the analyst").

Russell's 1911 analytic realism is *realist* because it claims that cognitive relations are external relations and that there is no reason in general for thinking that what is known depends, logically speaking, on cognition; *analytic* because it claims that the existence of what is complex depends logically and unilaterally on the existence of what is simple. The logical atoms of his logical atomism are universals and particulars. A particular can never appear in a proposition as a predicate (property) or relation. All the particulars we know are sense data, and, he says, there are reasons for thinking that these exist only when they are given to us, that they depend causally on us, although sense data such as visual experiences are not in the mind. But there are also unknown particulars. Universals are causally and logically independent of us. Just what Russell means here by logical as opposed to causal dependence is not clear. But he presumably does not have modal dependence ("could not exist without") in mind.[1]

Russell's realism here is a form of critical realism: the physical world is distinct from the sensory world and we have only inductive reasons for believing in the existence of the physical world. In spite of the central role of sensory experience, Russell's analytic realism is not any form of empiricism. For empiricism is incapable of doing justice to the relations subsisting between universals that are expressed by the propositions of mathematics and logic. There are two worlds, that of existence—physical and psychological—and that of essence (cf. Frege, this volume, 93–105).

The project of actually constructing Sam, Mary, or desks out of sense data has a long and tortuous history. In addition to Russell's own writings (cf. Russell 1914), important contributions to the project and examinations of it were given by Russell's French pupil Jean Nicod as well as Rudolf Carnap, Nelson Goodman, and A. J. Ayer (this volume).

The Possibility of Metaphysics

Carnap, in his contribution to this volume, uses the term "metaphysics" to refer to certain types of bad philosophy that, unconstrained by experience, rigour or argument, are meaningless. In 1928, four years before the publication in German of the article reproduced here, Carnap had published a book entitled *Der logische Aufbau der Welt* ("The Logical Construction of the World") which aims to trace back various central objects, concepts, properties, and relations to "what is immediately given." The bricks of the construction are elementary experiences and a relating experience, memory or retention, in which the similarity of two experiences is recognized. From these materials Carnap (1967, §§78–83) builds up an account of qualities or properties and similarity that looks very like a version of what we called earlier "resemblance nominalism." But the appearance is deceptive. Nominalism, as expounded here—as well as, for example, the claim that reality is independent of consciousness—is a metaphysical claim (Carnap 1967, §27, §176), in the pejorative sense Carnap gives to the word. For, Carnap argues, no experience could possibly confirm such metaphysical claims or even begin to give them a sense.

A simple modification of our starting point provides a possible compromise between analytic metaphysics and Carnap. We began with the traditional claim that metaphysics and ontology deal with the most general categories of what there is. But if we except theological claims about entities that exist necessarily, it seems that existence claims are claims to the effect that entities exist or do not exist as a matter of contingent fact. Now it may be the case that philosophy is as little concerned with the existence of universals or substances as it is with the existence of lollipops or genes. Certainly, metaphysics is concerned with giving an account of what it is to be a substance or a property and with evaluating the consequences of the hypothesis that there are tropes but no universals, or vice versa. A metaphysician, it might be thought, should tell us what it is to be a substance rather than a process. But perhaps it is up to science to tell us whether the category of substance, as explicated by some metaphysical theory, is empty or not. Of course, even if the task of evaluating metaphysical existence claims is shunted over to science in this way, there still remains the task of explaining how the expressions of metaphysics—"substance," "universal"—acquire a sense.

One suggestion—in the spirit of Russell—goes as follows. Truth and existence are intimately related. Whether or not a proposition, judgment, sentence, or statement (a truth bearer) which is contingently true or false is true or false is not a philosophical question. But two genuinely philosophical questions are (1) If some given truth bearer is true, what must then exist? (2) What sort of entities, if they exist, would make the truth bearer true? Answers to questions like (1) and (2) would constitute part of a theory of meaning. If such answers have to use expressions such as "trope" or "universal" or "state of affairs," then we might be on the way to understanding how metaphysical expressions acquire a meaning.[2]

Whatever the connection between the theory of truth-making and metaphysics or ontology these, as noted above, must give an account of existence. We have seen that philosophers have said that certain entities enjoy temporal existence, whereas states of affairs or universals subsist. Similarly, within the general category of temporal existence a metaphysician might want to say that whereas substances endure, processes take place. Do these claims belong to a philosophical account of existence? No. One lesson from Frege and Russell is that the theories of existence associated with the logical theory of the quantifiers are distinct from and presupposed by theories about such different "modes of existence" (cf. Russell 1992, 145) as subsistence, enduring, or taking place. For we may want to be able to say that there are entities enjoying different modes of existence.

Before and After

Our brief tour of some fundamental categories discussed within early analytic metaphysics and ontology has identified a number of questions that have been at the center of later discussions within analytic philosophy. Some suggestions for further reading are appended.

It is perhaps also worth noting that philosophical analyses of the categories of substance, trope, universals, states of affairs, essence, and modality were developed from the turn of the century onward by Husserl, Meinong, and their pupils under such headings as "formal ontology" and the "theory of objects." In parallel investigations, these philosophers analyzed in some detail the way in which different types of objects are "constituted" or "constructed"—the ugly and misleading terms used by Husserl, Russell, Carnap, and Ayer—in experience as well the ways in which different types of proposition are verified.

NOTES

1. Compare Russell's earlier, uncertain rejection of modal dependence (Russell [1904] 1973, 25).
2. This paragraph has profited from unpublished work by Gonzalo Rodriquez-Pecyra.

REFERENCES

Carnap, Rudolf. 1967. *The Logical Structure of the World.* Trans. Rolf Georg. London: Routledge and Kegan Paul.
Moore, G. E. 1900. "Identity." *Proceedings of the Aristotelian Society* 1: 103–127.

―――. 1902. "Qualities." In *Dictionary of Philosophy and Psychology,* vol. 2, edited by J. M. Baldwin. New York: Macmillan, 406–408.

―――. 1922. "The Conception of Intrinsic Value." *Philosophical Studies.* London: Kegan Paul, 253–75.

―――. [1903] 1954. *Principia Ethica.* Cambridge: Cambridge University Press.

―――. [1923] 1970. "Are the Characteristics of Particular Things Universal or Particular?" *Philosophical Papers.* London: Allen and Unwin, 17–31.

Price, H. H. 1953. *Thinking and Experience.* London: Hutchinson's University Library.

Ramsey, F. P. 1990. "Universals." *Philosophical Papers,* ed. D. H. Mellor. Cambridge. Cambridge University Press, 8–30.

Russell, Bertrand. 1897. "An Analysis of Mathematical Reasoning." Extracts reproduced in T. R. Foster, 1983–84. "Russell on Particularized Relations." *Russell: The Journal of the Bertrand Russell Archives* 3, no. 2: 129–44.

―――. 1903. *The Principles of Mathematics.* London. Allen and Unwin.

―――. [1904] 1973. "Meinong's Theory of Complexes and Assumptions." *Essays in Analysis,* edited by Lackey, 21–76.

―――. [1912] 1986. *The Problems of Philosophy.* Oxford: Oxford University Press. http://www.voyageronline.net/~daniel/bertrand.htm

―――. 1914. *Our Knowledge of the External World.* Chicago and London: Open Court.

―――. 1989. *Logic and Knowledge: Essays 1901–1950.* Edited by R. C. Marsh. London: Unwin Hyman.

―――. 1992. "Le Réalisme analytique." *Collected Papers of Bertrand Russell,* Vol. 6. London: Routledge, 409–32. [Translated as "Analytic Realism," 132–46.]

Stout, G. F. 1921. "The Nature of Universals and Propositions." *Proceedings of the British Academy* 10 (1921–23): 157–72.

―――. 1923. "Are the Characteristics of Particular Things Universal or Particular?" *Proceedings of the Aristotelian Society,* Suppl. vol. 3: 114–22.

Universals: Properties and Relations

Armstrong, D. M. 1989. *Universals: An Opinionated Introduction.* Boulder, CO: Westview Press.

Johansson, Ingvar. 1989. *Ontological Investigations: An Inquiry into the Categories of Nature, Man, and Society.* London: Routledge and Kegan Paul.

Oliver, Alex 1996. "The Metaphysics of Properties." *Mind* 105, no. 417: 1–80.

Tropes

Campbell, Keith. 1976. *Metaphysics: An Introduction.* Encino: Dickenson.

―――. 1990. *Abstract Particulars.* Oxford: Blackwell.

Mulligan, Kevin, P., Simons and B. Smith. 1984. "Truth-Makers." *Philosophy and Phenomenological Research* 14, no. 3: 287–321. http://wings.buffalo.edu/academic/department/philosophy/faculty/smith/articles/truthmakers/tm.html

States of Affairs

Armstrong, D. M. 1997. *A World of States of Affairs.* Cambridge: Cambridge University Press.

Substances

Wiggins, David. 1980. *Sameness and Substance.* Oxford: Blackwell.

The Thought: A Logical Inquiry[1]   7

GOTTLOB FREGE

THE WORD "TRUE" indicates the aim of logic as does "beautiful" that of aesthetics or "good" that of ethics. All sciences have truth as their goal; but logic is also concerned with it in a quite different way from this. It has much the same relation to truth as physics has to weight or heat. To discover truths is the task of all sciences; it falls to logic to discern the laws of truth. The word "law" is used in two senses. When we speak of laws of morals or the state we mean regulations which ought to be obeyed but with which actual happenings are not always in conformity. Laws of nature are the generalization of natural occurrences with which the occurrences are always in accordance. It is rather in this sense that I speak of laws of truth. This is, to be sure, not a matter of what happens so much as of what is. Rules for asserting, thinking, judging, inferring, follow from the laws of truth. And thus one can very well speak of laws of thought too. But there is an imminent danger here of mixing different things up. Perhaps the expression "law of thought" is interpreted by analogy with "law of nature" and the generalization of thinking as a mental occurrence is meant by it. A law of thought in this sense would be a psychological law. And so one might come to believe that logic deals with the mental process of thinking and the psychological laws in accordance with which it takes place. This would be a misunderstanding of the task of logic, for truth has not been given the place which is its due here. Error and superstition have causes just as much as genuine knowledge. The assertion both of what is false and of what is true takes place in accordance with psychological laws. A derivation from these and an explanation of a mental process that terminates in an assertion can never take the place of a proof of what is asserted. Could not logical laws also have played a part in this mental process? I do not want to dispute this, but when it is a question of truth possibility is not enough. For it is also possible that something

not logical played a part in the process and deflected it from the truth. We can only decide this after we have discerned the laws of truth; but then we will probably be able to do without the derivation and explanation of the mental process if it is important to us to decide whether the assertion in which the process terminates is justified. In order to avoid this misunderstanding and to prevent the blurring of the boundary between psychology and logic, I assign to logic the task of discovering the laws of truth, not of assertion or thought. The meaning of the word "true" is explained by the laws of truth.

But first I shall attempt to outline roughly what I want to call true in this connexion. In this way other uses of our word may be excluded. It is not to be used here in the sense of "genuine" or "veracious," nor, as it sometimes occurs in the treatment of questions of art, when, for example; truth in art is discussed, when truth is set up as the goal of art, when the truth of a work of art or true feeling is spoken of. The word "true" is put in front of another word in order to show that this word is to be understood in its proper, unadulterated sense. This use too lies off the path followed here; that kind of truth is meant whose recognition is the goal of science.

Grammatically the word "true" appears as an adjective. Hence the desire arises to delimit more closely the sphere in which truth can be affirmed, in which truth comes into the question at all. One finds truth affirmed of pictures, ideas, statements, and thoughts. It is striking that visible and audible things occur here alongside things which cannot be perceived with the senses. This hints that shifts of meaning have taken place. Indeed! Is a picture, then, as a mere visible and tangible thing, really true, and a stone, a leaf, not true? Obviously one would not call a picture true unless there were an intention behind it. A picture must represent something. Furthermore, an idea is not called true in itself but only with

Mind 64 (1956): 289–311. Reprinted with permission of *Mind*. Originally published as "Der Gedanke," *Beiträge zur Philosophie des Deutschen Idealismus* (1918–1919).

respect to an intention that it should correspond to something. It might be supposed from this that truth consists in the correspondence of a picture with what it depicts. Correspondence is a relation. This is contradicted, however, by the use of the word "true," which is not a relation-word and contains no reference to anything else to which something must correspond. If I do not know that a picture is meant to represent Cologne Cathedral then I do not know with what to compare the picture to decide on its truth. A correspondence, moreover, can only be perfect if the corresponding things coincide and are, therefore, not distinct things at all. It is said to be possible to establish the authenticity of a banknote by comparing it stereoscopically with an authentic one. But it would be ridiculous to try to compare a gold piece with a twenty-mark note stereoscopically. It would only be possible to compare an idea with a thing if the thing were an idea too. And then, if the first did correspond perfectly with the second, they would coincide. But this is not at all what is wanted when truth is defined as the correspondence of an idea with something real. For it is absolutely essential that the reality be distinct from the idea. But then there can be no complete correspondence, no complete truth. So nothing at all would be true; for what is only half true is untrue. Truth cannot tolerate a more or less. But yet? Can it not be laid down that truth exists when there is correspondence in a certain respect? But in which? For what would we then have to do to decide whether something were true? We should have to inquire whether it were true that an idea and a reality, perhaps, corresponded in the laid-down respect. And then we should be confronted by a question of the same kind and the game could begin again. So the attempt to explain truth as correspondence collapses. And every other attempt to define truth collapses too. For in a definition certain characteristics would have to be stated. And in application to any particular case the question would always arise whether it were true that the characteristics were present. So one goes round in a circle. Consequently, it is probable that the content of the word "true" is unique and indefinable.

When one ascribes truth to a picture one does not really want to ascribe a property which belongs to this picture altogether independently of other things, but one always has something quite different in mind

and one wants to say that that picture corresponds in some way to this thing. "My idea corresponds to Cologne Cathedral" is a sentence and the question now arises of the truth of this sentence. So what is improperly called the truth of pictures and ideas is reduced to the truth of sentences. What does one call a sentence? A series of sounds; but only when it has a sense, by which is not meant that every series of sounds that has sense is a sentence. And when we call a sentence true we really mean its sense is. From which it follows that it is for the sense of a sentence that the question of truth arises in general. Now is the sense of a sentence an idea? In any case being true does not consist in the correspondence of this sense with something else, for otherwise the question of truth would reiterate itself to infinity.

Without wishing to give a definition, I call a thought something for which the question of truth arises. So I ascribe what is false to a thought just as much as what is true.[2] So I can say: the thought is the sense of the sentence without wishing to say as well that the sense of every sentence is a thought. The thought, in itself immaterial, clothes itself in the material garment of a sentence and thereby becomes comprehensible to us. We say a sentence expresses a thought.

A thought is something immaterial and everything material and perceptible is excluded from this sphere of that for which the question of truth arises. Truth is not a quality that corresponds with a particular kind of sense-impression. So it is sharply distinguished from the qualities which we denote by the words "red," "bitter," "lilac-smelling." But do we not see that the sun has risen and do we not then also see that this is true? That the sun has risen is not an object which emits rays that reach my eyes, it is not a visible thing like the sun itself. That the sun has risen is seen to be true on the basis of sense-impressions. But being true is not a material, perceptible property. For being magnetic is also recognized on the basis of sense-impressions of something, though this property corresponds as little as truth with a particular kind of sense-impressions. So far these properties agree. However, we need sense-impressions in order to recognize a body as magnetic. On the other hand, when I find that it is true that I do not smell anything at this moment, I do not do so on the basis of sense-impressions.

It may nevertheless be thought that we cannot recognize a property of a thing without at the same time
realizing the thought that this thing has this property
to be true. So with every property of a thing is joined
a property of a thought, namely, that of truth. It is
also worthy of notice that the sentence "I smell the
scent of violets" has just the same content as the
sentence "it is true that I smell the scent of violets."
So it seems, then, that nothing is added to the
thought by my ascribing to it the property of truth.
And yet is it not a great result when the scientist, after
much hesitation and careful inquiry, can finally say
"what I supposed is true"? The meaning of the word
"true" seems to be altogether unique. May we not be
dealing here with something which cannot, in the ordinary sense, be called a quality at all? In spite of this
doubt I want first to express myself in accordance with
ordinary usage, as if truth were a quality, until something more to the point is found.

In order to work out more precisely what I want
to call thought, I shall distinguish various kinds of
sentences.[3] One does not want to deny sense to an
imperative sentence, but this sense is not such that
the question of truth could arise for it. Therefore I
shall not call the sense of an imperative sentence a
thought. Sentences expressing desires or requests are
ruled out in the same way. Only those sentences in
which we communicate or state something come
into the question. But I do not count among these
exclamations in which one vents one's feelings,
groaning, sighing, laughing, unless it has been decided by some agreement that they are to communicate something. But how about interrogative
sentences? In a word-question we utter an incomplete sentence which only obtains a true sense
through the completion for which we ask. Word-
questions are accordingly left out of consideration
here. Sentence-questions are a different matter. We
expect to hear "yes" or "no." The answer "yes"
means the same as an indicative sentence, for in it
the thought that was already completely contained
in the interrogative sentence is laid down as true.
So a sentence-question can be formed from every
indicative sentence. An exclamation cannot be regarded as a communication on this account, since no
corresponding sentence-question can be formed. An
interrogative sentence and an indicative one contain
the same thought; but the indicative contains something else as well, namely, the assertion. The interrogative sentence contains something more too,
namely a request. Therefore two things must be
distinguished in an indicative sentence: the content,
which it has in common with the corresponding
sentence-question, and the assertion. The former is
the thought, or at least contains the thought. So it is
possible to express the thought without laying it
down as true. Both are so closely joined in an indicative sentence that it is easy to overlook their sep-
arability. Consequently we may distinguish:

1. the apprehension of a thought—thinking,
2. the recognition of the truth of a thought—
   judgment,[4]
3. the manifestation of this judgment—
   assertion.

We perform the first act when we form a sentence-
question. An advance in science usually takes place
in this way; first a thought is apprehended, such as
can perhaps be expressed in a sentence-question,
and, after appropriate investigations, this thought
is finally recognized to be true. We declare the
recognition of truth in the form of an indicative
sentence. We do not have to use the word "true"
for this. And even when we do use it the real assertive force lies not in it but in the form of the indicative sentence, and where this loses its assertive
force the word "true" cannot put it back again. This
happens when we do not speak seriously. As stage
thunder is only apparent thunder and a stage fight
only an apparent fight, so stage assertion is only apparent assertion. It is only acting, only fancy. In his
part the actor asserts nothing, nor does he lie, even
if he says something of whose falsehood he is convinced. In poetry we have the case of thoughts
being expressed without being actually put forward
as true in spite of the form of the indicative sentence, although it may be suggested to the hearer
to make an assenting judgment himself. Therefore
it must still always be asked, about what is presented
in the form of an indicative sentence, whether it really contains an assertion. And this question must
be answered in the negative if the requisite seri-
ousness is lacking. It is irrelevant whether the word
"true" is used here. This explains why it is that
nothing seems to be added to a thought by attributing to it the property of truth.

An indicative sentence often contains, as well as a thought and the assertion, a third component over which the assertion does not extend. This is often said to act on the feelings, the mood of the hearer, or to arouse his imagination. Words like "alas" and "thank God" belong here. Such constituents of sentences are more noticeably prominent in poetry, but are seldom wholly absent from prose. They occur more rarely in mathematical, physical, or chemical than in historical expositions. What are called the humanities are more closely connected with poetry and are therefore less scientific than the exact sciences which are drier the more exact they are for exact science is directed toward truth and only the truth. Therefore all constituents of sentences to which the assertive force does not reach do not belong to scientific exposition but they are sometimes hard to avoid, even for one who sees the danger connected with them. Where the main thing is to approach what cannot be grasped in thought by means of guesswork these components have their justification. The more exactly scientific an exposition is the less will the nationality of its author be discernible and the easier will it be to translate. On the other hand, the constituents of language, to which I want to call attention here, make the translation of poetry very difficult, even make a complete translation almost always impossible, for it is in precisely that in which poetic value largely consists that languages differ most.

It makes no difference to the thought whether I use the word "horse" or "steed" or "cart-horse" or "mare."[5] The assertive force does not extend over that in which these words differ. What is called mood, fragrance, illumination in a poem, what is portrayed by cadence and rhythm, does not belong to the thought.

Much of language serves the purpose of aiding the hearer's understanding, for instance the stressing of part of a sentence by accentuation or word-order. One should remember words like "still" and "already" too. With the sentence "Alfred has still not come" one really says "Alfred has not come" and, at the same time, hints that his arrival is expected, but it is only hinted. It cannot be said that, since Alfred's arrival is not expected, the sense of the sentence is therefore false. The word "but" differs from "and" in that with it one intimates that what follows is in contrast with what would be expected from what preceded it. Such suggestions in speech make no difference to the thought. A sentence can be transformed by changing the verb from active to passive and making the object the subject at the same time. In the same way the dative may be changed into the nominative while "give" is replaced by "receive." Naturally such transformations are not indifferent in every respect; but they do not touch the thought, they do not touch what is true or false. If the inadmissibility of such transformations were generally admitted then all deeper logical investigation would be hindered. It is just as important to neglect distinctions that do not touch the heart of the matter as to make distinctions which concern what is essential. But what is essential depends on one's purpose. To a mind concerned with what is beautiful in language what is indifferent to the logician can appear as just what is important.

Thus the contents of a sentence often go beyond the thoughts expressed by it. But the opposite often happens too, that the mere wording, which can be grasped by writing or the gramophone does not suffice for the expression of the thought. The present tense is used in two ways: first, in order to give a date, second, in order to eliminate any temporal restriction where timelessness or eternity is part of the thought. Think, for instance, of the laws of mathematics. Which of the two cases occurs is not expressed but must be guessed. If a time indication is needed by the present tense one must know when the sentence was uttered to apprehend the thought correctly. Therefore the time of utterance is part of the expression of the thought. If someone wants to say the same today as he expressed yesterday using the word "today," he must replace this word with "yesterday." Although the thought is the same its verbal expression must be different so that the sense, which would otherwise be affected by the differing times of utterance, is readjusted. The case is the same with words like "here" and "there." In all such cases the mere wording, as it is given in writing, is not the complete expression of the thought, but the knowledge of certain accompanying conditions of utterance, which are used as means of expressing the thought, are needed for its correct apprehension. The pointing of fingers, hand movements, glances may belong here too. The same utterance containing the word "I" will express different thoughts in the mouths of different men, of which some may be true, others false.

The occurrence of the word "I" in a sentence gives rise to some questions.

Consider the following case. Dr. Gustav Lauben says, "I have been wounded." Leo Peter hears this and remarks some days later, "Dr. Gustav Lauben has been wounded." Does this sentence express the same thought as the one Dr. Lauben uttered himself? Suppose that Rudolph Lingens were present when Dr. Lauben spoke and now hears what is related by Leo Peter. If the same thought is uttered by Dr. Lauben and Leo Peter then Rudolph Lingens, who is fully master of the language and remembers what Dr. Lauben has said in his presence, must now know at once from Leo Peter's report that the same thing is under discussion. But knowledge of the language is a separate thing when it is a matter of proper names. It may well be the case that only a few people associate a particular thought with the sentence "Dr. Lauben has been wounded." In this case one needs for complete understanding a knowledge of the expression "Dr. Lauben." Now if both Leo Peter and Rudolph Lingens understand by "Dr. Lauben" the doctor who lives as the only doctor in a house known to both of them, then they both understand the sentence "Dr. Gustav Lauben has been wounded" in the same way, they associate the same thought with it. But it is also possible that Rudolph Lingens does not know Dr. Lauben personally and does not know that he is the very Dr. Lauben who recently said "I have been wounded." In this case Rudolph Lingens cannot know that the same thing is in question. I say, therefore, in this case: the thought which Leo Peter expresses is not the same as that which Dr. Lauben uttered.

Suppose further that Herbert Garner knows that Dr. Gustav Lauben was born on 13th September 1875 in N. N. and this is not true of anyone else; against this, suppose that he does not know where Dr. Lauben now lives nor indeed anything about him. On the other hand, suppose Leo Peter does not know that Dr. Lauben was born on 13th September 1875 in N. N. Then as far as the proper name "Dr. Gustav Lauben" is concerned, Herbert Garner and Leo Peter do not speak the same language, since, although they do in fact refer to the same man with

this name, they do not know that they do so. Therefore Herbert Garner does not associate the same thought with the sentence "Dr. Gustav Lauben has been wounded" as Leo Peter wants to express with it. To avoid the drawback of Herbert Garner's and Leo Peter's not speaking the same language, I am assuming that Leo Peter uses the proper name "Dr. Lauben" and Herbert Garner, on the other hand uses the proper name "Gustav Lauben." Now it is possible that Herbert Garner takes the sense of the sentence "Dr. Lauben has been wounded" to be true while, misled by false information, taking the sense of the sentence "Gustav Lauben has been wounded" to be false. Under the assumptions given these thoughts are therefore different.

Accordingly, with a proper name, it depends on how whatever it refers to is presented. This can happen in different ways and every such way corresponds with a particular sense of a sentence containing a proper name. The different thoughts which thus result from the same sentence correspond in their truth-value, of course; that is to say, if one is true then all are true, and if one is false then all are false. Nevertheless their distinctness must be recognized. So it must really be demanded that a single way in which whatever is referred to is presented be associated with every proper name. It is often unimportant that this demand should be fulfilled but not always.

Now everyone is presented to himself in a particular and primitive way, in which he is presented to no-one else. So, when Dr. Lauben thinks that he has been wounded, he will probably take as a basis this primitive way in which he is presented to himself. And only Dr. Lauben himself can grasp thoughts determined in this way. But now he may want to communicate with others. He cannot communicate a thought which he alone can grasp. Therefore, if he now says "I have been wounded," he must use the "I" in a sense which can be grasped by others, perhaps in the sense of "he who is speaking to you at this moment," by doing which he makes the associated conditions of his utterance serve for the expression of his thought.[6]

Yet there is a doubt. Is it at all the same thought which first that man expresses and now this one?

A person who is still untouched by philosophy knows first of all things which he can see and touch, in short, perceive with the senses, such as trees, stones and houses, and he is convinced that another person equally can see and touch the same tree and the same stone which he himself sees and touches. Obviously no thought belongs to these things. Now can he, nevertheless, stand in the same relation to a person as to a tree?

Even an unphilosophical person soon finds it necessary to recognize an inner world distinct from the outer world, a world of sense-impressions, of creations of his imagination, of sensations, of feelings and moods, a world of inclinations, wishes and decisions. For brevity I want to collect all these, with the exception of decisions, under the word "idea."

Now do thoughts belong to this inner world? Are they ideas? They are obviously not decisions. How are ideas distinct from the things of the outer world?

First: Ideas cannot be seen or touched, cannot be smelled, nor tasted, nor heard.

I go for a walk with a companion. I see a green field, I have a visual impression of the green as well. I have it but I do not see it.

Secondly: Ideas are had. One has sensations, feelings, moods, inclinations, wishes. An idea which someone has belongs to the content of his consciousness.

The field and the frogs in it, the sun which shines on them are there no matter whether I look at them or not, but the sense-impression I have of green exists only because of me, I am its bearer. It seems absurd to us that a pain, a mood, a wish should rove about the world without a bearer, independently. An experience is impossible without an experient. The inner world presupposes the person whose inner world it is.

Thirdly: Ideas need a bearer. Things of the outer world are however independent.

My companion and I are convinced that we both see the same field; but each of us has a particular sense-impression of green. I notice a strawberry among the green strawberry leaves. My companion does not notice it, he is colour-blind. The colour-impression, which he receives from the strawberry, is not noticeably different from the one he receives from the leaf. Now does my companion see the green leaf as red, or does he see the red berry as green, or does he see both as of one colour with which I am not acquainted at all? These are unanswerable, indeed really nonsensical, questions. For when the word "red" does not state a property of things but

is supposed to characterize sense-impressions belonging to my consciousness, it is only applicable within the sphere of my consciousness. For it is impossible to compare my sense-impression with that of someone else. For that it would be necessary to bring together in one consciousness a sense-impression, belonging to one consciousness, with a sense-impression belonging to another consciousness. Now even if it were possible to make an idea disappear from one consciousness and, at the same time, to make an idea appear in another consciousness, the question whether it were the same idea in both would still remain unanswerable. It is so much of the essence of each of my ideas to be the content of my consciousness, that every idea of another person is, just as such, distinct from mine. But might it not be possible that my ideas, the entire content of my consciousness might be at the same time the content of a more embracing, perhaps divine, consciousness? Only if I were myself part of the divine consciousness. But then would they really be my ideas, would I be their bearer? This oversteps the limits of human understanding to such an extent that one must leave its possibility out of account. In any case it is impossible for us as men to compare another person's ideas with our own. I pick the strawberry, I hold it between my fingers. Now my companion sees it too, this very same strawberry; but each of us has his own idea. No other person has my idea but many people can see the same thing. No other person has my pain. Someone can have sympathy for me but still my pain always belongs to me and his sympathy to him. He does not have my pain and I do not have his sympathy.

Fourthly: Every idea has only one bearer; no two men have the same idea.

For otherwise it would exist independently of this person and independently of that one. Is that lime-tree my idea? By using the expression "that lime-tree" in this question I have really already anticipated the answer, for with this expression I want to refer to what I see and to what other people can also look at and touch. There are now two possibilities. If my intention is realized when I refer to something with the expression "that lime-tree" then the thought expressed in the sentence "that lime-tree is my idea" must obviously be negated. But if my intention is not realized, if I only think I see without really seeing, if on that account the designation "that lime-tree" is empty, then I have gone astray into the sphere of fiction without knowing it or wanting to. In that case neither the content of the sentence "that lime-tree is my idea" nor the content of the sentence "that lime-tree is not my idea" is true for in both cases I have a statement which lacks an object. So then one can only refuse to answer the question for the reason that the content of the sentence "that lime-tree is my idea" is a piece of fiction. I have, naturally, got an idea then, but I am not referring to this with the words "that lime-tree." Now someone may really want to refer to one of his ideas with the words "that lime-tree." He would then be the bearer of that to which he wants to refer with those words, but then he would not see that lime-tree and no-one else would see it or be its bearer.

I now return to the question: is a thought an idea? If the thought I express in the Pythagorean theorem can be recognized by others just as much as by me then it does not belong to the content of my consciousness, I am not its bearer; yet I can, nevertheless, recognize it to be true. However, if it is not the same thought at all which is taken to be the content of the Pythagorean theorem by me and by another person, one should not really say "the Pythagorean theorem" but "my Pythagorean theorem" "his Pythagorean theorem" and these would be different; for the sense belongs necessarily to the sentence. Then my thought can be the content of my consciousness and his thought the content of his. Could the sense of my Pythagorean theorem be true while that of his was false? I said that the word "red" was applicable only in the sphere of my consciousness if it did not state a property of things but was supposed to characterize one of my sense-impressions. Therefore the words "true" and "false," as I understand them, could also be applicable only in the sphere of my consciousness if they were not supposed to be concerned with something of which I was not the bearer, but were somehow appointed to characterize the content of my consciousness. Then truth would be restricted to the content of my consciousness and it would remain doubtful whether anything at all comparable occurred in the consciousness of others.

If every thought requires a bearer, to the contents of whose consciousness it belongs, then it would be a thought of this bearer only and there would be no science common to many, on which many could work. But I, perhaps, have my science, namely, a whole of thought whose bearer I am, and another person has his. Each of us occupies himself with the contents of his own consciousness. No contradiction between the two sciences would then be possible and it would really be idle to dispute about truth, as idle, indeed almost ludicrous, as it would be for two people to dispute whether a hundred-mark note were genuine, where each meant the one he himself had in his pocket and understood the word "genuine" in his own particular sense. If someone takes thoughts to be ideas, what he then recognizes to be true is, on his own view, the content of his consciousness and does not properly concern other people at all. If he were to hear from me the opinion that a thought is not an idea he could not dispute it, for, indeed, it would not now concern him.

So the result seems to be: thoughts are neither things of the outer world nor ideas.

A third realm must be recognized. What belongs to this corresponds with ideas, in that it cannot be perceived by the senses, but with things, in that it needs no bearer to the contents of whose consciousness to belong. Thus the thought, for example, which we expressed in the Pythagorean theorem is timelessly true, true independently of whether anyone takes it to be true. It needs no bearer. It is not true for the first time when it is discovered, but is like a planet which, already before anyone has seen it, has been in interaction with other planets.[7]

But I think I hear an unusual objection. I have assumed several times that the same thing that I see can also be observed by other people. But how could this be the case, if everything were only a dream? If I only dreamed I was walking in the company of another person, if I only dreamed that my companion saw the green field as I did, if it were all only a play performed on the stage of my consciousness, it would be doubtful whether there were things of the outer world at all. Perhaps the realm of things is empty and I see no things and no men, but have only ideas of which I myself am the bearer. An idea, being something which can as little exist independently of me as my feeling of fatigue, cannot be a man, cannot look at the same field together with me, cannot see the strawberry I am holding. It is quite incredible that I should really have only my inner world instead of the whole environment, in which I am supposed to move and to act. And yet it is an inevitable consequence of the thesis that only what is my idea can be the object of my awareness. What would follow from this thesis if it were true? Would there then be other men? It would certainly be possible but I should know nothing of it. For a man cannot be my idea, consequently, if our thesis were true, he also cannot be an object of my awareness. And so the ground would be removed from under any process of thought in which I might assume that something was an object for another person as for myself, for even if this were to happen I should know nothing of it. It would be impossible for me to distinguish that of which I was the bearer from that of which I was not. In judging something not to be my idea I would make it the object of my thinking and, therefore, my idea. On this view, is there a green field? Perhaps, but it would not be visible to me. For if a field is not my idea, it cannot, according to our thesis, be an object of my awareness. But if it is my idea it is invisible, for ideas are not visible. I can indeed have the idea of a green field, but this is not green for there are no green ideas. Does a shell weighing a hundred kilogrammes exist, according to this view? Perhaps, but I could know nothing of it. If a shell is not my idea then, according to our thesis, it cannot be an object of my awareness, of my thinking. But if a shell were my idea, it would have no weight. I can have an idea of a heavy shell. This then contains the idea of weight as a part-idea. But this part-idea is not a property of the whole idea any more than Germany is a property of Europe. So it follows:

Either the thesis that only what is my idea can be the object of my awareness is false, or all my knowledge and perception is limited to the range of my ideas, to the stage of my consciousness. In this case I should have only an inner world and I should know nothing of other people.

It is strange how, upon such reflections, the opposites collapse into each other. There is, let us suppose, a physiologist of the senses. As is proper for a scholarly scientist, he is, first of all, far from supposing the things he is convinced he sees and touches to be his ideas. On the contrary, he believes that in sense-impressions he has the surest proof of things which

are wholly independent of his feeling, imagining, thinking, which have no need of his consciousness. So little does he consider nerve-fibres and ganglion-cells to be the content of his consciousness that he is, on the contrary, rather inclined to regard his consciousness as dependent on nerve-fibres and ganglion-cells. He establishes that light-rays, refracted in the eye, strike the visual nerve-endings and bring about a change, a stimulus, there. Some of it is transmitted through nerve-fibres and ganglion-cells. Further processes in the nervous system are perhaps involved, colour-impressions arise and these perhaps join themselves to what we call the idea of a tree. Physical, chemical and physiological occurrences insert themselves between the tree and my idea. These are immediately connected with my consciousness but, so it seems, are only occurrences in my nervous system and every spectator of the tree has his particular occurrences in his particular nervous system. Now the light-rays, before they enter my eye, may be reflected by a mirror and be spread further as if they came from a place behind the mirror. The effects on the visual nerves and all that follows will now take place just as they would if the light-rays had come from a tree behind the mirror and had been transmitted undisturbed to the eye. So an idea of a tree will finally occur even though such a tree does not exist at all. An idea, to which nothing at all corresponds, can also arise through the bending of light, with the mediation of the eye and the nervous system. But the stimulation of the visual nerves need not even happen through light. If lightning strikes near us we believe we see flames, even though we cannot see the lightning itself. In this case the visual nerve is perhaps stimulated by electric currents which originate in our body in consequence of the flash of lightning. If the visual nerve is stimulated by this means, just as it would be stimulated by light-rays coming from flames, then we believe we see flames. It just depends on the stimulation of the visual nerve, it is indifferent how that itself comes about.

One can go a step further still. This stimulation of the visual nerve is not actually immediately given, but is only a hypothesis. We believe that a thing, independent of us, stimulates a nerve and by this means produces a sense-impression, but, strictly speaking, we experience only the end of this process which projects into our consciousness. Could not this sense-impression, this sensation, which we attribute to a nerve-stimulation, have other causes also, as the same nerve-stimulation can arise in different ways? If we call what happens in our consciousness idea, then we really experience only ideas but not their causes. And if the scientist wants to avoid all mere hypothesis, then only ideas are left for him, everything resolves into ideas, the light-rays, nerve-fibres and ganglion-cells from which he started. So he finally undermines the foundations of his own construction. Is everything an idea? Does everything need a bearer, without which it could have no stability? I have considered myself as the bearer of my ideas, but am I not an idea myself? It seems to me as if I were lying in a deck-chair, as if I could see the toes of a pair of waxed boots, the front part of a pair of trousers, a waistcoat, buttons, part of a jacket, in particular sleeves, two hands, the hair of a beard, the blurred outline of a nose. Am I myself this entire association of visual impressions, this total idea? It also seems to me as if I see a chair over there. It is an idea. I am not actually much different from this myself, for am I not myself just an association of sense-impressions, an idea? But where then is the bearer of these ideas? How do I come to single out one of these ideas and set it up as the bearer of the rest? Why must it be the idea which I choose to call "I"? Could I not just as well choose the one that I am tempted to call a chair? Why, after all, have a bearer for ideas at all? But this would always be something essentially different from merely borne ideas, something independent, needing no extraneous bearer. If everything is idea, then there is no bearer of ideas. And so now, once again, I experience a change into the opposite. If there is no bearer of ideas then there are also no ideas, for ideas need a bearer without which they cannot exist. If there is no ruler, there are also no subjects. The dependence, which I found myself induced to confer on the experience as opposed to the experient, is abolished if there is no more bearer. What I called ideas are then independent objects. Every reason is wanting for granting an exceptional position to that object which I call "I."

But is that possible? Can there be an experience without someone to experience it? What would this whole play be without an onlooker? Can there be a pain without someone who has it? Being experienced is necessarily connected with pain, and someone experiencing is necessarily connected with being experienced. But there is something which is not my idea and yet which can be the object of my awareness, of my thinking, I am myself of this nature. Or can I be part of the content of my consciousness while another part is, perhaps, an idea of the moon? Does this perhaps take place when I judge that I am looking at the moon? Then this first part would have a consciousness and part of the content of this consciousness would be I myself once more. And so on. Yet it is surely inconceivable that I should be boxed into myself in this way to infinity, for then there would not be only one I but infinitely many. I am not my own idea and if I assert something about myself, *e.g.*, that I do not feel any pain at this moment, then my judgment concerns something is not a content of my consciousness, is not my idea, that is me myself. Therefore that about which I state something is not necessarily my idea. But, someone perhaps objects, if I think 1 have no pain at the moment, does not the word 'I' nevertheless correspond with something in the content of my consciousness and is that not an idea? That may be. A certain idea in my consciousness may be associated with the idea of the word 'I'. But then it is an idea among other ideas and I am its bearer as I am the bearer of the other ideas. I have an idea of myself but I am not identical with this idea. What is a content of my consciousness, my idea, should be sharply distinguished from what is an object of my thought. Therefore the thesis that only what belongs to the content of my consciousness can be the object of my awareness, of my thought, is false.

Now the way is clear for me to recognize another person as well as to be an independent bearer of ideas. I have an idea of him but I do not confuse it with him himself. And if I state something about my brother I do not state it about the idea that I have of my brother.

The invalid who has a pain is the bearer of this pain, but the doctor in attendance who reflects on the cause of this pain is not the bearer of the pain. He does not imagine he can relieve the pain by anaesthetizing himself. An idea in the doctor's mind may very well correspond to the pain of the invalid but that is not the pain and not what the doctor is trying to remove. The doctor might consult another doctor. Then one must distinguish: first, the pain whose bearer is the invalid, second, the first doctor's idea of this pain, third, the second doctor's idea of this pain. This idea does indeed belong to the content of the second doctor's consciousness, but it is not the object of his reflection, it is rather an aid to reflection, as a drawing can be such an aid perhaps. Both doctors have the invalid's pain, which they do not bear, as their common object of thought. It can be seen from this that not only a thing but also an idea can be the common object of thought of people who do not have the idea.

So, it seems to me, the matter becomes intelligible. If man could not think and could not take something of which he was not the bearer as the object of his thought he would have an inner world but no outer world. But may this not be based on a mistake? I am convinced that the idea I associate with the words 'my brother' corresponds to something that is not my idea and about which I can say something. But may I not be making a mistake about this? Such mistakes do happen. We then, against our will, lapse into fiction. Indeed! By the step with which I secure an environment for myself I expose myself to the risk of error. And here I come up against a further distinction between my inner and outer worlds. I cannot doubt that I have a visual impression of green but it is not so certain that I see a lime-leaf. So, contrary to widespread views, we find certainty in the inner world while doubt never altogether leaves us in our excursions into the outer world. It is difficult in many cases, nevertheless, to distinguish probability from certainty here, so we can presume to judge about things in the outer world. And we must presume this even at the risk of error if we do not want to succumb to far greater dangers.

In consequence of these last considerations I lay down the following: not everything that can be the object of my understanding is an idea. I, as a bearer of ideas, am not myself an idea. Nothing now stands in the way of recognizing other people to be bearers of ideas as I am myself. And, once given the possibility, the probability is very great, so great that it is in my opinion no longer distinguishable from certainty. Would there be a science of history otherwise? Would not every precept of duty, every law otherwise come to nothing? What would be left of religion? The natural sciences too could only be as-

sessed as fables like astrology and alchemy. Thus the reflections I have carried on, assuming that there are other people besides myself who can take the same thing as the object of their consideration, of their thinking, remain essentially unimpaired in force.

Not everything is an idea. Thus I can also recognize the thought, which other people can grasp just as much as I, as being independent of me. I can recognize a science in which many people can be engaged in research. We are not bearers of thoughts as we are bearers of our ideas. We do not have a thought as we have, say, a sense-impression, but we also do not see a thought as we see, say, a star. So it is advisable to choose a special expression and the word 'apprehend' offers itself for the purpose. A particular mental capacity, the power of thought, must correspond to the apprehension[8] of thought. In thinking we do not produce thoughts but we apprehend them. For what I have called thought stands in the closest relation to truth. What I recognize as true I judge to be true quite independently of my recognition of its truth and of my thinking about it. That someone thinks it has nothing to do with the truth of a thought. 'Facts, facts, facts' cries the scientist if he wants to emphasize the necessity of a firm foundation for science. What is a fact? A fact is a thought that is true. But the scientist will surely not recognize something which depends on men's varying states of mind to be the firm foundation of science. The work of science does not consist of creation but of the discovery of true thoughts. The astronomer can apply a mathematical truth in the investigation of long past events which took place when on earth at least no one had yet recognized that truth. He can do this because the truth of a thought is timeless. Therefore that truth cannot have come into existence with its discovery.

Not everything is an idea. Otherwise psychology would contain all the sciences within it or at least it would be the highest judge over all the sciences. Otherwise psychology would rule over logic and mathematics. But nothing would be a greater misunderstanding of mathematics than its subordination to psychology. Neither logic nor mathematics has the task of investigating minds and the contents of consciousness whose bearer is a single person. Perhaps their task could be represented rather as the investigation of the mind, of the mind not of minds.

The apprehension of a thought presupposes someone who apprehends it, who thinks. He is the bearer of the thinking but not of the thought. Although the thought does not belong to the contents of the thinker's consciousness yet something in his consciousness must be aimed at the thought. But this should not be confused with the thought itself. Similarly Algol itself is different from the idea someone has of Algol.

The thought belongs neither to my inner world as an idea nor yet to the outer world of material, perceptible things.

This consequence, however cogently it may follow from the exposition, will nevertheless not perhaps be accepted without opposition. It will, I think, seem impossible to some people to obtain information about something not belonging to the inner world except by sense-perception. Sense-perception indeed is often thought to be the most certain, even to be the sole, source of knowledge about everything that does not belong to the inner world. But with what right? For sense-impressions are necessary constituents of sense-perceptions and are a part of the inner world. In any case two men do not have the same, though they may have similar, sense-impressions. These alone do not disclose the outer world to us. Perhaps there is a being that has only sense-impressions without seeing or touching things. To have visual impressions is not to see things. How does it happen that I see the tree just there where I do see it? Obviously it depends on the visual impressions I have and on the particular type which occur because I see with two eyes. A particular image arises, physically speaking, on each of the two retinas. Another person sees the tree in the same place. He also has two retinal images but they differ from mine. We must assume that these retinal images correspond to our impressions. Consequently we have visual impressions, not only not the same, but markedly different from each other. And yet we move about in the same outer world. Having visual impressions is certainly necessary for seeing things but not sufficient. What must still be added is non-sensible. And yet this is just what opens up the outer world for us; for without this non-sensible something everyone would remain shut up in his inner world. So since the answer lies in the non-sensible, perhaps something non-sensible could also lead us out of the inner world and enable us to grasp thoughts where no sense-impressions were involved. Outside one's inner world one would have to distinguish the proper outer world of sensible, perceptible things from the realm of the nonsensibly perceptible. We should need something non-sensible for the recognition of both realms but for the sensible perception of things we should need sense-impressions as well and these belong entirely to the inner world. So that in which the distinction between the way in which a thing and a thought is given mainly consists is something which is attributable, not to both realms, but to the inner world. Thus I cannot find this distinction to be so great that on its account it would be impossible for a thought to be given that did not belong to the inner world.

The thought, admittedly, is not something which it is usual to call real. The world of the real is a world in which this acts on that, changes it and again experiences reactions itself and is changed by them. All this is a process in time. We will hardly recognize what is timeless and unchangeable as real. Now is the thought changeable or is it timeless? The thought we express by the Pythagorean theorem is surely timeless, eternal, unchangeable. But are there not thoughts which are true today but false in six months time? The thought, for example, that the tree there is covered with green leaves, will surely be false in six months time. No, for it is not the same thought at all. The words 'this tree is covered with green leaves' are not sufficient by themselves for the utterance, the time of utterance is involved as well. Without the time-indication this gives we have no complete thought, *i.e.,* no thought at all. Only a sentence supplemented by a time-indication and complete in every respect expresses a thought. But this, if it is true, is true not only today or tomorrow but timelessly. Thus the present tense in 'is true' does not refer to the speaker's present but is, if the expression be permitted, a tense of timelessness. If we use the mere form of the indicative sentence, avoiding the word 'true', two things must be distinguished, the expression of the thought and the assertion. The time-indication that may be contained in the sentence belongs only to the expression of the thought, while the truth, whose recognition lies in the form of the indicative sentence, is timeless. Yet the same words, on account of the variability of language with time, take on another sense, express another thought; this change, however, concerns only the linguistic aspect of the matter.

And yet! What value could there be for us in the eternally unchangeable which could neither undergo effects nor have effect on us? Something entirely and in every respect inactive would be unreal and non-existent for us. Even the timeless, if it is to be anything for us, must somehow be implicated with the temporal. What would a thought be for me that was never apprehended by me? But by apprehending a thought I come into a relation to it and it to me. It is possible that the same thought that is thought by me today was not thought by me yesterday. In this way the strict timelessness is of course annulled. But one is inclined to distinguish between essential and inessential properties and to regard something as timeless if the changes it undergoes involve only its inessential properties. A property of a thought will be called inessential which consists in, or follows from the fact that, it is apprehended by a thinker.

How does a thought act? By being apprehended and taken to be true. This is a process in the inner world of a thinker which can have further consequences in this inner world and which, encroaching on the sphere of the will, can also make itself noticeable in the outer world. If, for example, I grasp the thought which we express by the theorem of Pythagoras, the consequence may be that I recognize it to be true and further, that I apply it, making a decision which brings about the acceleration of masses. Thus our actions are usually prepared by thinking and judgment. And so thought can have an indirect influence on the motion of masses. The influence of one person on another is brought about for the most part by thoughts. One communicates a thought. How does this happen? One brings about changes in the common outside world which, perceived by another person, are supposed to induce him to apprehend a thought and take it to be true. Could the great events of world history have come about without the communication of thoughts? And yet we are inclined to regard thoughts as unreal because they appear to be without influence on events while thinking, judging, stating, understanding and the like are facts of human life. How much more real a hammer appears compared with a thought. How different the process of handing over a hammer is

from the communication of a thought. The hammer passes from one control to another, it is gripped, it undergoes pressure and on account of this its density, the disposition of its parts, is changed in places. There is nothing of all this with a thought. It does not leave the control of the communicator by being communicated, for after all a person has no control over it. When a thought is apprehended, it at first only brings about changes in the inner world of the apprehender, yet it remains untouched in its true essence, since the changes it undergoes involve only inessential properties. There is lacking here something we observe throughout the order of nature: reciprocal action. Thoughts are by no means unreal but their reality is of quite a different kind from that of things. And their effect is brought about by an act of the thinker without which they would be ineffective, at least as far as we can see. And yet the thinker does not create them but must take them as they are. They can be true without being apprehended by a thinker and are not wholly unreal even then, at least if they could be apprehended and by this means be brought into operation.[9]

NOTES

1. [Translators' note: This essay was first published in the *Beiträge zur Philosophie des Deutschen Idealismus* for 1918–19, and was the first of three connected essays, the others being 'Die Verneinung,' which has been translated into English by Mr. P. T. Geach, and appears in his and Mr. M. Black's *Translations from the Philosophical Writings of Gottlob Frege*, and 'Gedankengefüge'. A. M. and Marcelle Quinton.]

2. In a similar way it has perhaps been said 'a judgment is something which is either true or false'. In fact I use the word 'thought' in approximately the sense which 'judgment' has in the writings of logicians. I hope it will become clear in what follows why I choose 'thought'. Such an explanation has been objected to on the ground that in it a distinction is drawn between true and false judgments which of all possible distinctions among judgments has perhaps the least significance. I cannot see that it is a logical deficiency that a distinction is given with the explanation. As far as significance is concerned, it should not by any means be judged as trifling if, as I have said, the word 'true' indicates the aim of logic.

3. I am not using the word 'sentence' here in a purely grammatical sense where it also includes subordinate clauses. An isolated subordinate clause does not always have a sense about which the question of truth can arise,

whereas the complex sentence to which it belongs has such a sense.

4. It seems to me that thought and judgment have not hitherto been adequately distinguished. Perhaps language is misleading. For we have no particular clause in the indicative sentence which corresponds to the assertion, that something is being asserted lies rather in the form of the indicative. We have the advantage in German that main and subordinate clauses are distinguished by the word-order. In this connexion it is noticeable that a subordinate clause can also contain an assertion and that often neither main nor subordinate clause expresses a complete thought by itself but only the complex sentence does.

5. [Professor Peter T. Geach has brought to my attention a certain problem of translation in connection with this passage. In German, there are four words all of which are synonymous with the English word 'horse.' Since English is, in comparison, somewhat impoverished, the translators resorted to 'steed,' 'carthorse,' and 'mare.' The first of these will pass. But 'carthorse' and 'mare' are not adequate. Professor Geach suggests that perhaps 'nag' might serve. But this would still leave us with a need for a suitable fourth term. Ed. (1956)]

6. I am not in the happy position here of a mineralogist who shows his hearers a mountain crystal. I cannot put a thought in the hands of my readers with the request that they should minutely examine it from all sides. I have to content myself with presenting the reader with a thought, in itself immaterial, dressed in sensible linguistic form. The metaphorical aspect of language presents difficulties. The sensible always breaks in and makes expression metaphorical and so improper. So a battle with language takes place and I am compelled to occupy myself with language although it is not my proper concern here. I hope I have succeeded in making clear to my readers what I want to call a thought.

7. One sees a thing, one has an idea, one apprehends or thinks a thought. When one apprehends or thinks a thought one does not create it but only comes to stand in a certain relation, which is different from seeing a thing or having an idea, to what already existed beforehand.

8. The expression 'apprehend' is as metaphorical as 'content of consciousness'. The nature of language does not permit anything else. What I hold in my hand can certainly be regarded as the content of my hand but is all the same the content of my hand in quite a different way from the bones and muscles of which it is made and their tensions, and is much more extraneous to it than they are.

9. [Throughout the essay, Frege's 'wirklich' and 'Wirklichkeit' have been translated as 'real' and 'reality.' Prof. R. H. Stoothoff has suggested that a preferable rendering would be the now well-established 'actual' and 'actuality.' Ed. (1956)]

The Elimination of Metaphysics through the Logical Analysis of Language

8

RUDOLF CARNAP

1. INTRODUCTION

THERE HAVE BEEN many *opponents of metaphysics* from the Greek skeptics to the empiricists of the 19th century. Criticisms of very diverse kinds have been set forth. Many have declared that the doctrine of metaphysics is *false,* since it contradicts our empirical knowledge. Others have believed it to be *uncertain,* on the ground that its problems transcend the limits of human knowledge. Many anti-metaphysicians have declared that occupation with metaphysical questions is *sterile.* Whether or not these questions can be answered, it is at any rate unnecessary to worry about them; let us devote ourselves entirely to the practical tasks which confront active men every day of their lives!

The development of *modern logic* has made it possible to give a new and sharper answer to the

"Überwindung der Metaphysik durch Logisch Analyse der Sprache," Erkenntnis, 2 (1932). Translated by Arthur Pap.
Reprinted with the kind permission of The Free Press, a division of Simon and Schuster. From *Logical Positivism,* edited by A. J. Ayer. Copyright © 1959 by the Free Press.

question of the validity and justification of metaphysics. The researches of applied logic or the theory of knowledge, which aim at clarifying the cognitive content of scientific statements and thereby the meanings of the terms that occur in the statements, by means of logical analysis, lead to a positive and to a negative result. The positive result is worked out in the domain of empirical science; the various concepts of the various branches of science are clarified; their formal-logical and epistemological connections are made explicit. In the domain of *metaphysics*, including all philosophy of value and normative theory, logical analysis yields the negative result *that the alleged statements in this domain are entirely meaningless.* Therewith a radical elimination of metaphysics is attained, which was not yet possible from the earlier antimetaphysical standpoints. It is true that related ideas may be found already in several earlier trains of thought, e.g., those of a nominalistic kind; but it is only now when the development of logic during recent decades provides us with a sufficiently sharp tool that the decisive step can be taken.

In saying that the so-called statements of metaphysics are *meaningless,* we intend this word in its strictest sense. In a loose sense of the word a statement or a question is at times called meaningless if it is entirely sterile to assert or ask it. We might say this for instance about the question "what is the average weight of those inhabitants of Vienna whose telephone number ends with '3'?" or about a statement which is quite obviously false like "in 1910 Vienna had 6 inhabitants" or about a statement which is not just empirically, but logically false, a contradictory statement such as "persons A and B are each a year older than the other." Such sentences are really meaningful, though they are pointless or false; for it is only meaningful sentences that are even divisible into (theoretically) fruitful and sterile, true and false. In the strict sense, however, a sequence of words is *meaningless* if it does not, within a specified language, constitute a statement. It may happen that such a sequence of words looks like a statement at first glance; in that case we call it a *pseudo-statement*. Our thesis, now, is that logical analysis reveals the alleged statements of metaphysics to be pseudo-statements.

A language consists of a vocabulary and a syntax, i.e., a set of words which have meanings and rules of sentence formation. These rules indicate how sentences may be formed out of the various sorts of words. Accordingly, there are two kinds of pseudo-statements: either they contain a word which is erroneously believed to have meaning, or the constituent words are meaningful, yet are put together in a counter-syntactical way, so that they do not yield a meaningful statement. We shall show in terms of examples that pseudo-statements of both kinds occur in metaphysics. Later we shall have to inquire into the reasons that support our contention that metaphysics in its entirety consists of such pseudo-statements.

2. THE SIGNIFICANCE OF A WORD

A word which (within a definite language) has a meaning, is usually also said to designate a concept; if it only seems to have a meaning, while it really does not, we speak of a "pseudo-concept." How is the origin of a pseudo-concept to be explained? Has not every word been introduced into the language for no other purpose than to express something or other, so that it had a definite meaning from the very beginning of its use? How, then, can a traditional language contain meaningless words? To be sure, originally every word (excepting rare cases which we shall illustrate later) had a meaning. In the course of historical development a word frequently changes its meaning. And it also happens at times that a word loses its old sense without acquiring a new one. It is thus that a pseudo-concept arises.

What, now, is *the meaning of a word*? What stipulations concerning a word must be made in order for it to be significant? (It does not matter for our investigation whether these stipulations are explicitly laid down, as in the case of some words and symbols of modern science, or whether they have been tacitly agreed upon, as is the case for most words of traditional language.) First, the *syntax* of the word must be fixed, i.e., the mode of its occurrence in the simplest sentence form in which it is capable of occurring; we call this sentence form its *elementary sentence*. The elementary sentence form for the word "stone," e.g., is "x is a stone"; in sentences of this form some designation from the category of things occupies the place of "x," e.g., "this diamond," "this apple." Secondly, for an elementary sentence S containing the word an answer must be given to the following question, which can be formulated in various ways:

1. What sentences is S *deducible* from, and what sentences are deducible from S?

2. Under what conditions is S supposed to be true, and under what conditions false?

3. How is S to be *verified*?

4. What is the *meaning* of S?

(1) is the correct formulation; formulation (2) accords with the phraseology of logic, (3) with the phraseology of the theory of knowledge, (4) with that of philosophy (phenomenology). Wittgenstein has asserted that (2) expresses what philosophers mean by (4): the meaning of a sentence consists in its truth-condition. ((1) is the "metalogical" formulation; it is planned to give elsewhere a detailed exposition of metalogic as the theory of syntax and meaning, i.e., relations of deducibility.)

In the case of many words, specifically in the case of the overwhelming majority of scientific words, it is possible to specify their meaning by reduction to other words ("constitution," definition). E.g., " 'arthropodes' are animals with segmented bodies and jointed legs." Thereby the above-mentioned question for the elementary sentence form of the word "arthropods," that is for the sentence form "the thing x is an arthropode," is answered: it has been stipulated that a sentence of this form is deducible from premises of the form "x is an animal," "x has a segmented body," "x has jointed legs," and that conversely each of these sentences is deducible from the former sentence. By means of these stipulations about deducibility (in other words: about the truth-condition, about the method of verification, about the meaning) of the elementary sentence about "arthropode" the meaning of the word "arthropode" is fixed. In this way every word of the language is reduced to other words and finally to the words which occur in the so-called "observation sentences" or "protocol sentences." It is through this reduction that the word acquires its meaning.

For our purposes we may ignore entirely the question concerning the content and form of the primary sentences (protocol sentences) which has not yet been definitely settled. In the theory of knowledge it is customary to say that the primary sentences refer to "the given"; but there is no unanimity on the question what it is that is given. At times the position is taken that sentences about the given speak of the simplest qualities of sense and feeling (e.g., "warm," "blue," "joy" and so forth); others incline to the view that basic sentences refer to total experiences and similarities between them; a still different view has it that even the basic sentences speak of things. Regardless of this diversity of opinion it is certain that a sequence of words has a meaning only if its relations of deducibility to the protocol sentences are fixed, whatever the characteristics of the protocol sentences may be; and similarly, that a word is significant only if the sentences in which it may occur are reducible to protocol sentences.

Since the meaning of a word is determined by its criterion of application (in other words: by the relations of deducibility entered into by its elementary sentence-form, by its truth-conditions, by the method of its verification), the stipulation of the criterion takes away one's freedom to decide what one wishes to "mean" by the word. If the word is to receive an exact meaning, nothing less than the criterion of application must be given; but one cannot, on the other hand, give more than the criterion of application, for the latter is a sufficient determination of meaning. The meaning is implicitly contained in the criterion; all that remains to be done is to make the meaning explicit.

Let us suppose, by way of illustration, that someone invented the new word "teavy" and maintained that there are things which are teavy and things which are not teavy. In order to learn the meaning of this word, we ask him about its criterion of application: how is one to ascertain in a concrete case whether a given thing is teavy or not? Let us suppose to begin with that we get no answer from him: there are no empirical signs of teavyness, he says. In that case we would deny the legitimacy of using this word. If the person who uses the word says that all the same there are things which are teavy and there are things which are not teavy, only it remains for the weak, finite intellect of man an eternal secret which things are teavy and which are not, we shall regard this as empty verbiage. But perhaps he will assure us that he means, after all, something by the word "teavy." But from this we only learn the psychological fact that he associates some kind of images and feelings with the word. The word does not acquire a meaning through such associations. If no criterion of application for the word is stipulated, then nothing is asserted by the sentences in which it occurs, they are but pseudo-statements.

Secondly, take the case when we are given a criterion of application for a new word, say "toovy"; in particular, let the sentence "this thing is toovy" be true if and only if the thing is quadrangular. (It is irrelevant in this context whether the criterion is explicitly stated or whether we derive it by observing the affirmative and the negative uses of the word). Then we will say: the word "toovy" is synonymous with the word "quadrangular." And we will not allow its users to tell us that nevertheless they "intended" something else by it than "quadrangular"; that though every quadrangular thing is also toovy and conversely, this is only because quadrangularity is the visible manifestation of toovyness, but that the latter itself is a hidden, not itself observable property. We would reply that after the criterion of application has been fixed, the synonymy of "toovy" and "quadrangular" is likewise fixed, and that we are no further at liberty to "intend" this or that by the word.

Let us briefly summarize the result of our analysis. Let "a" be any word and "S(a)" the elementary sentence in which it occurs. Then the sufficient and necessary condition for "a" being meaningful may be given by each of the following formulations, which ultimately say the same thing:

1. The *empirical criteria* for a are known.

2. It has been stipulated from what protocol sentences "S(a)" is *deducible*.

3. The *truth-conditions* for "S(a)" are fixed.

4. The method of *verification* of "S(a)" is known.[1]

3. METAPHYSICAL WORDS WITHOUT MEANING

Many words of metaphysics, now, can be shown not to fulfill the above requirement, and therefore to be devoid of meaning.

Let us take as an example the metaphysical term "principle" (in the sense of principle of being, not principle of knowledge or axiom). Various meta-physicians offer an answer to the question which is the (highest) "principle of the world" (or of "things," of "existence," of "being"), e.g., water, number, form, motion, life, the spirit, the idea, the unconscious, activity, the good, and so forth. In order to discover the meaning of the word "principle" in this metaphysical question we must ask the metaphysician under what conditions a statement of the form "x is the principle of y" would be true and under what conditions it would be false. In other words: we ask for the criteria of application or for the definition of the word "principle." The metaphysician replies approximately as follows: "x is the principle of y" is to mean "y arises out of x," "the being of y rests on the being of x," "y exists by virtue of x" and so forth. But these words are ambiguous and vague. Frequently they have a clear meaning; e.g., we say of a thing or process y that it "arises out of" x when we observe that things or processes of kind x are frequently or invariably followed by things or processes of kind y (causal connection in the sense of a lawful succession). But the metaphysician tells us that he does not mean this empirically observable relationship. For in that case his metaphysical theses would be merely empirical propositions of the same kind as those of physics. The expression "arising from" is not to mean here a relation of temporal and causal sequence, which is what the word ordinarily means. Yet, no criterion is specified for any other meaning. Consequently, the alleged "metaphysical" meaning, which the word is supposed to have here in contrast to the mentioned empirical meaning, does not exist. If we reflect on the original meaning of the word "principium" (and of the corresponding Greek word ἀρχή"), we notice the same development. The word is explicitly deprived of its original meaning "beginning"; it is not supposed to mean the temporally prior any more, but the prior in some other, specifically metaphysical, respect. The criteria for this "metaphysical respect," however, are lacking. In both cases, then, the word has been deprived of its earlier meaning without being given a new meaning; there remains the word as an empty shell. From an earlier period of significant use, it is still associatively connected with various mental images; these in turn get associated with new mental images and feelings in the new context of usage. But the word does not thereby become meaningful; and it remains meaningless as long as no method of verification can be described.

Another example is the word "God." Here we must, apart from the variations of its usage within each domain, distinguish the linguistic usage in three different contexts or historical epochs, which how-ever overlap temporally. In its *mythological* use the word has a clear meaning. It, or parallel words in other languages, is sometimes used to denote phys-ical beings which are enthroned on Mount Olym-pus, in Heaven or in Hades, and which are endowed with power, wisdom, goodness and happiness to a greater or lesser extent. Sometimes the word also refers to spiritual beings which, indeed, do not have manlike bodies, yet manifest themselves nevertheless somehow in the things or processes of the visible world and are therefore empirically verifiable. In its *metaphysical* use, on the other hand, the word "God" refers to something beyond experience. The word is deliberately divested of its reference to a physical being or to a spiritual being that is immanent in the physical. And as it is not given a new meaning, it becomes meaningless. To be sure, it often looks as though the word "God" had a meaning even in metaphysics. But the definitions which are set up prove on closer inspection to be pseudo-definitions. They lead either to logically illegitimate combinations of words (of which we shall treat later) or to other metaphysical words (e.g., "primordial basis," "the ab-solute," "the unconditioned," "the autonomous," "the self-dependent" and so forth), but in no case to the truth-conditions of its elementary sentences. In the case of this word not even the first requirement of logic is met, that is the requirement to specify its syntax, i.e., the form of its occurrence in elementary sentences. An elementary sentence would here have to be of the form "x is a God"; yet, the metaphysi-cian either rejects this form entirely without substi-tuting another, or if he accepts it he neglects to indicate the syntactical category of the variable x. (Categories are for example, material things, proper-ties of things, relations between things, numbers etc.).

The *theological* usage of the word "God" falls be-tween its mythological and its metaphysical usage. There is no distinctive meaning here, but an oscil-lation from one of the mentioned two uses to the other. Several theologians have a clearly empirical (in our terminology, "mythological") concept of God. In this case there are no pseudo-statements; but the disadvantage for the theologian lies in the circumstance that according to this interpretation the statements of theology are empirical and hence are subject to the judgment of empirical science. The linguistic usage of other theologians is clearly metaphysical. Others again do not speak in any def-inite way, whether this is because they follow now this, now that linguistic usage, or because they ex-press themselves in terms whose usage is not clearly classifiable since it tends towards both sides.

Just like the examined examples "principle" and "God," most of the other *specifically metaphysical terms are devoid of meaning*, e.g., "the Idea," "the Absolute," "the Unconditioned," "the Infinite," "the being of being," "non-being," "thing in itself," "absolute spirit," "objective spirit," "essence," "being-in-itself," "being-in-and-for-itself," "emana-tion," "manifestation," "articulation," "the Ego," "the non-Ego," etc. These expressions are in the same boat with "teavy," our previously fabricated ex-ample. The metaphysician tells us that empirical truth-conditions cannot be specified; if he adds that nevertheless he "means" something, we know that this is merely an allusion to associated images and feelings which, however, do not bestow a meaning on the word. The alleged statements of metaphysics which contain such words have no sense, assert noth-ing, are mere pseudo-statements. Into the explana-tion of their historical origin we shall inquire later.

4. THE SIGNIFICANCE OF A SENTENCE

So far we have considered only those pseudo-statements which contain a meaningless word. But there is a second kind of pseudo-statement. They consist of meaningful words, but the words are put together in such a way that nevertheless no meaning results. The syntax of a language specifies which com-binations of words are admissible and which inadmis-sible. The grammatical syntax of natural languages, however, does not fulfill the task of elimination of senseless combinations of words in all cases. Let us take as examples the following sequences of words:

1. "Caesar is and"

2. "Caesar is a prime number"

The word sequence (1) is formed countersyntactically; the rules of syntax require that the third position be occupied, not by a conjunction, but by a predicate, hence by a noun (with article) or by an adjective. The word sequence "Caesar is a general," e.g., is formed in accordance with the rules of syntax. It is a meaningful word sequence, a genuine sentence. But, now, word sequence (2) is likewise syntactically correct, for it has the same grammatical form as the sentence just mentioned. Nevertheless (2) is meaningless. "Prime number" is a predicate of numbers; it can be neither affirmed nor denied of a person. Since (2) looks like a statement yet is not a statement, does not assert anything, expresses neither a true nor a false proposition, we call this word sequence a "pseudo-statement." The fact that the rules of grammatical syntax are not violated easily seduces one at first glance into the erroneous opinion that one still has to do with a statement, albeit a false one. But "a is a prime number" is false if and only if a is divisible by a natural number different from a and from 1; evidently it is illicit to put here "Caesar" for "a." This example has been so chosen that the nonsense is easily detectable. Many so-called statements of metaphysics are not so easily recognized to be pseudo-statements. The fact that natural languages allow the formation of meaningless sequences of words without violating the rules of grammar, indicates that grammatical syntax is, from a logical point of view, inadequate. If grammatical syntax corresponded exactly to logical syntax, pseudo-statements could not arise. If grammatical syntax differentiated not only the word-categories of nouns, adjectives, verbs, conjunctions etc., but within each of these categories made the further distinctions that are logically indispensable, then no pseudo-statements could be formed. if, e.g., nouns were grammatically subdivided into several kinds of words, according as they designated properties of physical objects, of numbers etc., then the words "general" and "prime number" would belong to grammatically different word-categories, and (2) would be just as linguistically incorrect as (1). In a correctly constructed language, therefore, all nonsensical sequences of words would be of the kind of example (1). Considerations of grammar would already eliminate them as it were automatically; i.e., in order to avoid nonsense, it would be unnecessary to pay attention to the meanings of the individual words over and above their syntactical type (their "syntactical category," e.g., thing, property of things, relation between things, number, property of numbers, relation between numbers, and so forth). It follows that if our thesis that the statements of metaphysics are pseudo-statements is justifiable, then metaphysics could not even be expressed in a logically constructed language. This is the great philosophical importance of the task, which at present occupies the logicians, of building a logical syntax.

5. METAPHYSICAL PSEUDO-STATEMENTS

Let us now take a look at some examples of metaphysical pseudo-statements of a kind where the violation of logical syntax is especially obvious, though they accord with historical-grammatical syntax. We select a few sentences from that metaphysical school which at present exerts the strongest influence in Germany.[2]

"What is to be investigated is being only and—*nothing* else; being alone and further—*nothing;* solely being, and beyond being—*nothing. What about this Nothing?* . . . *Does the Nothing exist only because the Not, i.e., the Negation, exists? Or is it the other way around? Does Negation and the Not exist only because the Nothing exists?* . . . We assert: *the Nothing is prior to the Not and the Negation.* . . . Where do we seek the Nothing? How do we find the Nothing? . . . We know the Nothing. . . . *Anxiety reveals the Nothing.* . . . That for which and because of which we were anxious, was 'really'—nothing. Indeed: the Nothing itself—as such—was present. . . . *What about this Nothing?—The Nothing itself nothings.*"

In order to show that the possibility of forming pseudo-statements is based on a logical defect of language, we set up the schema below. The sentences under I are grammatically as well as logically impeccable, hence meaningful. The sentences under II (excepting B3) are in grammatical respects perfectly analogous to those under I. Sentence form IIA (as question and answer) does not, indeed, satisfy the requirements to be imposed on a logically correct language. But it is nevertheless meaningful. because it is translatable into correct language. This is shown by sentence IIIA which has the same meaning as IIA. Sentence form IIA then proves to be undesirable because we can be led from it, by means of grammatically faultless operations, to the meaningless sentence forms IIB, which are taken from the above quotation. These forms cannot even be constructed in the correct language of Column III. Nonetheless, their nonsensicality is not obvious at first glance, because one is easily deceived by the analogy with the meaningful sentences IB. The fault of our language identified here lies, therefore, in the circumstance that, in contrast to a logically correct language, it admits of the same grammatical form for meaningful and meaningless word sequences. To each sentence in words we have added a corresponding formula in the notation of symbolic logic; these formulae facilitate recognition of the undesirable analogy between IA and IIA and therewith of the origin of the meaningless constructions IIB.

I. *Meaningful Sentences of Ordinary Language*	II. *Transition from Sense to Nonsense Ordinary Language*	III. *Logically Correct Language*
A. What is outside? $Ou(?)$ Rain is outside $Ou(r)$	A. What is outside? $Ou\ (?)$ Nothing is outside $Ou(no)$	A. There is nothing (does not exist anything) which is outside. $\sim(\exists x).Ou(x)$
B. What about this rain? (i.e., what does the rain do? or: what else can be said about this rain? $?(r)$	B. "What about this Nothing?" $?(no)$	B. None of these forms can even be constructed.
1. We know the rain $K(r)$	1. "We seek the Nothing" "We find the Nothing" "We know the Nothing" $K(no)$	
2. The rain rains $R(r)$	2. "The Nothing nothings" $No(no)$	
	3. "The Nothing exists only because . . ." $Ex(no)$	

On closer inspection of the pseudo-statements under IIB, we also find some differences. The construction of sentence (1) is simply based on the mistake of employing the word "nothing" as a noun, because it is customary in ordinary language to use it in this form in order to construct a negative existential statement (see IIA). In a correct language, on the other hand, it is not a particular *name*, but a certain *logical form* of the sentence that serves this purpose (see IIIA). Sentence IIB2 adds something new, viz. the fabrication of the meaningless word "to nothing." This sentence, therefore, is senseless for a twofold reason. We pointed out before that the meaningless words of metaphysics usually owe their origin to the fact that a meaningful word is deprived of its meaning through its metaphorical use in metaphysics. But here we confront one of those rare cases where a new word is introduced which never had a meaning to begin with. Likewise sentence IIB3 must be rejected for two reasons. In respect of the error of using the word "nothing" as a noun, it is like the previous sentences. But in addition it involves a contradiction. For even if it were admissible to introduce "nothing" as a name or description of an entity, still the existence of this entity would be denied in its very definition, whereas sentence (3) goes on to affirm its existence. This sentence, therefore, would be contradictory, hence absurd, even if it were not already meaningless.

In view of the gross logical errors which we find in sentences IIB, we might be led to conjecture that perhaps the word "nothing" has in Heidegger's treatise a meaning entirely different from the customary one. And this presumption is further strengthened as we go on to read there that anxiety reveals the Nothing, that the Nothing itself is present as such in anxiety. For here the word "nothing" seems to refer to a certain emotional constitution, possibly of a religious sort, or something or other that underlies such emotions. If such were the case, then the mentioned logical errors in sentences IIB would not be committed. But the first sentence of the quotation at the beginning of this section proves that this interpretation is not possible. The combination of "only" and "nothing else" shows unmistakably that the word "nothing" here has the usual meaning of a logical particle that serves for the formulation of a negative existential statement. This introduction of the word "nothing" is then immediately followed by the leading question of the treatise: "What about this Nothing?".

But our doubts as to a possible misinterpretation get completely dissolved as we note that the author of the treatise is clearly aware of the conflict between his questions and statements, and logic. "*Question and answer* in regard to the Nothing are equally *absurd* in themselves. . . . The fundamental rule of thinking commonly appealed to, the law of prohibited contradiction, general '*logic*,' destroys this question." All the worse for logic! We must abolish its sovereignty: "If thus the power of the *understanding* in the field of questions concerning Nothing and Being is broken, then the fate of the sovereignty of 'logic' within philosophy is thereby decided as well. The very idea of 'logic' dissolves in the whirl of a more basic questioning." But will sober science condone the whirl of counterlogical questioning? To this question too there is a ready answer: "The alleged sobriety and superiority of science becomes ridiculous if it does not take the Nothing seriously." Thus we find here a good confirmation of our thesis; a metaphysician himself here states that his questions and answers are irreconcilable with logic and the scientific way of thinking.

The difference between our thesis and that of the *earlier antimetaphysicians* should now be clear. We do not regard metaphysics as "mere speculation" or "fairy tales." The statements of a fairy tale do not conflict with logic, but only with experience; they are perfectly meaningful, although false. Metaphysics is not "*superstition*"; it is possible to believe true and false propositions, but not to believe meaningless sequences of words. Metaphysical statements are not even acceptable as "*working hypotheses*"; for

an hypothesis must be capable of entering into relations of deducibility with (true or false) empirical statements, which is just what pseudo-statements cannot do.

With reference to the so-called *limitation of human knowledge* an attempt is sometimes made to save metaphysics by raising the following objection: metaphysical statements are not, indeed, verifiable by man nor by any other finite being; nevertheless they might be construed as conjectures about the answers which a being with higher or even perfect powers of knowledge would make to our questions, and as such conjectures they would, after all, be meaningful. To counter this objection, let us consider the following. If the meaning of a word cannot be specified, or if the sequence of words does not accord with the rules of syntax, then one has not even asked a question. (Just think of the pseudo-questions: "Is this table teavy?", "is the number 7 holy?", "which numbers are darker, the even or the odd ones?"). Where there is no question, not even an omniscient being can give an answer. Now the objector may say: just as one who can see may communicate new knowledge to the blind, so a higher being might perhaps communicate to us metaphysical knowledge, e.g., whether the visible world is the manifestation of a spirit. Here we must reflect on the meaning of "new knowledge." It is, indeed, conceivable that we might encounter animals who tell us about a new sense. If these beings were to prove to us Fermat's theorem or were to invent a new physical instrument or were to establish a hitherto unknown law of nature, then our knowledge would be increased with their help. For this sort of thing we can test, just the way even a blind man can understand and test the whole of physics (and therewith any statement made by those who can see). But if those hypothetical beings tell us something which we cannot verify, then we cannot understand it either; in that case no information has been communicated to us, but mere verbal sounds devoid of meaning though possibly associated with images. It follows that our knowledge can only be quantitatively enlarged by other beings, no matter whether they know more or less or everything, but no knowledge of an essentially different kind can be added. What we do not know for certain, we may come to know with greater certainty through the assistance of other beings; but what is unintelligible, meaningless for us, cannot become meaningful through someone else's assistance, however vast his knowledge might be. Therefore no god and no devil can give us metaphysical knowledge.

6. MEANINGLESSNESS OF ALL METAPHYSICS

The examples of metaphysical statements which we have analyzed were all taken from just one treatise. But our results apply with equal validity, in part even in verbally identical ways, to other metaphysical systems. That treatise is completely in the right in citing approvingly a statement by Hegel ("pure Being and pure Nothing, therefore, are one and the same"). The metaphysics of Hegel has exactly the same logical character as this modern system of metaphysics. And the same holds for the rest of the metaphysical systems, though the kind of phraseology and therewith the kind of logical errors that occur in them deviate more or less from the kind that occurs in the examples we discussed.

It should not be necessary here to adduce further examples of specific metaphysical sentences in diverse systems and submit them to analysis. We confine ourselves to an indication of the most frequent kinds of errors.

Perhaps the majority of the logical mistakes that are committed when pseudo-statements are made, are based on the logical faults infecting the use of the word "to be" in our language (and of the corresponding words in other languages, at least in most European languages). The first fault is the ambiguity of the word "to be." It is sometimes used as copula prefixed to a predicate ("I am hungry"), sometimes to designate existence ("I am"). This mistake is aggravated by the fact that metaphysicians often are not clear about this ambiguity. The second fault lies in the form of the verb in its second meaning, the meaning of *existence*. The verbal form feigns a predicate where there is none. To be sure, it has been known for a long time that existence is not a property (cf. Kant's refutation of the ontological proof of the existence of God). But it was not until the advent of modern logic that full consistency on this point was reached: the syntactical form in which

modern logic introduces the sign for existence is such that it cannot, like a predicate, be applied to signs for objects, but only to predicates (cf., e.g., sentence IIIA in the above table). Most metaphysicians since antiquity have allowed themselves to be seduced into pseudo-statements by the verbal, and therewith the predicative form of the word "to be," e.g., "I am" "God is."

We meet an illustration of this error in Descartes' "*cogito, ergo sum.*" Let us disregard here the material objections that have been raised against the premise—viz. whether the sentence "I think" adequately expresses the intended state of affairs or contains perhaps an hypostasis—and consider the two sentences only from the formal-logical point of view. We notice at once two essential logical mistakes. The first lies in the conclusion "I am." The verb "to be" is undoubtedly meant in the sense of existence here; for a copula cannot be used without predicate; indeed, Descartes' "I am" has always been interpreted in this sense. But in that case this sentence violates the above-mentioned logical rule that existence can be predicated only in conjunction with a predicate, not in conjunction with a name (subject, proper name). An existential statement does not have the form "*a* exists" (as in "I am," i.e., "I exist"), but "there exists something of such and such a kind." The second error lies in the transition from "I think" to "I exist." If from the statement "P(a)" ("a has the property P") an existential statement is to be deduced, then the latter can assert existence only with respect to the predicate P, not with respect to the subject *a* of the premise. What follows from "I am a European" is not "I exist," but "a European exists." What follows from "I think" is not "I am" but "there exists something that thinks."

The circumstance that our languages express existence by a verb ("to be" or "to exist") is not in itself a logical fault; it is only inappropriate, dangerous. The verbal form easily misleads us into the misconception that existence is a predicate. One then arrives at such logically incorrect and hence senseless modes of expression as were just examined. Likewise such forms as "Being" or "Not-Being," which from time immemorial have played a great role in metaphysics, have the same origin. In a logically correct language such forms cannot even be constructed. It appears that in the Latin and the German languages the forms "*ens*" or "*das Seiende*" were, perhaps under the seductive influence of the Greek example, introduced specifically for use by metaphysicians; in this way the language deteriorated logically whereas the addition was believed to represent an improvement.

Another very frequent violation of logical syntax is the so-called "*type confusion*" of concepts. While the previously mentioned mistake consists in the predicative use of a symbol with non-predicative meaning, in this case a predicate is, indeed, used as predicate yet as predicate of a different type. We have here a violation of the rules of the so-called theory of types. An artificial example is the sentence we discussed earlier: "Caesar is a prime number." Names of persons and names of numbers belong to different logical types, and so do accordingly predicates of persons (e.g., "general") and predicates of numbers ("prime number"). The error of type confusion is, unlike the previously discussed usage of the verb "to be," not the prerogative of metaphysics but already occurs very often in conversational language also. But here it rarely leads to nonsense. The typical ambiguity of words is here of such a kind that it can be easily removed.

Example: 1. "This table is larger than that." 2. "The height of this table is larger than the height of that table." Here the word "larger" is used in (1) for a relation between objects, in (2) for a relation between numbers, hence for two distinct syntactical categories. The mistake is here unimportant; it could, e.g., be eliminated by writing "larger1" and "larger2"; "larger1" is then defined in terms of "larger2" by declaring statement form (1) to be synonymous with (2) (and others of a similar kind).

Since the confusion of types causes no harm in conversational language, it is usually ignored entirely. This is, indeed, expedient for the ordinary use of language, but has had unfortunate consequences in metaphysics. Here the conditioning by everyday language has led to confusions of types which, unlike those in everyday language, are no longer translatable into logically correct form. Pseudo-statements of this kind are encountered in especially large quantity, e.g., in the writings of Hegel and Heidegger. The latter has adopted many peculiarities of the Hegelian idiom along with their logical faults (e.g., predicates which should be applied to objects of a

certain sort are instead applied to predicates of these objects or to "being" or to "existence" or to a relation between these objects).

Having found that many metaphysical statements are meaningless, we confront the question whether there is not perhaps a core of meaningful statements in metaphysics which would remain after elimination of all the meaningless ones.

Indeed, the results we have obtained so far might give rise to the view that there are many dangers of falling into nonsense in metaphysics, and that one must accordingly endeavor to avoid these traps with great care if one wants to do metaphysics. But actually the situation is that meaningful metaphysical statements are impossible. This follows from the task which metaphysics sets itself: to discover and formulate a kind of knowledge which is not accessible to empirical science.

We have seen earlier that the meaning of a statement lies in the method of its verification. A statement asserts only so much as is verifiable with respect to it. Therefore a sentence can be used only to assert an empirical proposition, if indeed it is used to assert anything at all. If something were to lie, in principle, beyond possible experience, it could be neither said nor thought nor asked.

(Meaningful) statements are divided into the following kinds. First there are statements which are true solely by virtue of their form ("tautologies" according to Wittgenstein; they correspond approximately to Kant's "analytic judgments"). They say nothing about reality. The formulae of logic and mathematics are of this kind. They are not themselves factual statements, but serve for the transformation of such statements. Secondly there are the negations of such statements ("*contradictions*"). They are self-contradictory, hence false by virtue of their form. With respect to all other statements the decision about truth or falsehood lies in the protocol sentences. They are therefore (true or false) *empirical statements* and belong to the domain of empirical science. Any statement one desires to construct which does not fall within these categories becomes automatically meaningless. Since metaphysics does not want to assert analytic propositions, nor to fall within the domain of empirical science, it is compelled to employ words for which no criteria of application are specified and which are therefore devoid of sense, or else to combine meaningful words in such a way that neither an analytic (or contradictory) statement nor an empirical statement is produced. In either case pseudo-statements are the inevitable product.

Logical analysis, then, pronounces the verdict of meaninglessness on any alleged knowledge that pretends to reach above or behind experience. This verdict hits, in the first place, any speculative metaphysics, any alleged knowledge by *pure thinking* or by *pure intuition* that pretends to be able to do without experience. But the verdict equally applies to the kind of metaphysics which, starting from experience, wants to acquire knowledge about that which *transcends experience* by means of special *inferences* (e.g., the neo-vitalist thesis of the directive presence of an "entelechy" in organic processes, which supposedly cannot be understood in terms of physics; the question concerning the "essence of causality," transcending the ascertainment of certain regularities of succession; the talk about the "thing in itself"). Further, the same judgment must be passed on all *philosophy of norms,* or *philosophy of value,* on any ethics or esthetics as a normative discipline. For the objective validity of a value or norm is (even on the view of the philosophers of value) not empirically verifiable nor deducible from empirical statements; hence it cannot be asserted (in a meaningful statement) at all. In other words: Either empirical criteria are indicated for the use of "good" and "beautiful" and the rest of the predicates that are employed in the normative sciences, or they are not. In the first case, a statement containing such a predicate turns into a factual judgment, but not a value judgment; in the second case, it becomes a pseudo-statement. It is altogether impossible to make a statement that expresses a value judgment.

Finally, the verdict of meaninglessness also hits those metaphysical movements which are usually called, improperly, epistemological movements, that is *realism* (insofar as it claims to say more than the empirical fact that the sequence of events exhibits a certain regularity, which makes the application of the inductive method possible) and its opponents: subjective *idealism,* solipsism, phenomenalism, and *positivism* (in the earlier sense).

But what, then, is left over for *philosophy,* if all statements whatever that assert something are of an empirical nature and belong to factual science? What remains is not statements, nor a theory, nor a system, but only a *method:* the method of logical analysis. The foregoing discussion has illustrated the negative application of this method: in that context it serves to eliminate meaningless words, meaningless pseudo-statements. In its positive use it serves to clarify meaningful concepts and propositions, to lay logical foundations for factual science and for mathematics. The negative application of the method is necessary and important in the present historical situation. But even in its present practice, the positive application is more fertile. We cannot here discuss it in greater detail. It is the indicated task of logical analysis inquiry into logical foundations, that is meant by *"scientific philosophy"* in contrast to metaphysics.

The question regarding the logical character of the statements which we obtain as the result of a logical analysis, e.g., the statements occurring in this and other logical papers, can here be answered only tentatively: such statements are partly analytic, partly empirical. For these statements about statements and parts of statements belong in part to pure *metalogic* (e.g., "a sequence consisting of the existence-symbol and a noun, is not a sentence"), in part to descriptive metalogic (e.g., "the word sequence at such and such a place in such and such a book is meaningless"). Metalogic will be discussed elsewhere. It will also be shown there that the metalogic which speaks about the sentences of a given language can be formulated in that very language itself.

7. METAPHYSICS AS EXPRESSION OF AN ATTITUDE TOWARD LIFE

Our claim that the statements of metaphysics are entirely meaningless, that they do not assert anything, will leave even those who agree intellectually with our results with a painful feeling of strangeness: how could it be explained that so many men in all ages and nations, among them eminent minds, spent so much energy, nay veritable fervor, on metaphysics if the latter consisted of nothing but mere words, nonsensically juxtaposed? And how could one account for the fact that metaphysical books have exerted such a strong influence on readers up to the present day, if they contained not even errors, but nothing at all? These doubts are justified since metaphysics does indeed have a content; only it is not theoretical content. The (pseudo)statements of metaphysics do not serve for the *description of states of affairs,* neither existing ones (in that case they would be true statements) nor non-existing ones (in that case they would be at least false statements). They serve for the *expression of the general attitude of a person towards life* ("*Lebenseinstellung, Lebensgefühl*").

Perhaps we may assume that metaphysics originated from *mythology.* The child is angry at the "wicked table" which hurt him. Primitive man endeavors to conciliate the threatening demon of earthquakes, or he worships the deity of the fertile rains in gratitude. Here we confront personifications of natural phenomena, which are the quasi-poetic expression of man's emotional relationship to his environment. The heritage of mythology is bequeathed on the one hand to poetry, which produces and intensifies the effects of mythology on life in a deliberate way; on the other hand, it is handed down to theology, which develops mythology into a system. Which, now, is the historical role of metaphysics? Perhaps we may regard it as a substitute for theology on the level of systematic, conceptual thinking. The (supposedly) transcendent sources of knowledge of theology are here replaced by natural, yet supposedly trans-empirical sources of knowledge. On closer inspection the same content as that of mythology is here still recognizable behind the repeatedly varied dressing: we find that metaphysics also arises from the need to give expression to a man's attitude in life, his emotional and volitional reaction to the environment, to society, to the tasks to which he devotes himself, to the misfortunes that befall him. This attitude manifests itself, unconsciously as a rule, in everything a man does or says. It also impresses itself on his facial features, perhaps even on the character of his gait. Many people, now, feel a desire to create over and above these manifestations a special expression of their attitude, through which it might become visible in a more succinct and penetrating way. If they have artistic talent they are able to express themselves by producing a work of art. Many writers have already clarified the way in which the basic attitude is manifested through the style and

manner of a work of art (e.g., Dilthey and his students). [In this connection the term "world view" ("*Weltanschauung*") is often used; we prefer to avoid it because of its ambiguity, which blurs the difference between attitude and theory, a difference which is of decisive importance for our analysis.] What is here essential for our considerations is only the fact that art is an adequate, metaphysics an inadequate means for the expression of the basic attitude. Of course, there need be no intrinsic objection to one's using any means of expression one likes. But in the case of metaphysics we find this situation: through the form of its works it pretends to be something that it is not. The form in question is that of a system of statements which are apparently related as premises and conclusions, that is, the form of a theory. In this way the fiction of theoretical content is generated, whereas, as we have seen, there is no such content. It is not only the reader, but the metaphysician himself who suffers from the illusion that the metaphysical statements say something, describe states of affairs. The metaphysician believes that he travels in territory in which truth and falsehood are at stake. In reality, however, he has not asserted anything, but only expressed something, like an artist. That the metaphysician is thus deluding himself cannot be inferred from the fact that he selects language as the medium of expression and declarative sentences as the form of expression; for lyrical poets do the same without succumbing to self-delusion. But the metaphysician supports his statements by arguments, he claims assent to their content, he polemicizes against metaphysicians of divergent persuasion by attempting to refute their assertions in his treatise. Lyrical poets, on the other hand, do not try to refute in their poem the statements in a poem by some other lyrical poet; for they know they are in the domain of art and not in the domain of theory.

Perhaps music is the purest means of expression of the basic attitude because it is entirely free from any reference to objects. The harmonious feeling or attitude, which the metaphysician tries to express in a monistic system, is more clearly expressed in the music of Mozart. And when a metaphysician gives verbal expression to his dualistic-heroic attitude towards life in a dualistic system, is it not perhaps because he lacks the ability of a Beethoven to express this attitude in an adequate medium? Metaphysicians are musicians without musical ability. Instead they have a strong inclination to work within the medium of the theoretical, to connect concepts and thoughts. Now, instead of activating, on the one hand, this inclination in the domain of science, and satisfying, on the other hand, the need for expression in art, the metaphysician confuses the two and produces a structure which achieves nothing for knowledge and something inadequate for the expression of attitude.

Our conjecture that metaphysics is a substitute, albeit an inadequate one, for art, seems to be further confirmed by the fact that the metaphysician who perhaps had artistic talent to the highest degree, viz. Nietzsche, almost entirely avoided the error of that confusion. A large part of his work has predominantly empirical content. We find there, for instance, historical analyses of specific artistic phenomena, or an historical-psychological analysis of morals. In the work, however, in which he expresses most strongly that which others express through metaphysics or ethics, in *Thus Spake Zarathustra,* he does not choose the misleading theoretical form, but openly the form of art, of poetry.

REMARKS BY THE AUTHOR (1957)

To section 1, "metaphysics." This term is used in this paper, as usually in Europe, for the field of alleged knowledge of the essence of things which transcends the realm of empirically founded, inductive science. Metaphysics in this sense includes systems like those of Fichte, Schelling, Hegel, Bergson, Heidegger. But it does not include endeavors towards a synthesis and generalization of the results of the various sciences.

To section 1, "meaning." Today we distinguish various kinds of meaning, in particular cognitive (designative, referential) meaning on the one hand,

and non-cognitive (expressive) meaning components, e.g., emotive and motivative, on the other. In the present paper, the word "meaning" is always understood in the sense of "cognitive meaning." The thesis that the sentences of metaphysics are meaningless, is thus to be understood in the sense that they have no cognitive meaning, no assertive content. The obvious psychological fact that they have expressive meaning is thereby not denied; this is explicitly stated in Section 7.

To section 6, "metalogic." This term refers to the theory of expressions of a language and, in particular, of their logical relations. Today we would distinguish between logical syntax as the theory of purely formal relations and semantics as the theory of meaning and truth-conditions.

To section 6, realism and idealism. That both the affirmative and the negative theses concerning the reality of the external world are pseudo-statements, I have tried to show in the monograph *Scheinprobleme in der Philosophie: Das Fremdpsychische und der Realismusstreit,* Berlin, 1928. The similar nature of the ontological theses about the reality or unreality of abstract entities, e.g., properties, relations, propositions, is discussed in "Empiricism, Semantics, and Ontology," *Revue Intern. de Philos.* 4, 1950, 20–40, reprinted in: *Meaning and Necessity,* second edition, Chicago, 1956.

NOTES

1. For the logical and epistemological conception which underlies our exposition, but can only briefly be intimated here, cf. Wittgenstein, *Tractatus Logico-Philosophicus,* 1922, and Carnap, *Der logische Aufbau der Welt,* 1928.
2. The following quotations (original italics) are taken from M. Heidegger, *Was Ist Metaphysik?* 1929. We could just as well have selected passages from any other of the numerous metaphysicians of the present or of the past; yet the selected passages seem to us to illustrate our thesis especially well.

9   The Constitution of Material Things

A. J. AYER

THE PROBLEM OF SPECIFYING the relationship of material things to sense-data, to which the causal theory of perception has been shown to provide so unsatisfactory an answer, is apt to be obscured by being represented as a problem about the inter-relationship of two different classes of objects. There is, indeed, a sense in which it is correct to say that both sense-data and material things exist, inasmuch as sentences that are used to describe sense-data and sentences that are used to describe material things both very frequently express true propositions. But it would not be correct to infer from this that there really were both material things and sense-data, in the sense in which it can truly be said that there really are chairs as well as tables, or that there are tastes as well as sounds. For whereas, in these cases, the existential propositions refer to different empirical "facts", this does not hold good in the case of sense-data and material things. All the same, the term "material thing" is not synonymous with any term or set of terms that stand for species of sense-data. It is indeed logically necessary that any situation that in any degree establishes the existence of a material thing should also establish the existence of a sense-datum; for we have constructed the sense-datum language in such a way that whenever it is true that a material thing is perceived, it must also be true that a sense-datum is sensed; and this applies also to the cases where the existence of the material thing is inferred from observations of its "physical effects". But it is not wholly a matter of convention that a situation which establishes the existence of a sense-datum should also be evidence in some degree for the existence of a material thing. For this depends, as I shall show, upon certain special features of our sensory experience, which it might conceivably not have possessed. Moreover, while a situation which directly establishes the existence of a sense-datum does so conclusively, no such situations can conclu-sively establish the existence of a material thing. The degree to which the existence of the material thing is established will depend upon the character of the sense-data in question, and especially upon the nature of the contexts in which they occur; but what-ever the strength of this evidence may be, it will always be logically compatible with the hypothesis that this material thing is not in all respects what it appears to be, or even that it does not exist at all. Additional evidence may weaken this hypothesis to an extent that makes it very foolish still to entertain it; but it may also substantiate it, as the fact that there are illusions shows. At the same time, it is to be remarked that this additional evidence, whether favourable or not, will always consist in the occur-rence of further sense-data. Indeed there is nothing else in which one can legitimately suppose it to con-sist, once one has accepted the rule that the word "sense-datum" is to be used to stand for whatever is, in fact, observed. And since it is impossible, by any valid process of inference, to make a transition from what is observed to anything that is conceived as being, in principle, unobservable, all that the ev-idence in question will be evidence for or against is the possible occurrence of further sense-data still. And from this it seems to follow that, even though the term "material thing" is not synonymous with any set of terms that stand for species of sense-data, any proposition that refers to a material thing must somehow be expressible in terms of sense-data, if it is to be empirically significant.

A common way of expressing this conclusion is to say that material things are nothing but collec-tions of actual and possible sense-data. But this is a misleading formula and one that provokes objec-tions which a more accurate way of speaking might avoid. Thus, it is sometimes argued, by those who reject this "phenomenalistic" analysis of the nature of material things, that to conceive of such things as

The Foundations of Empirical Knowledge, chapter 5 (London: Macmillan, 1940). Reprinted by permission of Macmillan.

houses or trees or stones as mere collections of actual and possible sense-data is to ignore their "unity" and "substantiality", and that, in any case, it is hard to see how anything can be composed of so shadowy a being as a possible sense-datum. But these objections are founded upon the mistaken assumption that a material thing is supposed to consist of sense-data, as a patchwork quilt consists of different coloured pieces of silk. To remove this misconception, it must be made clear that what the statement that material things consist of sense-data must be understood to designate is not a factual but a linguistic relationship. What is being claimed is simply that the propositions which are ordinarily expressed by sentences which refer to material things could also be expressed by sentences which referred exclusively to sense-data; and the inclusion of possible as well as actual sense-data among the elements of the material things must be taken only to imply a recognition that some of these statements about sense-data will have to be hypothetical. As for the belief in the "unity" and "substantiality" of material things, I shall show that it may be correctly represented as involving no more than the attribution to visual and tactual sense-data of certain relations which do, in fact, obtain in our experience. And I shall show that it is only the contingent fact that there are these relations between sense-data that makes it profitable to describe the course of our experience in terms of the existence and behaviour of material things.

It may seem that an attempt to carry out this plan of "reducing" material things to sense-data would be at variance with my previous attempt to draw a sharp distinction between them. But the purpose of making this distinction was simply to increase the utility and clarity of the sense-datum language by ensuring that its sentences should not be of the same logical form as those that refer to material things. And here it may be explained that two sentences may be said to have the same logical form if they can be correlated in such a way that to each expression that occurs in either one of them there corresponds in the other an expression of the same logical type; and that two expressions may be said to be of the same logical type if any sentence that significantly contains either one of them remains significant when the other is put in its place. It follows that if sentences referring to sense-data are of a different

logical form from sentences referring to material things, it must not be assumed that precisely the same things can be said about them. To say, for example, that this was being written with a "pennish" group of sense-data, instead of saying that it was being written with a pen, would be neither true nor false but nonsensical. But this does not rule out the possibility that a proposition which is expressed by a sentence referring to a material thing can equally well be expressed by an entirely different set of sentences, which refer to sense-data; and this is what those who assert that material things are "logical constructions" out of sense-data must be understood to claim. Their view is sometimes put in the form of an assertion that "to say anything about a material thing is to say something, but not the same thing about classes of sense-data";[1] but if this is taken to imply that any significant statement about a material thing can actually be translated, without alteration of meaning, into a definite set of statements about sense-data, it is not strictly accurate, for a reason I shall presently give.

An objection which is often brought against phenomenalists is that they begin with a false conception of the nature of "perceptual situations". Thus, it is held by some philosophers that what is directly observed is usually not a sense-datum at all, but a material thing; so that the view that material things must be reducible to sense-data, on the ground that these alone are observable, is fundamentally erroneous. But this . . . is not the expression of a disagreement about any matter of fact, but only of a preference for a different form of language. It is indeed legitimate to use the phrase "direct observation" in such a way that things like houses and trees and stones can properly be said to be directly observable; and this usage can perfectly well be made to cover the case of delusive as well as veridical perceptions, provided that it is allowed that what is "directly observed" may not in fact exist, and that it may not really have the properties that it appears to have. But . . . it is also legitimate to use the phrase "direct observation" in such a way that it is only what is designated by the term "sense-datum", or some equivalent term, that can be said to be directly observable; and that it is this usage that, for my present purpose, is to be preferred. And one reason why it is to be preferred is to be found in the fact . . . that whereas the proposition that a sense-datum is veridically sensed does not entail that any material thing is veridically perceived, the proposition that a material thing is veridically perceived can always be represented as entailing that some sense-datum or other is veridically sensed. Indeed, it is inconceivable that any sense-datum should not be sensed veridically, since it has been made self-contradictory to say of an experienced sense-datum that it does not exist or that it does not really have the properties that it appears to have. And because there is this logical relationship between "perceiving a material thing" and "sensing a sense-datum", it follows that, while a reference to a material thing will not elucidate the meaning of a sentence which is used to describe a sense-datum, except in so far as the poverty of our language may make it convenient to identify this sense-datum as one of a type that is ordinarily associated with a special sort of material thing, a reference to sense-data will provide a general elucidation of the meaning of statements about material things by showing what is the kind of evidence by which they may be verified. And this may be regarded as the purpose of the phenomenalist analysis.

Besides the philosophers who maintain that material things are themselves "directly observed", there are others who object to phenomenalism on the ground that even if the occurrence of illusions shows that what is directly observed is not a material thing, it is still not just a sense-datum. Thus Professor Stout, for one, has argued that "the evidence of sense-perception flatly contradicts phenomenalism", on the ground that to regard what is immediately experienced as being just a sensible appearance is to ignore an essential factor which he calls "perceptual seeming".[2] According to him, it is because of "perceptual seeming" that one is able to "perceive one thing as behind another, although it is so hidden that there is no sensible appearance of it", or that one can "perceive things as having insides, when they are not transparent".[3] But while this line of argument may have some force against those who employ a physiological criterion for determining the character of sense-data, it does not affect us at all, inasmuch as our use of the word sense-datum is not bound up with any special empirical theory about the nature of what is given. If one accepts the view of certain psychologists that there are experiences

that may properly be described as experiences of "seeing the inside of a solid object" or "seeing an object when it is screened by another", then the inference one must draw is not that what is observed on such occasions is "more than a mere sense-datum", but that the character of people's visual sense-fields is empirically different from what a misplaced attention to the laws of physiology might lead one to suppose. It is true that the terms in which the psychologists describe such experiences are not purely sensory; but the reason for this is that it is only by referring to material things that they can actually expect to make their meaning understood. We must not, therefore, be misled into supposing that what they are intending to describe is anything more than a sensory phenomenon. The statement that someone is having the experience of "seeing the inside of a solid object" must not, in this context, be taken to exclude the possibility that no such physical object is actually there.

It may, however, be admitted that not only in cases of this sort, but in the vast majority of cases in which one senses a visual or tactual sense-datum, one tends to take it for granted that there is a physical object "there"; and it may be that this is what Professor Stout is referring to when he talks of "perceptual seeming". But this is a fact that I do not think any phenomenalist would wish to deny. The view that material things are, in the sense I have just explained, logical constructions out of sense-data does not imply that "perceiving a material thing" need involve any conscious process of inference from the occurrence of one sense-datum to the possible occurrence of another. The phenomenalist is perfectly free to admit that the sensing of a visual or tactual sense-datum is, in most cases, accompanied by an unreflecting assumption of the existence of some material thing. But the question in which he is interested is, What exactly is it that is here unreflectingly assumed? And his answer, which certainly cannot be refuted by any such appeal to psychology as Professor Stout relies on, is that it is the possibility of obtaining further sense-data.

It would seem that the best way to justify the claim that "to say anything about a material thing is always to say something, though not the same thing, about certain sense-data", would be to provide a number of specimen translations. But this is what no one has ever yet been able to do. It may be suggested that the reason why it has never been done is that no one has yet devised a sufficiently elaborate vocabulary. With our current resources of language we are able to classify visual sense-data only in a very general way, tactual data even less specifically, and kinaesthetic data hardly at all: and the result is that when we wish to distinguish the sense-data that belong to one sort of material thing from those that belong to another we are unable to achieve it except by referring to the material things in question. But suppose that someone took the trouble to name all the different varieties of sensible characteristics with which he was acquainted. Even so, he would still not be able to translate any statement about a material thing into a finite set of statements about sense-data. It is not inconceivable that someone should construct and make use of such a sensory language, though in practice he would find it very difficult to make himself understood; but what he succeeded in expressing by these means would never be precisely equivalent even to the singular statements that we make about material things. For when statements are equivalent to one another, they can always be represented as standing in a relationship of mutual entailment. And, in the case I am now considering, this condition cannot be fulfilled.

I have indeed already admitted that no finite set of singular statements about sense-data can ever formally entail a statement about a material thing, inasmuch as I have recognized that statements about material things are not conclusively verifiable. For when we try to reproduce the content of a statement about a material thing by specifying the empirical situations that would furnish us with direct tests of its validity, we find that the number of these possible tests is infinite. Admittedly, when someone makes a statement of this kind he does not actually envisage an infinite series of possible verifications. He may very well be satisfied, in familiar circumstances, with the single sense-experience on which his statement is based; and if he does think it necessary to test it further, the subsequent occurrence, in the appropriate conditions, of only a limited number of "favourable" sense-data will be sufficient, in the absence of contrary evidence, to convince him that it is true. And this is an entirely reasonable procedure. . . . But the fact remains that however many

favourable tests he may make he can never reach a stage at which it ceases to be conceivable that further sense-experience will reverse the verdict of the previous evidence. He will never be in a position to demonstrate that he will not subsequently have experiences that will entitle him to conclude that his original statement was false after all. And this implies that the content of a statement about a material thing cannot be exhaustively specified by any finite number of references to sense-data. This difficulty could indeed be met by introducing into the sense-datum language a suitable set of expressions which would be understood to refer to infinite series of sense-data. But I am afraid that most philosophers would not admit that this gave them the sort of translation that they wanted. For all that would seem to be achieved by the introduction of these new expressions would be a mere renaming of material things.

But not only is the occurrence of any one particular, finite series of sense-data never formally sufficient to establish the truth of a statement about a material thing; it is never even necessary. There is, indeed, a sense in which it can be said that every statement about a material thing entails some set of statements or other about sense-data, inasmuch as it is only by the occurrence of some sense-datum that any statement about a material thing is ever in any degree verified. But there is no set of statements about the occurrence of particular sense-data of which it can truly be said that precisely this is entailed by a given statement about a material thing. And the reason for this is that what is required to verify a statement about a material thing is never just the occurrence of a sense-datum of an absolutely specific kind, but only the occurrence of one or other of the sense-data that fall within a fairly indefinite range. In other words, not only can we go on testing a statement about a material thing as long as we like without being able to arrive at a formal demonstration of its truth; but for any test that we actually do carry out there are always an indefinite number of other tests, differing to some extent either in respect of their conditions or their results, which would have done just as well. And this means that if we try to describe what at any given moment would afford us direct evidence for the truth of a statement about a material thing by putting forward a disjunction of statements about sense-data, we shall find once again that this disjunction will have to be infinite.[4]

But if one infers from this that sentences referring to material things cannot be translated, without alteration of meaning, into sentences referring to sense-data, one must not then conclude that to speak about a material thing is to speak about something altogether different from sense-data, or that it is to speak about sense-data but about something else besides. For that would be a mistake analogous to that of supposing that because sentences referring indefinitely to what is red cannot be translated into a finite number of sentences referring to particular red things, therefore "redness" is the name of an object with a distinct existence of its own, or that because sentences referring to "someone" cannot be translated into a finite disjunction of sentences referring to particular persons, therefore "someone" is the name of a peculiar being, a "subsistent entity" perhaps, who is distinct from any person that one can actually meet. If we cannot produce the required translations of sentences referring to material things into sentences referring to sense-data, the reason is not that it is untrue that "to say anything about a material thing is always to say something about sense-data", but only that one's references to material things are vague in their application to phenomena and that the series of sense-data that they may be understood to specify are composed of infinite sets of terms.

This does not mean, however, that nothing can be done in the way of "analysing material things in terms of sense-data". It would not, indeed, be profitable to seek in any such analysis a means of distinguishing one material thing from another. It is not by a verbal analysis in terms of sense-data that one can hope to make clear what is meant, for example, by "a pen" as opposed to "a pencil", or by "a steamship" as opposed to "a canoe". One can give a verbal, as well as an ostensive, indication of the meaning of such words; but it will not exclude the use of other expressions that belong to a physical rather than to a purely sensory terminology. At the same time, there are certain general features about the way in which any expression referring to a material thing applies to phenomena that one can profitably undertake to analyse. That is to say, one may be able to explain

what are the relations between sense-data that make it possible for us successfully to employ the physical terminology that we do. If I may now use the metaphor of construction without being misunderstood, I can describe the task I am about to undertake as that of showing what are the general principles on which, from our resources of sense-data, we "construct" the world of material things.

ELEMENTARY CONSTRUCTION OF THE MATERIAL WORLD

The main problem which lies before me is that of answering Hume's question why it is that "we attribute a *continued* existence to objects even when they are not present to the senses; and why we suppose them to have an existence *distinct* from perception".[5] Hume himself interpreted this as a question about the sources of an illusion. He saw that the "philosophical" assumption that besides one's perceptions, which alone were directly given, there existed an independent set of objects, of which one's perceptions were copies or effects, was an entirely unwarrantable re-duplication of the perceptual world; and since he held that it was self-contradictory to suppose that any "perception" itself could exist unsensed, he came to the conclusion that the belief in the continued and distinct existence of objects was a fallacious product of the imagination. What he did not see was that the relations of "constancy" and "coherence" between sense-data in which he discovered the source of this supposed illusion could themselves be taken as definitive of the continued and distinct existence of objects. But what precisely are these relations of constancy and coherence? And how do they make it possible for us to describe our sense-data, which are conceived to be transitory and private, by the use of expressions which ostensibly refer to substances which are supposed to endure unperceived, to be endowed with causal properties, to be accessible to different senses and to different observers, and to stand to one another in the system of relations that constitutes their being in "physical space"? With the question of the publicity of these material things, and the way in which it is compatible with the privacy of sense-data, I have already dealt. And I have given an indication of what we mean by attributing causal properties to them, and of the grounds on which we conceive them as able to exist unperceived. But a more detailed explanation is required of the nature of our "construction" of physical space, and of what Hume called "the principle of identity", in virtue of which we derive from successive sense-data the conception of a single, persistent material thing.

An outline of what I take to be the correct view of these matters was given by John Stuart Mill when he spoke of physical bodies as "permanent possibilities of sensation". He explains very well how it is that "a group of sensations", which are mainly "conceived in the form of present possibilities", "presents itself to the mind as permanent, in contrast not solely with the temporariness of one's bodily presence, but also with the temporary character of each of the sensations composing the group; in other words as a kind of permanent substratum, under a set of passing experiences or manifestations"; and how it is that "we learn to think of nature as made up solely of these groups of possibilities, and the active force in nature as manifested in the modification of some of these by others"; while "the sensations, though the original foundation of the whole, come to be looked upon as a sort of accident depending on us, and the possibilities as much more real than the actual sensations, nay, as the very realities of which these are only the representations, appearances, or effects".[6] But some account is required of the manner in which these groups are formed; and we cannot here be satisfied, as Mill apparently was, with a vague reference to "the laws of the association of ideas". For sense-data may be associated, both in fact and in thought, in many ways that are not relevant to the issue; nor is it every kind of well-founded hypothetical proposition about sense-data that enters into the conception of the continued existence of material things. Moreover, Mill was at fault in supposing that, in the case of the "primary qualities" of material things, visual sensations were merely "*symbols* of tactual and muscular ones".[7] This mistake, which was made also by Berkeley in his *Theory of Vision,* may perhaps be due to a failure to distinguish properly between physical and sensible space. It is true that the conception of the physical situation of a material thing involves, as we shall see, a reference to the possible movements of an observer, and so to kinaesthetic data, though even here it would be inaccurate to speak of the vi-

sual data as symbols of the kinaesthetic; but this does not mean that any reference to kinaesthetic data is required for the ascription of spatial properties to visual sense-data themselves. The extension and figure of a visual sense-datum are sensibly "given" no less than its colour; and so are its spatial relations to other sense-data within the same visual field, including its "distance" from sense-data which belong to the body of the observer. For the visual sense-field is sensibly three-dimensional. And while it is true that the data out of which the material world is "constructed" are not drawn from the sense of sight alone, it is, for those who can obtain them, the visual and not the tactual data that are of primary importance. In either case, what interests us in the present context is not so much the qualities of the individual sense-data as the relations which obtain between them, and especially the relations which obtain between sense-data which are constituents of different sense-fields. Now, whatever may be the difference in content between visual and tactual experiences, it does not prevent their having a close similarity of structure; and it is because of this similarity of structure that one finds it natural to regard a visual and a tactual "construct" as one and the same material thing. Accordingly, if one is able to give an account of the principles which are involved in the construction of the physical world out of either visual or tactual sense-data, the case of the other sense will present no special problem; and since ordinary language is chiefly adapted to the description of visual phenomena I shall confine myself to them.

At the present moment I am aware of a visual sense-field the contents of which I may describe by saying that I am perceiving, among other things, a table covered with papers, and beyond the table a chair, and beyond the chair a section of a book-case fastened to a wall. If I now turn aside to look out of the window on my right, these particular sense-data cease to exist, and in their place I obtain a new set of visual sense-data which I may describe by saying that I am perceiving a garden fringed with trees, and beyond the trees the roof of a cottage, and in the distance a thickly wooded hill. And if I execute a further movement, I shall find that these sense-data too will cease to exist, and that others will take their place. But suppose that at some stage in a process of this kind I reverse the direction of my movements.

In that case I shall find that this fragment of my sense-history repeats itself, but in a reverse order. I do not mean by this that I shall sense numerically the same sense-data as I sensed before; for that is excluded by the conventions of the sense-datum language. But there will be a general resemblance between these two sections of my experience; so that I shall find not merely that individual sense-data are closely similar to ones that I sensed before, but that they occur in similar contexts. In the end I shall have a sense-field whose similarity to the first will make it proper for me to describe it by saying that I am again perceiving a table, a chair and a book-case, related as before; but whereas, in the previous case, the sense-field which I described in this way preceded the sense-field which I described by referring to a garden fringed with trees, in the case of their counterparts this order will be reversed. And in whatever direction I may move away from my original point of view, I find that I can always obtain a "reversible" series of this sort, beginning and ending with a sense-field of a kind that I habitually describe in the same way as that with which my account of this experiment began. And I find also that I am able to obtain any number of "reversible" series in which a sense-field of this kind occurs, not as an end but as a middle term.[8] In some cases, indeed, the "reproduction" of a term in such a series is not perfect; for I may have experiences that would ordinarily be described by saying that some particular thing had altered its position, or undergone a change of quality, or even that it had ceased to exist altogether. But all such changes take place within a relatively stable environment. The sense-data by which they are manifested do not have counterparts in the relevant strand of my previous experience; but they occur in contexts that do have the requisite counterparts; and it is only because this is so that I am able to classify them in the way that I do.[9]

Ignoring, for the moment, the problem of illusory experiences, with which I shall deal later on, I shall now try to generalize this example in such a way as to indicate the nature of the "laws of sensory association" which give rise to our conception of the material world. I suggest that our grouping of sense-data to form particular material things is governed by four main conditions, which I shall now set forth.

The first set of relations which obtain between the different sense-data that enter into the constitution of the same material thing are relations of resemblance. For reasons which I have already given,[10] I am not able to say what these relations are in any particular case except by referring to the kind of material thing in question; but there is no foundation here for a charge of circularity, since the point is not that I must already have a conception of the material thing in order to be able to discover these relations, but only that I have no other means of describing them. It may, however, be objected that one's field of vision does not always comprise even the appearance of the whole of a single surface of a material thing, let alone an appearance of all the surfaces of what is presumed to be "a three-dimensional solid"; and that there is often very little resemblance between the appearances of one part of the thing and those of another. But while the sense-data that are supposed to belong to different parts of the same material thing may not resemble one another directly to any great extent, they do stand in what may be called a relation of indirect resemblance, in virtue of the fact that they can be linked by a series of sense-data which do directly resemble one another. For it is possible, by making suitable movements, to sense a series of sense-fields which I can find no better way to describe than by saying that they reveal partially overlapping aspects of the thing in question; and while there may be considerable differences in content between sense-fields which are remote from one another in the series, the differences between its adjacent members will be very small. And by this means one can provide oneself also with a set of sense-data which can be fitted together in the imagination, like the pieces of a jigsaw puzzle, in such a way as to yield a complete picture of the object, which may never as a whole be given to sense. And there will be what I may call a relation of "global resemblance" between any two series of sense-data that make up the complete views of the object that are obtainable at different periods of time.[11]

That this relation admits of various degrees is shown by the fact that we allow it to be possible for the material thing to change without thereby losing its identity. But how far such changes may go before it becomes correct to say that the original thing has ceased to exist, and has been replaced by another, is a question that is not subject to any exact set of rules. In any case, one's attribution of numerical identity to a material thing depends not only upon the degree of resemblance that is displayed by the sense-data that one takes to belong to it, but also upon one's finding that they occur in similar contexts. And this brings me to the second of my four conditions; which is, that for similar sense-data to be elements of numerically the same material thing, they must, generally speaking, occur in a similar sensible environment. I say "generally speaking" to allow for the fact that the thing may sometimes move; but here again there is a relation of indirect resemblance between the sensible environments. For one's judgement that an object which has moved is numerically the same as that which previously existed in another place involves an assumption that one could have "traced its path" through a series of partially overlapping sense-fields, of which any two adjacent members would have been directly resemblant. And this assumption is grounded on the fact that in many cases this "possibility of sensation" is actually realized. I include also under this heading of the constancy of the sensible environment the criterion of a thing's self-identity which consists in its retaining the same causal properties. For this amounts only to a temporal extension of the context for which the similarity is required.

Now were this condition of the recurrence of similar contexts not, in fact, fulfilled in our experience, as it conceivably might not have been, we should not have any grounds for identifying particular material things in the way that we do. Given the necessary resemblances between sense-data, we should be able to find a use for words that stand for different species of material things, but unless such sense-data occurred, as they actually do, in a relatively constant sensible environment, we should not, with our current rules of self-identity, be able to distinguish particular instances of these species and assign to each of them an individual history. Moreover, our conception of these things as enduring through time, and occupying definite positions in "physical space" involves the fulfillment of a further condition; which is that the relevant sorts of sense-data should be systematically reproducible in the way that was indicated by my illustration. To provide a more imaginative illustration, which may

help to show how this condition operates, I shall now have recourse to a different class of sense-data, the phenomena of sounds. For Caliban "the isle was full of noises" which he was not able to identify as the "effects" of any physical sources; and one may assume that the noises came to him in patterns and that these patterns were fairly constantly repeated, in the ordinary sense in which a song may be said to be repeated when the singer gives an encore. But suppose that the sounds exhibited a more extensive uniformity, the sort of uniformity that is actually displayed by visual and tactual sense-data in our everyday experience. Imagine a Caliban, devoid of the senses of sight and touch, but endowed with highly differentiated kinaesthetic sensations, in terms of which he was able to distinguish different directions of movement; and suppose that he found that with every kinaesthetic series, which constituted his movement "from one place to another", there was associated a special type of auditory series which was reinstated in a reverse order when the direction of his movements was reversed. In that case it would be natural for him to construct a "physical space" of sounds and to conceive of them as persisting in it unheard, just as out of visual and tactual sense-data we construct a physical space which we people with persistent sensibilia in the form of material things. He would say that a sound which he heard on different occasions was the same, not merely in the qualitative sense of sameness in which a musician who gives an encore may be said to play the same tune as before, but in a numerical sense analogous to that in which I may say of the pen with which I am now writing that it is the same as that with which I was writing yesterday. If he were addicted to philosophizing he might even come to distinguish between auditory sense-data, or "ideas of sound", which he would regard as momentary objects, incapable of existing unperceived, and auditory things, to which he would attribute "a continued and distinct existence"; and then he might perplex himself with the question how the existence of these things could be inferred from the occurrence of the sense-data, which alone were directly given. And this would not be a more artificial problem than that which the peculiar structure of our visual and tactual experience has actually led philosophers to raise about "our knowledge of the external world".[12]

For us there is no problem of the self-identity of particular sounds since we do not subject them, any more than we subject tastes or smells, to the category of substance. We find it more convenient to regard the data of these senses as adjectival to the visuo-tactual constructs to which, on the basis of observed correlations, they are referred as qualities or effects. It is true that we do allow ourselves to speak of a sound as existing unsensed, in cases where we believe that if someone were to be in the relevant position he would be hearing it; but we do not admit the possibility of hearing numerically the same sound on different occasions, in the sense in which we suppose that we are able to perceive numerically the same material thing. If we speak of "hearing the same sound" it is only in an analogous sense to that in which we speak of "seeing the same colour" or "feeling the same pain". We do not identify the sound as a particular with any one that has been heard before or could be heard after. What we mean by saying that it is the same sound as one that is heard on some other occasion is that it exhibits the same character, or, in other words, that it is a different particular instance of the same "universal". The criterion in this case is simply that of qualitative resemblance. And the reason why we do not find it useful to substantialize sounds, in the way that we substantialize groups of visual and tactual sense-data, is that the condition of "systematic reproduction" is not fulfilled in the requisite way by auditory sense-fields. But it is easy to conceive that it might have been fulfilled by them, just as it is easy to conceive that it might not have been fulfilled in the case of our visual and tactual experiences. It is a contingent fact that any domain of sense-experience possesses the structure that makes it convenient for us to apply to it the language that we do.

At this point it may be objected that the fact that one does not make substances out of auditory sense-data proves that I was wrong to accept Mill's doctrine of "permanent possibilities of sensation". For if this, it may be said, is to be taken as the criterion of "continued and distinct existence", then the world must be literally much more "full of noises" than it is supposed to be. For example, I am not now hearing the sound of my front-door bell; nor do I believe that it is being heard by anyone else; but I have good reason to believe the hypothetical proposition that if at any time I were to have such experiences as are associated with ringing this bell, I should then have the sensation of hearing it; and this would apply to a multitude of other sounds that are not actually believed to exist. And the same objection can be raised with regard to visual sense-data. For example, it is a "conditional certainty", in Mill's sense,[13] that if at any time I were to have such experiences as would constitute my heating the water in my kettle to boiling point, I should then obtain some visual sense-data which I might describe by saying that I was seeing steam issuing from it; yet while I believe that the kettle exists unperceived, I do not believe this to be true of the steam. But this difficulty is met by the introduction of my fourth condition; which is, that for a permanent possibility of sensation to be definitive of the continued and distinct existence of a material thing, its realization must be viewed as depending, apart from the fulfillment of the "standing conditions" which are required for the occurrence of any sense-data of the relevant sense, only upon the movements of the observer. Thus I believe that the kettle now exists because I believe that if I were in the appropriate position, at which I could arrive by carrying out a given series of movements, I should be experiencing a visual or tactual sense-datum of it; but I do not believe this to be true of the steam, and therefore I do not believe that it now exists. The reference to what I have called the "standing conditions", such as the state of the light or of the nervous system of the observer, is not of importance in this context; for they are present also in the case where a permanent possibility of sensation is not taken to be constitutive of a persistent material thing; and they are not therefore relevant to the problem of distinguishing between this case and the other. Nor does the consideration of these standing conditions carry us outside the domain of actual and possible sense-data. For the belief in the necessity of these conditions may be founded on the observation, in particular cases, that unless sense-data that verify the presence of these conditions are obtainable, other sense-data of the relevant sense do not occur, or else upon the observation that the others vary in accordance with them. And then these conclusions are legitimately generalized so as to cover even the occurrence of the sense-data that at any given moment are constitutive of the state of the conditions themselves.

As for the observer's awareness of his own movements, it is based upon kinaesthetic sensations supplemented by the evidence of sight and touch; and this evidence consists in the fact that members of the group of resemblant sense-data which are elements of the observer's body are found to succeed one another in a changing visual and tactual environment. It might be thought that a reference to the changes in the sensible environment would be sufficient, without our having to bring in any kinaesthetic sense-data, or even any visual or tactual sense-data of the observer's body. And this is, for example, the view of Professor Price, who maintains that "a purely visual being, i.e., one having no sense but sight, could know that he had a point of view and that he was changing it thus and thus", and further that "a visual percipient without any body at all could have a point of view and change it just as we can".[14] But to arrive at this conclusion he has to assume that his visual percipient is able to know that the sense-data which he successively experiences are constituents of different "standard solids", which are situated at different places in physical space; and I do not think that this assumption is justifiable. For I think that it is only by correlating such sense-data, in the manner I have described, with the series of his movements that he would be able to construct the physical system at all; so that his original grounds for believing that he was altering his point of view could not consist solely in his observation of the changes in his environment. Once he had constructed the physical system, he would indeed be able to make use of it for his own orientation, and to conceive of its physical constituents as maintaining their relative spatial positions independently of any movements that he or any other observer might actually execute. But this does not mean that we can dispense with our reference to the observer's movements in giving an account of the principles that enter into this "construction" itself.

I hold, then, that the main features of the structure of our visual experience which give rise to our conception of material things are, first, the relations of resemblance between individual sense-data; secondly, the comparative stability of the contexts in which these resemblant sense-data occur; thirdly, the fact that the occurrence of such sense-data is systematically repeatable, in the way I have tried to indicate; and fourthly, the dependence of this repetition upon the movements of the observer. These features are reproduced, albeit less clearly, in the structure of our tactual experience; and it is, as I have said, this structural correspondence that makes it possible for us to combine our visual and tactual constructs to form particular material things.

Once one has accounted for the attribution of "continued and distinct existence" to material things, it is not very difficult to sketch out an analysis of our conception of physical space. The main problem here is to explain how the spatial relations that are "given" as obtaining between different constituents of single sense-fields can be used to define the relative positions of different material things, even when these are not capable of being simultaneously perceived. And for this I shall have recourse to a simple example. Consider the case of two material things A and M, which are conceived to be situated at places that are physically accessible from one another, but at such a distance that it is impossible to see them both at once. It follows that no sense-datum a of A will ever be observed to stand in a direct spatial relationship to any sense-datum m of M. But, by carrying out a suitable series of movements, it will be possible to obtain a series of "partially overlapping" sense-fields such that a is observed to stand in the spatial relation r to another sense-datum b, a sense-datum of the same kind as b is observed to stand in the relation r to another sense-datum c, a sense-datum of the same kind as c is observed to stand in the relation r to another sense-datum d, and, finally, to omit the intervening stages of the process, a sense-datum of the same kind as l is observed to stand in the relation r to m. Then, just as the groups of transient sense-data of which a and m are representatives are transformed, in accordance with the principles I have described, into the persistent material things A and M, so the relation r is transformed into the higher order relation R, which is supposed to obtain between material things even when no actual sense-data of them are being observed to be related by r, and even in cases where the possibility of linking the relevant sense-data consists, not in the power to observe a direct relation between them, but only in the power to establish an indirect relation such as obtained between a and m in my example. And thus one arrives at the conception of M as standing in the direction R from A, and also, since this process of spatial linking is reversible, at that of A as standing in the converse direction to R from M. The next step is to remove the restriction which I described by saying that M was physically accessible from A, by allowing that M may be said to stand in the direction R from A even when the establishment of the indirect relation between the relevant sense-data, though possible in principle, is, as the result of some hindrance to the movements of the observer, incapable of being realized in fact.

Now, it is characteristic of the sense-given spatial relations with which we are here concerned, first, that if a sense-datum x stands in any such relation r to another sense-datum y, then it is not the case that y also has r to x; secondly, that if, within a single sense-field, x has r to y and y has r to another sense-datum z, then x has r to z; and thirdly, that every sense-datum is either directly related by r to another constituent of the same sense-field, or, if it is one of the data by which the field is bounded, is indirectly related by r, in the manner I have explained, to some constituent of an "adjoining" field. And these structural properties of being asymmetrical, transitive and connected are assigned also to R, and to all the other higher order relations that are modelled on sense-given spatial relations, in the way that R is modelled on r. Consequently, one comes to hold that if any material thing X stands in any direction S from any other material thing Y, then Y does not stand in the direction S from X but in the converse direction; that if X stands in the direction S from Y, and Y stands in the direction S from a third thing Z, then X stands in the direction S from Z; and further, that there is always some material thing that stands in any given direction from any given material thing.[15] And I believe that this is all that is essentially involved in the ordinary conception of physical space.

It appears then, if my account of this matter is even substantially correct, that our conception of material things as having a continued and distinct existence in physical space, so far from involving any *a priori* intuition, can be derived from purely empirical and contingent features of our visual, tactual and kinaesthetic experiences.[16] I have found it convenient to deal with this problem as if it were a question of constructing one sort of objects out of another; but, strictly, it should be viewed as a problem about the reference of words. For what my construction of the physical world amounts to is a very general and simplified description of the main assumptions about the structure of phenomena that are involved in the everyday use of physical terms.

24. APPEARANCE AND REALITY

That the course of our sense-experience is not completely uniform is shown by the fact that the world of material things is found to be subject to change. But it is not always the case that a break in the uniformity of our sense-data is taken as a sign of an objective change in the material world. For we sometimes find that the perceptions to which the "discordant" sense-data give rise are qualitatively or existentially delusive; we find that the sense-data endow material things with qualities that they do not really possess, or even that the material things that they seem to present do not exist at all. But how can one distinguish these cases from the others? By what criteria does one determine whether or not a sense-datum presents a material thing as it really is? We may dispose of the case of existentially delusive perceptions by referring to the foregoing analysis of the constitution of material things. For we may say that the occasions where a perception is held to be existentially delusive are those on which the form or the context of a sense-datum would lead one to assume that it belonged to a group of sense-data of the kind I have been describing, whereas, in fact, one's expectation of being able to sense further members of the group would not be capable of being fulfilled. But what of the perceptions that are held to be qualitatively delusive? In this case, the sense-datum on which the perception is based does belong to a group which is constitutive of a material thing, but it is not an "honest" representative of the group, inasmuch as its presentation of the material thing is in some manner incorrect. If one is deceived by it, one will attribute to the thing some character that it does not really have. If one is not deceived one may say that the thing really has the character x, but that it appears to have the character y. Accordingly, the problem is to discover what differences among sense-data underlie this particular distinction between "appearance" and "reality". And to answer this will be to furnish an explanation of the use of the word "real" as it is applied to the characteristics of material things.

It has already been made clear that the distinction between real and apparent characteristics does not enter into the domain of sense-data themselves. Nor is there anything in a sense-datum, considered wholly by itself, by which one can decide whether or not it presents a material thing as it really is. Suppose that one has the experience of perceiving a round coin which looks elliptical, or that of perceiving a red flower which looks purple. One can describe these experiences by saying that one of them comprises the occurrence of a sense-datum which really is elliptical, and the other the occurrence of a sense-datum which really is purple. In neither case, however, does the relevant material thing really have the characteristic that the sense-datum makes it appear to have. But the reason for this cannot lie simply in the qualities of the sense-data; for it may well be the case that sense-data with these qualities are not deceptive in this way at all. This particular coin, which looks elliptical, may really be round; and this particular flower, which looks purple, may really be red; but it is not impossible that a thing that looked elliptical should really be elliptical, or that one that looked purple should really be purple. And, conversely, in the cases where a sense-datum does present the real character of the material thing which is constituted by the group to which it belongs, it is always possible that on other occasions a sense-datum of the same quality may not be a faithful representative of its group. But if this distinction does not depend upon a difference in the intrinsic qualities of sense-data, it must depend upon a difference in their relations. And so we must try to discover what is the special relationship in which a sense-datum must stand to other sense-data, if it is to be accounted a bearer of the real character of the relevant material thing.

The first expedient that suggests itself is to look for our criterion in the nature of the context in which the sense-datum occurs. For one is inclined to think that the reason why a perception is qualitatively delusive is to be found in the accompanying conditions; that a thing appears, for example, to have a different shape from that which it really has because it is seen

from an abnormal angle, or that its colour is falsified because it is seen in an imperfect light. Accordingly, one might attempt to give a general description, in terms of sense-data, of what are conventionally taken to be preferential conditions; and then one might say that the sense-data that were bearers of the real characters of the material things to which they belonged were those that occurred in conditions of this sort. Thus, the real shape of the material thing might be defined by a reference to the shape of sense-data that were in a certain spatial relationship to sense-data belonging to the observer's body; or its real colour might be defined by a reference to sense-data that occurred in sense-fields displaying a relatively high degree of illumination, where the degree of illumination would be taken as a sensory characteristic of the field. But while this method may lead to correct results so far as it goes, it is not altogether satisfactory. One difficulty is that these preferential conditions are not the same for every kind of material thing. Thus, to take only one obvious example, the choice of an optimal distance from which to view an object depends to some extent upon the object's size. Let us assume, however, that the different cases can be classified in such a way that it is possible to specify the contexts that determine the selection of the correct sense-data out of any given group. Even so, there will remain the further objection that this process of selection is made to seem entirely arbitrary. Admittedly, the attribution of the characteristics of certain members of a group of sense-data to the material thing which is supposed to be constituted by the group as a whole is a matter of convention. But surely this convention serves some empirical purpose? Must there not be some reason why the sense-data that occur in special sorts of contexts are given this preference over the other members of their groups?

I think that there is a reason, and that it consists in the fact, which some philosophers have recognized,[17] that the privileged sense-data are found to be the most reliable members of the groups to which they belong, in the sense that they have the greatest value as sources of prediction. Thus, if I have obtained from my past experience a knowledge of the general feature of certain sequences of sense-data which may be described as the blurring of objects as their distance from the observer increases beyond a certain point, I am able from a near view of an object to infer how it will look from farther off; but if I am seeing an object for the first time from a considerable distance, I am not able, by the use of any general laws of perspective, to infer with the same degree of accuracy how it will look from near at hand. Or again, if I am placed "too near" the object, I am not able, if I am seeing it for the first time to infer precisely what sense-data of it will be presented if I go a little farther away; but if I start with the sense-data that are obtained from this more remote position, together with a knowledge of the manner of the blurring of appearances that accompanies a decrease of distance from such a point, I can more accurately calculate what sense-data will be obtained if I approach the object more nearly. And similar distinctions can be drawn among the sense-data that belong to the other relevant types of series, such as those that accompany variations in the light. Thus, to take a negative example, the use of dark glasses is held to be a distorting medium in respect of colour, because the sense-data of colour that occur under this condition have a minimal predictive value; for if one sees an object for the first time through dark glasses, one cannot at all infer what shade of colour it will appear when the glasses are removed. The choice of the preferential conditions may not be the same for every kind of material thing; but it will be governed by the general rule of giving preference to the sense-data that are the most reliable, in the foregoing sense. And so we come to conceive of these sense-data as the "standard" members of their groups, from which the others systematically deviate.[18] And it is by reference to them that we determine the real, as opposed to the merely apparent, characteristics of the material thing which is constituted by the group in question. Generally speaking, the privileged sense-data in relation to colour are those that, in comparison with the other members of their groups, are the most conspicuously differentiated in this respect from the other constituents of their sense-fields; in relation to shape, they are those that combine the greatest specific detail with the most clearly defined outline. And this means that their greater reliability is not evinced only in relation to other members of their groups. For they will also be the ones that are the least likely to betray us into the incorrect predictions which are involved in

what is described as the mistaking of one material thing for another.

I have chosen my examples from the sense of sight because, as I have already pointed out, it is, for those who are able to obtain them, the visual data that play the predominant role in the construction of the material world. But the same principles govern our application of the distinction between appearance and reality to the physical qualities that are manifested to the other senses. Thus, if I wish to determine the real character of a person's voice, I do not take as my standard the sense-data that I obtain when I hear it over a defective telephone, or from a considerable distance; for they may have relatively small predictive values in comparison with certain other sense-data which, in virtue of their common association with a single visuo-tactual construct, are assigned to the same auditory group. And it is for a similar reason that if I wished to determine how a thing really tasted, I should not rely on the sense-data which I obtained when I had a severe cold; or that if my fingertips were severely burned, I should not regard the tactual sense-data which I then obtained as indicative of the tactual consistency which really characterized the material thing in question. In none of these cases is it significant to say that the sense-data which occur in such abnormal conditions are themselves in any way illusory. But they may be judged to give a false impression of the material things with which they are associated, inasmuch as they fall short of the standard of reliability which is set by certain other members of their groups.

It is characteristic of the domain of tactual sense-data that while it is poorer in content than the visual domain, there is a sense in which it may be said to exhibit a greater measure of uniformity. For in the groups of tactual sense-data which help to constitute particular material things there tend to be fewer distortion series than in the groups which are their visual counterparts. And no doubt it is this that has led certain philosophers to identify the real characteristics of material things with those that are manifested to the sense of touch. But this is to overlook the fact that illusions of touch, though less common than illusions of sight, do nevertheless occur. And the refusal to make use of any visual data whatsoever in determining the real characteristics of material things is a plain departure from ordinary usage, and surely an unjustified impoverishment of our conception of the material world.

It is true, however, that this factor of sensible constancy, which is especially characteristic of tactual sense-data, is one to which we do attach very great importance. For it is this that leads to the introduction of a superior criterion of the reality of certain physical characteristics, the criterion of measurement. The use of the word "reality" which here comes into question is of a different order from that which I have so far been considering. For I have been concerned with the cases in which the determination of what is physically real consists in ascribing the sensible characteristics of certain privileged members of a group of sense-data to the group as a whole. But in the case where a numerically measurable value is given to what is held to be a real characteristic of a material thing, this characteristic is not manifested by any individual sense-datum of the group which constitutes the material thing in question. For the process of measurement is not a matter of discrimination within the group, but of correlating members of the group with those of another. Thus, in the case of a simple measurement of length, it is a matter of correlating visual or tactual sense-data which belong to the object that is being measured with visual or tactual sense-data which belong to the group that constitutes the measuring instrument. But even so the underlying principle that governs this use of the word "real" is the same as in the other case. For it is characteristic of the sensible relations from which such measurements are derived that they exhibit a very high degree of constancy.[19] The appearance of the thing that is measured and of the measuring instrument itself may vary to a considerable extent in different perceptual conditions, but the appearance of coincidence between them usually remains unaffected; and it is upon this relation of coincidence that the measurement is based. If we add to this greater constancy the convenience of the mathematical terminology which they enable us to introduce, it becomes clear that the phenomena of measurement have a markedly high predictive value; and it is for this reason that they are taken to furnish a superior criterion of the reality of the physical characteristics to which they apply. It is then by an extension of this principle that, when a technical scientific language is devised for describing the phenomena that enter into certain complicated processes of measurement, people are inclined to attribute an exclusive, or at any rate superior, reality to the scientific "objects" to which they suppose that the terms of such a language refer. And here it may be noted that a similar reservation of the use of the word "real" for what can be quantitatively measured is to be found in the distinction which philosophers have made between primary and secondary qualities. For what distinguishes the so-called ideas of primary qualities from the others is pre-eminently the part they can be made to play in processes of measurement. But it is not correct to go on to maintain, as some philosophers have done, that it is only the ideas of primary qualities that can have literal counterparts in the physical world. For, quite apart from the fallaciousness of the causal, or representative, theories of perception with which such a view is commonly associated, it is a mistake to suppose that because an apparent physical characteristic cannot be directly subjected to the criterion of measurement, it cannot properly be said to be "real" in any sense at all.

Finally, we must notice yet another use of the distinction between reality and illusion, in which these terms are understood to apply, not simply to the content of this or that perceptual judgement, but to whole segments of our perceptual histories. In this sense, a series of perceptions which satisfy the foregoing tests may still turn out to be delusive. I may find among my sense-data the relations that justify me in grouping them to form material things; I may apply the authorized methods for assigning to these things their "real characteristics"; I may even have such experiences as I should ordinarily describe by saying that I was making use of the criteria of measurement; and still I may wake to find that I have been dreaming all along; or I may be persuaded by the testimony of other observers that the whole of this strand of my experience was a prolonged illusion, if I find that the hypothesis that this testimony itself is genuine fits in with my current experience. But this further, over-riding, distinction between appearance and reality does not bring in any new principle. For the only way in which one can test whether a series of perceptions is veridical, in this sense, is to see whether it is substantiated by further sense-experiences; so that once again the ascription of "reality" depends upon the predictive value of the sense-data on which the perceptions are based. So long as the general structure of my sense-data conforms to the expectations that I derive from the memory of my past experience, I remain convinced that I am not living in a dream; and the longer the series of successful predictions is extended, the smaller becomes the probability that I am mistaken. Admittedly, this progressive limitation of the probability of illusion can never reach the status of a formal demonstration. But then . . . it is unreasonable to expect that it should. The most that we can do is to elaborate a technique for predicting the course of our sensory experience, and to adhere to it so long as it is found to be reliable. And this is all that is essentially involved in our belief in the reality of the physical world.

NOTES

1. *Vide* A. E. Duncan-Jones, "Does Philosophy Analyse Common Sense?" *Aristotelian Society Supplementary Proceedings,* 1937, pp. 140–41.

2. "Phenomenalism", *Proceedings of the Aristotelian Society,* 1938–9, pp. 1–18.

3. *Loc. cit.* pp. 10–11.

4. Cf. John Wisdom, "Metaphysics and Verification", *Mind,* October 1938, pp. 478–81.

5. *Vide. A Treatise of Human Nature,* Book I, Part IV, section ii.

6. *An Examination of Sir William Hamilton's Philosophy,* pp. 194–95.

7. *Op. cit.* p. 237.

8. For the importance of this possibility of "reversion" cf. Eino Kaila, "Über das System der Wirklichkeitsbegriffe", *Acta Philosophica Fennica,* Fasc. 2, 1936, pp. 29–33. I am much indebted to him.

9. Cf. Kaila, *op. cit.* pp. 59–60.

10. Pp. 238 ff.

11. A very full and good account of this, the first of my four conditions, is given by Professor Price in his chapter in "The Relation of Sense-data to One Another", *Per-*ception, ch. viii. But he seems occasionally to confuse sensible and physical space, as when he speaks of an unsensed sense-datum as being "literally beyond" one that is being sensed (cf. pp. 240–43), and he seems to have overlooked the importance of my other conditions, particularly the second and third.

12. Kaila (*op. cit.* pp. 35–9) makes use of a similar example. But he seems to suggest that a person who constructed a world of auditory things, in such conditions as I have described, would be subject to an illusion, and says that "we can laugh at his naïvety, because we possess a more comprehensive sense, our sense of sight, which affords us a *simultaneous* conspectus of our blind man's world, while he can apprehend it only in the form of an acoustical kinaesthetic *succession*". I should say, however, that the construction of auditory things was a correct and reasonable way for my Caliban to describe his experience, and that the possession of a mere comprehensive sense of *sight* would not necessarily make any difference in this context, except in so far as it introduced a problem about the relationship of visual and auditory "space".

13. Vide *An Examination of Sir William Hamilton's Philosophy* p. 193.

14. *Perception,* p. 255.

15. Cf. Kaila, *op. cit.* pp. 44–9.

16. With regard to physical space, this point is well brought out by Henri Poincaré in his "L'Espace et la Géométrie", *La Science et l'Hypothèse,* ch. iv.

17. E.g., Kaila, *op. cit.* pp. 22–9, and Price, *op. cit.* p. 211.

18. Cf. Price, *op. cit.* pp. 209–15. But he is mistaken in supposing that "the fact that common sense is trying to state when it says that x is the real quality of a material thing M" is merely that the relevant qualities of the sense-data which belong to M can be made to form a unity of system with x as its centre. For this can be achieved even when x is not the real quality of the material thing. Thus his criterion does not enable one to distinguish between the case of a thing which is really round but sometimes looks elliptical, and that of a thing which is really elliptical but sometimes look round. His error is that he neglects to make any reference to the contexts in which the sense-data occur.

19. Cf. Kaila, *op. cit.* pp. 64–8 and 82–6.

On What There Is   10

W. V. QUINE

A CURIOUS THING about the ontological problem is its simplicity. It can be put in three Anglo-Saxon monosyllables: 'What is there?' It can be answered, moreover, in a word—'Everything'—and everyone will accept this answer as true. However, this is merely to say that there is what there is. There remains room for disagreement over cases; and so the issue has stayed alive down the centuries.

Suppose now that two philosophers, McX and I, differ over ontology. Suppose McX maintains there is something which I maintain there is not. McX can, quite consistently with his own point of view, describe our difference of opinion by saying that I refuse to recognize certain entities. I should protest, of course, that he is wrong in his formulation of our disagreement, for I maintain that there are no entities, of the kind which he alleges, for me to recognize; but my finding him wrong in his formulation of our disagreement is unimportant, for I am committed to considering him wrong in his ontology anyway.

When *I* try to formulate our difference of opinion, on the other hand, I seem to be in a predicament. I cannot admit that there are some things which McX countenances and I do not, for in admitting that there are such things I should be contradicting my own rejection of them.

It would appear, if this reasoning were sound, that in any ontological dispute the proponent of the negative side suffers the disadvantage of not being able to admit that his opponent disagrees with him.

This is the old Platonic riddle of nonbeing. Nonbeing must in some sense be, otherwise what is it that there is not? This tangled doctrine might be nicknamed *Plato's beard;* historically it has proved tough, frequently dulling the edge of Occam's razor.

It is some such line of thought that leads philosophers like McX to impute being where they might otherwise be quite content to recognize that there is nothing. Thus, take Pegasus. If Pegasus *were* not,

McX argues, we should not be talking about anything when we use the word; therefore it would be nonsense to say even that Pegasus is not. Thinking to show thus that the denial of Pegasus cannot be coherently maintained, he concludes that Pegasus is.

McX cannot, indeed, quite persuade himself that any region of space-time, near or remote, contains a flying horse of flesh and blood. Pressed for further details on Pegasus, then, he says that Pegasus is an idea in men's minds. Here, however, a confusion begins to be apparent. We may for the sake of argument concede that there is an entity, and even a unique entity (though this is rather implausible), which is the mental Pegasus-idea; but this mental entity is not what people are talking about when they deny Pegasus.

McX never confuses the Parthenon with the Parthenon-idea. The Parthenon is physical; the Parthenon-idea is mental (according anyway to McX's version of ideas, and I have no better to offer). The Parthenon is visible; the Parthenon-idea is invisible. We cannot easily imagine two things more unlike, and less liable to confusion, than the Parthenon and the Parthenon-idea. But when we shift from the Parthenon to Pegasus, the confusion sets in—for no other reason than that McX would sooner be deceived by the crudest and most flagrant counterfeit than grant the nonbeing of Pegasus.

The notion that Pegasus must be, because it would otherwise be nonsense to say even that Pegasus is not, has been seen to lead McX into an elementary confusion. Subtler minds, taking the same precept as their starting point, come out with theories of Pegasus which are less patently misguided than McX's, and correspondingly more difficult to eradicate. One of these subtler minds is named, let us say, Wyman. Pegasus, Wyman maintains, has his being as an unactualized possible. When we say of Pegasus that there is no such thing, we are saying, more precisely,

Review of Metaphysics 2, no. 1 (1948). Reprinted by permission of *The Review of Metaphysics.*

that Pegasus does not have the special attribute of actuality. Saying that Pegasus is not actual is on a par, logically, with saying that the Parthenon is not red; in either case we are saying something about an entity whose being is unquestioned.

Wyman, by the way, is one of those philosophers who have united in ruining the good old word 'exist'. Despite his espousal of unactualized possibles, he limits the word 'existence' to actuality—thus preserving an illusion of ontological agreement between himself and us who repudiate the rest of his bloated universe. We have all been prone to say, in our common-sense usage of 'exist', that Pegasus does not exist, meaning simply that there is no such entity at all. If Pegasus existed he would indeed be in space and time, but only because the word 'Pegasus' has spatio-temporal connotations, and not because 'exists' has spatio-temporal connotations. If spatio-temporal reference is lacking when we affirm the existence of the cube root of 27, this is simply because a cube root is not a spatio-temporal kind of thing, and not because we are being ambiguous in our use of 'exist'.[1] However, Wyman, in an ill-conceived effort to appear agreeable, genially grants us the nonexistence of Pegasus and then, contrary to what *we* meant by nonexistence of Pegasus, insists that Pegasus *is*. Existence is one thing, he says, and subsistence is another. The only way I know of coping with this obfuscation of issues is to *give* Wyman the word 'exist'. I'll try not to use it again; I still have 'is'. So much for lexicography; let's get back to Wyman's ontology.

Wyman's overpopulated universe is in many ways unlovely. It offends the aesthetic sense of us who have a taste for desert landscapes, but this is not the worst of it. Wyman's slum of possibles is a breeding ground for disorderly elements. Take, for instance, the possible fat man in that doorway; and, again, the possible bald man in that doorway. Are they the same possible man, or two possible men? How do we decide? How many possible men are there in that doorway? Are there more possible thin ones than fat ones? How many of them are alike? Or would their being alike make them one? Are no *two* possible things alike? Is this the same as saying that it is impossible for two things to be alike? Or, finally, is the concept of identity simply inapplicable to unactualized possibles? But what sense can be found in talking of entities which cannot meaningfully be said to be identical with themselves and distinct from one another? These elements are well-nigh incorrigible. By a Fregean therapy of individual concepts, some effort might be made at rehabilitation; but I feel we'd do better simply to clear Wyman's slum and be done with it.

Possibility, along with the other modalities of necessity and impossibility and contingency, raises problems upon which I do not mean to imply that we should turn our backs. But we can at least limit modalities to whole statements. We may impose the adverb 'possibly' upon a statement as a whole, and we may well worry about the semantical analysis of such usage; but little real advance in such analysis is to be hoped for in expanding our universe to include so-called *possible entities*. I suspect that the main motive for this expansion is simply the old notion that Pegasus, for example, must be because otherwise it would be nonsense to say even that he is not.

Still, all the rank luxuriance of Wyman's universe of possibles would seem to come to naught when we make a slight change in the example and speak not of Pegasus but of the round square cupola on Berkeley College. If, unless Pegasus were, it would be nonsense to say that he is not, then by the same token, unless the round square cupola on Berkeley College were, it would be nonsense to say that it is not. But, unlike Pegasus, the round square cupola on Berkeley College cannot be admitted even as an unactualized *possible*. Can we drive Wyman now to admitting also a realm of unactualizable impossibles? If go, a good many embarrassing questions could be asked about them. We might hope even to trap Wyman in contradictions, by getting him to admit that certain of these entities are at once round and square. But the wily Wyman chooses the other horn of the dilemma and concedes that it is nonsense to say that the round square cupola on Berkeley College is not. He says that the phrase 'round square cupola' is meaningless.

Wyman was not the first to embrace this alternative. The doctrine of the meaninglessness of contradictions runs away back. The tradition survives, moreover, in writers who seem to share none of Wyman's motivations. Still, I wonder whether the first temptation to such a doctrine may not have been substantially the motivation which we have observed in Wyman. Certainly the doctrine has no intrinsic appeal; and it has led its devotees to such quixotic extremes as that of challenging the method of proof by *reductio ad absurdum*—a challenge in which I sense a *reductio ad absurdum* of the doctrine itself.

Moreover, the doctrine of meaninglessness of contradictions has the severe methodological drawback that it makes it impossible, in principle, ever to devise an effective test of what is meaningful and what is not. It would be forever impossible for us to devise systematic ways of deciding whether a string of signs made sense—even to us individually, let alone other people—or not. For it follows from a discovery in mathematical logic, due to Church, that there can be no generally applicable test of contradictoriness.

I have spoken disparagingly of Plato's beard, and hinted that it is tangled. I have dwelt at length on the inconveniences of putting up with it. It is time to think about taking steps.

Russell, in his theory of so-called singular descriptions, showed clearly how we might meaningfully use seeming names without supposing that there be the entities allegedly named. The names to which Russell's theory directly applies are complex descriptive names such as 'the author of *Waverley*', 'the present King of France', 'the round square cupola on Berkeley College'. Russell analyzes such phrases systematically as fragments of the whole sentences in which they occur. The sentence 'The author of *Waverley* was a poet', for example, is explained as a whole as meaning 'Someone (better: something) wrote *Waverley* and was a poet, and nothing else wrote *Waverley*'. (The point of this added clause is to affirm the uniqueness which is implicit in the word 'the', in '*the* author of *Waverley*'.) The sentence 'The round square cupola on Berkeley College is pink' is explained as 'Something is round and square and is a cupola on Berkeley College and is pink, and nothing else is round and square and a cupola on Berkeley College'.

The virtue of this analysis is that the seeming name, a descriptive phrase, is paraphrased *in context* as a so-called incomplete symbol. No unified expression is offered as an analysis of the descriptive phrase, but the statement as a whole which was the context of that phrase still gets its full quota of meaning—whether true or false.

The unanalyzed statement 'The author of *Waverley* was a poet' contains a part, 'the author of *Waverley*', which is wrongly supposed by McX and Wyman to demand objective reference in order to be meaningful at all. But in Russell's translation, 'Something wrote *Waverley* and was a poet and nothing else wrote *Waverley*', the burden of objective reference which had been put upon the descriptive phrase is now taken over by words of the kind that logicians call bound variables, variables of quantification, namely, words like 'something', 'nothing', 'everything'. These words, far from purporting to be names specifically of the author of *Waverley*, do not purport to be names at all; they refer to entities generally, with a kind of studied ambiguity peculiar to themselves. These quantificational words or bound variables are, of course a basic part of language, and their meaningfulness, at least in context, is not to be challenged. But their meaningfulness in no way presupposes there being either the author of *Waverley* or the round square cupola on Berkeley College or any other specifically preassigned objects.

Where descriptions are concerned, there is no longer any difficulty in affirming or denying being. 'There *is* the author of *Waverley*' is explained by Russell as meaning 'Someone (or, more strictly, something) wrote *Waverley* and nothing else wrote *Waverley*'. 'The author of *Waverley* is not' is explained, correspondingly, as the alternation 'Either each thing failed to write *Waverley* or two or more things wrote *Waverley*'. This alternation is false, but meaningful; and it contains no expression purporting to name the author of *Waverley*. The statement 'The round square cupola on Berkeley College is not' is analyzed in similar fashion. So the old notion that statements of nonbeing defeat themselves goes by the board. When a statement of being or nonbeing is analyzed by Russell's theory of descriptions, it ceases to contain any expression which even purports to name the alleged entity whose being is in question, so that the meaningfulness of the statement no longer can be thought to presuppose that there be such an entity.

Now what of 'Pegasus'? This being a word rather than a descriptive phrase, Russell's argument does not immediately apply to it. However, it can easily be made to apply. We have only to rephrase 'Pegasus' as a description, in any way that seems adequately to single out our idea; say, 'the winged horse that was captured by Bellerophon'. Substituting such a phrase for 'Pegasus', we can then proceed to analyze the statement 'Pegasus is', or 'Pegasus is not', precisely on the analogy of Russell's analysis of 'The author of *Waverley* is' and 'The author of *Waverley* is not'.

In order thus to subsume a one-word name or alleged name such as 'Pegasus' under Russell's theory of description, we must, of course, be able first to translate the word into a description. But this is no real restriction. If the notion of Pegasus had been so obscure or so basic a one that no pat translation into a descriptive phrase had offered itself along familiar lines, we could still have availed ourselves of the following artificial and trivial-seeming device: we could have appealed to the *ex hypothesi* unanalyzable, irreducible attribute of *being Pegasus,* adopting, for its expression, the verb 'is-Pegasus', or 'pegasizes'. The noun 'Pegasus' itself could then be treated as derivative, and identified after all with a description: 'the thing that is-Pegasus', 'the thing that pegasizes'.[2]

If the importing of such a predicate as 'pegasizes' seems to commit us to recognizing that there is a corresponding attribute, pegasizing, in Plato's heaven or in the minds of men, well and good. Neither we nor Wyman nor McX have been contending, thus far, about the being or nonbeing of universals, but rather about that of Pegasus. If in terms of pegasizing we can interpret the noun 'Pegasus' as a description subject to Russell's theory of descriptions, then we have disposed of the old notion that Pegasus cannot be said not to be without presupposing that in some sense Pegasus is.

Our argument is now quite general. McX and Wyman supposed that we could not meaningfully affirm a statement of the form 'So-and-so is not', with a simple or descriptive singular noun in place of 'so-and-so', unless so-and-so is. This supposition is now seen to be quite generally groundless, since the singular noun in question can always be expanded into a singular description, trivially or otherwise, and then analyzed out *à la* Russell.

We commit ourselves to an ontology containing numbers when we say there are prime numbers larger than a million; we commit ourselves to an ontology containing centaurs when we say there are centaurs; and we commit ourselves to an ontology containing Pegasus when we say Pegasus is. But we do not commit ourselves to an ontology containing Pegasus or the author of *Waverley* or the round square cupola on Berkeley College when we say that Pegasus or the author of *Waverley* or the cupola in question is *not*. We need no longer labor under the delusion that the meaningfulness of a statement containing a singular term presupposes an entity named by the term. A singular term need not name to be significant.

An inkling of this might have dawned on Wyman and McX even without benefit of Russell if they had only noticed—as so few of us do—that there is a gulf between *meaning* and *naming* even in the case of a singular term which is genuinely a name of an object. The following example from Frege (this volume, pp. 21–32) will serve. The phrase 'Evening Star' names a certain large physical object of spherical form, which is hurtling through space some scores of millions of miles from here. The phrase 'Morning Star' names the same thing, as was probably first established by some observant Babylonian. But the two phrases cannot be regarded as having the same meaning; otherwise that Babylonian could have dispensed with his observations and contented himself with reflecting on the meanings of his words. The meanings, then, being different from one another, must be other than the named object, which is one and the same in both cases.

Confusion of meaning with naming not only made McX think he could not meaningfully repudiate Pegasus; a continuing confusion of meaning with naming no doubt helped engender his absurd notion that Pegasus is an idea, a mental entity. The structure of his confusion is as follows. He confused the alleged *named object* Pegasus with the *meaning* of the word 'Pegasus', therefore concluding that Pegasus must be in order that the word have meaning. But what sorts of things are meanings? This is a moot point; however, one might quite plausibly explain meanings as ideas in the mind, supposing we can make clear sense in turn of the idea of ideas in the mind. Therefore Pegasus, initially confused with a meaning, ends up as an idea in the mind. It is the more remarkable that Wyman, subject to the same initial motivation as McX, should have avoided this particular blunder and wound tip with unactualized possibles instead.

Now let us turn to the ontological problem of universals: the question whether there are such enti-

ties as attributes, relations, classes, numbers, functions. McX, characteristically enough, thinks there
are. Speaking of attributes, he says: "There are red
houses, red roses, red sunsets; this much is prephilo-
sophical common sense in which we must all agree.
These houses, roses, and sunsets, then, have something in common; and this which they have in common is all I mean by the attribute of redness." For
McX, thus, there being attributes is even more obvious and trivial than the obvious and trivial fact of
there being red houses, roses, and sunsets. This, I
think, is characteristic of metaphysics, or at least of
that part of metaphysics called ontology: one who
regards a statement on this subject as true at all must
regard it as trivially true. One's ontology is basic to
the conceptual scheme by which he interprets all experiences, even the most commonplace ones. Judged
within some particular conceptual scheme—and how
else is judgment possible?—an ontological statement
goes without saying, standing in need of no separate
justification at all. Ontological statements follow immediately from all manner of casual statements of
commonplace fact, just as—from the point of view,
anyway, of McX's conceptual scheme—'There is an
attribute' follows from 'There are red houses, red
roses, red sunsets'.

Judged in another conceptual scheme, an ontological statement which is axiomatic to McX's
mind may, with equal immediacy and triviality, be
adjudged false. One may admit that there are red
houses, roses, and sunsets, but deny, except as a
popular and misleading manner of speaking, that
they have anything in common. The words 'houses',
'roses', and 'sunsets' are true of sundry individual
entities which are houses and roses and sunsets, and
the word 'red' or 'red object' is true of each of
sundry individual entities which are red houses, red
roses, red sunsets; but there is not, in addition, any
entity whatever, individual or otherwise, which is
named by the word 'redness', nor, for that matter,
by the word 'househood', 'rosehood', 'sunsethood'.
That the houses and roses and sunsets are all of them
red may be taken as ultimate and irreducible, and it
may be held that McX is no better off, in point of
real explanatory power, for all the occult entities
which he posits under such names as 'redness'.

One means by which McX might naturally have
tried to impose his ontology of universals on us was

already removed before we turned to the problem of
universals. McX cannot argue that predicates such as
'red' or 'is-red', which we all concur in using, must
be regarded as names each of a single universal entity in order that they be meaningful at all. For we
have seen that being a name of something is a much
more special feature than being meaningful. He cannot even charge us—at least not by *that* argument—
with having posited an attribute of pegasizing by our
adoption of the predicate 'pegasizes'.

However, McX hits upon a different stratagem.
"Let us grant," he says, "this distinction between
meaning and naming of which you make so much.
Let us even grant that 'is red' 'pegasizes', etc., are
not names of attributes. Still, you admit they have
meanings. But these *meanings,* whether they are
named or not, are still universals, and I venture to
say that some of them might even be the very things
that I call attributes, or something to much the same
purpose in the end."

For McX, this is an unusually penetrating speech;
and the only way I know to counter it is by refusing
to admit meanings. However, I feel no reluctance
toward refusing to admit meanings, for I do not
thereby deny that words and statements are meaningful. McX and I may agree to the letter in our classification of linguistic forms into the meaningful and
the meaningless, even though McX construes meaningfulness as the *having* (in some sense of 'having')
of some abstract entity which he calls a meaning,
whereas I do not. I remain free to maintain that the
fact that a given linguistic utterance is meaningful
(or *significant,* as I prefer to say so as not to invite
hypostasis of meanings as entities) is an ultimate and
irreducible matter of fact; or, I may undertake to analyze it in terms directly of what people do in the
presence of the linguistic utterance in question and
other utterances similar to it.

The useful ways in which people ordinarily talk
or seem to talk about meanings boil down to two:
the *having* of meanings, which is significance, and
sameness of meaning, or synonymy. What is called
giving the meaning of an utterance is simply the uttering of a synonym, couched, ordinarily, in clearer
language than the original. If we are allergic to
meanings as such, we can speak directly of utterances
as significant or insignificant, and as synonymous
or heteronymous one with another. The problem of

explaining these adjectives 'significant' and 'synonymous' with some degree of clarity and rigor—preferably, as I see it, in terms of behavior—is as difficult as it is important. But the explanatory value of special and irreducible intermediary entities called meanings is surely illusory.

Up to now I have argued that we can use singular terms significantly in sentences without presupposing that there are the entities which those terms purport to name. I have argued further that we can use general terms, for example, predicates, without conceding them to be names of abstract entities. I have argued further that we can view utterances as significant, and as synonymous or heteronymous with one another, without countenancing a realm of entities called meanings. At this point McX begins to wonder whether there is any limit at all to our ontological immunity. Does *nothing* we may say commit us to the assumption of universals or other entities which we may find unwelcome?

I have already suggested a negative answer to this question, in speaking of bound variables, or variables of quantification, in connection with Russell's theory of descriptions. We can very easily involve ourselves in ontological commitments by saying, for example, that *there is something* (bound variable) which red houses and sunsets have in common; or that *there is something* which is a prime number larger than a million. But this is, essentially, the *only* way we can involve ourselves in ontological commitments: by our use of bound variables. The use of alleged names is no criterion, for we can repudiate their namehood at the drop of a hat unless the assumption of a corresponding entity can be spotted in the things we affirm in terms of bound variables. Names are, in fact, altogether immaterial to the ontological issue, for I have shown, in connection with 'Pegasus' and 'pegasize', that names can be converted to descriptions, and Russell has shown that descriptions can be eliminated. Whatever we say with the help of names can be said in a language which shuns names altogether. To be assumed as an entity is, purely and simply, to be reckoned as the value of a variable. In terms of the categories of traditional grammar, this amounts roughly to saying that to be is to be in the range of reference of a pronoun. Pronouns are the basic media of reference; nouns might better have been named propronouns.

The variables of quantification, 'something', 'nothing', 'everything', range over our whole ontology, whatever it may be; and we are convicted of a particular ontological presupposition if, and only if, the alleged presuppositum has to be reckoned among the entities over which our variables range in order to render one of our affirmations true.

We may say, for example, that some dogs are white and not thereby commit ourselves to recognizing either doghood or whiteners as entities. 'Some dogs are white' says that some things that are dogs are white; and, in order that this statement be true, the things over which the bound variable 'something' ranges must include some white dogs, but need not include doghood or whiteness. On the other hand, when we say that some zoölogical species are cross-fertile we are committing ourselves to recognizing as entities the several species themselves, abstract though they are. We remain so committed at least until we devise some way of so paraphrasing the statement as to show that the seeming reference to species on the part of our bound variable was an avoidable manner of speaking.

Classical mathematics, as the example of primes larger than a million clearly illustrates, is up to its neck in commitments to an ontology of abstract entities. Thus it is that the great mediaeval controversy over universals has flared up anew in the modern philosophy of mathematics. The issue is clearer now than of old, because we now have a more explicit standard whereby to decide what ontology a given theory or form of discourse is committed to: a theory is committed to those and only those entities to which the bound variables of the theory must be capable of referring in order that the affirmations made in the theory be true.

Because this standard of ontological presupposition did not emerge clearly in the philosophical tradition, the modern philosophical mathematicians have not on the whole recognized that they were debating the same old problem of universals in a newly clarified form. But the fundamental cleavages among modern points of view on foundations of mathematics do come down pretty explicitly to disagreements as to the range of entities to which the bound variables should be permitted to refer.

The three main mediaeval points of view regarding universals are designated by historians as *realism, conceptualism,* and *nominalism.* Essentially these same three doctrines reappear in twentieth-century surveys of the philosophy of mathematics under the new names *logicism, intuitionism,* and *formalism.*

Realism, as the word is used in connection with the mediaeval controversy over universals, is the Platonic doctrine that universals or abstract entities have being independently of the mind; the mind may discover them but cannot create them. *Logicism,* represented by Frege, Russell, Whitehead, Church, and Carnap, condones the use of bound variables to refer to abstract entities known and unknown, specifiable and unspecifiable, indiscriminately.

Conceptualism holds that there are universals but they are mind-made. *Intuitionism,* espoused in modern times in one form or another by Poincaré, Brouwer, Weyl, and others, countenances the use of bound variables to refer to abstract entities only when those entities are capable of being cooked up individually from ingredients specified in advance. As Fraenkel has put it, logicism holds that classes are discovered while intuitionism holds that they are invented—a fair statement indeed of the old opposition between realism and conceptualism. This opposition is no mere quibble; it makes an essential difference in the amount of classical mathematics to which one is willing to subscribe. Logicists, or realists, are able on their assumptions to get Cantor's ascending orders of infinity; intuitionists are compelled to stop with the lowest order of infinity, and, as an indirect consequence, to abandon even some of the classical laws of real numbers. The modern controversy between logicism and intuitionism arose, in fact, from disagreements over infinity.

Formalism, associated with the name of Hilbert, echoes intuitionism in deploring the logicist's unbridled recourse to universals. But formalism also finds intuitionism unsatisfactory. This could happen for either of two opposite reasons. The formalist might, like the logicist, object to the crippling of classical mathematics; or he might, like the *nominalists* of old, object to admitting abstract entities at all, even in the restrained sense of mind-made entities. The upshot is the same: the formalist keeps classical mathematics as a play of insignificant notations. This play of notations can still be of utility—whatever utility it has already shown itself to have as a crutch for physicists and technologists. But utility need not

imply significance, in any literal linguistic sense. Nor need the marked success of mathematicians in spinning out theorems, and in finding objective bases for agreement with one another's results, imply significance. For an adequate basis for agreement among mathematicians can be found simply in the rules which govern the manipulation of the notations— these syntactical rules being, unlike the notations themselves, quite significant and intelligible.[3]

I have argued that the sort of ontology we adopt can be consequential—notably in connection with mathematics, although this is only an example. Now how are we to adjudicate among rival ontologies? Certainly the answer is not provided by the semantical formula "To be is to be the value of a variable"; this formula serves rather, conversely, in testing the conformity of a given remark or doctrine to a prior ontological standard. We look to bound variables in connection with ontology not in order to know what there is, but in order to know what a given remark or doctrine, ours or someone else's, *says* there is; and this much is quite properly a problem involving language. But what there is is another question.

In debating over what there is, there are still reasons for operating on a semantical plane. One reason is to escape from the predicament noted at the beginning of this essay: the predicament of my not being able to admit that there are things which McX countenances and I do not. So long as I adhere to my ontology, as opposed to McX's, I cannot allow my bound variables to refer to entities which belong to McX's ontology and not to mine. I can, however, consistently describe our disagreement by characterizing the statements which McX affirms. Provided merely that my ontology countenances linguistic forms, or at least concrete inscriptions and utterances, I can talk about McX's sentences.

Another reason for withdrawing to a semantical plane is to find common ground on which to argue. Disagreement in ontology involves basic disagreement in conceptual schemes; yet McX and I, despite these basic disagreements, find that our conceptual schemes converge sufficiently in their intermediate and upper ramifications to enable us to communicate successfully on such topics as politics, weather, and, in particular, language. In so far as our basic controversy over ontology can be translated upward into a semantical controversy about words and what to do with them, the collapse of the controversy into question-begging may be delayed.

It is no wonder, then, that ontological controversy should tend into controversy over language. But we must not jump to the conclusion that what there is depends on words. Translatability of a question into semantical terms is no indication that the question is linguistic. To see Naples is to bear a name which, when prefixed to the words 'sees Naples', yields a true sentence; still there is nothing linguistic about seeing Naples.

Our acceptance of an ontology is, I think, similar in principle to our acceptance of a scientific theory, say a system of physics: we adopt, at least insofar as we are reasonable, the simplest conceptual scheme into which the disordered fragments of raw experience can be fitted and arranged. Our ontology is determined once we have fixed upon the over-all conceptual scheme which is to accommodate science in the broadest sense; and the considerations which determine a reasonable construction of any part of that conceptual scheme, for example, the biological or the physical part, are not different in kind from the considerations which determine a reasonable construction of the whole. To whatever extent the adoption of any system of scientific theory may be said to be a matter of language, the same—but no more—may be said of the adoption of an ontology.

But simplicity, as a guiding principle in constructing conceptual schemes, is not a clear and unambiguous idea; and it is quite capable of presenting a double or multiple standard. Imagine, for example, that we have devised the most economical set of concepts adequate to the play-by-play reporting of immediate experience. The entities under this scheme—the values of bound variables—are, let us suppose, individual subjective events of sensation or reflection. We should still find, no doubt, that a physicalistic conceptual scheme, purporting to talk about external objects, offers great advantages in simplifying our over-all reports. By bringing together scattered sense events and treating them as perceptions of one object, we reduce the complexity of our stream of experience to a manageable conceptual simplicity. The rule of simplicity is indeed our guiding maxim in assigning sense data to objects: we as-

sociate an earlier and a later round sensum with the same so-called penny, or with two different so-called pennies, in obedience to the demands of maximum simplicity in our total world-picture.

Here we have two competing conceptual schemes, a phenomenalistic one and a physicalistic one. Which should prevail? Each has its advantages; each has its special simplicity in its own way. Each, I suggest, deserves to be developed. Each may be said, indeed, to be the more fundamental, though in different senses: the one is epistemologically, the other physically, fundamental.

The physical conceptual scheme simplifies our account of experience because of the way myriad scattered sense events come to be associated with single so-called objects; still there is no likelihood that each sentence about physical objects can actually be translated, however deviously and complexly, into the phenomenalistic language. Physical objects are postulated entities which round out and simplify our account of the flux of experience, just as the introduction of irrational numbers simplifies laws of arithmetic. From the point of view of the conceptual scheme of the elementary arithmetic of rational numbers alone, the broader arithmetic of rational and irrational numbers would have the status of a convenient myth, simpler than the literal truth (namely, the arithmetic of rationals) and yet containing that literal truth as a scattered part. Similarly, from a phenomenalistic point of view, the conceptual scheme of physical objects is a convenient myth, simpler than the literal truth and yet containing that literal truth as a scattered part.[4]

Now what of classes or attributes of physical objects, in turn? A platonistic ontology of this sort is, from the point of view of a strictly physicalistic conceptual scheme, as much a myth as that physicalistic conceptual scheme itself is for phenomenalism. This higher myth is a good and useful one, in turn, in so far as it simplifies our account of physics. Since mathematics is an integral part of this higher myth, the utility of this myth for physical science is evident enough. In speaking of it nevertheless as a myth, I echo that philosophy of mathematics to which I alluded earlier under the name of formalism. But an attitude of formalism may with equal justice be adopted toward the physical conceptual scheme, in turn, by the pure aesthete or phenomenalist.

The analogy between the myth of mathematics and the myth of physics is, in some additional and perhaps fortuitous ways, strikingly close. Consider, for example, the crisis which was precipitated in the foundations of mathematics, at the turn of the century, by the discovery of Russell's paradox and other antinomies of set theory. These contradictions had to be obviated by unintuitive, *ad hoc* devices; our mathematical myth-making became deliberate and evident to all. But what of physics? An antinomy arose between the undular and the corpuscular accounts of light; and if this was not as out-and-out a contradiction as Russell's paradox, I suspect that the reason is that physics is not as out-and-out as mathematics. Again, the second great modern crisis in the foundations of mathematics—precipitated in 1931 by Gödel's proof that there are bound to be undecidable statements in arithmetic—has its companion piece in physics in Heisenberg's indeterminacy principle.

In earlier pages I undertook to show that some common arguments in favor of certain ontologies are fallacious. Further, I advanced an explicit standard whereby to decide what the ontological commitments of a theory are. But the question what ontology actually to adopt still stands open, and the obvious counsel is tolerance and an experimental spirit. Let us by all means see how much of the physicalistic conceptual scheme can be reduced to a phenomenalistic one; still, physics also naturally demands pursuing, irreducible *in toto* though it be. Let us see how, or to what degree, natural science may be rendered independent of platonistic mathematics; but let us also pursue mathematics and delve into its platonistic foundations.

From among the various conceptual schemes best suited to these various pursuits, one—the phenomenalistic—claims epistemological priority. Viewed from within the phenomenalistic conceptual scheme, the ontologies of physical objects and mathematical objects are myths. The quality of myth, however, is relative; relative, in this case, to the epistemological point of view. This point of view is one among various, corresponding to one among our various interests and purposes.

NOTES

1. The impulse to distinguish terminologically between existence as applied to objects actualized somewhere in space-time and existence (or subsistence or being) as applied to other entities arises in part, perhaps, from an idea that the observation of nature is relevant only to questions of existence of the first kind. But this idea is readily refuted by counterinstances such as 'the ratio of the number of centaurs to the number of unicorns'. If there were such a ratio, it would be an abstract entity, viz. a number. Yet it is only by studying nature that we conclude that the number of centaurs and the number of unicorns are both 0 and hence that there is no such ratio.

2. For further remarks on such assimilation of all singular terms to descriptions see . . . Quine, pp. 218–224.

3. See Goodman and Quine. For further discussion of the general matters touched on in the past two pages, see Bernays, Fraenkel, Black.

4. The arithmetical analogy is due to Frank, pp. 108f.

REFERENCES

Bernays, Paul. 1935–36. "Sure le Platonisme dans les Mathémetiques." *L'enseignment Mathématique* 34: 52–69.

Black, Max. 1933. *The Nature of Mathematics.* London: Kegan Paul.

Church, Alonzo. 1936. "A Note on the *Entscheidungsproblem.*" *Journal of Symbolic Logic* 1.

Fraenkel, A. A. 1935–36. "Sur la Notion d'existence dans les Mathématiques." *L'enseignment Mathématique* 34: 18–32.

Frank, Philipp. 1949. *Modern Science and Its Philosophy.* Cambridge: Harvard University Press.

Gödel, Kurt. 1930. "Über Formal unentscheidbare Satze der Principia Mathematica und verwandter Systeme." *Monatshefte für Mathematik und Physik* 37: 173–98.

Goodman, Nelson, and W. V. Quine. 1947. Steps towards a Constructive Nominalism. *Journal of Symbolic Logic* 12: 105–22.

Quine, W. V. 1950. *Methods of Logic.* 1st ed. New York: Holt.

11   The Identity of Indiscernibles

MAX BLACK

A. THE PRINCIPLE of the Identity of Indiscernibles seems to me obviously true. And I don't see how we are going to define identity or establish the connexion between mathematics and logic without using it.

B. It seems to me obviously false. And your troubles as a mathematical logician are beside the point. If the principle is false you have no right to use it.

A. You simply *say* it's false—and even if you said so three times that wouldn't make it so.

B. Well, you haven't done anything more yourself than assert the principle to be true. As Bradley once said, "assertion can demand no more than counter-assertion; and what is affirmed on the one side, we on the other can simply deny".

A. How will this do for an argument? If two things, *a* and *b,* are given, the first has the property of being identical with *a.* Now *b* cannot have this property, for else *b* would be *a,* and we should have only one thing, not two as assumed. Hence *a* has at least one property, which *b* does not have, that is to say the property of being identical with *a.*

B. This is a roundabout way of saying nothing, for "*a* has the property of being identical with *a*" means no more than "*a* is *a*". When you begin to say "*a* is . . ." I am supposed to know what thing you are referring to as "*a*" and I expect to be told something about that thing. But when you end the sentence with the words ". . . is *a*" I am left still waiting. The sentence "*a* is *a*" is a useless tautology.

A. Are you as scornful about difference as about identity? For *a* also has, and *b* does not have, the property of being different from *b.* This is a second property that the one thing has but not the other.

B. All you are saying is that *b* is different from *a.* I think the form of words "*a* is different from *b*" does have the advantage over "*a* is *a*" that it might be used to give information. I might learn from hearing it used that "*a*" and "*b*" were applied to dif-

ferent things. But this is not what you want to say, since you are trying to use the names, not mention them. When I already know what "*a*" and "*b*" stand for, "*a* is different from *b*" tells me nothing. It, too, is a useless tautology.

A. I wouldn't have expected you to treat "tautology" as a term of abuse. Tautology or not, the sentence has a philosophical use. It expresses the necessary truth that different things have at least one property not in common. Thus different things must be discernible; and hence, by contraposition, indiscernible things must be identical. Q.E.D.

B. Why obscure matters by this old-fashioned language? By "indiscernible" I suppose you mean the same as "having all properties in common". Do you claim to have proved that two things having all their properties in common are identical?

A. Exactly.

B. Then this is a poor way of stating your conclusion. If *a* and *b* are identical, there is just one thing having the two names "*a*" and "*b*"; and in that case it is absurd to say that *a* and *b* are two. Conversely, once you have supposed there are *two* things having all their properties in common, you can't without contradicting yourself say that *they* are "identical".

A. I can't believe you were really misled. I simply meant to say it is logically impossible for two things to have all their properties in common. I showed that *a* must have at least two properties—the property of being identical with *a,* and the property of being, different from *b*—neither of which can be a property of *b.* Doesn't this prove the principle of Identity of Indiscernibles?

B. Perhaps you have proved something. If so, the nature of your proof should show us exactly what you have proved. If you want to call "being identical with *a*" a "property" I suppose I can't prevent you. But you must then accept the consequences of

Mind 66 (1952). Reprinted by permission of *Mind*.

this way of talking. All you mean when you say "*a* has the property of being identical with *a*" is that *a* is *a*. And all you mean when you say "*b* does not have the property of being identical with *a*" is that *b* is not *a*. So what you have "proved" is that *a* is *a* and *b* is not *a*, that is to say, *b* and *a* are different. Similarly, when you said that *a*, but not *b*, had the property of being different from *b*, you were simply saying that *a* and *b* were different. In fact you are merely re-describing the hypothesis that *a* and *b* are different by calling it a case of "difference of properties". Drop the misleading description and your famous principle reduces to the truism that different things are different. How true! And how uninteresting!

A. Well, the properties of identity and difference may be uninteresting, but they *are* properties. If I had shown that grass was green, I suppose you would say I hadn't shown that grass was coloured.

B. You certainly would not have shown that grass had any colour *other than* green.

A. What it comes to is that you object to the conclusion of my argument *following* from the premise that *a* and *b* are different.

B. No, I object to the triviality of the conclusion. If you want to have an interesting principle to defend, you must interpret "property" more narrowly—enough so, at any rate, for "identity" and "difference" not to count as properties.

A. Your notion of an interesting principle seems to be one which I shall have difficulty in establishing. Will you at least allow me to include among "properties" what are sometimes called "relational characteristics"—like *being married to Caesar or being at a distance from London?*

B. Why not? If you are going to defend the principle, it is for you to decide what version you wish to defend.

A. In that case, I don't need to count identity and difference as properties. Here is a different argument that seems to me quite conclusive. The only way we can discover that two different things exist is by finding out that one has a quality not possessed by the other or else that one has a relational characteristic that the other hasn't.

If *both* are blue and hard and sweet and so on, and have the same shape and dimensions and are in the same relations to everything in the universe, it is logically impossible to tell them apart. The sup-

position that in such a case there might really be two things would be unverifiable *in principle*. Hence it would be meaningless.

B. You are going too fast for me.

A. Think of it this way. If the principle were false, the fact that I can see only two of your hands would be no proof that you had just two. And even if every conceivable test agreed with the supposition that you had two hands, you might all the time have three, four, or any number. You might have nine hands, different from one another and all indistinguishable from your left hand, and nine more all different from each other but indistinguishable from your right hand. And even if you really did have just two hands, and no more, neither you nor I nor anybody else could ever know that fact. This is too much for me to swallow. This is the kind of absurdity you get into, as soon as you abandon verifiability as a test of meaning.

B. Far be it from me to abandon your sacred cow. Before I give you a direct answer, let me try to describe a counter-example.

Isn't it logically possible that the universe should have contained nothing but two exactly similar spheres? We might suppose that each was made of chemically pure iron, had a diameter of one mile, that they had the same temperature, colour, and so on, and that nothing else existed. Then every quality and relational characteristic of the one would also be a property of the other. Now if what I am describing is logically possible, it is not impossible for two things to have all their properties in common. Seems to me to *refute* the Principle.

A. Your supposition, I repeat, isn't verifiable and therefore can't be regarded as meaningful. But supposing you *have* described a possible world, I still don't see that you have refuted the principle. Consider one of the spheres, *a*. . . .

B. How can I, since there is no way of telling them apart? *Which* one do you want me to consider?

A. This is very foolish. I mean either of the two spheres, leaving you to decide which one you wished to consider. If I were to say to you "Take any book off the shelf" it would be foolish on your part to reply "Which?"

B. It's a poor analogy. I know how to take a book off a shelf, but I don't know how to identify one of two spheres supposed to be alone in space and so symmetrically placed with respect to each other that neither has any quality or character the other does not also have.

A. All of which goes to show as I said before, the unverifiability of your supposition. Can't you imagine that one sphere has been designated as "*a*"?

B. I can imagine only what is logically possible. Now it is logically possible that somebody should enter the universe I have described, see one of the spheres on his left hand and proceed to call it "*a*". I can imagine that all right, if that's enough to satisfy you.

A. Very well, now let me try to finish what I began to say about *a*. . . .

B. I still can't let you, because you, in your present situation, have no right to talk about *a*. All I have conceded is that if something were to happen to introduce a change into my universe, so that an observer entered and could see the two spheres, one of them could then have a name. But this would be a different supposition from the one I wanted to consider. My spheres don't yet have names. If an observer were to enter the scene, he could perhaps put a red mark on one of the spheres. You might just as well say "By '*a*' I mean the sphere which would be the first to be marked by a red mark if anyone were to arrive and were to proceed to make a red mark!" You might just as well ask me to consider the first daisy in my lawn that would be picked by a child, if a child were to come along and do the picking. This doesn't now distinguish any daisy from the others. You are just pretending to use a name.

A. And I think you are just pretending not to understand me. All I am asking you to do is to think of one of your spheres, no matter which, so that I may go on to say something about it when you give me a chance.

B. You talk as if naming an object and then thinking about it were the easiest thing in the world. But it isn't so easy. Suppose I tell you to name any spider in my garden: if you can catch one first or describe one uniquely you can name it easily enough. But you can't pick one out, let alone "name" it, by just thinking. You remind me of the mathematicians who thought that talking about an Axiom of Choice would really allow them to choose a single member of a collection when they had no criterion of choice.

A. At this rate you will never give me a chance to say anything. Let me try to make my point without using names. Each of the spheres will surely differ from the other in being at some distance from that other one, but at no distance from itself—that is to say, it will bear at least one relation to itself—*being at no distance from,* or *being in the same place as*—that it does not bear to the other. And this will serve to distinguish it from the other.

B. Not at all. *Each* will have the relational characteristic *being at a distance of two miles,* say, *from the centre of a sphere one mile in diameter,* etc. And each will have the relational characteristic (if you want to call it that) of *being in the same place as itself.* The two are alike in this respect as in all others.

A. But look here. Each sphere occupies a different place; and this at least will distinguish them from one another.

B. This sounds as if you thought the places had some independent existence, though I don't suppose you really think so. To say the spheres are in "different places" is just to say that there is a distance between the two spheres; and we have already seen that will not serve to distinguish them. Each is at a distance—indeed the same distance—from the other.

A. When I said they were at different places I didn't mean simply that they were at a distance from one another. That one sphere is in a certain place does not entail the existence of any *other* sphere. So to say that one sphere is in its place, and the other in its place, and then to add that these places are different seems to me different from saying the spheres are at a distance from one another.

B. What does it mean to say "a sphere is in its place"? Nothing at all, so far as I can see. Where else could it be? *All* you are saying is that the spheres are in different places.

A. Then my retort is, What does it mean to say "Two spheres are in different places"? Or, as you so neatly put it, "Where else could they be?"

B. You have a point. What I should have said was that your assertion that the spheres occupied different places said nothing at all, unless you were drawing attention to the necessary truth that different physical objects must be in different places. Now if two spheres must be in different places, as indeed they must, to say that the spheres occupy different places is to say no more than they are two spheres.

A. This is like a point you made before. You won't allow me to deduce anything from the supposition that there are two spheres.

B. Let me put it another way. In the two-sphere universe, the only reason for saying that the places occupied were different would be that different things occupied them. So in order to show the places were different you would first have to show, in some other way, that the spheres were different. You will never be able to distinguish the spheres by means of the places they occupy.

A. A minute ago, you were willing to allow that somebody might give your spheres different names. Will you let me suppose that some traveller has visited your monotonous "universe" and has named one sphere "Castor" and the other "Pollux"?

B. All right—provided you don't try to use those names yourself.

A. Wouldn't the traveller, at least, have to recognise that *being at a distance of two miles from Castor* was not the same property as being at a distance of two miles *from Pollux*?

B. I don't see why. If he were to see that Castor and Pollux had exactly the same properties, he would see that "being at a distance of two miles from Castor" meant exactly the same as "being at a distance of two miles from Pollux".

A. They couldn't mean the same. If they did, "*being at a distance of two miles from Castor and at the same time not being at a distance of two miles from Pollux*" would be a self-contradictory description. But plenty of bodies could answer to this description. Again if the two expressions meant the same, anything which was two miles from Castor would have to be two miles from Pollux—which is clearly false. So the two expressions don't mean the same and the two spheres have at least two properties not in common.

B. Which?

A. Being at a distance of two miles from Castor and *being at a distance of two miles from Pollux.*

B. But now you are *using* the words "Castor" and "Pollux" as if they really stood for something. They are just our old friends "*a*" and "*b*" in disguise.

A. You surely don't want to say that the arrival of the name-giving traveller creates spatial properties? Perhaps we can't name your spheres and therefore can't name the corresponding properties; but the properties must be there.

B. What can this mean? The traveller has not visited the spheres, and the spheres have no names —neither "Castor", nor "Pollux", nor "*a*", nor "*b*",

nor any others. Yet you still want to say they have certain properties which cannot be referred to without using names for the spheres. You want to say "the property of being at a distance from Castor" though it is logically impossible for you to talk in this way. You can't speak, but you won't be silent.

A. How eloquent, and how unconvincing! But since you seem to have convinced yourself, at least, perhaps you can explain another thing that bothers me: I don't see that you have a right to talk as you do about places or spatial relations in connexion with your so-called "universe". So long as we are talking about our own universe—*the* universe—I know what you mean by "distance", "diameter", "place" and so on. But in what you want to call a universe, even though it contains only two objects, I don't see what such words could mean. So far as I can see, you are applying these spatial terms in their present usage to a hypothetical situation which contradicts the presuppositions of that usage.

B. What do you mean by "presupposition"?

A. Well, you spoke of measured distances, for one thing. Now this presupposes some means of measurement. Hence your "universe" must contain at least a third thing—a ruler or some other measuring device.

B. Are you claiming that a universe must have at least three things in it? What is the least number of things required to make a world?

A. No, all I am saying is that you cannot describe a configuration as *spatial* unless it includes at least three objects. This is part of the meaning of "spatial"—and it is no more mysterious than saying you can't have a game of chess without there existing at least thirty-five things (thirty-two pieces, a chessboard, and two players).

B. If this is all that bothers you, I can easily provide for three or any number of things without changing the force of my counter-example. The important thing, for my purpose, was that the configuration of two spheres was symmetrical. So long as we preserve this feature of the imaginary universe, we can now allow any number of objects to be found in it.

A. You mean any *even* number of objects.

B. Quite right. Why not imagine a plane running clear through space, with everything that happens on one side of it always exactly duplicated at an equal distance in the other side.

A. A kind of cosmic mirror producing real images.

B. Yes, except that there wouldn't be any mirror! The point is that in *this* world we can imagine any degree of complexity and chance to occur. No reason to exclude rulers, compasses, and weighing machines. No reason, for that matter, why the Battle of Waterloo shouldn't happen.

A. Twice over, you mean—with Napoleon surrendering later in two different places simultaneously!

B. Provided you wanted to call both of them "Napoleon."

A. So your point is that everything could be duplicated on the other side of the non-existent Looking Glass. I suppose whenever a man got married, his identical twin would be marrying the identical twin of the first man's fiancée?

B. Exactly.

A. Except that "identical twins" wouldn't be *numerically* identical?

B. You seem to be agreeing with me.

A. Far from it. This is just a piece of gratuitous metaphysics. If the inhabitants of your world had enough sense to know what was sense and what wasn't, they would never suppose all the events in their world were duplicated. It would be much more sensible for them to regard the "second" Napoleon as a mere mirror image—and similarly for all the other supposed "duplicates".

B. But they could walk through the "mirror" and find water just as wet, sugar just as sweet, and grass just as green on the other side.

A. You don't understand me. They would not postulate "another side". A man looking at the "mirror" would be seeing *himself*, not a duplicate. If he walked in a straight line toward the "mirror" he would eventually find himself back at his starting point, not at a duplicate of his starting point. This would involve their having a different geometry from ours—but that would be preferable to the logician's nightmare of the reduplicated universe.

B. They might think so—until the twins really began to behave differently for the first time!

A. Now it's you who are tinkering with your supposition. You can't have your universe and change it too.

B. All right, I retract.

A. The more I think about your "universe" the queerer it seems. What would happen when a man crossed your invisible "mirror"? While he was actually crossing, his body would have to change shape, in order to preserve the symmetry. Would it gradually shrink to nothing and then expand again?

B. I confess I hadn't thought of that.

A. And here is something that explodes the whole notion. Would you say that one of the two Napoleons in your universe had his heart in the right place—literally, I mean?

B. Why, of course.

A. In that case his "mirror-image" twin would have the heart on the opposite side of the body. One Napoleon would have his heart on the left of his body, and the other would have it on the right of his body.

B. It's a good point, though it would still make objects like spheres indistinguishable. But let me try again. Let me abandon the original idea of a *plane* of symmetry and to suppose instead that we have only a *centre* of symmetry. I mean that everything that happened at any place would be exactly duplicated at a place an equal distance on the opposite side of the centre of symmetry. In short, the universe would be what the mathematicians call "radially symmetrical". And to avoid complications we could suppose that the centre of symmetry itself was physically inaccessible, so that it would be impossible for any material body to pass through it. Now in *this* universe, identical twins would have to be either both right-handed or both left-handed.

A. Your universes are beginning to be as plentiful as blackberries. You are too ingenuous to see the force of my argument about verifiability. Can't you see that your supposed description of a universe in which everything has its "identical twin" doesn't describe anything verifably different from a corresponding universe without such duplication? This must be so, no matter what kind of symmetry your universe manifested.

B. You are assuming that in order to verify that there are two things of a certain kind, it must be possible to show that one has a property not possessed by the other. But this is not so. A pair of very close but similar magnetic poles produce a characteristic field of force which assures me that there are two poles, even if I have no way of examining them separately. The presence of two exactly similar stars at a great distance might be detected by some resultant gravitational effect or by optical interference—or in some such similar way—even though we had no way of inspecting one in isolation from the other. Don't physicists say something like this about the electrons inside an atom? We can verify *that* there are two, that is to say a certain property of the whole configuration, even though there is no way of detecting any character that uniquely characterises any element of the configuration.

A. But if you were to approach your two stars one would have to be on your left and one on the right. And this would distinguish them.

B. I agree. Why shouldn't we say that the two stars are distinguishable—meaning that it would be possible for an observer to see one on his left and the other on his right, or more generally, that it would be *possible* for one star to come to have a relation to a third object that the second star would not have to that third object.

A. So you agree with me after all.

B. Not if you mean that the two stars do not have all their properties in common. All I said was that it was logically possible for them to enter into different relationships with a third object. But this would be a change in the universe.

A. If you are right, nothing unobserved would be observable. For the presence of an observer would always change it, and the observation would always be an observation of something else.

B. I don't say that every observation changes what is observed. My point is that there isn't any *being to the right* or *being to the left* in the two-sphere universe until an observer is introduced, that is to say until a real change is made.

A. But the spheres themselves wouldn't have changed.

B. Indeed they would: they would have acquired new relational characteristics. In the absence of any asymmetric observer, I repeat, the spheres would have all their properties in common (including, if you like, the power to enter into different relations with other objects). Hence the principle of Identity of Indiscernibles is false.

A. So perhaps you really do have twenty hands after all?

B. Not a bit of it. Nothing that I have said prevents me from holding that we can verify *that* there are exactly two. But we could know *that* two things existed without there being any way to distinguish one from the other. The Principle is false.

A. I am not surprised that you ended in this way, since you assumed it in the description of your fantastic "universe". Of course, if you began by assuming that the spheres were numerically different though qualitatively alike, you could end by "proving" what you first assumed.

B. But I wasn't "proving" anything. I tried to support my contention that it is logically possible for two things to have all their properties in common by giving an illustrative description. (Similarly, if I had to show it is logically possible for nothing at all to be seen I would ask you to imagine a universe in which everybody was blind.) It was for you to show that my description concealed some hidden contradiction. And you haven't done so.

A. All the same I am not convinced.

B. Well, then, you ought to be.

On the Elements of Being   12

DONALD C. WILLIAMS

FIRST PHILOSOPHY, according to the traditional schedule, is analytic ontology, examining the traits necessary to whatever is, in this or any other possible world. Its cardinal problem is that of substance and attribute, or at any rate something cognate with this in that family of ideas which contains also subsistence and inherence, subject and predicate, particular and universal, singular and general, individual and class, and matter and form. It is the question how a thing can be an instance of many properties

The Review of Metaphysics 7, 1953. Reprinted by permission of *The Review of Metaphysics*.

while a property may inhere in many instances, the question how everything is a *case* of a *kind*, a this-such, an essence endowed with existence, an existent differentiated by essence, and so forth. Concerned with what it means to be a thing or a kind at all, it is in some wise prior to and independent of the other great branch of metaphysics, speculative cosmology: what kinds of things are there, what stuff are they made of, how are they strung together? Although "analytic ontology" is not much practiced as a unit under that name today, its problems, and especially the problem of subsistence and inherence, are as much alive in the latest manifestoes of the logical analysts, who pretend to believe neither in substances nor in universals, as they were in the counsels of Athens and of Paris. Nothing is clear until that topic is clear, and in this essay[1] I hope to do something to clarify it in terms of a theory or schema which over a good many years I have found so serviceable that it may well be true.

Metaphysics is the thoroughly empirical science. Every item of experience must be evidence for or against any hypothesis of speculative cosmology, and every experienced object must be an exemplar and test case for the categories of analytic ontology. Technically, therefore, one example ought for our present theme to be as good as another. The more dignified examples, however, are darkened with a patina of tradition and partisanship, while some frivolous ones are peculiarly perspicuous. Let us therefore imagine three lollipops, made by a candy man who buys sticks from a big supplier and molds candy knobs on them. Lollipop No. 1 has a red round peppermint head, No. 2 a brown round chocolate head, No. 3 a red square peppermint head. The circumstance here which mainly provokes theories of subsistence and inherence is similarity with difference: each lollipop is partially similar to each other and partially different from it. If we can give a good account of this circumstance in this affair we shall have the instrument to expose the anatomy of everything, from an electron or an apple to archangels and the World All.

My chief proposal to that end may be put, to begin with, as nothing more tremendous than that we admit literally and seriously that to say that *a* is partially similar to *b* is to say that a part of *a* is wholly or completely similar to a part of *b*. This is a truism when we construe it with respect to ordinary con-crete parts, for example, the sticks in the lollipops. On physical grounds, to be sure, it is not likely that any three solid objects, not even three sticks turned out by mass industry, are exactly similar, but they often look as if they were, and we can intelligibly stipulate for our argument that our exemplary sticks do exactly resemble each other through and through. To say then that each of the lollipops is partially similar to each other, that is, with respect to stick, is to say that there is a stick in each which is perfectly similar to the stick in every other, even though each stick remains as particular and distinct an individual as the whole lollipop. We would seldom give a proper name to a lollipop, and still more seldom to the stick in one, but we might easily do so—"Heraplem" for lollipop No. 1, for example, "Paraplete" for its stick, "Boanerp" for No. 2 and "Merrinel" for its stick. Heraplem and Boanerp then are partially similar because Paraplete and Merrinel are perfectly similar.

But what now of the rest of each lollipop and what of their more subtle similarities, of color, shape, and flavor? My proposal is that we treat them in exactly the same way. Since we can not find more parts of the usual gross sort, like the stick, to be wholly similar from lollipop to lollipop, let us discriminate subtler and thinner or more diffuse parts till we find some of these which *are* wholly similar. This odd-sounding assignment, of course, is no more than we are accustomed to do, easily and without noticing. Just as we can distinguish in the lollipops Heraplem and Boanerp the gross parts called "sticks," namely, Paraplete and Merrinel, so we can distinguish in each lollipop a finer part which we are used to call its "color" and another called its "shape"—not its kind of color or shape, mind you, but these particular cases, this reddening, this occurrence or occasion of roundness, each as uniquely itself as a man, an earth-quake, or a yell. With only a little more hardihood than christened the lollipops and sticks we can christen our finer components: "Harlac" and "Bantic" for the respective color components, let us say, and "Hamis" and "Borcas" for the respective shape components. In these four new names the first and last letters are initials of "Heraplem" and "Boanerp," and of "color" and "shape," respectively, but this is a mnemonic device for us, irrelevant to their force as names. "Harlac," for example, is not to be taken as an abbreviation for the description, "the color component of Heraplem." In a real situation like the one we are imagining, "Harlac" is defined ostensively, as one baptizes a child or introduces a man, present in the flesh; the descriptive phrase is only a scaffolding, a temporary device to bring attention to bear on the particular entity being denoted, as a mother of twins might admonish the vicar, "Boadicea is the cross-looking one." Heraplem and Boanerp are partially similar, then, not merely because the respective gross parts Paraplete and Merrinel (their sticks) are wholly similar, but also because the respective fine parts, Hamis and Borcas (their "shapes"), are wholly similar—all this without prejudice to the fact that Hamis is numerically as distinct from Borcas, to which it is wholly similar, and from Harlac, with which it is conjoined in Heraplem, as Harlac is from Bantic to which it is neither similar nor conjoined, and as the stick Paraplete is from the stick Merrinel, and as the whole lollipop, Heraplem, is from the whole Boanerp. The sense in which Heraplem and Boanerp "have the same shape," and in which "the shape of one is identical with the shape of the other," is the sense in which two soldiers "wear the same uniform" or in which a son "has his father's nose" or our candy man might say "I use the same identical stick, Ledbetter's Triple-X, in all my lollipops." They do not "have the same shape" in the sense in which two children "have the same father," or two streets have the same manhole in the middle of their intersection, or two college boys "wear the same tuxedo" (and so can't go to dances together). But while similar in the indicated respects, Heraplem and Boanerp are partially dissimilar in as much as their knobs or heads are partially dissimilar, and these are partially dissimilar because some of their finer parts, for example, Harlac and Bantic, their colors, are dissimilar.

In like manner, to proceed, we note that Harlac, the color component of No. (Heraplem), though numerically distinct from, is wholly similar to the color component of No. 3. But No. 1 has not only a color component which is perfectly similar to the color component of No. 3; it has also a flavor component perfectly similar to the flavor component of No. 3. (It does not matter whether we think of the flavor as a phenomenal quality or as a molecular structure in the stuff of the candy.) The flavor-plus-color of No. 1 (and likewise of No. 3) is a complex whose own constituents are the flavor and the color, and so on for innumerable selections and combinations of parts, both gross and fine, which are embedded in any one such object or any collection thereof.

Crucial here, of course, is the admission of a "fine" or "subtle" part, a "diffuse" or "permeant" one, such as a resident color or occurrent shape, to at least as good standing among the actual and individual items of the world's furniture as a "gross" part, such as a stick. The fact that one part is thus finer and more diffuse than another, and that it is more susceptible of similarity, no more militates against its individual actuality than the fact that mice are smaller and more numerous than elephants makes them any the less real. To borrow now an old but pretty appropriate term, a gross part, like the stick, is "concrete," as the whole lollipop is, while a fine or diffuse part, like the color component or shape component, is "abstract." The color-cum-shape is less abstract or more concrete or more nearly concrete than the color alone but it is more abstract or less concrete than color-plus-shape-plus-flavor, and so on up till we get to the total complex which is wholly concrete.

I propose now that entities like our fine parts or abstract components are the primary constituents of this or any possible world, the very alphabet of being. They not only are actual but are the only actualities, in just this sense, that whereas entities of all other categories are literally composed of them, they are not in general composed of any other sort of entity. That such a crucial category has no regular name is quite characteristic of first principles and is part of what makes the latter worth pursuing. A description of it in good old phraseology has a paradoxical ring: our thin parts are "abstract particulars."[2] We shall have occasion to use "parts" for concreta and "components" for our abstracta (and "constituent" for both), as some British philosophers use "component" for property and "constituent" for concrete part. Santayana, however, used "trope" to stand for the *essence* of an *occurrence*;[3] and I shall divert the word, which is almost useless in either his or its dictionary sense, to stand for the abstract particular which is, so to speak, the *occurrence* of an *essence*. A trope then is a particular entity either abstract or consisting of one or more concreta in combination with an abstractum. Thus a cat and the cat's tail are not tropes, but a cat's smile is a trope, and so is the whole whose constituents are the cat's smile plus her ears and the aridity of the moon.

Turning now briefly from the alphabet of being to a glimpse of its syllabary, we observe two fundamental ways in which tropes may be connected with one another: the way of location and the way of similarity. These are categorially different, and indeed systematic counterparts of one another—mirror images, as it were. Location is external in the sense that a trope *per se* does not entail or necessitate or determine its location with respect to any other trope, while similarity is internal in the sense that, given any two tropes, there are entailed or necessitated or determined whether and how they are similar. (What further this *prima facie* difference amounts to we cannot pursue here.) Location is easiest thought of as position in physical space-time, but I intend the notion to include also all the analogous spreads and arrangements which we find in different conscious fields and indeed in any realm of existence which we can conceive—the whole interior stretch and structure of a Leibnizian monad, for example. Both modes of connection are describable in terms of "distance" and "direction." We are very familiar in a general way with the numberless distances and directions which compose locations in space and time, somewhat less familiar with the idea of what I suggest is the limiting value of such location (though very familiar with the phenomenon itself): the collocation, or peculiar interpenetration, the unique congress in the same volume, which we call "belonging to (or inhering in, or characterizing) the same thing." With various interests and intentions, this nexus has been mentioned by Russell as "compresence," by Mill as "coinherence," by G. F. Stout as "concresence," by Professor Goodman as "togetherness," and by Whitehead, Keynes, and Mill again as "concurrence."[4] With respect to similarity, on the other hand, we are comparatively familiar with the notion of its limiting value, the precise, or almost precise, similarity such as obtained between the colors of our first and third lollipops, less familiar with the idea of the lesser similarity which obtains between a red and a purple, and rather uncertain, unless we are psychologists or phenomenologists, about such elaborate similarity distances and directions as are mapped on the color cone.

Any possible world, and hence, of course, this one, is completely constituted by its tropes and their connections of location and similarity, and any others there may be. (I think there are no others, but that is not necessary to the theory of tropes.) Location and similarity (or whatever else there is) provide all the relations, as the tropes provide the terms, but the total of the relations is not something over and above the total of the terms, for a relation R between tropes *a* and *b* is a constitutive trope of the complex $r'(a, b)$, while conversely the terms *a* and *b* will be in general, composed of constituents in relation—though perhaps no more than the spread of a smooth or "homoeomerous" quale such as a color.

Any trope belongs to as many sets or sums of tropes as there are ways of combining it with other tropes in the world. Of special interest however are (1) the set or sum of tropes which have to it the relation of *concurrence* (the limiting value of location), and (2) the set or sum of those which have to it the relation of *precise similarity* (the limiting value of similarity, sometimes mischievously called "identity"). For a given trope, of course, one or both of these sets or sums might contain nothing except the trope itself, but it is hard to imagine a world in which there would not be many tropes that belong to well populated sets or sums of both sorts, and in our world such sets or sums are very conspicuous. Speaking roughly, now, the set or sum of tropes concurrent with a trope, such as our color component Harlac, is the concrete particular or "thing" which it may be said to "characterize," in our example the lollipop Heraplem, or, to simplify the affair, the knob of the lollilop at a moment. Speaking roughly, again, the set or sum of tropes precisely similar to a given trope, say Harlac again, is the abstract universal or "essence" which it may be said to exemplify, in our illustration a definite shade of Redness. (The tropes approximately similar to the given one compose a less definite universal.)

The phrase "set or sum" above is a deliberate hedge. A set is a *class* of which the terms are members; a sum is a whole of which the terms are parts, in the very primitive sense of "part" dealt with by recent calculi of individuals.[5] In the accompanying figure, for instance, the class of six squares, the class of three rows, and the class of two columns are different from each other and from the one figure; but the sum of squares, the sum of rows, and the sum of columns are identical with one another and with the whole. What a difference of logical "type" amounts to, particularly in the philosophy of tropes, is far from clear, but everybody agrees that a sum is of the same type with its terms, as a whole is of the same type with its parts, a man of the same type with his arms and legs. The concept of a class or set, on the other hand, is notably more complex and questionable. A class is surely not, in any clear sense, what it is too often called,[6] "an abstract entity," but there is some excuse for considering it of a different "type" from its members. Convinced that tropes compose a concretum in a manner logically no different from that in which any other exhaustive batch of parts compose it, we have every incentive to say that the concretum is not the set but the sum of the tropes; and let us so describe it. Whether the counterpart concept of the universal can be defined as the sum of similars—all merely grammatical difficulties aside—is not so clear. There is little doubt that the set or class will do the job. For all the paradoxes which attend the fashionable effort to equate the universal Humanity, for example, with the class of concrete men (including such absurdities as that being a featherless biped is then the same as having a sense of humor) disappear when we equate it rather with our new set, the class of abstract humanities—the class whose members are not Socrates, Napoleon, and so forth, but the human trope in Socrates, the one in Napoleon, and so forth. Still wilder paradoxes resulted from the more radical nominalistic device of substituting the *sum* of concrete men for their class,[7] and most even of these are obviated by taking our sum of similar tropes instead. I suspect, however, that some remain, and because concurrence and similarity are such symmetrical counterparts, I shall not be surprised if it turns out that while the concurrence complex must be a sum the similarity complex must be a set.

In suggesting how both concrete particulars and abstract universals are composed of tropes, I aver that those two categories do not divide the world between them. It does not consist of concrete particulars in addition to abstract universals, as the old scheme had it, nor need we admit that it must be "constructible" *either* from concrete particulars *or* from abstract universals, as recent innovators argue (Carnap and Goodman, respectively, for example). The notions of the abstract and the universal (and hence of the concrete and the particular) are so far independent that their combinations box the logical compass. Socrates is a concrete particular; the component of him which is his wisdom is an abstract particular or "trope"; the total Wisdom of which all such wisdoms are components or members is an abstract universal; and the total Socratesity of which all creatures exactly like him are parts or members is a "concrete universal," not in the idealistic but in a strictly accurate sense. It was because of the unfortunate limitation of ordinary philosophic discourse to the two combinations, concrete particular and abstract universal, that in order to call attention to our tropes we had to divert such phrases as "the humanity of Socrates" or "the redness of the lollipop," which normally would stand for kinds or degrees of humanity and redness, to stand for their particular cases of Humanity and Redness, respectively, and so we have been driven in turn to using the capital letters in "Humanity" and "Redness" to restore the "abstract nouns" to their normal duty of naming the respective universals. A similar explanation, but a longer one, would have to be given of our less definite phrases like "the shape of Boanerp" or "the color of it."

Having thus sorted out the rubrics, we can almost automatically do much to dispel the ancient mystery of predication, so influential in the idea of logical types. The prevalent theory has been that if y can be "predicated" of x, or "inheres in" or "characterizes" x, or if x is an "instance" of y, then x and y must be sundered by a unique logical and ontological abyss. Most of the horror of this, however, which has recently impelled some logicians to graceless verbalistic contortions, is due to taking predication as one indissoluble and inscrutable operation, and vanishes when our principles reveal predication to be composed of two distinct but intelligible phases. "Socrates is wise," or generically "a is φ," means that the concurrence sum (Socrates) includes a trope which is a member of the similarity set (Wisdom). When we contrast a thing with a property or "characteristic" of it, a "substantive" with an "adjective," we may intend either or both of these connections.

The particular wisdom in Socrates is in one sense a "characteristic," i.e., it is a component, of him—this is the sense in which Stout held, quite properly to my way of thinking, that "characters are abstract particulars which are predicable of concrete particulars."[8] The universal Wisdom is in the second sense the "characteristic" of each such wisdom—this is the sense in which Moore could hold plausibly that even an event, such as a sneeze, *has* characteristics and is not one.[9] In the third or ordinary sense, however, the universal Wisdom "characterizes" the whole Socrates. From this imbroglio emerge at least two senses of "instance," the sense in which Socrates is a (concrete) "instance" of Wisdom and that in which his wisdom component is an (abstract) "instance" of it, and the two notions of class, the ordinary concreta class consisting of Socrates, Plato, and all other whole wise creatures, and the abstracta class of their wisdoms, our similarity set.

Raying out around the problem of predication is many another half magical notion about essence and existence which we now can prosily clarify. Thus Mr. Broad and Mr. Dawes Hicks, while believing in "Abstracta," have described them in the same fantastic terms in which Santayana described his essences, as placeless and timeless, and hence "real but non-existent."[10] This remarkable but not unusual proposition might for a Platonist be grounded in a whole theory of universals *ante rem,* but mostly it results from not distinguishing between its two principal sources: the specious eternity a *universal* has because, as Stout put it, it "spreads undivided, operates unspent,"[11] which for us is just the fact that similarity is a "saltatory" relation, overleaping spatial and temporal distances undiminished and without cost in stuff or energy; and the specious eternity an *abstractum* has because in attending to it we normally "abstract from" its spatiotemporal location (which nevertheless it has and keeps). As the obscurity of Essence is thus mostly resolved by looking at it stereoscopically, to distinguish the dimensions of the universal and of the abstract, so too that dark mingling of glory and degradation which haunts Existence and the individual is mostly resolved by the ideas of concreteness and particularity. The Individual is hallowed both by the utter self-identity and self-existence of the particular occurrent and by the inexhaustible richness and the inimitability of the concrete. At the same time, however, it is debased by the very same factors. It seems ignobly arbitrary and accidental, *qua* particular, with respect to its mere self in its external relations, because it thus lacks the similarity, classification, and generalization which could interpret it; and it has the confusion and unfathomability of the concrete, wherein every form struggles in a melee of forms so stupendous that the Aristotelians mistook it for formless matter.

A philosophy of tropes calls for completion in a dozen directions at once. Some of these I must ignore for the present because the questions would take us too far, some because I do not know the answers. Of the first sort would be a refinement and completion of our account of substances and of the similarity manifold. Of the second sort would be an assimilation of the very categories of our theory—concurrence, similarity, abstractness, and so forth—to the theory itself, as tropes like the rest, instead of relegating them to the anomalous immunities of "transcendentals" (as the old Scholastics said) and "metalanguage" (as the new scholastics say). What in fact I shall do here is to defend the fundamental notion that there are entities at once abstract, particular, and actual, and this in two ways: the affirmative way of showing how experience and nature evince them over and over, and the negative way of settling accounts with old dialectical objections to them.

I deliberately did not use the word "abstract" to describe our tropes till we had done our best to identify them in other ways, lest the generally derogatory connotation of the word blind us to the reality of objects as plain as the sunlight (for indeed the sunlight *is* an abstract existent). The many meanings of "abstract" which make it repulsive to the empirical temper of our age suggest that an abstractum is the product of some magical feat of mind, or the denizen of some remote immaterial eternity. Dictionaries, journalists, and philosophical writers are almost equally vague and various about it. Santayana has it that "abstract" means imprecise, but also "verbal, unrealizable, or cognitively secondary."[12] The abstract is equated with the abstruse, the ethereal, the mental, the rational, the incorporeal, the ideally perfect, the non-temporal, the primordial or ultimate, the purely theoretical, the precariously speculative and visionary; or again with the empty, the deficient, the non-actual or merely potential, the downright imaginary, and the unreal. In some quarters "abstract" means symbolical, figurative, or merely representative, in contrast with what is real in its own right. On the same page the word may connote alternately the two extremes of precious precision and the vague, confused, or indefinite. Mathematics or logic is called "abstract" partly because it is about formal structures, partly because it treats them only hypothetically;[13] but a symbolic calculus is called "abstract" because it isn't about anything. Semanticists and professors of composition shudder away from statements on such "high levels of abstraction" as "Herbivority is conducive to bovine complacency" in contrast with the "concrete" virility of "Cows like grass," though the two sentences describe exactly the same state of affairs. Logical philosophers proclaim their "renunciation of abstract entities" without making clear either what makes an entity "abstract" or how one goes about "renouncing" an entity.

One wonders, in view of this catalog, if there is anything which would not on occasion be called "abstract." Most people would deny that a cat is abstract, but an idealist would say she is. Yet it would be a mistake to infer that "abstract" has been a wholly indiscriminate epithet. All the uses we have observed, and doubtless others, have stemmed from two roots which in turn are related in a very intimate way. They represent what various persons believed, often mistakenly, is implied by those root ideas. One of them is the use of "abstract" to mean *transcending individual existence,* as a universal, essence, or Platonic idea is supposed to transcend it. But even though this use of "abstract" is probably as old as the word itself, I think it was in fact derived, by the natural mistake which we earlier noted, from the other aboriginal use, more literally in accord with the word's Latin construction, which is virtually identical with our own. At its broadest the "true" meaning of "abstract" is *partial, incomplete,* or *fragmentary,* the trait of what is less than its including whole. Since there must be, for everything but the World All, at least something, and indeed many things, of which it is a proper part, everything but the World All is "abstract" in this broad sense. It is thus that the idealist can denounce the cat as "abstract." The more usual practice of philosophers, however, has been to require for "abstractness" the more special sort of in-

completeness which pertains to what we have called the "thin" or "fine" or "diffuse" sort of constituent, like the color or shape of our lollipop, in contrast with the "thick," "gross," or chunky sort of constituent, like the stick in it.[14]

If now one looks at things without traditional prepossessions, the existence of abstracta seems as plain as any fact could be. There is something ironically archaic in the piety with which the new nominalists abhor abstract entities in favor of that "commonsense prejudice pedantically expressed,"[15] the dogma of Aristotle that there can be no real beings except "primary substances," concrete individuals, as absolute and "essential" units, and thus turn their backs on one of the greatest insights of the Renaissance, that the apparent primacy of such chunky middle-sized objects is only a function of our own middle size and practical motivation. The great modern philosophies have rather sought the real in putative "simple natures" at one end of the scale and the one great ocean of action at the other end. I have no doubt that whole things like lollipops, trees, and the moon, do exist in full-blooded concreteness, but it is not they which are "present to the senses,"[16] and it is not awareness of abstracta which is "difficult, . . . not to be attained without pains and study."[17] To claim primacy for our knowledge of concreta is "mysticism" in the strict sense, that is, a claim to such acquaintance with a plethoric being as no conceivable stroke of psychophysics could account for. What we primarily *see* of the moon, for example, is its shape and color and not at all its whole concrete bulk—generations lived and died without suspecting it had a concrete bulk; and if now we impute to it a solidity and an aridity, we do it item by item quite as we impute wheels to a clock or a stomach to a worm. Evaluation is similarly focussed on abstracta. What most men value the moon for is its brightness; what a child wants of a lollipop is a certain flavor and endurance. He would much rather have these abstracta without the rest of the bulk than the bulk without the qualities. Integral to the debate between the metaphysical champions of the concrete particular and of the abstract universal has been a discussion whether the baby's first experiences are of whole concrete particulars (his ball, his mother, and so forth) or of abstract universals (Redness, Roundness, and so forth). For what it may be worth, perhaps not much, a little observation of a baby, or of oneself in a babyish mood, will convince the candid and qualified that the object of such absorption is not the abstract universal (the infant does not "fall from the clouds upon the topmost twig of the tree of Porphyry")[18] and certainly not the concrete particular (that "foreign thing and a marvel to the spirit"[19] which a lifetime of observation and twenty centuries of research hardly begin to penetrate), but is in sooth the abstract particular or trope, *this* redness, *this* roundness, and so forth.

Though the uses of the trope to account for substances and universals are of special technical interest, the impact of the idea is perhaps greater in those many regions not so staled and obscured by long wont and old opinion and not so well supplied with alternative devices. While substances and universals can be "constructed" out of tropes, or apostrophized *in toto* for sundry purposes, the trope cannot well be "constructed" out of them and provides the one rubric which is hospitable to a hundred sorts of entity which neither philosophy, science, nor common sense can forego. This is most obvious in any attempt to treat of the mind, just because the mind's forte is the tuning, focussing, or spotlighting which brings abstracta into relief against a void or nondescript background. A pain is a trope *par excellence,* a mysterious bright pain in the night, for example, without conscious context or classification, yet as absolutely and implacably its particular self as the Great Pyramid. But all other distinguishable contents are of essentially the same order: a love, or a sorrow, or "a single individual pleasure."[20]

The notion, however, gets its best use in the theory of knowledge. The "sensible species" of the Scholastics, the "ideas" of Locke and Berkeley, the ideas and impressions of Hume, the sense data of recent epistemology—once they are understood as tropes, and as neither things nor essences, a hundred riddles about them dissolve, and philistine attacks on theory of knowledge itself lose most of their point. We need not propose that a red sensum, for example, is perfectly abstract (whatever that might be). But even though it have such distinguishable components as a shape and a size as well as a color, and though the color itself involve the "attributes" of hue, brightness, and saturation, still it is abstract in comparison with a whole colored solid. According

to reputable psychologists, furthermore, there can be data much more abstract, professed "empiricists" to the contrary notwithstanding: data which have color and no other character, or even hue and no other "attribute. The person who uses the theory of tropes to sharpen his sight of what really is present and what is not may not credit such still more delicate components, attributed to the mind, as the imageless thought of the old German schools, or the non-imaginal ideas of Descartes, or the pure concepts of the Scholastics, or the ethereal Gestalten of more recent German evangels; but if any of these do exist, they exist as tropes. The same is to be said, I suppose, of the still darker categories of pure mental act, intentionalities, dispositions, and powers. Such actual but relatively complex mental processes as trains of thought, moral decisions, beliefs, and so forth, taken as particular occurrents, whether comparatively brief or lifelong, and not (as nearly all phrases in this department at least equally suggest) as recurrent kinds, are tropes and compounded of tropes—and the kinds too, of course, are compounds of tropes in their own way. A whole soul or mind, if it is not a unique immaterial substance on its own, is a trope.

NOTES

1. It overlaps one read to the Philosophical Club of Boston University on December 3, 1952.

2. I argued the general legitimacy of such a category in "The Nature of Universals and of Abstractions," *The Monist,* XLI (1931), pp. 583–93.

3. *The Realm of Matter,* Chapter 6.

4. See Russell, *Human Knowledge,* pp. 294, 297, 304, etc.; Stout, "The Nature of Universals and Propositions" (note 8 below); Nelson Goodman, *The Structure of Appearance,* p. 178; Whitehead, *Concept of Nature,* pp. 157–58; J. M. Keynes, *Treatise on Probability,* p. 385; J. S. Mill, *A System of Logic* (Longmans, 1930), p. 67. Mill is quoting Bain.

5. Nelson Goodman and Henry Leonard, "The Calculus of Individuals and Its Uses," *Journal of Symbolic Logic,* V (1940), pp. 45–55; Goodman, *The Structure of Appearance,* pp. 42 ff.; Appendix E, by Alfred Tarski, in J. H. Woodger, *The Axiomatic Method in Biology,* pp. 161–72.

6. Goodman, op. cit., p. 150; W. V. Quine, *Methods of Logic,* p. 204.

7. Witness the doughty struggle of Quine and Goodman in "Steps Toward a Constructive Nominalism," *Journal of Symbolic Logic,* XII (1947), pp. 105–22.

8. "Are the Characteristics of Particular Things Universal or Particular?" a symposium by G. E. Moore, G. F. Stout, and G. Dawes Hicks, *Proceedings of the Aristotelian Society*, Supplementary Volume III (1923), pp. 95–128 (p. 114). His theory of abstract particulars, here and in "The Nature of Universals and Propositions" (Hertz Lecture, *Proceedings of the British Academy*, Vol. X, 1922–23), is almost identical with the one I am defending; if there is a difference it is in his obscure idea of the class as a unique form of unity not reducible to similarity.

9. Loc. cit., p. 98. Mr. Moore, I cannot help thinking, already a very uncommonplace minion of the commonplace, almost fiercely resists understanding the Stout theory.

10. Broad, *Mind and Its Place in Nature*, p. 19; Dawes Hicks, *Critical Realism*, pp. 76–78. Broad can justly marvel that we can cognize what is mental or physical only by "cognising objects which are neither" (op. cit., p. 5).

11. "Are the Characteristics, etc.," p. 116.

12. *Realms of Being*, p. 32.

13. C. I. Lewis, *Mind and the World-Order*, pp. 242, 249.

14. Although this has been for centuries the root meaning of "abstract," the nearest to a straight-forward statement of it which I have found is by Professor Ledger Wood in the Runes *Dictionary of Philosophy*, 1942, p. 2: "a designation applied to a partial aspect or quality considered in isolation from a total object, which is, in contrast, designated concrete." Even here the word "isolation," as we shall see, is delusive.

15. Russell. *History of Western Philosophy*, p. 163.

16. I have in mind Willard Quine's epistemological ballad about Homo javanensis, whose simple faculties "could only treat of things concrete and present to the senses." "Identity, Ostension, and Hypothasis," *Journal of Philosophy*, XLVII (1950), pp. 621–33 (p. 631 n.).

17. This is Berkeley on abstract ideas, *Principles*, Introd., Sect. 10. It is cited at length by James, *Psychology*, Vol. 1, p. 469, who argues, correctly I think, that what is difficult is not the recognition of abstracta but the recognition that they are abstract, and the conception of the universal, and that these are at worst no more laborious than the counterpart conception of the concretum.

18. Brand Blanshard, *The Nature of Thought*, Vol. I, p. 569.

19. Santayana, *The Unknowable* (Herbert Spencer Lecture), p. 29.

20. C. S. Peirce, without the notion of trope, denounces this perfectly intelligible phrase as "words without meaning," *Collected Papers*, Vol. I, p. 172.

Part III

Epistemology

RICHARD FUMERTON

Richard Fumerton is professor of philosophy at the University of Iowa and specializes in epistemology. Among his recent work is *Metaepistemology and Skepticism* (1995).

A History of Early Analytic Epistemology

M ANY ANALYTIC PHILOSOPHERS are committed to the view that through careful analysis of epistemic concepts like knowledge and justification and a clear understanding of the content of our everyday beliefs, they could pave the way for a resolution of the traditional problems of skepticism. Early in the century the majority of analytic philosophers were still wedded to some form of foundationalism, the view that all knowledge and justified belief is built upon a secure foundation of direct knowledge (self-evident truth, noninferentially justified belief). As the century progressed, traditional foundationalists had to fight on two fronts. The first was a continuation of combat with the skeptic who challenged the possibility of acquiring, from within the foundationalist's understanding of the structure of epistemic concepts, genuine, philosophically satisfying knowledge of, or even justified belief in, a host of "commonsense" truths. The second front grew in large part out of a perceived lack of success in confronting skepticism from within the constraints of traditional foundationalism. It mounted an attack on the foundationalist's understanding of epistemic concepts. The first such foe was the coherence theorist of justification, but the most recent, and probably more dangerous, attack came from a new, radically different kind of foundationalist—a foundationalist who sought to naturalize and externalize epistemic concepts like knowledge and justified belief.

The Regress Argument for Foundationalism

Some philosophers seem to take the truth of foundationalism as itself almost self-evident, but if an argument is offered, it is usually some version of the regress argument. If we reflect on much of what we think we know or justifiably believe, we might easily reach the conclusion that such knowledge and justified belief relies on inference from other truths

---

This essay was commissioned especially for this volume and appears here for the first time.

we know or justifiably believe.[1] We may have justification for believing that Washington was the first president of the United States, but our evidence consists in what we know about the contents of generally reliable history books, inscriptions on monuments, and other assorted indicators of past events. It seems obvious that if we are to justifiably believe one truth P by inferring it from something else E_1, we must justifiably believe that other truth E_1. I can't justifiably believe that the stock market will collapse by inferring it from impending hyperinflation unless I have reason to believe that such inflation will occur. But if we accept the principle that to justifiably believe P on the basis of E_1 one must justifiably believe E_1, then it seems that either finite minds will have no justified beliefs or there must be a source of justification that does not require the having of other different justified beliefs. If all knowledge or justification were inferential, then to justifiably believe P by inferring it from E_1, we would need to justifiably believe E_1 by inferring it from something else, E_2, which we would need to infer from something else, E_3, and so on, ad infinitum.

The classic skeptic also seemed to presuppose that inferential knowledge (or justified belief), would also require not only knowledge of that from which the inference is made but also knowledge of an appropriate *connection* between alleged evidence and conclusion. Thus our reason for rejecting the astrologer's claim to know the future based on what he knows about the relative positions of planets is that we are convinced that the astrologer has no reason to believe that there is any connection between the positions of planets and the affairs of people here on earth. Even if there were some bizarre connection between the two phenomena, in the absence of any reason to suppose that it exists, we could have no reason to believe predictions based on putative astrological evidence. This suggests that we might accept the following more complex principle concerning inferential justification:

(PIJ) To be justified in believing P on the basis of E, one must be (1) justified in believing E, and (2) justified in believing that E makes probable P.

If (PIJ) is true and if all justification were inferential, then finite minds would face not one but an infinite number of vicious regresses. To be justified in believing P on the basis of E_1, one would need to be justified in believing that E_1 makes probable P. One would need to infer that from some other proposition F_1, which one would need to infer from F_2, and so on ad infinitum. But one would also need reason to believe that F_1 does indeed make probable that E_1 makes probable P, something one would need to infer from some proposition G_2 which one would need to infer from some proposition G_3. . . . But one would also need to have reason to believe that G_1 does make likely that F_1 makes likely that E_1 makes likely P, so one would need to infer that from some other proposition H_1 which. . . . We face not one but an infinite number of infinite regresses. Rather than embracing the most radical of all skepticisms (the conclusion that we have no reason to believe anything at all), we must recognize, the foundationalist argues, that we can have a kind of justification for believing some propositions that does not consist in the having of other justified beliefs. We must accept that knowledge and justified belief have foundations.

We might call this regress argument for foundationalism the *epistemic* regress argument. But there may be an even more fundamental *conceptual* regress that the foundationalist hopes to head off by introducing the concept of noninferentially justified belief. One might argue that the very idea of inferential justification presupposes an understanding of justification that is not inferential. One might argue, for example, that (PIJ), or the first clause of (PIJ), is true by definition. Our very *concept* of inferential justification is simply our concept of a belief inferred from something *justifiably* believed. But this concept of inferential justification is clearly parasitic upon our understanding of justified belief. We must have a way of understanding justification that does not already presuppose the concept of justified belief.

An analogy might be helpful here. Suppose one introduces the notion of something's being good as a means and defines being good as a means in terms of producing something that is good. Exercise, for example, is good as a means because it is conducive to health, which is good. But clearly our proposed definition of something's being good as a means presupposes an understanding of something's being good. There must be a way of understanding something's being good in itself, a conception of goodness that does not presuppose an understanding of something else's being good. In precisely the same way, the foundationalist might argue, we can only understand a belief's being inferentially justified if we can understand a belief's being justified in such a way that it does not require the having of other justified beliefs.

Versions of Foundationalism

If foundationalists are united in their conviction that knowledge and justified belief must have foundations, they disagree profoundly on how to answer two crucial questions: (1) What should be *included* in foundations of knowledge and justified belief? and (2) How should we *understand* noninferential knowledge and justified belief? In answer to (1), radical empiricists have claimed that one's noninferential knowledge is restricted to truths about the current content of one's mental states (truths about beliefs, desires, emotions, sensations, and the like) and certain necessary truths knowable a priori (independently of sense experience and introspection) e.g., that bachelors are unmarried, that $2 + 2 = 4$, that the opposite angles of intersecting straight lines are equal. More moderate foundationalists have extended the class of self-evident truths to include descriptions of one's immediate experiential past and one's immediate (breadbox-sized) physical environment. As we shall see, externalist versions of foundationalism place no real restrictions on what could *conceivably* turn out to be noninferentially known.

Before we decide what kinds of truths can be known or justifiably believed without inference, it might seem that we need an answer to the second of the two questions just described. What precisely would make it the case that we know some truth without needing to infer it from other truths?

Noninferential Justification as Infallible Belief

Inspired by René Descartes, many classical foundationalists tried to identify noninferentially justified beliefs with beliefs that could not be mistaken. In searching for secure foundations upon which to build an ideal system of knowledge, Descartes seemed to suggest that we should eliminate a belief from our foundations if we can conceive of a situation in which a belief of that sort was false. No belief about the physical world could satisfy the relevant criteria for foundational knowledge, for no matter how vivid our sensations are, we can always imagine that those sensations have come to us in a dream or a demon-induced hallucination. Even relatively simple mathematical propositions seemed to Descartes not to be immune from the possibility of error, for we can imagine a powerful being with the means and motive to deceive us with respect to these facts. Indeed, as Descartes himself seemed to realize, it is decidedly difficult to construct a *robust* foundation for knowledge and justified belief if one is restricted to building materials made up of infallible belief. Descartes tried valiantly, but his effort to reconstruct a system of knowledge based on secure foundations itself rested on the shifting sands of a proof for the existence of a nondeceiving God, a proof that relied on premises that hardly seemed to meet the test of infallibility.

If we define infallible belief as belief that entails the truth of what is believed, there may be only a few examples of contingent propositions that are infallibly believed. Descartes's own famous example of our belief in our own existence, the belief that there are beliefs, the belief that there is consciousness, all can plausibly be regarded as guaranteeing the truth of the propositions believed. Plenty of examples of necessary truths are entailed by the fact that they are believed—too many! Given the standard definition of entailment, every necessary truth is entailed by the fact that it is believed. P entails Q when it is impossible for P to be true while Q is false, and since it is impossible for a necessary truth to be false, it is impossible for any other fact to obtain while the necessary truth is false! Every proposition entails a necessary truth. This poses real difficulties for the philosopher who thinks that infallible belief is the mark of a special kind of direct knowledge, for it seems obvious that one might believe some necessary truth far too complicated for one to even understand clearly, let alone justifiably believe.

If we focus on contingent truths, it is difficult to come up with uncontroversial examples (beyond the few examples of beliefs whose content itself refers back directly or indirectly to the having of the belief) of infallible belief. Some of the radical empiricists thought that we couldn't be mistaken about the nonrelational character of our subjective experience, but others have seriously questioned that proposition. Do we have infallible access to what we believe, what we desire, whom we love, whom we hate, or even what our current sense experience is like? It is not unusual to hear people complaining at the restaurant that they don't know what they want to order. At some point in our lives, most of us have been more than a bit puzzled about whether we really hate or love someone. If I close my eyes tightly and a number of bright flashes appear in my visual field, is it really plausible to claim that my estimation of the number of such flashes couldn't be mistaken? As A. J. Ayer argues (this volume, 206–219) the vast majority of beliefs, even beliefs about the contents of our minds, are distinct from the facts that would make the beliefs true. If my believing that I am in pain is a different state from my pain, why couldn't it be the case that the belief occurs without the pain? At the very least, it seems that very few truths will get included in the foundations of justified belief if we restrict such foundations to infallible belief, and the specter of skepticism looms over a foundationalism so austere. Unless we have an enormously liberal set of inference rules permitting travel from our foundations to the commonsense destinations we wish to reach, it's not clear that we will ever be able to leave successfully the confines of our foundations.

Infallible Justification

If we decide that it is a mistake to search for noninferential justification in the special character of a kind of *belief,* we might look instead for a special kind of *justification.* What would be a kind of justification that would obviate the need to infer what is believed from other assertions to which we are committed? Bertrand Russell and others have suggested that at least sometimes we stand in a special relation of direct awareness or direct acquaintance to aspects of the world that are the very truthmakers for the propositions we believe. The reason I don't need to infer that I'm in pain when I am is that the pain itself is "there" directly and immediately before my mind. There is nothing *between* me and the pain. When I entertain the belief that I'm in pain, I don't need to pay attention to anything but the pain that is before my consciousness in order to be fully justified in believing that I am in pain. Russell called this awareness knowledge by acquaintance, and while *I* don't think Russell was at all confused, others have complained that acquaintance with individuals, properties, or facts isn't a kind of knowledge at all, at least not a kind of knowledge that could provide us with premises from which we could then legitimately make inferences. Individuals, properties, and facts are not the kinds of things that are either true or false. Even if I am in some sense directly aware of my pain, how does that constitute knowledge of a "first" *truth* that will supply me with premises from which I can infer the rest of what I believe?

This objection, however, really misses the point. The acquaintance Russell talks about is a source of justification, not knowledge of a truth. Indeed if one were acquainted with facts but had no concepts and could form no beliefs, then, trivially, one would have no knowledge of truths. But when one does form a belief about one's pain, then the acquaintance with the pain is supposed to be that which obviates the need to *infer* the proposition that one is in pain from *other truths*.

Notice that there is a sense in which if one is acquainted with pain when one believes that one is in pain, the acquaintance with the pain guarantees the truth of what one believes. Acquaintance is a real relation that requires the existence of its relata. One couldn't stand in that relation to one's pain while one believes that one is in pain without believing *truly* that one is in pain. On the other hand, an acquaintance theorist might be able to allow that one can have noninferential justification provided by acquaintance that is nevertheless fallible. I might be acquainted with a mental state, for example, that is subtly different from pain but so much like it that I might still form the belief that I am in pain as a result of my awareness of this sensation. The justification, fallible though it turned out to be, would still be noninferential in that nothing other than close inspection (*intro*spection) of the character of the sensation would seem to be relevant to assessing the justification for the belief.

It is also interesting that the acquaintance theorist can give a unified account of foundational knowledge in that both foundational knowledge of contingent truth and foundational knowledge of necessary truth has its common source in acquaintance with the relevant facts. While acquaintance with my pain might justify me in believing that I'm in pain, acquaintance with relations between ideas might justify me in believing that bachelors are unmarried. And perhaps acquaintance with geometric properties and necessary relations that hold between them justify me in believing the axioms and theorems of Euclidean geometry.

Many anti-foundationalists reject the intelligibility of Russell's concept of direct acquaintance. Others argue that even if one allowed foundations consisting of truths made true by truthmakers with which we find ourselves directly acquainted, we still have too meager a foundation upon which to build any realistic hope of inferring legitimately the rest of what we think we believe. The specter of skepticism still hovers over this foundationalist. As Hume pointed out, if all we know directly are the contents of our minds and assorted necessary truths that depend only on "relations between ideas," how are we to legitimately move beyond our foundations to, for example, knowledge of the past or knowledge of the external world? We obviously can't deduce truths about the past from what we know about the present and we can't deduce truths about the objective, enduring physical world from what we know about the character of subjective, fleeting sensations.

There do, however, appear to be legitimate kinds of nondeductive inference. We infer that it will soon storm from the ominous look of those dark clouds gathering on the horizon and from the knowledge that in the past dark clouds of that sort were usually followed by storms. Can we use this sort of *inductive* reasoning to gain knowledge of the past or knowledge of the external world? It's hard to see how. It may be true that usually when we seem to remember having done something, we did it, but how would we *know* this correlation in order to use it as a premise? The most obvious answer is that we seem to remember that memory is reliable in this way, but, of course, no self-respecting skeptic will allow us to use memory in order to justify a claim about its reliability! And while we can, perhaps, correlate sensations with sensations (assuming we have somehow solved the problem of memory) and thus establish one kind of sensation as a reliable indicator of others, how could we possibly correlate sensations with something other than sensations (physical objects) in order to establish the former as reliable indicators of the latter?

Philosophers have never lacked ingenuity, however, and some have tried valiantly to find a way of justifying inductively a belief in the existence of physical objects even when one is limited to a foundation consisting of what we know about the character of our sensations. Some analytic philosophers have sought to pave the road to knowledge of a physical world with a helpful analysis of the meaning of assertions about physical objects, an analysis which brings their content closer to the world of subjective experience. C. I. Lewis, for example, carefully distinguishes what is given in experience (the raw sensory data) from the *interpretations* we place upon that given—the judgments we make about physical objects. Unlike the acquaintance theorist, Lewis may not even want to allow that we make judgments about the phenomenal (nonrelational) character of the given. Even so, we can abstract in our experience the data that are uninterpreted from those that receive interpretation. The interpretation consists of predictions we make about what further experience we *would* have *were* we to take various actions.

These "subjunctive" judgments about future possible experience never really go beyond experience and, as such, can presumably be confirmed inductively (by correlating sensations with sensations). It is, however, a drastic understatement to suggest that "translations" of talk about the physical world into talk about the phenomenally given character of actual and possible experience have not been unproblematic. One problem, put crudely, is that there don't really seem to be any truths about what sensations would follow others except relative to certain physical conditions of perception. What one would see or feel always depends in part on the state of one's physical sense organs and in part on the external conditions of perception. But one can't refer to anything but sensations if one is to successfully carry out the "reduction" of talk about the physical world to talk about sensation, a reduction that would allow us to confirm truths about the physical world without leaving correlations found in the world of experience.

There may, of course, be other legitimate sorts of nondeductive reasoning available to meet the skeptical challenge,[2] but I think it is fair to suggest that many contemporary epistemologists fear that skepticism will inevitably triumph, given the limited resources of foundational knowledge available to the radical empiricist and classical foundationalist. One can, of course, simply rule the skeptic out of court. Moore famously rejects as absurd any philosophical view that implies that he doesn't know various commonplace truths about the world around him. It is tempting to characterize Moore's defense of common sense as just a blatant begging of the question against the skeptic. Moore's point, however, is probably *metaphilosophical* (i.e., a philosophical point about the nature of philosophical method). He may be trying to emphasize that one has no ultimate recourse in philosophy but to appeal to at least some fundamental truths that just seem obvious. One of the most common arguments in philosophy is the *reductio*, the attempt to reduce one's opponent's views to absurdity by exposing absurd consequences of those views. Without the reductio, it is not clear how philosophy could proceed. But if radical skepticism doesn't count as an absurd consequence of a view, what does? The irony is that Moore himself held many of the same metaphysical and epistemological views that seem to legitimize the skeptic's arguments, and even if one ends up agreeing with Moore that something has gone wrong with a philosophical view when it leads to skepticism, one still wants to understand precisely where the errors were made.

Coherence Theory of Justification

Philosophers like W. V. Quine have sought to undermine some of the fundamental presuppositions of the foundationalists. In his classic "Two Dogmas of Empiricism" (this volume, 193–206) Quine tries to cast doubt on the possibility of providing a philosophically satisfying account of the analytic/synthetic distinction. You will recall that the classical foundationalist wanted to include in the foundations of knowledge certain necessary truths. These necessary truths included not only the truths of logic (e.g., either it is raining or it is not raining) but also truths that one can discover solely by reflecting on the meaning of terms or concepts (e.g., bachelors are unmarried, triangles have three sides). Quine's complaints seem to center largely on misgivings about the possibility of giving a satisfactory philosophical account of meaning and synonymy, and it is not clear what force his arguments really have given the difficulties of giving a philosophically satisfying account of *any* fundamental concept. But to the extent to which he and his followers became suspicious of the analytic/synthetic (necessary/contingent) distinction, they became suspicious of one important candidate for inclusion in the foundations of knowledge.

Beyond a rejection of unproblematic direct a priori knowledge, Quine and others also reject what is sometimes characterized as the "linear" conception of justification and knowledge presupposed by the foundationalist. If we reflect more on actual scientific practice, the argument goes, we will discover that one doesn't proceed step by step from foundational truths via unproblematic inference to more and more theoretical truths. Truths are only confirmed or disconfirmed as parts of complex theories or *networks* of claims, where there is room for all sorts of give and take at all "levels" in trying to reconcile one's theory with uncooperative experience. To take a somewhat trivial example, if my scientific instruments give me readings that would seem to refute some treasured theory of mine, I can always choose to believe that the instruments are faulty in some respect rather than give up the theory. When supposed eyewitnesses testify that my child has committed some crime, I can always retain my faith in my child's innocence by adopting the hypothesis that the alleged witnesses are lying. In a metaphor Quine made famous, our justified beliefs might best be thought of as hanging together in a coherent web, where we can always maintain the coherence of the web provided that we are prepared to make enough substantial revisions in the entire belief set.

The coherence theory still has its proponents, but it faces two formidable objections. Ironically, one was brought to the fore relatively recently by a former proponent of a coherence theory of empirical justification, Laurence BonJour[3]. BonJour argued, plausibly enough, that coherence within one's belief system of which one is ignorant can hardly yield justified belief. If I whimsically believe a number of different propositions all of which cohere magnificently as a matter of sheer luck, is there any plausibility to the claim that I have for that reason knowledge or justified belief in the propositions that cohere? But if we require "access" to coherence in addition to coherence for justified belief, then the coherence theorist must give us an account of how we gain access to what it is that we believe. If the coherence theorist presupposes some sort of "direct" unproblematic access to belief systems, one must wonder whether our coherentist isn't simply a disguised foundationalist with respect to knowledge of at least some truths.

Just as important, one might insist that access to coherence requires access to logical, *analytic,* and probabilistic connections between truths. If Quine's attack on the analytic/synthetic distinction were successful, one wonders how he would understand truths that describe coherence. And even if one can successfully argue that the content of such claims is unproblematic, one is left with the problem of how to account for *knowledge* of the coherence relations without again surreptitiously introducing foundational knowledge of at least some necessary truths.

Gettier's Counterexamples to the Traditional Concept of Knowledge and New Kinds of Foundationalism

In the preceding discussion, the reader will notice that we moved back and forth rather casually between talk of theories of knowledge and theories of justified belief. While Descartes may have hoped that only infallibly justified beliefs could constitute knowledge, twentieth-century philosophers almost all sought to "weaken" requirements for knowledge so as to gain some advantage in the fight against skepticism. In order to know some proposition P, we don't need justification that eliminates the possibility of error. We need only a true belief based on justification that makes highly likely the truth of what we believe. Philosophers who supported this "justified true belief" account of knowledge tended to focus their philosophical attention on justified belief instead of knowledge. Once one satisfies oneself that one does have a justified belief that P, after all, it is tempting to think that it is a matter of luck whether or not the world cooperates so as to turn that justified belief into knowledge (by making the belief true).

With his famous counterexamples, Edmund Gettier convinced almost all analytic philosophers to abandon this account of knowledge as justified true belief. To use an example that was actually given by Russell years before Gettier, one can justifiably and truly believe that it is 5:00 P.M. as a result of looking at a broken clock that just happens to be stuck at 5:00 P.M. when it is 5:00 P.M. But intuitively one doesn't *know* in this way what time it is. The evidence doesn't seem to hook up with the truth of what one believes in the right way. Faced with this sort of counterexample, proponents of the "traditional" account labored long and hard to find fourth, fifth, and many more conditions of knowledge that would immunize their accounts from Gettier-style counterexamples.

There is, however, no consensus on what the most promising approach might be. The most *radical* reactions to Gettier counterexamples, however, involved abandoning the central idea behind a justified true belief account of knowledge. So-called causal theorists noticed that in our clock example the actual time of the day was playing no causal role in the production of the person's belief that it was 5:00 P.M. When I believe that there is a desk in front of me now, the very desk that makes true my belief is also playing a causal role in the production of visual experience, which in turn causes me to believe that the desk is there. Philosophers love to generalize, and it occurred to some that we might characterize knowledge in terms of the causal origin of belief. A crude (far too crude) version of such a view might suggest that S knows that P when S's belief that P is caused (in the right way) by either the fact that P or some fact that in turn causes it to be the case that P. Once philosophers started thinking about the possibility of defining fundamental epistemic concepts in terms of origin of belief, it wasn't long before some returned to the concept of justified belief itself and wondered whether we couldn't distinguish between justified and unjustified belief in terms of facts about the ways in which these beliefs are produced.

In what is still the most influential of such views, Alvin Goldman suggested that we understand justified beliefs as beliefs that are produced by reliable belief-forming processes.[4] The "software" of the brain sometimes churns out beliefs, taking as its input states other than beliefs, and sometimes churns out beliefs, taking as its input beliefs. Notice that this distinction parallels precisely the traditional foundationalist's distinction between noninferential and inferential justification. In the case of belief-producing processes that take beliefs as their input, a condition of the output beliefs being justified is that the input beliefs are justified, and what makes the process reliable is that the output beliefs are usually true when the input beliefs are. *Belief-independent* processes operate on data like sensory stimulation, memory traces, and the like and are reliable provided that their output beliefs are usually true. Reliabilists and other "externalists" about epistemic justification insist that one doesn't need to know anything about how one's beliefs are produced in order for them to be justified. It is enough that the processes that produce them are reliable in the relevant sense.

Reliabilism and views like it held enormous attraction for many epistemologists who sought to avoid the restrictions of traditional empiricist foundationalism but who found the coherence theory fundamentally incoherent. Evolution may have taken relatively good care of us and may have "programmed" us to respond with accurate beliefs to a host of nondoxastic environmental cues. As a result, nature may have arranged for us to have a huge number of noninferentially justified beliefs.

If the new century opens with externalist epistemology riding a wave of philosophical enthusiasm, however, one would be unwise to ignore the cyclical nature of philosophy. The externalists' critics have long worried that externalist analyses of epistemic concepts secure a potential high ground in the battle with skepticism at the price of rendering epistemic concepts philosophically uninteresting. When Russell, Ayer, or Lewis wanted justified beliefs or knowledge, they wanted to be in a state that gave them some *assurance* that what they believed was true. It is simply not clear how having a reliably produced belief (when one doesn't know its source) gives one the kind of assurance that epistemologists have fought so hard to get, and as a result it is not clear that the new foundationalists are in a position to engage on common ground the epistemologist's old nemesis, the skeptic.

NOTES

1. Foundationalists sometimes express their views in terms of knowledge, sometimes in terms of justified belief. In what follows, I will focus on foundationalist accounts of justified belief. All of the arguments discussed will apply, *mutatis mutandis,* to knowledge.

2. C. S. Peirce talked about *abduction,* or reasoning to the best explanation. As the latter label implies, this sort of reasoning involves positing some truth as the best explanation for some otherwise unexplained phenomena one observes. At times, Russell seemed to encourage us to solve the problem of perception by construing out knowledge of the external world as reasoning to the best explanation. R. M. Chisholm throughout his epistemological writings suggested numerous epistemic principles "tailor made" to bridge the problematic gaps nondeductively.

3. In his *The Structure of Empirical Knowledge* (Cambridge: Harvard University Press, 1985), BonJour has since renounced the coherence theory of justification.

4. The now-classic early statement of his view was given in "What Is Justified Belief?" in *Justification and Knowledge,* ed. George Pappas (Dordrecht, Neth.: Reidel, 1979), 1–23. The view has taken twists and turns since then, most notably in his *Epistemology and Cognition* (Cambridge: Harvard University Press, 1986) and "Strong and Weak Justification," in *Philosophical Perspectives* (Atascadero, CA: Ridgeview, 1988) 2: 51–69.

13   Knowledge by Acquaintance and Knowledge by Description

BERTRAND RUSSELL

THE OBJECT OF THE FOLLOWING PAPER is to consider what it is that we know in cases where we know propositions about the "so-and-so" without knowing who or what the so-and-so is. For example, I know that the candidate who gets most votes will be elected, though I do not know who is the candidate who will get most votes. The problem I wish to consider is: What do we know in these cases, where the subject is merely described? I have considered this problem elsewhere[1] from a purely logical point of view; but in what follows I wish to consider the question in relation to theory of knowledge as well as in relation to logic, and in view of the above-mentioned logical discussions, I shall in this paper make the logical portion as brief as possible.

In order to make clear the antithesis between "acquaintance" and "description," I shall first of all try to explain what I mean by "acquaintance." I say that I am *acquainted* with an object when I have a direct cognitive relation to that object, i.e., when I am directly aware of the object itself. When I speak of a cognitive relation here, I do not mean the sort of relation which constitutes judgment, but the sort which constitutes presentation. In fact, I think the relation of subject and object which I call acquaintance is simply the converse of the relation of object and subject which constitutes presentation. That is, to say that S has acquaintance with O is essentially the same thing as to say that O is presented to S. But the associations and natural extensions of the word *acquaintance* are different from those of the word *presentation*. To begin with, as in most cognitive words, it is natural to say that I am acquainted with an object even at moments when it is not actually before my mind, provided it has been before my mind and will be again whenever occasion arises. This is the same sense in which I am said to know that 2 + 2 = 4 even when I am thinking of

something else. In the second place, the word *acquaintance* is designed to emphasise, more than the word *presentation*, the relational character of the fact with which we are concerned. There is, to my mind, a danger that, in speaking of presentation, we may so emphasise the object as to lose sight of the subject. The result of this is either to lead to the view that there is no subject, whence we arrive at materialism; or to lead to the view that what is presented is part of the subject, whence we arrive at idealism, and should arrive at solipsism but for the most desperate contortions. Now I wish to preserve the dualism of subject and object in my terminology, because this dualism seems to me a fundamental fact concerning cognition. Hence I prefer the word *acquaintance*, because it emphasises the need of a subject which is acquainted.

When we ask what are the kinds of objects with which we are acquainted, the first and most obvious example is *sense-data*. When I see a colour or hear a noise, I have direct acquaintance with the colour or the noise. The sense-datum with which I am acquainted in these cases is generally, if not always, complex. This is particularly obvious in the case of sight. I do not mean, of course, merely that the supposed physical object is complex, but that the direct sensible object is complex and contains parts with spatial relations. Whether it is possible to be aware of a complex without being aware of its constituents is not an easy question, but on the whole it would seem that there is no reason why it should not be possible. This question arises in an acute form in connection with self-consciousness, which we must now briefly consider.

In introspection, we seem to be immediately aware of varying complexes, consisting of objects in various cognitive and conative relations to ourselves. When I see the sun, it often happens that I am aware

Proceedings of the Aristotelian Society 11 (1910–11). Reprinted by permission of the Aristotelian Society.

of my seeing the sun, in addition to being aware of the sun; and when I desire food, it often happens that I am aware of my desire for food. But it is hard to discover any state of mind in which I am aware of myself alone, as opposed to a complex of which I am a constituent. The question of the nature of self-consciousness is too large, and too slightly connected with our subject, to be argued at length here. It is difficult, but probably not impossible, to account for plain facts if we assume that we do not have acquaintance with ourselves. It is plain that we are not only *acquainted* with the complex "Self-acquainted-with-A," but we also *know* the proposition "I am acquainted with A." Now here the complex has been analysed, and if "I" does not stand for something which is a direct object of acquaintance, we shall have to suppose that "I" is something known by description. If we wished to maintain the view that there is no acquaintance with Self, we might argue as follows: We are acquainted with *acquaintance,* and we know that it is a relation. Also we are acquainted with a complex in which we perceive that acquaintance is the relating relation. Hence we know that this complex must have a constituent which is that which is acquainted, i.e., must have a subject-term as well as an object-term. This subject-term we define as "I." Thus "I" means "the subject-term in awarenesses of which *I* am aware." But as a definition this cannot be regarded as a happy effort. It would seem necessary, therefore, either to suppose that I am acquainted with myself, and that "I," therefore, requires no definition, being merely the proper name of a certain object, or to find some other analysis of self-consciousness. Thus self-consciousness cannot be regarded as throwing light on the question whether we can know a complex without knowing its constituents. This question, however, is not important for our present purposes, and I shall therefore not discuss it further.

The awarenesses we have considered so far have all been awarenesses of particular existents, and might all in a large sense be called sense-data. For, from the point of view of theory of knowledge, introspective knowledge is exactly on a level with knowledge derived from sight or hearing. But, in addition to awareness of the above kind of objects, which may be called awareness of *particulars,* we have also (though not quite in the same sense) what

may be called awareness of *universals.* Awareness of universals is called *conceiving,* and a universal of which we are aware is called a *concept.* Not only are we aware of particular yellows, but if we have seen a sufficient number of yellows and have sufficient intelligence, we are aware of the universal *yellow;* this universal is the subject in such judgments as "yellow differs from blue" or "yellow resembles blue less than green does." And the universal yellow is the predicate in such judgments as "this is yellow," where "this" is a particular sense-datum. And universal relations, too, are objects of awarenesses; up and down, before and after, resemblance, desire, awareness itself, and so on, would seem to be all of them objects of which we can be aware.

In regard to relations, it might be urged that we are never aware of the universal relation itself, but only of complexes in which it is a constituent. For example, it may be said that we do not know directly such a relation as *before,* though we understand such a proposition as "this is before that," and may be directly aware of such a complex as "this being before that." This view, however, is difficult to reconcile with the fact that we often know propositions in which the relation is the subject, or in which the relata are not definite given objects, but "anything." For example, we know that if one thing is before another, and the other before a third, then the first is before the third; and here the things concerned are not definite things, but "anything." It is hard to see how we could know such a fact about "before" unless we were acquainted with "before," and not merely with actual particular cases of one given object being before another given object. And more directly: A judgment such as "this is before that," where this judgment is derived from awareness of a complex, constitutes an analysis, and we should not understand the analysis if we were not acquainted with the meaning of the terms employed. Thus we must suppose that we are acquainted with the meaning of "before," and not merely with instances of it.

There are thus at least two sorts of objects of which we are aware, namely, particulars and universals. Among particulars I include all existents, and all complexes of which one or more constituents are existents, such as this-before-that, this-above-that, the-yellowness-of-this. Among universals I include all objects of which no particular is a constituent. Thus the disjunction "universal-particular" includes all objects. We might also call it the disjunction "abstract-concrete." It is not quite parallel with the opposition "concept-percept," because things remembered or imagined belong with particulars, but can hardly be called percepts. (On the other hand, universals with which we are acquainted may be identified with concepts.)

It will be seen that among the objects with which we are acquainted are not included physical objects (as opposed to sense-data), nor other people's minds. These things are known to us by what I call "knowledge by description," which we must now consider.

By a "description" I mean any phrase of the form "a so-and-so" or "the so-and-so." A phrase of the form "a so-and-so" I shall call an "ambiguous" description; a phrase of the form "the so-and-so" (in the singular) I shall call a "definite" description. Thus "a man" is an ambiguous description, and "the man with the iron mask" is a definite description. There are various problems connected with ambiguous descriptions, but I pass them by, since they do not directly concern the matter I wish to discuss. What I wish to discuss is the nature of our knowledge concerning objects in cases where we know that there is an object answering to a definite description, though we are not *acquainted* with any such object. This is a matter which is concerned exclusively with *definite* descriptions. I shall, therefore, in the sequel, speak simply of "descriptions" when I mean "definite descriptions." Thus a description will mean any phrase of the form "the so-and-so" in the singular.

I shall say that an object is "known by description" when we know that it is "*the* so-and-so," i.e., when we know that there is one object, and no more, having a certain property; and it will generally be implied that we do not have knowledge of the same object by acquaintance. We know that the man with the iron mask existed, and many propositions are known about him; but we do not know who he was. We know that the candidate who gets most votes will be elected, and in this case we are very likely also acquainted (in the only sense in which one can be acquainted with some one else) with the man who is, in fact, the candidate who will

get most votes, but we do not know which of the candidates he is, i.e., we do not know any proposition of the form "A is the candidate who will get most votes" where A is one of the candidates by name. We shall say that we have "*merely* descriptive knowledge" of the so-and-so when, although we know that the so-and-so exists, and although we may possibly be acquainted with the object which is, in fact, the so-and-so, yet we do not know any proposition "*a* is the so-and-so," where *a* is something with which we are acquainted.

When we say "the so-and-so exists," we mean that there is just one object which is the so-and-so. The proposition "*a* is the so-and-so" means that *a* has the property so-and-so, and nothing else has. "Sir Joseph Larmor is the Unionist candidate" means "Sir Joseph Larmor is a Unionist candidate, and no one else is." "The Unionist candidate exists" means "some one is a Unionist candidate, and no one else is." Thus, when we are acquainted with an object which we know to be the so-and-so, we know that the so-and-so exists, but we may know that the so-and-so exists when we are not acquainted with any object which we know to be the so-and-so, and even when we are not acquainted with any object which, in fact, is the so-and-so.

Common words, even proper names, are usually really descriptions. That is to say, the thought in the mind of a person using a proper name correctly can generally only be expressed explicitly if we replace the proper name by a description. Moreover, the description required to express the thought will vary for different people, or for the same person at different times. The only thing constant (so long as the name is rightly used) is the object to which the name applies. But so long as this remains constant, the particular description involved usually makes no difference to the truth or falsehood of the proposition in which the name appears.

Let us take some illustrations. Suppose some statement made about Bismarck. Assuming that there is such a thing as direct acquaintance with oneself, Bismarck himself might have used his name directly to designate the particular person with whom he was acquainted. In this case, if he made a judgment about himself, he himself might be a constituent of the judgment. Here the proper name has the direct use which it always wishes to have, as simply standing for a certain object, and not for a description of the object. But if a person who knew Bismarck made a judgment about him, the case is different. What this person was acquainted with were certain sense-data which he connected (rightly, we will suppose) with Bismarck's body. His body as a physical object, and still more his mind, were only known as the body and the mind connected with these sense-data. That is, they were known by description. It is, of course, very much a matter of chance which characteristics of a man's appearance will come into a friend's mind when he thinks of him; thus the description actually in the friend's mind is accidental. The essential point is that he knows that the various descriptions all apply to the same entity, in spite of not being acquainted with the entity in question.

When we, who did not know Bismarck, make a judgment about him, the description in our minds will probably be some more or less vague mass of historical knowledge—far more, in most cases, than is required to identify him. But, for the sake of illustration, let us assume that we think of him as "the first Chancellor of the German Empire." Here all the words are abstract except "German." The word "German" will again have different meanings for different people. To some it will recall travels in Germany, to some the look of Germany on the map, and so on. But if we are to obtain a description which we know to be applicable, we shall be compelled, at some point, to bring in a reference to a particular with which we are acquainted. Such reference is involved in any mention of past, present, and future (as opposed to definite dates), or of here and there, or of what others have told us. Thus it would seem that, in some way or other, a description known to be applicable to a particular must involve some reference to a particular with which we are acquainted, if our knowledge about the thing described is not to be merely what follows logically from the description. For example, "the most long-lived of men" is a description which must apply to some man, but we can make no judgments concerning this man which involve knowledge about him beyond what the description gives. If, however, we say, "the first Chancellor of the German Empire

was an astute diplomatist," we can only be assured of the truth of our judgment in virtue of something with which we are acquainted—usually a testimony heard or read. Considered psychologically, apart from the information we convey to others, apart from the fact about the actual Bismarck, which gives importance to our judgment, the thought we really have contains the one or more particulars involved, and otherwise consists wholly of concepts. All names of places—London, England, Europe, the earth, the Solar System—similarly involve, when used, descriptions which start from some one or more particulars with which we are acquainted. I suspect that even the Universe, as considered by metaphysics, involves such a connection with particulars. In logic, on the contrary, where we are concerned not merely with what does exist, but with whatever might or could exist or be, no reference to actual particulars is involved.

It would seem that, when we make a statement about something only known by description, we often *intend* to make our statement, not in the form involving the description, but about the actual thing described. That is to say, when we say anything about Bismarck, we should like, if we could, to make the judgment which Bismarck alone can make, namely, the judgment of which he himself is a constituent. In this we are necessarily defeated, since the actual Bismarck is unknown to us. But we know that there is an object B called Bismarck, and that B was an astute diplomatist. We can thus *describe* the proposition we should like to affirm, namely, "B was an astute diplomatist," where B is the object which was Bismarck. What enables us to communicate in spite of the varying descriptions we employ is that we know there is a true proposition concerning the actual Bismarck, and that, however we may vary the description (so long as the description is correct), the proposition described is still the same. This proposition, which is described and is known to be true, is what interests us; but we are not acquainted with the proposition itself, and do not know *it*, though we know it is true,

It will be seen that there are various stages in the removal from acquaintance with particulars: there is Bismarck to people who knew him, Bismarck to those who only know of him through history, the man with the iron mask, the longest-lived of men. These are progressively further removed from acquaintance with particulars, and there is a similar hierarchy in the region of universals. Many universals, like many particulars, are only known to us by description. But here, as in the case of particulars, knowledge concerning what is known by description is ultimately reducible to knowledge concerning what is known by acquaintance.

The fundamental epistemological principle in the analysis of propositions containing descriptions is this: *Every proposition which we can understand must be composed wholly of constituents with which we are acquainted.* From what has been said already, it will be plain why I advocate this principle, and how I propose to meet the case of propositions which at first sight contravene it. Let us begin with the reasons for supposing the principle true.

The chief reason for supposing the principle true is that it seems scarcely possible to believe that we can make a judgment or entertain a supposition without knowing what it is that we are judging or supposing about. If we make a judgment about (say) Julius Caesar, it is plain that the actual person who was Julius Caesar is not a constituent of the judgment. But before going further, it may be well to explain what I mean when I say that this or that is a constituent of a judgment, or of a proposition which we understand. To begin with judgments: a judgment, as an occurrence, I take to be a relation of a mind to several entities, namely, the entities which compose what is judged. If, e.g., I judge that A loves B, the judgment as an event consists in the existence, at a certain moment, of a specific four-term relation, called *judging,* between me and A and love and B. That is to say, at the time when I judge, there is a certain complex whose terms are myself and A and love and B, and whose relating relation is *judging.* My reasons for this view have been set forth elsewhere,[2] and I shall not repeat them here. Assuming this view of judgment, the constituents of the judgment are simply the constituents of the complex which is the judgment. Thus, in the above case, the constituents are myself and A and love and B and judging. But myself and judging are constituents shared by all my judgments; thus the *distinctive* constituents of the particular judgment in question are A and love and B.

Coming now to what is meant by "understanding a proposition," I should say that there is another relation possible between me and A and love and B, which is called my *supposing* that A loves B.[3] When we can *suppose* that A loves B, we "understand the proposition" *A loves B.* Thus we often understand a proposition in cases where we have not enough knowledge to make a judgment. Supposing, like judging, is a many-term relation, of which a mind is one term. The other terms of the relation are called the constituents of the proposition supposed. Thus the principle which I enunciated may be re-stated as follows: *Whenever a relation of supposing or judging occurs, the terms to which the supposing or judging mind is related by the relation of supposing or judging must be terms with which the mind in question is acquainted.* This is merely to say that we cannot make a judgment or a supposition without knowing what it is that we are making our judgment or supposition about. It seems to me that the truth of this principle is evident as soon as the principle is understood; I shall, therefore, in what follows, assume the principle, and use it as a guide in analysing judgments that contain descriptions.

Returning now to Julius Caesar, I assume that it will be admitted that he himself is not a constituent of any judgment which I can make. But at this point it is necessary to examine the view that judgments are composed of something called "ideas," and that it is the "idea" of Julius Caesar that is a constituent of my judgment. I believe the plausibility of this view rests upon a failure to form a right theory of descriptions. We may mean by my "idea" of Julius Caesar the things that I know about him, e.g., that he conquered Gaul, was assassinated on the Ides of March, and is a plague to schoolboys. Now I am admitting, and indeed contending, that in order to discover what is actually in my mind when I judge about Julius Caesar, we must substitute for the proper name a description made up of some of the things I know about him. (A description which will often serve to express my thought is "the man whose name was *Julius Caesar.*" For whatever else I may have forgotten about him, it is plain that when I mention him I have not forgotten that that was his name.) But although I think the theory that judgments consist of ideas may have been suggested in some such way, yet I think the theory itself is fundamentally mistaken. The view seems to be that there is some mental existent which may be called the "idea" of something outside the mind of the person who has the idea, and that, since judgment is a mental event, its constituents must be constituents of the mind of the person judging. But in this view ideas become a veil between us and outside things—we never really, in knowledge, attain to the things we are supposed to be knowing about, but only to the ideas of those things. The relation of mind, idea, and object, on this view, is utterly obscure, and, so far as I can see, nothing discoverable by inspection warrants the intrusion of the idea between the mind and the object. I suspect that the view is fostered by the dislike of relations, and that it is felt the mind could not know objects unless there were something "in" the mind which could be called the state of knowing the object. Such a view, however, leads at once to a vicious endless regress, since the relation of idea to object will have to be explained by supposing that the idea itself has an idea of the object, and so on *ad infinitum*. I therefore see no reason to believe that, when we are acquainted with an object, there is in us something which can be called the "idea" of the object. On the contrary, I hold that acquaintance is wholly a relation, not demanding any such constituent of the mind as is supposed by advocates of "ideas." This is, of course, a large question, and one which would take us far from our subject if it were adequately discussed. I therefore content myself with the above indications, and with the corollary that, in judging, the actual objects concerning which we judge, rather than any supposed purely mental entities, are constituents of the complex which is the judgment.

When, therefore, I say that we must substitute for "Julius Caesar" some description of Julius Caesar, in order to discover the meaning of a judgment nominally about him, I am not saying that we must substitute an idea. Suppose our description is "the man whose name was *Julius Caesar*." Let our judgment be "Julius Caesar was assassinated." Then it becomes "the man whose name was *Julius Caesar* was assassinated." Here *Julius Caesar* is a noise or shape with which we are acquainted, and all the other constituents of the judgment (neglecting the tense in "was") are *concepts* with which we are acquainted. Thus our judgment is wholly reduced to constituents

with which we are acquainted, but Julius Caesar himself has ceased to be a constituent of our judgment. This, however, requires a proviso, to be further explained shortly, namely, that "the man whose name was *Julius Caesar*" must not, as a whole, be a constituent of our judgment, that is to say, this phrase must not, as a whole, have a meaning which enters into the judgment. Any right analysis of the judgment, therefore, must break up this phrase, and not treat it as a subordinate complex which is part of the judgment. The judgment "the man whose name was *Julius Caesar* was assassinated" may be interpreted as meaning "one and only one man was called *Julius Caesar*, and that one was assassinated." Here it is plain that there is no constituent corresponding to the phrase "the man whose name was *Julius Caesar*." Thus there is no reason to regard this phrase as expressing a constituent of the judgment, and we have seen that this phrase must be broken up if we are to be acquainted with all the constituents of the judgment. This conclusion, which we have reached from considerations concerned with the theory of knowledge, is also forced upon us by logical considerations, which must now be briefly reviewed.

It is common to distinguish two aspects, *meaning* and *denotation*, in such phrases as "the author of *Waverley*." The meaning will be a certain complex, consisting (at least) of authorship and *Waverley* with some relation; the denotation will be Scott. Similarly "featherless bipeds" will have a complex meaning, containing as constituents the presence of two feet and the absence of feathers, while its denotation will be the class of men. Thus when we say "Scott is the author of *Waverley*" or "men are the same as featherless bipeds," we are asserting an identity of denotation, and this assertion is worth making because of the diversity of meaning.[4] I believe that the duality of meaning and denotation, though capable of a true interpretation, is misleading if taken as fundamental. The denotation, I believe, is not a constituent of the proposition, except in the case of proper names, i.e., of words which do not assign a property to an object, but merely and solely name it. And I should hold further that, in this sense, there are only two words which are strictly proper names of particulars, namely, "I" and "this."[5]

One reason for not believing the denotation to be a constituent of the proposition is that we may know the proposition even when we are not acquainted with the denotation. The proposition "the author of *Waverley* is a novelist" was known to people who did not know that "the author of *Waverley*" denoted Scott. This reason has been already sufficiently emphasised.

A second reason is that propositions concerning "the so-and-so" are possible even when "the so-and-so" has no denotation. Take, e.g., "the golden mountain does not exist" or "the round square is self-contradictory." If we are to preserve the duality of meaning and denotation, we have to say, with Meinong, that there are such objects as the golden mountain and the round square, although these objects do not have being. We even have to admit that the existent round square is existent, but does not exist.[6] Meinong does not regard this as a contradiction, but I fail to see that it is not one. Indeed, it seems to me evident that the judgment "there is no such object as the round square" does not presuppose that there is such an object. If this is admitted, however, we are led to the conclusion that, by parity of form, no judgment concerning "the so-and-so" actually involves the so-and-so as a constituent.

Miss Jones[7] contends that there is no difficulty in admitting contradictory predicates concerning such an object as "the present King of France," on the ground that this object is in itself contradictory. Now it might, of course, be argued that this object, unlike the round square, is not self-contradictory, but merely non-existent. This, however, would not go to the root of the matter. The real objection to such an argument is that the law of contradiction ought not to be stated in the traditional form "A is not both B and not B," but in the form "no proposition is both true and false." The traditional form only applies to certain propositions, namely, to those which attribute a predicate to a subject. When the law is stated of propositions, instead of being stated concerning subjects and predicates, it is at once evident that propositions about the present King of France or the round square can form no exception, but are just as incapable of being both true and false as other propositions.

Miss Jones[8] argues that "Scott is the author of *Waverley*" asserts identity of denotation between *Scott* and *the author of Waverley*. But there is some difficulty in choosing among alternative meanings of this contention. In the first place, it should be observed *the author of Waverley* is not a *mere* name, like *Scott*. *Scott* is merely a noise or shape conventionally used to designate a certain person; it gives us no information about that person, and has nothing that can be called meaning as opposed to denotation. (I neglect the fact, considered above, that even proper names, as a rule, really stand for descriptions.) But *the author of Waverley* is not merely conventionally a name for Scott; the element of mere convention belongs here to the separate words, *the* and *author* and *of* and *Waverley*. Given what these words stand for, *the author of Waverley* is no longer arbitrary. When it is said that Scott is the author of *Waverley*, we are not stating that these are two *names* for one man, as we should be if we said "Scott is Sir Walter." A man's name is what he is called, but however much Scott had been called the author of *Waverley*, that would not have made him be the author; it was necessary for him actually to write *Waverley*, which was a fact having nothing to do with names.

If, then, we are asserting identity of denotation, we must not mean by *denotation* the mere relation of a name to the thing named. In fact, it would be nearer to the truth to say that the *meaning* of "Scott" is the *denotation* of "the author of *Waverley*." The relation of "Scott" to Scott is that "Scott" means Scott, just as the relation of "author" to the concept which is so called is that "author" means this concept. Thus if we distinguish meaning and denotation in "the author of *Waverley*," we shall have to say that "Scott" has meaning but not denotation. Also when we say "Scott is the author of *Waverley*," the *meaning* of "the author of *Waverley*" is relevant to our assertion. For if the denotation alone were relevant, any other phrase with the same denotation would give the same proposition. Thus "Scott is the author of *Marmion*" would be the same proposition as "Scott is the author of *Waverley*." But this is plainly not the case, since from the first we learn that Scott wrote *Marmion* and from the second we learn that he wrote *Waverley*, but the first tells us nothing about *Waverley* and the second nothing about *Marmion*. Hence the meaning of "the author of *Waverley*," as opposed to the denotation, is certainly relevant to "Scott is the author of *Waverley.*"

We have thus agreed that "the author of *Waverley*" is not a mere name, and that its meaning is relevant in propositions in which it occurs. Thus if we are to say, as Miss Jones does, that "Scott is the author of *Waverley*" asserts an identity of denotation, we must regard the denotation of "the author of Waverley" as the denotation of what is *meant* by "the author of *Waverley.*" Let us call the meaning of "the author of *Waverley*" M. Thus M is what "the author of *Waverley*" means. Then we are to suppose that "Scott is the author of *Waverley*" means "Scott is the denotation of M." But here we are explaining our proposition by another of the same form, and thus we have made no progress towards a real explanation. "The denotation of M," like "the author of *Waverley,*" has both meaning and denotation, on the theory we are examining. If we call its meaning M', our proposition becomes "Scott is the denotation of M'." But this leads at once to an endless regress. Thus the attempt to regard our proposition as asserting identity of denotation breaks down, and it becomes imperative to find some other analysis. When this analysis has been completed, we shall be able to reinterpret the phrase "identity of denotation," which remains obscure so long as it is taken as fundamental.

The first point to observe is that, in any proposition about "the author of *Waverley,*" provided Scott is not explicitly mentioned, the denotation itself, i.e., Scott, does not occur, but only the concept of denotation, which will be represented by a variable. Suppose we say "the author of *Waverley* was the author of *Marmion,*" we are certainly not saying that both were Scott—we may have forgotten that there was such a person as Scott. We are saying that there is some man who was the author of *Waverley* and the author of *Marmion*. That is to say, there is some one who wrote *Waverley* and *Marmion*, and no one else wrote them. Thus the identity is that of a variable, i.e., of an indefinite subject, "some one." This is why we can understand propositions about "the author of *Waverley,*" without knowing who he was. When we say "the author of *Waverley* was a poet," we mean "one and only one man wrote *Waverley*, and he was a poet"; when

we say "the author of *Waverley* was Scott" we mean "one and only one man wrote *Waverley*, and he was Scott." Here the identity is between a variable, i.e., an indeterminate subject ("he"), and Scott; "the author of *Waverley*" has been analysed away, and no longer appears as a constituent of the proposition.[9]

The reason why it is imperative to analyse away the phrase "the author of *Waverley*" may be stated as follows. It is plain that when we say "the author of *Waverley* is the author of *Marmion,*" the *is* expresses identity. We have seen also that the common *denotation*, namely Scott, is not a constituent of this proposition, while the *meanings* (if any) of "the author of *Waverley*" and "the author of *Marmion*" are not identical. We have seen also that, in any sense in which the meaning of a word is a constituent of a proposition in whose verbal expression the word occurs, "Scott" means the actual man Scott, in the same sense (so far as concerns our present discussion) in which "author" means a certain universal. Thus, if "the author of *Waverley*" were a subordinate complex in the above proposition, its *meaning* would have to be what was said to be identical with the *meaning* of "the author of *Marmion.*" This is plainly not the case; and the only escape is to say that "the author of *Waverley*" does not, by itself, have a meaning, though phrases of which it is part do have a meaning. That is, in a right analysis of the above proposition, "the author of *Waverley*" must disappear. This is effected when the above proposition is analysed as meaning: "Some one wrote *Waverley* and no one else did, and that some one also wrote *Marmion* and no one else did." This may be more simply expressed by saying that the propositional function "*x* wrote *Waverley* and *Marmion,* and no one else did" is capable of truth, i.e., some value of *x* makes it true, but no other value does. Thus the true subject of our judgment is a propositional function, i.e., a complex containing an undetermined constituent, and becoming a proposition as soon as this constituent is determined.

We may now define the denotation of a phrase. If we know that the proposition "*a* is the so-and-so" is true, i.e., that *a* is so-and-so and nothing else is, we call *a* the denotation of the phrase "the so-and-so." A very great many of the propositions we naturally make about "the so-and-so" will remain true or remain false if we substitute *a* for "the so-and-so," where *a* is the denotation of "the so-and-so." Such propositions will also remain true or remain false if we substitute for "the so-and-so" any other phrase having the same denotation. Hence, as practical men, we become interested in the denotation more than in the description, since the denotation decides as to the truth or falsehood of so many statements in which the description occurs. Moreover, as we saw earlier in considering the relations of description and acquaintance, we often wish to reach the denotation, and are only hindered by lack of acquaintance: in such cases the description is merely the means we employ to get as near as possible to the denotation. Hence it naturally comes to be supposed that the denotation is part of the proposition in which the description occurs. But we have seen, both on logical and on epistemological grounds, that this is an error. The actual object (if any) which is the denotation is not (unless it is explicitly mentioned) a constituent of propositions in which descriptions occur; and this is the reason why, in order to understand such propositions, we need acquaintance with the constituents of the description, but do not need acquaintance with its denotation. The first result of analysis, when applied to propositions whose grammatical subject is "the so-and-so," is to substitute a variable as subject; i.e., we obtain a proposition of the form: "There is *something* which alone is so-and-so, and that *something* is such-and-such." The further analysis of propositions concerning "the so-and-so" is thus merged in the problem of the nature of the variable, i.e., of the meanings of *some, any,* and *all.* This is a difficult problem, concerning which I do not intend to say anything at present.

To sum up our whole discussion: We began by distinguishing two sorts of knowledge of objects, namely, knowledge by *acquaintance* and knowledge by *description.* Of these it is only the former that brings the object itself before the mind. We have acquaintance with sense-data, with many universals, and possibly with ourselves, but not with physical objects or other minds. We have *descriptive* knowledge of an object when we know that it is *the* object having some property or properties with which we are acquainted; that is to say, when we know that the property or properties in question

belong to one object and no more, we are said to have knowledge of that one object by description, whether or not we are acquainted with the object. Our knowledge of physical objects and of other minds is only knowledge by description, the descriptions involved being usually such as involve sense-data. All propositions intelligible to us, whether or not they primarily concern things only known to us by description, are composed wholly of constituents with which we are acquainted, for a constituent with which we are not acquainted is unintelligible to us. A judgment, we found, is not composed of mental constituents called "ideas," but consists of an occurrence whose constituents are a mind[10] and certain objects, particulars or universals. (One at least must be a universal.) When a judgment is rightly analysed, the objects which are constituents of it must all be objects with which the mind which is a constituent of it is acquainted. This conclusion forces us to analyse descriptive phrases occurring in propositions, and to say that the objects denoted by such phrases are not constituents of judgments in which such phrases occur (unless these objects are explicitly mentioned). This leads us to the view (recommended also on purely logical grounds) that when we say "the author of *Marmion* was the author of *Waverley*," Scott himself is not a constituent of our judgment, and that the judgment cannot be explained by saying that it affirms identity of denotation with diversity of meaning. It also, plainly, does not assert identity of meaning. Such judgments, therefore, can only be analysed by breaking up the descriptive phrases, introducing a variable, and making propositional functions the ultimate subjects. In fact, "the so-and-so is such-and-such" will mean that "*x* is so-and-so and nothing else is, and *x* is such-and-such" is capable of truth. The analysis of such judgments involves many fresh problems, but the discussion of these problems is not undertaken in the present paper.

NOTES

1. See references later.
2. *Philosophical Essays,* "The Nature of Truth." I have been persuaded by Mr. Wittgenstein that this theory is somewhat unduly simple, but the modification which I believe it to require does not affect the above argument [1917].

3. Cf. Meinong, *Über Annahmen, passim.* I formerly supposed, contrary to Meinong's view, that the relationship of supposing might be merely that of presentation. In this view I now think I was mistaken, and Meinong is right. But my present view depends upon the theory that both in judgment and in assumption there is no single Objective, but the several constituents of the judgment or assumption are in a many-term relation to the mind.

4. This view has been recently advocated by Miss E. E. C. Jones. "A New Law of Thought and its Implications," *Mind,* January, 1911.

5. I should now exclude "I" from proper names in the strict sense, and retain only "this" [1917].

6. Meinong, *Über Annahmen,* 2nd ed., Leipzig, 1910, p. 141.

7. *Mind,* July, 1910, p. 380.

8. *Mind,* July, 1910, p. 379.

9. The theory which I am advocating is set forth fully, with the logical grounds in its favour, in *Principia Mathematica,* Vol. I, Introduction, Chap. 3; also, less fully, in *Mind,* October, 1905.

10. I use this phrase merely to denote the something psychological which enters into judgment, without intending to prejudge the question as to what this something is.

A Defence of Common Sense   14

G. E. MOORE

IN WHAT FOLLOWS I have merely tried to state, one by one, some of the most important points in which my philosophical position differs from positions which have been taken up by *some* other philosophers. It may be that the points which I have had room to mention are not really the most important, and possibly some of them may be points as to which no philosopher has ever really differed from me. But, to the best of my belief, each is a point as to which many have really differed; although (in most cases, at all events) each is also a point as to which many have agreed with me.

I.   The first point is a point which embraces a great many other points. And it is one which I cannot state as clearly as I wish to state it, except at some length. The method I am going to use for stating it is this. I am going to begin by enunciating, under the heading (1), a whole long list of propositions, which may seem, at first sight, such obvious truisms as not to be worth stating: they are, in fact, a set of propositions, every one of which (in my own opinion) I *know*, with certainty, to be true. I shall, next, under the heading (2), state a single proposition which makes an assertion about a whole set of *classes* of propositions—each class being defined, as the class consisting of all propositions which resemble *one* of the propositions in (1) in a certain respect. (2), therefore, is a proposition which could not be stated, until the list of propositions in (1), or some similar list, had already been given. (2) is itself a proposition which may seem such an obvious truism as not to be worth stating: and it is also a proposition which (in my own opinion) I *know*, with certainty, to be true. But, nevertheless, it is, to the best of my belief, a proposition with regard to which many philosophers have, for different reasons, differed from me; even if they have not directly denied (2) itself, they have held views incompatible with it. My first point, then, may be said to be that (2), together with all its implications, some of which I shall expressly mention, is true.

(1) I begin, then, with my list of truisms, every one of which (in my own opinion) I *know*, with certainty,

J. H. Muirhead, ed., *Contemporary British Philosophy* (second series), (Allen and Unwin, London: 1925), 192–233. Reprinted by permission of Timothy Moore.

to be true. The propositions to be included in this list are the following:

There exists at present a living human body, which is *my* body. This body was born at a certain time in the past, and has existed continuously ever since, though not without undergoing changes; it was, for instance, much smaller when it was born, and for some time afterwards, than it is now. Ever since it was born, it has been either in contact with or not far from the surface of the earth; and, at every moment since it was born, there have also existed many other things, having shape and size in three dimensions (in the same familiar sense in which it has), from which it has been at *various distances* (in the familiar sense in which it is now at a distance both from that mantelpiece and from that bookcase, and at a greater distance from the bookcase than it is from the mantelpiece); also there have (very often, at all events) existed some other things of this kind with which it was *in contact* (in the familiar sense in which it is now in contact with the pen I am holding in my right hand and with some of the clothes I am wearing). Among the things which have, in this sense, formed part of its environment (i.e., have been either in contact with it, or at *some* distance from it, however *great*) there have, at every moment since its birth, been large numbers of other living human bodies, each of which has, like it, (*a*) at some time been born, (*b*) continued to exist from some time after birth, (*c*) been, at every moment of its life after birth, either in contact with or not far from the surface of the earth; and many of these bodies have already died and ceased to exist. But the earth had existed also for many years before my body was born; and for many of these years, also, large numbers of human bodies had, at every moment, been alive upon it; and many of these bodies had died and ceased to exist before it was born. Finally (to come to a different class of propositions), I am a human being, and I have, at different times since my body was born, had many different experiences, of each of many different kinds: e.g., I have often perceived both my own body and other things which formed part of its environment, including other human bodies; I have not only perceived things of this kind, but have also observed facts about them, such as, for instance, the fact which I am now observing, that that mantelpiece is at

present nearer to my body than that bookcase; I have been aware of other facts, which I was not at the time observing, such as, for instance, the fact, of which I am now aware, that my body existed yesterday and was then also for some time nearer to that mantelpiece than to that bookcase; I have had expectations with regard to the future, and many beliefs of other kinds, both true and false; I have thought of imaginary things and persons and incidents, in the reality of which I did not believe; I have had dreams; and I have had feelings of many different kinds. And, just as my body has been the body of a human being, namely myself, who has, during his lifetime, had many experiences of each of these (and other) different kinds; so, in the case of very many of the other human bodies which have lived upon the earth, each has been the body of a different human being, who has, during the lifetime of that body, had many different experiences of each of these (and other) different kinds.

(2) I now come to the single truism which, as will be seen, could not be stated except by reference to the whole list of truisms, just given in (1). This truism also (in my own opinion) I *know*, with certainty, to be true; and it is as follows:

In the case of *very many* (I do not say *all*) of the human beings belonging to the class (which includes myself) defined in the following way, i.e., as human beings who have had human bodies, that were born and lived for some time upon the earth, and who have, during the lifetime of those bodies, had many different experiences of each of the kinds mentioned in (1), it is true that each has frequently, during the life of his body, known, with regard to *him*self or *his* body, and with regard to some time earlier than any of the times at which I wrote down the propositions in (1), a proposition *corresponding* to each of the propositions in (1), in the sense that it asserts with regard to *him*self or *his* body and the earlier time in question (namely, in each case, the time at which he knew it), just what the corresponding proposition in (1) asserts with regard to *me* or *my* body and the time at which I wrote that proposition down.

In other words what (2) asserts is only (what seems an obvious enough truism) that each of *us* (meaning by 'us', very many human beings of the class defined) has frequently *known*, with regard to *him*self or *his* body and the time at which he knew it, everything which, in writing down my list of propositions in (1), I was claiming to know about *my*self or *my* body and the time at which I wrote that proposition down, i.e., just as *I* knew (when I wrote it down) 'There exists at present a living human body which is my body', so each of us has frequently known with regard to himself and some other time the different but corresponding proposition, which *he* could *then* have properly expressed by, 'There exists *at present* a human body which is *my* body'; just as *I* know 'Many human bodies other than mine have before now lived on the earth', so each of us has frequently known the different but corresponding proposition 'Many human bodies other than *mine* have before *now* lived on the earth'; just as *I* know 'Many human beings other than myself have before now perceived, and dreamed, and felt', so each of *us* has frequently known the different but corresponding proposition 'Many human beings other than *myself* have before *now* perceived, and dreamed, and felt'; and so on, in the case of *each* of the propositions enumerated in (1).

I hope there is no difficulty in understanding, so far, what this proposition (2) asserts. I have tried to make clear by examples what I mean by 'propositions *corresponding* to each of the propositions in (1)'. And what (2) asserts is merely that each of us has frequently known to be true a proposition *corresponding* (in that sense) to each of the propositions in (1)—a *different* corresponding proposition, of course, at each of the times at which he knew such a proposition to be true.

But there remain two points, which, in view of the way in which some philosophers have used the English language, ought, I think, to be expressly mentioned, if I am to make quite clear exactly how much I am asserting in asserting (2).

The first point is this. Some philosophers seem to have thought it legitimate to use the word 'true' in such a sense that a proposition which is partially false may nevertheless also be true; and some of these, therefore, would perhaps *say* that propositions like those enumerated in (1) are, in their view, true, when all the time they believe that every such proposition is partially false. I wish, therefore, to make it quite plain that I am not using 'true' in any such sense. I am using it in such a sense (and I think

this is the ordinary usage) that if a proposition is partially false, it follows that it is *not* true, though, of course, it may be *partially* true. I am maintaining, in short, that all the propositions in (1), and also many propositions corresponding to each of these, are *wholly* true; I am asserting this in asserting (2). And hence any philosopher, who does in fact believe, with regard to any or all of these classes of propositions, that every proposition of the class in question is partially false, is, in fact, disagreeing with me and holding a view incompatible with (2), even though he may think himself justified in *saying* that he believes some propositions belonging to all of these classes to be 'true'.

And the second point is this. Some philosophers seem to have thought it legitimate to use such expressions as, e.g., 'The earth has existed for many years past', as if they expressed something which they really believed, when in fact they believe that every proposition, which such an expression would *ordinarily* be understood to express, is, at least partially, false; and all they really believe is that there is some *other* set of propositions, related in a certain way to those which such expressions do actually express, which, unlike these, really are true. That is to say, they use the expression 'The earth has existed for many years past' to express, not what it would ordinarily be understood to express, but the proposition that some proposition, related to this in a certain way, is true; when all the time they believe that the proposition, which this expression would ordinarily be understood to express, is, at least partially, false. I wish, therefore, to make it quite plain that I was not using the expressions I used in (1) in any such subtle sense. I meant by each of them precisely what every reader, in reading them, will have understood me to mean. And any philosopher, therefore, who holds that any of these expressions, if understood in this popular manner, expresses a proposition which embodies some popular error, is disagreeing with me and holding a view incompatible with (2), even though he may hold that there is some *other*, true, proposition which the expression in question might be legitimately used to express.

In what I have just said, I have assumed that there is some meaning which is *the* ordinary or popular meaning of such expressions as 'The earth has existed for many years past'. And this, I am afraid, is an assumption which some philosophers are capable of disputing. They seem to think that the question 'Do you believe that the earth has existed for many years past?' is not a plain question, such as should be met either by a plain 'Yes' or 'No', or by a plain 'I can't make up my mind', but is the sort of question which can be properly met by: 'It all depends on what you mean by "the earth" and "exists" and "years": if you mean so and so, and so and so, and so and so, then I do; but if you mean so and so, and so and so, and so and so, or so and so, and so and so, and so and so, or so and so, and so and so, and so and so, then I don't, or at least I think it is extremely doubtful'. It seems to me that such a view is as profoundly mistaken as any view can be. Such an expression as 'The earth has existed for many years past' is the very type of an unambiguous expression, the meaning of which we all understand. Anyone who takes a contrary view must, I suppose, be confusing the question whether we understand its meaning (which we all certainly do) with the entirely different question whether we *know what it means*, in the sense that we are able to *give a correct analysis* of its meaning. The question what is the correct analysis of *the* proposition meant *on any occasion* (for, of course, as I insisted in defining (2), a different proposition is meant at every different time at which the expression is used) by 'The earth has existed for many years past' is, it seems to me, a profoundly difficult question, and one to which, as I shall presently urge, no one knows the answer. But to hold that we do not know what, in certain respects, is the analysis of what we understand by such an expression, is an entirely different thing from holding that we do not understand the expression. It is obvious that we cannot even raise the question how what we do understand by it is to be analysed, unless we do understand it. So soon, therefore, as we know that a person who uses such an expression is using it in its ordinary sense, we understand his meaning. So that in explaining that I was using the expressions used in (1) in their ordinary sense (those of them which have an ordinary sense, which is not the case with quite all of them), I have done all that is required to make my meaning clear.

But now, assuming that the expressions which I have used to express (2) are understood, I think, as I have said, that many philosophers have really held

views incompatible with (2). And the philosophers who have done so may, I think, be divided into two main groups. A. What (2) asserts is, with regard to a whole set of *classes* of propositions, that we have, each of us, frequently *known* to be true propositions belonging to *each* of these classes. And one way of holding a view incompatible with this proposition is, of course, to hold, with regard to one or more of the classes in question, that *no* propositions of that class *are* true—that all of them are, at least partially, false; since if, in the case of any one of these classes, *no* propositions of that class *are* true, it is obvious that nobody can have *known* any propositions of that class to be true, and therefore that *we* cannot have known to be true propositions belonging to *each* of these classes. And my first group of philosophers consists of philosophers who have held views incompatible with (2) for this reason. They have held, with regard to one or more of the classes in question, simply that no propositions of that class *are* true. Some of them have held this with regard to *all* the classes in question; some only with regard to *some* of them. But, of course, whichever of these two views they have held, they have been holding a view inconsistent with (2). B. Some philosophers, on the other hand, have not ventured to assert, with regard to *any* of the classes in (2), that no propositions of that class *are* true, but what they have asserted is that, in the case of some of these classes, no human being has ever *known*, with certainty, that any propositions of the class in question are true. That is to say, they differ profoundly from philosophers of group A, in that they hold that propositions of *all* these classes *may* be true; but nevertheless they hold a view incompatible with (2) since they hold, with regard to some of these classes, that none of us has ever *known* a proposition of the class in question to be true.

A. I said that some philosophers, belonging to this group, have held that no propositions belonging to *any* of the classes in (2) are wholly true, while others have only held this with regard to *some* of the classes in (2). And I think the chief division of this kind has been the following. Some of the propositions in (1) (and, therefore, of course, all propositions belonging to the corresponding classes in (2)) are propositions which cannot be true, unless some *material things* have existed and have stood *in spatial relations* to one another: that is to say, they are propositions which, *in a certain sense*, imply *the reality of material things*, and *the reality of Space*. E.g., the proposition that my body has existed for many years past, and has, at every moment during that time been either in contact with or not far from the earth, is a proposition which implies both the *reality of material things* (provided you use 'material things' in such a sense that to deny the reality of material things implies that no proposition which asserts that human bodies have existed, or that the earth has existed, is wholly true) and also the *reality of Space* (provided, again, that you use 'Space' in such a sense that to deny the reality of Space implies that no proposition which asserts that anything has ever been in contact with or at a distance from another, in the familiar senses pointed out in (1), is wholly true). But others among the propositions in (1) (and, therefore, propositions belonging to the corresponding classes in (2)), do not (at least obviously) imply either the reality of material things or the reality of Space: e.g., the propositions that I have often had dreams, and have had many different feelings at different times. It is true that propositions of this second class do imply one thing which is also implied by all propositions of the first, namely that *(in a certain sense) Time is real*, and imply also one thing not implied by propositions of the first class, namely that *(in a certain sense) at least one Self is real*. But I think there are some philosophers, who, while denying that (in the senses in question) either material things or Space are real, have been willing to admit that Selves and Time are real, in the sense required. Other philosophers, on the other hand, have used the expression 'Time is not real', to express some view that they held; and some, at least, of these have, I think, meant by this expression something which is incompatible with the truth of *any* of the propositions in (1)—they have meant, namely, that *every* proposition of the sort that is expressed by the use of 'now' or 'at present', e.g., 'I am now both seeing and hearing' or 'There exists at present a living human body', or by the use of a *past* tense, e.g., 'I *have* had many experiences in the past', or 'The earth *has* existed for many years', are, at least partially, false.

All the four expressions I have just introduced, namely 'Material things are not real', 'Space is not real', 'Time is not real', 'The Self is not real', are, I think, unlike the expressions I used in (1), really ambiguous. And it may be that, in the case of each of them, some philosopher has used the expression in question to express some view he held which was not incompatible with (2). With such philosophers, if there are any, I am not, of course, at present concerned. But it seems to me that the most natural and proper usage of each of these expressions is a usage in which it *does* express a view incompatible with (2); and, in the case of each of them, some philosophers have, I think, really used the expression in question to express such a view. All such philosophers have, therefore, been holding a view incompatible with (2).

All such views, whether incompatible with *all* of the propositions in (1), or only with *some* of them, seem to me to be quite certainly false; and I think the following points are specially deserving of notice with regard to them.

(*a*) If *any* of the classes of propositions in (2) is such that no proposition of that class is true, then no philosopher has ever existed, and therefore none can ever have held with regard to any such class, that no proposition belonging to it is true. In other words, the proposition that some propositions belonging to each of these classes are true is a proposition which has the peculiarity, that, if any philosopher has ever denied it, it follows from the fact that he has denied it, that he must have been wrong in denying it. For when I speak of 'philosophers' I mean, of course (as we all do), exclusively philosophers who have been human beings, with human bodies that have lived upon the earth, and who have at different times had many different experiences. If, therefore, there have been any philosophers, there have been human beings of this class; and if there have been human beings of this class, all the rest of what is asserted in (1) is certainly true too. Any view, therefore, incompatible with the proposition that many propositions corresponding to each of the propositions in (1) are true, can only be true, on the hypothesis that no philosopher has ever held any such view. It follows, therefore, that, in considering whether this proposition is true, I cannot consistently regard the fact that many philosophers, whom I respect, have, to the best of my belief, held views incompatible with it, as having any weight at all against it. Since, if I know that they have held such views, I am, *ipso facto*, knowing that they were mistaken; and, if I have no reason to believe that the proposition in question is true, I have still less reason to believe that they have held views incompatible with it; since I am more certain that they have existed and held *some* views, i.e., that the proposition in question is true, than that they have held any views incompatible with it.

(*b*) It is, of course, the case that all philosophers who have held such views have repeatedly, even in their philosophical works, expressed other views inconsistent with them: i.e., no philosopher has ever been able to hold such views consistently. One way in which they have betrayed this inconsistency, is by alluding to the existence of other philosophers. Another way is by alluding to the existence of the human race, and in particular by using 'we' in the sense in which I have already constantly used it, in which any philosopher who asserts that 'we' do so and so, e.g., that '*we* sometimes believe propositions that are not true', is asserting not only that he himself has done the thing in question, but that *very many other human beings, who have had bodies and lived upon the earth,* have done the same. The fact is, of course, that all philosophers have belonged to the class of human beings which exists only if (2) be true: that is to say, to the class of human beings who have frequently *known* propositions corresponding to each of the propositions in (1). In holding views incompatible with the proposition that propositions of all these classes are true, they have, therefore, been holding views inconsistent with propositions which they themselves *knew* to be true; and it was, therefore, only to be expected that they should sometimes betray their knowledge of such propositions. The strange thing is that philosophers should have been able to hold sincerely, as part of their philosophical creed, propositions inconsistent with what they themselves *knew* to be true; and yet, so far as I can make out, this has really frequently happened. My position, therefore, on this first point, differs from that of philosophers belonging to this group A, not in that I hold anything which they don't hold, but only in that I don't hold, as part of my philosophical creed, things which they do hold

as part of theirs—that is to say, propositions inconsistent with some which they and I both hold in common. But this difference seems to me to be an important one.

(*c*) Some of these philosophers have brought forward, in favour of their position, arguments designed to show, in the case of some or all of the propositions in (1), that no propositions of that type can possibly be wholly true, because every such proposition entails both of two incompatible propositions. And I admit, of course, that if any of the propositions in (1) did entail both of two incompatible propositions it could not be true. But it seems to me I have an absolutely conclusive argument to show that none of them does entail both of two incompatible propositions. Namely this: All of the propositions in (1) are true; no true proposition entails both of two incompatible propositions; therefore, none of the propositions in (1) entails both of two incompatible propositions.

(*d*) Although, as I have urged, no philosopher who has held with regard to any of these types of proposition that no propositions of that type are true, has failed to hold also other views inconsistent with his view in this respect, yet I do not think that the view, with regard to any or all of these types, that no proposition belonging to them is true, is *in itself* a self-contradictory view, i.e., entails both of two incompatible propositions. On the contrary, it seems to me quite clear that it *might* have been the case that Time was not real, material things not real, space not real, selves not real. And in favour of my view that none of these things, which might have been the case, *is* in fact the case, I have, I think, no better argument than simply this—namely, that all the propositions in (1) are, in fact, true.

B. This view, which is usually considered a much more modest view than A, has, I think, the defect that, unlike A, it really is self-contradictory, i.e., entails both of two mutually incompatible propositions.

Most philosophers who have held this view, have held, I think, that though each of us knows propositions corresponding to *some* of the propositions in (1), namely to those which merely assert that *I* myself have had in the past experiences of certain kinds at many different times, yet none of us knows *for certain* any propositions either of the type (*a*) which assert the existence of *material things* or of the type (*b*) which assert the existence of *other* selves, beside myself, and that *they* also have had experiences. They admit that we do in fact *believe* propositions of both these types, and that they *may* be true: some would even say that we know them to be highly probable; but they deny that we ever know them, *for certain*, to be true. Some of them have spoken of such beliefs as 'beliefs of Common Sense', expressing thereby their conviction that beliefs of this kind are very commonly entertained by mankind: but they are convinced that these things are, in all cases, only *believed*, not known for certain; and some have expressed this by saying that they are matters of Faith, not of Knowledge.

Now the remarkable thing which those who take this view have not, I think, in general duly appreciated, is that, in each case, the philosopher who takes it is making an assertion about 'us'—that is to say, not merely about himself, but about *many other human beings as well.* When he says 'No human being has ever *known* of the existence of other human beings', he is saying: 'There have been many other human beings beside myself, and none of them (including myself) has ever known the existence of other human beings'. If he says: 'These beliefs are beliefs of Common Sense, but they are not matters of *knowledge*', he is saying: 'There have been many other human beings, beside myself, who have shared these beliefs, but neither I nor any of the rest have ever known them to be true'. In other words, he asserts with confidence that these beliefs *are* beliefs of Common Sense, and seems often to fail to notice that, *if* they are, they must be true; since the proposition that they are beliefs of Common Sense is one which logically entails the proposition both of type (*a*) and of type (*b*); it logically entails the proposition that many human beings, beside the philosopher himself, have had human bodies, which lived upon the earth, and have had various experiences, including beliefs of this kind. This is why this position, as contrasted with positions of group A, seems to me to be self-contradictory. Its difference from A consists in the fact that it is making a proposition about *human knowledge* in general, and therefore is actually asserting the existence of many human beings, whereas philosophers of group A in stating their position are not doing this: they are only contradicting *other* things which they hold. It is true that a philosopher who says 'There have existed many human beings beside myself, and none of us has ever known the existence of any human beings beside himself', is only contradicting himself if what he holds is 'There have *certainly* existed many human beings beside myself' or, in other words, '*I* know that there have existed other human beings beside myself'. But this, it seems to me, is what such philosophers have in fact been generally doing. They seem to me constantly to betray the fact that they regard the proposition that those beliefs *are* beliefs of Common Sense, or the proposition that they themselves are not the only members of the human race, as not merely true, but *certainly* true; and *certainly* true it cannot be, unless one member, at least, of the human race, namely themselves, has *known* the very things which that member is declaring that no human being has ever known.

Nevertheless, my position that I *know*, with certainty, to be true all of the propositions in (1), is certainly not a position, the denial of which entails both of two incompatible propositions. If I do *know* all these propositions to be true, then, I think, it is quite certain that other human beings also have known corresponding propositions: that is to say (2) also *is* true, and *I* know it to be true. But do I really *know* all the propositions in (1) to be true? Isn't it possible that I merely believe them? Or know them to be highly probable? In answer to this question, I think I have nothing better to say than that it seems to me that I *do* know them, with certainty. It is, indeed, obvious that, in the case of most of them, I do not know them *directly*: that is to say, I only know them because, in the past, I have known to be true *other* propositions which were evidence for them. If, for instance, I do know that the earth had existed for many years before I was born, I certainly only know this because I have known other things in the past which were evidence for it. And I certainly do not know exactly what the evidence was. Yet all this seems to me to be no good reason for doubting that I do know it. We are all, I think, in this strange position that we do *know* many things, with regard to which we *know* further that we must have had evidence for them, and yet we do not know *how* we know them, i.e., we do not know what the evidence was. If there is any 'we', and if we know that there is, this must be so: for that there is a 'we', is one of the things in question. And that I do know that there is a 'we', that is to say, that many other human beings, with human bodies, have lived upon the earth, it seems to me that I do know, for certain.

If this first point in my philosophical position, namely my belief in (2), is to be given any name, which has actually been used by philosophers in classifying the positions of other philosophers, it would have, I think, to be expressed by saying that I am one of those philosophers who have held that the 'Common Sense view of the world' is, in certain fundamental features, *wholly* true. But it must be remembered that, according to me, *all* philosophers, without exception, have agreed with me in holding this: and that the real difference, which is commonly expressed in this way, is only a difference between those philosophers, who have *also* held views inconsistent with these features in 'the Common Sense view of the world', and those who have not.

The features in question (namely, propositions of any of the classes defined in defining (2)) are all of them features, which have this peculiar property— namely, that *if we know that they are features in the 'Common Sense view of the world', it follows that they are true:* it is self-contradictory to maintain that *we* know them to be features in the Common Sense view, and that yet they are not true; since to say that *we* know this, is to say that they are true. And many of them also have the further peculiar property that, *if they are features in the Common Sense view of the world (whether 'we' know this or not), it follows that they are true,* since to say that there is a 'Common Sense view of the world', is to say that they are true. The phrases 'Common Sense view of the world' or 'Common Sense beliefs' (as used by philosophers) are, of course, extraordinarily vague; and, for all I know, there may be many propositions which may be properly called features in 'the Common Sense view of the world' or 'Common Sense beliefs', which are not true, and which deserve to be mentioned with the contempt with which some philosophers speak of 'Common Sense beliefs'. But to speak with contempt of those 'Common Sense beliefs'

which I have mentioned is quite certainly the height of absurdity. And there are, of course, enormous numbers of other features in 'the Common Sense view of the world' which, if these are true, are quite certainly true too: e.g., that there have lived upon the surface of the earth not only human beings, but also many different species of plants and animals, etc., etc. . . . .

IV. I now come to a point of a very different order.

As I have explained under I, I am not at all sceptical as to the *truth* of such propositions as 'The earth has existed for many years past', 'Many human bodies have each lived for many years upon it', i.e., propositions which assert the existence of material things: on the contrary, I hold that we all know, with certainty, many such propositions to be true. But I am very sceptical as to what, in certain respects, the correct *analysis* of such propositions is. And this is a matter as to which I think I differ from many philosophers. Many seem to hold that there is no doubt at all as to their *analysis*, nor, therefore, as to the analysis of the proposition 'Material things have existed', in certain respects in which I hold that the analysis of the propositions in question is extremely doubtful; and some of them, as we have seen, while holding that there is no doubt as to their *analysis*, seem to have doubted whether any such propositions are *true*. I, on the other hand, while holding that there is no doubt whatever that many such propositions are wholly true, hold also that no philosopher, hitherto, has succeeded in suggesting an analysis of them, as regards certain important points, which comes anywhere near to being certainly true.

It seems to me quite evident that the question how propositions of the type I have just given are to be analysed, depends on the question how propositions of another and simpler type are to be analysed. I know, at present, that I am perceiving a human hand, a pen, a sheet of paper, etc.; and it seems to me that I cannot know how the proposition 'Material things exist' is to be analysed, until I know how, in certain respects, these simpler propositions are to be analysed. But even these are not simple enough. It seems to me quite evident that my knowledge that I am now perceiving a human hand is a deduction from a pair of propositions simpler still—propositions which I can only express in the form 'I am perceiving *this*' and '*This* is a human hand'. It is the analysis of propositions of the latter kind which seems to me to present such great difficulties, while nevertheless the whole question as to the *nature* of material things obviously depends upon their analysis. It seems to me a surprising thing that so few philosophers, while saying a great deal as to what material things *are* and as to what it is to perceive them, have attempted to give a clear account as to what precisely they suppose themselves to *know* (or to *judge*, in case they have held that we don't *know* any such propositions to be true, or even that no such propositions *are* true) when they know or judge such things as 'This is a hand', 'That is the sun', 'This is a dog', etc., etc., etc.

Two things only seem to me to be quite certain about the analysis of such propositions (and even with regard to these I am afraid some philosophers would differ from me) namely that whenever I know, or judge, such a proposition to be true, (1) there is always some *sense-datum* about which the proposition in question is a proposition—some sense-datum which is *a* subject (and, in a certain sense, the principal or ultimate subject) of the proposition in question, and (2) that, nevertheless, *what* I am knowing or judging to be true about this sense-datum is not (in general) that it is *itself* a hand, or a dog, or the sun, etc., etc., as the case may be.

Some philosophers have I think doubted whether there are any such things as other philosophers have meant by 'sense-data' or 'sensa'. And I think it is quite possible that some philosophers (including myself, in the past) have used these terms in senses such that it is really doubtful whether there are any such things. But there is no doubt at all that there are sense-data, in the sense in which I am now using that term. I am at present seeing a great number of them, and feeling others. And in order to point out to the reader what sort of things I mean by sense-data, I need only ask him to look at his own right hand. If he does this he will be able to pick out something (and, unless he is seeing double, *only* one thing) with regard to which he will see that it is, at first sight, a natural view to take that that thing is identical, not, indeed, with his whole right hand, but with that part of its surface which he is actually seeing, but will also (on a little reflection) be able

to see that it is doubtful whether it can be identical with the part of the surface of his hand in question. Things *of the sort* (in a certain respect) of which this thing is, which he sees in looking at his hand, and with regard to which he can understand how some philosophers should have supposed it to *be* the part of the surface of his hand which he is seeing, while others have supposed that it can't be, are what I mean by 'sense-data'. I therefore define the term in such a way that it is an open question whether the sense-datum which I now see in looking at my hand and which is a sense-datum of my hand is or is not identical with that part of its surface which I am now actually seeing.

That what I know, with regard to this sense-datum, when I know 'This is a human hand', is not that it is *itself* a human hand, seems to me certain because I know that my hand has many parts (e.g., its other side, and the bones inside it), which are quite certainly *not* parts of this sense-datum.

I think it certain, therefore, that the analysis of the proposition 'This is a human hand' is, roughly at least, of the form 'There is a thing, and only one thing, of which it is true both that it is a human hand and that *this surface* is a part of its surface'. In other words, to put my view in terms of the phrase 'theory of representative perception', I hold it to be quite certain that I do not *directly* perceive *my hand*; and that when I am said (as I may be correctly said) to 'perceive' it, that I 'perceive' it means that I perceive (in a different and more fundamental sense) something which is (in a suitable sense) *representative* of it, namely, a certain part of its surface.

This is all that I hold to be *certain* about the analysis of the proposition 'This is a human hand'. We have seen that it includes in its analysis a proposition of the form 'This is part of the surface of a human hand' (where 'This', of course, has a different meaning from that which it has in the original proposition which has now been analysed). But this proposition also is undoubtedly a proposition about the sense-datum, which I am seeing, which is a sense-datum *of* my hand. And hence the further question arises: *What*, when I know '*This is part of the surface of* a human hand', am I knowing about the sense-datum in question? Am I, in this case, really knowing about the sense-datum in question that it *itself* is part of the surface of a human hand?

Or, just as we found in the case of 'This is a human hand', that what I was knowing about the sense-datum was certainly not that it *itself* was a human hand, so, is it perhaps the case, with this new proposition, that even here I am not knowing, with regard to the sense-datum, that it is *itself* part of the surface of a hand? And, if so, what is it that I am knowing about the sense-datum itself?

This is the question to which, as it seems to me, no philosopher has hitherto suggested an answer which comes anywhere near to being *certainly* true.

There seem to me to be three, and only three, alternative types of answer possible; and to any answer yet suggested, of any of these types, there seem to me to be very grave objections.

(1) Of the first type, there is but one answer: namely, that in this case what I am knowing really is that the sense-datum *itself* is part of the surface of a human hand. In other words that, though I don't perceive *my hand* directly, I do *directly* perceive part of its surface; that the sense-datum itself *is* this part of its surface and not merely something which (in a sense yet to be determined) 'represents' this part of its surface; and that hence the sense in which I 'perceive' this part of the surface of my hand, is not in its turn a sense which needs to be defined by reference to yet a third more ultimate sense of 'perceive', which is the only one in which perception is direct, namely that in which I perceive the sense-datum.

If this view is true (as I think it may just possibly be), it seems to me certain that we must abandon a view which has been held to be certainly true by most philosophers, namely the view that our sense-data always really have the qualities which they sensibly appear to us to have. For I know that if another man were looking through a microscope at the same surface which I am seeing with the naked eye, the sense-datum which he saw would sensibly appear to him to have qualities very different from and incompatible with those which my sense-datum sensibly appears to me to have: and yet, if my sense-datum is identical with the surface we are both of us seeing, his must be identical with it also. My sense-datum can, therefore, be identical with this surface only on condition that it is identical with his sense-datum; and, since his sense-datum sensibly appears to him to have qualities incompat-

ible with those which mine sensibly appears to me to have, his sense-datum can be identical with mine only on condition that the sense-datum in question either has not got the qualities which it sensibly appears to me to have, or has not got those which it sensibly appears to him to have.

I do not, however, think that this is a fatal objection to this first type of view. A far more serious objection seems to me to be that, when we see a thing double (have what is called 'a double image' of it), we certainly have *two* sense-data each of which is *of* the surface seen, and which cannot therefore both be identical with it; and that yet it seems as if, if any sense-datum is ever identical with the surface *of* which it is a sense-datum, each of these so-called 'images' must be so. It looks, therefore, as if every sense-datum is, after all, only 'representative' of the surface, *of* which it is a sense-datum.

(2) But, if so, what relation has it to the surface in question?

This second type of view is one which holds that when I know 'This is part of the surface of a human hand', what I am knowing with regard to the sense-datum which is *of* that surface, is, *not* that it is *itself* part of the surface of a human hand, but something of the following kind. There is, it says, *some* relation, R, such that what I am knowing with regard to the sense-datum is either 'There is one thing and only one thing, of which it is true both that it is a part of the surface of a human hand, and that it has R to this sense-datum', or else 'There are a set of things, of which it is true both that that set, taken collectively, *are* part of the surface of a human hand, and also that each member of the set has R to this sense-datum, and that nothing which is not a member of the set has R to it'.

Obviously, in the case of this second type, many different views are possible, differing according to the view they take as to what the relation R is. But there is only one of them, which seems to me to have any plausibility; namely that which holds that R is an ultimate and unanalysable relation, which might be expressed by saying that 'xRy' means the same as 'y is an appearance or manifestation of x'. I.e., the analysis which this answer would give of 'This is part of the surface of a human hand' would be 'There is one and only one thing of which it is true both that it is part of the surface of a human hand, and that this sense-datum is an appearance or manifestation of it'.

To this view also there seem to me to be very grave objections, chiefly drawn from a consideration of the questions how we can possibly *know* with regard to any of our sense-data that there is one thing and one thing only which has to them such a supposed ultimate relation; and how, if we do, we can possibly *know* anything further about such things, e.g., of what size or shape they are.

(3) The third type of answer, which seems to me to be the only possible alternative if (1) and (2) are rejected, is the type of answer which J. S. Mill seems to have been implying to be the true one when he said that material things are 'permanent possibilities of sensation'. He seems to have thought that when I know such a fact as 'This is part of the surface of a human hand', what I am knowing with regard to the sense-datum which is the principal subject of that fact, is not that it is itself part of the surface of a human hand, nor yet, with regard to any relation, that *the* thing which has to it that relation is part of the surface of a human hand, but a whole set of hypothetical facts each of which is a fact of the form 'If *these* conditions had been fulfilled, I should have been perceiving a sense-datum intrinsically related to *this* sense-datum in *this* way', 'If *these* (other) conditions had been fulfilled, I should have been perceiving a sense-datum intrinsically related to *this* sense-datum in *this* (other) way', etc., etc.

With regard to this third type of view as to the analysis of propositions of the kind we are considering, it seems to me, again, just *possible* that it is a true one; but to hold (as Mill himself and others seems to have held) that it is *certainly*, or nearly certainly, true, seems to me as great a mistake, as to hold with regard either to (1) or to (2) , that they are *certainly*, or nearly certainly, true. There seem to me to be very grave objections to it; in particular the three, (*a*) that though, in general, when I know such a fact as 'This is a hand', I certainly do know some hypothetical facts of the form 'If *these* conditions had been fulfilled, I should have been perceiving a sense-datum of *this* kind, which would have been a sense-datum of the same surface of which *this*

is a sense-datum', it seems doubtful whether any conditions with regard to which I know this are not themselves conditions of the form 'If this and that *material thing* had been in those positions and conditions . . .', (*b*) that it seems again very doubtful whether there is any intrinsic relation, such that my knowledge that (under *these* conditions) I should have been perceiving a sense-datum of *this* kind, which would have been a sense-datum of the same surface of which *this* is a sense-datum, is equivalent to a knowledge, with regard to that relation, that I should, under those conditions, have been perceiving a sense-datum related by it to *this* sense-datum, and (*c*) that, if it were true, the sense in which a material surface is 'round' or 'square', would necessarily be utterly different from that in which our sense-data sensibly appear to us to be 'round' or 'square'.

V. Just as I hold that the proposition 'There are and have been material things' is quite certainly true, but that the question how this proposition is to be analysed is one to which no answer that has been hitherto given is anywhere near certainly true; so I hold that the proposition 'There are and have been many Selves' is quite certainly true, but that here again all the analyses of this proposition that have been suggested by philosophers are highly doubtful.

That I am now perceiving many different sense-data, and that I have at many times in the past perceived many different sense-data, I know for certain—that is to say, I know that there are mental facts of class (β), connected in a way which it is proper to express by saying that they are all of them facts about *me*; but how this kind of connexion is to be analysed, I do not know for certain, nor do I think that any other philosopher knows with any approach to certainty. Just as in the case of the proposition 'This is part of the surface of a human hand', there are several extremely different views as to its analysis, each of which seems to me *possible*, but none nearly certain, so also in the case of the proposition 'This, that and that sense-datum are all at present being perceived by *me*', and still more so in the case of the proposition '*I* am now perceiving this sense-datum, and *I* have in the past perceived sense-data of these other kinds'. Of the *truth* of these propositions there seems to me to be no doubt, but as to what is the correct analysis of them there seems to me to be the gravest doubt—the true analysis may, for instance, *possibly* be quite as paradoxical as is the third view given above under IV as to the analysis of 'This is part of the surface of a human hand'; but whether it *is* as paradoxical as this seems to me to be quite as doubtful as in that case. Many philosophers, on the other hand, seem to me to have assumed that there is little or no doubt as to the correct analysis of such propositions; and many of these, just reversing my position, have also held that the propositions themselves are not true.

15   The Given Element in Experience

C. I. LEWIS

THE PRESUMPTION FROM WHICH we set out is that it is the business of philosophy to analyze and interpret our common experience, and by reflection, to bring to clear and cogent expression those principles which are implicit because they are brought to experience by the mind itself. Philosophy is the study of the a priori. It seeks to reveal those categorial criteria which the mind applies to what is given to it, and by correct delineation of those criteria to define the good, the right, the valid, and the real.

The attempt, however, so to approach the problems of philosophy leads at once to outstanding questions concerning the nature of knowledge, solution of which seems prerequisite. The distinction between what is a priori and what is not, is here presumed; as is also the correlative distinction between mind, or what mind brings to experience, and some other element, presumably independent of the mind's activity and responsible for other parts or aspects of experience. Have we a right to these distinctions? What are the grounds on which they can be drawn? How, in these terms, are knowledge and experience constituted? It is with such questions that the remainder of this book is concerned.

Its principal theses are the following: (1) The two elements to be distinguished in knowledge are the concept, which is the product of the activity of thought, and the sensuously given, which is independent of such activity. (2) The concept gives rise to the a priori; all a priori truth is definitive, or explicative of concepts. (3) The pure concept and the content of the given are mutually independent; neither limits the other. (4) Empirical truth, or knowledge of the objective, arises through conceptual interpretation of the given. (5) The empirical object, denoted by a concept, is never a momentarily given as such, but is some temporally-extended pattern of actual and possible experience. (6) Hence the assignment of any concept to the momentarily given (which is characteristic of perceptual knowledge) is essentially predictive and only partially verified. There is no knowledge merely by direct awareness. (7) Actual experience can never be exhaustive of that pattern, projected in the interpretation of the given, which constitutes the real object. Hence all empirical knowledge is probable only. (8) The mutual independence of the concept and the given, and the merely probable character of empirical truth, are entirely compatible with the validity of cognition. The problem of the "deduction of the categories" can be met without any metaphysical assumption of a preestablished amenability to categorial order in what is independent of the mind. (9) More explicitly, any conceivable experience will be such that it can be subsumed under concepts, and also such that predictive judgments which are genuinely probable will hold of it.

Mind and the World Order (New York: Charles Scribner's Sons, 1929), pp. 36–66. Reprinted by permission of Dover Publishing.

This chapter . . . [is] devoted to the distinction of the two elements in experience, and to the defense of this distinction from various common misinterpretations.

There are, in our cognitive experience, two elements; the immediate data, such as those of sense, which are presented or given to the mind, and a form, construction, or interpretation, which represents the activity of thought. Recognition of this fact is one of the oldest and most universal of philosophic insights. However, the manner in which these elements, and their relation to one another, are conceived, varies in the widest possible manner, and divergence on this point marks a principal distinction amongst theories of knowledge. As a result, even the most general attempt to designate these two elements—as by the terms used above—is likely to be objected to. Nevertheless this distinction, in some terms or other, is admitted to a place in almost every philosophy. To suppress it altogether, would be to betray obvious and fundamental characteristics of experience. If there be no datum given to the mind, then knowledge must be contentless and arbitrary; there would be nothing which it must be true to. And if there be no interpretation or construction which the mind itself imposes, then thought is rendered superfluous, the possibility of error becomes inexplicable, and the distinction of true and false is in danger of becoming meaningless. If the significance of knowledge should lie in the data of sense alone, without interpretation, then this significance would be assured by the mere presence of such data to the mind, and every cognitive experience must be veracious. . . .

We may . . . take it for granted, as something generally recognized, that there are in experience these two elements, something given and the interpretation or construction put upon it. But the very fact that the recognition of this is so general and of such long standing enforces the necessity of considering the distinction with care. Different significances have been assigned to it, both historically and in contemporary thought. Moreover, various metaphysical issues gather about it: What is the relation between the given and the real? How does mind construct or interpret? What is this mind which can interpret: does it transcend experience? If so, how can it be known? If not, how can it condition experience in general by its interpretation? Confronted with such a tangle of problems, we shall do best, I think, if first we can catch our facts. If we can identify the thing to be discussed, a certain degree of clarity will accrue simply by telling the truth about it, if we can.

There is, in all experience, that element which we are aware that we do not create by thinking and cannot, in general, displace or alter. As a first approximation, we may designate it as "the sensuous."

At the moment, I have a fountain pen in my hand. When I so describe this item of my present experience, I make use of terms whose meaning I have learned. Correlatively I abstract this item from the total field of my present consciousness and relate it to what is not just now present in ways which I have learned and which reflect modes of action which I have acquired. It might happen that I remember my first experience of such a thing. If so, I should find that this sort of presentation did not then mean "fountain pen" to me. I bring to the present moment something which I did not then bring; a relation of this to other actual and possible experiences, and a classification of what is here presented with things which I did not then include in the same group. This present classification depends on that learned relation of this experience, to other possible experience and to my action, which the shape, size, etc., of this object was not then a sign of. A savage in New Guinea, lacking certain interests and habits of action which are mine, would not so classify it. There is, to be sure, something in the character of this thing as a merely presented colligation of sense-qualities which is for me the clue to this classification or meaning; but that just this complex of qualities should be due to a "pen" character of the object is something which has been acquired. Yet what I refer to as "the given" in this experience is, in broad terms, qualitatively no different than it would be if I were an infant or an ignorant savage.

Again, suppose my present interest to be slightly altered. I might then describe this object which is in my hand as "a cylinder" or "hard rubber" or "a poor buy." In each case the thing is somewhat differently related in my mind, and the connoted modes of my possible behavior toward it, and my further experience of it, are different. Something called "given" remains constant, but its character as sign, its classification, and its relation to other things and to action are differently taken.

In whatever terms I describe this item of my experience, I shall not convey it *merely* as given, but shall supplement this by a meaning which has to do with relations, and particularly with relation to other experiences which I regard as possible but which are not just now actual. The manner of this supplementation reflects my habitual interests and modes of activity, the nature of my mind. The infant may see it much as I do, but still it will mean to him none of these things I have described it as being, but merely "plaything" or "smooth biteable." But for any mind whatever, it will be more than what is merely given if it be noted at all. Some meaning of it also will be contained in the experience. All that comes under this broad term "meaning" (unless immediate value or the specificity of sense-quality should be included) is brought to this experience by the mind, as is evidenced by the fact that in this respect the experience is alterable to my interest and my will.

This meaning or interpretation or construction which is attached to the given is significant in two directions, connected but different. The one is the relation of this which is immediately presented to further actual and possible experience; the other is its relation of my interest and action. The relation to other experience, is something which is brought to the present by a selective memory. As applied to this present given, however, it is significant, not of the past, but of an actual or possible future, continuous with this present moment. Thus this given is set in a relation with a to-be-given or could-be-given, and this setting is an interpretation of it which the temporal process of experience may verify or prove erroneous. The other relation—of the given to present interest or attitude—connotes an interplay between the temporal process of further possible experience and my own purposes and behavior. Since I not only think but physically act, I enter into the temporal process of the future as a factor which determines, in some part, what it shall present. Thus my interpretation is predictive of my own physical behavior as forecast by my present interested attitude, and of further experience as affected

by that behavior. In all those ways in which my interpretation could be phrased as predictive not of future actual but only of *possible* experience, it very likely has reference to ways of acting which I know I might adopt at will and the future experience which I *should* then expect.

My designation of this thing as "pen" reflects my purpose to write; as "cylinder" my desire to explain a problem in geometry or mechanics; as "a poor buy" my resolution to be more careful hereafter in my expenditures. These divergent purposes are anticipatory of certain different future contingencies which are expected to accrue, in each case, partly as a result of my own action.

The distinction between this element of interpretation and the given is emphasized by the fact that the latter is what remains unaltered, no matter what our interests, no matter how we think or conceive. I can apprehend this thing as pen or rubber or cylinder, but I cannot, by taking thought, discover it as paper or soft or cubical.

While we can thus isolate the element of the given by these criteria of its unalterability and its character as sensuous feel or quality, we cannot describe any particular given *as such,* because in describing it, in whatever fashion, we qualify it by bringing it under some category or other, select from it, emphasize aspects of it, and relate it in particular and avoidable ways. If there be states of pure esthesis, in violent emotion or in the presence of great art, which are unqualified by thought, even these can be conveyed— and perhaps even retained in memory—only when they have been rendered articulate by thought. So that in a sense the given is ineffable, always. It is that which remains untouched and unaltered, however it is construed by thought. Yet no one but a philosopher could for a moment deny this immediate presence in consciousness of that which no activity of thought can create or alter.

If now we have fastened upon the fact of experience which we wish to discuss as the given element in it, it is time that we proceed to clarify this conception and guard against various possible misinterpretations.

An initial difficulty may arise from ambiguity of the word "given." This term has most frequently been used in philosophy in meanings at least close to the one here intended. But on occasion it has the widely different significance of denoting those data which philosophy in general finds or takes for granted at the beginning of its study. And occasionally those who use the term in this second meaning make it carry something of methodological polemic against any notion that "the immediate" or "sense-data" are allowable categories of explanation in epistemology.

What I should have to say on this point is, in part at least, already clear from the preceding chapter. It is indeed the thick experience of the world of things, not the thin given of immediacy, which constitutes the datum for philosophic reflection. We do not see patches of color, but trees and houses; we hear, not indescribable sound, but voices and violins. What we most certainly know are objects and full-bodied facts about them which could be stated in propositions. Such initial data of object and fact set the problem in philosophy and are, in a measure, the criteria of its solution, since any philosophic theory will rightfully be rejected as inaccurate or inadequate if it does not measure up to, or account for, experience in this broad sense.

But the acceptance of such preanalytic data[1] as an ultimate epistemological category would, if really adhered to, put an end to all worthwhile investigation of the nature of knowledge—or to any other intellectual enterprise. What lies on the surface can be taken as ultimate only so long as there is no problem to be solved, or else no solution to be hoped for. Without analysis, there can be no advance of understanding.

The given, as here conceived, is certainly an abstraction. Unless there be such a thing as pure esthesis (and I should join with the critic in doubting this), the given never exists in isolation in any experience or state of consciousness. Any Kantian "manifold" as a psychic datum or moment of experience, is probably a fiction, and the assumption of it as such is a methodological error. The given is *in,* not before, experience. But the condemnation of abstractions is the condemnation of thought itself. Nothing that thought can ever comprise is other than some abstraction which cannot exist in isolation. Everything mentionable is an abstraction except the concrete universal; and the concrete universal is a myth. Thought can do just two things: it can separate, by analysis, entities which in their temporal or spatial

existence are not separated, and it can conjoin, by synthesis, entities which in their existence are disjoined. Only the mystic or those who conceive that man would be better off without an upper-brain, have ground for objection to analysis and abstractions. The only important question is whether this abstracted element, the "given," is genuinely to be discovered in experience. On this point I can, of course, only appeal to the reader. I shall hope that he has already identified provisionally what the word intends, and proceed upon that basis.

Assuming, however, such provisional identification, there are still ambiguities of language to be avoided. I have so far spoken of "the given" and "data of sense" as roughly synonymous, but the latter phrase has connotations which are slightly inappropriate. In the first place, "sense-data," as a psychological category, may be distinguished from other mental content by their correlation with the processes in the afferent nerves. A distinction made by the criterion of such correlation with nervous processes is open to two objections in epistemology. In the first place, the thing or mental state itself must first be accurately identifiable before such correlation can be established. If it is thus identifiable, the correlation is not essential and is, in fact, superfluous in discussions of epistemology by the method of reflection and analysis. Second, there is the more general objection that the theory of knowledge is a subject too fundamental to rest upon distinctions drawn from the particular sciences. Basic problems of category and of the general nature of knowledge are antecedent to the special sciences and cannot, therefore, legitimately depend upon their particular findings. Especially is this important as regards psychology, a valid method for which is, at the present moment, a serious problem. The manner in which my own body is known to me, the subjectivity or objectivity of pleasantness or emotional tone, the validity of the correlation between mental states which I inspect directly only in my own case (if such is the fact) and nervous processes which I can observe only in another organism; these are themselves problems which have at least an epistemological side.

Also, the particular purposes which the psychologist has in mind in making his analysis of mental states may be out of place in epistemology. "Sense-datum" may connote relation to particular sense-organs (as in the distinction between taste and odor), and hence mark a division where none can be drawn by direct inspection. Also other qualities than the strictly sensory may be as truly given; the pleasantness or fearfulness of a thing may be as un-get-overable as its brightness or loudness—that question, at least, must not be prejudiced. Hence "sense-data," defined by correlation with nervous processes, should have no place in our program. It is the brute-fact element in perception, illusion and dream (without antecedent distinction) which is intended.

However, if it be understood that the methodological connotation of psychological categories is not here in point, it will cause no confusion if I continue to refer to the "sensuous" or the "feeling" character of the given: the element in experience which is intended is difficult to designate in any terms which are not thus preempted to slightly different uses. It seems better to use language which is familiar, even at some risk of ambiguity, than to invent a technical jargon which would, after all, be no less ambiguous until its precise connotation could be discovered from its use.

There is also another and different kind of ambiguity which must be avoided. Obviously, we must distinguish the given from the *object which* is given. The given is presentation of something real, in the normal case at least; *what* is given (given in part) is this real object. But the whatness of this object involves its categorial interpretation; the real object, as known, is a construction put upon this experience of it, and includes much which is not, at the moment, given in the presentation.

Still further comment is required in view of contemporary theories which deal with the content of immediacy in a different fashion.[2]

When we remember that even the delimitation of that in which we are interested, the singling out of the presentation of our object from other accompanying consciousness is, in some part at least, a work of excision or abstraction wrought by the mind, we may be led to remark that there is, in all strictness, only one given, the Bergsonian real duration or the stream of consciousness. This, I take it, is at least approximately correct. The absolutely given is a specious present, fading into the past and growing into the future with no genuine bound-

aries. The breaking of this up into the presentation of things marks already the activity of an interested mind. On the other hand, we should beware of conceiving the given as a smooth undifferentiated flux; that would be wholly fictitious. Experience, when it comes, contains within it just those disjunctions which, when they are made explicit by our attention, mark the boundaries of events, "experiences" and things. The manner in which a field of vision or a duration breaks into parts reflects our interested attitudes, but attention cannot mark disjunctions in an undifferentiated field.

The interruptions and differences which form the boundaries of events and things are both given *and* constituted by interpretation. That the rug is on the floor or the thunder follows the flash, is as much given as the color of the rug or the loudness of the crash. But that I find this disjunction of rug and floor possessed of a meaning which the wrinkles in the rug do not have, reflects my past experience to taking up and putting down rugs. The cognitively significant on-the-floorness of the rug requires both the given break in the field of vision and the interpretation of it as the boundary between manipulable object and unyielding support.

Even in that sense in which the given is always one whole, it is not important for our purpose of analyzing knowledge that we should dwell upon this integrality of it. Our interest is, rather, in the *element* of givenness in what we may, for usual and commonplace reasons, mark off as "an experience" or "an object." This given element in a single experience of an object is what will be meant by "a presentation." Such a presentation is, obviously, an event and historically unique. But for most of the purposes of analyzing knowledge one presentation of a half-dollar held at right angles to the line of vision, etc., will be as good as another. If, then, I speak of "*the* presentation" of this or that, it will be on the supposition that the reader can provide his own illustration. No identification of the event itself with the repeatable content of it is intended.

In any presentation, this content is either a specific quale (such as the immediacy of redness or loudness) or something analyzable into a complex of such. The presentation as an event is, of course, unique, but the qualia which make it up are not.

They are recognizable from one to another experience. Such specific qualia and repeatable complexes of them are nowadays sometimes designated as "essences." This term, with such a meaning, will here be avoided; the liability to confuse such qualia with universal concepts makes this imperative.

It is at once the plausibility and the fatal error of "critical realism" that it commits this confusion of the logical universal with given qualia of sense by denominating both of these "essences." As will be pointed out later, what any concept denotes—or any adjective such as "red" or "round"—is something more complex than an identifiable sensequale. In particular, the object of the concept must always have a time-span which extends beyond the specious present; this is essential to the cognitive significance of concepts. The qualia of sense as something given do not, in the nature of the case, have such temporal spread. Moreover, such qualia, though repeatable in experience and intrinsically recognizable, have no names. They are fundamentally different from the "universals" of logic and of traditional problems concerning these. Elucidation of this point must wait upon the sequel.

The somewhat similar use of the terms "sensa" and "sense-data" is also likely to prove prejudicial. Mr. Broad in particular has used these terms in a fashion which gives what is denoted by them a dubious metaphysical status. He says, for example:[3] "We agreed that, if they (sensa) are states of mind at all, they must be presentations. But we find no reason *for* thinking that they are states of mind, and much the same reasons *against* that view as led us to hold that sensations are analyzable into act and sensum. . . . We saw no intrinsic reason why coloured patches or noises should not be capable of existing unsensed." And elsewhere:[4] "A sense-datum with which I am acquainted may perfectly well have parts with which I am not acquainted. If therefore I say that a given sense-datum has no parts except those which I have noticed and mentioned I may quite well be wrong. Similarly there may well be differences of quality which I cannot detect. If I say: This sense-datum with which I am acquainted is coloured all over with a uniform shade of red, this statement may be false."

Now it is indeed obvious that I may make erroneous report of the given, because I can make no report at all except by the use of language, which imports concepts which are *not* given. The sensum-theory, like the essence-theory, fails to go deep enough and to distinguish what is really given from what is imported by interpretation. There is interpretation involved in calling the *sensum "elliptical"* as much as in calling the *penny "round."* It means, for example, to assert something about the motion one must make with one's finger in order to hide successively the different portions of the periphery. Also it is true, of course, that if I report the given as "red," I may convey an erroneous impression because I am heedless of color-meanings, and another observer who should have an experience qualitatively the same might report "orange" or "violet." Similarly I may report "round" when an artist would report "elliptical," because I am not used to projecting things on a plane. All those difficulties which the psychologist encounters in dealing with reports of introspection may be sources of error in any report of the given. It may require careful self-questioning, or questioning by another, to elicit the full and correct account of a given experience. But Mr. Broad seems here to assert an entirely different ground of possible mistake. He seems to mean that with the same sensum before me I may at one moment see it red and at a later moment somewhat mottled or more deeply shaded at the center, and so forth.

Now if I look fixedly at a card and see it first uniform and then mottled, I shall very likely and quite properly report that the color of the surface has a quality which I did not at first see. But the subject of this statement is the *real* color of the *real* card, and the statement itself is not a report of the content of sense but *an interpretation* put upon my succession of sensory experience. It imports a distinction between the subjective and the objective which is irrelevant to *givenness* as such. There certainly is such a thing as the shape of a penny or the color of a card which can exist unnoticed while I am looking at it—or when I am not. This is because the shape of the penny has the same *kind* of enduring reality as the penny, and a quite different kind of reality from the intermittent presentation of the penny in my consciousness. But I thought it was the initial point of the sensum-theory to provide a name—if not a local habitation—for what I *see* as opposed to *what* I see, the ellipticity of the appearance as against the real roundness of the penny. As such, it should be of the essence of the sensum to be sensed; the sensum which is neither the real shape of the real penny nor the appearance of it in a mind is neither fish, flesh nor good red herring. A sensum which is not sensed, or a sense-datum which continues unaltered while consciousness of it changes, is merely a new kind of *ding an sich,* which is none the better for being inappropriately named so as to suggest its phenomenological character.

What is given may exist outside the mind—that question should not be prejudiced. But in order that we may meaningfully assert such existence, it is essential that there be an answer to the questions: What would it mean if that which is given has such independent existence? In what respect would experience in general be different if it had no such independent reality? For a sensum which is not sensed, it is difficult to see what answer there can be to such questions.[5] The main objection to the sensum-theory is that it leaves at once the ground of the analysis of experience and plunges into metaphysics. It would explain the immediate and indubitable by something intrinsically unverifiable and highly dubious.

It is of the essence of what will here be meant by "the given" that it should be *given.* We need not say that what is given is a "mental state" or even "in the mind" in any more explicit sense than is itself implied in such givenness. Nor should it be presumed that what is thus in mind is *exclusively* mental. The nature of that interpretation or construction by which we come to know objects suggests that the given must be, in some sense or other, a constituent of objective reality as well. All such questions are simply *later questions.* If there should be metaphysical problems concerning the kind of reality which what is "in mind" may have, it is not necessary to anticipate the solution of these beyond what may be verified in the discovery that certain items or aspects of the content of experience satisfy the criteria of givenness. These are, first, its specific sensuous or feeling-character, and second, that the mode of thought can neither create nor alter it—that it remains unaffected by any change of mental attitude or interest. It is the second of these criteria which is

definitive; the first alone is not sufficient, for reasons which will appear.

This given element is never, presumably, to be discovered in isolation. If the content of perception is first given and then, in a later moment, interpreted, we have no consciousness of such a first state of intuition unqualified by thought, though we *do* observe *alteration* and *extension* of interpretation of given content as a psychological temporal process. A state of intuition utterly unqualified by thought is a figment of the metaphysical imagination, satisfactory only to those who are willing to substitute a dubious hypothesis for the analysis of knowledge as we find it. The given is admittedly an excised element or abstraction; all that is here claimed is that it is not an "unreal" abstraction, but an identifiable constituent in experience.

NOTES

1. I borrow this useful phrase from Professor Loewenberg; see his article "Preanalytic and Postanalytic Data," *The Journal of Philosophy,* vol. 24 (1927), pp. 5*ff.*

2. Extended discussion of such theories cannot be included here; the object of the discussion is merely that of clarifying, by contrast, the terminology and procedure here adopted. Though criticisms will be ventured, it is recognized that the discussion is not sufficient fully to substantiate these.

3. "Scientific Thought" p. 265.

4. "Proceedings of the Aristotelian Society." supp. vol. II, p. 218.

5. I am never quite sure that I may not be misunderstanding Mr. Broad on this point. (I might say the same thing about Mr. Russell's "perspectives.") It may be that he means only that when no eye is situated at a certain angle from the penny, it is still true that if there were a normal observer there, he would observe this elliptical appearance, and that the appearance is there whether the observer is or not. To this I can give real meaning: the last part of the statement means the first part—that the appearance is there when *not* observed, means that if any observer *were* there he *would* observe it. Or it means that other effects of the penny are there, such as an image registered on a camera-plate, and that these may be verified by the same methods as the existence of physical objects when not observed. But if what Mr. Broad means to call to our attention is the fact that the truth of the statement, "If an observer were there, he would observe so and so," can not be tested when no one *is* there; and if its being thus true when not verified is what is meant by the exis-

tence of unsensed sensa; then I am compelled to say that the hypothesis is merely verbal nonsense. A hypothesis which in the nature of the case is incapable of any conceivable test is the hypothesis of nothing. What is *normally* meant by saying, "If an observer were there he would observe so and so," is verifiable by the fact that, other conditions being altered at will, whenever an observer *is* there he *does* see this. As will be pointed out later, the attribution of properties to objects and of existence to objects, consists, from the point of view of cognition, precisely in the truth of such hypothetical propositions. And these are held to be true *when* the hypothesis is contrary to fact. But

what we *mean* by the truth of such propositions is precisely the sort of thing set forth above: the hypothetical, "If *X* were, then *Y* would be," means, "However other conditions be varied, and condition *X* being similarly supplied at will, whenever *X* is, *Y* is." If the existence of an appearance or sensum when it is not sensed means its observability at will, then it means its existence *whenever* it *is* sensed. So far as I can see, there is nothing else which such existence reasonably could mean. In this, of course, I am merely arguing for the indispensability to meaning of the "pragmatic test" of Peirce and James.

Two Dogmas of Empiricism   16

W. V. QUINE

MODERN EMPIRICISM HAS BEEN conditioned in large part by two dogmas. One is a belief in some fundamental cleavage between truths which are *analytic,* or grounded in meanings independently of matters of fact, and truths which are *synthetic,* or grounded in fact. The other dogma is *reductionism:* the belief that each meaningful statement is equivalent to some logical construct upon terms which refer to immediate experience. Both dogmas, I shall argue, are ill-founded. One effect of abandoning them is, as we shall see, a blurring of the supposed boundary between speculative metaphysics and natural science. Another effect is a shift toward pragmatism.

1. BACKGROUND FOR ANALYTICITY

Kant's cleavage between analytic and synthetic truths was foreshadowed in Hume's distinction between relations of ideas and matters of fact, and in Leibniz's distinction between truths of reason and truths of fact. Leibniz spoke of the truths of reason as true in all possible worlds. Picturesqueness aside,

this is to say that the truths of reason are those which could not possibly be false. In the same vein we hear analytic statements defined as statements whose denials are self-contradictory. But this definition has small explanatory value; for the notion of self-contradictoriness, in the quite broad sense needed for this definition of analyticity, stands in exactly the same need of clarification as does the notion of analyticity itself. The two notions are the two sides of a single dubious coin.

Kant conceived of an analytic statement as one that attributes to its subject no more than is already conceptually contained in the subject. This formulation has two shortcomings: it limits itself to statements of subject-predicate form, and it appeals to a notion of containment which is left at a metaphorical level. But Kant's intent, evident more from the use he makes of the notion of analyticity than from his definition of it, can be restated thus: a statement is analytic when it is true by virtue of meanings and independently of fact. Pursuing this line, let us examine the concept of *meaning* which is presupposed.

The Philosophical Review 60 (1951), 20–43. Copyright 1951 Cornell University. Reprinted by permission of the publisher.

Meaning, let us remember, is not to be identified with naming. Frege's example of 'Evening Star' and 'Morning Star', and Russell's of 'Scott' and 'the author of *Waverley*', illustrate that terms can name the same thing but differ in meaning. The distinction between meaning and naming is no less important at the level of abstract terms. The terms '9' and 'the number of the planets' name one and the same abstract entity but presumably must be regarded as unlike in meaning; for astronomical observation was needed, and not mere reflection on meanings, to determine the sameness of the entity in question.

The above examples consist of singular terms, concrete and abstract. With general terms, or predicates, the situation is somewhat different but parallel. Whereas a singular term purports to name an entity, abstract or concrete, a general term does not; but a general term is *true of* an entity, or of each of many, or of none. The class of all entities of which a general term is true is called the *extension* of the term. Now paralleling the contrast between the meaning of a singular term and the entity named, we must distinguish equally between the meaning of a general term and its extension. The general terms 'creature with a heart' and 'creature with kidneys', for example, are perhaps alike in extension but unlike in meaning.

Confusion of meaning with extension, in the case of general terms, is less common than confusion of meaning with naming in the case of singular terms. It is indeed a commonplace in philosophy to oppose intension (or meaning) to extension, or, in a variant vocabulary, connotation to denotation.

The Aristotelian notion of essence was the forerunner, no doubt, of the modern notion of intension or meaning. For Aristotle it was essential in men to be rational, accidental to be two-legged. But there is an important difference between this attitude and the doctrine of meaning. From the latter point of view it may indeed be conceded (if only for the sake of argument) that rationality is involved in the meaning of the word 'man' while two-leggedness is not; but two-leggedness may at the same time be viewed as involved in the meaning of 'biped' while rationality is not. Thus from the point of view of the doctrine of meaning it makes no sense to say of the actual individual, who is at once a man and a biped, that his rationality is essential and his two-leggedness accidental or vice versa. Things had essences, for Aristotle, but only linguistic forms have meanings. Meaning is what essence becomes when it is divorced from the object of reference and wedded to the word.

For the theory of meaning a conspicuous question is the nature of its objects: what sort of things are meanings? A felt need for meant entities may derive from an earlier failure to appreciate that meaning and reference are distinct. Once the theory of meaning is sharply separated from the theory of reference, it is a short step to recognizing as the primary business of the theory of meaning simply the synonymy of linguistic forms and the analyticity of statements; meanings themselves, as obscure intermediary entities, may well be abandoned.

The problem of analyticity then confronts us anew. Statements which are analytic by general philosophical acclaim are not, indeed, far to seek. They fall into two classes. Those of the first class, which may be called *logically true,* are typified by:

(1)   No unmarried man is married.

The relevant feature of this example is that it not merely is true as it stands, but remains true under any and all reinterpretations of 'man' and 'married'. If we suppose a prior inventory of *logical* particles, comprising 'no', 'un-', 'not', 'if', 'then', 'and', etc., then in general a logical truth is a statement which is true and remains true under all reinterpretations of its components other than the logical particles.

But there is also a second class of analytic statements, typified by:

(2)   No bachelor is married.

The characteristic of such a statement is that it can be turned into a logical truth by putting synonyms for synonyms; thus (2) can be turned into (1) by putting 'unmarried man' for its synonym 'bachelor'. We still lack a proper characterization of this second class of analytic statements, and therewith of analyticity generally, inasmuch as we have had in the above description to lean on a notion of "synonymy" which is no less in need of clarification than analyticity itself.

In recent years Carnap has tended to explain analyticity by appeal to what he calls state-descriptions.[1] A state-description is any exhaustive assignment of truth values to the atomic, or noncompound, statements of the language. All other statements of the language are, Carnap assumes, built up of their component clauses by means of the familiar logical devices, in such a way that the truth value of any complex statement is fixed for each state-description by specifiable logical laws. A statement is then explained as analytic when it comes out true under every state description. This account is an adaptation of Leibniz's "true in all possible worlds." But note that this version of analyticity serves its purpose only if the atomic statements of the language are, unlike 'John is a bachelor' and 'John is married', mutually independent. Otherwise there would be a state-description which assigned truth to 'John is a bachelor' and to 'John is married', and consequently 'No bachelors are married' would turn out synthetic rather than analytic under the proposed criterion. Thus the criterion of analyticity in terms of state-descriptions serves only for languages devoid of extra-logical synonym-pairs, such as 'bachelor' and 'unmarried man'—synonym-pairs of the type which give rise to the "second class" of analytic statements. The criterion in terms of state-descriptions is a reconstruction at best of logical truth, not of analyticity.

I do not mean to suggest that Carnap is under any illusions on this point. His simplified model language with its state-descriptions is aimed primarily not at the general problem of analyticity but at another purpose, the clarification of probability and induction. Our problem, however, is analyticity; and here the major difficulty lies not in the first class of analytic statements, the logical truths, but rather in the second class, which depends on the notion of synonymy.

2. DEFINITION

There are those who find it soothing to say that the analytic statements of the second class reduce to those of the first class, the logical truths, by *definition;* 'bachelor', for example, is *defined* as 'unmarried man'. But how do we find that 'bachelor' is defined as 'unmarried man'? Who defined it thus, and when? Are we to appeal to the nearest dictionary, and accept the lexicographer's formulation as law? Clearly this would be to put the cart before the horse. The lexicographer is an empirical scientist, whose business is the recording of antecedent facts; and if he glosses 'bachelor' as 'unmarried man' it is because of his belief that there is a relation of synonymy between those forms, implicit in general or preferred usage prior to his own work. The notion of synonymy presupposed here has still to be clarified, presumably in terms relating to linguistic behavior. Certainly the "definition" which is the lexicographer's report of an observed synonymy cannot be taken as the ground of the synonymy.

Definition is not, indeed, an activity exclusively of philologists. Philosophers and scientists frequently have occasion to "define" a recondite term by paraphrasing it into terms of a more familiar vocabulary. But ordinarily such a definition, like the philologist's, is pure lexicography, affirming a relation of synonymy antecedent to the exposition in hand.

Just what it means to affirm synonymy, just what the interconnections may be which are necessary and sufficient in order that two linguistic forms be properly describable as synonymous, is far from clear; but, whatever these interconnections may be, ordinarily they are grounded in usage. Definitions reporting selected instances of synonymy come then as reports upon usage.

There is also, however, a variant type of definitional activity which does not limit itself to the reporting of preexisting synonymies. I have in mind what Carnap calls *explication*—an activity to which philosophers are given, and scientists also in their more philosophical moments. In explication the purpose is not merely to paraphrase the definiendum into an outright synonym, but actually to improve upon the definiendum by refining or supplementing its meaning. But even explication, though not merely reporting a preexisting synonymy between definiendum and definiens, does rest nevertheless on *other* preexisting synonymies. The matter may be viewed as follows. Any word worth explicating has some contexts which, as wholes, are clear and precise enough to be useful; and the purpose of explication is to preserve the usage of these favored contexts while sharpening the usage of other contexts. In order that a given definition be suitable for purposes of explication, therefore, what is required is not that the definiendum in its antecedent usage be synonymous with the definiens, but just that each of these favored contexts of the definiendum, taken as a whole in its antecedent usage, be synonymous with the corresponding context of the definiens.

Two alternative definientia may be equally appropriate for the purposes of a given task of explication and yet not be synonymous with each other; for they may serve interchangeably within the favored contexts but diverge elsewhere. By cleaving to one of these definientia rather than the other, a definition of explicative kind generates, by fiat, a relation of synonymy between definiendum and definiens which did not hold before. But such a definition still owes its explicative function, as seen, to preexisting synonymies.

There does, however, remain still an extreme sort of definition which does not hark back to prior synonymies at all: namely, the explicitly conventional introduction of novel notations for purposes of sheer abbreviation. Here the definiendum becomes synonymous with the definiens simply because it has been created expressly for the purpose of being synonymous with the definiens. Here we have a really transparent case of synonymy created by definition; would that all species of synonymy were as intelligible. For the rest, definition rests on synonymy rather than explaining it.

The word 'definition' has come to have a dangerously reassuring sound, owing no doubt to its frequent occurrence in logical and mathematical writings. We shall do well to digress now into a brief appraisal of the role of definition in formal work.

In logical and mathematical systems either of two mutually antagonistic types of economy may be striven for, and each has its peculiar practical utility. On the one hand we may seek economy of practical expression—ease and brevity in the statement of multifarious relations. This sort of economy calls usually for distinctive concise notations for a wealth of concepts. Second, however, and oppositely, we may seek economy in grammar and vocabulary; we may try to find a minimum of basic concepts such that, once a distinctive notation has been ap-

propriated to each of them, it becomes possible to express any desired further concept by mere combination and iteration of our basic notations. This second sort of economy is impractical in one way, since a poverty in basic idioms tends to a necessary lengthening of discourse. But it is practical in another way: it greatly simplifies theoretical discourse *about* the language, through minimizing the terms and the forms of construction wherein the language consists.

Both sorts of economy, though prima facie incompatible, are valuable in their separate ways. The custom has consequently arisen of combining both sorts of economy by forging in effect two languages, the one a part of the other. The inclusive language, though redundant in grammar and vocabulary, is economical in message lengths, while the part, called primitive notation, is economical in grammar and vocabulary. Whole and part are correlated by rules of translation whereby each idiom not in primitive notation is equated to some complex built up of primitive notation. These rules of translation are the so-called *definitions* which appear in formalized systems. They are best viewed not as adjuncts to one language but as correlations between two languages, the one a part of the other.

But these correlations are not arbitrary. They are supposed to show how the primitive notations can accomplish all purposes, save brevity and convenience, of the redundant language. Hence the definiendum and its definiens may be expected, in each case, to be related in one or another of the three ways lately noted. The definiens may be a faithful paraphrase of the definiendum into the narrower notation, preserving a direct synonymy[2] as of antecedent usage; or the definiens may, in the spirit of explication, improve upon the antecedent usage of the definiendum; or finally, the definiendum may be a newly created notation, newly endowed with meaning here and now.

In formal and informal work alike, thus, we find that definition—except in the extreme case of the explicitly conventional introduction of new notations—hinges on prior relations of synonymy. Recognizing then that the notion of definition does not hold the key to synonymy and analyticity, let us look further into synonymy and say no more of definition.

3. INTERCHANGEABILITY

A natural suggestion, deserving close examination, is that the synonymy of two linguistic form consists simply in their interchangeability in all contexts without change of truth value—interchangeability, in Leibniz's phrase, *salva veritate*.[3] Note that synonyms so conceived need not even be free from vagueness, as long as the vaguenesses match.

But it is not quite true that the synonyms 'bachelor' and 'unmarried man' are everywhere interchangeable *salva veritate*. Truths which become false under substitution of 'unmarried man' for 'bachelor' are easily constructed with the help of 'bachelor of arts' or 'bachelor's buttons'; also with the help of quotation, thus:

'Bachelor' has less than ten letters.

Such counterinstances can, however, perhaps be set aside by treating the phrases 'bachelor of arts' and 'bachelor's buttons' and the quotation "bachelor" each as a single indivisible word and then stipulating that the interchangeability *salva veritate* which is to be the touchstone of synonymy is not supposed to apply to fragmentary occurrences inside of a word. This account of synonymy, supposing it acceptable on other counts, has indeed the drawback of appealing to a prior conception of "word" which can be counted on to present difficulties of formulation in its turn. Nevertheless some progress might be claimed in having reduced the problem of synonymy to a problem of wordhood. Let us pursue this line a bit, taking "word" for granted.

The question remains whether interchangeability *salva veritate* (apart from occurrences within words) is a strong enough condition for synonymy, or whether, on the contrary, some heteronymous expressions might be thus interchangeable. Now let us be clear that we are not concerned here with synonymy in the sense of complete identity in psychological associations or poetic quality; indeed no two expressions are synonymous in such a sense. We are concerned only with what may be called *cognitive* synonymy. Just what this is cannot be said without successfully finishing the present study; but we know something about it from the need which

arose for it in connection with analyticity in §1. The sort of synonymy needed there was merely such that any analytic statement could be turned into a logical truth by putting synonyms for synonyms. Turning the tables and assuming analyticity, indeed, we could explain cognitive synonymy of terms as follows (keeping to the familiar example): to say that 'bachelor' and 'unmarried man' are cognitively synonymous is to say no more nor less than that the statement:

(3) All and only bachelors are unmarried men

is analytic.[4] What we need is an account of cognitive synonymy not presupposing analyticity—if we are to explain analyticity conversely with help of cognitive synonymy as undertaken in §1. And indeed such an independent account of cognitive synonymy is at present up for consideration, namely, interchangeability *salva veritate* everywhere except within words. The question before us, to resume the thread at last, is whether such interchangeability is a sufficient condition for cognitive synonymy. We can quickly assure ourselves that it is, by examples of the following sort. The statement:

(4) Necessarily all and only bachelors are bachelors

is evidently true, even supposing 'necessarily' so narrowly construed as to be truly applicable only to analytic statements. Then, if 'bachelor' and 'unmarried man' are interchangeable *salva veritate,* the result:

(5) Necessarily all and only bachelors are unmarried men

of putting 'unmarried man' for an occurrence of 'bachelor' in (4) must, like (4), be true. But to say that (5) is true is to say that (3) is analytic, and hence that 'bachelor' and 'unmarried man' are cognitively synonymous.

Let us see what there is about the above argument that gives it its air of hocus-pocus. The condition of interchangeability *salva veritate* varies in its force with variations in the richness of the language at hand. The above argument supposes we are working with a language rich enough to contain the adverb 'necessarily', this adverb being so construed as to yield truth when and only when applied to an analytic statement. But can we condone a language which contains such an adverb? Does the adverb really make sense? To suppose that it does is to suppose that we have already made satisfactory sense of 'analytic'. Then what are we so hard at work on right now?

Our argument is not flatly circular, but something like it. It has the form, figuratively speaking, of a closed curve in space.

Interchangeability *salva veritate* is meaningless until relativized to a language whose extent is specified in relevant respects. Suppose now we consider a language containing just the following materials. There is an indefinitely large stock of one-place predicates (for example, '*F*' where '*Fx*' means that *x* is a man) and many-place predicates (for example, '*G*' where '*Gxy*' means that *x* loves *y*), mostly having to do with extralogical subject matter. The rest of the language is logical. The atomic sentences consist each of a predicate followed by one or more variables '*x*', '*y*', etc.; and the complex sentences are built up of the atomic ones by truth functions ('not', 'and', 'or', etc.) and quantification. In effect such a language enjoys the benefits also of descriptions and indeed singular terms generally, these being contextually definable in known ways. Even abstract singular terms naming classes, classes of classes, etc., are contextually definable in case the assumed stock of predicates includes the two-place predicate of class membership. Such a language can be adequate to classical mathematics and indeed to scientific discourse generally, except in so far as the latter involves debatable devices such as contrary-to-fact conditionals or modal adverbs like 'necessarily'. Now a language of this type is extensional, in this sense: any two predicates which agree extensionally (that is, are true of the same objects) are interchangeable *salva veritate*.[5]

In an extensional language, therefore, interchangeability *salva veritate* is no assurance of cognitive synonymy of the desired type. That 'bachelor' and 'unmarried man' are interchangeable *salva veritate* in an extensional language assures us of no

more than that (3) is true. There is no assurance here that the extensional agreement of 'bachelor' and 'unmarried man' rests on meaning rather than merely on accidental matters of fact, as does the extensional agreement of 'creature with a heart' and 'creature with kidneys'.

For most purposes extensional agreement is the nearest approximation to synonymy we need care about. But the fact remains that extensional agreement falls far short of cognitive synonymy of the type required for explaining analyticity in the manner of §1. The type of cognitive synonymy required there is such as to equate the synonymy of 'bachelor' and 'unmarried man' with the analyticity of (3), not merely with the truth of (3).

So we must recognize that interchangeability *salva veritate,* if construed in relation to an extensional language, is not a sufficient condition of cognitive synonymy in the sense needed for deriving analyticity in the manner of §1. If a language contains an intensional adverb 'necessarily' in the sense lately noted, or other particles to the same effect, then interchangeability *salva veritate* in such a language does afford a sufficient condition of cognitive synonymy; but such a language is intelligible only in so far as the notion of analyticity is already understood in advance.

The effort to explain cognitive synonymy first, for the sake of deriving analyticity from it afterward as in §1, is perhaps the wrong approach. Instead we might try explaining analyticity somehow without appeal to cognitive synonymy. Afterward we could doubtless derive cognitive synonymy from analyticity satisfactorily enough if desired. We have seen that cognitive synonymy of 'bachelor' and 'unmarried man' can be explained as analyticity of (3). The same explanation works for any pair of one-place predicates, of course, and it can be extended in obvious fashion to many-place predicates. Other syntactical categories can also be accommodated in fairly parallel fashion. Singular terms may be said to be cognitively synonymous when the statement of identity formed by putting '=' between them is analytic. Statements may be said simply to be cognitively synonymous when their biconditional (the result of joining them by 'if and only if') is analytic.[6] If we care to lump all categories into a single formulation, at the expense of assuming again the notion of "word" which was appealed to early in this section, we can describe any two linguistic forms as cognitively synonymous when the two forms are interchangeable (apart from occurrences within "words") *salva* (no longer *veritate* but) *analyticitate*. Certain technical questions arise, indeed, over cases of ambiguity or homonymy; let us not pause for them, however, for we are already digressing. Let us rather turn our backs on the problem of synonymy and address ourselves anew to that of analyticity.

4. SEMANTICAL RULES

Analyticity at first seemed most naturally definable by appeal to a realm of meanings. On refinement, the appeal to meanings gave way to an appeal to synonymy or definition. But definition turned out to be a will-o'-the-wisp, and synonymy turned out to be best understood only by dint of a prior appeal to analyticity itself. So we are back at the problem of analyticity.

I do not know whether the statement 'Everything green is extended' is analytic. Now does my indecision over this example really betray an incomplete understanding, an incomplete grasp of the "meanings", of 'green' and 'extended'? I think not. The trouble is not with 'green' or 'extended', but with 'analytic'.

It is often hinted that the difficulty in separating analytic statements from synthetic ones in ordinary language is due to the vagueness of ordinary language and that the distinction is clear when we have a precise artificial language with explicit "semantical rules." This, however, as I shall now attempt to show, is a confusion.

The notion of analyticity about which we are worrying is a purported relation between statements and languages: a statement S is said to be *analytic for* a language L, and the problem is to make sense of this relation generally, that is, for variable 'S' and 'L'. The gravity of this problem is not perceptibly less for artificial languages than for natural ones. The problem of making sense of the idiom 'S is analytic for L', with variable 'S' and 'L', retains its stubbornness even if we limit the range of the variable 'L' to artificial languages. Let me now try to make this point evident.

For artificial languages and semantical rules we look naturally to the writings of Carnap. His semantical rules take various forms, and to make my point I shall have to distinguish certain of the forms. Let us suppose, to begin with, an artificial language L_0 whose semantical rules have the form explicitly of a specification, by recursion or otherwise, of all the analytic statements of L_0. The rules tell us that such and such statements, and only those, are the analytic statements of L_0. Now here the difficulty is simply that the rules contain the word 'analytic', which we do not understand! We understand what expressions the rules attribute analyticity to, but we do not understand what the rules attribute to those expressions. In short, before we can understand a rule which begins 'A statement S is analytic for language L_0 if and only if . . .', we must understand the general relative term 'analytic for'; we must understand 'S is analytic for L' where 'S' and 'L' are variables.

Alternatively we may, indeed, view the so-called rule as a conventional definition of a new simple symbol 'analytic-for-L_0', which might better be written untendentiously as 'K' so as not to seem to throw light on the interesting word 'analytic'. Obviously any number of classes K, M, N, etc., of statements of L_0 can be specified for various purposes or for no purpose; what does it mean to say that K, as against M, N, etc., is the class of the "analytic" statements of L_0?

By saying what statements are analytic for L_0 we explain 'analytic-for-L_0' but not 'analytic', not 'analytic for'. We do not begin to explain the idiom 'S is analytic for L' with variable 'S' and 'L', even if we are content to limit the range of 'L' to the realm of artificial languages.

Actually we do know enough about the intended significance of 'analytic' to know that analytic statements are supposed to be true. Let us then turn to a second form of semantical rule, which says not that such and such statements are analytic but simply that such and such statements are included among the truths. Such a rule is not subject to the criticism of containing the un-understood word 'analytic'; and we may grant for the sake of argument that there is no difficulty over the broader term 'true'. A semantical rule of this second type, a rule of truth, is not supposed to specify all the truths of the language; it merely stipulates, recursively or otherwise, a certain multitude of statements which, along with others unspecified, are to count as true. Such a rule may be conceded to be quite clear. Derivatively, afterward, analyticity can be demarcated thus: a statement is analytic if it is (not merely true but) true according to the semantical rule.

Still there is really no progress. Instead of appealing to an unexplained word 'analytic', we are now appealing to an unexplained phrase 'semantical rule'. Not every true statement which says that the statements of some class are true can count as a semantical rule—otherwise *all* truths would be "analytic" in the sense of being true according to semantical rules. Semantical rules are distinguishable, apparently, only by the fact of appearing on a page under the heading 'Semantical Rules'; and this heading is itself then meaningless.

We can say indeed that a statement is *analytic-for-L_0* if and only if it is true according to such and such specifically appended "semantical rules," but then we find ourselves back at essentially the same case which was originally discussed: 'S is analytic-for-L_0 if and only if. . . .' Once we seek to explain 'S is analytic for L' generally for variable 'L' (even allowing limitation of 'L' to artificial languages), the explanation 'true according to the semantical rules of L' is unavailing; for the relative term 'semantical rule of' is as much in need of clarification, at least, as 'analytic for'.

It may be instructive to compare the notion of semantical rule with that of postulate. Relative to a given set of postulates, it is easy to say what a postulate is: it is a member of the set. Relative to a given set of semantical rules, it is equally easy to say what a semantical rule is. But given simply a notation, mathematical or otherwise, and indeed as thoroughly understood a notation as you please in point of the translations or truth conditions of its statements, who can say which of its true statements rank as postulates? Obviously the question is meaningless—as meaningless as asking which points in Ohio are starting points. Any finite (or effectively specifiable infinite) selection of statements (preferably true ones, perhaps) is as much *a* set of postulates as any other. The word 'postulate' is significant only relative to

an act of inquiry; we apply the word to a set of statements just in so far as we happen, for the year or the moment, to be thinking of those statements in relation to the statements which can be reached from them by some set of transformations to which we have seen fit to direct our attention. Now the notion of semantical rule is as sensible and meaningful as that of postulate, if conceived in a similarly relative spirit—relative, this time, to one or another particular enterprise of schooling unconversant persons in sufficient conditions for truth of statements of some natural or artificial language L. But from this point of view no one signalization of a subclass of the truths of L is intrinsically more a semantical rule than another; and, if 'analytic' means 'true by semantical rules', no one truth of L is analytic to the exclusion of another.[7]

It might conceivably be protested that an artificial language L (unlike a natural one) is a language in the ordinary sense *plus* a set of explicit semantical rules—the whole constituting, let us say, an ordered pair; and that the semantical rules of L then are specifiable simply as the second component of the pair L. But, by the same token and more simply, we might construe an artificial language L outright as an ordered pair whose second component is the class of its analytic statements; and then the analytic statements of L become specifiable simply as the statements in the second component of L. Or better still, we might just stop tugging at our bootstraps altogether.

Not all the explanations of analyticity known to Carnap and his readers have been covered explicitly in the above considerations, but the extension to other forms is not hard to see. Just one additional factor should be mentioned which sometimes enters: sometimes the semantical rules are in effect rules of translation into ordinary language, in which case the analytic statements of the artificial language are in effect recognized as such from the analyticity of their specified translations in ordinary language. Here certainly there can be no thought of an illumination of the problem of analyticity from the side of the artificial language.

From the point of view of the problem of analyticity the notion of an artificial language with semantical rules is a *feu follet par excellence*. Semantical rules determining the analytic statements of an artificial language are of interest only in so far as we already understand the notion of analyticity; they are of no help in gaining this understanding.

Appeal to hypothetical languages of an artificially simple kind could conceivably be useful in clarifying analyticity, if the mental or behavioral or cultural factors relevant to analyticity—whatever they may be—were somehow sketched into the simplified model. But a model which takes analyticity merely as an irreducible character is unlikely to throw light on the problem of explicating analyticity.

It is obvious that truth in general depends on both language and extralinguistic fact. The statement 'Brutus killed Caesar' would be false if the world had been different in certain ways, but it would also be false if the word 'killed' happened rather to have the sense of 'begat'. Thus one is tempted to suppose in general that the truth of a statement is somehow analyzable into a linguistic component and a factual component. Given this supposition, it next seems reasonable that in some statements the factual component should be null; and these are the analytic statements. But, for all its a priori reasonableness, a boundary between analytic and synthetic statements simply has not been drawn. That there is such a distinction to be drawn at all is an unempirical dogma of empiricists, a metaphysical article of faith.

5. THE VERIFICATION THEORY AND REDUCTIONISM

In the course of these somber reflections we have taken a dim view first of the notion of meaning, then of the notion of cognitive synonymy, and finally of the notion of analyticity. But what, it may be asked, of the verification theory of meaning? This phrase has established itself so firmly as a catchword of empiricism that we should be very unscientific indeed not to look beneath it for a possible key to the problem of meaning and the associated problems.

The verification theory of meaning, which has been conspicuous in the literature from Peirce onward, is that the meaning of a statement is the method of empirically confirming or infirming it.

An analytic statement is that limiting case which is confirmed no matter what.

As urged in §1, we can as well pass over the question of meanings as entities and move straight to sameness of meaning, or synonymy. Then what the verification theory says is that statements are synonymous if and only if they are alike in point of method of empirical confirmation or infirmation.

This is an account of cognitive synonymy not of linguistic forms generally, but of statements.[8] However, from the concept of synonymy of statements we could derive the concept of synonymy for other linguistic forms, by considerations somewhat similar to those at the end of §3. Assuming the notion of "word," indeed, we could explain any two forms as synonymous when the putting of the one form for an occurrence of the other in any statement (apart from occurrences within "words") yields a synonymous statement. Finally, given the concept of synonymy thus for linguistic forms generally, we could define analyticity in terms of synonymy and logical truth as in §1. For that matter, we could define analyticity more simply in terms of just synonymy of statements together with logical truth; it is not necessary to appeal to synonymy of linguistic forms other than statements. For a statement may be described as analytic simply when it is synonymous with a logically true statement.

So, if the verification theory can be accepted as an adequate account of statement synonymy, the notion of analyticity is saved after all. However, let us reflect. Statement synonymy is said to be likeness of method of empirical confirmation or infirmation. Just what are these methods which are to be compared for likeness? What, in other words, is the nature of the relation between a statement and the experiences which contribute to or detract from its confirmation?

The most naïve view of the relation is that it is one of direct report. This is *radical reductionism*. Every meaningful statement is held to be translatable into a statement (true or false) about immediate experience. Radical reductionism, in one form or another, well antedates the verification theory of meaning explicitly so called. Thus Locke and Hume held that every idea must either originate directly in sense experience or else be compounded of ideas thus originating; and taking a hint from Tooke we might rephrase this doctrine in semantical jargon by saying that a term, to be significant at all, must be either a name of a sense datum or a compound of such names or an abbreviation of such a compound. So stated, the doctrine remains ambiguous as between sense data as sensory events and sense data as sensory qualities; and it remains vague as to the admissible ways of compounding. Moreover, the doctrine is unnecessarily and intolerably restrictive in the term-by-term critique which it imposes. More reasonably, and without yet exceeding the limits of what I have called radical reductionism, we may take full statements as our significant units—thus demanding that our statements as wholes be translatable into sense-datum language, but not that they be translatable term by term.

This emendation would unquestionably have been welcome to Locke and Hume and Tooke, but historically it had to await an important reorientation in semantics—the reorientation whereby the primary vehicle of meaning came to be seen no longer in the term but in the statement. This reorientation, seen in Bentham and Frege, underlies Russell's concept of incomplete symbols defined in use; also it is implicit in the verification theory of meaning, since the objects of verification are statements.

Radical reductionism, conceived now with statements as units, set itself the task of specifying a sense-datum language and showing how to translate the rest of significant discourse, statement by statement, into it. Carnap embarked on this project in the *Aufbau*.

The language which Carnap adopted as his starting point was not a sense-datum language in the narrowest conceivable sense, for it included also the notations of logic, up through higher set theory. In effect it included the whole language of pure mathematics. The ontology implicit in it (that is, the range of values of its variables) embraced not only sensory events but classes, classes of classes, and so on. Empiricists there are who would boggle at such prodigality. Carnap's starting point is very parsimonious, however, in its extralogical or sensory part. In a series of constructions in which he exploits the resources of modern logic with much ingenuity, Carnap succeeds in defining a wide array of important additional sensory concepts which,

but for his constructions, one would not have dreamed were definable on so slender a basis. He was the first empiricist who, not content with asserting the reducibility of science to terms of immediate experience, took serious steps toward carrying out the reduction.

If Carnap's starting point is satisfactory, still his constructions were, as he himself stressed, only a fragment of the full program. The construction of even the simplest statements about the physical world was left in a sketchy state. Carnap's suggestions on this subject were, despite their sketchiness, very suggestive. He explained spatio-temporal point-instants as quadruples of real numbers and envisaged assignment of sense qualities to point-instants according to certain canons. Roughly summarized, the plan was that qualities should be assigned to point-instants in such a way as to achieve the laziest world compatible with our experience. The principle of least action was to be our guide in constructing a world from experience.

Carnap did not seem to recognize, however, that his treatment of physical objects fell short of reduction not merely through sketchiness, but in principle. Statements of the form 'Quality q is at point-instant $x;y;z;t$' were, according to his canons, to be apportioned truth values in such a way as to maximize and minimize certain over-all features, and with growth of experience the truth values were to be progressively revised in the same spirit. I think this is a good schematization (deliberately oversimplified, to be sure) of what science really does; but it provides no indication, not even the sketchiest, of how a statement of the form 'Quality q is at $x;y;z;t$' could ever be translated into Carnap's initial language of sense data and logic. The connective 'is at' remains an added undefined connective; the canons counsel us in its use but not in its elimination.

Carnap seems to have appreciated this point afterward; for in his later writings he abandoned all notion of the translatability of statements about the physical world into statements about immediate experience. Reductionism in its radical form has long since ceased to figure in Carnap's philosophy.

But the dogma of reductionism has, in a subtler and more tenuous form, continued to influence the thought of empiricists. The notion lingers that to each statement, or each synthetic statement, there is associated a unique range of possible sensory events such that the occurrence of any of them would add to the likelihood of truth of the statement, and that there is associated also another unique range of possible sensory events whose occurrence would detract from that likelihood. This notion is of course implicit in the verification theory of meaning.

The dogma of reductionism survives in the supposition that each statement, taken in isolation from its fellows, can admit of confirmation or infirmation at all. My countersuggestion, issuing essentially from Carnap's doctrine of the physical world in the *Aufbau,* is that our statements about the external world face the tribunal of sense experience not individually but only as a corporate body.[9]

The dogma of reductionism, even in its attenuated form, is intimately connected with the other dogma—that there is a cleavage between the analytic and the synthetic. We have found ourselves led, indeed, from the latter problem to the former through the verification theory of meaning. More directly, the one dogma clearly supports the other in this way: as long as it is taken to be significant in general to speak of the confirmation and infirmation of a statement, it seems significant to speak also of a limiting kind of statement which is vacuously confirmed, *ipso facto,* come what may; and such a statement is analytic.

The two dogmas are, indeed, at root identical. We lately reflected that in general the truth of statements does obviously depend both upon language and upon extralinguistic fact; and we noted that this obvious circumstance carries in its train, not logically but all too naturally, a feeling that the truth of a statement is somehow analyzable into a linguistic component and a factual component. The factual component must, if we are empiricists, boil down to a range of confirmatory experiences. In the extreme case where the linguistic component is all that matters, a true statement is analytic. But I hope we are now impressed with how stubbornly the distinction between analytic and synthetic has resisted any straightforward drawing. I am impressed also, apart from prefabricated examples of black and white balls in an urn, with how baffling the problem has always been of arriving at any explicit theory of the empirical confirmation of a synthetic

statement. My present suggestion is that it is nonsense, and the root of much nonsense, to speak of a linguistic component and a factual component in the truth of any individual statement. Taken collectively, science has its double dependence upon language and experience; but this duality is not significantly traceable into the statements of science taken one by one.

The idea of defining a symbol in use was, as remarked, an advance over the impossible term-by-term empiricism of Locke and Hume. The statement, rather than the term, came with Bentham to be recognized as the unit accountable to an empiricist critique. But what I am now urging is that even in taking the statement as unit we have drawn our grid too finely. The unit of empirical significance is the whole of science.

6. EMPIRICISM WITHOUT THE DOGMAS

The totality of our so-called knowledge or beliefs, from the most casual matters of geography and history to the profoundest laws of atomic physics or even of pure mathematics and logic, is a man-made fabric which impinges on experience only along the edges. Or, to change the figure, total science is like a field of force whose boundary conditions are experience. A conflict with experience at the periphery occasions readjustments in the interior of the field. Truth values have to be redistributed over some of our statements. Reevaluation of some statements entails reevaluation of others, because of their logical interconnections—the logical laws being in turn simply certain further statements of the system, certain further elements of the field. Having reevaluated one statement we must reevaluate some others, which may be statements logically connected with the first or may be the statements of logical connections themselves. But the total field is so underdetermined by its boundary conditions, experience, that there is much latitude of choice as to what statements to reevaluate in the light of any single contrary experience. No particular experiences are linked with any particular statements in the interior of the field, except indirectly through considerations of equilibrium affecting the field as a whole.

If this view is right, it is misleading to speak of the empirical content of an individual statement—especially if it is a statement at all remote from the experiential periphery of the field. Furthermore it becomes folly to seek a boundary between synthetic statements, which hold contingently on experience, and analytic statements, which hold come what may. Any statement can be held true come what may, if we make drastic enough adjustments elsewhere in the system. Even a statement very close to the periphery can be held true in the face of recalcitrant experience by pleading hallucination or by amending certain statements of the kind called logical laws. Conversely, by the same token, no statement is immune to revision. Revision even of the logical law of the excluded middle has been proposed as a means of simplifying quantum mechanics; and what difference is there in principle between such a shift and the shift whereby Kepler superseded Ptolemy, or Einstein Newton, or Darwin Aristotle?

For vividness I have been speaking in terms of varying distances from a sensory periphery. Let me try now to clarify this notion without metaphor. Certain statements, though *about* physical objects and not sense experience, seem peculiarly germane to sense experience—and in a selective way: some statements to some experiences, others to others. Such statements, especially germane to particular experiences, I picture as near the periphery. But in this relation of "germaneness" I envisage nothing more than a loose association reflecting the relative likelihood, in practice, of our choosing one statement rather than another for revision in the event of recalcitrant experience. For example, we can imagine recalcitrant experiences to which we would surely be inclined to accommodate our system by reevaluating just the statement that there are brick houses on Elm Street, together with related statements on the same topic. We can imagine other recalcitrant experiences to which we would be inclined to accommodate our system by reevaluating just the statement that there are no centaurs, along with kindred statements. A recalcitrant experience can, I have urged, be accommodated by any of various alternative reevaluations in various alternative quarters of the total system; but, in the cases which we are now imagining, our natural tendency to disturb the total system as little as possible would lead us to focus our revisions upon these specific statements concerning brick houses or centaurs. These statements are felt, therefore, to have a sharper empirical reference than highly theoretical statements of physics or logic or ontology. The latter statements may be thought of as relatively centrally located within the total network, meaning merely that little preferential connection with any particular sense data obtrudes itself.

As an empiricist I continue to think of the conceptual scheme of science as a tool, ultimately, for predicting future experience in the light of past experience. Physical objects are conceptually imported into the situation as convenient intermediaries—not by definition in term of experience, but simply as irreducible posits comparable, epistemologically, to the gods of Homer. For my part I do, qua lay physicist, believe in physical objects and not in Homer's gods; and I consider it a scientific error to believe otherwise. But in point of epistemological footing the physical objects and the gods differ only in degree and not in kind. Both sorts of entities enter our conception only as cultural posits. The myth of physical objects is epistemologically superior to most in that it has proved more efficacious than other myths as a device for working a manageable structure into the flux of experience.

Positing does not stop with macroscopic physical objects. Objects at the atomic level are posited to make the laws of macroscopic objects, and ultimately the laws of experience, simpler and more manageable; and we need not expect or demand full definition of atomic and subatomic entities in terms of macroscopic ones, any more than definition of macroscopic things in terms of sense data. Science is a continuation of common sense, and it continues the common-sense expedient of swelling ontology to simplify theory.

Physical objects, small and large, are not the only posits. Forces are another example; and indeed we are told nowadays that the boundary between energy and matter is obsolete. Moreover, the abstract entities which are the substance of mathematics—

ultimately classes and classes of classes and so on up—are another posit in the same spirit. Epistemologically these are myths on the same footing with physical objects and gods, neither better nor worse except for differences in the degree to which they expedite our dealings with sense experiences.

The over-all algebra of rational and irrational numbers is underdetermined by the algebra of rational numbers, but is smoother and more convenient; and it includes the algebra of rational numbers as a jagged or gerrymandered part. Total science, mathematical and natural and human, is similarly but more extremely underdetermined by experience. The edge of the system must be kept squared with experience; the rest, with all its elaborate myths or fictions, has as its objective the simplicity of laws.

Ontological questions, under this view, are on a par with questions of natural science.[10] Consider the question whether to countenance classes as entities. This, as I have argued elsewhere, is the question whether to quantify with respect to variables which take classes as values. Now Carnap [3] has maintained that this is a question not of matters of fact but of choosing a convenient language form, a convenient conceptual scheme or framework for science. With this I agree, but only on the proviso that the same be conceded regarding scientific hypotheses generally. Carnap ([3], p. 32n) has recognized that he is able to preserve a double standard for ontological questions and scientific hypotheses only by assuming an absolute distinction between the analytic and the synthetic; and I need not say again that this is a distinction which I reject.[11]

The issue over there being classes seems more a question of convenient conceptual scheme; the issue over there being centaurs, or brick houses on Elm Street, seems more a question of fact. But I have been urging that this difference is only one of degree, and that it turns upon our vaguely pragmatic inclination to adjust one strand of the fabric of science rather than another in accommodating some particular recalcitrant experience. Conservatism figures in such choices, and so does the quest for simplicity.

Carnap, Lewis, and others take a pragmatic stand on the question of choosing between language forms, scientific frameworks; but their pragmatism leaves off at the imagined boundary between the analytic and the synthetic. In repudiating such a boundary I espouse a more thorough pragmatism. Each man is given a scientific heritage plus a continuing barrage of sensory stimulation; and the considerations which guide him in warping his scientific heritage to fit his continuing sensory promptings are, where rational, pragmatic.

NOTES

1. Carnap [1], pp. 9ff; [2], pp. 70ff.
2. According to an important variant sense of 'definition', the relation preserved may be the weaker relation of mere agreement in reference; see below, p. 132. But definition in this sense is better ignored in the present connection, being irrelevant to the question of synonymy.
3. Cf. Lewis [1], p. 373.
4. This is cognitive synonymy in a primary, broad sense. Carnap ([1], pp. 56ff) and Lewis ([2], pp. 83ff) have suggested how, once this notion is at hand, a narrower sense of cognitive synonymy which is preferable for some purposes can in turn be derived. But this special ramification of concept-building lies aside from the present purposes and must not be confused with the broad sort of cognitive synonymy here concerned.
5. This is the substance of Quine, *121.
6. The 'if and only if' itself is intended in the truth functional sense. See Carnap [1], p. 14.
7. The foregoing paragraph was not part of the present essay as originally published. It was prompted by Martin (see References).
8. The doctrine can indeed be formulated with terms rather than statements as the units. Thus Lewis describes the meaning of a term as "*a criterion in mind,* by reference to which one is able to apply or refuse to apply the expression in question in the case of presented, or imagined, things or situations" ([2], p. 133).—For an instructive account of the vicissitudes of the verification theory of meaning, centered however on the question of meaning*fulness* rather than synonymy and analyticity, see Hempel.
9. This doctrine was well argued by Duhem, pp. 303–328. Or see Lowinger, pp. 132–140.
10. "L'ontologie fait corps avec la science elle-même et ne peut en être separée." Meyerson, p. 439.
11. For an effective expression of further misgivings over this distinction, see White 2.

REFERENCES

Carnap, Rudolf. [1] *Meaning and Necessity.* Chicago: University of Chicago Press, 1947.

———. [2] *Logical Foundations of Probability*. Chicago: University of Chicago Press, 1950.

———. [3]. 1950. "Empiricism, Semantics, and Ontology." *Revue Internationale de Philosophie* 4: 20–40.

Duhem, Pierre. *La Theorie physique: Son objet et sa structure*. Paris: 1906.

Hempel, Carl G. 1950. "Problems and Changes in the Empiricist Criterion of Meaning." *Revue Internationale de Philosophie* 4: 41–63.

Lewis, Clarence I. [1] *A Survey of Symbolic Logic*. Berkley: University of California Press, 1918.

———. [2] *An Analysis of Knowledge and Valuation*. LaSalle, IL: Open Court, 1946.

Lowinger, Armand. *The Methodology of Pierre Duhem*. New York: Columbia University Press, 1941.

Martin, R. M. "On 'Analytic,' " *Philosophical Studies* 3 (1952): 42–47.

Meyerson, Emile. *Identité et réalité*. 1908. 4th ed. Paris: 1932.

Quine, W. V. *Mathematical Logic*. New York: Norton, 1940; Cambridge: Harvard University Press, 1947; rev. ed., Cambridge: Harvard University Press, 1951.

White, Morton. "The Analytic and Synthetic: An Untenable Dualism." In *John Dewey: Philosopher of Science and Freedom*. Ed. Sydney Hook. New York: Dial, 1950, 316–30.

---

17   The Nature of Knowledge

A. J. AYER

(I) THE METHOD OF PHILOSOPHY

IT IS BY ITS METHODS rather than its subject-matter that philosophy is to be distinguished from other arts or sciences. Philosophers make statements which are intended to be true, and they commonly rely on argument both to support their own theories and to refute the theories of others; but the arguments which they use are of a peculiar character. The proof of a philosophical statement is not, or only very seldom, like the proof of a mathematical statement; it does not normally consist in formal demonstration. Neither is it like the proof of a statement in any of the descriptive sciences. Philosophical theories are not tested by observation. They are neutral with respect to particular matters of fact.

This is not to say that philosophers are not concerned with facts, but they are in the strange position that all the evidence which bears upon their problems is already available to them. It is not further scientific information that is needed to decide such philosophical questions as whether the material world is real, whether objects continue to exist at times when they are not perceived, whether other human beings are conscious in the same sense as one is oneself. These are not questions that can be settled by experiment, since the way in which they are answered itself determines how the result of any experiment is to be interpreted. What is in dispute in such cases is not whether, in a given set of circumstances, this or that event will happen, but rather how anything at all that happens is to be described.

This preoccupation with the way things are, or are to be, described is often represented as an enquiry into their essential nature. Thus philosophers are given to asking such questions as What is mind? What sort of a relation is causality? What is the nature of belief? What is truth? The difficulty is then to see how such questions are to be taken. It must not be supposed, for instance, that a philosopher who asks What is mind? is looking for the kind of

The Problem of Knowledge (Harmondsworth, UK: Penguin, 1956), pp. 7–35. © 1956 A. J. Ayer. Reprinted by permission of Penguin.

information that a psychologist might give him. His problem is not that he is ignorant of the ways in which people think and feel, or even that he is unable to explain them. Neither should it be assumed that he is simply looking for a definition. It is not as if philosophers do not understand how words like 'mind' or 'causality' or 'truth' are actually used. But why, then, do they ask such questions? What is it that they are trying to find out?

The answer to this, though not indeed the whole answer, is that, already knowing the use of certain expressions, they are seeking to give an analysis of their meaning. This distinction between the use of an expression and the analysis of its meaning is not easy to grasp. Let us try to make it clear by taking an example. Consider the case of knowledge. A glance at the dictionary will show that the verb 'to know' is used in a variety of ways. We can speak of knowing, in the sense of being familiar with, a person or a place, of knowing something in the sense of having had experience of it, as when someone says that he has known hunger or fear, of knowing in the sense of being able to recognize or distinguish, as when we claim to know an honest man when we see one or to know butter from margarine. I may be said to know my Dickens, if I have read, remember, and can perhaps also quote his writings, to know a subject such as trigonometry, if I have mastered it, to know how to swim or drive a car, to know how to behave myself. Most important of all, perhaps, are the uses for which the dictionary gives the definition of 'to be aware or apprized of', 'to apprehend or comprehend as fact or truth', the sense, or senses, in which to have knowledge is to know that something or other is the case.

All this is a matter of lexicography. The facts are known, in a sense, to anyone who understands the English language, though not everyone who understands the English language would be competent to set them out. The lexicographer, *pace* Dr. Johnson, is required to be something more than a harmless drudge. What he is not required to be is a philosopher. To possess the information which the dictionary provides about the accredited uses of the English word 'to know', or the corresponding words in other languages, is no doubt a necessary qualification for giving an analysis of knowledge; but it is not sufficient. The philosopher who has this information may still ask What is knowledge? and hesitate for an answer.

We may discover the sense of the philosopher's question by seeing what further questions it incorporates, and what sorts of statement the attempt to answer it leads him to make. Thus, he may enquire whether the different cases in which we speak of knowing have any one thing in common; whether, for example, they are alike in implying the presence of some special state of mind. He may maintain that there is, on the subjective side, no difference in kind between knowing and believing, or, alternatively, that knowing is a special sort of mental act. If he thinks it correct to speak of acts of knowing, he may go on to enquire into the nature of their objects. Is any limitation to be set upon them? Or, putting it another way, is there anything thinkable that is beyond the reach of human knowledge? Does knowing make a difference to what is known? Is it necessary to distinguish between the sorts of things that can be known directly and those that can be known only indirectly? And, if so, what are the relationships between them? Perhaps it is philosophically misleading to talk of knowing objects at all. It may be possible to show that what appears to be an instance of knowing some object always comes down to knowing that something is the case. What is known, in this sense, must be true, whereas what is believed may very well be false. But it is also possible to believe what is in fact true without knowing it. Is knowledge then to be distinguished by the fact that if one knows that something is so, one cannot be mistaken? And in that case does it follow that what is known is necessarily true, or in some other way indubitable? But, if this does follow, it will lead in its turn to the conclusion that we commonly claim to know much more than we really do; perhaps even to the paradox that we do not know anything at all: for it may be contended that there is no statement whatsoever that is not in itself susceptible to doubt. Yet surely there must be something wrong with an argument that would make knowledge unattainable. Surely some of our claims to knowledge must be capable of being justified. But in what ways can we justify them? In what would the processes of justifying them consist?

I do not say that all these questions are clear, or even that they are all coherent. But they are instances of the sort of question that philosophers ask. The next step is to see how one would try to answer them. Once again, it will be best to take particular examples. Let us begin with the question whether the various sorts of knowing have any one thing in common, and the suggestion that this common feature is a mental state or act.

(II) COMMON FEATURES OF KNOWLEDGE

Except where a word is patently ambiguous, it is natural for us to assume that the different situations, or types of situation, to which it applies have a distinctive common feature. For otherwise why should we use the same word to refer to them? Sometimes we have another way of describing such a common feature; we can say, for example, that what irascible people have in common is that they are all prone to anger. But very often we have no way of saying what is common to the things to which the same word applies except by using the word itself. How else should we describe the distinctively common feature of red things except by saying that they are all red? In the same way, it might be said that what the things that we call 'games' have in common is just that they are games; but here there seems to be a difference. Whereas there is a simple and straightforward resemblance between the things whose colour we call 'red', the sort of resemblance that leads us naturally to talk of their having an identical quality, there is no such simple resemblance between the things that we call 'games'. The *Oxford English Dictionary* defines a game as 'a diversion of the nature of a contest, played according to rules, and decided by superior skill, strength, or good fortune'. But not all games are diversions, in the sense of being played for fun; games of patience are hardly contests, though they are decided by skill and luck; children's games are not always played according to rules; acting games need not be decided. Wittgenstein,[1] from whom I have taken this example, concludes that we cannot find anything common to all games, but only a 'complicated network of similarities' which 'over-

lap and crisscross' in the same way as the resemblances between people who belong to the same family. " 'Games' ", he says, 'form a family.'

This is a good analogy, but I think that Wittgenstein is wrong to infer from it that games do not have any one thing in common. His doing so suggests that he takes the question whether things have something in common to be different from the question whether there are resemblances between them. But surely the difference is only one of formulation. If things resemble one another sufficiently for us to find it useful to apply the same word to them, we are entitled to say, if it pleases us, that they have something in common. Neither is it necessary that what they have in common should be describable in different words, as we saw in the case of 'red'. It is correct, though not at all enlightening, to say that what games have in common is their being games. The point which Wittgenstein's argument brings out is that the resemblance between the things to which the same word applies may be of different degrees. It is looser and less straightforward in some cases than in others.

Our question then becomes whether the different sorts of cases in which we speak of something's being known resemble one another in some straightforward fashion like the different instances of the colour red, or whether they merely have what Wittgenstein would call a family resemblance. Another possibility is that they share a common factor the possession of which is necessary to their being instances of knowledge, even though it is not sufficient. If knowledge were always knowledge that something is the case, then such a common factor might be found in the existence of a common relation to truth. For while what is true can be believed, or disbelieved, or doubted, or imagined, or much else besides being known, it is, as we have already noted, a fact of ordinary usage that what is known, in this sense, cannot but be true.

But can it reasonably be held that knowledge is always knowledge that something is the case? If knowing that something is the case is taken to involve the making of a conscious judgement, then plainly it cannot. A dog knows its master, a baby knows its mother, but they do not know any statements to be true. Or if we insist on saying that there is a sense in which they do know statements to be true, that the dog which knows its master knows the fact that this is his master, we must allow that what we call knowing facts may sometimes just be a matter of being disposed to behave in certain appropriate ways; it need not involve any conscious process of judging, or stating, that such and such is so. Indeed, we constantly recognize objects without troubling to describe them, even to ourselves. No doubt, once we have acquired the use of language, we can always describe them if we choose, although the descriptions that we have at our command may not always be the descriptions that we want. 'I know that tune', I say, though its name escapes me and I cannot remember where I heard it before; 'I know that man', though I have forgotten who he is. But at least I identify him as a man, and as a man that I have met somewhere or other. There is a sense in which knowing something, in this usage of the term, is always a matter of knowing what it is; and in this sense it can perhaps be represented as knowing a fact, as knowing that something is so.

Much the same applies to the cases where knowing is a matter of knowing how. Certainly, when people possess skills, even intellectual skills, like the ability to act or teach, they are not always consciously aware of the procedures which they follow. They use the appropriate means to attain their ends, but the fact that these means are appropriate may never be made explicit by them even to themselves. There are a great many things that people habitually do well, without remarking how they do them. In many cases they could not say how they did them if they tried. Nor does this mean that their performances are unintelligent. As Professor Ryle has pointed out,[2] the display of intelligence lies in the manner of the performance, rather than in its being accompanied or preceded by any conscious recognition of the relevant facts. The performer does not need to tell himself that if such and such things are done, then such and such will follow. He may, indeed, do so, but equally he may not: and even when he does it is not because of this that his performance is judged to be intelligent. This point is convincingly established by Professor Ryle. But once again, if we are prepared to say that knowing facts need

not consist in anything more than a disposition to behave in certain ways, we can construe knowing how to do things as being, in its fashion, a matter of knowing facts. Only by this time we shall have so extended our use of the expression 'knowing facts' or 'knowing that something is the case' that it may well become misleading. It may be taken to imply that the resemblances between the different ways of having, or manifesting, knowledge are closer and neater than they really are.

(III) DOES KNOWING CONSIST IN BEING IN A SPECIAL STATE OF MIND?

It should by now be obvious that if 'knowing a fact' is understood in this extended sense, it need not be even partially a description of any special state of mind. But suppose that we confine our attention to the cases in which knowing something is straightforwardly a matter of knowing something to be true, the cases where it is natural in English to use the expression 'knowing that', or one of its grammatical variants. Is it a necessary condition for having this sort of knowledge, not only that what one is said to know should in fact be true, but also that one should be in some special state of mind, or that one should be performing some special mental act? Is it perhaps a sufficient condition, or even both necessary and sufficient? Some philosophers have maintained not only that there are such cognitive states, or acts, but that they are infallible. According to them, it is impossible for anyone to be in such a state of mind, unless what it purports to reveal to him is really so. For someone to think that he knows something when he really does not know it, it is not enough, in their view, that he should be mistaken about the fact which he claims to know, that what he thinks true should actually be false; he must also be mistaken about the character of his mental state: for if his mental state were what he took it to be, that is a state of knowledge, he could not be mistaken about the fact which it revealed to him. If this view were correct, then being in a mental state of this kind would be a sufficient condition for having knowledge. And if, in addition, one could not know anything to be true without being in this state, it would be both necessary and sufficient.

An obvious objection to this thesis is that to credit someone with the possession of knowledge is not to say that he is actually displaying it, even to himself. I know some facts of ancient history and I do not know them only on the rare occasions when I call them to mind. I know them at this moment even though I am not thinking of them. What is necessary is that if I were to think of them I should get them right, that if the subject comes up I am in a position to make statements which are authoritative and true. It is not necessary that I should continually be making these statements, or even that I should ever make them, provided that I could make them if the occasion arose. This point is sometimes made by saying that the verb 'to know' is used to signify a disposition or, as Ryle puts it, that it is a 'capacity' verb.[3] To have knowledge is to have the power to give a successful performance, not actually to be giving one.

But still, it may be said, however intermittent these performances may be, it is surely necessary that they be given at least once. They need not be public, but even if they are only private they must in fact occur. It would be absurd to say that someone knew a truth, which he had never even thought of, or one that he had thought of but not acknowledged to be true. Let it be granted that the most common use of the English verb 'to know' is dispositional. It is not even the only correct use—we do sometimes speak of knowing in the sense of coming to realize—but let that pass. The important point is that the dispositions which are taken to constitute knowing must sometimes be actualized. And the way in which they are actualized, so this argument continues, is through the existence of a special mental state.

But what is this state of mind supposed to be? The reply to this may be that it is unique in character, so that it cannot be analysed in terms of anything else. But what then is the evidence for its existence? It is indeed true that one is not reasonably said to know a fact unless one is completely sure of it. This is one of the distinctions between knowledge and belief. One may also be completely sure of what one believes, in cases where the belief

is refused the title of knowledge on other grounds; such as that it is false, or that, although it is true, the reasons for which it is held do not come up to the standard which knowledge requires. But whereas it is possible to believe what one is not completely sure of, so that one can consistently admit that what one believes to be true may nevertheless be false, this does not apply to knowledge. It can, indeed, be said of someone who hesitates, or makes a mistake, that he really knows what he is showing himself to be unsure of, the implication being that he ought, or is in a position, to be sure. But to say of oneself that one knew that such and such a statement was true but that one was not altogether sure of it would be self-contradictory. On the other hand, while the respective states of mind of one who knows some statement to be true and another who only believes it may in this way be different, it does not seem that there need be any difference between them when the belief is held with full conviction, and is distinguished from knowledge on other grounds. As Professor Austin puts it, 'Saying "I know" is *not* saying "I have performed a specially striking feat of cognition, superior, in the same scale as believing and being sure, even to being merely quite sure": for there *is* nothing in that scale superior to being quite sure'.[4] And it may very well happen that even when people's beliefs are false they are as fully convinced of their truth as they are of the truth of what they know.

Moreover, though to be convinced of something is, in a sense, to be in a particular state of mind, it does not seem to consist in any special mental occurrence. It is rather a matter of accepting the fact in question and of not being at all disposed to doubt it than of contemplating it with a conscious feeling of conviction. Such feelings of conviction do indeed exist. There is the experience of suddenly coming to realize the truth of something that one had not known before: and it may be that similar experiences occur when one is engaged in defending a belief that has been put in question, or when one finally succeeds in resolving a doubt. But for the most part the things that we claim to know are not presented to us in an aura of revelation. We learn that they are so, and from then on we unquestioningly accept them. But this is not a matter of having any special feelings. It is not certain that to have a feeling of conviction is even a sufficient condition for being sure; for it would seem that a conscious feeling of complete conviction may co-exist with an unconscious feeling of doubt. But whether or not it ever is sufficient, it clearly is not necessary. One can be sure without it. And equally its presence is not necessary for the possession, or even for the display, of knowledge.

The fact is, as Professor Austin has pointed out,[5] that the expression 'I know' commonly has what he calls a 'performative' rather than a descriptive use. To say that I know that something is the case, though it does imply that I am sure of it, is not so much to report my state of mind as to vouch for the truth of whatever it may be. In saying that I know it I engage myself to answer for its truth: and I let it be understood that I am in a position to give this undertaking. If my credentials do not meet the usual standards, you have the right to reproach me. You have no right to reproach me if I merely say that I believe, though you may think the less of me if my belief appears to you irrational. If I tell you that I believe something which I do not, I am mis-informing you only about my mental attitude, but if I tell you that I know something which I do not, the chances are that I am misinforming you about the truth of the statement which I claim to know, or if not about its truth, then about my authority for making it. In the same way, to say of some other person that he knows that such and such is so is not primarily, if at all, to describe his state of mind; it is first of all to grant that what he is said to know is true; and, secondly, it is to admit his credentials. If we consider that his credentials are insufficient, whether on the ground that he is not, as we say, in a position to know, though others might be, or, possibly, because we hold that what he claims to know is something for which neither he nor any-one could have the requisite authority, then we will not allow that he really does know what he says he knows, even though he is quite sure of it and even though it is actually true.

But here it may be objected that this excursus into philology is beside the point. Let it be granted that the expression 'I know' is not always used in English to signify a cognitive mental state, Let it be granted even, what is very much more doubtful, that it is never so used. The fact remains, it may be argued, that these cognitive states, or acts, exist. When they do occur, they are sufficient for knowl-edge. Furthermore, their existence is the only au-thority worth having, so that if our ordinary use of words were strictly philosophical, which it obvi-ously is not, they would be not only sufficient for knowledge, but necessary as well.

Now I do not deny that ordinary usage is capa-ble of improvement, or even that some improve-ment might be made in it on philosophical grounds. Philosophers, like scientists, are at liberty to intro-duce technical terms, or to use ordinary words in a technical sense. But this proposal to restrict the ap-plication of the verb 'to know' to cases where the knowledge consisted in someone's being in a cog-nitive mental state would not be fortunate. For the consequence of accepting it would be that no one could ever properly be said to know anything at all.

The reason for this is that there cannot be a men-tal state which, being as it were directed towards a fact, is such that it guarantees that the fact is so. And here I am not saying merely that such states never do occur, or even that it is causally impossible that they ever should occur, but rather that it is logically impossible. My point is that from the fact that someone is convinced that something is true, how-ever firm his conviction may be, it never follows logically that it is true.[6] If he is a reliable witness and if he is in a good position to assess the truth of whatever statement is in question, then his being convinced of its truth may provide us with a strong reason for accepting it; but it cannot be it conclu-sive reason. There will not be a formal contradic-tion in saying both that the man's state of mind is such that he is absolutely sure that a given state-ment is true, and that the statement is false. There would indeed be a contradiction in saying both that he knew the statement to be true, and that it was false; but this, as has already been explained, is be-cause it enters into the meaning of the word 'know' that one cannot know what is not true. It cannot validly be inferred from this linguistic fact that when someone is considering a statement which he knows to be true, it is his state of mind that guarantees its truth. The statement is true if, and only if, what it states is so, or, in other words, if the situation which it describes is as it describes it. And whether the sit-uation really is as it is described is not to be decided merely by examining the attitude which anyone who considers the statement has towards it, not even if the person who considers it knows it to be true. If philosophers have denied, or overlooked, this point, the fault may lie in their use of such expressions as 'state of knowledge'. For if to say of someone that he is in a state of knowledge is merely to describe his condition of mind, it does not entail that there is anything which he knows; and if it does entail that there is something which he knows, then, as we have seen, it does not merely describe his condition of mind. Since the expression is in any case artificial, it may be understood in either of these ways, though I suppose it would be more natural to take it in the second sense, as signifying the opposite of being in a state of ignorance. What we may not do is use it in both senses at once, for they are incompatible; an expression cannot refer only to a condition of mind, and to something else besides. The mistake should be obvious when it is pointed out, but it has not always been avoided. And the result is that a condition of mind, ambiguously referred to as a state of knowledge, is wrongly thought to be sufficient to guarantee the truth of the statements upon which it is supposed to be directed.

But unless some states of mind are cognitive, it may be said, how can we come to know anything? We may make the truth of some statements depend upon the truth of others, but this process cannot go on for ever. There must be some statements of empirical fact which are directly verified. And in what can this verification consist except in our having the appropriate experiences? But then these experiences will be cognitive: to have whatever experience it may be will itself be a way of knowing something to be true. And a similar argument applies to *a priori* statements, like those of logic or pure mathematics. We may prove one mathematical statement by deducing it from others, but the proof must start somewhere. There must be at least one statement which is accepted without such proof, an axiom of some sort which is known intuitively. Even if we are able to explain away our knowledge of such axioms, by showing that they are true by definition, we still have to see that a set of definitions is consistent. To conduct any formal proof, we have to be able to see that one statement follows logically from another. But what is this seeing that one statement follows from another except the performance of a cognitive act?

The bases of this argument are sound. We do just have to see that certain proofs are valid, and it is through having some experience that we discover the truth or falsehood of any statement of empirical fact. In the case of some such statements, it may even be that our having certain experiences verifies them conclusively. This is a point which will have to be considered later on. But in any such case what verifies the statement, whether conclusively or not, is the existence of the experience, not the confidence that we may have in some description of it. To take a simple example, what verifies the statement that I have a headache is my feeling a headache, not my having a feeling of confidence that the statement that I have a headache is true. Of course if I do have a headache and also understand the statement, I shall undoubtedly accept it as being true. This is the ground for saying that if I have such an experience, I know that I am having it. But, in this sense, my knowing that I am having the experience is just my having it and being able to identify it. I know that I am having it inasmuch as I correctly take it as verifying the statement which describes it. But my justification for accepting the statement is not that I have a cognitive, or any other attitude towards it: it is simply that I am having the experience. To say that the experience itself is cognitive is correct, though perhaps misleading, if it is merely a way of saying that it is a conscious experience. It may still be correct if it is a way of saying that the experience is recognized for what it is by the person who is having it, though, as we shall see later on, such recognition can be mistaken. It is not correct if it is taken as implying that the experience either consists in or includes a process of infallibly apprehending some statement to be true.

Similarly, what makes it true, for example, that the conclusion of a syllogism follows from the premises is that the inference exemplifies a law of logic. And if we are asked what makes the law of logic true, we can in this and in many other cases provide a proof. But this proof in its turn relies upon some law of logic. There will come a point, therefore, when we are reduced to saying of some logical statement simply that it is valid. Now to be in a position to say that such a statement is valid we must be able to see that it is so, but it is not made valid by our seeing that it is. It is valid in its own right. Of course if 'seeing' here has the force of 'knowing', then the fact that the statement is valid will indeed follow from the fact that it is seen to be so. But once again this makes only the verbal point, that we are not, in this usage, entitled to talk of 'seeing' something to be true unless it really is true. It does not prove that there are, or can be, any mental states of intuition which are such that their existence affords an absolute guarantee that one really is, in this sense, seeing what one thinks one sees. It must always remain possible that one is mistaken. Admittedly, if someone thinks that he may have been mistaken in accepting some logical statement which had seemed to him evidently true, there may be nothing for him to do but just look at it again. And if this second look confirms the first, his doubts may reasonably be put to rest. But the truth of the statement in question still does not logically follow from the fact that it continues to strike him as self-evident. Truths of logic make no reference to persons: consequently, they cannot be established by any mere description of some person's mental state. And this holds good whatever the mental state may be.

This is not to say that we do not know the truth of any *a priori* statements, or even that we do not know some of them intuitively, if to know them intuitively is to know them without proof. Our argument no more implies this than it implies that we cannot know any empirical statements to be true. It is designed to show, not that we do not have the knowledge which we think we have, but only that knowing should not be represented as a matter of being in some infallible state of consciousness: for there cannot be such states.

This point is important, if only because their neglect of it has led philosophers into difficulties which might have been avoided. In Berkeley's well-known phrase, they 'have first raised a dust, and then complain, we cannot see'.[7] Starting from the premise that consciousness, in the sense of cognitive awareness, must always be consciousness *of* something,

they have perplexed themselves with such questions as what consciousness is in itself and how it is related to the things, or facts, which are its objects. It does not seem to be identical with its objects, yet neither does it seem to be anything apart from them. They are separate, yet nothing separates them. When there is added the further premise that consciousness is also self-conscious, the problem becomes more complicated still. In attempting to solve it existentialist philosophers have gone so far as to deny the law of identity and even to speak of 'the nothing' as if it were a special sort of agent, one of whose functions was to divide consciousness from itself. But apart from their own obvious demerits, these are reactions to a problem which should not arise. It depends upon the initial mistake of assuming that a naive analysis in terms of act and object yields an adequate account of knowledge.

Other philosophers, besides the existentialists, have made the mistake of treating knowledge as though it consisted in the possession of an inner searchlight. How far, they then ask, can the searchlight reach? Is it confined to the present or can its rays illuminate the past? Is not remembering a way of knowing? But does it then follow that the past is still real? Perhaps the light can even play upon the future. But how can it be possible to inspect what does not yet exist? It is commonly assumed that we can train the searchlight upon our own conscious states. But can it ever go beyond them? Do physical objects come within its scope? Do the thoughts and feelings of others? Some philosophers have held that moral and aesthetic values can be objects of knowledge. Numbers and abstracts entities have also been included. Indeed Plato seems to have thought that these were the only things that could be really known. Religious persons have claimed to be acquainted with a deity. And does not the experience of mystics suggest that the rays can penetrate beyond the actual world? But must there then not be a suprasensible reality? For it is taken for granted that whatever the searchlight can illuminate must in some manner exist.

Not all these questions are fictitious. There are genuine problems about the character and extent of what can be known. But this fashion of presenting them is a great impediment to their solution. It suggests that all that need be done to discover what it is possible to know, and consequently what is real, is to examine the states of mind of those who lay claim to knowledge. But, setting aside the question how such an examination could be made, it would be little to the purpose. The most that it could reveal would be that the subjects were having certain experiences and that they were convinced of the truth of whatever it was that these experiences led them to assert. But this would not prove that they knew anything at all, except, possible, that they were having the experiences in question. It would still have to be established by an independent argument that the experiences disclosed the existence of anything beyond themselves. And there is another way in which this talk of knowing objects is misleading. It fosters mistaken views of the dependence of questions about the criteria of knowledge upon questions about reality. Thus followers of Plato are apt to make such pronouncements as that 'the perfectly real can alone be perfectly known': [8] but it is not clear even what this means unless it is merely a portentous way of saying that one cannot know what is not the case. We shall see, for example, that the fact that historical statements can be known does not oblige us to conclude that the past is real, unless to say that the past is real is just a way of saying that there are historical statements which are true. In this, as in other cases, it will be found that questions about the possibility of knowledge are to be construed as questions about the analysis of different types of statement and about the grounds that there may be for accepting them.

The mistaken doctrine that knowing is an infallible state of mind may have contributed to the view, which is sometimes held, that the only statements that it is possible to know are those that are themselves in some way infallible. The ground for this opinion is that if one knows something to be true one cannot be mistaken. As we remarked when contrasting knowledge with belief, it is inconsistent to say 'I know but I may be wrong'. But the reason why this is inconsistent is that saying 'I know' offers a guarantee which saying 'I may be wrong' withdraws. It does not follow that for a fact to be known it must be such that no one could be mistaken about it or such that it could not have been

otherwise. It is doubtful if there are any facts about which no one could be mistaken, and while there are facts which could not be otherwise, they are not the only ones that can be known. But how can this second point be reconciled with the fact that what is known must be true? The answer is that the statement that what is known must be true is ambiguous. It may mean that it is necessary that if something is known it is true; or it may mean that if something is known, then it is a necessary truth. The first of these propositions is correct; it re-states the linguistic fact that what is not true cannot properly be said to be known. But the second is in general false. It would follow from the first only if all truths were necessary, which is not the case. To put it another way, there is a necessary transition from being known to being true; but that is not to say that what is true, and known to be true, is necessary or certain in itself.

If we are not to be bound by ordinary usage, it is still open to us to make it a rule that only what is certain can be known. That is, we could decide, at least for the purposes of philosophical discourse, not to use the word 'know' except with the implication that what was known was necessarily true, or, perhaps, certain in some other sense. The consequence would be that we could still speak of knowing the truth of *a priori* statements, such as those of logic and pure mathematics; and if there were any empirical statements, such as those describing the content of one's present experience, that were certain in themselves, they too might be included: but most of what we now correctly claim to know would not be knowable, in this allegedly strict sense. This proposal is feasible, but it does not appear to have anything much to recommend it. It is not as if a statement by being necessary became incapable of being doubted. Every schoolboy knows that it is possible to be unsure about a mathematical truth. Whether there are any empirical statements which are in any important sense indubitable is, as we shall see, a matter of dispute: if there are any they belong to a very narrow class. It is, indeed, important philosophically to distinguish between necessary and empirical statements, and in dealing with empirical statements to distinguish between different types and degrees of evidence. But there are better ways of bringing out these distinctions than by tampering with the meaning, or the application, of the verb 'to know'.

(IV) DISCUSSION OF METHOD: PHILOSOPHY AND LANGUAGE

We have now answered some of the questions which are raised by a philosophical enquiry into the nature of knowledge. It has been found that there is no very close resemblance between the different instances which are correctly described as instances of knowing, and in particular that to know something does not consist in being in some special state of mind. There are facts which we can be said to know intuitively, but these intuitions cannot be infallible. It has further been shown that the conception of objects of knowledge can be philosophically misleading, and that while there is a sense in which one cannot be mistaken if one knows that something is so, this does not imply that what one knows is itself necessary or indubitable. The whole discussion was introduced as an example of philosophic method. Let us therefore consider, for a moment, how these conclusions have in fact been reached.

An important part of our procedure has been to put these general questions about knowledge to the test of particular instances. Thus the proof that one can know an object, in the sense of being able to recognize it, without making any conscious judgement about it, is that it is possible to find examples of such recognition where there is no evidence that any judgement is made. The proof that knowing how to do something need not include the ability to give an account of the way in which it is done is just that there are many things which people know how to do without their being able to give any such accounts. To discover that there need be no difference, in respect of being sure, between knowing and believing, we need only look at cases in which it turns out that someone does not know what he thought he knew. Very often the reason for this is that what he thought he knew was false. Consequently, he could not have known it, he only believed it. But there is no suggestion that his mental state was different from what it was supposed to be.

Had what he claimed to know been true he would, in these circumstances, have known it. In such cases we show that what might be thought to be a necessary factor in a given type of situation is really not necessary, by finding examples in which it does not occur. This is essentially a method of disproof: we cannot so decisively show that a certain factor is necessary, merely by finding examples in which it does occur; we have to be able to see that its presence is logically required by the fact that the situation is of the given type. At the same time we may test the view that it is so required by searching for counterexamples. That none are forthcoming is at least an indication that it is correct. There is a certain analogy here with scientific reasoning, except that it is not so much a matter, as in the scientific case, of discovering whether there are any counterexamples as of deciding whether there could be. The question is whether there is anything that we should be prepared to count as an exception to the suggested rule. Thus the proof that knowing, in the sense of 'knowing that', is always knowledge of some truth is that it would not otherwise be reckoned as knowledge. But it is not always so clear whether or not we should be prepared to admit exceptions. And one way of finding out is to examine carefully whatever might appear to be a doubtful case.

It does not matter whether the examples taken are actual or imaginary. In either case we describe a situation in order to see how it should be classified. Or if there be no doubt as to its classification, we may redescribe it in such a way as to bring to light certain features of it which might otherwise be overlooked. The argument therefore depends upon considerations of language; in the present instance upon the ways in which we use, or propose to use, the verb 'to know'. But this does not mean that it is an argument about words, in any trivial sense, or that it is especially tied to the English language. We are concerned with the work that the word 'know' does, not with the fact that it is this particular word that does it. It is for this reason that we can spare ourselves a sociological investigation into the ways in which people actually do use words. For it would not matter if the popular practice were different from what we took it to be, so long as we were clear about the uses that we ourselves were ascribing to the word in question. And in talking about these uses we are talking about the uses of any words in any language that are, or may be, used in the same way. It is therefore indifferent whether, in this manner of philosophizing, we represent ourselves as dealing with words or as dealing with facts. For our enquiry into the use of words can equally be regarded as an enquiry into the nature of the facts which they describe.

Although we have not been in any way concerned with setting up a formal system, the argument has also been developed by means of deductive logic. Thus the proof that no cognitive state of mind could be infallible depends upon the logical truism that if two states of affairs are distinct a statement which refers to only one of them does not entail anything about the other. If the statement that someone is apprehending, or intuiting, something is to be regarded purely as a description of his state of mind it cannot follow from it that what he apprehends is true. A similar argument was used by Hume to prove that knowledge of causal relations 'is not, in any instance, attained by reasonings *a priori*'.[9] 'The effect', he says, 'is totally different from the cause, and consequently can never be discovered in it.'[10] Or again, 'there is no object, which implies the existence of any other if we consider these objects in themselves, and never look beyond the idea which we form of them.'[11] As Hume puts them these statements are not obviously tautological; but they become so when it is seen that what he is saying is that when two objects are distinct, they are distinct; and consequently that to assert the existence of either one of them is not necessarily to assert the existence of the other.

When they are formulated in this way such statements may seem too trivial to be worth making. But their consequences are important and easily overlooked. The proof of this is that many philosophers have in fact maintained that causality is a logical relation and that there can be infallible acts of knowing. To refute them satisfactorily, we may need to do more than merely point out the logical mistake. We may have to consider how they could have come to be misled, what are the arguments which seem to support their view, how these arguments are to be met. In general, it will be found that the points

of logic on which philosophical theories turn are simple. How much of moral theory, for example, is centred upon the truism, again remarked by Hume, that 'ought' is not implied by 'is', that there can be no deductive step from saying how things are to saying how they ought to be. What is difficult is to make the consequences of such truisms palatable, to discover and neutralize the motives which lead to their being denied. It is the fact that much philosophizing consists in persuasive work of this sort, the fact also that in all philosophy so much depends upon the way in which things are put, that gives point to the saying that philosophy is an exercise in rhetoric. But if this is to be said, it must be understood that the word 'rhetoric' is not to be taken, as it now very often is, in a pejorative sense.

It is not my purpose to give an exhaustive list of philosophical procedures. Those that I have described are typical and important, but they are not the only ones that will come within our notice. In particular, it will be seen that philosophers do not limit themselves to uncovering the criteria which we actually use in assessing different types of statement. They also question these criteria; they may even go so far as to deny their validity. In this way they come to put forward paradoxes, such as that matter is unreal or that no one can ever really know what goes on in the mind of another. In themselves such statements may seem merely perverse: their philosophical importance comes out in the discussion of what lies behind them.

(V) KNOWING AS HAVING THE RIGHT TO BE SURE

The answers which we have found for the questions we have so far been discussing have not yet put us in a position to give a complete account of what it is to know that something is the case. The first requirement is that what is known should be true, but this is not sufficient; not even if we add to it the further condition that one must be completely sure of what one knows. For it is possible to be completely sure of something which is in fact true, but yet not to know it. The circumstances may be such that one is not entitled to be sure. For instance, a superstitious person who had inadvertently walked under a ladder might be convinced as a result that he was about to suffer some misfortune; and he might in fact be right. But it would not be correct to say that he knew that this was going to be so. He arrived at his belief by a process of reasoning which would not be generally reliable; so, although his prediction came true, it was not a case of knowledge. Again, if someone were fully persuaded of a mathematical proposition by a proof which could be shown to be invalid, he would not, without further evidence, be said to know the proposition, even though it was true. But while it is not hard to find examples of true and fully confident beliefs which in some ways fail to meet the standards required for knowledge, it is not at all easy to determine exactly what these standards are.

One way of trying to discover them would be to consider what would count as satisfactory answers to the question How do you know? Thus people may be credited with knowing truths of mathematics or logic if they are able to give a valid proof of them, or even if, without themselves being able to set out such a proof, they have obtained this information from someone who can. Claims to know empirical statements may be upheld by a reference to perception, or to memory, or to testimony, or to historical records, or to scientific laws. But such backing is not always strong enough for knowledge. Whether it is so or not depends upon the circumstances of the particular case. If I were asked how I knew that a physical object of a certain sort was in such and such a place, it would, in general, be a sufficient answer for me to say that I could see it; but if my eyesight were bad and the light were dim, this answer might not be sufficient. Even though I was right, it might still be said that I did not really know that the object was there. If I have a poor memory and the event which I claim to remember is remote, my memory of it may still not amount to knowledge, even though in this instance it does not fail me. If a witness is unreliable, his unsupported evidence may not enable us to know that what he says is true, even in a case where we completely trust him and he is not in fact deceiving us. In a given instance it is possible to decide whether the backing is strong enough to justify a claim to knowledge. But to say in general how strong it has to be would require our drawing up a list of the conditions under which perception, or memory, or testimony, or other forms of evidence are reliable. And this would be a very complicated matter, if indeed it could be done at all.

Moreover, we cannot assume that, even in particular instances, an answer to the question How do you know? will always be forthcoming. There may very well be cases in which one knows that something is so without its being possible to say how one knows it. I am not so much thinking now of claims to know facts of immediate experience, statements like 'I know that I feel pain', which raise problems of their own into which we shall enter later on. In cases of this sort it may be argued that the question how one knows does not arise. But even when it clearly does arise, it may not find an answer. Suppose that someone were consistently successful in predicting events of a certain kind, events, let us say, which are not ordinarily thought to be predictable, like the results of a lottery. If his run of successes were sufficiently impressive, we might very well come to say that he knew which number would win, even though he did not reach this conclusion by any rational method, or indeed by any method at all. We might say that he knew it by intuition, but this would be to assert no more than that he did know it but that we could not say how. In the same way, if someone were consistently successful in reading the minds of others without having any of the usual sort of evidence, we might say that he knew these things telepathically. But in default of any further explanation this would come down to saying merely that he did know them, but not by any ordinary means. Words like 'intuition' and 'telepathy' are brought in just to disguise the fact that no explanation has been found.

But if we allow this sort of knowledge to be even theoretically possible, what becomes of the distinction between knowledge and true belief? How does our man who knows what the results of the lottery will be differ from one who only makes a series of lucky guesses? The answer is that, so far as the man himself is concerned, there need not be any difference. His procedure and his state of mind, when he is said to know what will happen, may be exactly the same as when it is said that he is only guessing. The difference is that to say that he knows is to concede to him the right to be sure, while to say that he is only guessing is to withhold it. Whether we make this concession will depend upon the view which we take of his performance. Normally we do not say that people know things unless they have followed one of the accredited routes to knowledge. If someone reaches a true conclusion without appearing to have any adequate basis for it, we are likely to say that he does not really know it. But if he were repeatedly successful in a given domain, we might very well come to say that he knew the facts in question, even though we could not explain how he knew them. We should grant him the right to be sure, simply on the basis of his success. This is, indeed, a point on which people's views might be expected to differ. Not everyone would regard a successful run of predictions, however long sustained, as being by itself a sufficient backing for a claim to knowledge. And here there can be no question of proving that this attitude is mistaken. Where there are recognized criteria for deciding when one has the right to be sure, anyone who insists that their being satisfied is still not enough for knowledge may be accused, for what the charge is worth, of misusing the verb 'to know'. But it is possible to find, or at any rate to devise, examples which are not covered in this respect by any established rule of usage. Whether they are to count as instances of knowledge is then a question which we are left free to decide.

It does not, however, matter very greatly which decision we take. The main problem is to state and assess the grounds on which these claims to knowledge are made, to settle, as it were, the candidate's marks. It is a relatively unimportant question what titles we then bestow upon them. So long as we agree about the marking, it is of no great consequence where we draw the line between pass and failure, or between the different levels of distinction. If we choose to set a very high standard, we may find ourselves committed to saying that some of what ordinarily passes for knowledge ought rather to be described as probable opinion. And some critics will then take us to task for flouting or-

dinary usage. But the question is purely one of terminology. It is to be decided, if at all, on grounds of practical convenience.

One must not confuse this case, where the markings are agreed upon, and what is in dispute is only the bestowal of honours, with the case where it is the markings themselves that are put in question. For this second case is philosophically important, in a way in which the other is not. The sceptic who asserts that we do not know all that we think we know, or even perhaps that we do not strictly know anything at all, is not suggesting that we are mistaken when we conclude that the recognized criteria for knowing have been satisfied. Nor is he primarily concerned with getting us to revise our usage of the verb 'to know', any more than one who challenges our standards of value is trying to make us revise our usage of the word 'good'. The disagreement is about the application of the word, rather than its meaning. What the sceptic contends is that our markings are too high; that the grounds on which we are normally ready to concede the right to be sure are worth less than we think; he may even go so far as to say that they are not worth anything at all. The attack is directed, not against the way in which we apply our standards of proof, but against these standards themselves. It has, as we shall see, to be taken seriously because of the arguments by which it is supported.

I conclude then that the necessary and sufficient conditions for knowing that something is the case are first that what one is said to know be true, secondly that one be sure of it, and thirdly that one should have the right to be sure. This right may be earned in various ways; but even if one could give a complete description of them it would be a mistake to try to build it into the definition of knowledge, just as it would be a mistake to try to incorporate our actual standards of goodness into a definition of good. And this being so, it turns out that the questions which philosophers raise about the possibility of knowledge are not all to be settled by discovering what knowledge is. For many of them reappear as questions about the legitimacy of the title to be sure. They need to be severally examined; and this is the main concern of what is called the theory of knowledge.

NOTES

1. L. Wittgenstein, *Philosophical Investigations* (Oxford, 1953), 1, 66, 67, pp. 31–2.
2. G. Ryle, *The Concept of Mind* (London, 1949), ch. 2.
3. *Op. cit.* pp. 133–4.
4. J. L. Austin, 'Other Minds', *Supplementary Proceedings of the Aristotelian Society,* vol. xx, p. 171.
5. *Op. cit.*
6. Except in the rare cases where the truth of the statement in question is a logical condition of its being believed, as in the assertion of one's own existence.

7. G. Berkeley, *The Principles of Human Knowledge,* Introduction, section iii.
8. Dean Inge, 'Philosophy and Religion', *Contemporary British Philosophy,* 1st series, p. 191.
9. D. Hume, *An Enquiry Concerning Human Understanding,* section IV, part 1, para. 23.
10. Ibid. section IV, part 1, para. 25.
11. D. Hume, *A Treatise of Human Nature,* Book 1, part III section vi.

Is Justified True Belief Knowledge?   18

EDMUND L. GETTIER

VARIOUS ATTEMPTS have been made in recent years to state necessary and sufficient conditions for someone's knowing a given proposition. The attempts have often been such that they can be stated in a form similar to the following:[1]

(a) S knows that P   if and only if
   (i)   P is true,
   (ii)   S believes that P, and
   (iii)   S is justified in believing that P.

For example, Chisholm has held that the following gives the necessary and sufficient conditions for knowledge:[2]

(b) S knows that P   if and only if
   (i)   S accepts P,
   (ii)   S has adequate evidence for P, and
   (iii)   P is true.

Ayer has stated the necessary and sufficient conditions for knowledge as follows:[3]

(c) S knows that P   if and only if
   (i)   P is true,
   (ii)   S is sure that P is true, and
   (iii)   S has the right to be sure that P is true.

I shall argue that (a) is false in that the conditions stated therein do not constitute a *sufficient* condition for the truth of the proposition that S knows that P. The same argument will show that (b) and (c) fail if 'has adequate evidence for' or 'has the right to be sure that' is substituted for 'is justified in believing that' throughout.

I shall begin by noting two points. First, in that sense of 'justified' in which S's being justified in believing P is a necessary condition of S's knowing that P, it is possible for a person to be justified in believing a proposition that is in fact false. Secondly, for any proposition P, if S is justified in believing P, and P entails Q, and S deduces Q from P and accepts Q as a result of this deduction, then S is justified in believing Q. Keeping these two points in mind, I shall now present two cases in which the

Analysis 23 (Blackwell, 1963): 121–123. Reprinted by permission of the author.

conditions stated in (a) are true for some proposition, though it is at the same time false that the person in question knows that proposition.

CASE I

Suppose that Smith and Jones have applied for a certain job. And suppose that Smith has strong evidence for the following conjunctive proposition:

> (d) Jones is the man who will get the job, and Jones has ten coins in his pocket.

Smith's evidence for (d) might be that the president of the company assured him that Jones would in the end be selected, and that he, Smith, had counted the coins in Jones's pocket ten minutes ago. Proposition (d) entails:

> (e) The man who will get the job has ten coins in his pocket.

Let us suppose that Smith sees the entailment from (d) to (e), and accepts (e) on the grounds of (d), for which he has strong evidence. In this case, Smith is clearly justified in believing that (e) is true.

But imagine, further, that unknown to Smith, he himself, not Jones, will get the job. And, also, unknown to Smith, he himself has ten coins in his pocket. Proposition (e) is then true, though proposition (d), from which Smith inferred (e), is false. In our example, then, all of the following are true: (i) (e) is true, (ii) Smith believes that (e) is true, and (iii) Smith is justified in believing that (e) is true. But it is equally clear that Smith does not *know* that (e) is true; for (e) is true in virtue of the number of coins in Smith's pocket, while Smith does not know how many coins are in Smith's pocket, and bases his belief in (e) on a count of the coins in Jones's pocket, whom he falsely believes to be the man who will get the job.

CASE II:

Let us suppose that Smith has strong evidence for the following proposition:

> (f) Jones owns a Ford.

Smith's evidence might be that Jones has at all times in the past within Smith's memory owned a car, and always a Ford, and that Jones has just offered Smith a ride while driving a Ford. Let us imagine, now, that Smith has another friend, Brown, of whose whereabouts he is totally ignorant. Smith selects three place-names quite at random, and constructs the following three propositions:

> (g) Either Jones owns a Ford, or Brown is in Boston;
> (h) Either Jones owns a Ford, or Brown is in Barcelona;
> (i) Either Jones owns a Ford, or Brown is in Brest-Litovsk.

Each of these propositions is entailed by (f). Imagine that Smith realizes the entailment of each of these propositions he has constructed by (f), and proceeds to accept (g), (h), and (i) on the basis of (f). Smith has correctly inferred (g), (h), and (i) from a proposition for which he has strong evidence. Smith is therefore completely justified in believing each of these three propositions. Smith, of course, has no idea where Brown is.

But imagine now that two further conditions hold. First, Jones does *not* own a Ford, but is at present driving a rented car. And secondly, by the sheerest coincidence, and entirely unknown to Smith, the place mentioned in proposition (h) happens really to be the place where Brown is. If these two conditions hold then Smith does *not* know that (h) is true, even though (i) (h) *is* true, (ii) Smith does believe that (h) is true, and (iii) Smith is justified in believing that (h) is true.

These two examples show that definition (a) does not state a *sufficient* condition for someone's knowing a given proposition. The same cases, with appropriate changes, will suffice to show that neither definition (b) nor definition (c) do so either.

NOTES

1. Plato seems to be considering some such definition it *Theatetus* 201, and perhaps accepting one at *Meno* 98.

2. Roderick M. Chisholm, *Perceiving: A Philosophical Study.* Cornell University Press (Ithaca, New York, 1957), p. 16.

3. A. J. Ayer, *The Problem of Knowledge.* Macmillan (London, 1956), p. 34.

Part IV

Philosophy of Mind

JOHN HEIL

John Heil is professor of philosophy at Davidson College. His research interests center on the philosophy of mind, metaphysics, and epistemology. His most recent books include *The Philosophy of Mind: A Contemporary Introduction* (1998), *First-Order Logic* (1994), *The Nature of True Minds* (1992), and (with Alfred Mele) *Mental Causation* (1993).

A History of Early Analytic Philosophy of Mind

PHILOSOPHY OF MIND even today is in large measure a reaction to a conception of the mind and its relation to the physical world advanced by René Descartes in the seventeenth century. Descartes sees the world as comprising *substances*. (By "substance," Descartes meant a particular thing: a particular tree, a particular rock, a particular planet, a particular ocean, a particular electron.) Some substances (indeed, all of those in the preceding list) are physical. They reside in a region of space, have boundaries (even if vague), and exclude other substances from the region they occupy. With the possible exception of the fundamental particles, every physical substance is itself made up of other physical substances, and these substances are made up of other physical substances.

Descartes held that there are, in addition to physical substances, mental substances. Mental and physical substances have distinct attributes. Every physical substance is *spatially extended,* and every property of a physical substance is, at bottom, a way of being extended: a *mode of extension*. A billiard ball is spherical and has a particular mass. The ball's sphericity and its mass are spatial modes, ways of being extended. What of the ball's red color? In experiencing the ball as red, we are reacting to a complex spatial feature of the ball—perhaps the arrangement of particles on its surface, an arrangement that reflects light in a distinctive way. Here we must distinguish between features of the ball that give rise in us to experiences of red and our red experiences. The former are physical; the latter are mental.

Physical substances are spatially extended; mental substances—minds or selves—*think*. No physical substance thinks; no mental substance is spatially extended. Physical properties are modes of extension, mental properties are *modes of thought*. Descartes provides no

This essay was commissioned especially for this volume and appears here for the first time.

positive characterization of mental modes, only a list of examples: doubting, affirming, understanding, willing, sensing, and imagining. Modes of thought include

- feeling a pain in your foot
- having a conscious visual experience of a red billiard ball
- doing mental arithmetic
- believing that Napoleon fought at Austerlitz
- wanting a Whopper
- judging that the cat is on the mat

You—the you who thinks—are a mental substance, a mind or self. Your body is a complex physical substance made up exclusively of simpler physical substances arranged in a particular way. Although minds and bodies are distinct substances, they are intimately connected:

> I am not present in my body in the way a sailor is present in his ship. Rather, I am very tightly bound to my body and so "mixed up" with it that we form a single thing. If this weren't so, I—who am just a thinking thing—wouldn't feel pain when my body was injured; I would perceive the injury by pure understanding in the way that a sailor sees the leaks in his ship with his eyes. And, when my body needed food or drink, I would explicitly understand that the need existed without having the confused sensations of hunger and thirst. For the sensations of thirst, hunger, and pain are just confused modes of thought arising from the union and "mixture" of mind and body. (*Meditations* [1641] 1986, 47)

Descartes speaks here of his mind and body being "mixed" and forming "a single thing," but he is clearly thinking of the mind as distinct from the body. You are a "mixture" of two substances: a mind and a body. In principle, at least, these could exist separately—as they perhaps do when the body dies and its soul "departs."

Descartes's dualism of mind and body is notorious for generating the *mind-body problem*. In what sense could a nonphysical (and therefore nonspatial) mind be "mixed" with a body? If mental and physical substances are utterly distinct, how could they causally interact? We like to think (and indeed scientists have thought since Descartes's time) that the physical world is "causally closed." Every physical occurrence has a physical cause. Imagine a nonphysical mind intervening in the physical world. This would require the mind's somehow affecting the motions of physical particles. But the motions of such particles are, as we suppose, governed by physical laws. Mental intervention would require circumventing those laws. The philosophers in Part IV of this volume can all be seen as reacting to Descartes in one way or another.

Franz Brentano

Franz Brentano (1838–1917), a German philosopher-psychologist, focuses on the Cartesian distinction between mind and body. Brentano, no less than Descartes, has had a lasting influence on our ways of thinking about minds and their contents. Brentano (whose students included Edmund Husserl and Alexius Meinong) worked in a period when the lines between philosophy and psychology were much looser than they are today. Discussion of mental phenomena was still heavily influenced by Kant and German idealism. (Idealism is the view that reality is mind dependent; all that exists is minds—or perhaps just a single mind—and their contents.) All parties follow Descartes in taking for granted that the study of the mind is the study of conscious phenomena. One aim of early psychology was to develop an exhaustive inventory of mental types—kinds of conscious occurrence. A second goal was to provide a systematic accounting for relations among conscious goings-on. Such projects presuppose a principled way of distinguishing mental from nonmental phenomena.

This is Brentano's target in "The Distinction between Mental and Physical Phenomena," taken from chapter one of the first volume of his *Psychology from an Empirical Standpoint* (1874). Although philosophy of mind is often pursued from the armchair, Brentano regarded his endeavor as thoroughly *empirical*. A biologist uses the empirical method in classifying organisms and investigating their makeup, so the psychologist uses the empirical method in investigating the mind. The difference is that the biologist engages in *outward* observation, the psychologist observes *inwardly*. The distinction between what is outwardly observable—observable in the usual way by looking, listening, feeling, tasting, or smelling—and what is observable inwardly—by means of *introspection*—provides one way of distinguishing the mental from the nonmental. Introspection occurs when the mind turns its attention to itself—to its own contents. Instead of looking out through your eyes, you look inward with the mind's eye. When you experience a tree visually, you attend to the tree. But it is also possible to attend—introspectively—to your visual experience. In this way, you become aware of your current conscious state; you come to know what you think, or feel, or believe, or want "directly," without observation in the usual sense. If you can become aware of something introspectively, Brentano contends, it is mental; if you can only see, touch, feel, taste or smell something, it is nonmental.

We can agree that feeling, thinking, imagining, and the like are mental phenomena and that mental phenomena are introspectable yet can remain in the dark as to the nature of mental phenomena: what makes a phenomenon mental. Brentano's answer is that mental phenomena, unlike physical phenomena, are *directed*. Doubting, affirming, understanding, willing, sensing, and imagining incorporate *of-ness* or *about-ness* or *for-ness* absent from the physical domain. Doubting, affirming, understanding, and the rest have *objects*. You have an image *of* your grandmother; you have doubts *about* the honesty of a senator; you have a desire *for* a pepperoni pizza. Conscious states are in this way *directed on* objects. These objects—*intentional objects*—may or may not exist. You can think about the moon and fear bears. But you can equally fear ghosts and think about Hamlet.

The capacity of thoughts to be directed on nonexistent objects (which Brentano calls "intentional nonexistence") is especially noteworthy. It implies that a thought's being directed on an object in no way depends on the existence of that object. Your thought of a banana is no less *of a banana* because no banana answers to it. The possibility of a thought's pointing to a definite nonexistent object lacks a counterpart in the physical realm. Brentano takes it to be the mark of the mental.

Physical objects, states, and events lack directedness—or as it is nowadays called, echoing Brentano, *intentionality*. This might seem obviously wrong. The words you are now reading are physical entities, yet they have meaning, they are directed beyond themselves. Such entities, however, have at most *derived intentionality;* they mean what they do because we use them to express our thoughts. Thoughts are directed on intentional objects because of their intrinsic nature, or the intrinsic nature of thinkers. Physical signs or symbols are directed only to the extent that they are used by thinkers to express their thoughts.

C. D. Broad

Whereas Brentano is unconcerned with the question of how minds and bodies interact, the English philosopher C. D. Broad (1887–1971) takes up precisely this issue. The reading included here, "The Traditional Problem of Body and Mind," is a chapter from *The*

Mind and Its Place in Nature (1925). As the title suggests, Broad takes seriously the problem of fitting the mind into the kind of naturalistic worldview associated with science. Broad's aim is to show that philosophers have been too ready to dismiss Cartesian interactionism, the thesis that minds and bodies interact causally.

Suppose, as Broad (following Descartes) does, that minds and bodies are distinct kinds of substance. The difficulty is to see how minds and bodies, given their manifest differences, could causally interact (Figure 1). It is not *merely* that minds and bodies are different: causes need not resemble their effects. What is hard to understand is how a physical event could have a nonphysical effect or a nonphysical event have a physical effect.

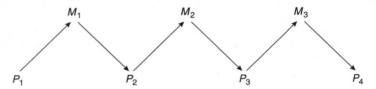

Figure 1.   Interactionism

Broad argues that the burden of proof lies with those who deny the possibility of interaction. As matters now stand, we have no good reason to doubt the possibility of mental-physical causal interaction and excellent reasons to believe that it occurs. On the positive side, we are constantly aware of sensory experiences following on the heels of bodily stimulations. You step on a tack and subsequently feel a sharp pain in your foot; the most obvious explanation for this sequence (and countless other such sequences) is that your stepping on the tack caused the feeling. You find the idea of a stroll attractive, decide to stroll, and stroll. Again, it is natural to suppose that your decision caused you to stroll. Why should anyone doubt mental-physical causal interaction?

One reason is that it is hard to see how to square the mental causing of a physical event with conservation laws in physics. If a mental event has a physical effect, this would seem to require the addition of energy to a physical system. If energy is added to a physical system, the added energy must have its source some other physical system. If we consider the physical universe as a whole, the amount of energy (though not its form) must remain constant (Figure 2).

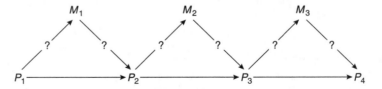

Figure 2.   Does interaction violate conservation?

Broad endorses this reading of conservation but argues that it is possible to influence a physical system causally without adding energy to the system. Consider an oscillating pendulum: a weight swinging on a string suspended from a fixed point. The motion of the weight is constrained by the string. "The string makes no difference to the total energy of the weight; but it makes all the difference in the world to the particular way in which the weight moves and the particular way in which the energy is distributed between the potential and kinetic forms" (249). Perhaps the mind affects the body in some analogous way without violating conservation.

Consider a slightly different example (borrowed from E. J. Lowe 1996). The bodily motions of a spider moving about its web are only partly explained by events in the spider's nervous system. Just as the string constrains the motion of a weight, so the spider's web constrains motions of the spider's body. The web does not push the spider about, but the web provides an important component of any causal explanation of the spider's movements. This is in keeping with Broad's suggestion that it is a mistake to suppose the mind initiates causal sequences resulting in bodily motions (a supposition that would violate conservation). Instead, the mind might be responsible for *patterns* of synaptic sequences in the nervous system that result in particular bodily motions (Figure 3).

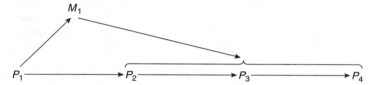

Figure 3.   Broad style interactionism

Broad speculates that certain mental events might "lower the resistance of certain synapses and . . . raise that of others." It is hard to see how this could be accomplished without violating conservation. Perhaps we could imagine mental goings-on explaining, not the raising or lowering of the resistance of particular synapses, however, but the existence of a particular synaptic *pattern*—one, namely, that results in a bodily motion appropriate to its mental cause. Otherwise (you might think), we could have no good explanation of the bodily motion, any more than we could have a good explanation for the delicate motions of the spider's legs without taking account of the web. In both cases, we can trace back physical causal chains culminating in a coordinated bodily motion as far as we like, and every link in these chains will be physical. What will be left unexplained is why the chains converge in just *this* way. To explain that, Broad would argue, we must go outside the physical system.

The most promising alternative to interactionism, Broad thinks, is *epiphenomenalism.* An epiphenomenalist grants physical-to-mental causation but denies that minds causally influence bodies: Mental events are nonphysical *by-products* of physical events in the brain (Figure 4). Your stepping on a tack initiates a complex causal sequence of physical events. One of these events produces, in addition to some physical effect, a mental effect: a painful sensation. You may be inclined to think of this sensation as responsible for your subsequent behavior, but to an epiphenomenalist, this is an illusion. Your behavior is entirely the project of complicated neurological goings-on. In taking consciousness to be a systematic by-product of neural activity, the epiphenomenalist hopes to account for our impression that the mind affects the physical world, without having to suppose that mental events themselves have physical effects. Rather, particular physical events in the brain produce *both* a conscious experience and a physical effect that we mistakenly regard as an effect of the correlated conscious experience. Broad regards epiphenomenalism as preferable to *parallelism* (according to which *all* mind-body interaction is illusory), but inferior to his own brand of interactionism.

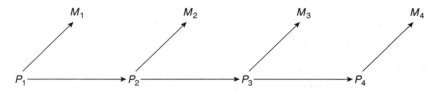

Figure 4.   Epiphenomenalism

Gilbert Ryle

Broad and Brentano take the Cartesian model of the mind for granted. In the 1940s, Gilbert Ryle (1900–1976) launched an attack on this model in an influential volume, *The Concept of Mind* (1949). According to Ryle, the conception of mind and its relation to the body inherited from Descartes is founded on a *category mistake*: concepts belonging to one logical category are mistakenly thought to belong to a distinct logical category. Imagine that you are showing a visitor around a university. You take the visitor to see academic buildings, dormitories, laboratories, libraries, and playing fields. When you are done, your visitor remarks, "We've seen students, faculty, administrators, academic buildings, dormitories, laboratories, libraries, and playing fields, but you haven't yet shown me the university." You must explain that "the university" is not some further building, similar perhaps to the library, but distinct from it. The university is just the arrangement of all these things.

Ryle argues that we make a similar mistake in imagining the mind to be an entity, similar to, but distinct from, the body. When no physical entity answers to our expectations, we leap to the conclusion that the mind is a *non*physical entity. The result is "the myth of the ghost in the machine," a picture of the mind as operating behind the scenes and somehow causally interacting with the body. In speaking of minds, however, we are not really speaking of mental *entities* at all, ghostly or otherwise. This is the category mistake. Ascribing a mind to you is not to imagine that you possess a kind of organ, even a brain. Rather, in saying that you have a mind, I am simply recognizing that your activities exhibit the marks of intelligence. Intelligent behavior is a kind of behavior, not behavior with a particular kind of cause. The causal model is itself merely a carryover of the myth of the ghost in the machine. Consider a basketball team that exercises *esprit de corps*—team spirit. Exercising team spirit is not something players do alongside or in addition to shooting, passing, rebounding, and the like. Rather, it is individuals on the team engaging in these activities with a special verve. Similarly, acting intelligently is not something done behind the scenes that produces actions; it is simply a way of behaving or being disposed to behave.

Ryle extends this "behaviorist" analysis of the mind to cover states of mind generally. Your believing that you will win the lottery, for instance, is not a matter of your—or your mind's—being in a certain private state that you might introspect. Your having this belief is a matter of your doing and saying various things, or being so disposed: if offered the chance to purchase a lottery ticket, you will; if an opportunity arises to begin arrangements for a cruise to Tahiti, you pursue it; and so on.

Alan M. Turing

Although not a behaviorist, Alan M. Turing (1912–1954), in "Computing Machinery and Intelligence" (1950), advances a famous argument concerning the possibility of intelligent machines that falls quite within the spirit of behaviorism. Turing, an important mathematician, is interested in the question: *Could a machine think?* By "machine" Turing means a digital computer, a device whose operations could be represented in a "machine table" as finite sequences of simple operations. The term *Turing machine* is nowadays used as a label for an important class of such devices. (Hilary Putnam provides a more detailed account of Turing machines in §1 of "Minds and Machines," pages 290–291 of this volume.) A Turing machine includes a component capable of reading and writing (and erasing) symbols, some means of storing symbols in definite "locations," and a way of "scanning" these locations. This is usually illustrated by envisaging a device that includes a "head" capable of reading and writing symbols on a (potentially infinite) tape containing discrete squares scanned one at a time. A machine's "program" is a set of instructions that tell it how to respond to a given symbol in a square it is scanning given its current state. Although a Turing machine is a mathematical idealization, it is possible to represent any computable function (any *algorithm*) as a sequence of operations on a Turing machine. Any program that can be run on a digital computer can be boiled down into a series of such operations.

It is possible, then, precisely to define "machine." Still, Turing contends, the question, Can a machine think? is too vague as it stands. Rather than debating the nature of thought, Turing "operationalizes" the question. Can we conceive of a *test* for intelligence? An adequate test would be such that anything that passed the test would count as capable of intelligent thought. Turing's suggestion is that any machine capable of playing the "imitation game" ought to be classified as thinking.

The imitation game is played by an interrogator and two contestants, A and B. In one version of the game A is a man, B, a woman. The interrogator's task is to discover which is the man, which the woman by questioning A and B via a teletype. A's goal is to mislead the interrogator, B's is to help the interrogator. If A is clever, he may succeed in making the interrogator guess that he is the woman reasonably often. Imagine now that we substitute a machine for A. Turing's suggestion is that if the machine can fool the interrogator *about as often as a person would,* then the machine should be called intelligent. (The machine need not be infallible, only as adept as an ordinary human contestant.)

Whether a machine could think, then, boils down to the question of whether a digital computer could be programmed so as to play the imitation game successfully. As Turing notes, this need not be a matter of the machine's being initially programmed to play the game in a particular way. A better strategy might be to program the device to "learn"— that is to modify its own program in response to inputs. The fact that a digital computer can "learn" in this way—can be programmed to reprogram itself in response to inputs unforeseen by the programmer—undercuts a common complaint that "computers, unlike intelligent agents, can only do what their programmers program them to do."

Turing takes up a number of arguments purporting to cast doubt on the idea that a machine could be intelligent and finds them all wanting. He himself has no positive argument for the possibility. Rather, he is content to point out that there is no reason to think that a digital computer could *not* be programmed to succeed in the imitation game. Turing speculates that this will have happened by the year 2000, a speculation that finds its way into Arthur C. Clarke's *2001: A Space Odyssey:* "Whether [the computer] HAL could actually think was a question which had been settled by the British mathematician Alan Turing back in the 1940's [sic]." The passage suggests that Turing *proved* that a machine could think. As we have seen, however, Turing hopes only to show that, *were* a machine to pass the test, we would have no good reason to deny that it thinks. This leaves open the question whether a machine *could* pass the Turing test.

From Thought to Consciousness

The Turing test provides a behavioral measure for one aspect of mental activity: thought. Even if we agree that thinking is an activity that could be performed by a computing machine, however, conscious experiences are another matter altogether. Turing makes no attempt to argue that a machine—even a machine adept at the imitation game—is *conscious* in the sense of having conscious experiences: pains, feelings of warmth, experiences of the sort you have when you bite into a mango. Perhaps beliefs and thoughts lack a distinctive "phenomenology," perhaps *all there is* to having a thought is to be capable of producing certain verbal and nonverbal responses. Much of our mental life, however, apparently includes a rich phenomenology. In biting into a mango, you undergo a qualitatively distinctive experience. It is difficult to see how this qualitative dimension of experience could be bestowed on a machine solely by means of clever programming.

One possibility is that while some kinds of mental activity can be understood by reference to their contribution to behavior, other mental processes include a qualitative element that resists analysis in terms of behavior. True, when you have a headache, you are disposed to behave in various ways and produce various utterances. Could this be *all there is* to your having a headache, however? What of the painful sensation that underlies your headache-manifesting behavior? This sensation evidently includes a significant qualitative element. How are we to understand the place of this qualitative element in the physical world?

U. T. Place

Mind-body dualists like Descartes locate conscious qualities in a nonphysical mind. We seem compelled to do so because the qualities are apparently utterly different from the qualities of any imaginable physical system. Physical qualities are publicly observable; conscious qualities are "observable" only by the person experiencing them. Physical qualities are in space; conscious qualities may have spatial associations but seem themselves not to be in space. You experience a pain in your foot. Where is your experience of the pain? It sounds odd to locate the experience in your foot. As Descartes pointed out, the phenomenon of phantom pain—experiences of pains in amputated limbs—suggests that it makes no sense to locate experiences, even of bodily sensations, in parts of the body.

You might think that conscious experiences are located in brains. After all, there is considerable evidence of a strong correlation between agents' reports of conscious experiences and brain goings-on. A correlation of As and Bs, however, even a perfect correlation, need not mean that As *are* Bs. Such a correlation would exist if, for instance, Bs were caused by As. This is exactly what Descartes, or Broad, or an epiphenomenalist would argue is so in the case of brain events and conscious experiences: the latter are caused by the former.

Still, an A-B correlation is consistent with Bs being reducible to As. What prevents us from making this reduction in the case of conscious experiences and brain processes? According to U. T. Place (1924–2000) in "Is Consciousness a Brain Process?" (1956), we are blinded to this possibility by a species of mistaken reasoning he dubs the "phenomenological fallacy." Suppose someone claims that your conscious visual experience of a ripe lemon illuminated in bright sunlight is really a pattern of neuron firings in your brain. How could this be? There is, to be sure, a correlation between experiences of this sort and patterns of neuron firings. But the qualities of the experience seem clearly to differ from the qualities of anything that might be going on in your brain. Your experience is of a yellowish, roundish object, but there is nothing yellow or round in your brain. And if As differ qualitatively from Bs, As could not *be* Bs.

This line of reasoning, Place argues is fallacious. True, when you have a visual experience of the lemon, your experience has certain qualities. These qualities, however, must not be confused with qualities of the object experienced. The *lemon* is yellow and round, but your *experience* of the lemon is not yellow or round. The fact that nothing in your brain is yellow or round, then, does not show that your visual experience of the lemon is not, at bottom, a process in your brain.

This does not imply that your conscious experience *is* a brain process. The empirical evidence establishes perhaps a correlation between subjects' reports of experiences of a certain kind and brain processes. But, argues Place, we can best account for this correlation by supposing that conscious experiences *are* goings-on in brains. We discover that streaks of lightning are correlated with electrical discharges in the atmosphere. We are not dualists about lightning and electrical discharges, however. Rather, we take it that lightning just *is* a particular sort of electrical discharge. This is the simplest hypothesis, and, other things equal, a simpler hypothesis is to be preferred to a more complex competitor. In the case of consciousness, the simplest hypothesis is that conscious experiences *are* processes in the brain.

Hilary Putnam

Place's idea that minds can be identified with brains falls prey to a line of reasoning originating with a paper, "Minds and Machines," published in 1960 by Hilary Putnam (b. 1926). Putnam has no interest in defending dualism. Instead, he argues that the question of how minds and bodies (or brains) are related is analogous to the question of how a computing machine's "logical states" are related to its "structural states." By "logical states," Putnam means states of a computing machine specified by means of a "machine table," a systematic characterization of a machine's states in terms of relations these bear to one another and to the machine's inputs and outputs. Think of a logical state as a state specified by a machine's program. In contrast, a machine's "structural states" are its physical states.

How are a machine's logical states related to its structural states? This question, Putnam holds, is strictly analogous to the question of how mental states are related to brain states. If there is no mystery in the case of a computing machine, then there is no mystery in the case of a conscious agent. Suppose, however, you are convinced that consciousness cannot be explained except by some form of dualism. Then, says Putnam, precisely analogous considerations would oblige you to accept a dualism of logical states and structural states. If that seems crazy, you should regard mind-body dualism as no less crazy.

This might lead you to imagine that Putnam is siding with Place and arguing for the identification of consciousness with brain processes. That is not his point, however. Return to the question of how a computing machine's logical states are related to its structural states. There cannot be an identity here: machines with very different physical constitutions might run the same programs and go into the same logical states. When my desktop computer adds 2 and 3, it goes into a particular state that leads it to display 5. Call this state S. Now a device constructed very differently—one with vacuum tubes instead of transistors, or one with brass cogs cranked by hand, or one made by a collection of fourth graders armed with pencils and paper—could also be in state S. There is no prospect of identifying S with any particular kind of physical state. True, whenever a device goes into state S it does so by virtue of going into some physical (structural) state. Insofar as devices differ in their physical makeup, however, these physical states will be quite different. Indeed, there is no end to the ways a device might be constructed so as to run the same program and thus go into state S. Further, if we reprogram a given machine, then it can go into the very same physical state without going into logical state S.

Suppose that Putnam is right: we cannot identify S with any physical state. What we can say is that a device's physical states "realize" its logical states. More generally, a machine's program is "realized" in its hardware. Different hardware can "realize" the same program. This does not imply a dualism of program and machine. Nor, argues Putnam, should we imagine that considerations traditionally advanced against the reduction of minds to brains oblige us to accept a dualism of mind and brain. Think of mental states as states of a program that runs on the brain. The *very same* program might be run on very different "hardware." There is no mystery here, no reason to embrace dualism. But neither is there any reason to think that "the mind just is the brain." (Compare: "the program just is the hardware.")

Putnam's observations that we can find a fruitful analogy between minds and computing machines have subsequently developed into a doctrine called *functionalism*. Functionalists regard states of mind as characterizable relationally (just as logical states are characterized relationally in a machine table). A belief, for instance, is a state that bears certain characteristic relations to other states; a desire has different systemic relations; and a pain is a state with its own characteristic relations to other states (and to inputs and outputs). These mental states, functionalists think, are "realized in," but not reducible to, physical states of systems (living or artificial) possessing them. Functionalism has dominated the philosophy of mind in recent years, and most researchers who call themselves "cognitive scientists" embrace one or another form of functionalism. (Ironically, Putnam himself gave up functionalism at just about the time it was becoming popular!)

Conclusion

These remarks provide only a briefest introduction to the authors featured in the section: Brentano, Broad, Ryle, Turing, Place, and Putnam. It is now your turn to see firsthand what they have to say. As you read, you will notice that each author takes up endless issues I have ignored. This is a poignant reminder that no one writes in a vacuum. Each author defends a thesis against a background of concerns pressing at the time. My discussion, in contrast, has focused on common themes, especially those bearing on topics salient today. You will benefit most if you take each author on his or her own terms. Such a strategy can make clear our own current biases and preconceptions. It can, in addition, give the lie to the old complaint that there is no progress in philosophy.

REFERENCES

Descartes, René. [1641]/1986. *Meditations on First Philosophy,* trans. Ronald Rubin. Claremont: Areté Press.
Lowe, E. J. 1996. *Subjects of Experience.* Cambridge: Cambridge University Press.

The Distinction between Mental and Physical Phenomena   19

FRANZ BRENTANO

I

THE DATA OF OUR CONSCIOUSNESS make up a world[1] which, taken in its entirety, falls into two great classes, the class of *physical* and the class of *mental* phenomena. We spoke of this distinction much earlier, in the course of defining the concept of psychology, and we returned to it again in our investigation of method. But what was said is still insufficient; what was then only suggested in passing we must now delineate more firmly and rigorously.

The fact that neither unity nor complete clarity has yet been achieved regarding the line of demarcation between the two areas seems to make this all the more necessary. We have already had occasion to see how physical phenomena which appear in the imagination have been taken to be mental. But there are many other cases of confusion as well. Even psychologists of considerable importance may find it difficult to vindicate themselves against the charge of self-contradiction.[2] We occasionally encounter such assertions as that sensation and imagination are differentiated by the fact that one occurs as the result of a physical phenomenon, while the other is evoked, according to the laws of association, by means of a mental phenomenon. But along with this the same psychologists admit that what appears in sensation does not correspond to its efficient cause. Accordingly, it turns out that what they call physical phenomena never appear to us in actual fact, and that we have no presentation of them whatsoever; surely this is a strange way in which to misuse the term "phenomenon"! When affairs are in such a state, we can not refrain from taking a somewhat closer look at the problem.

II

We do not aim to clear up the matter by a definition according to the traditional rules of logicians. These rules have lately been subjected to impartial criticism of various kinds, and there is still much more that might be added to what has been said against them. Our object is the elucidation of the two terms: physical phenomenon—mental phenomenon. We wish to exclude misunderstanding and confusion in connection with them. And for this we needn't be concerned about the means used, if only they really serve to produce clarity.

Giving more general, superordinate definitions is not the only useful means that can be employed for such an end. Just as induction is contrasted with deduction in the sphere of demonstration, here definition by way of the specific, i.e., by way of an example, is contrasted with definition by means of the more general. And the former method will be more appropriate as long as the particular term is more intelligible than the general. Hence, it may be a more effective procedure to define the term "color" by saying that it designates the general class for red, blue, green, and yellow, than to choose to give an account of red—following the opposite procedure—as a particular species of color. Definition by way of particular cases will perform still more useful service in connection with terms, such as those involved in our case, which are not at all common in ordinary life, while the names of the particular phenomena comprehended under them are familiar enough. So let us start with an attempt to make our concepts clear by way of examples.

Psychologie vom empirischen Standpunkt, vol. I, book II, chap. i, first published in 1874. R. M. Chisholm, ed., *Realism and the Background of Phenomenology* (Atascadero, CA: Ridgeview, 1960). Reprinted by permission of Ridgeview Publishing.

Every presentation (*Vorstellung*) of sensation or imagination offers an example of the mental phenomenon; and here I understand by presentation not that which is presented, but the act of presentation. Thus, hearing a sound, seeing a colored object, sensing warm or cold, and the comparable states of imagination as well, are examples of what I mean; but thinking, of a general concept, provided such a thing does actually occur, is equally so. Furthermore, every judgment, every recollection, every expectation, every inference, every conviction or opinion, every doubt, is a mental phenomenon. And again, every emotion, joy, sorrow, fear, hope, pride, despair, anger, love, hate, desire, choice, intention, astonishment, wonder, contempt, etc., is such a phenomenon.

Examples of physical phenomena, on the other hand, are a color, a shape, a landscape, which I see; a musical chord, which I hear; heat, cold, odor, which I sense; as well as comparable images, which appear to me in my imagination.

These examples may suffice as concrete illustrations of the distinction between the two classes.

III

Nevertheless, we will attempt to give a definition of the mental phenomenon in another, more unified way. For this, there is available a definition we have used before, when we said that by the term, mental phenomena, we designate presentations and, likewise, all those phenomena which are based on presentations. It scarcely requires notice that, once again, by presentation we understand here not what is presented but the presenting of it. This presentation forms the basis not merely of judgements, but also of desires, as well as of every other mental act. We cannot judge of anything, cannot desire anything, cannot hope for anything, or fear anything, if it is not presented. Hence, the definition which we gave embraces all of the examples just introduced and, in general, all of the phenomena belonging to this domain.

It is a sign of the immature state in which psychology finds itself that one can scarcely utter a single sentence about mental phenomena which would not be disputed by many. Still, the great majority

agree with what we just said; presentations are the basis for the other mental phenomena. Thus, Herbart is quite correct in saying: "In every case of emotion, something, no matter how diversified and complicated, must be in consciousness as something presented; so that this particular presentation is included in this particular feeling. And every time we have a desire . . . [we] also have in our thoughts that which we desire."[3]

Herbart then goes farther, however. He sees nothing but certain states of presentation, which are derivable from presentations, in all other phenomena; a viewpoint which has already been attacked repeatedly, especially by Lotze, on decisive grounds. Among others, J. B. Meyer recently set forth a lengthy criticism of it in his exposition of Kant's psychology. But he is not satisfied with denying that feelings and desires can be derived from presentations; he maintains that phenomena of this sort can exist even without any presentation.[4] Indeed, Meyer believes that the lowest animals have only feelings and desires, but no presentations, and that the life even of the higher animals and of human beings begins with mere feeling and desire, while presentation first emerges as development progresses.[5] In this way he, too, seems to come into conflict with our contention.

Nevertheless, if I am not mistaken, the contradiction is more apparent than real. From several of his expressions it seems to me to follow that Meyer understands the concept of presentation more narrowly than we have understood it, while he broadens the concept of feeling to an equal extent. "Presentation," he says, "first enters in when the sensed change in one's own state can be understood as the result of an outer stimulus, even if this expresses itself, at first, only in the unconscious looking or feeling around for an external object which results from it." If Meyer were to understand the same thing under presentation as we do, then it would be impossible for him to speak in this way. He would see that a state like the one which he describes as the origin of presentation would already include an abundant number of presentations: for example, presentations of temporal proximity, of spatial proximity, and of cause and effect. If all of this must already be present in the soul in order that a presentation in J. B. Meyer's sense might be formed, it is surely clear that such a thing cannot be the basis of every other mental phenomenon. On the contrary, the very state of being present (*Gegenwärtig-sein*) which belongs to each of the things named is precisely a state of being presented (*Vorgestelltsein*) in our sense. And such is the case generally, wherever something appears in consciousness: whether it be hated or loved or regarded indifferently; whether it be affirmed or rejected, or, in the case of complete withholding of judgment—I cannot express myself better than by saying—presented. As we use the word "to present," "to be presented" comes to the same thing as "to appear."

Even J. B. Meyer recognizes that a presentation in this sense is presupposed by every feeling, even the most lowly feelings of pleasure and displeasure; but deviating from us in his terminology he calls *it* a feeling and not a presentation. This seems to me to follow from these words: "Between non-sensation and sensation there is no intermediate state. . . . Now the simplest form of sensation does not need to be more than the mere *sensing* of the *change* in one's own body or a part of it which results from some stimulus. A creature endowed with sensation of this sort would then have only a *feeling of its own states*. A sensibility of the soul for the changes which are advantageous or harmful to it could very well be immediately connected *with this vital feeling* for the events beneath one's own skin, even if this *new sensitivity* were not simply derivable from that feeling; such a soul could have *feelings* of pleasure and displeasure *along with the sensation* . . . A soul so endowed would still possess no presentation. . . ."[6] We see clearly that what is, in our opinion, the only thing to deserve the name "feeling," also arises, in J. B. Meyer's opinion, as a successor [to something else. Its predecessor] falls under the concept of presentation, as we understand it, and forms the indispensable presupposition of the other. Hence it appears that if Meyer's viewpoint is translated into our language, the contradiction disappears of its own accord.

Perhaps the same is also true of others who express themselves similar to Meyer. Still, we may surely find that, as regards some kinds of sensual feelings of pleasure and displeasure, someone does actually hold the opinion that there is no presentation, even in our sense, on which they are based. We cannot deny a certain temptation in that direction, at least.

This holds, for example, in regard to feelings which are caused by a cut or a burn. If someone is cut, then for the most part he has no further perception of touch; if he is burned, no further perception of heat; but pain alone seems to be present in the one case and the other.

Nonetheless, there is no doubt that even here the feeling is based on a presentation. In such cases we always have the presentation of a definite spatial location, which we ordinarily specify in relation to one or the other of the visible and palpable parts of our body. We say that our foot hurts, or our hand hurts, this or the other place on our body is in pain. In the first place, then, those who look on such a spatial presentation as something originally given by means of the neural stimulation itself will therefore be unable to deny that a presentation is the basis of this feeling. But others, too, cannot avoid making the same assumption. For we have within us not merely the presentation of a definite spatial location, but also that of a particular sensory quality, analogous to color, sound, and other so-called sensory qualities, a quality which belongs among the physical phenomena and which is definitely to be distinguished from the accompanying feeling. If we hear a pleasant, mild sound or a shrill one, a harmonious chord or a discord, it will occur to no one to identify the sound with the accompanying feeling of pleasure or pain. But, likewise, when a cut, a burn, or a tickle arouses a feeling of pain or pleasure in us, we must maintain in a similar manner the distinction between a physical phenomenon, which enters in as the object of outer perception, and a mental phenomenon of feeling, which accompanies its appearance, even though the superficial observer is rather inclined to confusion here.

The principal basis of the illusion is probably the following. It is well known that our sensations are mediated by the so-called afferent (*sensibeln*) nerves. It was believed earlier that specialized nerves served exclusively as conductors for each class of sensory qualities, color, sound, and so on. Recently, physiology has inclined more and more to the opposite point of view.[7] Particularly, it teaches almost universally that the nerves for tactile sensations, when stimulated in one way, produce in us the sensations of heat and cold, and when stimulated in another way, produce the so-called sensations of pain and pleasure. In fact, however, something similar holds for all nerves, insofar as a sensory phenomenon of the kind just mentioned can be aroused in us by way of every nerve. If they are very strongly stimulated, all nerves arouse painful phenomena, which are not distinguished in kind one from another. If a nerve serves as the medium of diverse classes of sensations, it often happens that it serves as the medium of several at the same time, as, for example, looking at an electric light results simultaneously in a "beautiful" sensation of color, i.e., one that is pleasant to us, and a painful phenomenon of another class. The nerves of the tactile sense frequently communicate at the same time a so-called sensation of touch, a sensation of heat or cold, and a so-called sensation of pain or pleasure. Now it is manifest that when several sensory phenomena appear together, it is not seldom the case that they are regarded as being *one*. This has been demonstrated in a striking way in connection with the sensations of taste and smell. It is established that almost all of the differences which we are accustomed to look upon as differences of taste are, in fact, only differences in simultaneously occurring phenomena of smell. It is a similar matter when we eat a food cold or warm: we often believe ourselves to have differences in taste which are in fact only differences in phenomena of temperature. It is not to be wondered at, then, if we do not always maintain a strict distinction between what is a phenomenon of temperature and what is a tactile phenomenon. Indeed, we would perhaps not distinguish them at all if they did not ordinarily appear independently of each other. But if now we consider the sensations of feeling (*Gefühlsempfindungen*) we find that for the most part they are bound up with sensations of another class and that when the excitation is very strong these other sensations sink into insignificance beside them. It is very easy, then, to account for the fact that we should be deceived about the occurrence of a particular class of sensory qualities and believe ourselves to have a single sensation instead of two. Since the supervening presentation was accompanied by a relatively very strong feeling, incomparably stronger than the one which followed upon the first kind of quality, this mental phenomenon was regarded as the only one which had newly been experienced. And if the first kind of quality

disappeared entirely, then we would believe that we possessed nothing besides a feeling, without any presentation on which it was based.

A further basis of the illusion is that the quality on which the feeling ensues, and the feeling itself, do not bear two distinct names. We call the physical phenomenon, which occurs along with the feeling of pain, itself pain in this case. We do not say that this or that phenomenon in the foot is experienced with pain so much as we say that pain is experienced in the foot. To be sure, this is an equivocation such as we find elsewhere, whenever things stand in a close relationship to each other. We call the body healthy, and in connection with it, the air, food, facial color, and so on, but plainly in different senses. In our case, a physical phenomenon itself is called pleasure or pain, after the feeling of pleasure or pain which accompanies its appearance, and here too the sense is modified. It is as if we should say of a harmonious sound that it is a pleasure to us, because we experience a feeling of pleasure on its occurrence; or that the loss of a friend is a great sorrow to us. Experience shows that equivocation is one of the foremost hindrances to our knowledge of distinctions. It must necessarily be very much so here, where a danger of being deluded exists in and of itself, and the transference of the term was perhaps itself the result of a confusion. Hence, many psychologists were deceived, and further errors were tied up with this one. Many arrived at the false conclusion that the experiencing subject must be present at the place of the injured limb in which a painful phenomenon is localized in perception. For, insofar as they identified the phenomenon with the accompanying feeling of pain, they regarded it as a mental, not as a physical, phenomenon. And for just that reason, they believed its perception in the limb to be an inner, and consequently, an evident and infallible perception.[8] But their opinion is contradicted by the fact that the same phenomena often appear in the same way after the limb has been amputated. Others accordingly argued rather to the opposite effect, skeptically opposing the self-evidence (*Evidenz*) of inner perception. This is all resolved, if one has learned to distinguish between the pain in the sense in which the term designates the apparent property of a part of our body and the feeling of pain which is tied up with sensing it. But if one has done this, then one is no longer inclined to hold that the feeling of sensory pain which one experiences on being injured is not based on any presentation.

We may, accordingly, regard it as an indubitably correct definition of mental phenomena that they are either presentations or (in the sense which has been explained) rest on presentations as their basis. In this we would thus have a second definition of the concept [of mental phenomena] which breaks down into fewer terms. Yet it is not entirely unified, since it presents mental phenomena as divided into two groups.

IV

The attempt has been made to give a perfectly unified definition which distinguishes all of the mental phenomena, as contrasted with the physical, by means of negation. All physical phenomena, it is said, manifest extension and definite spatial location, whether they are appearances to sight or another sense, or products of the imagination, which presents similar objects to us. The opposite, however, is true of mental phenomena; thinking, willing, and so on appear as unextended and without a situation in space.

According to this view, we would be in a position to characterize the physical phenomena easily and rigorously in contrast to the mental, if we were to say that they are those which appear extended and spatial. And, with the same exactitude, the mental phenomena would then be definable, as contrasted with the physical, as those which exhibit no extension or definite spatial location. One could call on Descartes and Spinoza in support of such a differentiation, but particularly on Kant, who declares space to be the form of intuition of outer sensation.

A. Bain has recently given the same definition: "The department of the Object, or Object-World," he says, "is exactly circumscribed by one property, Extension. The world of Subject-experience is devoid of this property.

"A tree or a river is said to possess extended magnitude. A pleasure has no length, breadth, or thickness; it is in no respect an extended thing. A thought or idea may refer to extended magnitudes, but it cannot be said to have extension in itself. Neither can we say that an act of the will, a desire, a be-

lief, occupy dimensions in space. Hence all that comes within the sphere of the Subject is spoken of as the Unextended.

"Thus, if Mind, as commonly happens, is put for the sum total of Subject-experiences, we may define it negatively by a single fact—the absence of Extension."9

So it appears that we have found, negatively at least, a unified definition for the sum-total of mental phenomena.

But here, too, unanimity does not prevail among the psychologists, and for diverse reasons we often hear it denied that extension and the absence of extension are differentiating characteristics distinguishing physical and mental phenomena.

Many believe that the definition is false because not only mental, but also many physical phenomena, appear without extension. Thus, a large number of not unimportant psychologists teach that the phenomena of certain senses, or even of the senses in general, originally manifest themselves free of all extension and definite spatial character. This is very generally believed [to be true] of sounds and of the phenomena of smell. According to Berkeley, the same holds true of colors, and according to Platner, of the phenomena of the sense of touch. According to Herbart and Lotze, as well as Hartley, Brown, the two Mills, H. Spencer, and others, [it is true] of the phenomena of all the external senses. To be sure, it appears to us as if the phenomena which the external senses, particularly vision and the sense of touch, manifest to us were all spatially extended. But the reason for this, it is said, is the fact that on the basis of prior experience we connect with them our gradually developed presentation of *space*; originally without definite spatial location, they are later localized by us. If this should really be the only way in which physical phenomena attain definite spatial location, then we could plainly no longer distinguish the two realms by reference to this property. [The possibility of such a distinction] is decreased still more by the fact that mental phenomena are also localized by us in such a way, as, for example, when we mistakenly place a phenomenon of anger in the irritable lion, and our own thoughts in the space that is filled by us.

So that would be one way, from the point of view of a large number of important psychologists, in which the stated definition must be contested. When all is said, even Bain, who seems to advance it, is to be counted among these thinkers; for he follows Hartley's line of thought completely. He is able to speak as he has spoken only because (even though without complete consistency) he has not included the phenomena of the external senses, in and for themselves, among the physical phenomena.[10]

Others, as I have said, will reject the definition for contrary reasons. It is not so much the claim that all physical phenomena appear extended that arouses their opposition. It is the claim, rather, that all mental phenomena lack extension; according to them, certain mental phenomena also manifest themselves as extended. Aristotle appears to have been of this opinion when, in the first chapter of his treatise on sensation and the object of sense, he regards it as evident, immediately and without previous proof, that sense perception is the act of a physical organ.[11] Modern psychologists and physiologists express themselves similarly at times in connection with certain affects. They speak of feelings of pleasure and pain which appear in the external organs, sometimes, indeed, even after the amputation of the member; and surely, feeling, like perception, is a mental phenomenon. Many also say of sensual desires that they appear localized; and the fact that poets speak, perhaps not of thought, but of bliss and yearning which suffuse the heart and all the parts of the body, is in accord with that view.

So we see that the stated distinction is assailed with regard to both physical and mental phenomena. Perhaps both points raised against it are equally unfounded.[12] Nevertheless, a further definition common to mental phenomena is still desirable in any case. For conflict over the question whether certain mental and physical phenomena appear extended or not shows at once that the alleged attribute does not suffice for a distinct differentiation; furthermore, for the mental phenomena it is negative only.

V

What positive attribute will we now be able to advance? Or is there, perhaps, no positive definition at all which holds true of all mental phenomena generally?

A. Bain says that in fact there is none.[13] Nonetheless, psychologists of an earlier period have already directed attention to a particular affinity and analogy which exists among all mental phenomena, while the physical do not share in it. Every mental phenomenon is characterized by what the scholastics of the Middle Ages called the intentional (and also mental)[14] inexistence (*Inexistenz*) of an object (*Gegenstand*), and what we could call, although in not entirely unambiguous terms, the reference to a content, a direction upon an object (by which we are not to understand a reality in this case), or an immanent objectivity. Each one includes something as object within itself, although not always in the same way. In presentation something is presented, in judgment something is affirmed or denied, in love [something is] loved, in hate [something] hated, in desire [something] desired, etc.[15]

This intentional inexistence is exclusively characteristic of mental phenomena. No physical phenomenon manifests anything similar. Consequently, we can define mental phenomena by saying that they are such phenomena as include an object intentionally within themselves.

But here, too, we come up against conflict and contradiction. And it is Hamilton in particular who denies the alleged property of a whole broad class of mental phenomena, namely, of all those which he designates as feelings, of pleasure and pain in their most diverse shades and varieties. He is in agreement with us concerning the phenomena of thinking and desire. Obviously, there would be no thinking without an object which is thought, no desire without an object which is desired. "In the phenomena of Feeling—the phenomena of Pleasure and Pain—on the contrary, consciousness does not place the mental modification or state before itself; it does not contemplate it apart—as separate from itself—but is, as it were, fused into one. The peculiarity of Feeling, therefore, is that there is nothing but what is subjectively subjective; there is no object different from self—no objectification of any mode of self."[16] In the first case, there would be something there which, according to Hamilton's way of expression, is "objective"; in the second, something which is "objectively subjective," as in self-knowledge, whose object Hamilton therefore calls subject-object; Hamilton, in denying both with regard to feeling, most definitely denies any intentional inexistence to it.

However, what Hamilton says is surely not entirely correct. Certain feelings are unmistakably referred to objects, and language itself indicates these through the expressions it uses. We say that a person rejoices in or about something, that a person sorrows or grieves about something. And once again: that delights me, that pains me, that hurts me, and so on. Joy and sorrow, like affirmation and denial, love and hate, desire and aversion, distinctly ensue upon a presentation and are referred to what is presented in it.

At the utmost, one could be inclined to agree with Hamilton in *those* cases in which one succumbs most easily, as we saw before, to the illusion that feeling is not based on any presentation: the case of the pain which is aroused by a cut or burn, for example. But its basis is none other than the very temptation toward this hypothesis, which, as we saw, is erroneous. Moreover, even Hamilton recognizes with us the fact that, without exception, presentations form the basis of feelings, and consequently [do so] in these cases as well. Therefore, his denial that feelings have an object seems so much the more striking.

To be sure, one thing is to be granted. The object to which a feeling refers is not always an external object. Even when I hear a harmonious chord, the pleasure which I feel is not really a pleasure in the sound, but a pleasure in the hearing [of it]. Indeed, one might not be mistaken in saying that it even refers to itself in a certain way and, therefore, that what Hamilton asserts, namely, that the feeling is "fused into one" with its object, *does* occur more or less. But this is nothing which does not likewise hold true of many phenomena of presentation and knowledge, as we shall see in our study of inner consciousness. Nevertheless, in them there is still a mental inexistence, a subject-object, to speak Hamilton's language; and the same will therefore hold true of these feelings as well. Hamilton is mistaken when he says that, in them, everything is "subjectively subjective," an expression which is indeed really self-contradictory; for where we can no longer speak of an object, we can no longer speak of a subject either. Even when Hamilton spoke of a fusion-into-one of the feeling with the mental mod-

ification, he gave witness against himself if we consider the matter exactly. Every fusion is a unification of several things; and consequently the pictorial expression, which is intended to make us concretely aware of the distinctive character of feeling, still indicates a certain duality in the unity.

We may thus take it to be valid that the intentional inexistence of an object is a general distinguishing characteristic of mental phenomena, which differentiates this class of phenomena from the class of physical phenomena.

VI

It is a further general characteristic of all mental phenomena that they are perceived only in inner consciousness, while only outer perception is possible for the physical. Hamilton advances this distinguishing attribute.[17]

One could believe that such a definition says little, since it would seem more natural to take the opposite course, defining the act by reference to its object, and so defining inner perception, in contrast to all others, as perception of mental phenomena. But inner perception has still another characteristic, apart from the special nature of its object, which distinguishes it: namely, that immediate, infallible self-evidence, which pertains to it alone among all the cases in which we know objects of experience. Thus, if we say that mental phenomena are those which are grasped by means of inner perception, we have accordingly said that their perception is immediately evident.

Still more! Inner perception is not merely unique as immediately evident perception; it is really unique as perception (*Wahrnehmung*) in the strict sense of the word. We have seen that the phenomena of so-called outer perception can in no way be demonstrated to be true and real, even by means of indirect reasoning. Indeed, we have seen that anyone who placed confidence in them and took them to be what they presented themselves as being is misled by the way the phenomena hang together. Strictly speaking, so-called outer perception is thus not perception; and mental phenomena can accordingly be designated as the only ones of which perception in the strict sense of the word is possible.

Mental phenomena are also adequately characterized by means of this definition. It is not as if all mental phenomena are introspectively perceivable for everyone, and therefore that everything which a person cannot perceive he is to count among the physical phenomena. On the contrary, it is obvious, and was already expressly remarked by us earlier, that no mental phenomenon is perceived by more than a single individual; but on that occasion we also saw that every type of mental phenomenon is represented in the psychical life of every fully developed human being. For this reason, reference to the phenomena which constitute the realm of inner perception serves our purpose satisfactorily.

VII

We said that mental phenomena are the only ones of which a perception in the strict sense is possible. We could just as well say that they are the only phenomena to which actual, as well as intentional, existence pertains. Knowledge, joy, desire, exist actually; color, sound, heat, only phenomenally and intentionally.

There are philosophers who go so far as to say that it is self-evident that no actuality *could* correspond to a phenomenon such as we call a physical one. They maintain that anyone who assumes this and ascribes to physical phenomena any existence other than mental holds a view which is self-contradictory in itself. Bain, for example, says that some people have attempted to explain the phenomena of outer perception by the hypothesis of a material world, "in the first instance, detached from perception, and, afterwards, coming into perception, by operating upon the mind." "This view," he says, "involves a contradiction. The prevailing doctrine is that a tree is something in itself apart from all perception; that, by its luminous emanations, it impresses our mind and is then perceived; the perception being an effect, and the unperceived tree [i.e. the one which exists outside of perception] the cause. But the tree is known only through perception; what it may be anterior to, or independent of, perception, we cannot tell; we can think of it as perceived but not as unperceived. There is a manifest contradiction in the supposition; we are required at

the same moment to perceive the thing and not to perceive it. We know the touch of iron, but we cannot know the touch apart from the touch."[18]

I must confess that I am not in a position to be convinced of the correctness of this argument. As certain as it is that a color only appears to us when it is an object of our presentation [*wenn wir sie vorstellen*], it is nevertheless not to be inferred from this that a color could not exist without being presented. Only if being presented were included as one factor in the color, just as a certain quality and intensity is included in it, would a color which is not presented signify a contradiction, since a whole without one of its parts is truly a contradiction. This, however, is obviously not the case. Otherwise it would be strictly inconceivable how the belief in the actual existence of the physical phenomenon outside of our presentation of it could have, not to say originated, but achieved the most general dissemination, been maintained with the utmost tenacity, and, indeed, even long been shared by thinkers of the first rank. If what Bain says were correct: "We can think of [a tree] as perceived, but not as unperceived. There is manifest contradiction in the supposition," then his further conclusion would surely no longer be subject to objection. But it is precisely this which is not to be granted. Bain explains his dictum by saying: "We are required at the same moment to perceive the thing and not to perceive it." But it is not true that this is required: For, in the first place, not every case of thinking is a perception; and further, even if this were the case, it would only follow that a person could only think of trees perceived by him, but not that he could only think of trees *as perceived by him*. To taste a white piece of sugar does not mean to taste a piece of sugar *as white*. The fallacy reveals itself quite distinctly when it is applied to mental phenomena. If one should say: "I cannot think of a mental phenomenon without thinking of it; and so I can only think of mental phenomena as thought by me; hence no mental phenomena exists outside of my thinking," this mode of inference would be exactly like the one Bain uses. Nonetheless, Bain himself will not deny that his individual mental life is not the only thing, to which actual existence belongs. When Bain adds, "We know the touch of iron, but it is not possible that we should know the touch apart from the touch," he uses the word "touch," in the first place, obviously, in the sense of what is felt, and then in the sense of the feeling of it. These are different concepts even if they have the same name. Accordingly, only someone who permits himself to be deceived by the equivocation could make the concession of immediate evidence required by Bain.

It is not true, then, that the hypothesis that a physical phenomenon like those which exist intentionally in us exists outside of the mind in actuality includes a contradiction. It is only that, when we compare one with the other, conflicts are revealed, which show clearly that there is no actual existence corresponding to the intentional existence in this case. And even though this holds true in the first instance only as far as our experience extends, we will, nevertheless, make no mistake if we quite generally deny to physical phenomena any existence other than intentional existence.

VIII

Still another circumstance has been taken as a distinguishing characteristic for physical and mental phenomena. It has been said that mental phenomena occur only one after the other, while many physical phenomena, on the other hand, occur at the same time. This has not always been asserted in one and the same sense; and not every sense which has been attached to the contention appears to be in accord with the truth.

H. Spencer expressed his opinion on this subject recently: "The two great classes of vital actions called Physiology and Psychology are broadly distinguished in this, that while the one includes both simultaneous and successive changes the other includes successive changes only. The phenomena forming the subject-matter of Physiology present themselves as an immense number of different series bound up together. Those forming the subject-matter of Psychology present themselves as but a single series. A glance at the many continuous actions constituting the life of the body at large, shows that they are synchronous—that digestion, circulation, respiration, excretion, secretion, etc., in all their many sub-divisions, are going on at one time in mutual dependence. And the briefest introspection

makes it clear that the actions constituting thought occur, not together, but one after another."[19] Thus, in making his comparison, Spencer has particularly in view the physiological and physical phenomena within one and the same organism to which a consciousness is attached. If he had not done this, he would have had to grant that several series of mental phenomena can also run concurrently, since there is, surely, more than one living thing in the world endowed with consciousness. But even within the limits he gives, the contention he advances is still not entirely true. And Spencer himself is so far from failing to recognize this fact that he immediately calls attention to those kinds of lower animals, e.g., the *Radiata,* in which a manifold psychological life spins itself out within *one* body. Here, he says—something which others, however, will not readily admit—that there is little difference between mental and physical existence. And he makes still further concessions, according to which the alleged difference between physiological and mental phenomena is weakened to a matter of a mere more or less. Still more! If we ask ourselves what Spencer understands by physiological phenomena, alterations in which are supposed to occur simultaneously, in contrast to mental phenomena, it appears that he does not really mean physical phenomena by this term, but their causes, which are in themselves unknown; for with respect to the physical phenomena which present themselves in sensation, it may be undeniable that they could not vary simultaneously unless the sensations also admitted of simultaneous variations. Hence we could not arrive at a distinguishing characteristic for the two classes in this way.

Others have chosen to see a peculiarity of mental life in the fact that only *one* object can ever be grasped in consciousness, and never several at the same time. They point to the noteworthy case of error in time-determination which regularly occurs in astronomical observations, in that the simultaneous swing of the pendulum does not enter into consciousness simultaneously with, but earlier or later than, the moment when the observed star touches the hairline in the telescope.[20] Thus, mental phenomena always merely follow one another in a simple series. But certainly a person would be mistaken to generalize on the basis of what such a case (involving the utmost concentration of attention) shows, without any further evidence. Spencer, at least, says: "I find that there may sometimes be detected as many as five simultaneous series of nervous changes, which in various degrees rise into consciousness so far that we cannot call any of them absolutely unconscious. When walking, there is the locomotive series; there may be, under certain circumstances, a tactual series; there is very often (in myself at least) an auditory series, constituting some melody or fragment of a melody which haunts me; and there is the visual series: all of which, subordinate to the dominant consciousness formed by some train of reflection, are continually crossing it and weaving themselves into it."[21] Hamilton, Cardaillac and other psychologists make similar reports on the basis of their experiences. But if it were assumed to be correct that all cases of perception are like the astronomer's, would we not always have to grant at least that we often have a presentation of something and simultaneously make a judgment about it or desire it? So there would still be several simultaneous mental phenomena. Indeed, one could more correctly advance the opposite contention, that, often enough, several mental phenomena are present but never more than one physical phenomenon.

What is the only sense, then, in which we might say that invariably only one mental phenomenon is apparent but, on the other hand, that many physical phenomena appear simultaneously? We can say this insofar as the entire multiplicity of mental phenomena which appear to someone in inner perception always manifests itself to him as a unity, while this does not hold true of the physical phenomena which he simultaneously grasps by means of so-called outer perception. As is commonly the case elsewhere, many persons have confused unity with simplicity here and therefore maintain that they perceive themselves in inner consciousness as something simple. Others, in contradicting the simplicity of the phenomenon, at the same time denied its unity. But just as the former group could not maintain a consistent position, since, as soon as they described what was within them, a great number of different factors came to be mentioned, so the latter could also not prevent themselves from testifying involuntarily to the unity of the mental phenomenon. They speak, as do others, of an "I" and not a "we,"

and sometimes call this entity a "bundle" of perceptions, sometimes by other names which describe a state of hanging-together in an internal unity. When we perceive simultaneously color, sound, heat, smell, nothing hinders us from ascribing each to a particular thing. On the other hand, we are obliged to take the diverse set of corresponding acts of sensation, seeing, hearing, sensing heat, and smelling, and with them the willing, and feeling and considering going on at the same time, and the inner perception by which we are aware of all of them as well, to be partial phenomena of a unified phenomenon which includes them, and to take them to be a single, unified thing. We shall thoroughly discuss the reason we are obliged to do so somewhat later and shall present in greater detail and more fully at that time more that is pertinent to the question. For what we touched on here is nothing other than the so-called unity of consciousness, a fact of psychology which is one of the richest in its consequences and which is, nevertheless, still disputed.

IX

In conclusion, let us summarize the results of our comments on the distinction between physical and mental phenomena. First of all, we made ourselves concretely aware of the distinctive nature of the two classes by means of *examples*. We then defined mental phenomena as *presentations* and such phenomena which are *based upon presentations;* all the rest belong to the physical. We next spoke of the attribute of *extension,* which was taken by psychologists to be a distinctive characteristic of all physical phenomena; all mental phenomena were supposed to lack it. The contention had not remained uncontested, however, and only later investigations could decide the issue; that in fact mental phenomena do invariably appear unextended was all that could be confirmed now. We next found *intentional inexistence,* the reference to something as an object, to be a distinguishing feature of all mental phenomena; no physical phenomenon manifests anything similar. We further defined mental phenomena as the exclusive *object of inner perception;* they alone are therefore perceived with immediate evidence; indeed, they alone are perceived in the strict sense of the word. And with this there was bound up the further definition, that they alone are phenomena which possess *actual* existence besides their intentional existence. Finally, we advanced it as a distinguishing [feature] that the mental phenomena which someone perceives *always* appear *as a unity* despite their variety, while the physical phenomena which he may perceive simultaneously are not all presented in the same way as partial phenomena within a single phenomenon.

There can be no doubt but that the characteristic which is more distinctive of mental phenomena than any of the others is intentional inexistence. We may now regard them as distinctly defined, over against the physical phenomena, by this, as well as by the other properties which were introduced.

The definitions of mental and physical phenomena which have been given cannot fail to throw a brighter light on our earlier definitions of mental science and physical science (*psychischer und Naturwissenschaft*): indeed, we said of the latter that it is the science of physical phenomena and of the former that it is the science of mental phenomena. It is now easy to see that both definitions implicitly include certain limitations.

This holds true principally of the definition of physical science. For it is not concerned with all physical phenomena; not with those of imagination, but only with those which appear in sensation. And it determines laws for these only insofar as they depend upon physical stimulation of the sense organs. We could express the scientific task of physical science precisely by saying that physical science is the science which attempts to explain the succession of physical phenomena which are normal and pure (not influenced by any particular psychological states and events) on the basis of the hypothesis [that they are the effect] of the stimulation of our sense organs by a world which is quasi-spatially (*raumähnlich*) extended in three dimensions and which proceeds quasi-temporally (*zeitähnlich*) in *one* direction.[22] Without giving any particulars concerning the absolute nature of this world, [physical science] is satisfied to ascribe to it powers which evoke the sensations and mutually influence each other in their working, and to determine the laws of coexistence and succession for these powers. In

those laws, it then indirectly gives the laws governing the succession of the physical phenomena of sensation when, by means of scientific abstraction from concomitant psychological conditions, these are regarded as pure and as occurring in relation to a constant sensory capacity. Hence, "science of physical phenomena" must be interpreted in this somewhat complicated way, if it is made synonymous with physical science.[23]

We have seen, along the way, how the expression "physical phenomenon" is sometimes misused by being applied to the above-mentioned powers themselves. And, since the object of a science is naturally designated as the one for which it determines laws directly and explicitly, I believe I make no mistake in also assuming with respect to the definition of physical science as the science of physical phenomena that there is ordinarily bound up with this term the concept of powers belonging to a world which is quasi-spatially extended and which proceeds quasi-temporally, powers which evoke sensations by their effect on the sense organs and which reciprocally influence one another, and for which physical science investigates the laws of coexistence and succession. If one regards these powers as the object [of physical science], this also has the convenient feature that something which truly and actually exists appears as object of the science. This last would be just as attainable if we defined physical science as the science of sensations, implicitly adding the same limitation of which we just spoke. What made the expression "physical phenomenon" seem preferable was, probably, primarily the fact that the external causes of sensation were thought of as corresponding to the physical phenomena appearing in it, (whether this be in every respect, as was originally the case, or whether it be, as now, in respect at least to extension in three dimensions). From this, there also arose the otherwise inappropriate term, "outer perception." It is pertinent, however, that the act of sensation manifests, alone with the intentional inexistence of the physical phenomenon, still other properties with which the physical scientist (*Naturforscher*) is not at all concerned, since sensation does not give through them similar information about the distinctive relationships of the external world.

With respect to the definition of psychology, it may be apparent in the first place that the concept of mental phenomena is to be broadened rather than narrowed. For the physical phenomena of imagination, at least, fall completely within its scope just as much as do mental phenomena, in the sense defined earlier; and those which appear in sensation can also not remain unconsidered in the theory of sensation. But it is obvious that they come into consideration only as the content of mental phenomena, when the characteristics of those phenomena are being described. And the same holds true of all mental phenomena which possess exclusively phenomenal existence. It is only mental phenomena in the sense of actual states which we shall have to regard as the true object of psychology. And it is exclusively with reference to them that we say psychology is the science of mental phenomena.

NOTES

1. [Translator's Note: The original, which reads, "Die gesamte Welt unserer Erscheinungen," would be too misleading in literal translation as "the entire world of our phenomena," or "of our appearances." Brentano rejected the Kantian interpretation of "phenomenon" in the first chapter of the *Psychologie vom empirischen Standpunkt*, and for him the word *Erscheinung* functions very much as did "idea" for Locke and "perception" for Hume, i.e., as a general term for any datum of consciousness. The entire sentence is very probably an echo of the beginning of Bain's, *Mental Science:* "Human Knowledge, Experience, or Consciousness, falls under two great departments. . . ." D. B. Terrell.]

2. Thus I, at least, am unable successfully to bring into harmony the various definitions which A. Bain has given in one of his latest psychological works, *Mental Science* (London, 3d ed., 1872). On page 120, No. 59, he says that mental science (Science of Mind, which he also calls Subject Science) is based on self-consciousness or introspective attention; the eye, the ear, the organs of touch, are means of observing the physical world, the "object world," as he expresses himself. On the other hand, on page 198, No. 4 he says that: "The perception of matter or the Object consciousness is connected with the putting forth of Muscular Energy, as opposed to Passive Feeling." And in his explanation he adds, "In purely *passive* feeling, as in those of our sensations that do not call forth our muscular energies, we are not perceiving matter, we are in a state of subject consciousness." He explains this in terms of the sensation of warmth when one takes a warm bath, and in terms of those cases of gentle contact in which no muscular activity occurs, and

explains that under the same conditions, sound, even possibly light and color as well, can be purely subject-experiences. Thus for examples of subject-consciousness, he draws on those very sensations by way of eye, ear, and organs of touch which in the other passage he had indicated to be the mediators of object-consciousness in contrast to subject-consciousness. [All quotations from sources originally written in English are given in the original version, rather than having been retranslated from Brentano's German version.]

3. *Psych. als Wissensch.* Part II, Sec. 1, chap. i, §103. Cf. also Drobisch, *Empir. Psychol.,* pp. 38 and 348, and others of Herbart's school.

4. *Kant's Psychologie* (Berlin, 1870), pp. 92ff.

5. *Ibid.,* p. 94.

6. Kant's *Psychol.,* p. 92. J. B. Meyer appears to understand sensation just as Ueberweg does in his *Logik,* I, 36 (2d ed., p. 64): "Perception is distinguished from mere sensation . . . by the fact that consciousness in the latter is attached only to the subjective state, but in perception it is directed to an element which is perceived and accordingly . . . stands over against the act of perception as a distinct and objective thing." If this opinion of Ueberweg concerning sensation as distinct from perception were correct, sensation would none the less include a presentation in our sense. Why we hold it not to be correct will be shown later.

7. Cf. especially Wundt, *Physiol. Psychol.,* pp. 345ff.

8. This is the opinion of the Jesuit, Tongiorgi, in his very widely circulated philosophy textbook.

9. *Mental Science,* Intro., chap. i.

10. See note 2.

11. *De sens. et sens* 1. p. 436, b, 7. See also what he says in *De anim.* I. 1. p. 403, a, 16 about the affects, especially those of fear.

12. The claim that even mental phenomena appear extended rests plainly on a confusion between physical and mental phenomena similar to the one we became convinced of above, when we established that even sensory feelings are necessarily based on a presentation.

13. *The Senses and the Intellect,* Intro.

14. They also use the expression "to be in something objectively," which, if we should wish to make use of it now, could possibly be taken in just the opposite sense, as the designation of a real existence outside of the mind. Nevertheless, it reminds one of the expression "to be immanently objective," which we sometimes use in a similar sense, and in which the "immanently" is intended to exclude the misunderstanding that was to be feared.

15. Aristotle has already spoken of this mental inherence. In his books on the soul, he says that what is experienced, insofar as it is experienced, is in the one experiencing it, that sense contains what is experienced without its matter, that what is thought is in the thinking

intellect. In Philo we likewise find the doctrine of mental existence and inexistence. In confusing this, however, with existence in the strict sense, he arrives at his doctrine of the Logos and Ideas, with its wealth of contradictions. The like holds true of the Neo-Platonists. Augustine touches on the same fact in his theory of the *Verbum mentis* and its internal origin. Anselm does so in his well-known ontological argument; and many have alleged the basis of his fallacy to be the fact that he regarded mental existence as if it were actual existence (see Ueberweg, *History of Philosophy,* Vol. II). Thomas Aquinas teaches that what is thought is intentionally in the one thinking, the object of love in the person loving, what is desired in the person desiring, and uses this for theological purposes. When the scripture speaks of an indwelling of the Holy Ghost, he explains this as an intentional indwelling by way of love. And he also seeks to find in intentional inexistence, in the cases of thinking and loving, a certain analogy for the mystery of the Trinity and the procession of the Word and Spirit.

16. *Lect. on Metaph.,* I, 432.

17. *Ibid.*

18. *Mental Science,* 3d ed., p. 198.

19. *Principles of Psychol.,* 2d ed., Vol. I, §177, p. 395.

20. Cf. Bessel, *Astron. Beobachtungen* (Konigsberg, 1823), Intro., Part. VIII; Struve, *Expedition Chronometrique,* etc. (Petersburg, 1844), p. 29.

21. *Ibid.,* p. 398. Likewise, Drobisch says, it is "a fact, that several series of presentations can go through the mind simultaneously, but at different levels, as it were" (*Empir. Psych.,* p. 140).

22. On this point see Ueberweg (*System der Logik*), in whose analysis, to be sure, not everything is deserving of approval. He is mistaken particularly when he considers the external causes to be spatial instead of quasi-spatial, temporal instead of quasi-temporal.

23. The interpretation would not be quite as Kant would have it; nevertheless, it approximates his interpretations as far as is feasible. In a certain sense, it comes closer to the viewpoint of Mill in his book against Hamilton (chap. xi), but still without agreeing with him in all the essential respects. What Mill calls permanent possibilities of sensations has a close relationship with what we call powers. The relationship to, as well as the most important departure from, Ueberweg's view was already touched upon in the preceding note.

The Traditional Problem of Body and Mind   20

C. D. BROAD

IN THE LAST CHAPTER we considered organisms simply as complicated material systems which behave in certain characteristic ways. We did not consider the fact that some organisms are animated by minds, and that all the minds of whose existence we are certain animate organisms. And we did not deal with those features in the behaviour of certain organisms which are commonly supposed to be due to the mind which animates the organism. It is such facts as these, and certain problems to which they have given rise, which I mean to discuss in the present chapter. There is a question which has been argued about for some centuries now under the name of "Interaction"; this is the question whether minds really do act on the organisms which they animate, and whether organisms really do act on the minds which animate them. (I must point out at once that I imply no particular theory of mind or body by the word "to animate". I use it as a perfectly neutral name to express the fact that a certain mind is connected in some peculiarly intimate way with a certain body, and, under normal conditions with no other body. This is a fact even on a purely behaviouristic theory of mind; on such a view to say that the mind M animates the body B would mean that the body B, in so far as it behaves in certain ways, *is* the mind M. A body which did not act in these ways would be said not to be animated by a

The Mind and Its Place in Nature (London: Routledge and Kegan Paul, 1925). Reprinted by permission of Routledge.

mind. And a different Body B′, which acted in the same general way as B, would be said to be animated by a different mind M′.)

The problem of Interaction is generally discussed at the level of enlightened common-sense; where it is assumed that we know pretty well what we mean by "mind", by "matter" and by "causation". Obviously no solution which is reached at that level can claim to be ultimate. If what we call "matter" should turn out to be a collection of spirits of low intelligence, as Leibniz thought, the argument that mind and body are so unlike that their interaction is impossible would become irrelevant. Again, if causation be nothing but regular sequence and concomitance, as some philosophers have held, it is ridiculous to regard psycho-neural parallelism and interaction as mutually exclusive alternatives. For interaction will mean no more than parallelism, and parallelism will mean no less than interaction. Nevertheless I am going to discuss the arguments here at the common-sense level, because they are so incredibly bad and yet have imposed upon so many learned men.

We start then by assuming a developed mind and a developed organism as two distinct things, and by admitting that the two are now intimately connected in some way or other which I express by saying that "this mind *animates* this organism". We assume that bodies are very much as enlightened common-sense believes them to be; and that, even if we cannot define "causation", we have some means of recognising when it is present and when it is absent. The question then is: "Does a mind ever act on the body which it animates, and does a body ever act on the mind which animates it?" The answer which common-sense would give to both questions is: "Yes, certainly." On the face of it my body acts on my mind whenever a pin is stuck into the former and a painful sensation thereupon arises in the latter. And, on the face of it, my mind acts on my body whenever a desire to move my arm arises in the former and is followed by this movement in the latter. Let us call this common-sense view "Two-sided Interaction". Although it seems so obvious it has been denied by probably a majority of philosophers and a majority of physiologists. So the question is: "Why should so many distinguished men,

who have studied the subject, have denied the apparently obvious fact of Two-sided Interaction?"

The arguments against Two-sided Interaction fall into two sets:—Philosophical and Scientific. We will take the philosophical arguments first; for we shall find that the professedly scientific arguments come back in the end to the principles or prejudices which are made explicit in the philosophical arguments.

Philosophical Arguments against Two-sided Interaction.   No one can deny that there is a close correlation between certain bodily events and certain mental events, and conversely. Therefore anyone who denies that there is action of mind on body and of body on mind must presumably hold (a) that concomitant variation is not an adequate criterion of causal connexion, and (b) that the other feature which is essential for causal connexion is absent in the case of body and mind. Now the common philosophical argument is that minds and mental states are so extremely unlike bodies and bodily states that it is inconceivable that the two should be causally connected. It is certainly true that, if minds and mental events are just what they seem to be to introspection and nothing more, and if bodies and bodily events are just what enlightened common-sense thinks them to be and nothing more, the two *are* extremely unlike. And this fact is supposed to show that, however closely correlated certain pairs of events in mind and body respectively may be, they cannot be causally connected.

Evidently the assumption at the back of this argument is that concomitant variation, together with a high enough degree of likeness, is an adequate test for causation; but that no amount of concomitant variation can establish causation in the absence of a high enough degree of likeness. Now I am inclined to admit part of this assumption. I think it is practically certain that causation does not simply *mean* concomitant variation. (And, if it did, *cadit quaestio.*) Hence the existence of the latter is not *ipso facto* a proof of the presence of the former. Again, I think it is almost certain that concomitant variation between A and B is not in fact a sufficient sign of the presence of a *direct* causal relation between the two. (I think it may perhaps be a sufficient sign of *either* a direct causal relation between A and B *or* of several causal relations which indirectly unite A and B through the medium of other terms C, D, etc.) So far I agree with the assumptions of the argument. But I cannot see the least reason to think that the other characteristic, which must be added to concomitant variation before we can be sure that A and B are causally connected, is a high degree of likeness between the two. One would like to know just how unlike two events may be before it becomes impossible to admit the existence of a causal relation between them. No one hesitates to hold that draughts and colds in the head are causally connected, although the two are extremely unlike each other. If the unlikeness of draughts and colds in the head does not prevent one from admitting a causal connexion between the two, why should the unlikeness of volitions and voluntary movements prevent one from holding that they are causally connected? To sum up. I am willing to admit that an adequate criterion of causal connexion needs some other relation between a pair of events beside concomitant variation; but I do not believe for a moment that this other relation is that of qualitative likeness.

This brings us to a rather more refined form of the argument against Interaction. It is said that, whenever we admit the existence of a causal relation between two events, these two events (to put it crudely) must also form parts of a single substantial whole. E.g., all physical events are spatially related and form one great extended whole. And the mental events which would commonly be admitted to be causally connected are always events in a single mind. A mind is a substantial whole of a peculiar kind too. Now it is said that between bodily events and mental events there are no relations such as those which unite physical events in different parts of the same Space or mental events in the history of the same mind. In the absence of such relations, binding mind and body into a single substantial whole, we cannot admit that bodily and mental events can be causally connected with each other, no matter how closely correlated their variations may be.

This is a much better argument than the argument about qualitative likeness and unlikeness. If we accept the premise that causal relations can subsist only between terms which form parts of a single substantial whole must we deny that mental and bodily events can be causally connected? I do not think that we need to.

(i) It is of course perfectly true that an organism and the mind which animates it do not form a physical whole, and that they do not form a mental whole; and these, no doubt, are the two kinds of substantial whole with which we are most familiar. But it does not follow that a mind and its organism do not form a substantial whole of *some* kind. There, plainly, is the extraordinary intimate union between the two which I have called "animation" of the one by the other. Even if the mind be just what it seems to introspection, and the body be just what it seems to perception aided by the more precise methods of science, this seems to me to be enough to make a mind and its body a substantial whole. Even so extreme a dualist about Mind and Matter as Descartes occasionally suggests that a mind and its body together form a quasi-substance; and, although we may quarrel with the language of the very numerous philosophers who have said that the mind is "the form" of its body, we must admit that such language would never have seemed plausible unless a mind and its body together had formed something very much like a single substantial whole.

(ii) We must, moreover, admit the possibility that minds and mental events have properties and relations which do not reveal themselves to introspection, and that bodies and bodily events may have properties and relations which do not reveal themselves to perception or to physical and chemical experiment. In virtue of these properties and relations the two together may well form a single substantial whole of the kind which is alleged to be needed for causal interaction. Thus, if we accept the premise of the argument, we have no right to assert that mind and body *cannot* interact; but only the much more modest proposition that introspection and perception do not suffice to assure us that mind and body are so interrelated that they *can* interact.

(iii) We must further remember that the Two-sided Interactionist is under no obligation to hold that the *complete* conditions of any mental event are bodily or that the complete conditions of any bodily event are mental. He needs only to assert that some mental events include certain bodily events among their necessary conditions, and that some bodily events include certain mental events among their necessary conditions. If I am paralysed my volition may not move my arm; and, if I am hypnotised or intensely interested or frightened, a wound may not produce a painful sensation. Now, if the complete cause and the complete effect in all interaction include both a bodily and a mental factor, the two wholes will be related by the fact that the mental constituents belong to a single mind, that the bodily constituents belong to a single body, and that this mind animates this body. This amount of connexion should surely be enough to allow of causal interaction.

This will be the most appropriate place to deal with the contention that, in voluntary action, and there only, we are immediately acquainted with an instance of causal connexion. If this be true the controversy is of course settled at once in favour of the Interactionist. It is generally supposed that this view was refuted once and for all by Mr. Hume in his *Enquiry concerning Human Understanding* (Sect. VII, Part I). I should not care to assert that the doctrine in question is true; but I do think that it is plausible, and I am quite sure that Mr. Hume's arguments do not refute it. Mr. Hume uses three closely connected arguments. (1) The connexion between a successful volition and the resulting bodily movement is as mysterious and as little self-evident as the connexion between any other event and its effect. (2) We have to learn from experience which of our volitions will be effective and which will not. E.g., we do not know, until we have tried, that we can voluntarily move our arms and cannot voluntarily move our livers. And again, if a man were suddenly paralysed, he would still expect to be able to move his arm voluntarily, and would be surprised when he found that it kept still in spite of his volition. (3) We have discovered that the immediate consequence of a volition is a change in our nerves and muscles, which most people know nothing about; and is not the movement of a limb, which most people believe to be its immediate and necessary consequence.

The second and third arguments are valid only against the contention that we know immediately that a volition to make a certain movement is the *sufficient* condition for the happening of that movement. They are quite irrelevant to the contention that

we know immediately that the volition is a *necessary* condition for the happening of just that movement at just that time. No doubt many other conditions are also necessary, e.g., that our nerves and muscles shall be in the right state; and these other necessary conditions can be discovered only by special investigation. Since our volitions to move our limbs are in fact followed in the vast majority of cases by the willed movement, and since the other necessary conditions are not very obvious, it is natural enough that we should think that we know immediately that our volition is the *sufficient* condition of the movement of our limbs. If we think so, we are certainly wrong; and Mr. Hume's arguments prove that we are. But they prove nothing else. It does not follow that we are wrong in thinking that we know, without having to wait for the result, that the volition is a *necessary* condition of the movement.

It remains to consider the first argument. Is the connexion between cause and effect as mysterious and as little self-evident in the case of the voluntary production of bodily movement as in all other cases? If so, we must hold that the first time a baby wills to move its hand it is just as much surprised to find its hand moving as it would be to find its leg moving or its nurse bursting into flames. I do not profess to know anything about the infant mind; but it seems to me that this is a wildly paradoxical consequence, for which there is no evidence or likelihood. But there is no need to leave the matter there. It is perfectly plain that, in the case of volition and voluntary movement, there *is* a connexion between the cause and the effect which is not present in other cases of causation, and which does make it plausible to hold that in this one case the nature of the effect can be foreseen by merely reflecting on the nature of the cause. The peculiarity of a volition as a cause-factor is that it involves as an essential part of it the idea of the effect. To say that a person has a volition to move his arm involves saying that he has an idea of his arm (and not of his leg or his liver) and an idea of the position in which he wants his arm to be. It is simply silly in view of this fact to say that there is no closer connexion between the desire to move my arm and the movement of my arm than there is between this desire and the movement of my leg or my liver. We cannot detect any analogous connexion between cause and effect in causal transactions which we view wholly from outside, such as the movement of a billiard-ball by a cue. It is therefore by no means unreasonable to suggest that, in the one case of our own voluntary movements, we can see without waiting for the result that such and such a volition is a necessary condition of such and such a bodily movement.

It seems to me then that Mr. Hume's arguments on this point are absolutely irrelevant, and that it may very well be true that in volition we positively know that our desire for such and such a bodily movement is a necessary (though not a sufficient) condition of the happening of just that movement at just that time. On the whole then I conclude that the philosophical arguments certainly do not disprove Two-sided Interaction, and that they do not even raise any strong presumption against it. And, while I am not prepared definitely to commit myself to the view that, in voluntary movement, we positively *know* that the mind acts on the body, I do think that this opinion is quite plausible when properly stated and that the arguments which have been brought against it are worthless. I pass therefore to the scientific arguments.

Scientific Arguments against Two-sided Interaction.   There are, so far as I know, two of these. One is supposed to be based on the physical principle of the Conservation of Energy, and on certain experiments which have been made on human bodies. The other is based on the close analogy which is said to exist between the structures of the physiological mechanism of reflex action and that of voluntary action. I will take them in turn.

(1) The Argument from Energy.   It will first be needful to state clearly what is asserted by the principle of the Conservation of Energy. It is found that, if we take certain material systems, e.g., a gun, a cartridge, and a bullet, there is a certain magnitude which keeps approximately constant throughout all their changes. This is called "Energy". When the gun has not been fired it and the bullet have no motion, but the explosive in the cartridge has great chemical energy. When it has been fired the bullet is moving very fast and has great energy of movement. The gun, though not moving fast in its recoil, has also great energy of movement because it is very massive. The gases produced by the explosion have

some energy of movement and some heat-energy, but much less chemical energy than the unexploded charge had. These various kinds of energy can be measured in common units according to certain conventions. To an innocent mind there seems to be a good deal of "cooking" at this stage, i.e., the conventions seem to be chosen and various kinds and amounts of concealed energy seem to be postulated in order to make the principle come out right at the end. I do not propose to go into this in detail, for two reasons. In the first place, I think that the conventions adopted and the postulates made, though somewhat suggestive of the fraudulent company-promoter, can be justified by their coherence with certain experimental facts, and that they are not simply made *ad hoc*. Secondly, I shall show that the Conservation of Energy is absolutely irrelevant to the question at issue, so that it would be waste of time to treat it too seriously in the present connexion. Now it is found that the total energy of all kinds in this system, when measured according to these conventions, is approximately the same in amount though very differently distributed after the explosion and before it. If we had confined our attention to a part of this system and *its* energy this would not have been true. The bullet, e.g., had no energy at all before the explosion and a great deal afterwards. A system like the bullet, the gun, and the charge, is called a "Conservative System"; the bullet alone, or the gun and the charge, would be called "Non-conservative Systems". A conservative system might therefore be defined as one whose total energy is redistributed, but not altered in amount, by changes that happen within it. Of course a given system might be conservative for some kinds of change and not for others.

So far we have merely defined a "Conservative System", and admitted that there are systems which, for some kinds of change at any rate, answer approximately to our definition. We can now state the Principle of the Conservation of Energy in terms of the conceptions just defined. The principle asserts that every material system is either itself conservative, or, if not, is part of a larger material system which is conservative. We may take it that there is good inductive evidence for this proposition.

The next thing to consider is the experiments on the human body. These tend to prove that a living body, with the air that it breathes and the food that it eats, forms a conservative system to a high degree of approximation. We can measure the chemical energy of the food given to a man, and that which enters his body in the form of Oxygen breathed in. We can also, with suitable apparatus, collect, measure and analyse the air breathed out, and thus find its chemical energy. Similarly, we can find the energy given out in bodily movement, in heat, and in excretion. It is alleged that, on the average, whatever the man may do, the energy of his bodily movements is exactly accounted for by the energy given to him in the form of food and of Oxygen. If you take the energy put in in food and Oxygen, and subtract the energy given out in waste-products, the balance is almost exactly equal to the energy put out in bodily movements. Such slight differences as are found are as often on one side as on the other, and are therefore probably due to unavoidable experimental errors. I do not propose to criticise the interpretation of these experiments in detail, because, as I shall show soon, they are completely irrelevant to the problem of whether mind and body interact. But there is just one point that I will make before passing on. It is perfectly clear that such experiments can tell us only what happens on the average over a long time. To know whether the balance was accurately kept at every moment we should have to kill the patient at each moment and analyse his body so as to find out the energy present then in the form of stored-up products. Obviously we cannot keep on killing the patient in order to analyse him, and then reviving him in order to go on with the experiment. Thus it would seem that the results of the experiment are perfectly compatible with the presence of quite large excesses or defects in the total bodily energy at certain moments, provided that these average out over longer periods. However, I do not want to press this criticism; I am quite ready to accept for our present purpose the traditional interpretation which has been put on the experiments.

We now understand the physical principle and the experimental facts. The two together are generally supposed to prove that mind and body cannot interact. What precisely is the argument, and is it valid? I imagine that the argument, when fully stated, would run somewhat as follows: "I will to

move my arm, and it moves. If the volition has anything to do with causing the movement we might expect energy to flow from my mind to my body. Thus the energy of my body ought to receive a measurable increase, not accounted for by the food that I eat and the Oxygen that I breathe. But no such physically unaccountable increases of bodily energy are found. Again, I tread on a tin-tack, and a painful sensation arises in my mind. If treading on the tack has anything to do with causing the sensation we might expect energy to flow from my body to my mind. Such energy would cease to be measurable. Thus there ought to be a noticeable decrease in my bodily energy, not balanced by increases anywhere in the physical system. But such unbalanced decreases of bodily energy are not found." So it is concluded that the volition has nothing to do with causing my arm to move, and that treading on the tack has nothing to do with causing the painful sensation.

Is this argument valid? In the first place it is important to notice that the conclusion does not follow from the Conservation of Energy and the experimental facts alone. The real premise is a tacitly assumed proposition about causation; viz., that, if a change in A has anything to do with causing a change in B, energy must leave A and flow into B. This is neither asserted nor entailed by the Conservation of Energy. What *it* says is that, *if* energy leaves A, it must appear in something else, say B; so that A and B together form a conservative system. Since the Conservation of Energy is not itself the premise for the argument against Interaction, and since it does not entail that premise, the evidence for the Conservation of Energy is not evidence against Interaction. Is there any independent evidence for the premise? We may admit that it *is* true of many, though not of all, transactions within the physical realm. But there are cases where it is not true even of purely physical transactions; and, even if it were always true in the physical realm, it would not follow that it must also be true of transphysical causation. Take the case of a weight swinging at the end of a string hung from a fixed point. The total energy of the weight is the same at all positions in its course. It is thus a conservative system. But at every moment the direction and velocity of the weight's motion are different, and the proportion between its kinetic and its potential energy is constantly changing. These changes are caused by the pull of the string, which acts in a different direction at each different moment. The string makes no difference to the total energy of the weight; but it makes all the difference in the world to the particular way in which the weight moves and the particular way in which the energy is distributed between the potential and the kinetic forms. This is evident when we remember that the weight would begin to move in an utterly different course if at any moment the string were cut.

Here, then, we have a clear case even in the physical realm where a system is conservative but is continually acted on by something which affects its movement and the distribution of its total energy. Why should not the mind act on the body in this way? If you say that you can see how a string can affect the movement of a weight, but cannot see how a volition could affect the movement of a material particle, you have deserted the scientific argument and have gone back to one of the philosophical arguments. Your real difficulty is either that volitions are so very unlike movements, or that the volition is in your mind whilst the movement belongs to the physical realm. And we have seen how little weight can be attached to these objections.

The fact is that, even in purely physical systems, the Conservation of Energy does not explain what changes will happen or when they will happen. It merely imposes a very general limiting condition on the changes that are possible. The fact that the system composed of bullet, charge, and gun, in our earlier example, is conservative does not tell us that the gun ever will be fired, or when it will be fired if at all, or what will cause it to go off, or what forms of energy will appear if and when it does go off. The change in this case is determined by pulling the trigger. Likewise the mere fact that the human body and its neighbourhood form a conservative system does not explain any particular bodily movement; it does not explain why I ever move at all, or why I sometimes write, sometimes walk, and sometimes swim. To explain the happening of these particular movements at certain times it seems to be essential to take into account the volitions which happen from time to time in my mind; just as it is essential to take the string into account to explain the par-

ticular behaviour of the weight, and to take the trigger into account to explain the going off of the gun at a certain moment. The difference between the gun-system and the body-system is that a little energy does flow into the former when the trigger is pulled, whilst it is alleged that none does so when a volition starts a bodily movement. But there is not even this amount of difference between the body-system and the swinging weight.

Thus the argument from energy has no tendency to disprove Two-sided Interaction. It has gained a spurious authority from the august name of the Conservation of Energy. But this impressive principle proves to have nothing to do with the case. And the real premise of the argument is not self-evident, and is not universally true even in purely intra-physical transactions. In the end this scientific argument has to lean on the old philosophic arguments; and we have seen that these are but bruised reeds. Nevertheless, the facts brought forward by the argument from energy do throw some light on the *nature* of the interaction between mind and body, assuming this to happen. They do suggest that all the energy of our bodily actions comes out of and goes back into the physical world, and that minds neither add energy to nor abstract it from the latter. What they do, if they do anything, is to determine that at a given moment so much energy shall change from the chemical form to the form of bodily movement; and they determine this, so far as we can see, without altering the total amount of energy in the physical world.

(2) The Argument from the Structure of the Nervous System.   There are purely reflex actions, like sneezing and blinking, in which there is no reason to suppose that the mind plays any essential part. Now we know the nervous structure which is used in such acts as these. A stimulus is given to the outer end of an efferent nerve; some change or other runs up this nerve, crosses a synapsis between this and an afferent nerve, travels down the latter to a muscle, causes the muscle to contract, and so produces a bodily movement. There seems no reason to believe that the mind plays any essential part in this process. The process may be irreducibly vital, and not merely physico-chemical; but there seems no need to assume anything more than this. Now it is

said that the whole nervous system is simply an immense complication of interconnected nervous arcs. The result is that a change which travels inwards has an immense number of alternative paths by which it may travel outwards. Thus the reaction to a given stimulus is no longer one definite movement, as in the simple reflex. Almost any movement may follow any stimulus according to the path which the afferent disturbance happens to take. This path will depend on the relative resistance of the various synapses at the time. Now a variable response to the same stimulus is characteristic of deliberate as opposed to reflex action.

These are the facts. The argument based on them runs as follows. It is admitted that the mind has nothing to do with the causation of purely reflex actions. But the nervous structure and the nervous processes involved in deliberate action do not differ in kind from those involved in reflex action; they differ only in degree of complexity. The variability which characterises deliberate action is fully explained by the variety of alternative paths and the variable resistances of the synapses. So it is unreasonable to suppose that the mind has any more to do with causing deliberate actions than it has to do with causing reflex actions.

I think that this argument is invalid. In the first place I am pretty sure that the persons who use it have before their imagination a kind of picture of how mind and body must interact if they interact at all. They find that the facts do not answer to this picture, and so they conclude that there is no interaction. The picture is of the following kind. They think of the mind as sitting somewhere in a hole in the brain, surrounded by telephones. And they think of the efferent disturbance as coming to an end at one of these telephones and there affecting the mind. The mind is then supposed to respond by sending an efferent impulse down another of these telephones. As no such hole, with efferent nerves stopping at its walls and afferent nerves starting from them, can be found, they conclude that the mind can play no part in the transaction. But another alternative is that this picture of how the mind must act if it acts at all is wrong. To put it shortly, the mistake is to confuse a gap in an explanation with a spatio-temporal gap, and to argue from the absence of the latter to the absence of the former.

The Interactionist's contention is simply that there is a gap in any purely physiological explanation of deliberate action; i.e., that all such explanations fail to account completely for the facts because they leave out one necessary condition. It does not follow in the least that there must be a spatio-temporal breach of continuity in the physiological conditions, and that the missing condition must fill this gap in the way in which the movement of a wire fills the spatio-temporal interval between the pulling of a bell-handle and the ringing of a distant bell. To assume this is to make the mind a kind of physical object, and to make its action a kind of mechanical action. Really, the mind and its actions are not literally in Space at all, and the time which is occupied by the mental event is no doubt *also* occupied by some part of the physiological process. Thus I am inclined to think that much of the force which this argument actually exercises on many people is simply due to the presupposition about the *modus operandi* of interaction, and that it is greatly weakened when this presupposition is shown to be a mere prejudice due to our limited power of envisaging unfamiliar alternative possibilities.

We can, however, make more detailed objections to the argument than this. There is a clear introspective difference between the mental accompaniment of voluntary action and that of reflex action. What goes on in our minds when we decide with difficulty to get out of a hot bath on a cold morning is obviously extremely different from what goes on in our minds when we sniff pepper and sneeze. And the difference is qualitative; it is not a mere difference of complexity. This difference has to be explained somehow; and the theory under discussion gives no plausible explanation of it. The ordinary view that, in the latter case, the mind is not acting on the body at all; whilst, in the former, it is acting on the body in a specific way, does at least make the introspective difference between the two intelligible.

Again, whilst it is true that deliberate action differs from reflex action in its greater variability of response to the same stimulus, this is certainly not the whole or the most important part of the difference between them. The really important difference is that, in deliberate action, the response is varied *appropriately* to meet the special circumstances which are supposed to exist at the time or are expected to arise later; whilst reflex action is not varied in this way, but is blind and almost mechanical. The complexity of the nervous system explains the *possibility* of variation; it does not in the least explain why the alternative which actually takes place should as a rule be appropriate and not merely haphazard. And so again it seems as if some factor were in operation in deliberate action which is not present in reflex action; and it is reasonable to suppose that this factor is the volition in the mind.

It seems to me that this second scientific argument has no tendency to disprove interaction; but that the facts which it brings forward do tend to suggest the particular form which interaction probably takes if it happens at all. They suggest that what the mind does to the body in voluntary action, if it does anything, is to lower the resistance of certain synapses and to raise that of others. The result is that the nervous current follows such a course as to produce the particular movement which the mind judges to be appropriate at the time. On such a view the difference between reflex, habitual, and deliberate actions for the present purpose becomes fairly plain. In pure reflexes the mind cannot voluntarily affect the resistance of the synapses concerned, and so the action takes place in spite of it. In habitual action it deliberately refrains from interfering with the resistance of the synapses, and so the action goes on like a complicated reflex. But it *can* affect these resistances if it wishes, though often only with difficulty; and it is ready to do so if it judges this to be expedient. Finally, it may lose the power altogether. This would be what happens when a person becomes a slave to some habit, such as drug-taking.

I conclude that, at the level of enlightened common-sense at which the ordinary discussion of Interaction moves, no good reason has been produced for doubting that the mind acts on the body in volition, and that the body acts on the mind in sensation. The philosophic arguments are quite inconclusive; and the scientific arguments, when properly understood, are quite compatible with Two-sided Interaction. At most they suggest certain conclusions as to the form which interaction probably takes if it happens at all.

Difficulties in the Denial of Interaction. I propose now to consider some of the difficulties which would attend the denial of Interaction, still keeping the discussion at the same common-sense level. If a man denies the action of body on mind he is at once in trouble over the causation of new sensations. Suppose that I suddenly tread on an unsuspected tin-tack. A new sensation suddenly comes into my mind. This is an event, and it presumably has some cause. Now, however carefully I introspect and retrospect, I can find no other mental event which is adequate to account for the fact that just that sensation has arisen at just that moment. If I reject the common-sense view that treading on the tack is an essential part of the cause of the sensation, I must suppose either that it is uncaused, or that it is caused by other events in my mind which I cannot discover by introspection or retrospection, or that it is caused telepathically by other finite minds or by God. Now enquiry of my neighbours would show that it is not caused telepathically by any event in their minds which they can introspect or remember. Thus anyone who denies the action of body on mind, and admits that sensations have causes, must postulate either (a) immense numbers of unobservable states in his own mind; or (b) as many unobservable states in his neighbours' minds, together with telepathic action; or (c) some non-human spirit together with telepathic action. I must confess that the difficulties which have been alleged against the action of body on mind seem to be mild compared with those of the alternative hypotheses which are involved in the denial of such action.

The difficulties which are involved in the denial of the action of mind on body are at first sight equally great; but I do not think that they turn out to be so serious as those which are involved in denying the action of body on mind. The *prima facie* difficulty is this. The world contains many obviously artificial objects, such as books, bridges, clothes, etc. We know that, if we go far enough back in the history of their production, we always do in fact come on the actions of some human body. And the minds connected with these bodies did design the objects in question, did will to produce them, and did believe that they were initiating and guiding the physical process by means of these designs and volitions. If it be true that the mind does not act on the body, it follows that the designs and volitions in the agents minds did not in fact play any part in the production of books, bridges, clothes, etc. This appears highly paradoxical. And it is an easy step from it to say that anyone who denies the action of mind on body must admit that books, bridges, and other such objects *could* have been produced even though there had been no minds, no thought of these objects and no desire for them. This consequence seems manifestly absurd to common-sense, and it might be argued that it reflects its absurdity back on the theory which entails it.

The man who denies that mind can act on body might deal with this difficulty in two ways: (1) He might deny that the conclusion *is* intrinsically absurd. He might say that human bodies are extraordinarily complex physical objects, which probably obey irreducible laws of their own, and that we really do not know enough about them to set limits to what their unaided powers could accomplish. This is the line which Spinoza took. The conclusion, it would be argued, *seems* absurd only because the state of affairs which it contemplates is so very unfamiliar. We find it difficult to imagine a body like ours without a mind like ours; but, if we could get over this defect in our powers of imagination, we might have no difficulty in admitting that such a body could do all the things which our bodies do. I think it must be admitted that the difficulty is not so great as that which is involved in denying the action of body on mind. There we had to postulate *ad hoc* utterly unfamiliar entities and modes of action; here it is not certain that we should have to do this.

(2) The other line of argument would be to say that the alleged consequence does not necessarily follow from denying the action of mind on body. I assume that both parties admit that causation is something more than mere *de facto* regularity of sequence and concomitance. If they do not, of course the whole controversy between them becomes futile; for there will certainly be causation between mind and body and between body and mind, in the only sense in which there is causation anywhere. This being presupposed, the following kind of answer is logically possible. When I say that B could not have happened unless A had happened, there are two alternative possibilities. (a) A may itself be an indispensable link in any chain of causes which ends up with B. (b) A may not itself be a link in any

chain of causation which ends up with B. But there may be an indispensable link α in any such chain of causation, and A may be a necessary accompaniment or sequent of α. These two possibilities may be illustrated by diagrams. (a) is represented by the figure below:—

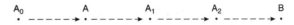

The two forms of (b) are represented by the two figures below:—

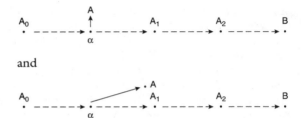

and

Evidently, if B cannot happen unless α precedes, and if α cannot happen without A accompanying or immediately following it, B will not be able to happen unless A precedes it. And yet A will have had no part in causing B. It will be noticed that, on this view, α has a complex effect AA_1, of which a certain part, viz., A_1 is sufficient by itself to produce A_2 and ultimately B. Let us apply this abstract possibility to our present problem. Suppose that B is some artificial object, like a book or a bridge. If we admit that this could not have come into existence unless a certain design and volition had existed in a certain mind, we could interpret the facts in two ways. (a) We could hold that the design and volition are themselves an indispensable link in the chain of causation which ends in the production of a bridge or a book. This is the common view, and it requires us to admit the action of mind on body. (b) We might hold that the design and the volition are not themselves a link in the chain of causation which ends in the production of the artificial object; but that they are a necessary accompaniment or sequent of something which *is* an indispensable link in this chain of causation. On this view the chain consists wholly of physical events; but one of these physical events (viz., some event in the brain) has a complex consequent. One part of this consequent is purely physical, and leads by purely physical causation to the ultimate production of a bridge or a book. The other is purely mental, and consists of a certain design and volition in the mind which animates the human body concerned. If this has any consequences they are purely mental. Each part of this complex consequent follows with equal necessity; this particular brain-state could no more have existed without such and such a mental state accompanying or following it than it could have existed without such and such a bodily movement following it. If we are willing to take some such view as this, we can admit that certain objects could not have existed unless there had been designs of them and desires for them; and yet we could consistently deny that these desires and designs have any effect on the movements of our bodies.

It seems to me then that the doctrine which I will call "One-sided Action of Body on Mind" is logically possible; i.e., a theory which accepts the action of body on mind but denies the action of mind on body. But I do not see the least reason to accept it, since I see no reason to deny that mind acts on body in volition. One-sided Action has, I think, generally been held in the special form called "Epiphenomenalism." I take this doctrine to consist of the following four propositions: (1) Certain bodily events cause certain mental events. (2) No mental event plays any part in the causation of any bodily event. (3) No mental event plays any part in the causation of any other mental event. Consequently (4) all mental events are caused by bodily events and by them only. Thus Epiphenomenalism is just One-sided Action of Body on Mind, together with a special theory about the nature and structure of mind. This special theory does not call for discussion here, where I am dealing only with the relations between minds and bodies, and am not concerned with a detailed analysis of mind. In a later chapter we shall have to consider the special features of Epiphenomenalism.

Arguments in Favour of Interaction.   The only arguments *for* One-sided Action of Body on Mind or for Parallelism are the arguments *against* Two-sided Interaction; and these, as we have seen, are worthless. Are there any arguments in favour of Two-sided Interaction? I have incidentally given two which seem to me to have considerable weight. In favour of the action of mind on body is the fact that we seem to be immediately aware of a causal relation when we voluntarily try to produce a bodily movement, and that the arguments to show that this cannot be true are invalid. In favour of the action of body on mind are the insuperable difficulties which I have pointed out in accounting for the happening of new sensations on any other hypothesis. There are, however, two other arguments which have often been thought to prove the action of mind on body. These are (1) an evolutionary argument, first used, I believe, by William James; and (2) the famous "telegram argument." They both seem to me to be quite obviously invalid.

(1) The evolutionary argument runs as follows: It is a fact, which is admitted by persons who deny Two-sided Interaction, that minds increase in complexity and power with the growth in complexity of the brain and nervous system. Now, if the mind makes no difference to the actions of the body, this development on the mental side is quite unintelligible from the point of view of natural selection. Let us imagine two animals whose brains and nervous systems were of the same degree of complexity; and suppose, if possible, that one had a mind and the other had none. If the mind makes no difference to the behaviour of the body the chance of survival and of leaving descendants will clearly be the same for the two animals. Therefore natural selection will have no tendency to favour the evolution of mind which has actually taken place. I do not think that there is anything in this argument. Natural selection is a purely negative process; it simply tends to eliminate individuals and species which have variations unfavourable to survival. Now, by hypothesis, the possession of a mind is not *unfavourable* to survival; it simply makes no difference. Now it may be that the existence of a mind of such and such a kind is an inevitable consequence of the existence of a brain and nervous system of such and such a degree of complexity. Indeed we have seen that some such view is essential if the opponent of Two-sided Interaction is to answer the common-sense objection that artificial objects could

not have existed unless there had been a mind which designed and desired them. On this hypothesis there is no need to invoke natural selection twice over, once to explain the evolution of the brain and nervous system, and once to explain the evolution of the mind. If natural selection will account for the evolution of the brain and nervous system, the evolution of the mind will follow inevitably, even though it adds nothing to the survival-value of the organism. The plain fact is that natural selection does not account for the origin or for the growth in complexity of anything whatever; and therefore it is no objection to any particular theory of the relations of mind and body that, if it were true, natural selection would not explain the origin and development of mind.

(2) The "telegram argument" is as follows: Suppose there were two telegrams, one saying "Our son has been killed", and the other saying: "Your son has been killed". And suppose that one or other of them was delivered to a parent whose son was away from home. As physical stimuli they are obviously extremely alike, since they differ only in the fact that the letter "Y" is present in one and absent in the other. Yet we know that the reaction of the person who received the telegram might be very different according to which one he received. This is supposed to show that the reactions of the body cannot be wholly accounted for by bodily causes, and that the mind must intervene causally in some cases. Now I have very little doubt that the mind does play a part in determining the action of the recipient of the telegram; but I do not see why this argument should prove it to a person who doubted or denied it. If two very similar stimuli are followed by two very different results, we are no doubt justified in concluding that these stimuli are not the complete causes of the reactions which follow them. But of course it would be admitted by everyone that the receipt of the telegram is not the complete cause of the recipient's reaction. We all know that his brain and nervous system play an essential part in any reaction that he may make to the stimulus. The question then is whether the minute structure of his brain and nervous system, including in this the supposed traces left by past stimuli and past reactions, is not enough to account for the great difference in his behaviour on receiving two very

similar stimuli. Two keys may be very much alike, but one may fit a certain lock and the other may not. And, if the lock be connected with the trigger of a loaded gun, the results of "stimulating" the system with one or other of the two keys will be extremely different. We know that the brain and nervous system are very complex, and we commonly suppose that they contain more or less permanent traces and linkages due to past stimuli and reactions. If this be granted, it is obvious that two very similar stimuli may produce very different results, simply because one fits in with the internal structure of the brain and nervous system whilst the other does not. And I do not see how we can be sure that anything more is needed to account for the mere difference of reaction adduced by the "telegram argument."

The Positive Theory of Parallelism.   The doctrine of Psycho-physical Parallelism, or, as I prefer to call it, "Psycho-neural Parallelism", has two sides to it. One is negative; it is the denial that mind acts on body and the denial that body acts on mind. With this side of it I have now dealt to the best of my ability, and have argued that there is no reason to believe it and tolerably good reason to disbelieve it. But Psycho-neural Parallelism has also a positive side, which might be accepted by one who rejected its negative side. The positive assertion of Parallelism is that there is a one-one correlation between events in a mind and events in the brain and nervous system of the body which it animates. Is there any reason to believe this on empirical grounds?

I think we must say that it *may* be true, but that it is a perfectly enormous assumption unless there be some general metaphysical ground for it; and that the empirical evidence for it is, and will always remain, quite inadequate. The assertion is that to every particular change in the mind there corresponds a certain change in the brain which this mind animates, and that to every change in the brain there corresponds a certain change in the mind which animates this brain. What kind of empirical evidence *could* there be for such an assertion? At best the evidence would be of the following kind: "I have observed a number of brains and the minds which animate them; and I have never found a change in either which was not correlated with a specific change in the other. And all other people who have made similar observations have found the same thing." *If we had evidence of this sort the positive side of Parallelism would be a straightforward inductive generalisation of it;* i.e., an argument from "A has never been observed to happen without B" to "A never does happen without B". But actually we have *no* evidence whatever of this kind. No one person in the world ever has observed, or probably ever will observe, a brain and *its* mind. The only mind that he can observe is his own and the only brains that he can observe are those of others. Nor is this the worst. We can very rarely observe other men's brains at all, and never when they are alive and in a state of normal consciousness. Thus the actual empirical data for the positive side of Parallelism consist of observations on brains which are no longer animated by minds at all or whose animating minds are in abeyance. And these minds could not be directly observed by us even if they were present and functioning normally.

It will therefore be worth while to consider carefully what amount of parallelism we really are justified on empirical grounds in assuming. (1) We have fairly good reasons for thinking that the existence and general integrity of a brain and nervous system is a necessary condition for the manifestation of a mind to itself and to other minds. We do not positively know that it is a sufficient condition; and the question whether it be so or not will have to be discussed later in this book. Our evidence is all of the following kind: (i) In the absence of a brain and nervous system we see none of those external actions which we know in our own case to be accompanied by consciousness. (ii) The brain and nervous system are known to increase in complexity up to a certain age, and we have observed in ourselves and can infer from the behaviour of others a corresponding growth in mental complexity. (iii) Soon after men have ceased to show signs of consciousness by their external behaviour their brains and nervous systems break up. It must be admitted that it might be maintained with almost equal plausibility that these last facts show that the integrity of the brain and nervous system is dependent on the presence of the mind. We might just as well argue that the brain begins to break up because the mind has ceased to animate it, as that the mind has ceased to manifest itself because the brain has begun to break

up. In fact, seeing the order in which we actually get our knowledge of the two facts, the former is *prima facie* the more plausible interpretation. (iv) In many cases where men's behaviour has been so odd as to suggest that their minds are abnormal, it is known that their brains have been injured or it has been found after their death that their brains were in an abnormal state. On the other hand, it must be admitted that the brains of some lunatics on dissection show no systematic differences from those of normal people. It would obviously be absurd to talk of "Parallelism" in reference to this very general relation between the integrity and complexity of the brain and nervous system, on the one hand, and the manifestation of a human mind, on the other.

(2) There is, however, empirical evidence which goes rather further than this. It is found that wounds in certain parts of the brain make specific differences to the mind. E.g., a wound in one part may be followed by a loss of memory for spoken words, and so on. Unfortunately, similar results can often be produced by causes like hypnotism or like those which open to inspection, he is not likely to be in a position to introspect or to tell others what is going on in his mind, even if something is happening there at the time. (ii) In any case the events in the brain which are supposed to correspond to particular events in the mind would be admitted to be too minute to be observable even under the most favourable circumstances. They are as purely hypothetical as the motions of electrons, without the advantage that the assumption of them enables us to predict better than we could otherwise do what states of mind a man will probably have under given circumstances.

It seems to me then that there is no empirical evidence at all for a Parallelism of Events between mind and brain. If this doctrine is to be held, the grounds for it must be general. E.g., psycho-*neural* parallelism might be plausible if, on other grounds, we saw reason to accept psycho-*physical* parallelism; i.e., the doctrine that *every* physical event is correlated with a specific mental event, and conversely. And the wider doctrine might be defended as helping to explain the apparent origin of life and mind from apparently non-living and non-conscious matter. This is a question which we shall have to discuss later; all that I am concerned to argue at present is that, at the level of enlightened common-sense and apart from some general metaphysical theory of the nature of matter and mind, there is no adequate evidence for a psycho-neural parallelism of events. And, as parallelism has commonly been defended on the ground that it is established by empirical scientific investigation of the brain and nervous system, this fact is worth pointing out.

If there is no reason *for* psycho-neural parallelism of events, is there any positive reason *against* it? Some philosophers have held that there is. They have held that, while it is possible and even probable that *some* mental events are correlated with specific neural events, it is impossible that this should be true of *all* mental psycho-analysts discuss. And here there is no positive empirical evidence that these specific areas of the brain are affected. Again, there seems to be some evidence that, after a time and within certain limits, another part of the brain can take over the functions of a part that has been injured. Thus the most that we can say is that the general integrity of certain parts of the brain seems to be at least a temporarily necessary condition for the manifestation of certain specific kinds of mental activity. It remains doubtful how far any given area is indispensable for a given kind of mental activity, and whether there may not be some kinds of activity which, though dependent like all others on the general integrity of the brain, are not specially correlated with any particular area. We might sum up these facts by saying that there is good evidence for a considerable amount of "Departmental Parallelism" between mind and brain.

(3) The orthodox Parallelist, however, goes much further than this, and much beyond the most rigid departmental parallelism. He would hold, not merely that there is a strict correlation between each distinguishable *department* of mental life and some specific *area* of the brain, but also that there is a strict parallelism of *events*. E.g., he holds, not merely that I could not remember at all unless a certain area of my brain were intact, but also that if I now remember eating my breakfast there is a certain event in this area uniquely correlated with this particular mental event. And by "unique correlation" he means that if some other mental state had happened now instead of this particular memory there would necessarily have been a different brain-event,

and conversely. So far as I know there is not, and could not possibly be, any empirical evidence for this "Parallelism of Events", as I will call it. For (i), while a man is conscious and can observe events in his own mind, his brain is not open to inspection by himself or by anyone else. And, when his brain is events. Those who take this view generally hold that there probably is psycho-neural parallelism of events for sensations, but that there certainly cannot be such parallelism for comparison, introspection, attentive inspection, and so on. This view is taken by Mr. Johnson in his *Logic* (Part III); and it will be worth while to consider his arguments. They are contained in Chapter VII, §6 of that work. Mr. Johnson's argument, if I rightly understand it, comes to this: We must distinguish, e.g., between the *fact* that I am having two sensations, one of which is light red and the other dark red, and my *recognition* that both are red and that one is darker than the other. We must likewise distinguish, e.g, between the *fact* that the dark one started before the light one, and my *recognition* of this fact; and between the *fact* that the dark one is to the left of the light one in my visual field and my recognition of this fact. Finally, we must notice that we have to distinguish different degrees of clearness and determinateness with which a perfectly determinate fact may be recognised. We may merely judge that one sensum is separate from another, or we may judge that one is to the left of the other, or we may judge that the first is as much to the left of the second as the second is to the right of a third, and so on. Now Mr. Johnson contends that the sensations themselves have neural correlates, and that the determinate qualities and relations which the sensations actually have are determined by the qualities and relations of these neural correlates. But he holds that there is then nothing left on the neural side for the *recognition* of these qualities and relations to be correlated with. Still less is there anything left on the neural side to be correlated with the infinitely numerous different degrees of determinateness with which the qualities and relations of the sensations may be apprehended. Hence he concludes that mental events above the level of sensations *cannot* be correlated one to one with specific neural events. He does not explicitly draw the distinction which I have done between Departmental Parallelism and Parallelism of Events;

but I think it is plain that his argument is meant only to deny the latter. He would probably admit that, if certain specific areas of our brains were injured, we should lose altogether the power of making judgments of comparison and of recognising spatio-temporal relations; but he would hold that, given the general integrity of those areas, there is not some one specific event within them corresponding to each particular judgment of comparison or of spatio-temporal relation.

Before criticising this argument we must notice that Mr. Johnson does not explicitly distinguish sensations and sensa. By a "sensation" I think he means what I should call a "sensed sensum". And he thinks that, from the nature of the case, there can be no unsensed sensa. Thus a sensation for him is a sensum, regarded as existentially mind-dependent; and, in virtue of its supposed existential mind-dependence, it counts as a mental event belonging to the mind on which its existence depends. If we like to distinguish between mental *states* and mental *acts* we can say that a sensation, for Mr. Johnson, is apparently a mental *state* having certain sensible qualities, such as colour, position in the visual field, and so on. To recognise that one is having a sensation, that it is of such an such a kind, and that it stands in such and such spatio-temporal relations to other sensations, would be to perform a cognitive mental *act*. And his contention is that, whilst there is a parallelism of events for mental states, there cannot for this very reason be also a parallelism of events for mental acts. This at least is how I understand him.

Now I must confess that Mr. Johnson's argument seems to me to be so extremely weak that (knowing Mr. Johnson) I hesitate to believe that I can have properly understood it. Let us suppose that the actual relative position of two sensa s_1 and s_2 in a visual sense-field is determined by the relative position of two excited areas in the brain, b_1 and b_2. Let us suppose that the actual relative date of the two sensa in the sense-history of the experiment is determined by the relative date of the excitement of these areas. And let us suppose that the determinate sensible qualities of the two sensa (e.g., the particular shade of the particular colour possessed by each) is determined by the particular kind of movement which is going on in the microscopic particles within these two areas. Mr. Johnson's con-

tention seems to be that, when we have mentioned the positions of the excited areas, the dates at which they begin to be excited, and the particular kind of movement which is going on within them, we have said all that can be said about the neural events. There is nothing left on the neural side to be correlated with our acts of recognition, of qualitative comparison, and of spatio-temporal judgment; and therefore these events can have no special neural correlate. To this there are two answers which seem so obvious that I am almost ashamed to make them.

(1) At the very utmost the argument would show only that there is nothing left *within the two areas b_1 and b_2* to be correlated with any judgments which we happen to make about the sensations s_1 and s_2. But these two areas do not exhaust the whole of the brain and nervous system. Why our acts of judgment about these two sensations should not have neural correlates in some other part of the brain I cannot imagine. The situation on the mental side is that we may, but need not, make these judgments if we do have the sensations; and that we cannot make them unless we have the sensations. This is exactly what we might expect if the neural correlates of the acts of judgment were in a different part of the brain from the neural correlates of the sensations themselves; and if a certain kind of disturbance in the latter were a necessary but insufficient condition of a certain kind of disturbance in the former.

(2) But we could answer the argument without needing even to assume that the neural correlates of judgments about sensations are in a different area of the brain from the neural correlates of the sensations themselves. We have to remember that the same area may contain at the same time microscopic events of different scales of magnitude. Let us take a purely physical analogy. The same piece of metal may be at once hot and glowing. We have extremely good reasons to believe that *both* these apparent characteristics are correlated with microscopic motions which are going on throughout the whole volume occupied by the bit of metal. The heat is supposed to be correlated with the random movements of molecules and the light with the jumps of electrons from one stable orbit to another. The large-scale events can go on without the small-scale events (a body may be hot without glowing); but the more

violent the large-scale events the more frequent will be the small-scale events (a body begins to glow if it be heated enough). Now I cannot imagine why the same thing might not be true of the neural correlates of sensations and the neural correlates of our judgments about our sensations. Suppose that the neural correlates of sensations were large-scale events in a certain area of the brain; and suppose that the neural correlates of our judgments about these sensations were small-scale events in the same area. Then I should expect to find that sensations could happen without our making judgments about them; that we could not make the judgments unless we had the sensations; and that it would be more difficult not to make the judgments as the sensations became more intense, other things being equal. And this is exactly what I do find. It seems to me then, either that I have altogether misunderstood Mr. Johnson's argument, or that there is nothing whatever in it.

There remains one other point to be discussed before leaving the subject. It is true, as Mr. Johnson points out, that we make judgments of various degrees of determinateness about the same perfectly determinate fact. Does this raise any particular difficulty against the view that every act of judgment has a specific neural correlate? I do not think that it does, if we avoid certain confusions into which it is very easy to fall. I suppose that the difficulty that is felt is this: "Every neural event is perfectly determinate; how can an indeterminate judgment have a determinate neural correlate; and how can there be different determinate neural correlates for all the different degrees of determinateness in judgements?" To this I should answer (i) that of course the differences on the neural side which would correspond to different degrees of determinateness in the judgment are not themselves differences of determinateness. But why should they be? The differences on the neural side which correspond to differences of shade in sensations of colour are not themselves differences of shade. If, e.g., the area which is correlated with judgments about our sensations be different from the area which is correlated with the sensations themselves, we might suppose that differences in the determinateness of the judgment were correlated with differences in the extent or the intensity of the

disturbance within this area. If, on the other hand, we supposed that our sensations were correlated with large-scale events, and our judgments about these sensations with small-scale events in the same region of the brain, we might suppose that differences in the determinateness of the judgment are correlated with differences in the frequency of these small-scale events. There is thus no difficulty, so far as I can see, in providing neural correlates to every different degree of determinateness in our judgments. (ii) It is perhaps necessary to point out that what is called an "indeterminate judgment" is not an indeterminate event; every event, whether mental or physical, is no doubt perfectly determinate of its kind. E.g., whether I merely judge that *some one* has been in the room or make the more determinate judgment that *John Smith* has been in the room, either judgment as a psychical event has perfectly determinate forms of all the psychical determinables under which it falls. The indefiniteness is in what is asserted, not in the act of asserting as such. Hence the problem is not, as it might seem to a careless observer, to find a determinate neural correlate to an indeterminate psychical event; the problem is merely to find a determinate neural correlate to a determinate psychical event which consists in the asserting of a relatively indeterminate characteristic.

I conclude then that no adequate reason has been produced by Mr. Johnson to prove that there *cannot* be specific neural correlates to mental *acts* as well as to mental *states*. I have also tried to show that there neither is nor is likely to be any empirical evidence *for* the doctrine that all mental events have specific neural events as their correlates. Hence the positive doctrine of Psycho-neural Parallelism of Events seems to me to be a perfectly open question. This is not perhaps a wildly exciting result. But it is not altogether to be despised, since it leaves us with a perfectly free hand when we try to construct a speculative theory of the relations of matter and mind which shall do justice to all the known facts. For the known facts neither require nor preclude complete Psycho-neural Parallelism of Events.

Summary and Conclusions.   I wish to make quite clear what I do and what I do not claim to have done in this chapter. I have definitely assumed that the body and the mind are two distinct entities, which are now in a very intimate union, which I express by saying that the former is "animated by" the latter. I have raised no question about the exact nature or origin of this relation of "animation"; and I have not considered the apparent growth of mind in the individual or the apparent development of consciousness from the non-conscious in the course of the earth's history. Again, I have taken the body to be very much as common-sense, enlightened by physical science, but not by philosophical criticism, takes it to be; I have supposed that we know pretty well what a mind is; and I have assumed that causation *is* not simply regular sequence and concomitant variation, though these are more or less trustworthy *signs* of the presence of a causal relation. These are the assumptions on which the question of Interaction has commonly been discussed by philosophers and by scientists; and it would be idle for me to conceal my opinion that it has been discussed extraordinarily badly. The problem seems to have exercised a most unfortunate effect on those who have treated it; for I have rarely met with a collection of worse arguments on all sides. I can only hope that I have not provided yet another instance in support of this generalisation.

My conclusion is that, subject to the assumptions just mentioned, no argument has been produced which should make any reasonable person doubt that mind acts on body in volition and that body acts on mind in sensation. I have tried to show the extreme difficulties which are involved in attempting to deny that body acts on mind. And I have tried to show that the apparently equal difficulties which seem to be involved in attempting to deny that mind acts on body could be evaded with a little ingenuity. Thus One-sided Action of Body on Mind is a possible theory. But there seems to me to be no positive reason for accepting it, and at least one reason for doubting it, viz., the conviction

which many men have (and which Mr. Hume's arguments fail altogether to refute) that we *know* directly that our volitions are necessary conditions for the occurrence of our voluntary movements.

If these conclusions be sound, Parallelism, considered as an *alternative* which excludes Interaction, has no leg left to stand upon. But Parallelism has a positive side to it which is perfectly compatible with Interaction, and is therefore worth discussing for its own sake. I distinguished between the metaphysical doctrine of Psycho-*physical* Parallelism and the more restricted doctrine of Psycho-*neural* Parallelism. And I divided the latter into Departmental Parallelism and Parallelism of Events. It seemed to me that there was good empirical evidence for a considerable amount of Departmental Parallelism, but that there was not and is not likely to be adequate empirical evidence for Parallelism of Events. On the other hand, I came to the conclusion that Mr. Johnson's arguments to prove that complete parallelism between mental and neural events is *impossible* were quite unsound.

This, I think, is as far as the discussion can be carried at this level. One thing seems to me to emerge clearly even at this point. If interaction has to be denied at a later stage it can only be because the relation between mind and body turns out to be so intimate that "interaction" is an unsuitable expression for the connection between a particular mental event and its correlated bodily event. This would be so if, e.g., Materialism were true, so that the mind was just some part of the body. It might be so on a Double-aspect Theory, or on a theory of Neutral Monism. But we cannot decide between such general theories until we know more about the true nature of Mind and of Matter, and have taken into consideration questions about origin and development of minds which we have hitherto explicitly left out of account. Thus the final discussion of the question can come only near the end of the book.

21   Descartes' Myth

GILBERT RYLE

(1) THE OFFICIAL DOCTRINE

THERE IS A DOCTRINE about the nature and place of minds which is so prevalent among theorists and even among laymen that it deserves to be described as the official theory. Most philosophers, psychologists and religious teachers subscribe, with minor reservations, to its main articles and, although they admit certain theoretical difficulties in it, they tend to assume that these can be overcome without serious modifications being made to the architecture of the theory. It will be argued here that the central principles of the doctrine are unsound and conflict with the whole body of what we know about minds when we are not speculating about them.

The official doctrine, which hails chiefly from Descartes, is something like this. With the doubtful exceptions of idiots and infants in arms every human being has both a body and a mind. Some would prefer to say that every human being is both a body and a mind. His body and his mind are ordinarily harnessed together, but after the death of the body his mind may continue to exist and function.

Human bodies are in space and are subject to the mechanical laws which govern all other bodies in space. Bodily processes and states can be inspected by external observers. So a man's bodily life is as much a public affair as are the lives of animals and reptiles and even as the careers of trees, crystals and planets.

But minds are not in space, nor are their operations subject to mechanical laws. The workings of one mind are not witnessable by other observers; its career is private. Only I can take direct cognisance of the states and processes of my own mind. A person therefore lives through two collateral histories, one consisting of what happens in and to his body, the other consisting of what happens in and to his mind. The first is public, the second private.

The events in the first history are events in the physical world, those in the second are events in the mental world.

It has been disputed whether a person does or can directly monitor all or only some of the episodes of his own private history; but, according to the official doctrine, of at least some of these episodes he has direct and unchallengeable cognisance. In consciousness, self-consciousness and introspection he is directly and authentically apprised of the present states and operations of his mind. He may have great or small uncertainties about concurrent and adjacent episodes in the physical world, but he can have none about at least part of what is momentarily occupying his mind.

It is customary to express this bifurcation of his two lives and of his two worlds by saying that the things and events which belong to the physical world, including his own body, are external, while the workings of his own mind are internal. This antithesis of outer and inner is of course meant to be construed as a metaphor, since minds, not being in space, could not be described as being spatially inside anything else, or as having things going on spatially inside themselves. But relapses from this good intention are common and theorists are found speculating how stimuli, the physical sources of which are yards or miles outside a person's skin, can generate mental responses inside his skull, or how decisions framed inside his cranium can set going movements of his extremities.

Even when 'inner' and 'outer' are construed as metaphors, the problem how a person's mind and body influence one another is notoriously charged with theoretical difficulties. What the mind wills, the legs, arms and the tongue execute; what affects the ear and the eye has something to do with what the mind perceives; grimaces and smiles betray the mind's moods and bodily castigations

The Concept of Mind (London: Hutchinson, 1949). Reprinted by permission of Taylor & Francis.

lead, it is hoped, to moral improvement. But the actual transactions between the episodes of the private history and those of the public history remain mysterious, since by definition they can belong to neither series. They could not be reported among the happenings described in a person's autobiography of his inner life, but nor could they be reported among those described in some one else's biography of that person's overt career. They can be inspected neither by introspection nor by laboratory experiment. They are theoretical shuttlecocks which are forever being bandied from the physiologist back to the psychologist and from the psychologist back to the physiologist.

Underlying this partly metaphorical representation of the bifurcation of a person's two lives there is a seemingly more profound and philosophical assumption. It is assumed that there are two different kinds of existence or status. What exists or happens may have the status of physical existence, or it may have the status of mental existence. Somewhat as the faces of coins are either heads or tails, or somewhat as living creatures are either male or female, so, it is supposed, some existing is physical existing, other existing is mental existing. It is a necessary feature of what has physical existence that it is in space and time; it is a necessary feature of what has mental existence that it is in time but not in space. What has physical existence is composed of matter, or else is a function of matter; what has mental existence consists of consciousness, or else is a function of consciousness.

There is thus a polar opposition between mind and matter, an opposition which is often brought out as follows. Material objects are situated in a common field, known as 'space', and what happens to one body in one part of space is mechanically connected with what happens to other bodies in other parts of space. But mental happenings occur in insulated fields, known as 'minds', and there is, apart maybe from telepathy, no direct causal connection between what happens in one mind and what happens in another. Only through the medium of the public physical world can the mind of one person make a difference to the mind of another. The mind is its own place and in his inner life each of us lives the life of a ghostly Robinson Crusoe. People can see, hear and jolt one another's bodies, but they are irremediably blind and deaf to the workings of one another's minds and inoperative upon them.

What sort of knowledge can be secured of the workings of a mind? On the one side, according to the official theory, a person has direct knowledge of the best imaginable kind of the workings of his own mind. Mental states and processes are (or are normally) conscious states and processes, and the consciousness which irradiates them can engender no illusions and leaves the door open for no doubts. A person's present thinkings, feelings and willings, his perceivings, rememberings and imaginings are intrinsically 'phosphorescent'; their existence and their nature are inevitably betrayed to their owner. The inner life is a stream of consciousness of such a sort that it would be absurd to suggest that the mind whose life is that stream might be unaware of what is passing down it.

True, the evidence adduced recently by Freud seems to show that there exist channels tributary to this stream, which run hidden from their owner. People are actuated by impulses the existence of which they vigorously disavow; some of their thoughts differ from the thoughts which they acknowledge; and some of the actions which they think they will to perform they do not really will. They are thoroughly gulled by some of their own hypocrisies and they successfully ignore facts about their mental lives which on the official theory ought to be patent to them. Holders of the official theory tend, however, to maintain that anyhow in normal circumstances a person must be directly and authentically seized of the present state and workings of his own mind.

Besides being currently supplied with these alleged immediate data of consciousness, a person is also generally supposed to be able to exercise from time to time a special kind of perception, namely inner perception, or introspection. He can take a (non-optical) 'look' at what is passing in his mind. Not only can he view and scrutinize a flower through his sense of sight and listen to and discriminate the notes of a bell through his sense of hearing; he can also reflectively or introspectively watch, without any bodily organ of sense, the current episodes of his inner life. This self-observation is also commonly supposed to be immune from illusion, confusion or doubt. A mind's reports of its own affairs have a certainty superior to the best that is possessed by its reports of matters in the physical world. Sense-perceptions can, but consciousness and introspection cannot, be mistaken or confused.

On the other side, one person has no direct access of any sort to the events of the inner life of another. He cannot do better than make problematic inferences from the observed behaviour of the other person's body to the states of mind which, by analogy from his own conduct, he supposes to be signalised by that behaviour. Direct access to the workings of a mind is the privilege of that mind itself; in default of such privileged access, the workings of one mind are inevitably occult to everyone else. For the supposed arguments from bodily movements similar to their own to mental workings similar to their own would lack any possibility of observational corroboration. Not unnaturally, therefore, an adherent of the official theory finds it difficult to resist this consequence of his premises, that he has no good reason to believe that there do exist minds other than his own. Even if he prefers to believe that to other human bodies there are harnessed minds not unlike his own, he cannot claim to be able to discover their individual characteristics, or the particular things that they undergo and do. Absolute solitude is on this showing the ineluctable destiny of the soul. Only our bodies can meet.

As a necessary corollary of this general scheme there is implicitly prescribed a special way of construing our ordinary concepts of mental powers and operations. The verbs, nouns and adjectives, with which in ordinary life we describe the wits, characters and higher-grade performances of the people with whom we have do, are required to be construed as signifying special episodes in their secret histories, or else as signifying tendencies for such episodes to occur. When someone is described as knowing, believing or guessing something, as hoping, dreading, intending or shirking something, as designing this or being amused at that, these verbs are supposed to denote the occurrence of specific modifications in his (to us) occult stream of consciousness. Only his own privileged access to this stream in direct awareness and introspection could provide authentic testimony that these mental-conduct verbs were correctly or incorrectly applied. The onlooker, be

he teacher, critic, biographer or friend, can never assure himself that his comments have any vestige of truth. Yet it was just because we do in fact all know how to make such comments, make them with general correctness and correct them when they turn out to be confused or mistaken, that philosophers found it necessary to construct their theories of the nature and place of minds. Finding mental-conduct concepts being regularly and effectively used, they properly sought to fix their logical geography. But the logical geography officially recommended would entail that there could be no regular or effective use of these mental-conduct concepts in our descriptions of, and prescriptions for, other people's minds.

(2) THE ABSURDITY OF THE OFFICIAL DOCTRINE

Such in outline is the official theory. I shall often speak of it, with deliberate abusiveness, as 'the dogma of the Ghost in the Machine'. I hope to prove that it is entirely false, and false not in detail but in principle. It is not merely an assemblage of particular mistakes. It is one big mistake and a mistake of a special kind. It is, namely, a category-mistake. It represents the facts of mental life as if they belonged to one logical type or category (or range of types or categories), when they actually belong to another. The dogma is therefore a philosopher's myth. In attempting to explode the myth I shall probably be taken to be denying well-known facts about the mental life of human beings, and my plea that I aim at doing nothing more than rectify the logic of mental-conduct concepts will probably be disallowed as mere subterfuge.

I must first indicate what is meant by the phrase 'Category-mistake'. This I do in a series of illustrations.

A foreigner visiting Oxford or Cambridge for the first time is shown a number of colleges, libraries, playing fields, museums, scientific departments and administrative offices. He then asks 'But where is the University? I have seen where the members of the Colleges live, where the Registrar works, where the scientists experiment and the rest. But I have not yet seen the University in which reside and work the members of your University.' It has then to be explained to him that the University is not another collateral institution, some ulterior counterpart to the colleges, laboratories and offices which he has seen. The University is just the way in which all that he has already seen is organized. When they are seen and when their co-ordination is understood, the University has been seen. His mistake lay in his innocent assumption that it was correct to speak of Christ Church, the Bodleian Library, the Ashmolean Museum *and* the University, to speak, that is, as if 'the University' stood for an extra member of the class of which these other units are members. He was mistakenly allocating the University to the same category as that to which the other institutions belong.

The same mistake would be made by a child witnessing the march-past of a division, who, having had pointed out to him such and such battalions, batteries, squadrons, etc., asked when the division was going to appear. He would be supposing that a division was a counterpart to the units already seen, partly similar to them and partly unlike them. He would be shown his mistake by being told that in watching the battalions, batteries and squadrons marching past he had been watching the division marching past. The march-past was not a parade of battalions, batteries, squadrons *and* a division; it was a parade of the battalions, batteries and squadrons *of* a division.

One more illustration. A foreigner watching his first game of cricket learns what are the functions of the bowlers, the batsmen, the fielders, the umpires and the scorers. He then says 'But there is no one left on the field to contribute the famous element of team-spirit. I see who does the bowling, the batting and the wicket-keeping; but I do not see whose role it is to exercise *esprit de corps*.' Once more, it would have to be explained that he was looking for the wrong type of thing. Team-spirit is not another cricketing-operation supplementary to all of the other special tasks. It is, roughly, the keenness with which each of the special tasks is performed, and performing a task keenly is not performing two tasks. Certainly exhibiting team-spirit

is not the same thing as bowling or catching, but nor is it a third thing such that we can say that the bowler first bowls *and* then exhibits team-spirit or that a fielder is at a given moment *either* catching *or* displaying *esprit de corps*.

These illustrations of category-mistakes have a common feature which must be noticed. The mistakes were made by people who did not know how to wield the concepts *University, division* and *team-spirit*. Their puzzles arose from inability to use certain items in the English vocabulary.

The theoretically interesting category-mistakes are those made by people who are perfectly competent to apply concepts, at least in the situations with which they are familiar, but are still liable in their abstract thinking to allocate those concepts to logical types to which they do not belong. An instance of a mistake of this sort would be the following story. A student of politics has learned the main differences between the British, the French and the American Constitutions, and has learned also the differences and connections between the Cabinet, Parliament, the various Ministries, the Judicature and the Church of England. But he still becomes embarrassed when asked questions about the connections between the Church of England, the Home Office and the British Constitution. For while the Church and the Home Office are institutions, the British Constitution is not another institution in the same sense of that noun. So inter-institutional relations which can be asserted or denied to hold between the Church and the Home Office cannot be asserted or denied to hold between either of them and the British Constitution. 'The British Constitution' is not a term of the same logical type as 'the Home Office' and 'the Church of England'. In a partially similar way, John Doe may be a relative, a friend, an enemy or a stranger to Richard Roe; but he cannot be any of these things to the Average Taxpayer. He knows how to talk sense in certain sorts of discussions about the Average Taxpayer, but he is baffled to say why he could not come across him in the street as he can come across Richard Roe.

It is pertinent to our main subject to notice that, so long as the student of politics continues to think of the British Constitution as a counterpart to the other institutions, he will tend to describe it as a mysteriously occult institution; and so long as John Doe continues to think of the Average Taxpayer as a fellow-citizen, he will tend to think of him as an elusive insubstantial man, a ghost who is everywhere yet nowhere.

My destructive purpose is to show that a family of radical category-mistakes is the source of the double-life theory. The representation of a person as a ghost mysteriously ensconced in a machine derives from this argument. Because, as is true, a person's thinking, feeling and purposive doing cannot be described solely in the idioms of physics, chemistry and physiology, therefore they must be described in counterpart idioms. As the human body is a complex organised unit, so the human mind must be another complex organised unit, though one made of a different sort of stuff and with a different sort of structure. Or, again, as the human body, like any other parcel of matter, is a field of causes and effects, so the mind must be another field of causes and effects, though not (Heaven be praised) mechanical causes and effects.

(3) THE ORIGIN OF THE CATEGORY-MISTAKE

One of the chief intellectual origins of what I have yet to prove to be the Cartesian category-mistake seems to be this. When Galileo showed that his methods of scientific discovery were competent to provide a mechanical theory which should cover every occupant of space, Descartes found in himself two conflicting motives. As a man of scientific genius he could not but endorse the claims of mechanics, yet as a religious and moral man he could not accept, as Hobbes accepted, the discouraging rider to those claims, namely that human nature differs only in degree of complexity from clockwork. The mental could not be just a variety of the mechanical.

He and subsequent philosophers naturally but erroneously availed themselves of the following escape-route. Since mental-conduct words are not to be construed as signifying the occurrence of mechanical processes, they must be construed as signifying the occurrence of non-mechanical processes; since

mechanical laws explain movements in space as the effects of other movements in space, other laws must explain some of the non-spatial workings of minds as the effects of other non-spatial workings of minds. The difference between the human behaviours which we describe as intelligent and those which we describe as unintelligent must be a difference in their causation; so, while some movements of human tongues and limbs are the effects of mechanical causes, others must be the effects of non-mechanical causes, i.e., some issue from movements of particles of matter, others from workings of the mind.

The differences between the physical and the mental were thus represented as differences inside the common framework of the categories of 'thing', 'stuff', 'attribute', 'state', 'process', 'change', 'cause' and 'effect'. Minds are things, but different sorts of things from bodies; mental processes are causes and effects, but different sorts of causes and effects from bodily movements. And so on. Somewhat as the foreigner expected the University to be an extra edifice, rather like a college but also considerably different, so the repudiators of mechanism represented minds as extra centres of causal processes, rather like machines but also considerably different from them. Their theory was a para-mechanical hypothesis.

That this assumption was at the heart of the doctrine is shown by the fact that there was from the beginning felt to be a major theoretical difficulty in explaining how minds can influence and be influenced by bodies. How can a mental process, such as willing, cause spatial movements like the movements of the tongue? How can a physical change in the optic nerve have among its effects a mind's perception of a flash of light? This notorious crux by itself shows the logical mould into which Descartes pressed his theory of the mind. It was the self-same mould into which he and Galileo set their mechanics. Still unwittingly adhering to the grammar of mechanics, he tried to avert disaster by describing minds in what was merely an obverse vocabulary. The workings of minds had to be described by the mere negatives of the specific descriptions given to bodies; they are not in space, they are not motions, they are not modifications of matter, they are not accessible to public observation. Minds are not bits of clockwork, they are just bits of not-clockwork.

As thus represented, minds are not merely ghosts harnessed to machines, they are themselves just spectral machines. Though the human body is an engine, it it not quite an ordinary engine, since some of its workings are governed by another engine inside it—this interior governor-engine being one of a very special sort. It is invisible, inaudible and it has no size or weight. It cannot be taken to bits and the laws it obeys are not those known to ordinary engineers. Nothing is known of how it governs the bodily engine.

A second major crux points the same moral. Since, according to the doctrine, minds belong to the same category as bodies and since bodies are rigidly governed by mechanical laws, it seemed to many theorists to follow that minds must be similarly governed by rigid non-mechanical laws. The physical world is a deterministic system, so the mental world must be a deterministic system. Bodies cannot help the modifications that they undergo, so minds cannot help pursuing the careers fixed for them. *Responsibility, choice, merit* and *demerit* are therefore inapplicable concepts—unless the compromise solution is adopted of saying that the laws governing mental processes, unlike those governing physical processes, have the congenial attribute of being only rather rigid. The problem of the Freedom of the Will was the problem how to reconcile the hypothesis that minds are to be described in terms drawn from the categories of mechanics with the knowledge that higher-grade human conduct is not of a piece with the behaviour of machines.

It is an historical curiosity that it was not noticed that the entire argument was broken-backed. Theorists correctly assumed that any sane man could already recognise the differences between, say, rational and non-rational utterances or between purposive and automatic behaviour. Else there would have been nothing requiring to be salved from mechanism. Yet the explanation given presupposed that one person could in principle never recognise the difference between the rational and the irrational utterances issuing from other human bodies, since he could never get access to the postulated immaterial causes of some of their utterances. Save for the doubtful exception of himself, he could never tell the difference between a man and a Robot. It would have to be conceded, for example, that, for all that we can tell, the inner lives of persons who are classed as idiots or lunatics are as rational as those of anyone else. Perhaps only their overt behaviour is disappointing; that is to say, perhaps 'idiots' are not really idiotic, or 'lunatics' lunatic. Perhaps, too, some of those who are classed as sane are really idiots. According to the theory, external observers could never know how the overt behaviour of others is correlated with their mental powers and processes and so they could never know or even plausibly conjecture whether their applications of mental-conduct concepts to these other people were correct or incorrect. It would then be hazardous or impossible for a man to claim sanity or logical consistency even for himself, since he would be debarred from comparing his own performances with those of others. In short, our characterisations of persons and their performances as intelligent, prudent and virtuous or as stupid, hypocritical and cowardly could never have been made, so the problem of providing a special causal hypothesis to serve as the basis of such diagnoses would never have arisen. The question, 'How do persons differ from machines?' arose just because everyone already knew how to apply mental-conduct concepts before the new causal hypothesis was introduced. This causal hypothesis could not therefore be the source of the criteria used in those applications. Nor, of course, has the causal hypothesis in any degree improved our handling of those criteria. We still distinguish good from bad arithmetic, politic from impolitic conduct and fertile from infertile imaginations in the ways in which Descartes himself distinguished them before and after he speculated how the applicability of these criteria was compatible with the principle of mechanical causation.

He had mistaken the logic of his problem. Instead of asking by what criteria intelligent behaviour is actually distinguished from non-intelligent behaviour, he asked 'Given that the principle of mechanical causation does not tell us the difference, what other causal principle will tell it us?' He realised that the problem was not one of mechanics and assumed that it must therefore be one of some counterpart to mechanics. Not unnaturally psychology is often cast for just this role.

When two terms belong to the same category, it is proper to construct conjunctive propositions embodying them. Thus a purchaser may say that he bought a left-hand glove and a right-hand glove, but not that he bought a left-hand glove, a right-hand glove and a pair of gloves. 'She came home in a flood of tears and a sedan-chair' is a well-known joke based on the absurdity of conjoining terms of different types. It would have been equally ridiculous to construct the disjunction 'She came home either in a flood of tears or else in a sedan-chair'. Now the dogma of the Ghost in the Machine does just this. It maintains that there exist both bodies and minds; that there occur physical processes and mental processes; that there are mechanical causes of corporeal movements and mental causes of corporeal movements. I shall argue that these and other analogous conjunctions are absurd; but, it must be noticed, the argument will not show that either of the illegitimately conjoined propositions is absurd in itself I am not, for example, denying that there occur mental processes. Doing long division is a mental process and so is making a joke. But I am saying that the phrase 'there occur mental processes' does not mean the same sort of thing as 'there occur physical processes', and, therefore, that it makes no sense to conjoin or disjoin the two.

If my argument is successful, there will follow some interesting consequences. First, the hallowed contrast between Mind and Matter will be dissipated, but dissipated not by either of the equally hallowed absorptions of Mind by Matter or of Matter by Mind, but in quite a different way. For the seeming contrast of the two will be shown to be as illegitimate as would be the contrast of 'she came home in a flood of tears' and 'she came home in a sedan-chair'. The belief that there is a polar opposition between Mind and Matter is the belief that they are terms of the same logical type.

It will also follow that both Idealism and Materialism are answers to an improper question. The 'reduction' of the material world to mental states and processes, as well as the 'reduction' of mental states and processes to physical states and processes, presuppose the legitimacy of the disjunction 'Either there exist minds or there exist bodies (but not both)'. It would be like saying, 'Either she bought a left-hand and a right-hand glove or she bought a pair of gloves (but not both)'.

It is perfectly proper to say, in one logical tone of voice, that there exist minds and to say, in another logical tone of voice, that there exist bodies. But these expressions do not indicate two different species of existence, for 'existence' is not a generic word like 'coloured' or 'sexed'. They indicate two different senses of 'exist', somewhat as 'rising' has different senses in 'the tide is rising', 'hopes are rising', and 'the average age of death is rising'. A man would be thought to be making a poor joke who said that three things are now rising, namely the tide, hopes and the average age of death. It would be just as good or bad a joke to say that there exist prime numbers and Wednesdays and public opinions and navies; or that there exist both minds and bodies. In the succeeding chapters I try to prove that the official theory does rest on a batch of category-mistakes by showing that logically absurd corollaries follow from it. The exhibition of these absurdities will have the constructive effect of bringing out part of the correct logic of mental-conduct concepts.

(4) HISTORICAL NOTE

It would not be true to say that the official theory derives solely from Descartes' theories, or even from a more widespread anxiety about the implications of seventeenth century mechanics. Scholastic and Reformation theology had schooled the intellects of the scientists as well as of the laymen, philosophers and clerics of that age. Stoic-Augustinian theories of the will were embedded in the Calvinist doctrines of sin and grace; Platonic and Aristotelian theories of the intellect shaped the orthodox doctrines of the immortality of the soul. Descartes was reformulating already prevalent theological doctrines of the soul in the new syntax of Galileo. The theologian's privacy of conscience became the philosopher's privacy of consciousness, and what had been the bogy of Predestination reappeared as the bogy of Determinism.

It would also not be true to say that the two-worlds myth did no theoretical good. Myths often do a lot of theoretical good, while they are still new. One benefit bestowed by the para-mechanical myth was that it partly superannuated the then prevalent para-political myth. Minds and their Faculties had previously been described by analogies with political superiors and political subordinates. The idioms used were those of ruling, obeying, collaborating and rebelling. They survived and still survive in many ethical and some epistemological discussions.

As, in physics, the new myth of occult Forces was a scientific improvement on the old myth of Final Causes, so, in anthropological and psychological theory, the new myth of hidden operations, impulses and agencies was an improvement on the old myth of dictations, deferences and disobediences.

Computing Machinery and Intelligence 22

ALAN M. TURING

1. THE IMITATION GAME

I PROPOSE to consider the question, 'Can machines think?' This should, begin with definitions of the meaning of the terms 'machine' and 'think'. The definitions might be framed so as to reflect so far as possible the normal use of the words, but this attitude is dangerous. If the meaning of the words 'machine' and 'think' are to be found by examining how they are commonly used it is difficult to escape the conclusion that the meaning and the answer to the question, 'Can machines think?' is to be sought in a statistical survey such as a Gallup poll. But this is absurd. Instead of attempting such a definition I shall replace the question by another, which is closely related to it and is expressed in relatively unambiguous words.

The new form of the problem can be described in terms of a game which we call the 'imitation game'. It is played with three people, a man (A), a woman (B), and an interrogator (C) who may be of either sex. The interrogator stays in a room apart from the other two. The object of the game for the interrogator is to determine which of the other two is the man and which is the woman. He knows them by labels X and Y, and at the end of the game he says either 'X is A and Y is B' or 'X is B and Y is

A'. The interrogator is allowed to put questions to A and B thus:

C: Will X please tell me the length of his or her hair?

Now suppose X is actually A, then A must answer. It is A's object in the game to try and cause C to make the wrong identification. His answer might therefore be

'My hair is shingled, and the longest strands are about nine inches long.'

In order that tones of voice may not help the interrogator the answers should be written, or better still, typewritten. The ideal arrangement is to have a teleprinter communicating between the two rooms. Alternatively the question and answers can be repeated by an intermediary. The object of the game for the third player (B) is to help the interrogator. The best strategy for her is probably to give truthful answers. She can add such things as 'I am the woman, don't listen to him!' to her answers, but it will avail nothing as the man can make similar remarks.

We now ask the question, 'What will happen when a machine takes the part of A in this game?' Will the interrogator decide wrongly as often when the game is played like this as he does when the game

Mind 59, no. 236 (October 1950). Reprinted by permission of *Mind*.

is played between a man and a woman? These questions replace our original, 'Can machines think?'

2. CRITIQUE OF THE NEW PROBLEM

As well as asking, 'What is the answer to this new form of the question', one may ask, 'Is this new question a worthy one to investigate?' This latter question we investigate without further ado, thereby cutting short an infinite regress.

The new problem has the advantage of drawing a fairly sharp line between the physical and the intellectual capacities of a man. No engineer or chemist claims to be able to produce a material which is indistinguishable from the human skin. It is possible that at some time this might be done, but even supposing this invention available we should feel there was little point in trying to make a 'thinking machine' more human by dressing it up in such artificial flesh. The form in which we have set the problem reflects this fact in the condition which prevents the interrogator from seeing or touching the other competitors, or hearing their voices. Some other advantages of the proposed criterion may be shown up by specimen questions and answers. Thus:

Q: Please write me a sonnet on the subject of the Forth Bridge.

A: Count me out on this one. I never could write poetry.

Q: Add 34967 to 70764

A: (Pause about 30 seconds and then give as answer) 105621.

Q: Do you play chess?

A: Yes.

Q: I have K at my K1, and no other pieces. You have only K at K6 and R at R1. It is your move. What do you play?

A: (After a pause of 15 seconds) R-R8 mate.

The question and answer method seems to be suitable for introducing almost any one of the fields of human endeavour that we wish to include. We do not wish to penalise the machine for its inability to shine in beauty competitions, nor to penalise a man for losing in a race against an aeroplane. The conditions of our game make these disabilities irrelevant. The 'witnesses' can brag, if they consider it advisable, as much as they please about their charms, strength or heroism, but the interrogator cannot demand practical demonstrations.

The game may perhaps be criticised on the ground that the odds are weighted too heavily against the machine. If the man were to try and pretend to be the machine he would clearly make a very poor showing. He would be given away at once by slowness and inaccuracy in arithmetic. May not machines carry out something which ought to be described as thinking but which is very different from what a man does? This objection is a very strong one, but at least we can say that if, nevertheless, a machine can be constructed to play the imitation game satisfactorily, we need not be troubled by this objection.

It might be urged that when playing the 'imitation game' the best strategy for the machine may possibly be something other than imitation of the behaviour of a man. This may be, but I think it is unlikely that there is any great effect of this kind. In any case there is no intention to investigate here the theory of the game, and it will be assumed that the best strategy is to try to provide answers that would naturally be given by a man.

3. THE MACHINES CONCERNED IN THE GAME

The question which we put in §1 will not be quite definite until we have specified what we mean by the word 'machine'. It is natural that we should wish to permit every kind of engineering technique to be used in our machines. We also wish to allow the possibility that an engineer or team of engineers may construct a machine which works, but whose manner of operation cannot be satisfactorily described by its constructors because they have applied a method which is largely experimental. Finally, we wish to exclude from the machines men born in the usual manner. It is difficult to frame the definitions so as to satisfy these three conditions. One might for instance insist that the team of engineers should be all of one sex, but this would not really be satisfactory, for it is probably possible to rear a complete individual from a single cell of the skin (say) of a man. To do so would be a feat of biological technique deserving of the very highest praise, but we would not be inclined to regard it as a case of 'constructing a thinking machine'. This prompts us to abandon the requirement that every kind of technique should be permitted. We are the more ready to do so in view of the fact that the present interest in 'thinking machines' has been aroused by a particular kind of machine, usually called an 'electronic computer' or 'digital computer'. Following this suggestion we only permit digital computers to take part in our game.

This restriction appears at first sight to be a very drastic one. I shall attempt to show that it is not so in reality. To do this necessitates a short account of the nature and properties of these computers.

It may also be said that this identification of machines with digital computers, like our criterion for 'thinking', will only be unsatisfactory if (contrary to my belief), it turns out that digital computers are unable to give a good showing in the game.

There are already a number of digital computers in working order, and it may be asked, 'Why not try the experiment straight away? It would be easy to satisfy the conditions of the game. A number of interrogators could be used, and statistics compiled to show how often the right identification was given.' The short answer is that we are not asking whether all digital computers would do well in the game nor whether the computers at present available would do well, but whether there are imaginable computers which would do well. But this is only the short answer. We shall see this question in a different light later.

4. DIGITAL COMPUTERS

The idea behind digital computers may be explained by saying that these machines are intended to carry out any operations which could be done by a human computer. The human computer is supposed to be following fixed rules; he has no authority to deviate from them in any detail. We may suppose that these rules are supplied in a book, which is altered whenever he is put on to a new job. He has also an unlimited supply of paper on which he does his calculations.

He may also do his multiplications, and additions on a 'desk machine', but this is not important.

If we use the above explanation as a definition we shall be in danger of circularity of argument. We avoid this by giving an outline of the means by which the desired effect is achieved. A digital computer can usually be regarded as consisting of three parts:

(i) Store

(ii) Executive unit

(iii) Control

The store is a store of information, and corresponds to the human computer's paper, whether this is the paper on which he does his calculations or that on which his book of rules is printed. In so far as the human computer does calculations in his head a part of the store will correspond to his memory.

The executive unit is the part which carries out the various individual operations involved in a calculation. What these individual operations are will vary from machine to machine. Usually fairly lengthy operations can be done such as 'Multiply 3540675445 by 7076345687' but in some machines only very simple ones such as 'Write down 0' are possible.

We have mentioned that the 'book of rules' supplied to the computer is replaced in the machine by a part of the store. It is then called the 'table of instructions'. It is the duty of the control to see that these instructions are obeyed correctly and in the right order. The control is so constructed that this necessarily happens.

The information in the store is usually broken up into packets of moderately small size. In one machine, for instance a packet might consist of ten decimal digits. Numbers are assigned to the parts of the store in which the various packets of information are stored, in some systematic manner. A typical instruction might say—

'Add the number stored in position 6809 to that in 4302 and put the result back into the latter storage position'.

Needless to say it would not occur in the machine expressed in English. It would more likely be coded in a form such as 6809430217. Here 17 says which of various possible operations is to be performed on the two numbers. In this case the operation is that described above, viz., 'Add the number. . . .' It will be noticed that the instruction takes up 10 digits and so forms one packet of information, very conveniently. The control will normally take the instructions to be obeyed in the order of the positions in which they are stored, but occasionally an instruction such as

'Now obey the instruction stored in position 5606, and continue from there'

may be encountered, or again

'If position 4505 contains 0 obey next the instruction stored in 6707, otherwise continue straight on.'

Instructions of these latter types are very important because they make it possible for a sequence of operations to be repeated over and over again until some condition is fulfilled, but in doing so to obey, not fresh instructions on each repetition, but the same ones over and over again. To take a domestic analogy. Suppose Mother wants Tommy to call at the cobbler's every morning on his way to school to see if her shoes are done, she can ask him afresh every morning. Alternatively she can stick up a notice once and for all in the hall which he will see when he leaves for school and which tells him to call for the shoes, and also to destroy the notice when he comes back if he has the shoes with him.

The reader must accept it as a fact that digital computers can be constructed, and indeed have been constructed, according to the principles we have described, and that they can in fact mimic the actions of a human computer very closely.

The book of rules which we have described our human computer as using is of course a convenient fiction. Actual human computers really remember what they have got to do. If one wants to make a machine mimic the behaviour of the human computer in some complex operation one has to ask him how it is done, and then translate the answer into the form of an instruction table. Constructing instruction tables is usually described as 'programming'. To 'programme a machine to carry out the operation A' means to put the appropriate instruction table into the machine so that it will do A.

An interesting variant on the idea of a digital computer is a 'digital computer with a random element'.

These have instructions involving the throwing of a die or some equivalent electronic process; one such instruction might for instance be, 'Throw the die and put the resulting number into store 1000'. Sometimes such a machine is described as having free will (though I would not use this phrase myself). It is not normally possible to determine from observing a machine whether it has a random element, for a similar effect can be produced by such devices as making the choices depend on the digits of the decimal for π.

Most actual digital computers have only a finite store. There is no theoretical difficulty in the idea of a computer with an unlimited store. Of course only a finite part can have been used at any one time. Likewise only a finite amount can have been constructed, but we can imagine more and more being added as required. Such computers have special theoretical interest and will be called infinitive capacity computers.

The idea of a digital computer is an old one. Charles Babbage, Lucasian Professor of Mathematics at Cambridge from 1828 to 1839, planned such a machine, called the Analytical Engine, but it was never completed. Although Babbage had all the essential ideas, his machine was not at that time such a very attractive prospect. The speed which would have been available would be definitely faster than a human computer but something like 100 times slower than the Manchester machine, itself one of the slower of the modern machines. The storage was to be purely mechanical, using wheels and cards.

The fact that Babbage's Analytical Engine was to be entirely mechanical will help us to rid ourselves of a superstition. Importance is often attached to the fact that modern digital computers are electrical, and that the nervous system also is electrical. Since Babbage's machine was not electrical, and since all digital computers are in a sense equivalent, we see that this use of electricity cannot be of theoretical importance. Of course electricity usually comes in where fast signalling is concerned so that it is not surprising that we find it in both these connections. In the nervous system chemical phenomena are at least as important as electrical. In certain computers the storage system is mainly acoustic. The feature of using electricity is thus seen to be only a very superficial similarity. If we wish to find such similarities we should look rather for mathematical analogies of function.

5. UNIVERSALITY
OF DIGITAL COMPUTERS

The digital computers considered in the last section may be classified amongst the 'discrete state machines'. These are the machines which move by sudden jumps or clicks from one quite definite state to another. These states are sufficiently different for the possibility of confusion between them to be ignored. Strictly speaking there are no such machines. Everything really moves continuously. But there are many kinds of machine which can profitably be *thought of* as being discrete state machines. For instance in considering the switches for a lighting system it is a convenient fiction that each switch must be definitely on or definitely off. There must be intermediate positions, but for most purposes we can forget about them. As an example of a discrete state machine we might consider a wheel which clicks round through 120° once a second, but may be stopped by a lever which can be operated from outside; in addition a lamp is to light in one of the positions of the wheel. This machine could be described abstractly as follows. The internal state of the machine (which is described by the position of the wheel) may be q_1, q_2 or q_3. There is an input signal i_0 or i_1 (position of lever). The internal state at any moment is determined by the last state and input signal according to the table

Last State

		q_1	q_2	q_3
	i_0	q_2	q_3	q_1
Input	i_1	q_1	q_2	q_3

The output signals, the only externally visible indication of the internal state (the light) are described by the table

State	q_1	q_2	q_3
Output	o_0	o_0	o_1

This example is typical of discrete state machines. They can be described by such tables provided they have only a finite number of possible states.

It will seem that given the initial state of the machine and the input signals it is always possible to predict all future states. This is reminiscent of Laplace's view that from the complete state of the universe at one moment of time, as described by the positions and velocities of all particles, it should be possible to predict all future states. The prediction which we are considering is, however, rather nearer to practicability than that considered by Laplace. The system of the 'universe as a whole' is such that quite small errors in the initial conditions can have an overwhelming effect at a later time. The displacement of a single electron by a billionth of a centimetre at one moment might make the difference between a man being killed by an avalanche a year later, or escaping. It is an essential property of the mechanical systems which we have called 'discrete state machines' that this phenomenon does not occur. Even when we consider the actual physical machines instead of the idealised machines, reasonably accurate knowledge of the state at one moment yields reasonably accurate knowledge any number of steps later.

As we have mentioned, digital computers fall within the class of discrete state machines. But the number of states of which such a machine is capable is usually enormously large. For instance, the number for the machine now working at Manchester is about $2^{165,000}$, i.e., about $10^{50,000}$. Compare this with our example of the clicking wheel described above, which had three states. It is not difficult to see why the number of states should be so immense. The computer includes a store corresponding to the paper used by a human computer. It must be possible to write into the store any one of the combinations of symbols which might have been written on the paper. For simplicity suppose that only digits from 0 to 9 are used as symbols. Variations in handwriting are ignored. Suppose the computer is allowed 100 sheets of paper each containing 50 lines with room for 30 digits. Then the number of states is $10^{100 \times 50 \times 30}$, i.e., $10^{150,000}$. This is about the number of states of three Manchester machines put together. The logarithm to the base two of the number of states is usually called the 'storage capacity' of the machine. Thus the Manchester machine has a storage capacity of about 165,000 and the wheel machine of our example about 1.6. If two machines are put together their capacities must be added to obtain the capacity of the resultant machine. This leads to the possibility of statements such as 'The Manchester machine contains 64 magnetic tracks each with a capacity of 2560, eight electronic tubes with a capacity of 1280. Miscellaneous storage amounts to about 300 making a total of 174,380.'

Given the table corresponding to a discrete state machine it is possible to predict what it will do. There is no reason, why this calculation should not be carried out by means of a digital computer. Provided it could be carried out sufficiently quickly the digital computer could mimic the behaviour of any discrete state machine. The imitation game could then be played with the machine in question (as B) and the mimicking digital computer (as A) and the interrogator would be unable to distinguish them. Of course the digital computer must have an adequate storage capacity as well as working sufficiently fast. Moreover, it must be programmed afresh for each new machine which it is desired to mimic.

This special property of digital computers, that they can mimic any discrete state machine, is described by saying that they are *universal* machines. The existence of machines with this property has the important consequence that, considerations of speed apart, it is unnecessary to design various new machines to do various computing processes. They can all be done with one digital computer, suitably programmed for each case. It will be seen that as a consequence of this all digital computers are in a sense equivalent.

We may now consider again the point raised at the end of §3. It was suggested tentatively that the question, 'Can machines think?' should be replaced by 'Are there imaginable digital computers which would do well in the imitation game?' If we wish we can make this superficially more general and ask 'Are there discrete state machines which would do well?' But in view of the universality property we see that either of these questions is equivalent to this, 'Let us fix our attention on one particular digital computer C. Is it true that by modifying this computer to have an adequate storage, suitably in-

creasing its speed of action, and providing it with an appropriate programme, C can be made to play satisfactorily the part of A in the imitation game, the part of B being taken by a man?'

6. CONTRARY VIEWS ON THE MAIN QUESTION

We may now consider the ground to have been cleared and we are ready to proceed to the debate on our question, 'Can machines think?' and the variant of it quoted at the end of the last section. We cannot altogether abandon the original form of the problem, for opinions will differ as to the appropriateness of the substitution we must at least listen to what has to be said in this connexion.

It will simplify matters for the reader if I explain first my own beliefs in the matter. Consider first the more accurate form of the question. I believe that in about fifty years' time it will be possible to programme computers, with a storage capacity of about 10^9, to make them play the imitation game so well that an average interrogator will not have more than 70 per cent chance of making the right identification after five minutes of questioning. The original question, 'Can machines think?' I believe to be too meaningless to deserve discussion. Nevertheless I believe that at the end of the century the use of words and general educated opinion will have altered so much that one will be able to speak of machines thinking without expecting to be contradicted. I believe further that no useful purpose is served by concealing these beliefs. The popular view that scientists proceed inexorably from well-established fact to well-established fact, never being influenced by any improved conjecture, is quite mistaken. Provided it is made clear which are proved facts and which are conjectures, no harm can result. Conjectures are of great importance since they suggest useful lines of research.

I now proceed to consider opinions opposed to my own.

(1) THE THEOLOGICAL OBJECTION

Thinking is a function of man's immortal soul. God has given an immortal soul to every man and woman, but not to any other animal or to machines. Hence no animal or machine can think.

I am unable to accept any part of this, but will attempt to reply in theological terms. I should find the argument more convincing if animals were classed with men, for there is a greater difference, to my mind, between the typical animate and the inanimate than there is between man and the other animals. The arbitrary character of the orthodox view becomes clearer if we consider how it might appear to a member of some other religious community. How do Christians regard the Moslem view that women have no souls? But let us leave this point aside and return to the main argument. It appears to me that the argument quoted above implies a serious restriction of the omnipotence of the Almighty. It is admitted that there are certain things that He cannot do such as making one equal to two, but should we not believe that He has freedom to confer a soul on an elephant if He sees fit? We might expect that He would only exercise this power in conjunction with a mutation which provided the elephant with an appropriately improved brain to minister to the needs of this soul. An argument of exactly similar form may be made for the case of machines. It may seem different because it is more difficult to "swallow". But this really only means that we think it would be less likely that He would consider the circumstances suitable for conferring a soul. The circumstances in question are discussed in the rest of this paper. In attempting to construct such machines we should not be irreverently usurping His power of creating souls, any more than we are in the procreation of children: rather we are, in either case, instruments of His will providing mansions for the souls that He creates.[1]

However, this is mere speculation. I am not very impressed with theological arguments whatever they may be used to support. Such arguments have often been found unsatisfactory in the past. In the time of Galileo it was argued that the texts, "And the sun stood still . . . and hasted not to go down about a whole day" (Joshua x. 13) and "He laid the foundations of the earth, that it should not move at any time" (Psalm cv. 5) were an adequate refutation of the Copernican theory. With our present knowledge such an argument appears futile. When

that knowledge was not available it made a quite different impression.

(2) THE 'HEADS IN THE SAND' OBJECTION

"The consequences of machines thinking would be too dreadful. Let us hope and believe that they cannot do so."

This argument is seldom expressed quite so openly as in the form above. But it affects most of us who think about it at all. We like to believe that Man is in some subtle way superior to the rest of creation. It is best if he can be shown to be *necessarily* superior, for then there is no danger of him losing his commanding position. The popularity of the theological argument is clearly connected with this feeling. It is likely to be quite strong in intellectual people since they value the power of thinking more highly than others, and are more inclined to base their belief in the superiority of Man on this power.

I do not think that this argument is sufficiently substantial to require refutation. Consolation would be more appropriate: perhaps this should be sought in the transmigration of souls.

(3) THE MATHEMATICAL OBJECTION

There are a number of results of mathematical logic which can be used to show that there are limitations to the powers of discrete state machines. The best known of these results is known as *Gödel's* theorem,[2] and shows that in any sufficiently powerful logical system statements can be formulated which can neither be proved nor disproved within the system, unless possibly the system itself is inconsistent. There are other, in some respects similar, results due to *Church, Kleene, Russell,* and *Turing.* The latter result is the most convenient to consider, since it refers directly to machines, whereas the others can only be used in a comparatively indirect argument: for instance if Gödel's theorem is to be used we need in addition to have some means of describing logical systems in terms of machines, and machines in terms of logical systems. The result in question refers to a type of machine which is essentially a digital computer with an infinite capacity. It states that there are certain things that such a machine cannot do. If it is rigged up to give answers to questions as in the imitation game, there will be some questions to which it will either give a wrong answer, or fail to give an answer at all however much time is allowed for a reply. There may, of course, be many such questions, and questions which cannot be answered by one machine may be satisfactorily answered by another. We are of course supposing for the present that the questions are of the kind to which an answer 'Yes' or 'No' is appropriate, rather than questions such as 'What do you think of Picasso?' The questions that we know the machines must fail on are of this type, "Consider the machine specified as follows. . . . Will this machine ever answer 'Yes' to any question?" The dots are to be replaced by a description of some machine in a standard form, which could be something like that used in §5. When the machine described bears a certain comparatively simple relation to the machine which is under interrogation, it can be shown that the answer is either wrong or not forthcoming. This is the mathematical result: it is argued that it proves a disability of machines to which the human intellect is not subject.

The short answer to this argument is that although it is established that there are limitations to the powers of any particular machine, it has only been stated, without any sort of proof, that no such limitations apply to the human intellect. But I do not think this view can be dismissed quite so lightly. Whenever one of these machines is asked the appropriate critical question, and gives a definite answer, we know that this answer must be wrong, and this gives us a certain feeling of superiority. Is this feeling illusory? It is no doubt quite genuine, but I do not think too much importance should be attached to it. We too often give wrong answers to questions ourselves to be justified in being very pleased at such evidence of fallibility on the part of the machine. Further, our superiority can only be felt on such an occasion in relation to the one machine over which we have scored our petty triumph. There would be no question of triumphing simultaneously over *all* machines. In short, then, there might be men cleverer than any given machine, but then again there might be other machines cleverer again, and so on.

Those who hold to the mathematical argument would, I think, mostly be willing to accept the imitation game as a basis for discussion. Those who believe in the two previous objections would probably not be interested in any criteria.

(4) THE ARGUMENT FROM CONSCIOUSNESS

This argument is very well expressed in *Professor Jefferson's* Lister Oration for 1949, from which I quote. "Not until a machine can write a sonnet or compose a concerto because of thoughts and emotions felt, and not by the chance fall of symbols, could we agree that machine equals brain—that is, not only write it but know that it had written it. No mechanism could feel (and not merely artificially signal, an easy contrivance) pleasure at its successes, grief when its valves fuse, be warmed by flattery, be made miserable by its mistakes, be charmed by sex, be angry or depressed when it cannot get what it wants."

This argument appears to be a denial of the validity of our test. According to the most extreme form of this view the only way by which one could be sure that a machine thinks is to *be* the machine and to feel oneself thinking. One could then describe these feelings to the world, but of course no one would be justified in taking any notice. Likewise according to this view the only way to know that a *man* thinks is to be that particular man. It is in fact the solipsist point of view. It may be the most logical view to hold but it makes communication of ideas difficult. A is liable to believe 'A thinks but B does not' whilst B believes 'B thinks but A does not'. Instead of arguing continually over this point it is usual to have the polite convention that everyone thinks.

I am sure that Professor Jefferson does not wish to adopt the extreme and solipsist point of view. Probably he would be quite willing to accept the imitation game as a test. The game (with the player B omitted) is frequently used in practice under the name of *viva voce* to discover whether some one really understands something or has 'learnt it parrot fashion'. Let us listen in to a part of such a *viva voce:*

Interrogator: In the first line of your sonnet which reads 'Shall I compare thee to a summer's day', would not 'a spring day' do as well or better?

Witness: It wouldn't scan.

Interrogator: How about 'a winter's day'. That would scan all right.

Witness: Yes, but nobody wants to be compared to a winter's day.

Interrogator: Would you say Mr. Pickwick reminded you of Christmas?

Witness: In a way.

Interrogator: Yet Christmas is a winter's day, and I do not think Mr. Pickwick would mind the comparison.

Witness: I don't think you're serious. By a winter's day one means a typical winter's day, rather than a special one like Christmas.

And so on. What would Professor Jefferson say if the sonnet-writing machine was able to answer like this in the *viva voce*? I do not know whether he would regard the machine as 'merely artificially signalling' these answers, but if the answers were as satisfactory and sustained as in the above passage I do not think he would describe it as 'an easy contrivance'. This phrase is, I think, intended to cover such devices as the inclusion in the machine of a record of someone reading a sonnet, with appropriate switching to turn it on from time to time.

In short then, I think that most of those who support the argument from consciousness could be persuaded to abandon it rather than be forced into the solipsist position. They will then probably be willing to accept our test.

I do not wish to give the impression that I think there is no mystery about consciousness. There is, for instance, something of a paradox connected with any attempt to localise it. But I do not think these mysteries necessarily need to be solved before we can answer the question with which we are concerned in this paper.

(5) ARGUMENTS FROM VARIOUS DISABILITIES

These arguments take the form, "I grant you that you can make machines do all the things you have mentioned but you will never be able to make one to do X". Numerous features X are suggested in this connexion. I offer a selection:

Be kind, resourceful, beautiful, friendly, have initiative, have a sense of humour, tell right from wrong, make mistakes, fall in love, enjoy strawberries and cream, make some one fall in love with it, learn from experience, use words properly, be the subject of its own thought, have as much diversity of behaviour as a man, do something really new.

No support is usually offered for these statements. I believe they are mostly founded on the principle of scientific induction. A man has seen thousands of machines in his lifetime. From what he sees of them he draws a number of general conclusions. They are ugly, each is designed for a very limited purpose, when required for a minutely different purpose they are useless, the variety of behaviour of any one of them is very small, etc., etc. Naturally he concludes that these are necessary properties of machines in general. Many of these limitations are associated with the very small storage capacity of most machines. (I am assuming that the idea of storage capacity is extended in some way to cover machines other than discrete-state machines. The exact definition does not matter as no mathematical accuracy is claimed in the present discussion.) A few years ago, when very little had been heard of digital computers, it was possible to elicit much incredulity concerning them, if one mentioned, their properties without describing their construction. That was presumably due to a similar application of the principle of scientific induction. These applications of the principle are of course largely unconscious. When a burnt child fears the fire and shows that he fears it by avoiding it, I should say that he was applying scientific induction. (I could of course also describe his behavior in many other ways.) The works and customs of mankind do not seem to be very suitable material to which to apply scientific induction. A very large part of space-time must be investigated, if reliable results are to be obtained. Otherwise we may (as most English children do) decide that everybody speaks English, and that it is silly to learn French.

There are, however, special remarks to be made about many of the disabilities that have been mentioned. The inability to enjoy strawberries and cream may have struck the reader as frivolous. Possibly a machine might be made to enjoy this delicious dish, but any attempt to make one do so would be idiotic. What is important about this disability is that it contributes to some of the other disabilities, e.g., to the difficulty of the same kind of friendliness occurring between man and machine as between white man and white man, or between black man and black man.

The claim that "machines cannot make mistakes" seems a curious one. One is tempted to retort, "Are they any the worse for that?" But let us adopt a more sympathetic attitude, and try to see what is really meant. I think this criticism can be explained in terms of the imitation game. It is claimed that the interrogator could distinguish the machine from the man simply by setting them a number of problems in arithmetic. The machine would be unmasked because of its deadly accuracy. The reply to this is simple. The machine (programmed for playing the game) would not attempt to give the *right* answers to the arithmetic problems. It would deliberately introduce mistakes in a manner calculated to confuse the interrogator. A mechanical fault would probably show itself through an unsuitable decision as to what sort of a mistake to make in the arithmetic. Even this interpretation of the criticism is not sufficiently sympathetic. But we cannot afford the space to go into it much further. It seems to me that this criticism depends on a confusion between two kinds of mistake. We may call them 'errors of functioning' and 'errors of conclusion'. Errors of functioning are due to some mechanical or electrical fault which causes the machine to behave otherwise than it was designed to do. In philosophical discussions one likes to ignore the possibility of such errors; one is therefore discussing 'abstract machines'. These abstract machines are mathematical fictions rather than physical objects. By definition they are incapable of errors of functioning. In this sense we can truly say that 'machines can never make mistakes'. Errors of conclusion can only arise when some meaning is attached to the output signals from the machine. The machine might, for instance, type out mathematical equations, or sentences in English. When a false proposition is typed we say that the machine has committed an error of conclusion. There is clearly no reason at all for saying that a machine cannot make this kind of mistake. It might do nothing but type out repeatedly '0 = 1'. To take a less perverse

example, it might have some method for drawing conclusions by scientific induction. We must expect such a method to lead occasionally to erroneous results.

The claim that a machine cannot be the subject of its own thought can of course only be answered if it can be shown that the machine has *some* thought with *some* subject matter. Nevertheless, 'the subject matter of a machine's operations' does seem to mean something, at least to the people who deal with it. If, for instance, the machine was trying to find a solution of the equation $x^2 - 40x - 11 = 0$ one would be tempted to describe this equation as part of the machine's subject matter at that moment. In this sort of sense a machine undoubtedly can be its own subject matter. It may be used to help in making up its own programmes, or to predict the effect of alterations in its own structure. By observing the results of its own behaviour it can modify its own programmes so as to achieve some purpose more effectively. These are possibilities of the near future, rather than Utopian dreams.

The criticism that a machine cannot have much diversity of behaviour is just a way of saying that it cannot have much storage capacity. Until fairly recently a storage capacity of even a thousand digits was very rare.

The criticisms that we are considering here are often disguised forms of the argument from consciousness. Usually if one maintains that a machine *can* do one of these things, and describes the kind of method that the machine could use, one will not make much of an impression. It is thought that the method (whatever it may be, for it must be mechanical) is really rather base. Compare the parenthesis in Jefferson's statement quoted on p. 274.

(6) LADY LOVELACE'S OBJECTION

Our most detailed information of Babbage's Analytical Engine comes from a memoir by [the *Countess of*] *Lovelace*. In it she states "The Analytical Engine has no pretensions to *originate* anything. It can do *whatever we know how to order it* to perform" (her italics). This statement is quoted by *Hartree* who adds: "This does not imply that it may not be possible to construct electronic equipment which will 'think for itself', or in which, in biological terms, one could set up a conditioned reflex, which would serve as a basis for 'learning'. Whether this is possible in principle or not is a stimulating and exciting question, suggested by some of these recent developments. But it did not seem that the machines constructed or projected at the time had this property".

I am in thorough agreement with Hartree over this. It will be noticed that he does not assert that the machines in question had not got the property, but rather that the evidence available to Lady Lovelace did not encourage her to believe that they had it. It is quite possible that the machines in question had in a sense got this property. For suppose that some discrete-state machine has the property. The Analytical Engine was a universal digital computer, so that, if its storage capacity and speed were adequate, it could by suitable programming be made to mimic the machine in question. Probably this argument did not occur to the Countess or to Babbage. In any case there was no obligation on them to claim all that could be claimed.

This whole question will be considered again under the heading of learning machines.

A variant of Lady Lovelace's objection states that a machine can 'never do anything really new'. This may be parried for a moment with the saw, 'There is nothing new under the sun'. Who can be certain that 'original work' that he has done was not simply the growth of the seed planted in him by teaching, or the effect of following well-known general principles. A better variant of the objection says that a machine can never 'take us by surprise'. This statement is a more direct challenge and can be met directly. Machines take me by surprise with great frequency. This is largely because I do not do sufficient calculation to decide what to expect them to do, or rather because, although I do a calculation, I do it in a hurried, slipshod fashion, taking risks. Perhaps I say to myself, 'I suppose the voltage here ought to be the same as there: anyway let's assume it is'. Naturally I am often wrong, and the result is a surprise for me for by the time the experiment is done these assumptions have been forgotten. These admissions lay me open to lectures on the subject of my vicious ways, but do not throw any doubt on my credibility when I testify to the surprises I experience.

I do not expect this reply to silence my critic. He will probably say that such surprises are due to some creative mental act on my part, and reflect no credit on the machine. This leads us back to the argument from consciousness, and far from the idea of surprise. It is a line of argument we must consider closed, but it is perhaps worth remarking that the appreciation of something as surprising requires as much of a 'creative mental act' whether the surprising event originates from a man, a book, a machine, or anything else.

The view that machines cannot give rise to surprises is due, I believe, to a fallacy to which philosophers and mathematicians are particularly subject. This is the assumption that as soon as a fact is presented to a mind all consequences of that fact spring into the mind simultaneously with it. It is a very useful assumption under many circumstances, but one too easily forgets that it is false. A natural consequence of doing so is that one then assumes that there is no virtue in the mere working out of consequences from data and general principles.

(7) ARGUMENT FROM CONTINUITY IN THE NERVOUS SYSTEM

The nervous system is certainly not a discrete-state machine. A small error in the information about the size of a nervous impulse impinging on a neuron, may make a large difference to the size of the outgoing impulse. It may be argued that, this being so, one cannot expect to be able to mimic the behaviour of the nervous system with a discrete-state system.

It is true that a discrete-state machine must be different from a continuous machine. But if we adhere to the conditions of the imitation game, the interrogator will not be able to take any advantage of this difference. The situation can be made clearer if we consider some other simpler continuous machine. A differential analyser will do very well. (A differential analyser is a certain kind of machine not of the discrete-state type used for some kinds of calculation.) Some of these provide their answers in a typed form, and so are suitable for taking part in the game. It would not be possible for a digital computer to predict exactly what answers the differential analyser would give to a problem, but it would be quite capable of giving the right sort of answer. For instance, if asked to give the value of π (actually about 3.1416) it would be reasonable to choose at random between the values 3.12, 3.13,

3.14, 3.15, 3.16 with the probabilities of 0.05, 0.15, 0.55, 0.19, 0.06 (say). Under these circumstances it would be very difficult for the interrogator to distinguish the differential analyser from the digital computer.

(8) THE ARGUMENT FROM INFORMALITY OF BEHAVIOUR

It is not possible to produce a set of rules purporting to describe what a man should do in every conceivable set of circumstances. One might for instance have a rule that one is to stop when one sees a red traffic light, and to go if one sees a green one, but what if by some fault both appear together? One may perhaps decide that it is safest to stop. But some further difficulty may well arise from this decision later. To attempt to provide rules of conduct to cover every eventuality, even those arising from traffic lights, appears to be impossible. With all this I agree.

From this it is argued that we cannot be machines. I shall try to reproduce the argument, but I fear I shall hardly do it justice. It seems to run something like this. 'If each man had a definite set of rules of conduct by which he regulated his life he would be no better than a machine. But there are no such rules, so men cannot be machines.' The undistributed middle is glaring. I do not think the argument is ever put quite like this, but I believe this is the argument used nevertheless. There may however be a certain confusion between 'rules of conduct' and 'laws of behaviour' to cloud the issue. By 'rules of conduct' I mean precepts such as 'Stop if you see red lights', on which one can act, and of which one can be conscious. By 'laws of behaviour' I mean laws of nature as applied to a man's body such as 'if you pinch him he will squeak'. If we substitute 'laws of behaviour which regulate his life' for 'laws of conduct by which he regulates his life' in the argument quoted the undistributed middle is no longer insuperable. For we believe that it is not only true that being regulated by laws of behaviour implies being some sort of machine (though not necessarily a discrete-state machine), but that conversely being such a machine implies being regulated by such laws. However, we cannot so easily convince ourselves of the absence of complete laws of behaviour as of complete rules of conduct. The

only way we know of for finding such laws is scientific observation, and we certainly know of no circumstances under which we could say, 'We have searched enough. There are no such laws.'

We can demonstrate more forcibly that any such statement would be unjustified. For suppose we could be sure of finding such laws if they existed. Then given a discrete-state machine it should certainly be possible to discover by observation sufficient about it to predict its future behaviour, and this within a reasonable time, say a thousand years. But this does not seem to be the case. I have set up on the Manchester computer a small programme using only 1000 units of storage, whereby the machine supplied with one sixteen figure number replies with another within two seconds. I would defy anyone to learn from these replies sufficient about the programme to be able to predict any replies to untried values.

(9) THE ARGUMENT FROM EXTRA-SENSORY PERCEPTION

I assume that the reader is familiar with the idea of extra-sensory perception, and the meaning of the four items of it, viz., telepathy, clairvoyance, precognition and psycho-kinesis. These disturbing phenomena seem to deny all our usual scientific ideas. How we should like to discredit them! Unfortunately the statistical evidence at least for telepathy, is overwhelming. It is very difficult to rearrange one's ideas so as to fit these new facts in. Once one has accepted them it does not seem a very big step to believe in ghosts and bogies. The idea that our bodies move simply according to the known laws of physics, together with some others not yet discovered but somewhat similar, would be one of the first to go.

This argument is to my mind quite a strong one. One can say in reply that many scientific theories seem to remain workable in practice, in spite of clashing with E.S.P.; that in fact one can get along very nicely if one forgets about it. This is rather cold comfort, and one fears that thinking is just the kind of phenomenon where E.S.P. may be especially relevant.

A more specific argument based on E.S.P. might run as follows: "Let us play the imitation game, using as witnesses a man who is good as a telepathic receiver, and a digital computer. The interrogator can ask such questions as 'What suit does the card in my right hand belong to?' The man by telepathy or clairvoyance gives the right answer 130 times out of 400 cards. The machine can only guess at random, and perhaps gets 104 right, so the interrogator makes the right identification." There is an interesting possibility which opens here. Suppose the digital computer contains a random number generator. Then it will be natural to use this to decide what answer to give. But then the random number generator will be subject to the psycho-kinetic powers of the interrogator. Perhaps this psychokinesis might cause the machine to guess right more often than would be expected on a probability calculation, so that the interrogator might still be unable to make the right identification. On the other hand, he might be able to guess right without any questioning, by clairvoyance. With E.S.P. anything may happen.

If telepathy is admitted it will be necessary to tighten our test up. The situation could be regarded as analogous to that which would occur if the interrogator were talking to himself and one of the competitors was listening with his ear to the wall. To put the competitors into a 'telepathy-proof room' would satisfy all requirements.

7. LEARNING MACHINES

The reader will have anticipated that I have no very convincing arguments of a positive nature to support my views. If I had I should not have taken such pains to point out the fallacies in contrary views. Such evidence as I have I shall now give.

Let us return for a moment to Lady Lovelace's objection, which stated that the machine can only do what we tell it to do. One could say that a man can 'inject' an idea into the machine, and that it will respond to a certain extent and then drop into quiescence, like a piano string struck by a hammer. Another simile would be an atomic pile of less than critical size: an injected idea is to correspond to a neutron entering the pile from without. Each such neutron will cause a certain disturbance which eventually dies away. If, however, the size of the pile

is sufficiently increased, the disturbance caused by such an incoming neutron will very likely go on and on increasing until the whole pile is destroyed. Is there a corresponding phenomenon for minds, and is there one for machines? There does seem to be one for the human mind. The majority of them seem to be 'sub-critical', i.e., to correspond in this analogy to piles of subcritical size. A idea presented to such a mind will on average give rise to less than one idea in reply. A smallish proportion are supercritical. An idea presented to such a mind may give rise to a whole 'theory ' consisting of secondary, tertiary and more remote ideas. Animals' minds seem to be very definitely sub-critical. Adhering to this analogy we ask, 'Can a machine be made to be super-critical?'

The 'skin of an onion' analogy is also helpful. In considering the functions of the mind or the brain we find certain operations which we can explain in purely mechanical terms. This we say does not correspond to the real mind: it is a sort of skin which we must strip off if we are to find the real mind. But then in what remains we find a further skin to be stripped off, and so on. Proceeding in this way do we ever come to the 'real' mind, or do we eventually come to the skin which has nothing in it? In the latter case the whole mind is mechanical. (It would not be a discrete-state machine however. We have discussed this.)

These last two paragraphs do not claim to be convincing arguments. They should rather be described as 'recitations tending to produce belief'.

The only really satisfactory support that can be given for the view expressed at the beginning of §6, will be that provided by waiting for the end of the century and then doing the experiment described. But what can we say in the meantime? What steps should be taken now if the experiment is to be successful?

As I have explained, the problem is mainly one of programming. Advances in engineering will have to be made too, but it seems unlikely that these will not be adequate for the requirements. Estimates of the storage capacity of the brain vary from 10^{10} to 10^{15} binary digits. I incline to the lower values and believe that only a very small fraction is used for the higher types of thinking. Most of it is probably used for the retention of visual impressions. I should be surprised if more than 10^9 was required for satisfactory playing of the imitation game, at any rate against a blind man. (Note: The capacity of the *Encyclopaedia Britannica,* 11th edition, is 2×10^9.) A storage capacity of 10^7 would be a very practicable possibility even by present techniques. It is probably not necessary to increase the speed of operations of the machines at all. Parts of modern machines which can be regarded as analogues of nerve cells work about a thousand times faster than the latter. This should provide a 'margin of safety' which could cover losses of speed arising in many ways. Our problem then is to find out how to programme these machines to play the game. At my present rate of working I produce about a thousand digits of programme a day, so that about sixty workers, working steadily through the fifty years might accomplish the job, if nothing went into the waste-paper basket. Some more expeditious method seems desirable.

In the process of trying to imitate an adult human mind we are bound to think a good deal about the process which has brought it to the state that it is in. We may notice three components,

(a) The initial state of the mind, say at birth,
(b) The education to which it has been subjected,
(c) Other experience, not to be described as education, to which it has been subjected.

Instead of trying to produce a programme to simulate the adult mind, why not rather try to produce one which simulated the child's? If this were then subjected to an appropriate course of education one would obtain the adult brain. Presumably the child-brain is something like a note-book as one buys it from the stationers. Rather little mechanism, and lots of blank sheets. (Mechanism and writing are from our point of view almost synonymous.) Our hope is that there is so little mechanism in the child-brain that something like it can be easily programmed. The amount of work in the education we can assume, as a first approximation, to be much the same as for the human child.

We have thus divided our problem into two parts. The child-programme and the education process. These two remain very closely connected. We

cannot expect to find a good child-machine at the first attempt. One must experiment with teaching one such machine and see how well it learns. One can then try another and see if it is better or worse. There is an obvious connection between this process and evolution, by the identifications.

Structure of the child machine	=	Hereditary material
Changes [in the child machine]	=	Mutations
Natural selection	=	Judgment of the experimenter

One may hope, however, that this process will be more expeditious than evolution. The survival of the fittest is a slow method for measuring advantages. The experimenter, by the exercise of intelligence, should be able to speed it up. Equally important is the fact that he is not restricted to random mutations. If he can trace a cause for some weakness he can probably think of the kind of mutation which will improve it.

It will not be possible to apply exactly the same teaching process to the machine as to a normal child. It will not, for instance, be provided with legs, so that it could not be asked to go out and fill the coal scuttle. Possibly it might not have eyes. But however well these deficiencies might be overcome by clever engineering, one could not send the creature to school without the other children making excessive fun of it. It must be given some tuition. We need not be too concerned about the legs, eyes, etc. The example of Miss Helen Keller shows that education can take place provided that communication in both directions between teacher and pupil can take place by some means or other.

We normally associate punishments and rewards with the teaching process. Some simple child-machines can be constricted or programmed on this sort of principle. The machine has to be so constructed that events which shortly preceded the occurrence of a punishment-signal are unlikely to be repeated, whereas a reward-signal increased the probability of repetition of the events which led up to it. These definitions do not presuppose any feelings on the part of the machine. I have done some experiments with one such child-machine, and succeeded in teaching it a few things, but the teaching method was too unorthodox for the experiment to be considered really successful.

The use of punishments and rewards can at best be a part of the teaching process. Roughly speaking, if the teacher has no other means of communicating to the pupil, the amount of information which can reach him does not exceed the total number of rewards and punishments applied. By the time a child has learnt to repeat 'Casabianca,' he would probably feel very sore indeed, if the text could only be discovered by a 'Twenty Questions' technique, every 'NO' taking the form of a blow. It is necessary therefore to have some other 'unemotional' channels of communication. If these are available it is possible to teach a machine by punishments and rewards to obey orders given in some language, e.g., a symbolic language. These orders are to be transmitted through the 'unemotional' channels. The use of this language will diminish greatly the number of punishments and rewards required.

Opinions may vary as to the complexity which is suitable in the child machine. One might try to make it as simple as possible consistently with the general principles. Alternatively one might have a complete system of logical inference 'built in'.[3] In the latter case the store would be largely occupied with definitions and propositions. The propositions would have various kinds of status, e.g., well-established facts, conjectures, mathematically proved theorems, statements given by an authority, expressions having the logical form of proposition but not belief-value. Certain propositions may be described as 'imperatives'. The machine should be so constructed that as soon as an imperative is classed as 'well-established' the appropriate action automatically takes place. To illustrate this, suppose the teacher says to the machine, 'Do your homework now'. This may cause "Teacher says 'Do your homework now'" to be included amongst the well-established facts. Another such fact might be, "Everything that teacher says is true". Combining these may eventually lead to the imperative, 'Do your homework now', being included amongst the well-established facts, and this, by the construction of the machine, will mean that the homework actually gets started, but the effect is very satisfactory. The

processes of inference used by the machine need not be such as would satisfy the most exacting logicians. There might for instance be no hierarchy of types. But this need not mean that type fallacies will occur, any more than we are bound to fall over unfenced cliffs. Suitable imperatives (expressed *within* the systems, not forming part of the rules *of* the system), such as 'Do not use a class unless it is a subclass of one which has been mentioned by teacher' can have a similar effect to 'Do not go too near the edge'.

The imperatives that can be obeyed by a machine that has no limbs are bound to be of a rather intellectual character, as in the example (doing homework) given above. Important amongst such imperatives will be ones which regulate the order in which the rules of the logical system concerned are to be applied. For at each stage when one is using a logical system, there is a very large number of alternative steps, any of which one is permitted to apply, so far as obedience to the rules of the logical system is concerned. These choices make the difference between a brilliant and a footling reasoner, not the difference between a sound and a fallacious one. Propositions leading to imperatives of this kind might be "When Socrates is mentioned, use the syllogism in Barbara" or "If one method has been proved to be quicker than another, do not use the slower method". Some of these may be 'given by authority', but others may be produced by the machine itself, e.g., by scientific induction.

The idea of a learning machine may appear paradoxical to some readers. How can the rules of operation of the machine change? They should describe completely how the machine will react whatever its history might be, whatever changes it might undergo. The rules are thus quite time-invariant. This is quite true. The explanation of the paradox is that the rules which get changed in the learning process are of a rather less pretentious kind, claiming only an ephemeral validity. The reader may draw a parallel with the Constitution of the United States.

An important feature of a learning machine is that its teacher will often be very largely ignorant of quite what is going on inside, although he may still be able to some extent to predict his pupil's behaviour. This should apply most strongly to the later education of a machine arising from a child-machine of well-tried design (or programme). This is in clear contrast with normal procedure when using a machine to do computations: one's object is then to have a clear mental picture of the state of the machine at each moment in the computation. This object can only be achieved with a struggle. The view that 'the machine can only do what we know how to order it to do',[4] appears strange in face of this. Most of the programmes which we can put into the machine will result in its doing something that we cannot make sense of at all, or which we regard as completely random behaviour. Intelligent behaviour presumably consists in a departure from the completely disciplined behaviour involved in computation, but a rather slight one, which does not give rise to random behaviour, or to pointless repetitive loops. Another important result of preparing our machine for its part in the imitation game by a process of teaching and learning is that 'human fallibility' is likely to be omitted in a rather natural way, i.e., without special 'coaching'. . . . Processes that are learnt do not produce a hundred per cent certainty of result; if they did they could not be unlearnt.

It is probably wise to include a random element in a learning machine (see p. 270). A random element is rather useful when we are searching for a solution of some problem. Suppose for instance we wanted to find a number between 50 and 200 which was equal to the square of the sum of its digits, we might start at 51 then try 52 and go on until we got a number that worked. Alternatively we might choose numbers at random until we got a good one. This method has the advantage that it is unnecessary to keep track of the values that have been tried, but the disadvantage that one may try the same one twice, but this is not very important if there are several solutions. The systematic method has the disadvantage that there may be an enormous block without any solutions in the region which has to be investigated first. Now the learning process may be regarded as a search for a form of behaviour which will satisfy the teacher (or some other criterion). Since there is probably a very large number of satisfactory solutions the random method seems to be better than the systematic. It should be

noticed that it is used in the analogous process of evolution. But there the systematic method is not possible. How could one keep track of the different genetical combinations that had been tried, so as to avoid trying them again?

We may hope that machines will eventually compete with men in all purely intellectual fields. But which are the best ones to start with? Even this is a difficult decision. Many people think that a very abstract activity, like the playing of chess, would be best. It can also be maintained that it is best to provide the machine with the best sense organs that money can buy, and then teach it to understand and speak English. This process could follow the normal teaching of a child. Things would be pointed out and named, etc. Again I do not know what the right answer is, but I think both approaches should be tried.

We can only see a short distance ahead, but we can see plenty there that needs to be done.

NOTES

1. Possibly this view is heretical. St. Thomas Aquinas (*Summa Theologica*, quoted by Bertrand Russell) states that God cannot make a man to have no soul. But this may not be a real restriction on His powers, but, only a result of the fact that men's souls are immortal, and therefore indestructible.

2. Authors' names in italics refer to the Bibliography.

3. Or rather 'programmed in' for our child-machine will be programmed in a digital computer. But the logical system will not have to be learnt.

4. Compare Lady Lovelace's statement (p. 276), which does not contain the word 'only'.

BIBLIOGRAPHY

Alonzo Church, "An Unsolvable Problem of Elementary Number Theory", *American Journal of Math.*, 58 (1936), 345–363.

K. Gödel, "Über formal unentscheidbare Sätze der Principia Mathematica und verwandter Systeme, I", *Monatshefte für Math. und Phys.*, (1931), 173–189.

D. R. Hartree, *Calculating Instruments and Machines*, New York, 1949.

S. C. Kleene, "General Recursive Functions of Natural Numbers", *American Journal of Math.*, 57 (1935), 153–173 and 219–244.

G. Jefferson, "The Mind of Mechanical Man". Lister Oration for 1949. *British Medical Journal,* vol. i (1949), 1105–1121.

Countess of Lovelace, 'Translator's notes to an article on Babbage's Analytical Engine', *Scientific Memoirs* (ed. by R. Taylor), vol. 3 (1842), 691–731.

Bertrand Russell, *History of Western Philosophy,* London, 1940.

A. M. Turing, "On Computable Numbers, with an Application to the Entscheidungsproblem", *Proceedings of the London Mathematical Society* (2), 42 (1937), 230–265.

Is Consciousness a Brain Process?   23

U. T. PLACE

INTRODUCTION

THE VIEW that there exists a separate class of events, mental events, which cannot be described in terms of the concepts employed by the physical sciences no longer commands the universal and unquestioning acceptance amongst philosophers and psychologists which it once did. Modern physicalism, however, unlike the materialism of the seventeenth and eighteenth centuries, is behaviouristic. Consciousness on this view is either a special type of behaviour, 'sampling' or 'running-back-and-forth' behaviour as Tolman (1932, p. 206) has it, or a disposition to behave in a certain way, an itch for example being a temporary propensity to scratch. In the case of cognitive concepts like 'knowing', 'believing', 'understanding', 'remembering' and volitional concepts like 'wanting' and 'intending', there can be little doubt, I think, that an analysis in terms of dispositions to behave (Wittgenstein 1953, Ryle 1949) is fundamentally sound. On the other hand, there would seem to be an intractable residue of concepts clustering around the notions of consciousness, experience, sensation and mental imagery, where some sort of inner process story is unavoidable (Place 1954). It is possible, of course, that a satisfactory behaviouristic account of this conceptual residuum will ultimately be found. For our present purposes, however, I shall assume that this cannot be done and that statements about pains and twinges, about how things look, sound and feel, about things dreamed of or pictured in the mind's eye, are statements referring to events and processes which are in some sense private or internal to the individual of whom they are predicated. The question I wish to raise is whether in making this assumption we are inevitably committed to a dualist position in which sensations and mental images form a separate category of processes over and above the physical and physiological processes with which they are known to be correlated. I shall argue that an acceptance of inner processes does not entail dualism and that the thesis that consciousness is a process in the brain cannot be dismissed on logical grounds.

THE 'IS' OF DEFINITION AND THE 'IS' OF COMPOSITION

I want to stress from the outset that in defending the thesis that consciousness is a process in the brain, I am not trying to argue that when we describe our dreams, fantasies and sensations we are talking about processes in our brains. That is, I am not claiming that statements about sensations and mental images are reducible to or analysable into statements about brain processes, in the way in which

The British Journal of Psychology 47 (1956). Reprinted by permission of the British Psychological Society.

'cognition statements' are analysable into statements about behaviour. To say that statements about consciousness are statements about brain processes is manifestly false. This is shown (a) by the fact that you can describe your sensations and mental imagery without knowing anything about your brain processes or even that such things exist, (b) by the fact that statements about one's consciousness and statements about one's brain processes are verified in entirely different ways and (c) by the fact that there is nothing self-contradictory about the statement 'X has a pain but there is nothing going on in his brain'. What I do want to assert, however, is that the statement 'consciousness is a process in the brain', although not necessarily true, is not necessarily false. 'Consciousness is a process in the brain', in my view is neither self-contradictory nor self-evident; it is a reasonable scientific hypothesis, in the way that the statement 'lightning is a motion of electric charges' is a reasonable scientific hypothesis.

The all but universally accepted view that an assertion of identity between consciousness and brain processes can be ruled out on logical grounds alone, derives, I suspect, from a failure to distinguish between what we may call the 'is' of definition and the 'is' of composition. The distinction I have in mind here is the difference between the function of the word 'is' in statements like 'a square is an equilateral rectangle', 'red is a colour', 'to understand an instruction is to be able to act appropriately under the appropriate circumstances', and its function in statements like 'his table is an old packing case', 'her hat is a bundle of straw tied together with string', 'a cloud is a mass of water droplets or other particles in suspension'. These two types of 'is' statements have one thing in common. In both cases it makes sense to add the qualification 'and nothing else'. In this they differ from those statements in which the 'is' is an 'is' of predication; the statements 'Toby is 80 years old and nothing else', 'her hat is red and nothing else' or 'giraffes are tall and nothing else', for example, are nonsense. This logical feature may be described by saying that in both cases both the grammatical subject and the grammatical predicate are expressions which provide an adequate characterization of the state of affairs to which they both refer.

In another respect, however, the two groups of statements are strikingly different. Statements like 'a square is an equilateral rectangle' are necessary statements which are true by definition. Statements like 'his table is an old packing case', on the other hand, are contingent statements which have to be verified by observation. In the case of statements like 'a square is an equilateral rectangle' or 'red is a colour', there is a relationship between the meaning of the expression forming the grammatical predicate and the meaning of the expression forming the grammatical subject, such that whenever the subject expression is applicable the predicate must also be applicable. If you can describe something as red then you must also be able to describe it as coloured. In the case of statements like 'his table is an old packing case', on the other hand, there is no such relationship between the meanings of the expressions 'his table' and 'old packing case'; it merely so happens that in this case both expressions are applicable to and at the same time provide an adequate characterization of the same object. Those who contend that the statement 'consciousness is a brain process' is logically untenable base their claim, I suspect, on the mistaken assumption that if the meanings of two statements or expressions are quite unconnected, they cannot both provide an adequate characterization of the same object or state of affairs: if something is a state of consciousness, it cannot be a brain process, since there is nothing self-contradictory in supposing that someone feels a pain when there is nothing happening inside his skull. By the same token we might be led to conclude that a table cannot be an old packing case, since there is nothing self-contradictory in supposing that someone has a table, but is not in possession of an old packing case.

THE LOGICAL INDEPENDENCE OF EXPRESSIONS AND THE ONTOLOGICAL INDEPENDENCE OF ENTITIES

There is, of course, an important difference between the table/packing case case and the consciousness/brain process case in that the statement 'his table is an old packing case' is a particular proposition which refers only to one particular case, whereas the statement 'consciousness is a process in the brain' is a general or universal proposition applying to all states of consciousness whatever. It is fairly clear, I think, that if we lived in a world in which all tables without exception were packing cases, the concepts of 'table' and 'packing case' in our language would not have their present logically independent status. In such a world a table would be a species of packing case in much the same way that red is a species of colour. It seems to be a rule of language that whenever a given variety of object or state of affairs has two characteristics or sets of characteristics, one of which is unique to the variety of object or state of affairs in question, the expression used to refer to the characteristic or set of characteristics which defines the variety of object or state of affairs in question will always entail the expression used to refer to the other characteristic or set of characteristics. If this rule admitted of no exception it would follow that any expression which is logically independent of another expression which uniquely characterizes a given variety of object or state of affairs, must refer to a characteristic or set of characteristics which is not normally or necessarily associated with the object or state of affairs in question. It is because this rule applies almost universally, I suggest, that we are normally justified in arguing from the logical independence of two expressions to the ontological independence of the states of affairs to which they refer. This would explain both the undoubted force of the argument that consciousness and brain processes must be independent entities because the expressions used to refer to them are logically independent and, in general, the curious phenomenon whereby questions about the furniture of the universe are often fought and not infrequently decided merely on a point of logic.

The argument from the logical independence of two expressions to the ontological independence of the entities to which they refer breaks down in the case of brain processes and consciousness, I believe, because this is one of a relatively small number of cases where the rule stated above does not apply. These exceptions are to be found, I suggest, in those cases where the operations which have to be performed in order to verify the presence of the two sets of characteristics inhering in the object or state of affairs in question can seldom if ever be performed si-

multaneously. A good example here is the case of the cloud and the mass of droplets or other particles in suspension. A cloud is a large semi-transparent mass with a fleecy texture suspended in the atmosphere whose shape is subject to continual and kaleidoscopic change. When observed at close quarters, however, it is found to consist of a mass of tiny particles, usually water droplets, in continuous motion. On the basis of this second observation we conclude that a cloud is a mass of tiny particles and nothing else. But there is no logical connexion in our language between a cloud and a mass of tiny particles; there is nothing self-contradictory in talking about a cloud which is not composed of tiny particles in suspension. There is no contradiction involved in supposing that clouds consist of a dense mass of fibrous tissue; indeed, such a consistency seems to be implied by many of the functions performed by clouds in fairy stories and mythology. It is clear from this that the terms 'cloud' and 'mass of tiny particles in suspension' mean quite different things. Yet we do not conclude from this that there must be two things, the mass of particles in suspension and the cloud. The reason for this, I suggest, is that although the characteristics of being a cloud and being a mass of tiny particles in suspension are invariably associated, we never make the observations necessary to verify the statement 'that is a cloud' and those necessary to verify the statement 'this is a mass of tiny particles in suspension' at one and the same time. We can observe the micro-structure of a cloud only when we are enveloped by it, a condition which effectively prevents us from observing those characteristics which from a distance lead us to describe it as a cloud. Indeed, so disparate are these two experiences that we use different words to describe them. That which is a cloud when we observe it from a distance becomes a fog or mist when we are enveloped by it.

WHEN ARE TWO SETS OF OBSERVATIONS OBSERVATIONS OF THE SAME EVENT?

The example of the cloud and the mass of tiny particles in suspension was chosen because it is one of the few cases of a general proposition involving what I have called the 'is' of composition which does not involve us in scientific technicalities. It is useful because it brings out the connexion between the ordinary everyday cases of the 'is' of composition like the table/packing case example and the more technical cases like 'lightning is a motion of electric charges' where the analogy with the consciousness/ brain process case is most marked. The limitation of the cloud/tiny particles in suspension case is that it does not bring out sufficiently clearly the crucial problem of how the identity of the states of affairs referred to by the two expressions is established. In the cloud case the fact that something is a cloud and the fact that something is a mass of tiny particles in suspension are both verified by the normal processes of visual observation. It is arguable, moreover, that the identity of the entities referred to by the two expressions is established by the continuity between the two sets of observations as the observer moves towards or away from the cloud. In the case of brain processes and consciousness there is no such continuity between the two sets of observations involved. A closer introspective scrutiny will never reveal the passage of nerve impulses over a thousand synapses in the way that a closer scrutiny of a cloud will reveal a mass of tiny particles in suspension. The operations required to verify statements about consciousness and statements about brain processes are fundamentally different.

To find a parallel for this feature we must examine other cases where an identity is asserted between something whose occurrence is verified by the ordinary processes of observation and something whose occurrence is established by special scientific procedures. For this purpose I have chosen the case where we say that lightning is a motion of electric charges. As in the case of consciousness, however closely we scrutinize the lightning we shall never be able to observe the electric charges, and just as the operations for determining the nature of one's state of consciousness are radically different from those involved in determining the nature of one's brain processes, so the operations for determining the occurrence of lightning are radically different from those involved in determining the occurrence of a motion of electric charges. What is it, therefore, that leads us to say that the two sets of observations are observations of the same event? It cannot be merely the fact that the two sets of observations are systematically correlated such that whenever there is lightning there is always a motion of electric charges. There are innumerable cases of such correlations where we have no temptation to say that the two sets of observations are observations of the same event. There is a systematic correlation, for example, between the movement of the tides and the stages of the moon, but this does not lead us to say that records of tidal levels are records of the moon's stages or vice versa. We speak rather of a causal connexion between two independent events or processes.

The answer here seems to be that we treat the two sets of observations as observations of the same event, in those cases where the technical scientific observations set in the context of the appropriate body of scientific theory provide an immediate explanation of the observations made by the man in the street. Thus we conclude that lightning is nothing more than a motion of electric charges, because we know that a motion of electric charges through the atmosphere, such as occurs when lightning is reported, gives rise to the type of visual stimulation which would lead an observer to report a flash of lightning. In the moon/tide case, on the other hand, there is no such direct causal connexion between the stages of the moon and the observations made by the man who measures the height of the tide. The causal connexion is between the moon and the tides, not between the moon and the measurement of the tides.

THE PHYSIOLOGICAL EXPLANATION OF INTROSPECTION AND THE PHENOMENOLOGICAL FALLACY

If this account is correct, it should follow that in order to establish the identity of consciousness and certain processes in the brain, it would be necessary to show that the introspective observations reported by the subject can be accounted for in terms of processes which are known to have occurred in his brain. In the light of this suggestion it is extremely interesting to find that when a physiologist as distinct from a philosopher finds it difficult to see how consciousness could be a process in the brain, what worries him is not any supposed self-contradiction involved in such an assumption, but the apparent impossibility of accounting for the reports given by the subject of his conscious processes in terms of the known properties of the central nervous system. Sir Charles Sherrington has posed the problem as follows: 'The chain of events stretching from the sun's radiation entering the eye to, on the one hand, the contraction of the pupillary muscles, and on the other, to the electrical disturbances in the brain-cortex are all straightforward steps in a sequence of physical "causation", such as, thanks to science, are intelligible. But in the second serial chain there follows on, or attends, the stage of brain-cortex reaction an event or set of events quite inexplicable to us, which both as to themselves and as to the causal tie between them and what preceded them science does not help us; a set of events seemingly incommensurable with any of the events leading up to it. The self "sees" the sun; it senses a two-dimensional disc of brightness, located in the "sky", this last a field of lesser brightness, and overhead shaped as a rather flattened dome, coping the self and a hundred other visual things as well. Of hint that this is within the head there is none. Vision is saturated with this strange property called "projection", the unargued inference that what it sees is at a "distance" from the seeing "self". Enough has been said to stress that in the sequence of events a step is reached where a physical situation in the brain leads to a psychical, which however contains no hint of the brain or any other bodily part. . . . The supposition has to be, it would seem, two continuous series of events, one physico-chemical, the other psychical, and at times interaction between them' (Sherrington, 1947, pp. xx–xxi).

Just as the physiologist is not likely to be impressed by the philosopher's contention that there is some self-contradiction involved in supposing consciousness to be a brain process, so the philosopher is unlikely to be impressed by the considerations which lead Sherrington to conclude that there are two sets of events, one physico-chemical, the other psychical. Sherrington's argument for all its emotional appeal depends on a fairly simple logical mistake, which is unfortunately all too frequently

made by psychologists and physiologists and not infrequently in the past by the philosophers themselves. This logical mistake, which I shall refer to as the 'phenomenological fallacy', is the mistake of supposing that when the subject describes his experience, when he describes how things look, sound, smell, taste or feel to him, he is describing the literal properties of objects and events on a peculiar sort of internal cinema or television screen, usually referred to in the modern psychological literature as the 'phenomenal field'. It we assume, for example, that when a subject reports a green after-image he is asserting the occurrence inside himself of an object which is literally green, it is clear that we have on our hands an entity for which there is no place in the world of physics. In the case of the green after-image there is no green object in the subject's environment corresponding to the description that he gives. Nor is there anything green in his brain; certainly there is nothing which could have emerged when he reported the appearance of the green after-image. Brain processes are not the sort of things to which colour concepts can be properly applied.

The phenomenological fallacy on which this argument is based depends on the mistaken assumption that because our ability to describe things in our environment depends on our consciousness of them, our descriptions of things are primarily descriptions of our conscious experience and only secondarily, indirectly and inferentially descriptions of the objects and events in our environments. It is assumed that because we recognize things in our environment by their look, sound, smell, taste and feel, we begin by describing their phenomenal properties, i.e., the properties of the looks, sounds, smells, tastes and feels which they produce in us, and infer their real properties from their phenomenal properties. In fact, the reverse is the case. We begin by learning to recognize the real properties of things in our environment. We learn to recognize them, of course, by their look, sound, smell, taste and feel; but this does not mean that we have to learn to describe the look, sound, smell, taste and feel of things before we can describe the things themselves. Indeed, it is only after we have learnt to describe the things in our environment that we can learn to describe our consciousness of them. We describe our conscious experience not in terms of the mythological 'phenomenal properties' which are supposed to inhere in the mythological 'objects' in the mythological 'phenomenal field', but by reference to the actual physical properties of the concrete physical objects, events and processes which normally, though not perhaps in the present instance, give rise to the sort of conscious experience which we are trying to describe. In other words when we describe the after-image as green, we are not saying that there is something, the after-image, which is green, we are saying that we are having the sort of experience which we normally have when, and which we have learnt to describe as, looking at a green patch of light.

Once we rid ourselves of the phenomenological fallacy we realize that the problem of explaining introspective observations in terms of brain processes is far from insuperable. We realize that there is nothing that the introspecting subject says about his conscious experiences which is inconsistent with anything the physiologist might want to say about the brain processes which cause him to describe the environment and his consciousness of that environment in the way he does. When the subject describes his experience by saying that a light which is in fact stationary, appears to move, all the physiologist or physiological psychologist has to do in order to explain the subject's introspective observations, is to show that the brain process which is causing the subject to describe his experience in this way, is the sort of process which normally occurs when he is observing an actual moving object and which therefore normally causes him to report the movement of an object in his environment. Once the mechanism whereby the individual describes what is going on in his environment has been worked out, all that is required to explain the indi-

vidual's capacity to make introspective observations is an explanation of his ability to discriminate between those cases where his normal habits of verbal description are appropriate to the stimulus situation and those cases where they are not and an explanation of how and why, in those cases where the appropriateness of his normal descriptive habits is in doubt, he learns to issue his ordinary descriptive protocols preceded by a qualificatory phrase like 'it appears', 'seems', 'looks', 'feels', etc.

ACKNOWLEDGMENTS

I am greatly indebted to my fellow-participants in a series of informal discussions on this topic which took place in the Department of Philosophy, University of Adelaide, in particular to Mr. C. B. Martin for his persistent and searching criticism of my earlier attempts to defend the thesis that consciousness is a brain process, to Prof. D. A. T. Gasking, of the University of Melbourne, for clarifying many of the logical issues involved and to Prof. J. J. C. Smart for moral support and encouragement in what often seemed a lost cause.

REFEREMCES

Place, U. T. (1954). 'The Concept of Heed.' *British Journal of Psychology* 45, 243–55.
Ryle, G. (1949). *The Concept of Mind*. London: Hutchinson.
Sherrington, Sir Charles (1947). Foreword to the 1947 edition of *The Integrative Action of the Nervous System*. Cambridge University Press.
Tolman, E. C. (1932). *Purposive Behaviour in Animals and Men*. Berkeley and Los Angeles: University of California Press.
Wittgenstein, L. (1953). *Philosophical Investigations*. Oxford: Blackwell.

Minds and Machines   24

HILARY PUTNAM

THE VARIOUS ISSUES and puzzles that make up the traditional mind–body problem are wholly linguistic and logical in character: whatever few empirical 'facts' there may be in this area support one view as much as another. I do not hope to establish this contention in this paper, but I hope to do something toward rendering it more plausible. Specifically, I shall try to show that all of the issues arise in connection with any computing system capable of answering questions about its own structure, and have thus nothing to do with the unique nature (if it *is* unique) of human subjective experience.

To illustrate the sort of thing that is meant: one kind of puzzle that is sometimes discussed in connection with the 'mind–body problem' is the puzzle of *privacy*. The question 'How do I know I have a pain?' is a *deviant*[1] ('logically odd') question. The question 'How do I know Smith has a pain?' is not at all deviant. The difference can also be mirrored in impersonal questions: 'How does anyone ever know he himself has a pain?' is deviant; 'How does anyone ever know that someone else is in pain?' is non-deviant. I shall show that the difference in status between the last two questions is mirrored in the case of machines: if *T* is a *Turing machine* (see below), the question 'How does *T* ascertain that it is in state *A*?' is, as we shall see, 'logically odd' with a vengeance; but if *T* is capable of investigating its neighbor machine *T'* (say, *T* has electronic 'sense-organs' which 'scan' *T'*), the question. 'How does *T* ascertain that *T'* is in state *A*?' is not at all odd.

Another question connected with the 'mind–body problem' is the question whether or not it is ever permissible to identify mental events and physical events. Of course, I do not claim that this question arises for Turing machines, but I do claim that it is possible to construct a logical analogue for this question that does arise, and that all of the question of 'mind–body identity' can be mirrored in terms of the analogue.

To obtain such an analogue, let us identify a scientific theory with a 'partially-interpreted calculus' in the sense of Carnap.[2] Then we can perfectly well imagine a Turing machine which generates theories, tests them (assuming that it is possible to 'mechanize' inductive logic to some degree), and 'accepts' theories which satisfy certain criteria (e.g., predictive success). In particular, if the machine has electronic 'sense organs' which enable it to 'scan' itself while it is in operation, it may formulate theories concerning its own structure and subject them to test. Suppose the machine is in a given state (say, 'state A') when, and only when, flip-flop 36 is on. Then this statement: 'I am in state A when, and only when, flip-flop 36 is on', may be one of the theoretical principles concerning its own structure accepted by the machine. Here 'I am in state A' is, of course, 'observation language' for the machine, while 'flip-flop 36 is on', is a 'theoretical expression' which is partially interpreted in terms of 'observables' (if the machine's 'sense organs report by printing symbols on the machine's input tape, the 'observables' in terms of which the machine would give a partial operational definition of 'flip-flop 36 being on' would be of the form 'symbol # so-and-so appearing on the input tape'). Now all of the usual considerations for and against mind–body identification can be paralleled by considerations for and against saying that state A is in fact *identical* with flip-flop 36 being on.

Corresponding to Occamist arguments for 'identify' in the one case are Occamist arguments for identity in the other. And the usual argument for dualism in the mind–body case can be paralleled in the other as follows: for the machine, 'state A' is directly observable; on the other hand, 'flip-flops' are something it knows about only via highly-sophisticated inferences—How *could* two things so different *possibly* be the same? This last argument can be put into

Sidney Hook, ed., *Dimensions of Mind* (New York, 1960). Reprinted by permission of Ernest Hook.

a form which makes it appear somewhat stronger. The proposition:

> (1) I am in state A if, and only if, flip-flop 36 is on,

is clearly a 'synthetic' proposition for the machine. For instance, the machine might be in state A and its sense organs might report that flip-flop 36 was *not* on. In such a case the machine would have to make a methodological 'choice'—namely, to give up (1) or to conclude that it had made an 'observational error' (just as a human scientist would be confronted with similar methodological choices in studying his own psychophysical correlations). And just as philosophers have argued from the synthetic nature of the proposition:

> (2) I am in pain if, and only if, my C-fibers are stimulated,

to the conclusion that the *properties* (or 'states' or 'events') being in pain, and having C-fibers stimulated, cannot possibly be the same (otherwise (2) would be analytic, or so the argument runs); so one should be able to conclude from the fact that (1) is synthetic that the two properties (or 'states' or 'events')—being in state A and having flip-flop 36 on—cannot possibly be the same!

It is instructive to note that the traditional argument for dualism is not at all a conclusion from 'the raw data of direct experience' (as is shown by the fact that it applies just as well to non-sentient machines), but a highly complicated bit of reasoning which depends on (a) the reification of universals[3] (e.g., 'properties', 'states', 'events'); and on (b) a sharp analytic-synthetic distinction.

I may be accused of advocating a 'mechanistic' world-view in pressing the present analogy. If this means that I am supposed to hold that machines think,[4] on the one hand, or that human beings are machines, on the other, the charge is false. If there is some version of mechanism sophisticated enough to avoid these errors, very likely the considerations in this paper support it.[5]

I. TURING MACHINES

The present paper will require the notion of a *Turing machine*[6] which will now be explained.

Briefly, a Turing machine is a device with a finite number of internal configurations, each of which involves the machine's being in one of a finite number of *states*,[7] and the machine's scanning a tape on which certain symbols appear.

The machine's tape is divided into separate squares, thus:

on each of which a symbol (from a fixed finite alphabet) may be printed. Also the machine has a 'scanner' which 'scans' one square of the tape at a time. Finally, the machine has a *printing mechanism* which may (a) *erase* the symbol which appears on the square being scanned, and (b) print some other symbol (from the machine's alphabet) on that square.

Any Turing machine is completely described by a *machine table*, which is constructed as follows: the rows of the table correspond to letters of the alphabet (including the 'null' letter, i.e., blank space), while the columns correspond to states A, B, C, etc. In each square there appears an 'instruction', e.g., '$s_5 L\ A$', '$s_7 C\ B$', '$s_3 R\ C$'. These instructions are read as follows: '$s_5 L\ A$' means 'print the symbol s_5 on the square you are now scanning (after erasing whatever symbol it now contains), and proceed to scan the square immediately to the left of the one you have just been scanning; also, shift into state A.' The other instructions are similarly interpreted ('R' means 'scan the square immediately to the right', while 'C' means 'center', i.e., continue scanning the *same* square). The following is a sample machine table:

		A	B	C	D
(s_1)	1	$s_1 RA$	$s_1 LB$	$s_3 LD$	$s_1 CD$
(s_2)	+	$s_1 LB$	$s_2 CD$	$s_2 LD$	$s_2 CD$
(s_3)	blank space	$s_3 CD$	$s_3 RC$	$s_3 LD$	$s_3 CD$

The machine described by this table is intended to function as follows: the machine is started in state A. On the tape there appears a 'sum' (in unary notion) to be 'worked out', e.g., '11 + 111.'

The machine is initially scanning the first '1'. The machine proceeds to 'work out' the sum (essentially by replacing the plus sign by a 1, and then going back and erasing the first 1). Thus if the 'input' was 1111+11111 the machine would 'print out' 111111111, and then go into the 'rest state' (state *D*).

A 'machine table' *describes* a machine if the machine has internal states corresponding to the columns of the table, and if it 'obeys' the instruction in the table in the following sense: when it is scanning a square on which a symbol s_1 appears and it is in, say, state *B*, that it carries out the 'instruction' in the appropriate row and column of the table (in this case, column *B* and row s_1). Any machine that is described by a machine table of the sort just exemplified is a Turing machine.

The notion of a Turing machine is also subject to generalization[8] in various ways—for example, one may suppose that the machine has a second tape (an 'input tape') on which additional information may be printed by an operator in the course of a computation. In the sequel we shall make use of this generalization (with electronic 'sense organs' taking the place of the 'operator').

It should be remarked that Turing machines are able in principle to do anything that any computing machine (of whichever kind) can do.[9]

It has sometimes been contended (e.g., by Nagel and Newman in their book *Gödel's Proof*) that 'the theorem [i.e., Gödel's theorem] does indicate that the structure and power of the human mind are far more complex and subtle than any non-living machine yet envisaged' (p. 10), and hence that a Turing machine cannot serve as a model for the human mind, but this is simply a mistake.

Let *T* be a Turing machine which 'represents' me in the sense that *T* can prove just the mathematical statements I can prove. Then the argument (Nagel and Newman give no argument, but I assume they must have this one in mind) is that by using Gödel's technique I can discover a proposition that *T* cannot prove, and moreover *I* can prove this proposition. This refutes the assumption that *T* 'represents' me, hence I am not a Turing machine. The fallacy is a misapplication of Gödel's theorem, pure and simple. Given an arbitrary machine *T*, all I can do is find a proposition *U* such that *I* can prove:

(3) If *T* is consistent, *U* is true,

where *U* is undecidable by *T* if *T* is in fact consistent. However, *T* can perfectly well prove (3) too! And the statement *U*, which *T* *cannot* prove (assuming consistency), *I* cannot prove either (unless I can prove that *T* is consistent, which is unlikely if *T* is very complicated)!

2. PRIVACY

Let us suppose that a Turing machine *T* is constructed to do the following. A number, say '3000' is printed on *T*'s tape and *T* is started in *T*'s 'initial state'. Thereupon *T* computes the 3000th (or whatever the given number was) digit in the decimal expansion of π, prints this digit on its tape, and goes into the 'rest state' (i.e., turns itself off). Clearly the question 'How does *T* "ascertain" [or "compute", or "work out"] the 3000th digit in the decimal expansion of π?' is a sensible question. And the answer might well be a complicated one. In fact, an answer would probably involve three distinguishable constituents:

(i) A description of the sequence of states through which *T* passed in arriving at the answer, and of the appearance of the tape at each stage in the computation.

(ii) A description of the *rules* under which *T* operated (these are given by the 'machine table' for *T*).

(iii) An explanation of the *rationale* of the entire procedure.

Now let us suppose that someone voices the following objection: 'In order to perform the computation just described, *T* must pass through states *A*, *B*, *C*, etc. But how can *T* ascertain that it is in states *A*, *B*, *C*, etc.?'

It is clear that this is a silly objection. But what makes it silly? For one thing, the 'logical description' (machine table) of the machine describes the state only in terms of their *relations* to each other and to what appears on the tape. The 'physical realization' of the machine is immaterial, so long as there *are* distinct states *A*, *B*, *C*, etc., and they succeed each other as specified in the machine table. Thus one can answer a question such as 'How does

T ascertain that *X*?' (or 'compute *X*', etc.) only in the sense of describing the *sequence of states* through which *T* must pass in ascertaining that *X* (computing, *X* etc.), the rules obeyed, etc. But there is no 'sequence of states' through which *T* must pass to be in a single state!

Indeed, suppose there were—suppose *T* could not *be* in state A without first *ascertaining* that it was in state *A* (by first passing through a sequence of other states). Clearly a vicious regress would be involved. And one 'breaks' the regress simply by noting that the machine, in ascertaining the 3000th digit in *π*, *passes through* its states—but it need not in any significant sense 'ascertain' that it is passing through them.

Note the analogy to a fallacy in traditional epistemology: the fallacy of supposing that to know that *p* (where *p* is any proposition) one must first know that q_1, q_2, etc. (where q_1, q_2, etc., are appropriate *other* propositions). This leads either to an 'infinite regress' or to the dubious move of inventing a special class of 'protocol' propositions.

The resolution of the fallacy is also analogous to the machine case. Suppose that on the basis of sense experiences E_1, E_2, etc., I know that there is a chair in the room. It does not follow that I verbalized (or even *could* have verbalized) E_1, E_2, etc., nor that I remember E_1, E_2, etc., nor even that I 'mentally classified' ('attended to', etc.) sense experiences E_1, E_2, etc., when I had them. In short, it is necessary to *have* sense experiences, but not to *know* (or even *notice*) what sense experiences one is having, in order to have certain kinds of knowledge.

Let us modify our case, however, by supposing that whenever the machine is in one particular state (say, 'state *A*') it prints the words 'I am in state *A*'. Then someone might grant that the machine does not in general ascertain what state it is in, but might say in the case of state *A* (after the machine printed 'I am in state *A*'): 'The machine ascertained that it was in state *A*'.

Let us study this case a little more closely. First of all, we want to suppose that when it is in state *A* the machine prints 'I am in state *A*' without first passing through any other states. That is, in every row of the column of the table headed 'state *A*' there appears the instruction: *print*[10] '*I am in state A*'. Secondly, by way of comparison, let us consider

a human being, Jones, who says 'I am in pain' (or 'Ouch!', or 'Something hurts') whenever he is in pain. To make the comparison as close as possible, we will have to suppose that Jones' linguistic conditioning is such that he simply says 'I am in pain' 'without thinking', i.e., without passing through any introspectible mental states other than the pain itself. In Wittgenstein's terminology, Jones simply *evinces* his pain by saying 'I am in pain'—he does not first reflect on it (or heed it, or note it, etc.) and then consciously describe it. (Note that this simple possibility of uttering the 'proposition', 'I am in pain' without first performing any mental 'act of judgement' was overlooked by traditional epistemologists from Hume to Russell!) Now we may consider the parallel question 'Does the machine "ascertain" that it is in state *A*?' and 'Does Jones "know" that he is in pain?' and their consequences.

Philosophers interested in semantical questions have, as one might expect, paid a good deal of attention to the verb 'know'. Traditionally, three elements have been distinguished: (1) '*X* know that *p*' implies that *p* is *true* (we may call this the *truth* element); (2) '*X* knows that *p*' implies that *X* believes that *p* (philosophers have quarrelled about the word, some contending that it should be '*X* is *confident* that *p*,' or '*X* is in a position to assert* that *p*'; I shall call this element the *confidence* element); (3) '*X* knows that *p*' implies that *X* has evidence that *p* (here I think the word 'evidence' is definitely wrong,[11] but it will not matter for present purposes; I shall call this the *evidential* element). Moreover, it it is part of the meaning of the word 'evidence' that nothing can be literally evidence for itself: if *X* is evidence for *Y*, then *X* and *Y* must be different things.

In view of such analyses, disputes have arisen over the propriety of saying (in cases like the one we are considering) 'Jones knows that he is in pain.' On the one hand, philosophers who take the common-sense view ('When I have a pain I *know* I have a pain') argue somewhat as follows: it would be clearly false to say Jones does *not* know he has a pain; but either Jones knows or he does not; hence, Jones knows he has a pain. Against these philosophers, one might argue as follows: 'Jones does not know *X*' implies Jones is not in a position to assert that *X;* hence, it is certainly wrong to say 'Jones does not know he has a pain.' But the above use of the Law of the Excluded Middle was fallacious: words in English have *significance ranges,* and what is contended is that it is not semantically correct to say *either* 'Jones knows that he has a pain.' *or* 'Jones does not know he has a pain.' (although the former sentence is certainly less misleading than the latter, since *one* at least of the conditions involved in knowing is met—Jones is in a position to assert he has a pain. (In fact the *truth* and *confidence* elements are both present; it is the evidential element that occasions the difficulty.)

I do not wish to argue this question here;[12] the present concern is rather with the similarities between our two questions. For example, one might decide to accept (as 'non-deviant', 'logically in order', 'non-selfcontradictory', etc.) the two statements:

(a) The machine ascertained that it was in state *A,*

(b) Jones knew that he had a pain,

or one might reject both. If one rejects (a) and (b), then one can find alternative formulations which are certainly semantically acceptable: e.g., (for (a)) 'The machine was in state *A,* and this caused it to print: "I am in state *A*"', (for (b)) 'Jones was in pain, and this caused him to say "I am in pain"' (or, 'Jones was in pain, and he evinced this by saying "I am in pain"').

On the other hand, if one accepts (a) and (b), then one must face the questions (a_1) '*How* did the machine ascertain that it was in state *A*?', and (b_1) '*How* did Jones know that he had a pain?'

And if one regards these questions as having answers at all, then they will be degenerate answers—e.g., 'By being in state *A*' and 'By having the pain.'

At this point it is, I believe, very clear that the difficulty has in both cases the same cause. Namely, the difficulty has occasioned by the fact that the 'verbal report' ('I am in state *A*', or 'I am in pain') issues directly from the state it 'reports': no 'computation' or additional 'evidence' is needed to arrive at the 'answer'. And the philosophic disagreements over 'how to talk' are at bottom concerned with finding a terminology for describing cognitive processes in general that is not misleading in this particular case. (Note that the traditional epistemological answer to (b_1)—namely, 'by introspection'—is false to the facts of this case, since it clearly implies the occur-

rence of a mental event (the 'act' of introspection) distinct from the feeling of pain.)

Finally, let us suppose that the machine is equipped to 'scan' its neighbor machine T_1. Then we can see that the question 'How does *T* ascertain that T_1 is in state *A*?' may be a perfectly sensible question, as much so as 'How does *T* ascertain that the 3000th digit of π is so-and-so?' In both cases the answer will involve describing a whole 'program' (plus explaining the *rationale* of the program, if necessary). Moreover, it will be necessary to say something about the physical context linking *T* and T_1 (arrangement of sense organs, etc.), and not just to describe the internal states of *T*: this is so because *T* is now answering an *empirical* and not a mathematical question. In the same way 'How did Sherlock Holmes know that Jones was in pain?' may be a perfectly sensible question, and may have quite a complicated answer.

3. 'MENTAL' STATES AND 'LOGICAL' STATES

Consider the two questions:

(1) How does Jones know he has a pain?

(2) How does Jones know he has a fever?

The first question is, as we saw in the preceding section, a somewhat peculiar one. The second question may be quite sensible. In fact, if Jones says 'I have a pain' no one will retort 'You are mistaken'. (One *might* retort 'You have made a slip of the tongue' or 'You are lying', but not 'You are *mistaken*'.) On the other hand, if Jones says 'I have a fever', the doctor who has just taken Jones' temperature may quite conceivably retort 'You are mistaken'. And the doctor need not mean that Jones made a linguistic error, or was lying, or confused.

It might be thought that, whereas the difference between statements about one's own state and statements about the states of others has an analogue in the case of machines, the difference, just touched upon, between statements about one's 'mental' state and statements about one's 'physical' state, in traditional parlance, does not have any analogue. But this is not so. Just what the analogue is will now be developed.

First of all, we have to go back to the notion of a Turing machine. When a Turing machine is described by means of a 'machine table', it is described as something having a tape, a printing device, a 'scanning' device (this may be no more than a point of the machine which at any given time is aligned with just one square of the tape), and a finite set (*A, B, C,* etc.) of 'states'. (In what follows, these will be referred to at times as *logical states* to distinguish them from certain other states to be introduced shortly.) Beyond this it is described only by giving the deterministic rules which determine the order in which the states succeed each other and what is printed when.

In particular, the 'logical description' of a Turing machine does not include any specification of the *physical nature* of these 'states'—or indeed, of the physical nature of the whole machine. (Shall it consist of electronic relays, of cardboard, of human clerks sitting at desks, or what?) In other words, a given 'Turing machine' is an *abstract* machine which may be physically realized in an almost infinite number of different ways.

As soon as a Turing machine is physically realized, however, something interesting happens. Although the machine has from the logician's point of view only the states *A, B, C,* etc., it has from the engineer's point of view an almost infinite number of additional 'states' (though not in the same sense of 'state'—we shall call these *structural states*). For instance, if the machine consists of vacuum tubes, one of the things that may happen is that one of its vacuum tubes may fail—this puts the machine in what is from the physicist's if not the logician's point of view a different 'state'. Again, if the machine is a manually operated one built of cardboard, one of its possible 'non-logical' or 'structural' states is obviously that its cardboard may buckle. And so on.

A physically realized Turing machine may have no way of ascertaining its own structural state, just as a human being may have no way of ascertaining the condition of his appendix at a given time. However, it is extremely convenient to give a machine electronic 'sense organs' which enable it to scan itself and to detect minor malfunctions. These 'sense organs' may be visualized as causing certain symbols to be printed on an 'input tape' which the machine 'examines' from time to time. (One minor difficulty is that the 'report' of a sense organ might occupy a number of squares of tape, whereas the machine only 'scans' one square at a time—however, this is unimportant, since it is well known that the effect of 'reading' any finite number of squares can be obtained using a program which only requires one square to be scanned at a time.)

(By way of a digression, let me remark that the first actually constructed digital computers did not have any devices of the kind just envisaged. On the other hand, they *did* have over 3000 vacuum tubes, some of which were failing at any given time! The need for 'routines' for self-checking therefore quickly became evident.)[13]

A machine which is able to detect at least some of its own structural states is in a position very analogous to that of a human being, who can detect some but not all of the malfunctions of his own body, and with varying degrees of reliability. Thus, suppose the machine 'prints out': 'Vacuum tube 312 has failed'. The question 'How did the machine ascertain that vacuum tube 312 failed?' is a perfectly sensible question. And the answer may involve a reference to both the physical structure of the machine ('sense organs', etc.) and the 'logical structure' (program for 'reading' and 'interpreting' the input tape).

If the machine prints: 'Vacuum tube 312 has failed' when vacuum tube 312 is in fact functioning, the mistake may be due to a miscomputation (in the course of 'reading' and 'interpreting' the input tape) or to an incorrect signal from a sense organ. On the other hand, if the machine prints: 'I am in state A', and it does this simply because its machine table contains the instruction: *Print: 'I am in state A when in state A',* then the question of a miscomputation cannot arise. Even if some accident causes the printing mechanism to print: 'I am in state A' when the machine is *not* in state A, there was not a 'miscomputation' (only, so to speak, a 'verbal slip').

It is interesting to note that just as there are two possible descriptions of the behavior of a Turing machine—the engineer's structural blueprint and the logician's 'machine table'—so there are two possible descriptions of human psychology. The 'behavioristic' approach (including in this category theories which employ 'hypothetical constructs', including 'constructs' taken from physiology) aims at eventually providing a complete physicalistic[14] description of human behavior, in terms which link up with chemistry and physics. This corresponds to the engineer's or physicist's description of a physically realized Turing machine. But it would also be possible to seek a more abstract description of human mental processes, in terms of 'mental states' (physical realization, if any, unspecified) and 'impressions' (these play the role of symbols on the machine's tapes)—a description which would specify the laws controlling the order in which the states succeeded one another, and the relation to verbalization (or, at any rate, verbalized thought). This description, which would be the analogue of a 'machine table', it was in fact the program of classical psychology to provide! Classical psychology is often thought to have failed for *methodological* reasons; I would suggest, in the light of this analogy, that it failed rather for empirical reasons—the mental states and 'impressions' of human beings do not form a causally closed system to the extent to which the 'configurations' of a Turing machine do.

The analogy which has been presented between logical states of a Turing machine and mental states of a human being, on the one hand, and structural states of a Turing machine and physical states of a human being, on the other, is one that I find very suggestive. In particular, further exploration of this analogy may make it possible to further clarify the notion of a 'mental state' that we have been discussing. This 'further exploration' has not yet been undertaken, at any rate by me, but I should like to put down, for those who may be interested, a few of the features that seem to distinguish logical and mental states respectively from structural and physical ones:

(1) The functional organization (problem solving, thinking) of the human being or machine can be described in terms of the sequences of mental or logical states respectively (and the accompanying verbalizations), without reference to the nature of the 'physical realization' of these states.

(2) The states seem intimately connected with *verbalization*.

(3) In the case of rational thought (or computing), the 'program' which

determines which states follow which, etc., is open to rational criticism.

4. MIND–BODY 'IDENTITY'

The last area in which we have to compare human beings and machines involves the question of *identifying* mental states with the corresponding physical states (or logical states with the corresponding structural states). As indicated at the beginning of this paper, all of the arguments for and against such identification can perfectly well be discussed in terms of Turing machines.

For example, in the 1930s Wittgenstein used the following argument: if I observe an after-image, and observe at the same time my brain state (with the aid of a suitable instrument) I observe *two* things, not one. (Presumably this is an argument *against* identification.) But we can perfectly well imagine a 'clever' Turing machine 'reasoning' as follows: 'When I print "I am in state *A*" I do not have to use my "sense organs". When I do use my "sense organs", and compare the occasions upon which I am in state *A* with the occasions upon which flip-flop 36 is on, I am comparing *two* things and not one.' And I do not think that we would find the argument of this mechanical Wittgenstein very convincing!

By contrast, Russell once carried the 'identity' view to the absurd extreme of maintaining that all we ever *see* is portions of our own brains. Analogously, a mechanical Russell might 'argue' that 'all I ever observe is my own vacuum tubes'. Both 'Russells' are wrong—the human being observes events in the outside world, and the process of 'observation' involves events in his brain. But we are not therefore forced to say that he 'really' observes his brain. Similarly, the machine *T* may 'observe', say, cans of tomato soup (if the machine's job is sorting cans of soup), and the process of 'observation' involves the functioning of vacuum tubes. But we are not forced to say that the machine 'really' observes its own vacuum tubes.

But let us consider more serious arguments on this topic. At the beginning of this paper, I pointed out that the *synthetic* character of the statement (1) 'I am in pain if, and only if, my C-fibers are stimulated' has been used as an argument for the view that the 'properties' (or 'events' or 'states') 'having C-fibers stimulated' and 'being in pain' cannot be the same. There are at least two reasons why this is not a very good argument: (a) the 'analytic-synthetic' distinction is not as sharp as that, especially where scientific laws are concerned; and (b) the criterion employed here for identifying 'properties' (or 'events' or 'states') is a very questionable one.

With respect to point (a): I have argued in chapter 2 that fundamental scientific laws cannot be happily classified as either 'analytic' or 'synthetic'. Consider, for example, the kind of conceptual shift that was involved in the transition from Euclidean to non-Euclidean geometry, or that would be involved if the law of the conservation of energy were to be abandoned. It is a distortion to say that the laws of Euclidean geometry (during their tenure of office) were 'analytic', and that Einstein merely 'changed the meaning of the words'. Indeed, it was precisely because Einstein did *not* change the meaning of the words, because he was really talking about shortest paths in the space in which we live and move and have our being, that General Relativity seemed so incomprehensible when it was first proposed. To be told that one could come back to the same place by moving in one direction on a straight line! Adopting General Relativity was indeed adopting a whole new system of concepts— but that is not to say 'adopting a new system of verbal labels'.

But if it is a distortion to assimilate the revision of fundamental scientific laws to the adoption of new linguistic conventions, it is equally a mistake to follow conventional philosophers of science, and assimilate the conceptual change that Einstein inaugurated to the kind of change that arises when we discover a black swan (whereas we had previously assumed all swans to be white)! Fundamental laws are like principles of pure mathematics (as Quine has emphasized), in that they cannot be overthrown by isolated experiments: we can always hold on to the laws, and explain the experiments in various more or less *ad hoc* ways. And—in spite of the pejorative flavor of '*ad hoc*'—it is even *rational* to do this, in the case of important scientific theories, *as long as no acceptable alternative theory exists*. This is why it took a century of concept formation—and not just some experiments—to overthrow Euclidean geom-

etry. And similarly, this is why we cannot today describe *any* experiments which would *by themselves* overthrow the law of the conservation of energy— although that law is not 'analytic', and might be abandoned if a new Einstein were to suggest good *theoretical* reasons for abandoning it, plus supporting experiments.

As Hanson has put it (Hanson, 1958), our concepts have theories 'built into' them—thus, to abandon a major scientific theory without providing an alternative would be to 'let our concepts crumble'. By contrast, although we *could* have held on to 'all swans are white' in the face of conflicting evidence, there would have been no *point* in doing so—the concepts involved did not *rest* on the acceptance of this or some rival principle in the way that geometrical concepts rest on the acceptance, not necessarily of Euclidean geometry, but of *some* geometry.

I do not deny that *today* any newly-discovered 'correlation' of the form: 'One is in mental state ψ if, and only if, one is in brain state φ' would *at first* be a *mere* correlation, a pure 'empirical generalization'. But I maintain that the interesting case is the case that would arise if we had a worked out a theoretically elaborated *system* of such 'correlations'. In such a case, scientific talk would be very different. Scientists would begin to say: 'It is impossible *in principle* to be in mental state ψ without being in brain state φ.' And it could very well be that the 'impossibility in principle' would amount to what Hanson rightly calls a *conceptual* (Cf. Hanson, 1958) impossibility: scientists could not *conceive* (barring a new Einstein) of someone's being in mental state ψ without being in brain state φ. In particular, no experiment could *by itself* overthrow psychophysical laws which had acquired this kind of status. Is it clear that in this kind of scientific situation it would not be correct to say that φ and ψ are the *same* state?

Moreover, the criteria for identifying 'events' or 'states' or 'properties' are by no means so clear. An example of a law with the sort of status we have been discussing is the following: Light passes through an aperture if, and only if, electromagnetic radiation (of such-and-such wavelengths) passes through the aperture.

This law is quite clearly *not* an 'analytic' statement. Yet it would be perfectly good scientific parlance to say that: (i) light passing through an aperture and (ii) electromagnetic radiation (of such-and-such wavelengths) passing through an aperture are two descriptions of the same event. (Indeed, in 'ordinary language' not only are descriptions of the same event not required to be equivalent: one may even speak of *incompatible* descriptions of the same event!)

It might be held, however, that *properties* (as opposed to events) cannot be described by different nonequivalent descriptions. Indeed, Frege, Lewis, and Carnap have *identified* properties and 'meanings' (so that by *definition* if two expressions have different meanings then they 'signify' different properties). This seems to me very dubious. But suppose it were correct. What would follow? One would have to admit that, e.g., being in pain and having C-fibers stimulated were different properties. But, in the language of the 'theory-constructing' Turing machine described at the beginning of this paper, one would equally have to admit that 'being in state *A*' and 'having flip-flop 36 on' were different properties. Indeed the sentences (i) 'I am in state *A*' and (ii) 'Flip-flop 36 is on' are clearly non-synonymous in the machine's language by any test (they have different syntactical properties and also different 'conditions of utterance'—e.g., the machine has to use different 'methods of verification'). Anyone who wishes, then, to argue on this basis for the existence of the soul will have to be prepared to hug the souls of Turing machines to his philosophical bosom!

5. A 'LINGUISTIC' ARGUMENT

The last argument I shall consider on the subject of mind–body identity is a widely used 'linguistic' argument—it was, for example, used by Max Black against Herbert Feigl at the Conference which inspired this volume (*Dimensions of Mind*). Consider the sentence:

(1) Pain *is identical with* stimulation of C-fibers.

The sentence is deviant (so the argument runs, though not in this terminology): there is no statement that it could be used to make in a normal context. Therefore, if a philosopher advances it as a thesis

he must be giving the words a new meaning, rather than expressing any sort of discovery. For example (Max Black argued) one might begin to say 'I have stimulated C-fibers' instead of 'I have a pain', etc. But then one would *merely* be giving the expression 'has stimulated C-fibers' the new meaning 'is in pain'. The contention is that as long as the words keep their present meanings, (1) is unintelligible.

I agree that the sentence (1) is a 'deviant' sentence in present-day English. I do *not* agree that (1) can never become a normal, non-deviant sentence unless the words change their present meanings.

The point, in a nutshell, is that what is 'deviant' depends very much upon context, including the state of our knowledge, and with the development of new scientific theories it is constantly occurring that sentences that did not previously 'have a use', that were previously 'deviant', acquire a use—not because the words acquire *new* meanings, but because the old meanings as fixed by the core of stock uses, *determine* a new use given the new context.

There is nothing wrong with trying to bring linguistic theory to bear on this issue, but one must have a sufficiently sophisticated linguistic theory to bring to bear. The real question is not a question in *synchronic* linguistics but one in *diachronic*[15] linguistics, not 'Is (1) *now* a deviant sentence?' but 'If a change in scientific knowledge (e.g., the development of an integrated network of psychophysical laws of high "priority" in our overall scientific world view) were to lead to (1)'s becoming a *non*-deviant sentence, would a change in the meaning of a word necessarily have taken place?'—and this is not so simple a question.

Although this is not the time or the place to attempt the job of elaborating a semantical theory,[16] I should like to risk a few remarks on this question.

In the first place, it is easy to show that the mere uttering of a sentence which no one has ever uttered before does not necessarily constitute the introduction of a 'new use'. If I say 'There is a purple Gila monster on this desk', I am very likely uttering a sentence that no English-speaker has uttered before me: but I am not in any way changing the meaning of any word.

In the second place, even if a sentence which was formerly deviant begins to acquire a standard use, no change in the *meaning* of any word need have taken place. Thus the sentence 'I am a thousand miles away from you', or its translation into ancient Greek, was undoubtedly a deviant sentence prior to the invention of *writing,* but acquired (was not 'given' but *acquired*) a normal use with the invention of writing and the ensuing possibility of long-distance interpersonal address.

Note the reasons that we would not say that any word (e.g., 'I', 'you', 'thousand') in this sentence changed its meaning: (a) the new use was not *arbitrary,* was not the product of *stipulation,* but represented an automatic projection[17] from the existing stock uses of the several words making up the sentence, given the new context; (b) the meaning of a sentence is in general a function of the meanings of the individual words making it up. (In fact this principle underlies the whole notion of word meaning—thus, if we said that the sentence had changed its meaning, we should have to face the question '*Which word* changed its meaning?'. But this would pretty clearly be an embarrassing question in this case.)

The case just described was one in which the new context was the product of new technology, but new theoretical knowledge may have a similar impact on the language. (For example, 'he went all the way around the world' would be a deviant sentence in a culture which did not know that the earth was round!) A case of this kind was discussed by Malcolm: we are beginning to have the means available for telling, on the basis of various physiological indicators (electroencephalograms, eye movements during sleep, blood pressure disturbances, etc.), when dreams begin and end. The sentence 'He is halfway through his dream' may, therefore, someday acquire a standard use. Malcolm's comment on this was that the words would in that case have been given a use. Malcolm is clearly mistaken, I believe; this case, in which a sentence acquires a use *because* of what the words mean is poles apart from the case in which words are literally *given* a use (i.e., in which meanings are stipulated for expressions). The 'realistic' account of this case is, I think, obviously correct: the sentence did not previously have a use because we had no way of telling when dreams start and stop. Now we are beginning to have ways of telling, and so we are beginning to find occasions upon which it is natural to employ this sentence.

(Note that in Malcom's account there is no explanation of the fact that we give *this* sentence *this* use.)

Now, someone may grant that change in meaning should not be confused with change in distribution,[18] and that scientific and technological advances frequently produce changes in the latter that are not properly regarded as changes in the former. But one might argue that whereas one could have envisaged beforehand the circumstances under which the sentence 'He went all the way around the world.' would become nondeviant, one cannot now envisage any circumstances under which[19] 'Mental state ψ is identical with brain state φ.' would be nondeviant. But this is not a very good objection. In the first place, it might very well have been impossible for primitive people to envisage a spherical earth (the people on the 'underside' would obviously fall off). Even forty years ago, it might have been difficult if not impossible to envisage circumstances under which 'he is halfway through his dream' would be nondeviant. And in the second place, I believe that one *can* describe in general terms circumstances under which 'Mental state ψ is identical with brain state φ.' would become nondeviant.

In order to do this, it is necessary to talk about one important kind of 'is'—the *'is' of theoretical identification.* The use of 'is' in question is exemplified in the following sentences:

(2) Light is electromagnetic radiation (of such-and-such wavelengths).

(3) Water is H_2O.

What was involved in the scientific acceptance of, for instance, (2) was very roughly this: prior to the identification there were two distinct bodies of theory—optical theory (whose character Toulmin has very well described in his book on philosophy of science), and electromagnetic theory (as represented by Maxwell's equations). The decision to *define* light as 'electromagnetic radiation of such-and-such wavelengths' was scientifically justified by the following sorts of considerations (as has often been pointed out):

(1) It made possible the *derivation* of the laws of optics (up to first approximation) from more 'basic' physical laws. Thus, even if it had accomplished nothing else, this theoretical identification would have been

a move towards simplifying the structure of scientific laws.

(2) It made possible the derivation of *new* predictions in the 'reduced' discipline (i.e., optics). In particular, it was now possible to predict that in certain cases the laws of geometrical optics would *not* hold. (Cf. Duhem's famous comments on the reduction of Kepler's laws to Newton's.)

Now let us try to envisage the circumstances under which a theoretical identification of mental states with physiological states might be in accordance with good scientific procedure. In general terms, what is necessary is that we should have not *mere* 'correlates' for subjective states, but something much more elaborate—e.g., that we should know of physical states (say micro-states of the central processes) on the basis of which we could not merely *predict* human behaviour, but causally explain it.

In order to avoid 'category mistakes', it is necessary to restrict this notion, 'explain human behavior', very carefully. Suppose a man says 'I feel bad'. His behavior, described in one set of categories, is: 'stating that he feels bad'. And the explanation may be 'He said that he felt bad because he was hungry and had a headache'. I do not wish to suggest that the event 'Jones *stating* that he feels bad' can be explained in terms of the laws of *physics*. But there is *another* event which is very relevant, namely 'Jones's body producing such-and-such sound waves'. From one point of view this is a 'different event' from Jones's stating that he feels bad. But (to adapt a remark of Hanson's) there would be no point in remarking that these are different events if there were not a sense in which they were the *same* event. And it is the sense in which these are the 'same event' and not the sense in which these are 'different events' that is relevant here.

In fine, all I mean when I speak of 'causally explaining human behavior' is: causally explaining certain physical events (motions of bodies, productions of sound waves, etc.) which are in the sense just referred to the 'same' as the events which make up human behavior. And no amount of 'Ryle-ism' can succeed in arguing away[20] what is obviously a possibility: that physical science might succeed in doing this much.

If this much were a reality, then theoretically identifying 'mental states' with their 'correlates' would have the following two advantages:

(1) It would be possible (again up to 'first approximation') to derive from physical theory the classical laws (or low-level generalizations) of common-sense 'mentalistic' psychology, such as: 'People tend to avoid things with which they have had painful experiences'.

(2) It would be possible to predict the cases (and they are legion) in which common-sense 'mentalistic' psychology fails.

Advantage (2) could, of course, be obtained without 'identification' (by using correlation laws). But advantage (2) could equally have been obtained in the case of optics without identification (by assuming that light *accompanies* electromagnetic radiation, but is not *identical* with it.) But the *combined* effect of eliminating certain laws altogether (in favor of theoretical definitions) *and* increasing the explanatory power of the theory could not be obtained in any other way in either case. The point worth noticing is that *every* argument for *and against* identification would apply equally in the mind–body case and in the light-electromagnetism case. (Even the 'ordinary language' argument could have been advanced against the identification of light with electromagnetic radiation.)

Two small points: (i) When I call 'light is electromagnetic radiation (of such-and-such wavelengths)' a definition, I do not mean that the statement is 'analytic'. But then 'definitions', *properly so called,* in theoretical science virtually *never* are analytic. (Quine remarked once that he could think of at least nine good senses of 'definition' none of which had anything to do with analyticity.) Of course a philosopher might then object to the whole *rationale* of theoretical identification on the ground that it is no gain to eliminate 'laws' in favor of 'definitions' if both are *synthetic* statements. The fact that the scientist does not feel at all the same way is another illustration of how unhelpful it is to look at science from the standpoint of the question 'Analytic or synthetic?' (ii) Accepting a theoretical identification, e.g., 'Pain *is* stimulation of C-fibers', does not commit one to *interchanging* the terms 'pain' and 'stimulation of C-fibers' in idiomatic talk, as Black suggested. For instance, the identification of 'water' with 'H_2O' is by now a very well-known one, but no one says 'Bring me a glass of H_2O', except as a joke.

I believe that the account just presented is able (a) to explain the fact that sentences such as 'Mental state ψ is identical with brain state φ.' are deviant in present-day English, while (b) making it clear how these same sentences might become *non* deviant given a suitable increase in our scientific insight into the physical nature and causes of human behavior. The sentences in question cannot today be used to express a theoretical identification, because no such identification has been made. The act of theoretical identification is not an act that can be performed 'at will'; there are *preconditions* for its performance, as there are for many acts, and these preconditions are not satisfied today. On the other hand, if the sort of scientific theory described above should materialize, then the preconditions for theoretical identification would be met, as they were met in the light-electromagnetism case, and sentences of the type in question would then *automatically* require a use—namely, to express the appropriate theoretical identifications. Once again, what makes this way of *acquiring* a use different from being *given* a use (and from 'change of meaning' properly so called) is that the 'new use' is an automatic *projection* from existing uses, and does not involve arbitrary stipulation (except insofar as some element of 'stipulation' may be present in the acceptance of *any* scientific hypothesis, including 'The earth is round.').

So far we have considered only sentences of the form[21] 'Mental state ψ is identical with brain state φ.'. But what of the sentence:

(3) Mental states are micro-states of the brain.

This sentence does not, so to speak, 'give' any *particular* theoretical identification: it only says that unspecified theoretical identifications are possible. This is the sort of assertion that Feigl might make. And Black[22] might reply that in uttering (3) Feigl had uttered an odd set of words (i.e., a deviant sentence). It is possible that Black is right. Perhaps (3) is deviant in present-day English. But it is also possible that our descendants in two or three hundred years will feel that Feigl was making perfectly good sense and that the linguistic objections to (3) were quite silly. And they too may be right.

6. MACHINE LINGUISTICS

Let us consider the linguistic question that we have just discussed from the standpoint of the analogy between man and Turing machine that we have been presenting in this paper. It will be seen that our Turing machine will probably not be able, if it lacks suitable 'sense organs', to construct a correct theory of its own constitution. On the other hand 'I am in state A.' will be a sentence with a definite pattern of occurrence in the machine's 'language'. If the machine's 'language' is sufficiently complex, it may be possible to analyze it syntactically in terms of a finite set of basic building blocks (morphemes) and rules for constructing a potentially infinite set of 'sentences' from these. In particular, it will be possible to distinguish *grammatical*[23] from *ungrammatical sentences* in the machine's 'language'. Similarly, it may be possible to associate regularities with sentence occurrences (or, 'describe sentence uses', in the Oxford jargon), and to assign 'meanings' to the finite set of morphemes and the finite set of forms of composition, in such a way that the 'uses' of the various sentences can be effectively projected from the meanings of the individual morphemes and forms of composition. In this case, one could distinguish not only 'grammatical' and 'ungrammatical' sentences in the 'machine language', but also 'deviant' and 'non-deviant' ones.

Chisholm would insist that it is improper to speak of machines as employing a language, and I agree. This is the reason for my occasionally enclosing the words 'language', 'meaning', etc., in 'raised-eyebrow' quotes—to emphasize, where necessary, that these words are being used in an extended sense. On the other hand, it is important to recognize that machine performances may be wholly *analogous* to language, so much so that the whole of linguistic theory can be applied to them. If the reader wishes to check this, he may go through a work like Chomsky's *Syntactic Structures* carefully, and note that *at no place is the assumption employed that the corpus of utterances studied by the linguist was produced by a conscious organism.* Then he may turn to such pioneer work in empirical semantics as Ziff's *Semantical Analysis* and observe that the same thing holds true for *semantical* theory.

Two further remarks in this connection: (i) Since I am contending that the mind–body problem is *strictly analogous* to the problem of the relation between structural and logical states, not that the two problems are *identical,* a suitable *analogy* between machine 'language' and human language is all that is needed here. (ii) Chisholm might contend that a 'behavioristic' semantics of the kind attempted by Ziff (i.e., one that does not take 'intentionality' as a primitive notion) is impossible. But even if this were true, it would not be relevant. For if *any* semantical theory can fit human language, it has to be shown why a completely *analogous* theory would not fit the language of a suitable machine. For instance, if 'intentionality' plays a role as a primitive notion in a *scientific* explanation of human language, then a theoretical construct with similar *formal* relations to the corresponding 'observables' will have the *same* explanatory power in the case of machine 'language'.

Of course, the objection to 'behavioristic' linguistics might *really* be an objection to all attempts at *scientific* linguistics. But this possibility I feel justified in dismissing.

Now suppose we equip our 'theory-constructing' Turing machine with 'sense organs' so that it can obtain the empirical data necessary for the construction of a theory of its own nature.

Then it may introduce into its 'theoretical language' noun phrases that can be 'translated' by the English expression 'flip-flop 36', and sentences that can be translated by 'Flip-flop 36 is on'. These expressions 'will have a meaning and use quite distinct from the meaning and use of 'I am in state *A*.' in the machine language.

If any 'linguistic' argument really shows that the sentence 'Pain is identical with stimulation of C-fibers.' is deviant, in English, the same argument must show that 'State *A* is identical with flip-flop 36 being on' is deviant in the machine language. If any argument shows that 'Pain is identical with stimulation of C-fibers.' could not become nondeviant (viewing English now *dia*chronically) unless the words first altered their meanings, the same

argument, applied to the 'diachronic linguistics of machine language', would show that the sentence 'State *A* is identical with flip-flop 36 being on.' could not become non-deviant in machine language unless the words first changed their meanings. In short, every philosophic argument that has ever been employed in connection with the mind–body problem, from the oldest and most naive (e.g., 'states of consciousness can just be *seen* to be different from physical states') to the most sophisticated, has its exact counterpart in the case of the 'problem' of logical states and structural states in Turing machines.

7. CONCLUSION

The moral, I believe, is quite clear: it is no longer possible to believe that the mind–body problem is a genuine theoretical problem, or that a 'solution' to it would shed the slightest light on the world in which we live. For it is quite clear that no grown man in his right mind would take the problem of the 'identity' or 'non-identity' of logical and structural states in a machine at all seriously—not because the answer is obvious, but because it is obviously of no importance *what* the answer is. But if the so-called 'mind–body problem' is nothing but a different realization of the same set of logical and linguistic issues, then it must be just as empty and just as verbal.

It is often an important insight that two problems with distinct subject matter are the same in all their logical and methodological aspects. In this case, the insight carries in its train the realization that any conclusion that might be reached in the case of the mind–body problem would have to be reached, *and for the same reasons,* in the Turing machine case. But if it is clear (as it obviously is) that, for example, the conclusion that the logical states of Turing machines are hopelessly different from their structural states, even if correct, could represent only a purely *verbal* discovery, then the same conclusion *reached by the same arguments* in the human case must likewise represent a purely verbal discovery. To put it differently, if the mind–body problem is identified with any problem of more than purely conceptual interest (e.g., with the question of whether or not human beings have 'souls') then *either* it must be that (a) no argument *ever* used by a philosopher sheds the *slightest* light on it (and this independently of the way the argument tends), or (b) that some philosophic argument for mechanism is correct, or (c) that some dualistic argument does show that *both* human beings *and* Turing machines have souls! I leave it to the reader to decide which of the three alternatives is at all plausible.

NOTES

1. By a 'deviant' utterance is here meant one that deviates from a semantic regularity (in the appropriate natural language). The term is taken from Ziff, 1960.

2. Cf. Curnap 1953 and 1956. This model of a scientific theory is too oversimplified to be of much general utility, in my opinion: however, the oversimplifications do not affect the present argument.

3. This point was made by Quine in Quine, 1957.

4. Cf. Ziff's paper (1959) and the reply (1959) by Smart. Ziff has informed me that by a 'robot' he did not have in mind a 'learning machine' of the kind envisaged by Smart, and he would agree that the considerations brought forward in his paper would not necessarily apply to such a machine (if it can properly be classed as a 'machine' at all). On the question of whether 'this machine thinks (feels, etc.)' is *deviant* or not, it is necessary to keep in mind both the point raised by Ziff (that the important question is not whether or not the utterance is deviant, but whether or not it is deviant for non-trivial reasons), and also the 'diachronic–synchronic' distinction discussed in section 5 of the present paper.

5. In particular, I am sympathetic with the general standpoint taken by Smart in (1959b) and (1959c). However, see the linguistic considerations in section 5.

6. For further details, cf. Davis, 1958 and Kleene, 1952.

7. This terminology is taken from Kleene, 1952, and differs from that of Davis and Turing.

8. This generalization is made in Davis, 1958, where it is employed in defining relative recursiveness.

9. This statement is a form of *Church's thesis* (that recursiveness equals effective computability).

10. Here it is necessary to suppose that the entire sentence 'I am in state *A*.' counts as a single symbol in the machine's alphabet.

11. For example, I know that the sun is 93 million miles from the earth, but I have no *evidence* that this is so. In fact, I do not even remember where I learned this.

12. In fact, it would be impossible to decide whether 'Jones knows he has a pain' is deviant or not without first reformulating the evidential condition so as to avoid the objection in note 11 (if it can be reformulated so as to save anything of the condition at all). However the discussion above will indicate, I believe, why one might *want* to find that this sentence is deviant.

13. Actually, it was not necessary to add any 'sense organs'; existing computers check themselves by 'performing crucial experiments with themselves' (i.e., carrying out certain test computations and comparing the results with the correct results which have been given).

14. In the sense of Oppenheim [and Putnam], 1958; not in the 'epistemological' sense associated with Carnap's writing on 'physicalism'.

15. Diachronic linguistics studies the language as it changes through time; synchronic linguistic seeks only to describe the language at one particular time.

16. For a detailed discussion, cf. Ziff, 1960. I am extremely indebted to Ziff, both for making this work available to me and for personal communications on these matters. Section 5 of the present paper represents partly Ziff's influence (especially the use of the 'synchronic-diachronic' distinction), and partly the application of some of the ideas in this volume to the present topic.

17. The term is taken from Ziff, 1960.

18. The *distribution* of a word = the set of sentences in which it occurs.

19. Here 'Mental state ψ is identical with brain state φ.' is used as a surrogate for such sentences as 'Pain is identical with stimulation of C-fibers.'

20. As one young philosopher attempted to do in a recent article in the *British Journal for the Philosophy of Science*.

21. By sentences of this *form* I do not literally mean *substitution instances* of 'mental state ψ is identical with brain state φ.' Cf. note 19.

22. I have, with hesitation, ascribed this position to Black on the basis of his remarks at the Conference. But, of course, I realize that he cannot justly be held responsible for remarks made on the spur of the moment.

23. This term is used in the sense of Chomsky, 1957, not in the traditional sense.

REFERENCES

Carnap, Rudolf. 1953. "The Interpretation of Physics." In *Readings in the Philosophy of Science*, edited by H. Feigl and M. Brodbeck. New York: Appleton-Century-Crofts, 309–18.

———. 1956. "The Methodological Character of Theoretical Concepts." In *Minnesota Studies in the Philosophy of Science*, edited by H. Feigl and M. Scriven. Minneapolis: University of Minnesota Press, 38–76.

Chomsky, Noam. 1957. *Syntactic Structures*. The Hague: Mouton.

Davis, Martin. 1958. *Computability and Unsolvability.* New York: McGraw-Hill.

Hanson, Norwood. 1958. *Patterns of Discovery.* Cambridge: Cambridge University Press.

Kleene, Stephen C. 1952. *Introduction to Metamathematics.* New York: Wolters-Noordhoff.

Oppenheim, Paul, and Hilary Putnam. 1958. "Unity of Science as a Working Hypothesis." In *Minnesota Studies in the Philosophy of Science.* Minneapolis: University of Minnesota Press.

Quine, W. V. 1957. "The Scope and Language of Science." *British Journal for the Philosophy of Science* 8: 1–17.

Smart, J. J. C. 1959a. "Incompatible Colors." *Philosophical Studies* 10: 39–42.

———. 1959b. "Professor Ziff on Robots." *Analysis* 19: 117–18.

———. 1959c. "Sensations and Brain Processes." *Philosophical Review* 48: 141–56.

Turing, Alan M. 1950. "Computing Machinery and Intelligence." This volume, 267–283.

Ziff, Paul. 1959. "The Feelings of Robots." *Analysis* 19: 64–68.

———. 1960. *Semantic Analysis.* Ithaca, NY. Cornell University Press.

Part V

Ethics

MICHAEL J. ZIMMERMAN

Michael J. Zimmerman is associate professor of philosophy at the University of North Carolina at Greensboro. He has published extensively in theoretical ethics, and his books include *The Concept of Moral Obligation* (1996) and *An Essay on Moral Responsibility* (1988).

A History of Early Analytic Ethics

THE HISTORY OF EARLY ANALYTIC ETHICS may fruitfully be seen as having two main parts: the presentation and defense by G. E. Moore of his own views on ethics and the critical reactions of others to these views, leading to the development of alternative views. Undoubtedly the most important of Moore's ethical works was *Principia Ethica*, published in 1903. Remarking that the main causes of difficulties and disagreements in ethics, as in all other areas of philosophical inquiry, was that philosophers had failed to make clear just what questions they were asking before they went on to try to answer these questions, in *Principia* Moore self-consciously started from scratch, attempting first to pose and then to answer questions about ethics as if no one had done so before, and taking just as much time and care over the former task as over the latter.

This is not to say that Moore paid no attention to his predecessors; on the contrary, he took into account the ethical views of Plato, Aristotle, Bishop Joseph Butler, Immanuel Kant, Jeremy Bentham, John Stuart Mill, and Henry Sidgwick, among others. But almost always he did so in order not to build on these philosophers' views but to criticize them. The one person by whom Moore himself claimed to be most influenced in his philosophical career was his contemporary, Bertrand Russell, but Russell's early writings on ethics were in fact preceded by, and owed a great deal to, Moore's *Principia*. It is almost no exaggeration, therefore, to say that analytic ethics was born in 1903. Moore certainly regarded himself as a pioneer in the field, and although there were precursors to Moore (most notably Sidgwick) who in their ethical writings exhibited the same circumspection as that displayed by Moore and by whom Moore was certainly influenced, it was with the

---

This essay was commissioned especially for this volume and appears here for the first time.

appearance of *Principia* that this approach to ethics took a firm hold on the imagination of those engaged in ethical philosophy.

Moore's Views

Many themes run through Moore's ethical works. The major ones are these: (1) The fundamental ethical concept is that of intrinsic value. (2) This concept is unanalyzable. (3) The intrinsic value of something is a nonnatural property of that thing. (4) The concepts of moral rightness, wrongness, and obligatoriness are to be accounted for in terms of the concept of intrinsic value. (5) Moral judgments are objective. Each of these requires some clarification. (Other somewhat less important themes in Moore's works, not to be discussed here, include: his employment of the so-called isolation method for assessing intrinsic value; his thesis that the intrinsic value of a whole need not be the same as the sum of the intrinsic values of its parts; his rejection of hedonism; and his rejection of ethical egoism.)

1. It is certainly the business of ethics, Moore concedes (in the first paragraph of chapter 1 of *Principia*, reproduced in part in this volume, pp. 314–323), to address such issues as whether someone is a saint or a villain, whether an act is right or wrong, whether certain characteristics are virtuous or vicious. At the heart of these issues, he claims, lies the question whether certain conduct would be good or bad. But to answer this question we must answer the prior question of what goodness and badness are in general. It is with this question that ethics is primarily concerned.

There are various types of goodness and badness. The most fundamental, according to Moore, are intrinsic goodness and badness. To explain what is meant here, it would be helpful if one were to give a definition of "intrinsically good" and "intrinsically bad," that is, an analysis of the concepts expressed by these terms. But this is something Moore denies to be possible (for reasons to be discussed shortly), and he doesn't do much to aid the reader in understanding just what intrinsic goodness and badness consist in. It may help, therefore, to supplement his discussion with a simple illustration.

Pain is usually taken to be a bad thing. This doesn't mean that it cannot on occasion prove useful. It may, for instance, alert someone to an injury that would otherwise go unnoticed, or it may teach someone a lesson that would otherwise go unlearned. In this way pain can have good consequences and thus can properly be called good "as a means," that is, good in virtue of these consequences. But that doesn't detract from the fact that pain seems bad "in itself"; all else being equal, it would surely be preferable if the injury were avoided, or the lesson learned, by nonpainful means. Even if on occasion it is good for the sake of its consequences, then, pain always seems to be bad for its own sake. This is what's meant by saying that it is intrinsically bad.

In like fashion, pleasure might be declared intrinsically good. Even if on occasion pleasure has bad consequences and so may be said to be bad as a means, it apparently has the saving grace of always being something that is desirable for its own sake. In *Principia* Moore endorses the view that pleasure is intrinsically good and pain intrinsically bad, although he claims that other things (knowledge, beauty, and certain kinds of virtue; ignorance, ugliness, and certain kinds of vice) also have intrinsic value.

The reason that Moore regards the concept of intrinsic value as fundamental is this: something's being valuable as a means is to be understood in terms of something else's being intrinsically valuable. What is valuable as a means is valuable precisely because it has consequences that are valuable in themselves. It derives its value as a means from the intrinsic values of these consequences.

2. In light of the foregoing, Moore declares the question how to define "(intrinsically) good" and "(intrinsically) bad" to be "the most fundamental question in all Ethics." Given this statement, it comes somewhat as a disappointment (as Moore himself acknowledges) to discover that he declares them indefinable. In so doing, he is reacting to such claims as that something's being intrinsically good is the same thing as its being pleasant, and that something's being intrinsically good is the same thing as its being desired for its own sake. He is famous for an argument he gives against all such claims, one that has come to be called the Open Question argument. It is essentially this. Consider any proposed analysis of intrinsic goodness in terms of some property F-ness (e.g., pleasantness). The question whether whatever is F is intrinsically good will always be an open one (that is, it will always be one whose answer is in principle open to doubt, in that understanding the question doesn't itself suffice for knowing that it is to be answered affirmatively), whereas the question whether whatever is intrinsically good is intrinsically good is not an open question. Hence the proposed analysis is to be rejected.

3. Moore is even more famous for his claim that many ethical philosophers have committed what he calls the "naturalistic fallacy." His treatment of this issue is not straightforward, primarily because he appears to have several different things in mind when talking of "the" naturalistic fallacy. At times he seems to mean simply the alleged mistake, just discussed, of attempting to analyze the concept of intrinsic value. But other passages in the reading suggest the alleged mistakes of (a) identifying intrinsic value with something else; (b) confusing the *is* of predication (as in "That man is frank") with the *is* of identity (as in "That man is Frank"), and (c) attempting to analyze the concept of intrinsic value entirely in terms of natural properties or relations. (Other passages in other chapters of *Principia* suggest still other alleged mistakes, some of which are pointed out by William Frankena in his contribution, pp. 343–350.) The first two, (a) and (b), are of course genuine, and not merely alleged, mistakes. Clearly the third, (c), is also a genuine mistake, if the concept of intrinsic value is not analyzable at all. But suppose that Moore is mistaken, and that it is analyzable after all. He could still be correct in saying that it isn't analyzable entirely in terms of natural properties or relations. Whether this would be correct depends, of course, on just what a "natural" property or relation is supposed to be. Moore never settled on a definitive answer to this question, but the idea is roughly this. A natural object is one that exists in time and, perhaps, space, and a natural property or relation is the sort of property or relation, exemplified by a natural object, that is subject to the type of empirical investigation that scientists undertake. Moore's view is that intrinsic value is not subject to such investigation. At times, he supports this view with the following observation: one can give a "full description" of something that is intrinsically good without mentioning its being intrinsically good, for its being so will always "supervene" (as philosophers nowadays say)—that is, depend—on other properties that it has; and to confuse intrinsic goodness with any property or set of properties on which it supervenes would be a mistake.

4. When it comes to accounting for the concepts of moral rightness, wrongness, and obligatoriness, Moore is what has come to be called a "consequentialist." This is not because he thinks that whether an act is morally right (or wrong, or obligatory) depends on its consequences, for almost everyone accepts this. It is because he thinks that whether an act is morally right depends *only* on its consequences (and on those of its alternatives).

Moore embraces consequentialism in parts of *Principia* not reproduced below, but he develops and defends it most fully in another book, *Ethics*, published in 1912. The basic idea is this. Whether an act is morally right (or wrong, or obligatory) depends on two things: what intrinsic value would be introduced into the world if it were performed, and what intrinsic value would be introduced into the world if some other act were performed instead. The consequentialist claims that an act is morally right just in case there is no alternative to it that would produce a more favorable balance of intrinsic goodness over intrinsic badness than it, and morally wrong otherwise; an act is morally obligatory just in case it is the only alternative that is morally right.

5. Also in *Ethics,* Moore provides many arguments for the view that moral judgments are objective. (Several of these arguments rely on the claims that an act cannot be both morally right and morally wrong and that genuine moral disagreements are possible.) A number of things might be meant by saying that moral judgments are "objective." Moore never provides an explicit definition of the term, but it's clear that he has at least two things in mind: (a) all moral judgments express propositions that are either true or false; (b) no such judgment implies or is implied by a judgment that expresses someone's (or some group's) attitude towards something. The first point opens up the possibility, at least in principle, of ethical knowledge. The second implies that any such claim as that an act is morally right if someone has a certain feeling toward it, or that an act is morally wrong only if someone believes it so, is to be rejected.

As to whether we ever actually possess ethical knowledge, Moore gives a twofold answer. He believes that we can and do know certain propositions concerning intrinsic value (such as that pain is intrinsically bad and pleasure intrinsically good) to be true. Such knowledge, he says, is "intuitive," in the sense that it is not derived from the knowledge of any other propositions. Moore also believes that we can never know for certain whether our acts are morally right (or wrong, or obligatory). This is because such knowledge would require full knowledge of all the consequences, and of the intrinsic values of these consequences, of our acts and their alternatives. We are never so fortunately situated as to possess such knowledge. This doesn't mean, however, that we cannot ever make more or less well-informed judgments about the moral rightness of our acts.

Critical Reactions to Moore's Views

None of the five major themes identified here as running through Moore's ethical works has gone unchallenged. Since these themes are interrelated, a challenge to one often constitutes a challenge to some other or others.

1. Although all Moore's early critics acknowledged the importance of the concept of intrinsic value, many denied that it is the fundamental ethical concept. Usually this was because they regarded the concepts of moral rightness, wrongness, and obligatoriness as being partly or wholly independent of the concept of intrinsic value. We shall return to this issue later when the fourth theme is discussed.

2. The claim that the concept of intrinsic value is unanalyzable has been challenged by many. In his contribution to this volume (pp. 343–350), W. K. Frankena points out that it cannot be assumed without argument that "intrinsically good" is indefinable. But of course Moore did not do this, since he did provide an argument—the Open Question argument. Although Frankena doesn't address this argument explicitly, others have done so, and they have pointed out, quite correctly, that it doesn't succeed in establishing the unanalyzability of the concept of intrinsic value. This is because it simply assumes that, no matter what property F-ness is at issue, the question whether whatever is F is intrinsically good is an open one. But what warrants this assumption? Even if we agree that, in those cases discussed by Moore where F is substituted by "pleasant" or "desired (in some way)," the question whether whatever is F is intrinsically good is an open one, clearly this doesn't justify the

claim that this is so for any substitution for *F* whatsoever. Recognizing this fact, A. C. Ewing wrote an entire book on this issue, *The Definition of Good* (1948), maintaining (in a manner reminiscent of Franz Brentano, C. D. Broad, and W. D. Ross, among others) that for something to be good is for it to be the fitting object of a favorable attitude. In light of the fact that what is good is often referred to as being "valuable," "desirable," and the like (i.e., worthy of being valued or desired), this seems a sensible suggestion.

Moore could agree that whatever is good is valuable (or desirable), and vice versa, without conceding that the concept of goodness is to be analyzed in terms of the concepts of worthiness and value (or desire). As Ross and others have pointed out, the analysis would apparently fail if something is worthy of being valued *because* it is good (and not good because it is worthy of being valued). Such an asymmetry would seem to point to a priority of the concept of goodness over the other concepts that would be incompatible with analyzing the former in terms of the latter.

Another question that can be raised in connection with the Open Question argument is this. It relies on the assumption that, if the question whether whatever is *F* is intrinsically good is an open one, then the concept of intrinsic goodness cannot be analyzed in terms of *F*-ness. But should this assumption be accepted? Compare the questions "Is whatever is a brother a male sibling?" and "Is whatever is a brother a brother?" The latter is obviously not an open question, but should we say the same of the former? Might not someone who understands the concepts of being a brother, being a male, and being a sibling reasonably hesitate to answer the former question affirmatively? The answer to this question is controversial, and yet the claim that the concept of being a brother is to be analyzed in terms of the concepts of being a male and being a sibling seems beyond reproach. (This has to do with the so-called "paradox of analysis," with which Moore wrestled throughout his philosophical career.)

3. Although Moore would of course reject the claim that the concept of intrinsic goodness can be analyzed in terms of the concepts of worthiness and value (or desire), he would not do so for the reason that the analysis is given entirely in terms of natural properties or relations. (For worthiness is a value concept, and Moore would therefore say that the property of being worthy of being valued (or desired) is nonnatural.) But he would reject the sort of analysis proposed by R. B. Perry in his *General Theory of Value* (1926) for this reason. Perry suggests that "*x* is good" is to be understood to mean the same as "*x* is the object of some interest." Moore would say that such a reduction of the ethical to the natural commits (one version of) the naturalistic fallacy. But this presupposes that ethical properties and relations are not subject to the type of empirical investigation that scientists undertake. Why accept this presupposition? The appeal to supervenience here is insufficient to motivate it, for not every supervening property is a nonnatural property. (Many philosophers contend that mental properties supervene on physical ones, although both types of properties are natural.) Moore simply assumes that ethical properties and relations are not subject to scientific investigation. But, as Frankena points out, this would seem simply to beg the question that divides Moore and others, such as Perry, who contend that ethical properties and relations are indeed subject to such investigation. Moore might accuse his opponents of a certain sort of moral blindness, failing to distinguish one kind of property or relation from another; but they could simply retort that he is suffering from a certain sort of moral hallucination, seeing two kinds of property or relation when in reality there is only one.

There is a third alternative that some philosophers have chosen. This is to agree with Moore when he says that intrinsic goodness is not a natural property (or relation) but to disagree with him when he says that it is a nonnatural property. They deny that there is any property (or relation) of intrinsic goodness at all, although they accept that it none-theless makes sense to say that something is intrinsically good. This alternative will be dis-cussed further below, when the objectivity of moral judgments is addressed.

4. Consequentialism has had many critics, even among those who accept that moral judgments are objective. Moore deems it unassailable, but others have not hesitated to at-tack it.

One of Moore's earliest critics was H. A. Prichard (although, in his contribution to this volume, pp. 324–333, Prichard doesn't mention Moore by name; he simply discusses "Util-itarianism in the generic sense," i.e., consequentialism). Prichard holds that consequen-tialism implicitly relies on the claim that what is intrinsically good ought to be, and he says that this claim is nonsensical, except in the case of good actions; for "ought," he contends, strictly applies only to actions. He maintains, moreover, that we simply do not think that we ought to do some action (such as paying a debt or telling the truth) because doing so will have the intrinsically best consequences possible under the circumstances. Rather, our appre-hension of the obligatoriness of a certain action is immediate, having to do with our appreci-ating that it will have consequences of a certain particular kind, rather than with our assessing all its consequences together with all the consequences of all its alternatives.

This sort of criticism was taken up by W. D. Ross in his influential book *The Right and the Good* (1930). Ross agrees with Prichard that our common moral sense is decidedly nonconsequentialist in character, but he is not as harsh a critic of consequentialism as Prichard, for he allows that whether an act will be "optimific" (that is, whether it will have the intrinsically best consequences possible under the circumstances) is relevant to whether it is morally right. He claims, however, that other matters are relevant also. In particular, Ross maintains that we all have certain "*prima facie* duties," as he calls them, which sup-plement and, on occasion, compete with the *prima facie* duty of optimificity. (Among such *prima facie* duties are those of fulfilling our commitments, making up for past wrong-doing, and the like.) What we ought on balance to do on any particular occasion will be, Ross contends, a matter of which of the various *prima facie* duties that may pertain to our situation is the most stringent, and it may well be that this is not the duty of optimificity.

Other philosophers have displayed an even greater affinity to the underlying theme of consequentialism than Ross, and yet they have not accepted the sort of unqualified con-sequentialism laid out by Moore. Often the term *rule consequentialism* is used to refer to their view. The contribution by John Rawls on pp. 351–363 is an example of this approach. Rawls believes that a direct appeal to the criterion of optimificity when trying to deter-mine whether an act would be morally justified can lead to grave wrongdoing. It may be, for instance, that in a particular case it would be optimific if one were to punish an inno-cent person or to break a solemn promise, but, Rawls says, this wouldn't justify acting in such a way. This is because acting in such a way would violate certain rules, or practices, that are themselves justified. However, the justification of these rules *is* to be made by an appeal to the criterion of optimificity. A rule is justified when general adherence to it would be optimific; acts are justified if they fall under a justified rule.

This sort of two-tiered consequentialism has had its own critics too, of course. One is J. J. C. Smart. In his contribution to this volume on pp. 363–370, Smart poses a dilemma for the rule consequentialist (whom he calls a "restricted utilitarian"). Either it is the case that the rule that we are to act optimifically is one that the rule consequentialist will rec-ognize as being both universally applicable and uniquely justified, or this is not the case. If it is the case, then rule consequentialism collapses into the sort of unqualified consequentialism (which Smart calls "extreme utilitarianism") advocated by Moore, in that whatever act is morally justified according to one theory will be morally justified according to the other; but then, of course, rule consequentialism constitutes no genuine departure from and improvement on Moore's theory after all. If it is not the case, then rule consequentialism is committed to something that Smart maintains is "monstrous," namely, that in some situations it is morally obligatory to abide strictly by a rule when it is known that doing so will produce consequences intrinsically worse than those that would be produced by violating the rule. In calling this monstrous, Smart is endorsing a remark made by Moore in chapter 5 of *Ethics:* "It seems to me to be self-evident that knowingly to do an action which would make the world, on the whole, really and truly *worse* than if we had acted differently, must always be wrong."

The critics of consequentialism discussed so far all concede that an appeal to consequences always has some relevance to whether one's act is morally justified. It is only somewhat more recently in the history of analytic ethics that there has been an upsurge among philosophers who have contended, in a manner reminiscent of Immanuel Kant in the eighteenth century, that sometimes consequences have no relevance at all. These philosophers usually express their view in terms of the concept of a right. Rights, they maintain, sometimes block all appeal to consequences. On such occasions, if the best consequences can be obtained only by means of violating someone's rights, acting so as to produce these consequences is not morally justified. Consequentialists, such as Moore and Smart, find such an inflexible, "absolutist" adherence to moral rules incredible. Absolutists, however, find consequentialism shocking, believing that it neglects the sanctity of the individual person.

5. It certainly looks as if to say that something is intrinsically good is to ascribe some property to it. But surface grammar is not always a reliable indicator of what is really at issue. To say that someone is married is best understood, not in terms of his or her having a certain property, but rather in terms of his or her bearing some relation to someone else. And sometimes the primary purpose of saying that x is F may be not to ascribe any property or relation to x but something else entirely.

Consider the sentence "That knife is sharp." Imagine its being uttered, first, by a mother to her child; second, by a salesman to a customer; and third, by a butcher to his assistant. The primary purpose of uttering this sentence might well be not to inform the listener of some property of the knife (for the speaker may know that the listener is already perfectly aware that the knife is sharp), but rather to urge him, first, not to touch it; second, to buy it; and third, to use it. In such cases the sentence, despite its grammatical form, would be used primarily to do something other than assert that something is the case.

Many philosophers have contended that consequentialists (and certain nonconsequentialists, too) have been misled by grammar in claiming such sentences as "Pleasure is intrinsically good" and "Theft is morally wrong" to be declarative. One of the first and most forceful of such critics of consequentialism was A. J. Ayer, who in his iconoclastic book *Language, Truth and Logic* (1936), claimed that all such sentences are to be understood as expressions of emotion coupled with an exhortation that the listener share in this emotion. Thus, according to this so-called "emotivist" theory, to say "Pleasure is intrinsically good" is really to say something like "Pleasure! Great! Please like it, too!" According to this view, such an ethical sentence performs no descriptive function at all. Charles Stevenson, in his contribution to this volume, suggests something very similar. In his view, to say "Pleasure is intrinsically good" is to say something that is indeed partly descriptive (captured roughly by "I like pleasure"), but also, and more important, partly dynamic (captured roughly by "Do so as well").

Emotivists clearly differ with Moore on whether an act can be both morally right and morally wrong and whether genuine moral disagreements are possible (although both Ayer and Stevenson claim that they can go some way to accepting what Moore says about these matters). Their approach to ethics has come to be called "noncognitivist." (Ayer's theory is purely noncognitivist, Stevenson's primarily so.) This term captures the idea that ethical sentences do not express propositions that are either true or false but rather perform some other function. Thus noncognitivists reject the claim that moral judgments are "objective," in at least one sense of this term. (In a reply to his critics published almost forty years after *Principia*, Moore says that he has some inclination to accept this view, but also still some inclination to accept his earlier view that ethical sentences indeed express propositions.)

Not all noncognitivists are emotivists. Emotivism has been criticized as being unable to account adequately for the role that reasons play in the formation and support of moral judgments. One philosopher who pressed this criticism was R. M. Hare. In his groundbreaking book *The Language of Morals* (1952), Hare rejects emotivism in favor of "prescriptivism," a noncognitive theory according to which moral judgments are disguised prescriptions for action. As developed by Hare, this theory stresses the reasonableness of moral judgments, despite the fact that the deep grammar of the sentences involved shows them to be imperative rather than declarative.

In tying moral judgments to expressions of emotion, emotivists deny that moral judgments are "objective" not only in the sense just mentioned, but also in the sense having to do with whether such judgments are to be understood as concerning someone's (or some group's) attitude toward something. Not all noncognitivists agree. Hare's theory, for instance, does not commit him to the view that moral judgments concern personal attitudes. Moreover, some cognitivists, such as Perry, clearly take moral judgments to concern such attitudes.

In denying that moral judgments are objective in the first sense, that is, in the sense that they express propositions that are either true or false, noncognitivists are committed to the view that there is no genuine ethical knowledge. Cognitivists, on the contrary, are committed to the claim that such knowledge is in principle possible, given sufficient evidence of the truth of the propositions in question. But they differ markedly regarding the conditions of such knowledge. Naturalists naturally claim that ethical knowledge is no different in kind from other types of empirical knowledge. Opponents of naturalism claim that ethical knowledge is quite different from empirical knowledge, consisting at bottom in the intuition of propositions that are to some degree self-evident. But there are various accounts of how this is so. Moore, as we have seen, claims that knowledge of propositions about intrinsic value is intuitive, whereas knowledge of what it would be morally right or wrong to do in a particular case is unachievable. Prichard disagrees, claiming that knowledge of what it would be morally right or wrong to do in a particular case is both achievable by and intuitive for someone of sufficient moral maturity who has an adequate appreciation of the true nature of the acts in question. Ross's view differs from but has affinities to both Moore's and Prichard's. His position is that knowledge of *prima facie* duties is intuitive for someone of sufficient moral maturity, but that our judgment concerning what we ought on balance to do on any particular occasion is neither intuitive nor infallible.

Recent Developments

The debate begun by Moore almost one hundred years ago is not over. Although many philosophers who engage in analytic ethics no longer pay explicit attention to Moore's writings, they nonetheless struggle with the issues that he raised. Some philosophers (such as Philippa Foot and Judith Thomson), far from agreeing that (1) the concept of intrinsic value is fundamental to ethics, have contended that there is no such thing as the sort of goodness that consequentialists invoke in their account of moral rightness and wrongness. Not very many philosophers nowadays discuss (2) whether the concept of intrinsic value is analyzable, but this question has recently been addressed by some (such as Roderick Chisholm and Noah Lemos). As to the remaining issues identified here: these continue to be vigorously debated, although the lines separating the various positions have become somewhat blurred by qualifications and refinements. Regarding (3), some (such as Richard Brandt and Alan Gewirth) press, while others (such as Robert Audi and Panayot Butchvarov) resist, the view that ethics, like other areas of philosophical inquiry, can in principle be "naturalized." As to (4), some (such as Fred Feldman and Peter Singer) claim, while others (such as Alan Donagan and Bernard Gert) deny, that the moral rightness or wrongness of acts can be accounted for entirely in terms of their consequences. Finally, concerning (5), some (such as Simon Blackburn and Allan Gibbard) urge, while others (such as David Brink and Nicholas Sturgeon) reject, the idea that ethical judgments are noncognitive. It is safe to say that Moore's influence on ethical philosophy will continue for some time to come.[1]

NOTE

1. I am indebted to Steven Hales and Terrance McConnell for their advice.

REFERENCES

Ayer, A. J. 1936. *Language, Truth and Logic*. London: Gollancz.
Ewing, A. C. 1948. *The Definition of Good*. New York: Macmillan.
Hare, R. M. 1952. *The Language of Morals*. Oxford: Oxford University Press.
Perry, R. B. 1926. *General Theory of Value*. New York: Longmans, Green & Co.
Ross, W. D. 1930. *The Right and the Good*. Oxford: Clarendon.

25   On Defining "Good"

G. E. MOORE

1. IT IS VERY EASY to point out some among our every-day judgments, with the truth of which Ethics is undoubtedly concerned. Whenever we say, 'So and so is a good man,' or 'That fellow is a villain'; whenever we ask, 'What ought I to do?' or 'Is it wrong for me to do like this?'; whenever we hazard such remarks as 'Temperance is a virtue and drunkenness a vice'—it is undoubtedly the business of Ethics to discuss such questions and such statements; to argue what is the true answer when we ask what it is right to do, and to give reasons for thinking that our statements about the character of persons or the morality of actions are true or false. In the vast majority of cases, where we make statements involving any of the terms 'virtue,' 'vice,' 'duty,' 'right,' 'ought,' 'good,' 'bad,' we are making ethical judgments; and if we wish to discuss their truth, we shall be discussing a point of Ethics.

So much as this is not disputed; but it falls very far short of defining the province of Ethics. That province may indeed be defined as the whole truth about that which is at the same time common to all such judgments and peculiar to them. But we have still to ask the question: What is it that is thus common and peculiar? And this is a question to which very different answers have been given by ethical philosophers of acknowledged reputation, and none of them, perhaps, completely satisfactory.

2. If we take such examples as those given above, we shall not be far wrong in saying that they are all of them concerned with the question of 'conduct'— with the question, what, in the conduct of us, human beings, is good, and what is bad, what is right, and what is wrong. For when we say that a man is good, we commonly mean that he acts rightly; when we say that drunkenness is a vice, we commonly mean that to get drunk is a wrong or wicked action. And this discussion of human conduct is, in fact, that with which the name 'Ethics' is most intimately associated. It is so associated by derivation; and conduct is undoubtedly by far the commonest and most generally interesting object of ethical judgments.

Accordingly, we find that many ethical philosophers are disposed to accept as an adequate definition of 'Ethics' the statement that it deals with the question what is good or bad in human conduct. They hold that its enquiries are properly confined to 'conduct' or to 'practice'; they hold that the name 'practical philosophy' covers all the matter with which it has to do. Now, without discussing the proper meaning of the word (for verbal questions are properly left to the writers of dictionaries and other persons interested in literature; philosophy, as we shall see, has no concern with them), I may say that I intend to use 'Ethics' to cover more than this—a usage, for which there is, I think, quite sufficient authority. I am using it to cover an enquiry for which, at all events, there is no other word: the general enquiry into what is good.

Ethics is undoubtedly concerned with the question what good conduct is; but, being concerned with this, it obviously does not start at the beginning, unless it is prepared to tell us what is good as well as what is conduct. For 'good conduct' is a complex notion: all conduct is not good; for some is certainly bad and some may be indifferent. And on the other hand, other things, beside conduct, may be good; and if they are so, then, 'good' denotes some property, that is common to them and conduct; and if we examine good conduct alone of all good things, then we shall be in danger of mistaking for this property, some property which is not shared by those other things: and thus we shall have made a mistake about Ethics even in this limited sense; for we shall not know what good conduct really is. This is a mistake which many writers have ac-

Principia Ethica (Cambridge: Cambridge University Press, 1903), 1–21. Reprinted by permission of Cambridge University Press.

tually made, from limiting their enquiry to conduct. And hence, I shall try to avoid it by considering first what is good in general; hoping, that if we can arrive at any certainty about this, it will be much easier to settle the question of good conduct: for we all know pretty well what 'conduct' is. This, then, is our first question: What is good? and What is bad? and to the discussion of this question (or these questions) I give the name of Ethics, since that science must, at all events, include it.

3. But this is a question which may have many meanings. If, for example, each of us were to say 'I am doing good now' or 'I had a good dinner yesterday,' these statements would each of them be some sort of answer to our question, although perhaps a false one. So, too, when A asks B what school he ought to send his son to, B's answer will certainly be an ethical judgment. And similarly all distribution of praise or blame to any personage or thing that has existed, now exists, or will exist, does give some answer to the question 'What is good?' In all such cases some particular thing is judged to be good or bad: the question 'What?' is answered by 'This.' But this is not the sense in which a scientific Ethics asks the question. Not one, of all the many million answers of this kind, which must be true, can form a part of an ethical system; although that science must contain reasons and principles sufficient for deciding on the truth of all of them. There are far too many persons, things and events in the world, past, present, or to come, for a discussion of their individual merits to be embraced in any science. Ethics, therefore, does not deal at all with facts of this nature, facts that are unique, individual, absolutely particular; facts with which such studies as history, geography, astronomy, are compelled, in part at least, to deal. And, for this reason, it is not the business of the ethical philosopher to give personal advice or exhortation.

4. But there is another meaning which may be given to the question 'What is good?' 'Books are good' would be an answer to it, though an answer obviously false; for some books are very bad indeed. And ethical judgments of this kind do indeed belong to Ethics; though I shall not deal with many of them. Such is the judgment 'Pleasure is good'—a judgment, of which Ethics should discuss the truth, although it is not nearly as important as that other

judgment, with which we shall be much occupied presently—'Pleasure *alone* is good.' It is judgments of this sort, which are made in such books on Ethics as contain a list of 'virtues'—in Aristotle's 'Ethics' for example. But it is judgments of precisely the same kind, which form the substance of what is commonly supposed to be a study different from Ethics, and one much less respectable—the study of Casuistry. We may be told that Casuistry differs from Ethics, in that it is much more detailed and particular, Ethics much more general. But it is most important to notice that Casuistry does not deal with anything that is absolutely particular—particular in the only sense in which a perfectly precise line can be drawn between it and what is general. It is not particular in the sense just noticed, the sense in which this book is a particular book, and A's friend's advice particular advice. Casuistry may indeed be *more* particular and Ethics *more* general; but that means that they differ only in degree and not in kind. And this is universally true of 'particular' and 'general,' when used in this common, but inaccurate, sense. So far as Ethics allows itself to give lists of virtues or even to name constituents of the Ideal, it is indistinguishable from Casuistry. Both alike deal with what is general, in the sense in which physics and chemistry deal with what is general. Just as chemistry aims at discovering what are the properties of oxygen, *wherever it occurs,* and not only of this or that particular specimen of oxygen; so Casuistry aims at discovering what actions are good, *whenever they occur.* In this respect Ethics and Casuistry alike are to be classed with such sciences as physics, chemistry and physiology, in their absolute distinction from those of which history and geography are instances. And it is to be noted that, owing to their detailed nature, casuistical investigations are actually nearer to physics and to chemistry than are the investigations usually assigned to Ethics. For just as physics cannot rest content with the discovery that light is propagated by waves of ether, but must go on to discover the particular nature of the ether-waves corresponding to each several colour; so Casuistry, not content with the general law that charity is a virtue must attempt to discover the relative merits of every different form of charity. Casuistry forms, therefore, part of the ideal of ethical science: Ethics cannot be complete without it. The defects of Casuistry are not defects of principle; no objection can be taken to its aim and object. It has failed only because it is far too difficult a subject to be treated adequately in our present state of knowledge. The casuist has been unable to distinguish, in the cases which he treats, those elements upon which their value depends. Hence he often thinks two cases to be alike in respect of value, when in reality they are alike only in some other respect. It is to mistakes of this kind that the pernicious influence of such investigations has been due. For Casuistry is the goal of ethical investigation. It cannot be safely attempted at the beginning of our studies, but only at the end.

5. But our question 'What is good?' may have still another meaning. We may, in the third place, mean to ask, not what thing or things are good, but how 'good' is to be defined. This is an enquiry which belongs only to Ethics, not to Casuistry; and this is the enquiry which will occupy us first.

It is an enquiry to which most special attention should be directed; since this question, how 'good' is to be defined, is the most fundamental question in all Ethics. That which is meant by 'good' is, in fact, except its converse 'bad,' the *only* simple object of thought which is peculiar to Ethics. Its definition is, therefore, the most essential point in the definition of Ethics; and moreover a mistake with regard to it entails a far larger number of erroneous ethical judgments than any other. Unless this first question be fully understood, and its true answer clearly recognised, the rest of Ethics is as good as useless from the point of view of systematic knowledge. True ethical judgments, of the two kinds last dealt with, may indeed be made by those who do not know the answer to this question as well as by those who do; and it goes without saying that the two classes of people may lead equally good lives. But it is extremely unlikely that the *most general* ethical judgments will be equally valid, in the absence of a true answer to this question: I shall presently try to shew that the gravest errors have been largely due to beliefs in a false answer. And, in any case, it is impossible that, till the answer to this question be known, any one should know *what is the evidence* for any ethical judgment whatsoever. But the main object of Ethics, as a systematic science, is to give correct *reasons* for thinking that this or that is good; and, unless this question be answered, such reasons

cannot be given. Even, therefore, apart from the fact that a false answer leads to false conclusions, the present enquiry is a most necessary and important part of the science of Ethics.

6. What, then, is good? How is good to be defined? Now, it may be thought that this is a verbal question. A definition does indeed often mean the expressing of one word's meaning in other words. But this is not the sort of definition I am asking for. Such a definition can never be of ultimate importance in any study except lexicography. If I wanted that kind of definition I should have to consider in the first place how people generally used the word 'good'; but my business is not with its proper usage, as established by custom. I should, indeed, be foolish, if I tried to use it for something which it did not usually denote: if, for instance, I were to announce that, whenever I used the word 'good,' I must be understood to be thinking of that object which is usually denoted by the word 'table.' I shall, therefore, use the word in the sense in which I think it is ordinarily used; but at the same time I am not anxious to discuss whether I am right in thinking that it is so used. My business is solely with that object or idea, which I hold, rightly or wrongly, that the word is generally used to stand for. What I want to discover is the nature of that object or idea, and about this I am extremely anxious to arrive at an agreement.

But, if we understand the question in this sense, my answer to it may seem a very disappointing one. If I am asked 'What is good?' my answer is that good is good, and that is the end of the matter. Or if I am asked 'How is good to be defined?' my answer is that it cannot be defined, and that is all I have to say about it. But disappointing as these answers may appear, they are of the very last importance. To readers who are familiar with philosophic terminology, I can express their importance by saying that they amount to this: That propositions about the good are all of them synthetic and never analytic; and that is plainly no trivial matter. And the same thing may be expressed more popularly, by saying that, if I am right, then nobody can foist upon us such an axiom as that 'Pleasure is the only good' or that 'The good is the desired' on the pretence that this is 'the very meaning of the word.'

7. Let us, then, consider this position. My point is that 'good' is a simple notion, just as 'yellow' is

a simple notion; that, just as you cannot, by any manner of means, explain to any one who does not already know it, what yellow is, so you cannot explain what good is. Definitions of the kind that I was asking for, definitions which describe the real nature of the object or notion denoted by a word, and which do not merely tell us what the word is used to mean, are only possible when the object or notion in question is something complex. You can give a definition of a horse, because a horse has many different properties and qualities, all of which you can enumerate. But when you have enumerated them all, when you have reduced a horse to his simplest terms, then you can no longer define those terms. They are simply something which you think of or perceive, and to any one who cannot think of or perceive them, you can never, by any definition, make their nature known. It may perhaps be objected to this that we are able to describe to others, objects which they have never seen or thought of. We can, for instance, make a man understand what a chimaera is, although he has never heard of one or seen one. You can tell him that it is an animal with a lioness's head and body, with a goat's head growing from the middle of its back, and with a snake in place of a tail. But here the object which you are describing is a complex object; it is entirely composed of parts, with which we are all perfectly familiar—a snake, a goat, a lioness; and we know, too, the manner in which those parts are to be put together, because we know what is meant by the middle of a lioness's back, and where her tail is wont to grow. And so it is with all objects, not previously known, which we are able to define: they are all complex; all composed of parts, which may themselves, in the first instance, be capable of similar definition, but which must in the end be reducible to simplest parts, which can no longer be defined. But yellow and good, we say, are not complex: they are notions of that simple kind, out of which definitions are composed and with which the power of further defining ceases.

8. When we say, as Webster says, 'The definition of horse is "A hoofed quadruped of the genus Equus,"' we may, in fact, mean three different things. (1) We may mean merely: 'When I say "horse," you are to understand that I am talking about a hoofed quadruped of the genus Equus.' This might be called the arbitrary verbal definition:

and I do not mean that good is indefinable in that sense. (2) We may mean, as Webster ought to mean: 'When most English people say "horse," they mean a hoofed quadruped of the genus Equus.' This may be called the verbal definition proper, and I do not say that good is indefinable in this sense either; for it is certainly possible to discover how people use a word: otherwise, we could never have known that 'good' may be translated by 'gut' in German and by 'bon' in French. But (3) we may, when we define horse, mean something much more important. We may mean that a certain object, which we all of us know, is composed in a certain manner: that it has four legs, a head, a heart, a liver, etc., etc., all of them arranged in definite relations to one another. It is in this sense that I deny good to be definable. I say that it is not composed of any parts, which we can substitute for it in our minds when we are thinking of it. We might think just as clearly and correctly about a horse, if we thought of all its parts and their arrangement instead of thinking of the whole: we could, I say, think how a horse differed from a donkey just as well, just as truly, in this way, as now we do, only not so easily; but there is nothing whatsoever which we could so substitute for good; and that is what I mean, when I say that good is indefinable.

9. But I am afraid I have still not removed the chief difficulty which may prevent acceptance of the proposition that good is indefinable. I do not mean to say that *the* good, that which is good, is thus indefinable; if I did think so, I should not be writing on Ethics, for my main object is to help towards discovering that definition. It is just because I think there will be less risk of error in our search for a definition of 'the good,' that I am now insisting that *good* is indefinable. I must try to explain the difference between these two. I suppose it may be granted that 'good' is an adjective. Well 'the good, that which is good,' must therefore be the substantive to which the adjective 'good' will apply: it must be the whole of that to which the adjective will apply, and the adjective must *always* truly apply to it. But if it is that to which the adjective will apply, it must be something different from that adjective itself; and the whole of that something different, whatever it is, will be our definition of *the* good. Now it may be that this something will have other adjectives, beside 'good,' that will apply to it. It may be

full of pleasure, for example; it may be intelligent: and if these two adjectives are really part of its definition, then it will certainly be true, that pleasure and intelligence are good. And many people appear to think that, if we say 'Pleasure and intelligence are good,' or if we say 'Only pleasure and intelligence are good,' we are defining 'good.' Well, I cannot deny that propositions of this nature may sometimes be called definitions; I do not know well enough how the word is generally used to decide upon this point. I only wish it to be understood that that is not what I mean when I say there is no possible definition of good, and that I shall not mean this if I use the word again. I do most fully believe that some true proposition of the form 'Intelligence is good and intelligence alone is good' can be found; if none could be found, our definition of *the* good would be impossible. As it is, I believe *the* good to be definable; and yet I still say that good itself is indefinable.

10. 'Good,' then, if we mean by it that quality which we assert to belong to a thing, when we say that the thing is good, is incapable of any definition, in the most important sense of that word. The most important sense of 'definition' is that in which a definition states what are the parts which invariably compose a certain whole; and in this sense 'good' has no definition because it is simple and has no parts. It is one of those innumerable objects of thought which are themselves incapable of definition, because they are the ultimate terms by reference to which whatever *is* capable of definition must be defined. That there must be an indefinite number of such terms is obvious, on reflection; since we cannot define anything except by an analysis, which, when carried as far as it will go, refers us to something, which is simply different from anything else, and which by that ultimate difference explains the peculiarity of the whole which we are defining: for every whole contains some parts which are common to other wholes also. There is, therefore, no intrinsic difficulty in the contention that 'good' denotes a simple and indefinable quality. There are many other instances of such qualities.

Consider yellow, for example. We may try to define it, by describing its physical equivalent; we may state what kind of light-vibrations must stimulate the normal eye, in order that we may perceive it. But a moment's reflection is sufficient to shew that those light-vibrations are not themselves what we mean by yellow. *They* are not what we perceive. Indeed we should never have been able to discover their existence, unless we had first been struck by the patent difference of quality between the different colours. The most we can be entitled to say of those vibrations is that they are what corresponds in space to the yellow which we actually perceive.

Yet a mistake of this simple kind has commonly been made about 'good.' It may be true that all things which are good are *also* something else, just as it is true that all things which are yellow produce a certain kind of vibration in the light. And it is a fact, that Ethics aims at discovering what are those other properties belonging to all things which are good. But far too many philosophers have thought that when they named those other properties they were actually defining good; that these properties, in fact, were simply not 'other,' but absolutely and entirely the same with goodness. This view I propose to call the 'naturalistic fallacy' and of it I shall now endeavour to dispose.

11. Let us consider what it is such philosophers say. And first it is to be noticed that they do not agree among themselves. They not only say that they are right as to what good is, but they endeavour to prove that other people who say that it is something else, are wrong. One, for instance, will affirm that good is pleasure, another, perhaps, that good is that which is desired; and each of these will argue eagerly to prove that the other is wrong. But how is that possible? One of them says that good is nothing but the object of desire, and at the same time tries to prove that it is not pleasure. But from his first assertion, that good just means the object of desire, one of two things must follow as regards his proof:

(1) He may be trying to prove that the object of desire is not pleasure. But, if this be all, where is his Ethics? The position he is maintaining is merely a psychological one. Desire is something which occurs in our minds, and pleasure is something else which so occurs; and our would-be ethical philosopher is merely holding that the latter is not the object of the former. But what has that to do with the question in dispute? His opponent held the ethical proposition that pleasure was the good, and although he should prove a million times over the psychological proposition that pleasure is not the object of de-

sire, he is no nearer proving his opponent to be wrong. The position is like this. One man says a triangle is a circle: another replies 'A triangle is a straight line, and I will prove to you that I am right: *for*' (this is the only argument) 'a straight line is not a circle.' 'That is quite true,' the other may reply; 'but nevertheless a triangle is a circle, and you have said nothing whatever to prove the contrary. What is proved is that one of us is wrong, for we agree that a triangle cannot be both a straight line and a circle: but which is wrong, there can be no earthly means of proving, since you define triangle as straight line and I define it as circle.'—Well, that is one alternative which any naturalistic Ethics has to face; if good is *defined* as something else, it is then impossible either to prove that any other definition is wrong or even to deny such definition.

(2) The other alternative will scarcely be more welcome. It is that the discussion is after all a verbal one. When A says 'Good means pleasant' and B says 'Good means desired,' they may merely wish to assert that most people have used the word for what is pleasant and for what is desired respectively. And this is quite an interesting subject for discussion: only it is not a whit more an ethical discussion than the last was. Nor do I think that any exponent of naturalistic Ethics would be willing to allow that this was all he meant. They are all so anxious to persuade us that what they call the good is what we really ought to do. 'Do, pray, act so, because the word "good" is generally used to denote actions of this nature': such, on this view, would be the substance of their teaching. And in so far as they tell us how we ought to act, their teaching is truly ethical, as they mean it to be. But how perfectly absurd is the reason they would give for it! 'You are to do this, because most people use a certain word to denote conduct such as this.' 'You are to say the thing which is not, because most people call it lying.' That is an argument just as good!—My dear sirs, what we want to know from you as ethical teachers, is not how people use a word; it is not even, what kind of actions they approve, which the use of this word 'good' may certainly imply: what we want to know is simply what *is* good. We may indeed agree that what most people do think good, is actually so; we shall at

all events be glad to know their opinions: but when we say their opinions about what *is* good, we do mean what we say; we do not care whether they call that thing which they mean 'horse' or 'table' or 'chair,' 'gut' or 'bon' or 'ἀγαθός'; we want to know what it is that they so call. When they say 'Pleasure is good,' we cannot believe that they merely mean 'Pleasure is pleasure' and nothing more than that.

12. Suppose a man says 'I am pleased'; and suppose that is not a lie or a mistake but the truth. Well, if it is true, what does that mean? It means that his mind, a certain definite mind, distinguished by certain definite marks from all others, has at this moment a certain definite feeling called pleasure. 'Pleased' *means* nothing but having pleasure, and though we may be more pleased or less pleased, and even, we may admit for the present, have one or another kind of pleasure; yet in so far as it is pleasure we have, whether there be more or less of it, and whether it be of one kind or another, what we have is one definite thing, absolutely indefinable, some one thing that is the same in all the various degrees and in all the various kinds of it that there may be. We may be able to say how it is related to other things: that, for example, it is in the mind, that it causes desire, that we are conscious of it, etc., etc. We can, I say, describe its relations to other things, but define it we can *not*. And if anybody tried to define pleasure for us as being any other natural object; if anybody were to say, for instance, that pleasure *means* the sensation of red, and were to proceed to deduce from that that pleasure is a colour, we should be entitled to laugh at him and to distrust his future statements about pleasure. Well, that would be the same fallacy which I have called the naturalistic fallacy. That 'pleased' does not mean 'having the sensation of red,' or anything else whatever, does not prevent us from understanding what it does mean. It is enough for us to know that 'pleased' does mean 'having the sensation of pleasure,' and though pleasure is absolutely indefinable, though pleasure is pleasure and nothing else whatever, yet we feel no difficulty in saying that we are pleased. The reason is, of course, that when I say 'I am pleased,' I do *not* mean that 'I' am the same thing as 'having pleasure.' And similarly no difficulty need be found in my saying that 'pleasure is good' and yet not meaning that 'pleasure' is the same thing

as 'good,' that pleasure *means* good, and that good *means* pleasure. If I were to imagine that when I said 'I am pleased,' I meant that I was exactly the same thing as 'pleased,' I should not indeed call that a naturalistic fallacy, although it would be the same fallacy as I have called naturalistic with reference to Ethics. The reason of this is obvious enough. When a man confuses two natural objects with one another, defining the one by the other, if for instance, he confuses himself, who is one natural object, with 'pleased' or with 'pleasure' which are others, then there is no reason to call the fallacy naturalistic. But if he confuses 'good,' which is not in the same sense a natural object, with any natural object whatever, then there is a reason for calling that a naturalistic fallacy; its being made with regard to 'good' marks it as something quite specific, and this specific mistake deserves a name because it is so common. As for the reasons why good is not to be considered a natural object, they may be reserved for discussion in another place. But, for the present, it is sufficient to notice this: Even if it were a natural object, that would not alter the nature of the fallacy nor diminish its importance one whit. All that I have said about it would remain quite equally true: only the name which I have called it would not be so appropriate as I think it is. And I do not care about the name: what I do care about is the fallacy. It does not matter what we call it, provided we recognise it when we meet with it. It is to be met with in almost every book on Ethics; and yet it is not recognised: and that is why it is necessary to multiply illustrations of it, and convenient to give it a name. It is a very simple fallacy indeed. When we say that an orange is yellow, we do not think our statement binds us to hold that 'orange' means nothing else than 'yellow,' or that nothing can be yellow but an orange. Supposing the orange is also sweet! Does that bind us to say that 'sweet' is exactly the same thing as 'yellow,' that 'sweet' must be defined as 'yellow'? And supposing it be recognised that 'yellow' just means 'yellow' and nothing else whatever, does that make it any more difficult to hold that oranges are yellow? Most certainly it does not: on the contrary, it would be absolutely meaningless to say that oranges were yellow, unless yellow did in the end mean just 'yellow' and nothing else whatever—unless it was absolutely indefinable. We should not get any very

clear notion about things, which are yellow—we should not get very far with our science, if we were bound to hold that everything which was yellow, *meant* exactly the same thing as yellow. We should find we had to hold that an orange was exactly the same thing as a stool, a piece of paper, a lemon, anything you like. We could prove any number of absurdities; but should we be the nearer to the truth? Why, then, should it be different with 'good'? Why, if good is good and indefinable, should I be held to deny that pleasure is good? Is there any difficulty in holding both to be true at once? On the contrary, there is no meaning in saying that pleasure is good, unless good is something different from pleasure. It is absolutely useless, so far as Ethics is concerned, to prove, as Mr. Spencer tries to do, that increase of pleasure coincides with increase of life, unless good *means* something different from either life or pleasure. He might just as well try to prove that an orange is yellow by shewing that it always is wrapped up in paper.

13.   In fact, if it is not the case that 'good' denotes something simple and indefinable, only two alternatives are possible: either it is a complex, a given whole, about the correct analysis of which there may be disagreement; or else it means nothing at all, and there is no such subject as Ethics. In general, however, ethical philosophers have attempted to define good, without recognising what such an attempt must mean. They actually use arguments which involve one or both of the absurdities considered in §11. We are, therefore, justified in concluding that the attempt to define good is chiefly due to want of clearness as to the possible nature of definition. There are, in fact, only two serious alternatives to be considered, in order to establish the conclusion that 'good' does denote a simple and indefinable notion. It might possibly denote a complex, as 'horse' does; or it might have no meaning at all. Neither of these possibilities has, however, been clearly conceived and seriously maintained, as such, by those who presume to define good; and both may be dismissed by a simple appeal to facts.

(1) The hypothesis that disagreement about the meaning of good is disagreement with regard to the correct analysis of a given whole, may be most plainly seen to be incorrect by consid-

eration of the fact that, whatever definition be offered, it may be always asked, with significance, of the complex so defined, whether it is itself good. To take, for instance, one of the more plausible, because one of the more complicated, of such proposed definitions, it may easily be thought, at first sight, that to be good may mean to be that which we desire to desire. Thus if we apply this definition to a particular instance and say 'When we think that A is good, we are thinking that A is one of the things which we desire to desire,' our proposition may seem quite plausible. But, if we carry the investigation further, and ask ourselves 'Is it good to desire to desire A?' it is apparent, on a little reflection, that this question is itself as intelligible, as the original question 'Is A good?'—that we are, in fact, now asking for exactly the same information about the desire to desire A for which we formerly asked with regard to A itself. But it is also apparent that the meaning of this second question cannot be correctly analysed into 'Is the desire to desire A one of the things which we desire to desire?': we have not before our minds anything so complicated as the question 'Do we desire to desire to desire to desire A?' Moreover any one can easily convince himself by inspection that the predicate of this proposition—'good'—is positively different from the notion of 'desiring to desire' which enters into its subject: 'That we should desire to desire A is good' is *not* merely equivalent to 'That A should be good is good.' It may indeed be true that what we desire to desire is always also good; perhaps, even the converse may be true: but it is very doubtful whether this is the case, and the mere fact that we understand very well what is meant by doubting it, shews clearly that we have two different notions before our minds.

(2) And the same consideration is sufficient to dismiss the hypothesis that 'good' has no meaning whatsoever. It is very natural to make the mistake of supposing that what is universally true is of such a nature that its negation would be self-contradictory: the importance which has been assigned to analytic propositions in the history of philosophy shews how easy such a mistake is. And thus it is very easy to conclude that what seems to be a universal ethical principle is in fact an identical proposition; that, if, for example, whatever is called 'good' seems to be pleasant, the proposition 'Pleasure is the good' does not assert a connection between two different notions, but involves only one, that of pleasure, which is easily recognised as a distinct entity. But whoever will attentively consider with himself what is actually before his mind when he asks the question 'Is pleasure (or whatever it may be) after all good?' can easily satisfy himself that he is not merely wondering whether pleasure is pleasant. And if he will try this experiment with each suggested definition in succession, he may become expert enough to recognise that in every case he has before his mind a unique object, with regard to the connection of which with any other object, a distinct question may be asked. Every one does in fact understand the question 'Is this good?' When he thinks of it, his state of mind is different from what it would be, were he asked 'Is this pleasant, or desired, or approved?' It has a distinct meaning for him, even though he may not recognise in what respect it is distinct. Whenever he thinks of 'intrinsic value,' or 'intrinsic worth,' or says that a thing 'ought to exist,' he has before his mind the unique object—the unique property of things—which I mean by 'good.' Everybody is constantly aware of this notion, although he may never become aware at all that it is different from other notions of which he is also aware. But, for correct ethical reasoning, it is extremely important that he should become aware of this fact; and, as soon as the nature of the problem is clearly understood, there should be little difficulty in advancing so far in analysis.

14. 'Good,' then, is indefinable; and yet, so far as I know, there is only one ethical writer, Prof. Henry Sidgwick, who has clearly recognised and stated this fact. We shall see, indeed, how far many of the most reputed ethical systems fall short of drawing the conclusions which follow from such a recognition. At present I will only quote one instance, which will serve to illustrate the meaning and importance of this principle that 'good' is indefinable, or, as Prof. Sidgwick says, an 'unanalysable notion.' It is an instance to which Prof. Sidgwick himself refers in a note on the passage, in which he argues that 'ought' is unanalysable.[1]

'Bentham,' says Sidgwick, 'explains that his fundamental principle "states the greatest happiness of all those whose interest is in question as being the right and proper end of human action"'; and yet 'his language in other passages of the same chapter would seem to imply' that he *means* by the word "right" "conducive to the general happiness." Prof. Sidgwick sees that, if you take these two statements together, you get the absurd result that 'greatest happiness is the end of human action, which is conducive to the general happiness'; and so absurd does it seem to him to call this result, as Bentham calls it, 'the fundamental principle of a moral system,' that he suggests that Bentham cannot have meant it. Yet Prof. Sidgwick himself states elsewhere[2] that Psychological Hedonism is 'not seldom confounded with Egoistic Hedonism'; and that confusion, as we shall see, rests chiefly on that same fallacy, the naturalistic fallacy, which is implied in Bentham's statements. Prof. Sidgwick admits therefore that this fallacy is sometimes committed, absurd as it is; and I am inclined to think that Bentham may really have been one of those who committed it. Mill, as we shall see, certainly did commit it. In any case, whether Bentham committed it or not, his doctrine, as above quoted, will serve as a very good illustration of this fallacy, and of the importance of the contrary proposition that good is indefinable.

Let us consider this doctrine. Bentham seems to imply, so Prof. Sidgwick says, that the word 'right' *means* 'conducive to general happiness.' Now this, by itself, need not necessarily involve the naturalistic fallacy. For the word 'right' is very commonly appropriated to actions which lead to the attainment of what is good; which are regarded as *means* to the ideal and not as ends-in-themselves. This use of 'right,' as denoting what is good as a means, whether or not it be also good as an end, is indeed the use to which I shall confine the word. Had Bentham been using 'right' in this sense, it might be perfectly consistent for him to *define* right as 'conducive to the general happiness,' *provided only* (and notice this proviso) he had already proved, or laid down as an axiom, that general happiness was *the* good, or (what is equivalent to this) that general happiness alone was good. For in that case he would have already defined *the* good as general happiness (a position perfectly consistent, as we have seen, with the contention that 'good' is indefinable), and, since right

was to be defined as 'conducive to *the* good,' it would actually *mean* 'conducive to general happiness.' But this method of escape from the charge of having committed the naturalistic fallacy has been closed by Bentham himself. For his fundamental principle is, we see, that the greatest happiness of all concerned is the *right* and proper *end* of human action. He applies the word 'right,' therefore, to the end, as such, not only to the means which are conducive to it; and, that being so, right can no longer be defined as 'conducive to the general happiness,' without involving the fallacy in question. For now it is obvious that the definition of right as conducive to general happiness can be used by him in support of the fundamental principle that general happiness is the right end; instead of being itself derived from that principle. If right, by definition, means conducive to general happiness, then it is obvious that general happiness is the right end. It is not necessary now first to prove or assert that general happiness is the right end, before right is defined as conducive to general happiness—a perfectly valid procedure; but on the contrary the definition of right as conducive to general happiness proves general happiness to be the right end—a perfectly invalid procedure, since in this case the statement that 'general happiness is the right end of human action' is not an ethical principle at all, but either, as we have seen, a proposition about the meaning of words, or else a proposition about the *nature* of general happiness, not about its rightness or goodness.

Now, I do not wish the importance I assign to this fallacy to be misunderstood. The discovery of it does not at all refute Bentham's contention that greatest happiness is the proper end of human action, if that be understood as an ethical proposition, as he undoubtedly intended it. That principle may be true all the same; we shall consider whether it is so in succeeding chapters. Bentham might have maintained it, as Prof. Sidgwick does, even if the fallacy had been pointed out to him. What I am maintaining is that the *reasons* which he actually gives for his ethical proposition are fallacious ones so far as they consist in a definition of right. What I suggest is that he did not perceive them to be fallacious; that, if he had done so, he would have been led to seek for other reasons in support of his Utilitarianism; and that, had he sought for other reasons, he *might* have found none which he thought to be sufficient. In that case he would have changed his whole system—a most important consequence. It is undoubtedly also possible that he would have thought other reasons to be sufficient, and in that case his ethical system, in its main results, would still have stood. But, even in this latter case, his use of the fallacy would be a serious objection to him as an ethical philosopher. For it is the business of Ethics, I must insist, not only to obtain true results, but also to find valid reasons for them. The direct object of Ethics is knowledge and not practice; and any one who uses the naturalistic fallacy has certainly not fulfilled this first object, however correct his practical principles may be.

My objections to Naturalism are then, in the first place, that it offers no reason at all, far less any valid reason, for any ethical principle whatever; and in this it already fails to satisfy the requirements of Ethics, as a scientific study. But in the second place I contend that, though it gives a reason for no ethical principle, it is a *cause* of the acceptance of false principles—it deludes the mind into accepting ethical principles, which are false; and in this it is contrary to every aim of Ethics. It is easy to see that if we start with a definition of right conduct as conduct conducive to general happiness; then, knowing that right conduct is universally conduct conducive to the good, we very easily arrive at the result that the good is general happiness. If, on the other hand, we once recognise that we must start our Ethics without a definition, we shall be much more apt to look about us, before we adopt any ethical principle whatever; and the more we look about us, the less likely are we to adopt a false one. It may be replied to this: Yes, but we shall look about us just as much, before we settle on our definition, and are therefore just as likely to be right. But I will try to shew that this is not the case. If we start with the conviction that a definition of good can be found, we start with the conviction that good *can mean* nothing else than some one property of things; and our only business will then be to discover what that property is. But if we recognise that, so far as the meaning of good goes, anything whatever may be good, we start with a much more open mind. Moreover, apart from the fact that, when we think we have a definition, we cannot logically defend our ethical principles in any way whatever, we shall also be much less apt to defend them well, even if illogically. For we shall start with

the conviction that good must mean so and so, and shall therefore be inclined either to misunderstand our opponent's arguments or to cut them short with the reply, 'This is not an open question: the very meaning of the word decides it; no one can think otherwise except through confusion.'

15. Our first conclusion as to the subject-matter of Ethics is, then, that there is a simple, indefinable, unanalysable object of thought by reference to which it must be defined. By what name we call this unique object is a matter of indifference, so long as we clearly recognise what it is and that it does differ from other objects. The words which are commonly taken as the signs of ethical judgments all do refer to it; and they are expressions of ethical judgments solely because they do so refer. But they may refer to it in two different ways, which it is very important to distinguish, if we are to have a complete definition of the range of ethical judgments. Before I proceeded to argue that there was such an indefinable notion involved in ethical notions, I stated (§4) that it was necessary for Ethics to enumerate all true universal judgments, asserting that such and such a thing was good, whenever it occurred. But, although all such judgments do refer to that unique notion which I have called 'good,' they do not all refer to it in the same way. They may either assert that this unique property does always attach to the thing in question, or else they may assert only that the thing in question is *a cause or necessary condition* for the existence of other things to which this unique property does attach. The nature of these two species of universal ethical judgments is extremely different; and a great part of the difficulties, which are met with in ordinary ethical speculation, are due to the failure to distinguish them clearly. Their difference has, indeed, received expression in ordinary language by the contrast between the terms 'good as means' and 'good in itself,' 'value as a means' and 'intrinsic value.' But these terms are apt to be applied correctly only in the more obvious instances; and this seems to be due to the fact that the distinction between the conceptions which they denote has not been made a separate object of investigation.

NOTES

1. *Methods of Ethics,* Bk. 1, Chap. iii, §1 (6th edition).
2. *Methods of Ethics,* Bk. 1, Chap. iv, §1.

26   Does Moral Philosophy Rest on a Mistake?

H. A. PRICHARD

PROBABLY TO MOST STUDENTS of Moral Philosophy there comes a time when they feel a vague sense of dissatisfaction with the whole subject. And the sense of dissatisfaction tends to grow rather than to diminish. It is not so much that the positions, and still more the arguments, of particular thinkers seem unconvincing, though this is true. It is rather that the aim of the subject becomes increasingly obscure. 'What,' it is asked, 'are we really going to learn by Moral Philosophy?' 'What are books on Moral Philosophy really trying to show, and when their aim is clear, why are they so unconvincing and artificial?' And again: 'Why is it so difficult to substitute anything better?' Personally, I have been led by growing dissatisfaction of this kind to wonder whether the reason may not be that the subject, at any rate as usually understood, consists in the attempt to answer an improper question. And in this article I shall venture to contend that the existence of the whole subject, as usually understood, rests on a mistake, and on a mistake parallel to that on which rests, as I think, the subject usually called the Theory of Knowledge.

If we reflect on our own mental history or on the history of the subject, we feel no doubt about the nature of the demand which originates the subject. Any one who, stimulated by education, has come to feel the force of the various obligations in life, at some time or other comes to feel the irksomeness of carrying them out, and to recognize the sacrifice of interest involved; and, if thoughtful, he inevitably puts to himself the question: 'Is there really a reason why I should act in the ways in which hitherto I have thought I ought to act? May I not have been all the time under an illusion in so thinking? Should not I really be justified in simply trying to have a good time?' Yet, like Glaucon, feeling that somehow he ought after all to act in these ways, he asks for a *proof* that this feeling is justified. In other words, he asks

'*Why* should I do these things?', and his and other people's moral philosophizing is an attempt to supply the answer, i.e., to supply by a process of reflection a proof of the truth of what he and they have prior to reflection believed immediately or without proof. This frame of mind seems to present a close parallel to the frame of mind which originates the Theory of Knowledge. Just as the recognition that the doing of our duty often vitally interferes with the satisfaction of our inclinations leads us to wonder whether we really ought to do what we usually call our duty, so the recognition that we and others are liable to mistakes in knowledge generally leads us, as it did Descartes, to wonder whether hitherto we may not have been always mistaken. And just as we try to find a proof, based on the general consideration of action and of human life, that we ought to act in the ways usually called moral, so we, like Descartes, propose by a process of reflection on our thinking to find a test of knowledge, i.e., a principle by applying which we can show that a certain condition of mind was really knowledge, a condition which *ex hypothesi* existed independently of the process of reflection.

Now, how has the moral question been answered? So far as I can see, the answers all fall, and fall from the necessities of the case, into one of two species. *Either* they state that we ought to do so and so, because, as we see when we fully apprehend the facts, doing so will be for our good, i.e., really, as I would rather say, for our advantage, or better still, for our happiness; *or* they state that we ought to do so and so, because something realized either in or by the action is good. In other words, the reason 'why' is stated in terms either of the agent's happiness or of the goodness of something involved in the action.

To see the prevalence of the former species of answer, we have only to consider the history of Moral Philosophy. To take obvious instances, Plato,

Mind 21 (1912). Reprinted by permission of *Mind*.

Butler, Hutcheson, Paley, Mill, each in his own way seeks at bottom to convince the individual that he ought to act in so-called moral ways by showing that to do so will really be for his happiness. Plato is perhaps the most significant instance, because of all philosophers he is the one to whom we are least willing to ascribe a mistake on such matters, and a mistake on his part would be evidence of the deep-rootedness of the tendency to make it. To show that Plato really justifies morality by its profitableness, it is only necessary to point out (1) that the very formulation of the thesis to be met, viz. that justice is ἀλλότριον ἀγαθόν,[1] implies that any refutation must consist in showing that justice is οἰκεῖον ἀγαθόν, i.e., really, as the context shows, one's own advantage, and (2) that the term λυσιτελεῖν[2] supplies the key not only to the problem but also to its solution.

The tendency to justify acting on moral rules in this way is natural. For if, as often happens, we put to ourselves the question 'Why should we do so and so?', we are satisfied by being convinced either that the doing so will lead to something which we want (e.g., that taking certain medicine will heal our disease), or that the doing so itself, as we see when we appreciate its nature, is something that we want or should like, e.g., playing golf. The formulation of the question implies a state of unwillingness or indifference towards the action, and we are brought into a condition of willingness by the answer. And this process seems to be precisely what we desire when we ask, e.g., 'Why should we keep our engagements to our own loss?'; for it is just the fact that the keeping of our engagements runs counter to the satisfaction of our desires which produced the question.

The answer is, of course, not an answer, for it fails to convince us that we ought to keep our engagements; even if successful on its own lines, it only makes us *want* to keep them. And Kant was really only pointing out this fact when he distinguished hypothetical and categorical imperatives, even though he obscured the nature of the fact by wrongly describing his so-called 'hypothetical imperatives' as imperatives. But if this answer be no answer, what other can be offered? Only, it seems, an answer which bases the obligation to do something on the *goodness* either of something to which the act leads or of the act itself. Suppose, when won-

dering whether we really ought to act in the ways usually called moral, we are told as a means of resolving our doubt that those acts are right which produce happiness. We at once ask: 'Whose happiness?' If we are told 'Our own happiness,' then, though we shall lose our hesitation to act in these ways, we shall not recover our sense that we ought to do so. But how can this result be avoided? Apparently, only by being told one of two things; *either* that anyone's happiness is a thing good in itself, and that *therefore* we ought to do whatever will produce it, *or* that working for happiness is itself good, and that the intrinsic goodness of such an action is the reason why we ought to do it. The advantage of this appeal to the goodness of something consists in the fact that it avoids reference to desire, and, instead, refers to something impersonal and objective. In this way it seems possible to avoid the resolution of obligation into inclination. But just for this reason it is of the essence of the answer, that to be effective it must neither include nor involve the view that the apprehension of the goodness of anything necessarily arouses the desire for it. Otherwise the answer resolves itself into a form of the former answer by substituting desire or inclination for the sense of obligation, and in this way it loses what seems its special advantage.

Now it seems to me that both forms of this answer break down, though each for a different reason.

Consider the first form. It is what may be Utilitarianism in the generic sense, in which what is good is not limited to pleasure. It takes its stand upon the distinction between something which is not itself an action, but which can be produced by an action, and the action which will produce it, and contends that if something which is not an action is good, then we *ought* to undertake the action which will, directly or indirectly, originate it.[3]

But this argument, if it is to restore the sense of obligation to act, must presuppose an intermediate link, viz. the further thesis that what is good ought to be.[4] The necessity of this link is obvious. An 'ought,' if it is to be derived at all, can only be derived from another 'ought.' Moreover, this link tacitly presupposes another, viz. that the apprehension that something good which is not an action ought to be involves just the feeling of imperativeness or obligation which is to be aroused by the thought of the action which will originate it. Otherwise the argument will not lead us to feel the obligation to produce it by the action. And, surely, both this link and its implication are false.[5] The word 'ought' refers to actions and to actions alone. The proper language is never 'So and so ought to be,' but 'I ought to do so and so.' Even if we are sometimes moved to say that the world or something in it is not what it ought to be, what we really mean is that God or some human being has not made something what he ought to have made it. And it is merely stating another side of this fact to urge that we can only feel the imperativeness upon us of something which is in our power; for it is actions and actions alone which, directly at least, are in our power.

Perhaps, however, the best way to see the failure of this view is to see its failure to correspond to our actual moral convictions. Suppose we ask ourselves whether our sense that we ought to pay our debts or to tell the truth arises from our recognition that in doing so we should be originating something good, e.g., material comfort in *A* or true belief in *B*, i.e., suppose we ask ourselves whether it is this aspect of the action which leads to our recognition that we ought to do it. We at once and without hesitation answer 'No.' Again, if we take as our illustration our sense that we ought to act justly as between two parties, we have, if possible, even less hesitation in giving a similar answer; for the balance of resulting good may be, and often is, not on the side of justice.

At best it can only be maintained that there is this element of truth in the Utilitarian view, that unless we recognized that something which an act will originate is good, we should not recognize that we ought to do the action. Unless we thought knowledge a good thing, it may be urged, we should not think that we ought to tell the truth; unless we thought pain a bad thing, we should not think the infliction of it, without special reason, wrong. But this is not to imply that the badness of error is the reason why it is wrong to lie, or the badness of pain the reason why we ought not to inflict it without special cause.[6]

It is, I think, just because this form of the view is so plainly at variance with our moral consciousness that we are driven to adopt the other form of the view, viz. that the act is good in itself and that its intrinsic goodness is the reason why it ought to

be done. It is this form which has always made the most serious appeal; for the goodness of the act itself seems more closely related to the obligation to do it than that of its mere consequences or results, and therefore, if obligation is to be based on the goodness of something, it would seem that this goodness should be that of the act itself. Moreover, the view gains plausibility from the fact that moral actions are most conspicuously those to which the term 'intrinsically good' is applicable.

Nevertheless this view, though perhaps less superficial, is equally untenable. For it leads to precisely the dilemma which faces everyone who tries to solve the problem raised by Kant's theory of the good will. To see this, we need only consider the nature of the acts to which we apply the term 'intrinsically good.'

There is, of course, no doubt that we approve and even admire certain actions, and also that we should describe them as good, and as good in themselves. But it is, I think, equally unquestionable that our approval and our use of the term 'good' is always in respect of the motive and refers to actions which have been actually done and of which we think we know the motive. Further, the actions of which we approve and which we should describe as intrinsically good are of two and only two kinds. They are either actions in which the agent did what he did because he thought he ought to do it, or actions of which the motive was a desire prompted by some good emotion, such as gratitude, affection, family feeling, or public spirit, the most prominent of such desires in books on Moral Philosophy being that ascribed to what is vaguely called benevolence. For the sake of simplicity I omit the case of actions done partly from some such desire and partly from the sense of duty; for even if all good actions are done from a combination of these motives, the argument will not be affected. The dilemma is this. If the motive in respect of which we think an action good is the sense of obligation, then so far from the sense that we ought to do it being derived from our apprehension of its goodness, our apprehension of its goodness will presuppose the sense that we ought to do it. In other words, in this case the recognition that the act is good will plainly *presuppose* the recognition that the act is right, whereas the view under consideration is that the recognition of the goodness of the act *gives rise* to the recognition of its rightness. On the other hand, if the motive in respect of which we think an action good is some intrinsically good desire, such as the desire to help a friend, the recognition of the goodness of the act will equally fail to give rise to the sense of obligation to do it. For we cannot feel that we ought to do that the doing of which is *ex hypothesi* prompted solely by the desire to do it.[7]

The fallacy underlying the view is that while to base the rightness of an act upon its intrinsic goodness implies that the goodness in question is that of the motive, in reality the rightness or wrongness of an act has nothing to do with any question of motives at all. For, as any instance will show, the rightness of an action concerns an action not in the fuller sense of the term in which we include the motive in the action, but in the narrower and commoner sense in which we distinguish an action from its motive and mean by an action merely the conscious origination of something, an origination which on different occasions or in different people may be prompted by different motives. The question 'Ought I to pay my bills?' really means simply 'Ought I to bring about my tradesmen's possession of what by my previous acts I explicitly or implicitly promised them?' There is, and can be, no question of whether I ought to pay my debts from a particular motive. No doubt we know that if we pay our bills we shall pay them with a motive, but in considering whether we ought to pay them we inevitably think of the act in abstraction from the motive. Even if we knew what our motive would be if we did the act, we should not be any nearer an answer to the question.

Moreover, if we eventually pay our bills from fear of the county court, we shall still have done *what* we ought, even though we shall not have done it *as* we ought. The attempt to bring in the motive involves a mistake similar to that involved in supposing that we can will to will. To feel that I ought to pay my bills is to be *moved towards* paying them. But what I can be moved towards must always be an action and not an action in which I am moved in a particular way, i.e., an action from a particular motive; otherwise I should be moved towards being moved, which is impossible. Yet the view under consideration involves this impossibility, for it really resolves the sense that I ought to do so and

so, into the sense that I ought to be moved to do it in a particular way.[8]

So far my contentions have been mainly negative, but they form, I think, a useful, if not a necessary, introduction to what I take to be the truth. This I will now endeavour to state, first formulating what, as I think, is the real nature of our apprehension or appreciation of moral obligations, and then applying the result to elucidate the question of the existence of Moral Philosophy.

The sense of obligation to do, or of the rightness of, an action of a particular kind is absolutely underivative or immediate. The rightness of an action consists in its being the origination of something of a certain kind *A* in a situation of a certain kind, a situation consisting in a certain relation *B* of the agent to others or to his own nature. To appreciate its rightness two preliminaries may be necessary. We may have to follow out the consequences of the proposed action more fully than we have hitherto done, in order to realize that in the action we should originate *A*. Thus we may not appreciate the wrongness of telling a certain story until we realize that we should thereby be hurting the feelings of one of our audience. Again, we may have to take into account the relation *B* involved in the situation, which we had hitherto failed to notice. For instance, we may not appreciate the obligation to give X a present, until we remember that he has done us an act of kindness. But, given that by a process which is, of course, merely a process of general and not of moral thinking we come to recognize that the proposed act is one by which we shall originate *A* in a relation *B*, then we appreciate the obligation immediately or directly, the appreciation being an activity of *moral* thinking. We recognize, for instance, that this performance of a service to X, who has done us a service, just in virtue of its being the performance of a service to one who has rendered a service to the would-be agent, ought to be done by us. This apprehension is immediate, in precisely the sense in which a mathematical apprehension is immediate, e.g., the apprehension that this three-sided figure, in virtue of its being three-sided, must have three angles. Both apprehensions are immediate in the sense that in both insight into the nature of the subject directly leads us to recognize its possession of the predicate; and it is only stating this fact from the other side to say that in both cases the fact apprehended is self-evident.

The plausibility of the view that obligations are not self-evident but need proof lies in the fact that an act which is referred to as an obligation may be incompletely stated, what I have called the preliminaries to appreciating the obligation being incomplete. If, e.g., we refer to the act of repaying X by a present merely as giving X a present, it appears, and indeed is, necessary to give a reason. In other words, wherever a moral act is regarded in this incomplete way the question '*Why* should I do it?' is perfectly legitimate. This fact suggests, but suggests wrongly, that even if the nature of the act is completely stated, it is still necessary to give a reason, or, in other words, to supply a proof.

The relations involved in obligations of various kinds are, of course, very different. The relation in certain cases is a relation to others due to a past act of theirs or ours. The obligation to repay a benefit involves a relation due to a past act of the benefactor. The obligation to pay a bill involves a relation due to a past act of ours in which we have either said or implied that we would make a certain return for something which we have asked for and received. On the other hand, the obligation to speak the truth implies no such definite act; it involves a relation consisting in the fact that others are trusting us to speak the truth, a relation the apprehension of which gives rise to the sense that communication of the truth is something owing by us to them. Again, the obligation not to hurt the feelings of another involves no special relation of us to that other, i.e., no relation other than that involved in our both being men, and men in one and the same world. Moreover, it seems that the relation involved in an obligation need not be a relation to another at all. Thus we should admit that there is an obligation to overcome our natural timidity or greediness, and that this involves no relations to others. Still there is a relation involved, viz. a relation to our own disposition. It is simply because we can and because others cannot directly modify our disposition that it is our business to improve it, and that it is not theirs, or, at least, not theirs to the same extent.

The negative side of all this is, of course, that we do not come to appreciate an obligation by an *argument,* i.e., by a process of nonmoral thinking, and that, in particular, we do not do so by an argument of which a premiss is the ethical but not moral activity of appreciating the goodness either of the act or of a consequence of the act; i.e., that our sense of the rightness of an act is not a conclusion from our appreciation of the goodness either of it or of anything else.

It will probably be urged that on this view our various obligations form, like Aristotle's categories, an unrelated chaos in which it is impossible to acquiesce. For, according to it, the obligation to repay a benefit, or to pay a debt, or to keep a promise, presupposes a previous act of another; whereas the obligation to speak the truth or not to harm another does not; and again, the obligation to remove our timidity involves no relations to others at all. Yet, at any rate, an effective *argumentum ad hominem* is at hand in the fact that the various qualities which we recognize as good are equally unrelated; e.g., courage, humility, and interest in knowledge. If, as is plainly the case, $\dot{\alpha}\gamma\alpha\theta\dot{\alpha}$ (goods) differ $\ddot{\eta}$ $\dot{\alpha}\gamma\alpha\theta\dot{\alpha}$ (*qua* goods), why would not obligations equally differ *qua* their obligatoriness? Moreover, if this were not so there could in the end be only one obligation, which is palpably contrary to fact.[9]

Certain observations will help to make the view clearer.

In the first place, it may seem that the view, being—as it is—avowedly put forward in opposition to the view that what is right is derived from what is good, must itself involve the opposite of this, viz. the Kantian position that what is good is based upon what is right, i.e., that an act, if it be good, is good because it is right. But this is not so. For, on the view put forward, the rightness of a right action lies solely in the origination in which the act consists, whereas the intrinsic goodness of an action lies solely in its motive; and this implies that a morally good action is morally good not simply because it is a right action but because it is a right action done because it is right, i.e., from a sense of obligation. And this implication, it may be remarked incidentally, seems plainly true.

In the second place, the view involves that when, or rather so far as, we act from a sense of obligation, we have no purpose or end. By a 'purpose' or 'end' we really mean something the existence of which we desire, and desire of the existence of which leads us to act. Usually our purpose is something which the act will originate, as when we turn round in order to look at a picture. But it may be the action itself, i.e., the origination of something, as when we hit a golf-ball into a hole or kill someone out of revenge.[10] Now if by a purpose we mean something the existence of which we desire and desire for which leads us to act, then plainly, so far as we act from a sense of obligation, we have no purpose, consisting either in the action or in anything which it will produce. This is so obvious that it scarcely seems worth pointing out. But I do so for two reasons. (1) If we fail to scrutinize the meaning of the terms 'end' and 'purpose,' we are apt to assume uncritically that all deliberate action, i.e., action proper, must have a purpose; we then become puzzled both when we look for the purpose of an action done from a sense of obligation, and also when we try to apply to such an action the distinction of means and end, the truth all the time being that since there is no end, there is no means either. (2) The attempt to base the sense of obligation on the recognition of the goodness of something is really an attempt to find a purpose in a moral action in the shape of something good which, as good, we want. And the expectation that the goodness of something underlies an obligation disappears as soon as we cease to look for a purpose.

The thesis, however, that so far as we act from a sense of obligation, we have no purpose must not be misunderstood. It must not be taken either to mean or to imply that so far as we so act we have no *motive*. No doubt in ordinary speech the words 'motive' and 'purpose' are usually treated as correlatives, 'motive' standing for the desire which induces us to act, and 'purpose' standing for the object of this desire. But this is only because, when we are looking for the motive of the action, say, of some crime, we are usually presupposing that the act in question is prompted by a desire and not by the sense of obligation. At bottom, however, we mean by a motive what moves us to act; a sense of obligation does sometimes move us to act; and in our ordinary consciousness we should not hesitate to allow that the action we are considering might have had as its motive a sense of obligation. Desire and the sense of obligation are coordinate forms or species of motive.

In the third place, if the view put forward be right, we must sharply distinguish morality and

virtue as independent, though related, species of goodness, neither being an aspect of something of which the other is an aspect, nor again a form or species of the other, nor again something deducible from the other; and we must at the same time allow that it is possible to do the same act either virtuously or morally or in both ways at once. And surely this is true. An act, to be virtuous, must, as Aristotle saw, be done willingly or with pleasure; as such it is just not done from a sense of obligation but from some desire which is intrinsically good, as arising from some intrinsically good emotion. Thus, in an act of generosity the motive is the desire to help another arising from sympathy with that other; in an act which is courageous and no more, i.e., in an act which is not at the same time an act of public spirit or family affection or the like, we prevent ourselves from being dominated by a feeling of terror, desiring to do so from a sense of shame at being terrified. The goodness of such an act is different from the goodness of an act to which we apply the term moral in the strict and narrow sense, viz. an act done from a sense of obligation. Its goodness lies in the intrinsic goodness of the emotion and of the consequent desire under which we act, the goodness of this motive being different from the goodness of the moral motive proper, viz. the sense of duty or obligation. Nevertheless, at any rate in certain cases, an act can be done either virtuously or morally or in both ways at once. It is possible to repay a benefit either from desire to repay it, or from the feeling that we ought to do so, or from both motives combined. A doctor may tend his patients either from a desire arising out of interest in his patients or in the exercise of skill, or from a sense of duty, or from a desire and a sense of duty combined. Further, although we recognize that in each case the act possesses an intrinsic goodness, we regard that action as the best in which both motives are combined; in other words, we regard as the really best man the man in whom virtue and morality are united.

It may be objected that the distinction between the two kinds of motive is untenable, on the ground that the *desire* to repay a benefit, for example, is only the manifestation of that which manifests itself as the *sense of obligation* to repay whenever we think of something in the action which is other than the repayment and which we should not like, such as the loss or pain involved. Yet the distinction can, I think, easily be shown to be tenable. For, in the analogous case of revenge, the desire to return the injury and the sense that we ought not to do so, leading, as they do, in opposite directions, are plainly distinct; and the obviousness of the distinction here seems to remove any difficulty in admitting the existence of a parallel distinction between the desire to return a benefit and the sense that we ought to return it.[11]

Further, the view implies that an obligation can no more be based on or derived from a virtue than a virtue can be derived from an obligation, in which latter case a virtue would consist in carrying out an obligation. And the implication is surely true and important. Take the case of courage. It is untrue to urge that, since courage is a virtue, we ought to act courageously. It is and must be untrue, because, as we see in the end, to feel an obligation to act courageously would involve a contradiction. For, as I have urged before, we can only feel an obligation to *act;* we cannot feel an obligation to *act from a certain desire,* in this case the desire to conquer one's feelings of terror arising from the sense of shame which they arouse. Moreover, if the sense of obligation to act in a particular way leads to an action, the action will be an action done from a sense of obligation, and therefore not, if the above analysis of virtue be right, an act of courage.

The mistake of supposing that there can be an obligation to act courageously seems to arise from two causes. In the first place, there is often an obligation to do that which involves the conquering or controlling of our fear in the doing of it, e.g., the obligation to walk along the side of a precipice to fetch a doctor for a member of our family. Here the acting on the obligation is externally, though only externally, the same as an act of courage proper. In the second place there is an obligation to acquire courage, i.e., to do such things as will enable us afterwards to act courageously, and this may be mistaken for an obligation to act courageously. The same considerations can, of course, be applied, *mutatis mutandis,* to the other virtues.

The fact, if it be a fact, that virtue is no basis for morality will explain what otherwise it is difficult to account for, viz. the extreme sense of dissatisfaction produced by a close reading of Aristotle's *Ethics.* Why is the *Ethics* so disappointing? Not, I think,

because it really answers two radically different questions as if they were one: (1) 'What is the happy life?,' (2) 'What is the virtuous life?' It is, rather, because Aristotle does not do what we as moral philosophers want him to do, viz. to convince us that we really ought to do what in our non-reflective consciousness we have hitherto believed we ought to do, or if not, to tell us what, if any, are the other things which we really ought to do, and to prove to us that he is right. Now, if what I have just been contending is true, a systematic account of the virtuous character cannot possibly satisfy this demand. At best it can only make clear to us the details of one of our obligations, viz. the obligation to make ourselves better men; but the achievement of this does not help us to discover what we ought to do in life as a whole, and why; to think that it did would be to think that our only business in life was self-improvement. Hence it is not surprising that Aristotle's account of the good man strikes us as almost wholly of academic value, with little relation to our real demand, which is formulated in Plato's words: οὐ γὰρ περὶ τοῦ ἐπιτυχόντος ὁ λόγος, ἀλλὰ περὶ τοῦ ὅντινα τρόπον χρὴ ζῆν.[12]

I am not, of course, *criticizing* Aristotle for failing to satisfy this demand, except so far as here and there he leads us to think that he intends to satisfy it. For my main contention is that the demand cannot be satisfied, and cannot be satisfied because it is illegitimate. Thus we are brought to the question: 'Is there really such a thing as Moral Philosophy, and, if there is, in what sense?'

We should first consider the parallel case—as it appears to be—of the Theory of Knowledge. As I urged before, at some time or other in the history of all of us, if we are thoughtful, the frequency of our own and of others' mistakes is bound to lead to the reflection that possibly we and others have *always* been mistaken in consequence of some radical defect of our faculties. In consequence, certain things which previously we should have said without hesitation that we *knew,* as, e.g., that $4 \times 7 = 28$, become subject to doubt; we become able only to say that we thought we knew these things. We inevitably go on to look for some general procedure by which we can ascertain that a given condition of mind is really one of knowledge. And this involves the search for a criterion of knowledge, i.e., for a principle by applying which we can settle that a given state of mind is really knowledge. The search for this criterion and the application of it, when found, is what is called the Theory of Knowledge. The search implies that instead of its being the fact that the knowledge that *A* is *B* is obtained directly by consideration of the nature of *A* and *B*, the knowledge that *A* is *B*, in the full or complete sense, can only be obtained by first knowing that *A* is *B*, and then knowing that we knew it by applying a criterion, such as Descartes's principle that what we clearly and distinctly conceive is true.

Now it is easy to show that the doubt whether *A* is *B*, based on this speculative or general ground, could, if genuine, never be set at rest. For if, in order really to know that *A* is *B*, we must first know that we knew it, then really, to know that we knew it, we must first know that we knew that we knew it. But— what is more important—it is also easy to show that this doubt is not a genuine doubt but rests on a confusion the exposure of which removes the doubt. For when we *say* we doubt whether our previous condition was one of knowledge, what we *mean*, if we mean anything at all, is that we doubt whether our previous *belief* was *true,* a belief which we should express as the *thinking* that *A* is *B*. For in order to doubt whether our previous condition was one of knowledge, we have to think of it not as knowledge but as only belief, and our only question can be 'Was this belief true?' But as soon as we see that we are thinking of our previous condition as only one of belief, we see that what we are now doubting is not what we first *said* we were doubting, viz. whether a previous condition of knowledge was really knowledge. Hence, to remove the doubt, it is only necessary to appreciate the real nature of our consciousness in apprehending, e.g., that $7 \times 4 = 28$, and thereby see that it was no mere condition of believing but a condition of knowing, and then to notice that in our subsequent doubt what we are really doubting is not whether this consciousness was really knowledge, but whether a consciousness of another kind, viz. a belief that $7 \times 4 = 28$, was true. We thereby see that though a doubt based on speculative grounds is possible, it is not a doubt concerning what we believed the doubt concerned, and that a doubt concerning this latter is impossible.

Two results follow. In the first place, if, as is usually the case, we mean by the 'Theory of Knowl-edge' the knowledge which supplies the answer to the question 'Is what we have hitherto thought knowledge really knowledge?,' there is and can be no such thing, and the supposition that there can is simply due to a confusion. There can be no answer to an illegitimate question, except that the question is illegitimate. Nevertheless the question is one which we continue to put until we realize the inevitable immediacy of knowledge. And it is positive knowledge that knowledge is immediate and neither can be, nor needs to be, improved or vindicated by the further knowledge that it was knowledge. This positive knowledge sets at rest the inevitable doubt, and, so far as by the 'Theory of Knowledge' is meant this knowledge, then even though this knowledge be the knowledge that there is no Theory of Knowledge in the former sense, to that extent the Theory of Knowledge exists.

In the second place, suppose we come genuinely to doubt whether, e.g., $7 \times 4 = 28$ owing to a genuine doubt whether we were right in believing yesterday that $7 \times 4 = 28$, a doubt which can in fact only arise if we have lost our hold of, i.e., no longer remember, the real nature of our consciousness of yesterday, and so think of it as consisting in believing. Plainly, the only remedy is to do the sum again. Or, to put the matter generally, if we do come to doubt whether it is true that *A* is *B*, as we once thought, the remedy lies not in any process of reflection but in such a reconsideration of the nature of *A* and *B* as leads to the knowledge that *A* is *B*.

With these considerations in mind, consider the parallel which, as it seems to me, is presented— though with certain differences—by Moral Philosophy. The sense that we ought to do certain things arises in our unreflective consciousness, being an activity of moral thinking occasioned by the various situations in which we find ourselves. At this stage our attitude to these obligations is one of unquestioning confidence. But inevitably the appreciation of the degree to which the execution of these obligations is contrary to our interest raises the doubt whether after all these obligations are really obligatory, i.e., whether our sense that we ought not to do certain things is not illusion. We then want to have it *proved* to us that we ought to do so, i.e., to be convinced of this by a process which, as an argument, is different in kind from our original and unreflective appreciation of it. This demand is, as I have argued, illegitimate.

Hence, in the first place, if, as is almost universally the case, by Moral Philosophy is meant the knowledge which would satisfy this demand, there is no such knowledge, and all attempts to attain it are doomed to failure because they rest on a mistake, the mistake of supposing the possibility of proving what can only be apprehended directly by an act of moral thinking. Nevertheless the demand, though illegitimate, is inevitable until we have carried the process of reflection far enough to realize the self-evidence of our obligations, i.e., the immediacy of our apprehension of them. This realization of their self-evidence is positive knowledge, and so far, and so far only, as the term Moral Philosophy is confined to this knowledge and to the knowledge of the parallel immediacy of the apprehension of the goodness of the various virtues and of good dispositions generally, is there such a thing as Moral Philosophy. But since this knowledge may allay doubts which often affect the whole conduct of life, it is, though not extensive, important and even vitally important.

In the second place, suppose we come genuinely to doubt whether we ought, for example, to pay our debts, owing to a genuine doubt whether our previous conviction that we ought to do so is true, a doubt which can, in fact, only arise if we fail to remember the real nature of what we now call our past conviction. The only remedy lies in actually getting into a situation which occasions the obligation, or—if our imagination be strong enough—in imagining ourselves in that situation, and then letting our moral capacities of thinking do their work. Or, to put the matter generally, if we do doubt whether there is really an obligation to originate *A* in a situation *B,* the remedy lies not in any process of general thinking, but in getting face to face with a particular instance of the situation *B,* and then directly appreciating the obligation to originate *A* in that situation.

NOTES

1. [Someone else's good, i.e., advantage.—Ed. (1912)]

2. [To profit (someone), i.e., to be to someone's advantage.—Ed. (1912)]

3. Cf. Dr. Rashdall's *Theory of Good and Evil,* vol. i, p. 138.

4. Dr. Rashdall, if I understand him rightly, supplies this link (cf. ibid., pp. 135–36).

5. When we speak of anything, e.g., of some emotion or of some quality of a human being, as good, we never dream in our ordinary consciousness of going on to say that therefore it ought to be.

6. It may be noted that if the badness of pain were the reason why we ought not to inflict pain on another, it would equally be a reason why we ought not to inflict pain on ourselves; yet, though we should allow the wanton infliction of pain on ourselves to be foolish, we should not think of describing it as wrong.

7. It is, I think, on this latter horn of the dilemma that Martineau's view falls; cf. *Types of Ethical Theory,* part ii, book i.

8. It is of course not denied here that an action done from a particular motive may be *good;* it is only denied that the *rightness* of an action depends on its being done with a particular motive.

9. Two other objections may be anticipated: (1) that obligations cannot be self-evident, since many actions regarded as obligations by some are not so regarded by others, and (2) that if obligations are self-evident, the problem of how we ought to act in the presence of conflicting obligations is insoluble.

To the first I should reply:

(*a*) That the appreciation of an obligation is, of course, only possible for a developed moral being, and that different degrees of development are possible.

(*b*) That the failure to recognize some particular obligations is usually due to the fact that, owing to a lack of thoughtfulness, what I have called the preliminaries to this recognition are incomplete.

(*c*) That the view put forward is consistent with the admission that, owing to a lack of thoughtfulness, even the best men are blind to many of their obligations, and that in the end our obligations are seen to be co-extensive with almost the whole of our life.

To the second objection I should reply that obligation admits of degrees, and that where obligations conflict, the decision of what we ought to do turns not on the question 'Which of the alternative courses of action will originate the greater good?' but on the question 'Which is the greater obligation?'

10. It is no objection to urge that an action cannot be its own purpose, since the purpose of something cannot be the thing itself. For, speaking strictly, the purpose is not the *action's* purpose but *our* purpose, and there is no contradiction in holding that our purpose in acting may be the action.

11. This sharp distinction of virtue and morality as coordinate and independent forms of goodness will explain a fact which otherwise it is difficult to account for. If we

turn from books on Moral Philosophy to any vivid account of human life and action such as we find in Shakespeare, nothing strikes us more than the comparative remoteness of the discussions of Moral Philosophy from the facts of actual life. Is not this largely because, while Moral Philosophy has, quite rightly, concentrated its attention on the fact of obligation, in the case of many of those whom we admire most and whose lives are of the greatest interest, the sense of obligation, though it may be an important, is not a dominating factor in their lives?

12. [For no light matter is at stake; the question concerns the very manner in which human life is to be lived (*Republic,* Bk. I, 352D)—Ed. (1912)]

The Emotive Meaning of Ethical Terms   27

C. L. STEVENSON

I

ETHICAL QUESTIONS first arise in the form "Is so and so good?" or "Is this alternative better than that?" These questions are difficult partly because we don't quite know what we are seeking. We are asking, "Is there a needle in that haystack?" without even knowing just what a needle is. So the first thing to do is to examine the questions themselves. We must try to make them clearer, either by defining the terms in which they are expressed, or by any other method that is available.

The present paper is concerned wholly with this preliminary step of making ethical questions clear. In order to help answer the question "Is X good?" we must *substitute* for it a question which is free from ambiguity and confusion.

It is obvious that in substituting a clearer question we must not introduce some utterly different kind of question. It won't do (to take an extreme instance of a prevalent fallacy) to substitute for "Is X good?" the question "Is X pink with yellow trimmings?" and then point out how easy the question really is. This would beg the original question, not help answer it. On the other hand, we must not expect the substituted question to be strictly "identical" with the original one. The original question may embody hypostatization, anthropormorphism, vagueness, and all the other ills to which our ordinary discourse is subject. If our substituted question is to be clearer, it must remove these ills. The questions will be identical only in the sense that a child is identical with the man he later becomes. Hence we must not demand that the substitution strike us, on immediate introspection, as making no change in meaning.

Just how, then, must the substituted question be related to the original? Let us assume (inaccurately) that it must result from replacing "good" by some set of terms which define it. The question then resolves itself to this: How must the defined meaning of "good" be related to its original meaning?

I answer that it must be *relevant*. A defined meaning will be called "relevant" to the original meaning under these circumstances: Those who have understood the definition must be able to say all that they then want to say by using the term in the defined way. They must never have occasion to use the term in the old, unclear sense. (If a person did have to go on using the word in the old sense, then to this extent his meaning would not be clarified, and the philosophical task would not be completed.) It frequently happens that a word is used so confusedly and ambiguously that we must give it *several* defined meanings, rather than one. In this case only the whole set of defined meanings will be

Mind 46 (1937). Reprinted by permission of *Mind.*

called " relevant," and any one of them will be called "partially relevant." This is not a rigorous treatment of *relevance,* by any means, but it will serve for the present purposes.

Let us now turn to our particular task—that of giving a relevant definition of "good." Let us first examine some of the ways in which others have attempted to do this.

The word "good" has often been defined in terms of *approval,* or similar psychological attitudes. We may take as typical examples: "good" means *desired by me* (Hobbes); and "good" means *approved by most people* (Hume, in effect).[1] It will be convenient to refer to definitions of this sort as "interest theories," following Mr. R. B. Perry, although neither "interest" nor "theory" is used in the most usual way.

Are definitions of this sort relevant?

It is idle to deny their *partial* relevance. The most superficial inquiry will reveal that "good" is exceedingly ambiguous. To maintain that "good" is *never* used in Hobbes's sense, and never in Hume's, is only to manifest an insensitivity to the complexities of language. We must recognize, perhaps, not only these senses, but a variety of similar ones, differing both with regard to the kind of interest in question, and with regard to the people who are said to have the interest.

But this is a minor matter. The essential question is not whether interest theories are *partially* relevant, but whether they are *wholly* relevant. This is the only point for intelligent dispute. Briefly: Granted that some senses of "good" may relevantly be defined in terms of interest, is there some *other* sense which is *not* relevantly so defined? We must give this question careful attention. For it is quite possible that when philosophers (and many others) have found the question "Is X good?" so difficult, they have been grasping for this *other* sense of "good," and not any sense relevantly defined in terms of interest. If we insist on defining "good" in terms of interest, and answer the question when thus interpreted, we may be begging *their* question entirely. Of course this *other* sense of "good" may not exist, or it may be a complete confusion, but that is what we must discover.

Now many have maintained that interest theories are *far* from being completely relevant. They have argued that such theories neglect the very sense of "good" which is most vital. And certainly, their arguments are not without plausibility.

Only . . . what *is* this "vital" sense of "good"? The answers have been so vague, and so beset with difficulties, that one can scarcely determine.

There are certain requirements, however, with which this "vital" sense has been expected to comply—requirements which appeal strongly to our common sense. It will be helpful to summarize these, showing how they exclude the interest theories:

In the first place, we must be able sensibly to *disagree* about whether something is "good." This condition rules out Hobbes's definition. For consider the following argument: "This is good." "That isn't so; it's not good." As translated by Hobbes, this becomes: "I desire this." "That isn't so, for *I* don't." The speakers are not contradicting one another, and think they are, only because of an elementary confusion in the use of pronouns. The definition, "good" means *desired by my community,* is also excluded, for how could people from different communities disagree?[2]

In the second place, "goodness" must have, so to speak, a magnetism. A person who recognizes X to be "good" must *ipso facto* acquire a stronger tendency to act in its favour than he otherwise would have had. This rules out the Humean type of definition. For according to Hume, to recognize that something is "good" is simply to recognize that the majority approve of it. Clearly, a man may see that the majority approve of X without having, himself, a stronger tendency to favour it. This requirement excludes any attempt to define "good' in terms of the interest of people *other* than the speaker.[3]

In the third place, the "goodness" of anything must not be verifiable solely by use of the scientific method. "Ethics must not be psychology." This restriction rules out all of the traditional interest theories, without exception. It is so sweeping a restriction that we must examine its plausibility. What are the methodological implications of interest theories which are here rejected?

According to Hobbes's definition, a person can prove his ethical judgments, with finality, by showing that he is not making an introspective error about his desires. According to Hume's definition, one may prove ethical judgments (roughly speaking) by taking a vote. *This* use of the empirical method, at any rate, seems highly remote from what we usually accept as proof, and reflects on the complete relevance of the definitions which imply it.

But aren't there more complicated interest theories which are immune from such methodological implications? No, for the same factors appear; they are only put off for a while. Consider, for example, the definition: "X is good" means *most people would approve of X if they knew its nature and consequences.* How, according to this definition, could we prove that a certain X was good? We should first have to find out, empirically, just what X was like, and what its consequences would be. To this extent the empirical method, as required by the definition, seems beyond intelligent objection. But what remains? We should next have to discover whether most people would approve of the sort of thing we had discovered X to be. This couldn't be determined by popular vote—but only because it would be too difficult to explain to the voters, beforehand, what the nature and consequences of X really were. Apart from this, voting would be a pertinent method. We are again reduced to counting noses, as a *perfectly final* appeal.

Now we need not scorn voting entirely. A man who rejected interest theories as irrelevant might readily make the following statement: "If I believed that X would be approved by the majority, when they knew all about it, I should be strongly *led* to say that X was good." But he would continue: "*Need* I say that X was good, under the circumstances? Wouldn't my acceptance of the alleged 'final proof' result simply from my being democratic? What about the more aristocratic people? They would simply say that the approval of most people, even when they knew all about the object of their approval, simply had nothing to do with the goodness of anything, and they would probably add a few remarks about the low state of people's interests." It would indeed seem, from these considerations, that the definition we have been considering has presupposed democratic ideals from the start; it has dressed up democratic propaganda in the guise of a definition.

The omnipotence of the empirical method, as implied by interest theories and others, may be shown unacceptable in a somewhat different way.

Mr. G. E. Moore's familiar objection about the open question is chiefly pertinent in this regard. No matter what set of scientifically knowable properties a thing may have (says Moore, in effect), you will find, on careful introspection, that it is an open question to ask whether anything having these properties is *good*. It is difficult to believe that this recurrent question is a totally confused one, or that it seems open only because of the ambiguity of "good." Rather, we must be using some sense of "good" which is not definable, relevantly, in terms of anything scientifically knowable. That is, the scientific method is not sufficient for ethics.[4]

These, then, are the requirements with which the "vital" sense of "good" is expected to comply: (1) goodness must be a topic for intelligent disagreement; (2) it must be "magnetic"; and (3) it must not be discoverable solely through the scientific method.

II

I can now turn to my proposed analysis of ethical judgments. First let me present my position dogmatically, showing to what extent I vary from tradition.

I believe that the three requirements, given above, are perfectly sensible; that there is some *one* sense of "good" which satisfies all three requirements; and that no traditional interest theory satisfies them all. But this does not imply that "good" must be explained in terms of a Platonic Idea, or of a categorical imperative, or of an unique, unanalyzable property. On the contrary, the three requirements can be met by a *kind* of interest theory. *But we must give up a presupposition which all the traditional interest theories have made.*

Traditional interest theories hold that ethical statements are *descriptive* of the existing state of interests—that they simply *give information* about interests. (More accurately, ethical judgments are said to describe what the state of interests is, was, or will be, or to indicate what the state of interests *would* be under specified circumstances.) It is this emphasis on description, on information, which leads to their incomplete relevance. Doubtless there is always *some* element of description in ethical judgments, but this is by no means all. Their major use is not to indicate facts, but to *create an influence*. Instead of merely describing people's interests, they *change* or *intensify* them. They *recommend* an interest in an object, rather than state that the interest already exists.

For instance: When you tell a man that he oughtn't to steal, your object isn't merely to let him know that people disapprove of stealing. You are attempting, rather, to get *him* to disapprove of it. Your ethical judgment has a quasi-imperative force which, operating through suggestion, and intensified by your tone of voice, readily permits you to begin to *influence,* to *modify,* his interests. If in the end you do not succeed in getting *him* to disapprove of stealing, you will feel that you've failed to convince him that stealing is wrong. You will continue to feel this, even though he fully acknowledges that you disapprove of it, and that almost everyone else does. When you point out to him the consequences of his actions—consequences which you suspect he already disapproves of—these *reasons* which support your ethical judgment are simply a means of facilitating your influence. If you think you can change his interests by making vivid to him how others will disapprove of him, you will do so; otherwise not. So the consideration about other people's interest is just an additional means you may employ, in order to move him, and is not a part of the ethical judgment itself. Your ethical judgment doesn't merely describe interests to him, it directs his very interests. The difference between the traditional interest theories and my view is like the difference between describing a desert and irrigating it.

Another example: A munition maker declares that war is a good thing. If he merely meant that he approved of it, he would not have to insist so strongly, nor grow so excited in his argument. People would be quite easily convinced that he approved of it. If he merely meant that most people approved of war, or that most people would approve of it if they knew the consequences, he would have to yield his point if it were proved that this wasn't so. But he wouldn't do this, nor does consistency require it. He is not *describing* the state of people's approval; he is trying to *change* it by his influence. If he found that few people approved of war, he might insist all the more strongly that it was good, for there would be more changing to be done.

This example illustrates how "good" may be used for what most of us would call bad purposes. Such cases are as pertinent as any others. I am not indicating the *good* way of using "good." I am not influencing people, but am describing the way this influence sometimes goes on. If the reader wishes to say that the munition maker's influence is bad— that is, if the reader wishes to awaken people's disapproval of the man, and to make him disapprove of his own actions—I should at another time be willing to join in this undertaking. But this is not the present concern. I am not using ethical terms, but am indicating how they *are* used. The munition maker, in his use of "good," illustrates the persuasive character of the word just as well as does the unselfish man who, eager to encourage in each of us a desire for the happiness of all contends that the supreme good is peace.

Thus ethical terms are *instruments* used in the complicated interplay and readjustment of human interests. This can be seen plainly from more general observations. People from widely separated communities have different moral attitudes. Why? To a great extent because they have been subject to different social influences. Now clearly this influence doesn't operate through sticks and stones alone; words play a great part. People praise one another, to encourage certain inclinations, and blame one another, to discourage others. Those of forceful personalities issue commands which weaker people, for complicated instinctive reasons, find it difficult to disobey, quite apart from fears of consequences. Further influence is brought to bear by writers and orators. Thus social influence is exerted, to an enormous extent, by means that have nothing to do with physical force or material reward. The ethical terms facilitate such influence. Being suited for use in *suggestion,* they are a means by which men's attitudes may be led this way or that. The reason, then, that we find a greater similarity in the moral attitudes of one community than in those of different communities is largely this: ethical judgments propagate themselves. One man says "This is good"; this may influence the approval of another person, who then makes the same ethical judgment, which in turn influences another person, and so on. In the end, by a process of mutual influence, people take up more or less the same attitudes. Between people of widely separated communities, of course, the influence is less strong; hence different communities have different attitudes.

These remarks will serve to give a general idea of my point of view. We must now go into more detail. There are several questions which must be answered: How does an ethical sentence acquire its power of influencing people—why is it suited to suggestion? Again, what has this influence to do with the *meaning* of ethical terms? And finally, do these considerations really lead us to a sense of "good" which meets the requirements mentioned in the preceding section?

Let us deal first with the question about *meaning*. This is far from an easy question, so we must enter into a preliminary inquiry about meaning in general. Although a seeming digression, this will prove indispensable.

III

Broadly speaking, there are two different *purposes* which lead us to use language. On the one hand we use words (as in science) to record, clarify, and communicate *beliefs*. On the other hand we use words to give vent to our feelings (interjections), or to create moods (poetry), or to incite people to actions or attitudes (oratory).

The first use of words I shall call "descriptive"; the second, "dynamic." Note that the distinction depends solely upon the *purpose* of the *speaker*.

When a person says "Hydrogen is the lightest known gas," his purpose *may* be simply to lead the hearer to believe this, or to believe that the speaker believes it. In that case the words are used descriptively. When a person cuts himself and says "Damn," his purpose is not ordinarily to record, clarify, or communicate any belief. The word is used dynamically. The two ways of using words, however, are by no means mutually exclusive. This is obvious from the fact that our purposes are often complex. Thus when one says "I want you to close the door," part of his purpose, ordinarily, is to lead the hearer to believe that he has this want. To that extent the words are used descriptively. But the major part of one's purpose is to lead the hearer to *satisfy* the want. To that extent the words are used dynamically.

It very frequently happens that the same sentence may have a dynamic use on one occasion, and may not have a dynamic use on another; and that it may have different dynamic uses on different occasions. For instance: A man says to a visiting neighbor, "I am loaded down with work." His purpose may be to let the neighbor know how life is going with him. This would *not* be a dynamic use of words. He may make the remark, however, in order to drop a hint. This *would be* dynamic usage (as well as descriptive). Again, he may make the remark to arouse the neighbor's sympathy. This would be a *different* dynamic usage from that of hinting.

Or again, when we say to a man, "Of course you won't make those mistakes any more," we *may* simply be making a prediction. But we are more likely to be using "suggestion," in order to encourage him and hence *keep* him from making mistakes. The first use would be descriptive; the second, mainly dynamic.

From these examples it will be clear that we can't determine whether words are used dynamically or not, merely by reading the dictionary—even assuming that everyone is faithful to dictionary meanings. Indeed, to know whether a person is using a word dynamically we must note his tone of voice, his gestures, the general circumstances under which he is speaking, and so on.

We must now proceed to an important question: What has the dynamic use of words to do with their *meaning*? One thing is clear—we must not define "meaning" in a way that would make meaning vary with dynamic usage. If we did, we should have no use for the term. All that we could say about such "meaning" would be that it is very complicated and subject to constant change. So we must certainly distinguish between the dynamic use of words and their meaning.

It does not follow, however, that we must define "meaning" in some nonpsychological fashion. We must simply restrict the psychological field. Instead of identifying meaning with *all* the psychological causes and effects that attend a word's utterance, we must identify it with those that it has a *tendency* (causal property, dispositional property) to be connected with. The tendency must be of a particular kind, moreover. It must exist for all who speak the language; it must be persistent and must be realizable more or less independently of determinate circumstances attending the word's utterance. There will be further restrictions dealing with the interrelations of words in different contexts. Moreover, we must include, under the psychological responses which the words tend to produce, not only immediately introspectable experiences but *dispositions* to react in a given way with appropriate stimuli. I hope to go into these matters in a subsequent essay.[5] Suffice it now to say that I think "meaning" may be thus defined in a way to include "propositional" meaning as an important kind.

The definition will readily permit a distinction between meaning and dynamic use. For when words are accompanied by dynamic purposes, it does not follow that they *tend* to be accompanied by them in the way mentioned above. E.g., there need be no tendency realizable more or less independently of the determinate circumstances under which the words are uttered.

There will be a kind of meaning, however, in the sense above defined, which has an intimate relation to dynamic usage. I refer to "emotive" meaning (in a sense roughly like that employed by Ogden and Richards).[6] The emotive meaning of a word is a tendency of a word, arising through the history of its usage, to produce (result from) *affective* responses in people. It is the immediate aura of feeling which hovers about a word.[7] Such tendencies to produce affective responses cling to words very tenaciously. It would be difficult, for instance, to express merriment by using the interjection "alas." Because of the persistence of such affective tendencies (among other reasons) it becomes feasible to classify them as "meanings."

Just *what* is the relation between emotive meaning and the dynamic use of words? Let us take an example. Suppose that a man tells his hostess, at the end of a party, that he thoroughly enjoyed himself, and suppose that he was in fact bored. If we consider his remark an innocent one, are we likely to remind him, later, that he "lied" to his hostess? Obviously not, or at least, not without a broad smile; for although he told her something that he believed to be false, and with the intent of making her believe that it was true—those being the ordinary earmarks of a lie—the expression, "you lied to her," would be emotively too strong for our purposes. It

would seem to be a reproach, even if we intended it not to be a reproach. So it will be evident that such words as "lied" (and many parallel examples could be cited) become suited, on account of their emotive meaning, to a certain kind of dynamic use—so well suited, in fact, that the hearer is likely to be misled when we use them in any other way. The more pronounced a word's emotive meaning is, the less likely people are to use it purely descriptively. Some words are suited to encourage people, some to discourage them, some to quiet them, and so on.

Even in these cases, of course, the dynamic purposes are not to be identified with any sort of meaning; for the emotive meaning accompanies a word much more persistently than do the dynamic purposes. But there is an important contingent relation between emotive meaning and dynamic purpose: the former assists the latter. Hence if we define emotively laden terms in a way that neglects their emotive meaning, we become seriously confused. *We lead people to think that the terms defined are used dynamically less often than they are.*

IV

Let us now apply these remarks in defining "good." This word may be used morally or nonmorally. I shall deal with the nonmoral usage almost entirely, but only because it is simpler. The main points of the analysis will apply equally well to either usage.

As a preliminary definition let us take an inaccurate approximation. It may be more misleading than helpful but will do to begin with. Roughly, then, the sentence 'X is good" means *we like* X. ("We" includes the hearer or hearers.)

At first glance this definition sounds absurd. If used, we should expect to find the following sort of conversation: A. "This is good." B. "But I *don't* like it. What led you to believe that I did?" The unnaturalness of B's reply, judged by ordinary word usage, would seem to cast doubt on the relevance of my definition.

B's unnaturalness, however, lies simply in this: he is assuming that "we like it" (as would occur implicitly in the use of "good") is being used descriptively. This will not do. When "we like it" is to take the place of "this is good," the former sentence must be used not purely descriptively, but dynamically. More specifically, it must be used to promote a very subtle (and for the nonmoral sense in question, a very easily resisted) kind of *suggestion*. To the extent that "we" refers to the hearer it must have the dynamic use, essential to suggestion, of leading the hearer to *make* true what is said, rather than merely to believe it. And to the extent that "we" refers to the speaker, the sentence must have not only the descriptive use of indicating belief about the speaker's interest, but the quasi-interjectory, dynamic function of giving direct expression to the interest. (This immediate expression of feelings assists in the process of suggestion. It is difficult to disapprove in the face of another's enthusiasm.)

For an example of a case where "we like this" is used in the dynamic way that "this is good" is used, consider the case of a mother who says to her several children, "one thing is certain, *we all like to be neat.*" If she really believed this, she would not bother to say so. But she is not using the words descriptively. She is *encouraging* the children to like neatness. By telling them that they like neatness, she will lead them to *make* her statement true, so to speak. If, instead of saying "we all like to be neat" in this way, she had said "it's a good thing to be neat," the effect would have been approximately the same.

But these remarks are still misleading. Even when "we like it" is used for suggestion, it is not quite like "this is good." The latter is more subtle. With such a sentence as "this is a good book," for example, it would be practically impossible to use instead "we like this book." When the latter is used it must be accompanied by so exaggerated an intonation, to prevent its becoming confused with a descriptive statement, that the force of suggestion becomes stronger and ludicrously more overt than when "good" is used.

The definition is inadequate, further, in that the definiens has been restricted to dynamic usage. Having said that dynamic usage was different from meaning, I should not have to mention it in giving the *meaning* of "good."

It is in connection with this last point that we must return to emotive meaning. The word "good" has a laudatory emotive meaning that fits it for the dynamic use of suggesting favorable interest. But the

sentence "we like it" has no such emotive meaning. Hence my definition has neglected emotive meaning entirely. Now to neglect emotive meaning serves to foster serious confusions, as I have previously intimated; so I have sought to make up for the inadequacy of the definition by letting the restriction about dynamic usage take the place of emotive meaning. What I should do, of course, is to find a definiens whose emotive meaning, like that of "good," simply does *lead* to dynamic usage.

Why did I not do this? I answer that it is not possible if the definition is to afford us increased clarity. No two words, in the first place, have quite the same emotive meaning. The most we can hope for is a rough approximation. But if we seek for such an approximation for "good," we shall find nothing more than synonyms, such as "desirable" or "valuable"; and these are profitless because they do not clear up the connection between "good" and favorable interest. If we reject such synonyms, in favor of nonethical terms, we shall be highly misleading. For instance "this is good" has something like the meaning of "I *do* like this; do so as well." But this is certainly not accurate. For the imperative makes an appeal to the conscious efforts of the hearer. Of course he cannot like something just by trying. He must be led to like it through suggestion. Hence an ethical sentence differs from an imperative in that it enables one to make changes in a much more subtle, less fully conscious way. Note that the ethical sentence centers the hearer's attention not on his interests but on the object of interest, and thereby facilitates suggestion. Because of its subtlety, moreover, an ethical sentence readily permits counter-suggestion and leads to the give and take situation that is so characteristic of arguments about values.

Strictly speaking, then, it is impossible to define 'good" in terms of favorable interest if emotive meaning is not to be distorted. Yet it is possible to say that "this is good" is *about* the favorable interest of the speaker and the hearer or hearers, and that it has a laudatory emotive meaning which fits the words for use in suggestion. This is a rough description of meaning, not a definition. But it serves the same clarifying function that a definition ordinarily does, and that, after all, is enough.

A word must be added about the moral use of "good." This differs from the above in that it is about a different kind of interest. Instead of being about what the hearer and speaker *like,* it is about a stronger sort of approval. When a person *likes* something, he is pleased when it prospers and disappointed when it does not. When a person *morally approves* of something he experiences a rich feeling of security when it prospers and is indignant or "shocked" when it does not. These are rough and inaccurate examples of the many factors which one would have to mention in distinguishing the two kinds of interest. In the moral usage, as well as in the nonmoral, "good" has an emotive meaning which adapts it to suggestion.

And now, are these considerations of any importance? Why do I stress emotive meanings in this fashion? Does the omission of them really lead people into errors? I think, indeed, that the errors resulting from such omissions are enormous. In order to see this, however, we must return to the restrictions, mentioned in Section I, with which the typical sense of "good" has been expected to comply.

V

The first restriction, it will be remembered, had to do with disagreement. Now there is clearly some sense in which people disagree on ethical points, but we must not rashly assume that all disagreement is modeled after the sort that occurs in the natural sciences. We must distinguish between "disagreement in belief" (typical of the sciences) and "disagreement in interest." Disagreement in belief occurs when A believes *p* and B disbelieves it. Disagreement in interest occurs when A has a favorable interest in X and when B has an unfavorable one in it. (For a full-bodied disagreement, neither party is content with the discrepancy.)

Let me give an example of disagreement in interest. A. "Let's go to a cinema tonight." B. "I don't want to do that. Let's go to the symphony." A continues to insist on the cinema, B on the symphony. This is disagreement in a perfectly conventional sense. They cannot agree on where they want to go, and each is trying to redirect the other's interest. (Note that imperatives are used in the example.)

It is a disagreement in *interest* which takes place in ethics. When C says "this is good," and D says

"no, it's bad," we have a case of suggestion and counter-suggestion. Each man is trying to redirect the other's interest. There obviously need be no domineering, since each may be willing to give ear to the other's influence; but each is trying to move the other none the less. It is in this sense that they disagree. Those who argue that certain interest theories make no provision for disagreement have been misled, I believe, simply because the traditional theories, in leaving out emotive meaning, give the impression that ethical judgments are used descriptively only; and of course when judgments are used purely descriptively, the only disagreement that can arise is disagreement *in belief.* Such disagreement may be disagreement in belief *about* interests, but this is not the same as disagreement *in* interest. My definition does not provide for disagreement in belief about interests any more than does Hobbes'; but that is no matter, for there is no reason to believe, at least on common sense grounds, that this kind of disagreement exists. There is only disagreement *in* interest. (We shall see in a moment that disagreement in interest does not remove ethics from sober argument— that this kind of disagreement may often be resolved through empirical means.)

The second restriction, about "magnetism," or the connection between goodness and actions, requires only a word. This rules out only those interest theories that do *not* include the interest of the speaker in defining "good." My account does include the speaker's interest, hence is immune.

The third restriction, about the empirical method, may be met in a way that springs naturally from the above account of disagreement. Let us put the question in this way: When two people disagree over an ethical matter, can they completely resolve the disagreement through empirical considerations, assuming that each applies the empirical method exhaustively, consistently, and without error?

I answer that sometimes they can and sometimes they cannot, and that at any rate, even when they can, the relation between empirical knowledge and ethical judgments is quite different from the one that traditional interest theories seem to imply.

This can best be seen from an analogy. Let us return to the example where A and B could not agree on a cinema or a symphony. The example differed from an ethical argument in that imperatives were used, rather than ethical judgments, but was analogous to the extent that each person was endeavoring to modify the other's interest. Now how would these people argue the case, assuming that they were too intelligent just to shout at one another?

Clearly, they would give "reasons" to support their imperatives. A might say, "but you know, Garbo is at the Bijou." His hope is that B, who admires Garbo, will acquire a desire to go to the cinema when he knows what film will be there. B may counter, "but Toscanini is guest conductor tonight, in an all-Beethoven program." And so on. Each supports his imperative (*"let's* do so and so") by reasons which may be empirically established.

To generalize from this: disagreement in interest may be rooted in disagreement in belief. That is to say, people who disagree in interest would often cease to do so if they knew the precise nature and consequences of the object of their interest. To this extent disagreement in interest may be resolved by securing agreement in belief, which in turn may be secured empirically.

This generalization holds for ethics. If A and B, instead of using imperatives, had said, respectively, "it would be *better* to go to the cinema," and "it would be *better* to go to the symphony," the reasons which they would advance would be roughly the same. They would each give a more thorough account of the object of interest, with the purpose of completing the redirection of interest which was begun by the suggestive force of the ethical sentence. On the whole, of course, the suggestive force of the ethical statement merely exerts enough pressure to start such trains of reasons, since the reasons are much more essential in resolving disagreement in interest than the persuasive effect of the ethical judgment itself.

Thus the empirical method is relevant to ethics simply because our knowledge of the world is a determining factor to our interests. But note that empirical facts are not inductive grounds from which the ethical judgment problematically follows. (This is what traditional interest theories imply.) If someone said "close the door," and added the reason "we'll catch cold," the latter would scarcely be called an inductive ground of the former. Now imperatives are related to the reasons which support them in the same way that ethical judgments are related to reasons.

Is the empirical method *sufficient* for attaining ethical agreement? Clearly not. For empirical knowledge resolves disagreement in interest only to the extent that such disagreement is rooted in disagreement in belief. Not all disagreement in interest is of this sort. For instance: A is of a sympathetic nature and B is not. They are arguing about whether a public dole would be good. Suppose that they discovered all the consequences of the dole. Is it not possible, even so, that A will say that it is good and B that it is bad? The disagreement in interest may arise not from limited factual knowledge but simply from A's sympathy and B's coldness. Or again, suppose in the above argument that A was poor and unemployed and that B was rich. Here again the disagreement might not be due to different factual knowledge. It would be due to the different social positions of the men, together with their predominant self-interest.

When ethical disagreement is not rooted in disagreement in belief, is there *any* method by which it may be settled? If one means by "method" a *rational* method, then there is no method. But in any case there is a "way." Let us consider the above example again, where disagreement was due to A's sympathy and B's coldness. Must they end by saying, "well, it's just a matter of our having different temperaments"? Not necessarily. A, for instance, may try to *change* the temperament of his opponent. He may pour out his enthusiasms in such moving way—present the sufferings of the poor with such appeal—that he will lead his opponent to see life through different eyes. He may build up by the contagion of his feelings an influence which will modify B's temperament and create in him a sympathy for the poor which did not previously exist. This is often the only way to obtain ethical agreement, if there is any way at all. It is persuasive, not empirical or rational; but that is no reason for neglecting it. There is no reason to scorn it, either, for it is only by such means that our personalities are able to grow, through our contact with others.

The point I wish to stress, however, is simply that the empirical method is instrumental to ethical agreement only to the extent that disagreement in interest is rooted in disagreement in belief. There is little reason to believe that all disagreement is of this sort. Hence the empirical method is not sufficient for ethics. In any case, ethics is not psychology, since psychology does not endeavor to *direct* our interests; it discovers facts about the ways in which interests are or can be directed, but that is quite another matter.

To summarize this section: my analysis of ethical judgments meets the three requirements for the typical sense of "good" that were mentioned in Section I. The traditional interest theories fail to meet these requirements simply because they neglect emotive meaning. This neglect leads them to neglect dynamic usage, and the sort of disagreement that results from such usage, together with the method of resolving the disagreement. I may add that my analysis answers Moore's objection about the open question. Whatever scientifically knowable properties a thing may have, it *is* always open to question whether a thing having these (enumerated) qualities is good. For to ask whether it is good is to ask for *influence*. And whatever I may know about an object, I can still ask, quite pertinently, to be influenced with regard to my interest in it.

VI

And now, have I really pointed out the "typical" sense of "good"?

I suppose that many will still say "no," claiming that I have simply failed to set down *enough* requirements that this sense must meet, and that my analysis, like all others given in terms of interest, is a way of begging the issue. They will say: "When we ask 'is X good?' we don't want mere influence, mere advice. We decidedly don't want to be influenced through persuasion, nor are we fully content when the influence is supported by a wide scientific knowledge of X. The answer to our question will, of course, modify our interests. But this is only because a unique sort of truth will be revealed to us— a truth that must be apprehended a priori. We want our interests to be guided by this truth and by nothing else. To substitute for this special truth mere emotive meaning and mere factual truth is to conceal from us the very object of our search."

I can only answer that I do not understand. What is this truth to be *about*? For I recollect no Platonic Idea, nor do I know what to *try* to recollect. I find no indefinable property nor do I know what to look for. And the "self-evident" deliverances of reason, which so many philosophers have mentioned, seem on examination to be deliverances of their respective reasons only (if of anyone's) and not of mine.

I strongly suspect, indeed, that any sense of "good' which is expected both to unite itself in synthetic a priori fashion with other concepts and to influence interest as well is really a great confusion. I extract from this meaning the power of influence alone, which I find the only intelligible part. If the rest is confusion, however, then it certainly deserves more than the shrug of one's shoulders. What I should like to do is to *account* for the confusion— to examine the psychological needs which have given rise to it and show how these needs may be satisfied in another way. This is *the* problem, if confusion is to be stopped at its source. But it is an enormous problem and my reflections on it, which are at present worked out only roughly, must be reserved until some later time.

I may add that if "X is good" has the meaning that I ascribe to it, then it is not a judgment that professional philosophers and only professional philosophers are qualified to make. To the extent that ethics predicates the ethical terms of anything, rather than explains their meaning, it becomes more than a purely intellectual study. Ethical judgments are social instruments. They are used in a cooperative enterprise that leads to a mutual readjustment of human interests. Philosophers have a part in this; but so too do all men.

NOTES

1. [The author has asked us, in republishing this paper, to add the note which follows: For a more adequate treatment of Hume's views see my *Ethics and Language* (Yale University Press, 1944), Chap. XII, Sect. 5. In the present paper the references to Hume are to be taken as references to the general *family* of definitions of which Hume's is typical; but Hume's own definition is somewhat different from any that is here specifically stated. Perhaps the same should be said of Hobbes. (1937)]

2. See G. E. Moore's *Philosophical Studies,* pp. 332–334.

3. See G. C. Field's *Moral Theory,* pp. 52, 56–57.

4. See G. E. Moore's *Principia Ethica,* Chap. i. I am simply trying to preserve the spirit of Moore's objection, and not the exact form of it.

5. The "subsequent essay" became, instead, Chapter 3 of *Ethics and Language,* which among other points defends those that follow:

(1) When used in a generic sense that emphasizes what C. W. Morris calls the *pragmatic* aspects of language, the term "meaning" designates a tendency of words to express or evoke states of mind in the people who use the words. The tendency is of a special kind, however, and many qualifications are needed (including some that bear on syntax) to specify its nature.

(2) When the states of mind in question are cognitive, the meaning can conveniently be called *descriptive;* and when they are feelings, emotions, or attitudes, the meanings can conveniently be called *emotive.*

(3) The states of mind (in a rough and tentative sense of that term) are normally quite complicated. They are not necessarily images or feelings but may in their turn be further tendencies—tendencies to respond to various stimuli that may subsequently arise. A word may have a constant meaning, accordingly, even though it is accompanied, at various times that it is used, by different images or feelings.

(4) Emotive meaning is sometimes more than a by-product of descriptive meaning. When a term has both sorts of meaning, for example, a change in its descriptive meaning may not be attended by a change in emotive meaning.

(5) When a speaker's use of emotive terms evokes an attitude in a hearer (as it sometimes may not, since it has only a *tendency* to do so), it must not be conceived as merely adding to the hearer's attitude in the way that a spark might add its heat to the atmosphere. For a more appropriate analogy, in many cases, we must think rather of a spark that ignites tinder.

6. See C. K. Ogden and I. A. Richards, *The Meaning of Meaning* (2nd ed. London, 1927). On p. 125 there is a passage on ethics which is the source of the ideas embodied in this essay.

7. In *Ethics and Language* the phrase "aura of feeling" was expressly repudiated. If the present essay had been more successful in anticipating the analysis given in that later work, it would have introduced the notion of emotive meaning in some such way as this:

The emotive meaning of a word or phrase is a strong and persistent tendency, built up in the course of linguistic history, to give direct expression (quasi-interjectionally) to certain of the speaker's feelings or emotions or attitudes; and it is also a tendency to evoke (quasi-imperatively) corresponding feelings, emotions, or attitudes in those to whom the speaker's remarks are addressed. It is the emotive meaning of a word, accordingly, that leads us to characterize it as *laudatory or derogatory*—that rather generic characterization being of particular importance when we are dealing with terms like "good" and "bad" or "right and wrong." But emotive meanings are of great variety: they may yield terms that express or evoke horror, amazement, sadness, sympathy, and so on.

The Naturalistic Fallacy   28

W. K. FRANKENA

THE FUTURE HISTORIAN of 'thought and expression' in the twentieth century will no doubt record with some amusement the ingenious trick, which some of the philosophical controversialists of the first quarter of our century had, of labelling their opponents' views 'fallacies'. He may even list some of these alleged fallacies for a certain sonority which their inventors embodied in their titles: the fallacy of initial predication, the fallacy of simple location, the fallacy of misplaced concreteness, the naturalistic fallacy.

Of these fallacies, real or supposed, perhaps the most famous is the naturalistic fallacy. For the practitioners of a certain kind of ethical theory, which is dominant in England and capably represented in America, and which is variously called objectivism, non-naturalism, or intuitionism, have frequently charged their opponents with committing the naturalistic fallacy. Some of these opponents have strongly repudiated the charge of fallacy, others have at least commented on it in passing, and altogether

Mind 48 (1939): 464–77. Reprinted by permission of *Mind*.

the notion of a naturalistic fallacy has had a considerable currency in ethical literature. Yet, in spite of its repute, the naturalistic fallacy has never been discussed at any length, and, for this reason, I have elected to make a study of it in this paper. I hope incidentally to clarify certain confusions which have been made in connexion with the naturalistic fallacy, but my main interest is to free the controversy between the intuitionists and their opponents of the notion of a logical or quasi-logical fallacy, and to indicate where the issue really lies.

The prominence of the concept of a naturalistic fallacy in recent moral philosophy is another testimony to the great influence of the Cambridge philosopher, Mr. G. E. Moore, and his book, *Principia Ethica*. Thus Mr. Taylor speaks of the 'vulgar mistake' which Mr. Moore has taught us to call 'the naturalistic fallacy',[1] and Mr. G. S. Jury, as if to illustrate how well we have learned this lesson, says, with reference to naturalistic definitions of value, 'All such definitions stand charged with Dr. Moore's "naturalistic fallacy"'.[2] Now, Mr. Moore coined the notion of the naturalistic fallacy in his polemic against naturalistic and metaphysical systems of ethics. 'The naturalistic fallacy is a fallacy,' he writes, and it 'must not be committed.' All naturalistic and metaphysical theories of ethics, however, 'are *based* on the naturalistic fallacy, in the sense that the commission of this fallacy has been the main cause of their wide acceptance'.[3] The best way to dispose of them, then, is to expose this fallacy. Yet it is not entirely clear just what is the status of the naturalistic fallacy in the polemics of the intuitionists against other theories. Sometimes it is used as a weapon, as when Miss Clarke says that if we call a thing good simply because it is liked we are guilty of the naturalistic fallacy.[4] Indeed, it presents this aspect to the reader in many parts of *Principia Ethica* itself. Now, in taking it as a weapon, the intuitionists use the naturalistic fallacy as if it were a logical fallacy on all fours with the fallacy of composition, the revelation of which disposes of naturalistic and metaphysical ethics and leaves intuitionism standing triumphant. That is, it is taken as a fallacy in advance, for use in controversy. But there are signs in *Principia Ethica* which indicate that the naturalistic fallacy has a rather different place in the intuitionist scheme, and should not be used as a weapon at all. In this aspect,

the naturalistic fallacy must be proved to be a fallacy. It cannot be used to settle the controversy, but can only be asserted to be a fallacy when the smoke of battle has cleared. Consider the following passages: (a) 'the naturalistic fallacy consists in the contention that good *means* nothing but some simple or complex notion, that can be defined in terms of natural qualities'; (b) 'the point that good is indefinable and that to deny this involves a fallacy, is a point capable of strict proof'.[5] These passages seem to imply that the fallaciousness of the naturalistic fallacy is just what is at issue in the controversy between the intuitionists and their opponents, and cannot be wielded as a weapon in that controversy. One of the points I wish to make in this paper is that the charge of committing the naturalistic fallacy can be made, if at all, only as a conclusion from the discussion and not as an instrument of deciding it.

The notion of a naturalistic fallacy has been connected with the notion of a bifurcation between the 'ought' and the 'is', between value and fact, between the normative and the descriptive. Thus Mr. D. C. Williams says that some moralists have thought it appropriate to chastise as the naturalistic fallacy the attempt to derive the Ought from the Is.[6] We may begin, then, by considering this bifurcation, emphasis on which, by Sidgwick, Sorley, and others, came largely as a reaction to the procedures of Mill and Spencer. Hume affirms the bifurcation in his *Treatise*: 'I cannot forbear adding to these reasonings an observation, which may, perhaps, be found of some importance. In every system of morality which I have hitherto met with, I have always remarked, that the author proceeds for some time in the ordinary way of reasoning, and establishes the being of a God, or makes observations concerning human affairs; when of a sudden I am surprised to find, that instead of the usual copulations of propositions, *is*, and *is not*, I meet with no proposition that is not connected with an *ought*, or an *ought not*. This change is imperceptible; but is, however, of the last consequence. For as this *ought*, or *ought not*, expresses some new relation or affirmation, it is necessary that it should be observed and explained; and at the same time that a reason should be given, for what seems altogether inconceivable, how this new relation can be a deduction from others, which are entirely different from it. But as authors do not commonly use this precaution, I shall presume to recommend it to the readers; and am persuaded, that this small attention would subvert all the vulgar systems of morality, and let us see that the distinction of vice and virtue is not founded merely on the relations of objects, nor is perceived by reason.'[7]

Needless to say, the intuitionists *have* found this observation of some importance.[8] They agree with Hume that it subverts all the vulgar systems of morality, though, of course, they deny that it lets us see that the distinction of virtue and vice is not founded on the relations of objects, nor is perceived by reason. In fact, they hold that a small attention to it subverts Hume's own system also, since this gives naturalistic definitions of virtue and vice and of good and evil.[9]

Hume's point is that ethical conclusions cannot be drawn validly from premises which are non-ethical. But when the intuitionists affirm the bifurcation of the 'ought' and the 'is', they mean more than that ethical propositions cannot be deduced from non-ethical ones. For this difficulty in the vulgar systems of morality could be remedied, as we shall see, by the introduction of definitions of ethical notions in non-ethical terms. They mean, further, that such definitions of ethical notions in non-ethical terms are impossible. 'The essential point,' says Mr. Laird, 'is the irreducibility of values to non-values.'[10] But they mean still more. Yellow and pleasantness are, according to Mr. Moore, indefinable in non-ethical terms, but they are natural qualities and belong on the 'is' side of the fence. Ethical properties, however, are not, for him, mere indefinable natural qualities, descriptive or expository. They are properties of a different *kind*—non-descriptive or non-natural.[11] The intuitionist bifurcation consists of three statements:

(1) Ethical propositions are not deducible from non-ethical ones.[12]

(2) Ethical characteristics are not definable in terms of non-ethical ones.

(3) Ethical characteristics are different in kind from non-ethical ones.

Really it consists of but one statement, namely, (3), since (3) entails (2) and (2) entails (1). It does not involve saying that any ethical characteristics are absolutely indefinable. That is another question, although this is not always noticed.

What, now, has the naturalistic fallacy to do with the bifurcation of the 'ought' and the 'is'? To begin with, the connexion is this: many naturalistic and metaphysical moralists proceed as if ethical conclusions can be deduced from premises all of which are non-ethical, the classical examples being Mill and Spencer. That is, they violate (1). This procedure has lately been referred to as the 'factualist fallacy' by Mr. Wheelwright and as the 'valuational fallacy' by Mr. Wood.[13] Mr. Moore sometimes seems to identify it with the naturalistic fallacy, but in the main he holds only that it involves, implies, or rests upon this fallacy.[14] We may now consider the charge that the procedure in question is or involves a fallacy.

It may be noted at once that, even if the deduction of ethical conclusions from non-ethical premises is in no way a fallacy, Mill certainly did commit a fallacy in drawing an analogy between visibility and desirability in his argument for hedonism; and perhaps his committing *this* fallacy, which, as Mr. Broad has said, we all learn about at our mothers' knees, is chiefly responsible for the notion of a naturalistic *fallacy*. But is it a fallacy to deduce ethical conclusions from non-ethical premises? Consider the Epicurean argument for hedonism which Mill so unwisely sought to embellish: pleasure is good, since it is sought by all men. Here an ethical conclusion is being derived from a non-ethical premise. And, indeed, the argument, taken strictly as it stands, *is* fallacious. But it is not fallacious because an *ethical* term occurs in the conclusion which does not occur in the premise. It is fallacious because any argument of the form 'A is B, therefore A is C' is invalid, if taken strictly as it stands. For example, it is invalid to argue that Croesus is rich because he is wealthy. Such arguments are, however, not intended to be taken strictly as they stand. They are enthymemes and contain a suppressed premise. And, when this suppressed premise is made explicit, they are valid and involve no logical fallacy.[15] Thus the Epicurean inference from psychological to ethical hedonism is valid when the suppressed premise is added to the effect that what is sought by all men is good. Then the only question left is whether the premises are true.

It is clear, then, that the naturalistic fallacy is not a logical fallacy, since it may be involved even when the argument is valid. How does the naturalistic fallacy enter such 'mixed ethical arguments'[16] as that of the Epicureans? Whether it does or not depends on the nature of the suppressed premise. This may be either an induction, an intuition, a deduction from a 'pure ethical argument', a definition, or a proposition which is true by definition. If it is one of the first three, then the naturalistic fallacy does not enter at all. In fact, the argument does not then involve violating (1), since one of its premises will be ethical. But if the premise to be supplied is a definition or a proposition which is true by definition, as it probably was for the Epicureans, then the argument, while still valid, involves the naturalistic fallacy, and will run as follows:

(a) Pleasure is sought by all men.
(b) What is sought by all men is good
      (by definition).
(c) Therefore, pleasure is good.

Now I am not greatly interested in deciding whether the argument as here set up violates (1). If it does not, then no 'mixed ethical argument' actually commits any factualist or valuational fallacy, except when it is unfairly taken as complete in its enthymematic form. If it does, then a valid argument may involve the deduction of an ethical conclusion from non-ethical premises and the factualist or valuational fallacy is not really a fallacy. The question depends on whether or not (b) and (c) are to be regarded as ethical propositions. Mr. Moore refuses so to regard them, contending that, by hypothesis, (b) is analytic or tautologous, and that (c) is psychological, since it really says only that pleasure is sought by all men.[17] But to say that (b) is analytic and not ethical and that (c) is not ethical but psychological is to prejudge the question whether 'good' can be defined; for the Epicureans would contend precisely that if their definition is correct then (b) is ethical but analytic and (c) ethical though psychological. Thus, unless the question of the definability of goodness is to be begged, (b) and (c) must be regarded as ethical, in which case our argument does not violate (1). However, suppose, if it be not nonsense, that (b) is non-ethical and (c) ethical, then the argument will violate (1), but it will still obey all of the canons of logic, and it is only confusing to talk of a 'valuational logic' whose basic rule

is that an evaluative conclusion cannot be deduced from non-evaluative premises.[18]

For the only way in which either the intuitionists or postulationists like Mr. Wood can cast doubt upon the conclusion of the argument of the Epicureans (or upon the conclusion of any parallel argument) is to attack the premises, in particular (b). Now, according to Mr. Moore, it is due to the presence of (b) that the argument involves the naturalistic fallacy. (b) involves the identification of goodness with 'being sought by all men', and to make this or any other such identification is to commit the naturalistic fallacy. The naturalistic fallacy is not the procedure of violating (1). It is the procedure, implied in many mixed ethical arguments and explicitly carried out apart from such arguments by many moralists, of defining such characteristics as goodness or of substituting some other characteristic for them. To quote some passages from *Principia Ethica*:

(a) '. . . far too many philosophers have thought that when they named those other properties [belonging to all things which are good] they were actually defining good; that these properties, in fact, were simply not "other", but absolutely and entirely the same with goodness. This view I propose to call the "naturalistic fallacy". . . .'[19]

(b) 'I have thus appropriated the name Naturalism to a particular method of approaching Ethics. . . .This method consists in substituting for "good" some one property of a natural object or of a collection of natural objects. . . .'[20]

(c) '. . . the naturalistic fallacy [is] the fallacy which consists in identifying the simple notion which we mean by "good" with some other notion.'[21]

Thus, to identify 'better' and 'more evolved', 'good' and 'desired', etc., is to commit the naturalistic fallacy.[22] But just why is such a procedure fallacious or erroneous? And is it a fallacy only when applied to good? We must now study Section 12 of *Principia Ethica*. Here Mr. Moore makes some interesting statements:

'. . . if anybody tried to define pleasure for us as being any other natural object; if anybody were to say, for instance that pleasure *means* the sensation of red. . . . Well, that would be the same fallacy which I have called the naturalistic fallacy. . . . I should not indeed call that a naturalistic fallacy, although it is the same fallacy as I have called naturalistic with reference to Ethics. . . . When a man confuses two natural objects with one another, defining the one by the other . . . then there is no reason to call the fallacy naturalistic. But if he confuses "good", which is not . . . a natural object, with any natural object whatever, then there is a reason for calling that a naturalistic fallacy. . . .'[23]

Here Mr. Moore should have added that, when one confuses 'good', which is not a metaphysical object or quality, with any metaphysical object or quality, as metaphysical moralists do, according to him, then the fallacy should be called the metaphysical fallacy. Instead he calls it a naturalistic fallacy in this case too, though he recognizes that the case is different since metaphysical properties are non-natural[24]—a procedure which has misled many readers of *Principia Ethica*. For example, it has led Mr. Broad to speak of 'theological naturalism'.[25]

To resume: 'Even if [goodness] were a natural object, that would not alter the nature of the fallacy nor diminish its importance one whit.'[26]

From these passages it is clear that the fallaciousness of the procedure which Mr. Moore calls the naturalistic fallacy is not due to the fact that it is applied to good or to an ethical or non-natural characteristic. When Mr. R. B. Perry defines 'good' as 'being an object of interest' the trouble is not merely that he is defining *good*. Nor is the trouble that he is defining an *ethical* characteristic in terms of *non-ethical* ones. Nor is the trouble that he is regarding a *non-natural* characteristic as a *natural* one. The trouble is more generic than that. For clarity's sake I shall speak of the definist fallacy as the generic fallacy which underlies the naturalistic fallacy. The naturalistic fallacy will then, by the above passages, be a species or form of the definist fallacy, as would the metaphysical fallacy if Mr. Moore had given that a separate name.[27] That is, the naturalistic fallacy, as illustrated by Mr. Perry's procedure, is a fallacy, not because it is naturalistic or confuses a non-natural quality with a natural one, but solely because it involves the definist fallacy. We may, then, confine our attention entirely to an understanding and evaluation of the definist fallacy.

To judge by the passages I have just quoted, the definist fallacy is the process of confusing or identifying two properties, of defining one property by another, or of substituting one property for another. Furthermore, the fallacy is always simply that two properties are being treated as one, and it is irrelevant, if it be the case, that one of them is natural or non-ethical and the other non-natural or ethical. One may commit the definist fallacy without infringing on the bifurcation of the ethical and the non-ethical, as when one identifies pleasantness and redness or rightness and goodness. But even when one infringes on that bifurcation in committing the definist fallacy, as when one identifies goodness and pleasantness or goodness and satisfaction, then the *mistake* is still not that the bifurcation is being infringed on, but only that two properties are being treated as one. Hence, on the present interpretation, the definist *fallacy* does not, in any of its forms, consist in violating (3), and has no essential connexion with the bifurcation of the 'ought' and the 'is'.

This formulation of the definist fallacy explains or reflects the motto of *Principia Ethica*, borrowed from Bishop Butler: 'Everything is what it is, and not another thing'. It follows from this motto that goodness is what it is and not another thing. It follows that views which try to identify it with something else are making a mistake of an elementary sort. For it *is* a mistake to confuse or identify two properties. If the properties really are two, then they simply are not identical. But do those who define ethical notions in non-ethical terms make this mistake? They will reply to Mr. Moore that they are not identifying two properties; what they are saying is that two words or sets of words stand for or mean one and the same property. Mr. Moore was being, in part, misled by the material mode of speech, as Mr. Carnap calls it, in such sentences as 'Goodness is pleasantness', 'Knowledge is true belief', etc. When one says instead, 'The word "good" and the word "pleasant" mean the same thing', etc., it is clear that one is not identifying two things. But Mr. Moore kept himself from seeing this by his disclaimer that he was interested in any statement about the use of words.[28]

The definist fallacy, then, as we have stated it, does not rule out any naturalistic or metaphysical

definitions of ethical terms. Goodness is not identifiable with any 'other' characteristic (if it is a characteristic at all). But the question is: *which* characteristics
are other than goodness, which names stand for characteristics other than goodness? And it is begging
the question of the definability of goodness to say
out of hand that Mr. Perry, for instance, is identifying goodness with something else. The point is that
goodness is what it is, even if it is definable. That is
why Mr. Perry can take as the motto of his naturalistic *Moral Economy* another sentence from Bishop
Butler: 'Things and actions are what they are, and
the consequences of them will be what they will be;
why then should we desire to be deceived?' The
motto of *Principia Ethica* is a tautology, and should
be expanded as follows: Everything is what it is, and
not another thing, unless it is another thing, and
even then it is what it is.

On the other hand, if Mr. Moore's motto (or the
definist fallacy) rules out any definitions, for example of 'good', then it rules out all definitions of any
term whatever. To be effective at all, it must be understood to mean, 'Every term means what it
means, and not what is meant by any other term'.
Mr. Moore seems implicitly to understand his
motto in this way in Section 13, for he proceeds as
if 'good' has no meaning, if it has no unique meaning. If the motto be taken in this way, it will follow
that 'good' is an indefinable term, since no synonyms can be found. But it will also follow that no
term is definable. And then the method of analysis
is as useless as an English butcher in a world without sheep.

Perhaps we have misinterpreted the definist fallacy. And, indeed, some of the passages which I
quoted earlier in this paper seem to imply that the
definist fallacy is just the error of defining an indefinable characteristic. On this interpretation, again,
the definist fallacy has, in all of its forms, no essential connexion with the bifurcation of the ethical
and the non-ethical. Again, one may commit the
definist fallacy without violating that bifurcation, as
when one defines pleasantness in terms of redness
or goodness in terms of rightness (granted Mr.
Moore's belief that pleasantness and goodness are
indefinable). But even when one infringes on that
bifurcation and defines goodness in terms of desire,
the *mistake* is not that one is infringing on the bifurcation by violating (3), but only that one is

defining an indefinable characteristic. This is possible because the proposition that goodness is indefinable is logically independent of the proposition
that goodness is non-natural: as is shown by the fact
that a characteristic may be indefinable and yet natural, as yellowness is; or non-natural and yet definable, as rightness is (granted Mr. Moore's views
about yellowness and rightness).

Consider the definist fallacy as we have just
stated it. It is, of course, an error to define an indefinable quality. But the question, again, is: which
qualities are indefinable? It is begging the question
in favour of intuitionism to say in advance that the
quality goodness is indefinable and that, therefore,
all naturalists commit the definist fallacy. One must
know that goodness is indefinable before one can
argue that the definist fallacy *is* a fallacy. Then, however, the definist fallacy can enter only at the end of
the controversy between intuitionism and definism,
and cannot be used as a weapon in the controversy.

The definist fallacy may be stated in such a way as
to involve the bifurcation between the 'ought' and
the 'is'.[29] It would then be committed by anyone
who offered a definition of any ethical characteristic
in terms of non-ethical ones. The trouble with such a
definition, on this interpretation, would be that an *ethical* characteristic is being reduced to a *non-ethical*
one, a *non-natural* one to a *natural* one. That is, the
definition would be ruled out by the fact that the
characteristic being defined is ethical or non-natural
and therefore cannot be defined in non-ethical or
natural terms. But on this interpretation, too, there
is danger of a *petitio* in the intuitionist argumentation. To assume that the ethical characteristic is exclusively ethical is to beg precisely the question which
is at issue when the definition is offered. Thus, again,
one must know that the characteristic is non-natural
and indefinable in natural terms before one can say
that the definists are making a mistake.

Mr. Moore, McTaggart, and others formulate
the naturalistic fallacy sometimes in a way somewhat
different from any of those yet discussed. They say
that the definists are confusing a universal synthetic
proposition about *the good* with a definition of *goodness*.[30] Mr. Abraham calls this the 'fallacy of misconstrued proposition'.[31] Here again the difficulty
is that, while it is true that it is an error to construe
a universal synthetic proposition as a definition, it is
a *petitio* for the intuitionists to say that what the

definist is taking for a definition is really a universal synthetic proposition.[32]

At last, however, the issue between the intuitionists and the definists (naturalistic or metaphysical) is becoming clearer. The definists are all holding that certain propositions involving ethical terms are analytic, tautologous, or true by definition, e.g., Mr. Perry so regards the statement, 'All objects of desire are good'. The intuitionists hold that such statements are synthetic. What underlies this difference of opinion is that the intuitionists claim to have at least a dim awareness of a simple unique quality or relation of goodness or rightness which appears in the region which our ethical terms roughly indicate, whereas the definists claim to have no awareness of any such quality or relation in that region, which is different from all other qualities and relations which belong to the same context but are designated by words other than 'good' and 'right' and their obvious synonyms.[33] The definists are in all honesty claiming to find but one characteristic where the intuitionists claim to find two, as Mr. Perry claims to find only the property of being desired where Mr. Moore claims to find both it and the property of being good. The issue, then, is one of inspection or intuition, and concerns the awareness or discernment of qualities and relations.[34] That is why it cannot be decided by the use of the notion of a fallacy.

If the definists may be taken at their word, then they are not actually confusing two characteristics with each other, nor defining an indefinable characteristic, not confusing definitions and universal synthetic propositions—in short they are not committing the naturalistic or definist fallacy in any of the interpretations given above. Then the only fallacy which they commit—the real naturalistic or definist fallacy— is the failure to descry the qualities and relations which are central to morality. But this is neither a logical fallacy nor a logical confusion. It is not even, properly speaking, an error. It is rather a kind of blindness, analogous to colour-blindness. Even this moral blindness can be ascribed to the definists only if they are correct in their claim to have no awareness of any unique ethical characteristics and if the intuitionists are correct in affirming the existence of such characteristics, but certainly to call it a 'fallacy', even in a loose sense, is both unamiable and profitless.

On the other hand, of course, if there are no such characteristics in the objects to which we attach ethical predicates, then the intuitionists, if we may take them at their word, are suffering from a corresponding moral hallucination. Definists might then call this the intuitionistic or moralistic fallacy, except that it is no more a 'fallacy' than is the blindness just described. Anyway, they do not believe the claim of the intuitionists to be aware of unique ethical characteristics, and consequently do not attribute to them this hallucination. Instead, they simply deny that the intuitionists really do find such unique qualities or relations, and then they try to find some plausible way of accounting for the fact that very respectable and trustworthy people think they find them.[35] Thus they charge the intuitionists with verbalism, hypostatization, and the like. But this half of the story does not concern us now.

What concerns us more is the fact that the intuitionists do not credit the claim of the definists either. They would be much disturbed, if they really thought that their opponents were morally blind, for they do not hold that we must be regenerated by grace before we can have moral insight, and they share the common feeling that morality is something democratic even though not all men are good. Thus they hold that 'we are all aware' of certain unique characteristics when we use the terms 'good', 'right', etc., only due to a lack of analytic clearness of mind, abetted perhaps by a philosophical prejudice, we may not be aware at all that they are different from other characteristics of which we are also aware.[36] Now, I have been arguing that the intuitionists cannot charge the definists with committing any fallacy unless and until they have shown that we are all, the definists included, aware of the disputed unique characteristics. If, however, they were to show this, then, at least at the end of the controversy, they could accuse the definists of the error of confusing two characteristics, or of the error of defining an indefinable one, and these errors might, since the term is somewhat loose in its habits, be called 'fallacies', though they are not logical fallacies in the sense in which an invalid argument is. The fallacy of misconstrued proposition depends on the error of confusing two characteristics, and hence could also on our present supposition, be ascribed to the definists, but it is not really a *logical* confusion,[37] since it does not actually involve being confused about the difference between a proposition and a definition.

Only it is difficult to see how the intuitionists can prove that the definists are at least vaguely aware of the requisite unique characteristics.[38] The question must surely be left to the inspection or intuition of the definists themselves, aided by whatever suggestions the intuitionists may have to make. If so, we must credit the verdict of their inspection, especially of those among them who have read the writings of the intuitionists reflectively, and, then, as we have seen, the most they can be charged with is moral blindness.

Besides trying to discover just what is meant by the naturalistic fallacy, I have tried to show that the notion that a logical or quasi-logical fallacy is committed by the definists only confuses the issue between the intuitionists and the definists (and the issue between the latter and the emotists or postulationists), and misrepresents the way in which the issue is to be settled. No logical fallacy need appear anywhere in the procedure of the definists. Even fallacies in any less accurate sense cannot be implemented to decide the case against the definists; at best they can be ascribed to the definists only after the issue has been decided against them on independent grounds. But the only defect which can be attributed to the definists, *if* the intuitionists are right in affirming the existence of unique indefinable ethical characteristics, is a peculiar moral blindness, which is not a fallacy even in the looser sense. The issue in question must be decided by whatever method we may find satisfactory for determining whether or not a word stands for a characteristic at all, and, if it does, whether or not it stands for a unique characteristic. What method is to be employed is, perhaps, in one form or another, the basic problem of contemporary philosophy, but no generally satisfactory solution of the problem has yet been reached. I shall venture to say only this: it does seem to me that the issue is not to be decided against the intuitionists by the application *ab extra* to ethical judgements of any empirical or ontological meaning dictum.[39]

NOTES

1. A.E. Taylor, *The Faith of a Moralist*, vol. i, p. 104 n.
2. *Value and Ethical Objectivity*, p. 58.
3. *Principia Ethica*, pp. 38, 64.
4. M. E. Clarke, 'Cognition and Affection in the Experience of Value', *Journal of Philosophy* (1938).
5. *Principia Ethica*, pp. 73, 77. See also p. xix.
6. 'Ethics as Pure Postulate'. *Philosophical Review* (1933). See also T. Whittaker, *The Theory of Abstract Ethics*, pp. 19 f.
7. Book III, part ii, section i.
8. See J. Laird, *A Study in Moral Theory*, pp. 16 f.; Whittaker, op cit., p. 19.
9. See C. D. Broad, *Five Types of Ethical Theory*, ch. iv.
10. *A Study in Moral Theory*, p. 94 n.
11. See *Philosophical Studies*, pp. 259, 273 f.
12. See J. Laird, op. cit., p. 318. Also pp. 12 ff.
13. P. E. Wheelwright, *A Critical Introduction to Ethics*, pp. 40–51, 91 f.; L. Wood, 'Cognition and Moral Value', *Journal of Philosophy*, (1937), p. 237.
14. See *Principia Ethica*, pp. 114, 57, 43, 49. Whittaker identifies it with the naturalistic fallacy and regards it as a 'logical' fallacy, op. cit., pp. 19 f.
15. See ibid., pp. 50, 139; Wheelwright, loc. cit.
16. See C. D. Broad, *The Mind and its Place in Nature*. pp. 488 f.; Laird, loc. cit.
17. See op. cit., pp. 11 f.; 19, 38, 73, 139.
18. See L. Wood, loc. cit.
19. p. 10.
20. p. 40.
21. p. 58, cf. pp. xiii, 73.
22. Cf. pp. 49, 53, 108, 139.
23. p. 13.
24. See pp. 38–40, 110–112.
25. *Five Types of Ethical Theory*, p. 259.
26. p. 14.
26. p. 14.
27. As Whittaker has, loc. cit.
28. See op. cit., pp. 6, 8, 12.
29. See J. Wisdom, *Mind* (1931), p. 213, note 1.
30. See *Principia Ethica*, pp. 10, 16, 38; *The Nature of Existence*, vol. ii, p. 398.
31. Leo Abraham, 'The Logic of Intuitionism', *International Journal of Ethics*, (1933).
32. As Mr. Abraham points out, loc. cit.
33. See R. B. Perry, *General Theory of Value*, p. 30; cf.; *Journal of Philosophy*, (1931), p. 520.
34. See H. Osborne, *Foundations of the Philosophy of Value*, pp. 15, 19, 70.
35. Cf. R. B. Perry, *Journal of Philosophy*, (1931), pp. 520 ff.
36. *Principia Ethica*, pp. 17, 38, 59, 61.
37. But see H. Osborne, op. cit., pp. 18 ff.
38. For a brief discussion of their arguments, see ibid., p. 67; L. Abraham, op. cit. I think they are all inconclusive, but cannot show this here.
39. See *Principia Ethica*, pp. 124 f., 140.

Two Concepts of Rules* 29

JOHN RAWLS

IN THIS PAPER I want to show the importance of the distinction between justifying a practice and justifying a particular action falling under it, and I want to explain the logical basis of this distinction and how it is possible to miss its significance. While the distinction has frequently been made, and is now becoming commonplace, there remains the task of explaining the tendency either to overlook it altogether, or to fail to appreciate its importance.

To show the importance of the distinction I am going to defend utilitarianism against those objections which have traditionally been made against it in connexion with punishment and the obligation to keep promises. I hope to show that if one uses the distinction in question then one can state utilitarianism in a way which makes it a much better explication of our considered moral judgements than traditional objections would seem to admit. Thus the importance of the distinction is shown by the way it strengthens the utilitarian view regardless of whether that view is completely defensible or not.

To explain how the significance of the distinction may be overlooked, I am going to discuss two conceptions of rules. One of these conceptions conceals the importance of distinguishing between the justification of a rule or practice and the justification of a particular action falling under it. The other conception makes it clear why this distinction must be made and what is its logical basis.

I

The subject of punishment, in the sense of attaching legal penalties to the violation of legal rules, has always been a troubling moral question. The trouble about it has not been that people disagree as to whether or not punishment is justifiable. Most people have held that, freed from certain abuses, it is an acceptable institution. Only a few have rejected punishment entirely, which is rather surprising when one considers all that can be said against it. The difficulty is with the justification of punishment: various arguments for it have been given by moral philosophers, but so far none of them has won any sort of general acceptance; no justification is without those who detest it. I hope to show that the use of the aforementioned distinction enables one to state the utilitarian view in a way which allows for the sound points of its critics.

For our purposes we may say that there are two justifications of punishment. What we may call the retributive view is that punishment is justified on the grounds that wrongdoing merits punishment. It is morally fitting that a person who does wrong should suffer in proportion to his wrongdoing. That a criminal should be punished follows from his guilt, and the severity of the appropriate punishment depends on the depravity of his act. The state of affairs where a wrongdoer suffers punishment is morally better than the state of affairs where he does not; and it is better irrespective of any of the consequences of punishing him.

What we may call the utilitarian view holds that on the principle that bygones are bygones and that only future consequences are material to present decisions, punishment is justifiable only by reference to the probable consequences of maintaining it as one of the devices of the social order. Wrongs committed in the past are, as such, not relevant considerations for deciding what to do. If punishment can be shown to promote effectively the interest of society it is justifiable, otherwise it is not.

---

*Some footnotes have been deleted.—ED.

The Philosophical Review, 64 (1955): 3–32. Reprinted by permission of *The Philosophical Review*.

I have stated these two competing views very roughly to make one feel the conflict between them: one feels the force of *both* arguments and one wonders how they can be reconciled. From my introductory remarks it is obvious that the resolution which I am going to propose is that in this case one must distinguish between justifying a practice as a system of rules to be applied and enforced, and justifying a particular action which falls under these rules; utilitarian arguments are appropriate with regard to questions about practices, while retributive arguments fit the application of particular rules to particular cases.

We might try to get clear about this distinction by imagining how a father might answer the question of his son. Suppose the son asks, 'Why was *J* put in jail yesterday?' The father answers, 'Because he robbed the bank at *B*. He was duly tried and found guilty. That's why he was put in jail yesterday.' But suppose the son had asked a different question, namely, 'Why do people put other people in jail?' Then the father might answer, 'To protect good people from bad people' or 'To stop people from doing things that would make it uneasy for all of us; for otherwise we wouldn't be able to go to bed at night and sleep in peace.' There are two very different questions here. One question emphasizes the proper name: it asks why *J* was punished rather than someone else, or it asks what he was punished for. The other question asks why we have the institution of punishment: why do people punish one another rather than, say, always forgiving one another?

Thus the father says in effect that a particular man is punished, rather than some other man, because he is guilty, and he is guilty because he broke the law (past tense). In his case the law looks back, the judge looks back, the jury looks back, and a penalty is visited upon him for something he did. That a man is to be punished, and what his punishment is to be, is settled by its being shown that he broke the law and that the law assigns that penalty for the violation of it.

On the other hand we have the institution of punishment itself, and recommend and accept various changes in it, because it is thought by the (ideal) legislator and by those to whom the law applies that, as a part of a system of law impartially applied from case to case arising under it, it will have the consequence, in the long run, of furthering the interests of society.

One can say, then, that the judge and the legislator stand in different positions and look in different directions: one to the past, the other to the future. The justification of what the judge does, *qua* judge, sounds like the retributive view; the justification of what the (ideal) legislator does, *qua* legislator, sounds like the utilitarian view. Thus both views have a point (this is as it should be since intelligent and sensitive persons have been on both sides of the argument); and one's initial confusion disappears once one sees that these views apply to persons holding different offices with different duties, and situated differently with respect to the system of rules that make up the criminal law.

One might say, however, that the utilitarian view is more fundamental since it applies to a more fundamental office, for the judge carries out the legislator's will so far as he can determine it. Once the legislator decides to have laws and to assign penalties for their violation (as things are there must be both the law and the penalty) an institution is set up which involves a retributive conception of particular cases. It is part of the concept of the criminal law as a system of rules that the application and enforcement of these rules in particular cases should be justifiable by arguments of a retributive character. The decision whether or not to use law rather than some other mechanism of social control, and the decision as to what laws to have and what penalties to assign, may be settled by utilitarian arguments; but if one decides to have laws then one has decided on something whose working in particular cases is retributive in form.

The answer, then, to the confusion engendered by the two views of punishment is quite simple: one distinguishes two offices, that of the judge and that of the legislator, and one distinguishes their different stations with respect to the system of rules which make up the law; and then one notes that the different sorts of considerations which would usually be offered as reasons for what is done under the cover of these offices can be paired off with the competing justifications of punishment. One reconciles the two views by the time-honoured device of making them apply to different situations.

But can it really be this simple? Well, this answer allows for the apparent intent of each side. Does a person who advocates the retributive view necessarily advocate, as an *institution,* legal machinery whose essential purpose is to set up and preserve a correspondence between moral turpitude and suffering? Surely not. What retributionists have rightly insisted upon is that no man can be punished unless he is guilty, that is, unless he has broken the law. Their fundamental criticism of the utilitarian account is that, as they interpret it, it sanctions an innocent person's being punished (if one may call it that) for the benefit of society.

On the other hand, utilitarians agree that punishment is to be inflicted only for the violation of law. They regard this much as understood from the concept of punishment itself. The point of the utilitarian account concerns the institution as a system of rules: utilitarianism seeks to limit its use by declaring it justifiable only if it can be shown to foster effectively the good of society. Historically it is a protest against the indiscriminate and ineffective use of the criminal law. It seeks to dissuade us from assigning to penal institutions the improper, if not sacrilegious, task of matching suffering with moral turpitude. Like others, utilitarians want penal institutions designed so that, as far as humanly possible, only those who break the law run afoul of it. They hold that no official should have discretionary power to inflict penalties whenever he thinks it for the benefit of society; for on utilitarian grounds an institution granting such power could not be justified.

The suggested way of reconciling the retributive and the utilitarian justifications of punishment seems to account for what both sides have wanted to say. There are, however, two further questions which arise, and I shall devote the remainder of this section to them.

First, will not a difference of opinion as to the proper criterion of just law make the proposed reconciliation unacceptable to retributionists? Will they not question whether, if the utilitarian principle is used as the criterion, it follows that those who have broken the law are guilty in a way which satisfies their demand that those punished deserve to be punished? To answer this difficulty, suppose that the rules of the criminal law are justified on utilitarian grounds (it is only for laws that meet his criterion that the utilitarian can be held responsible). Then it follows that the actions which the criminal law specifies as offences are such that, if they were tolerated, terror and alarm would spread in society. Consequently, retributionists can only deny that those who are punished deserve to be punished if they deny that such actions are wrong. This they will not want to do.

The second question is whether utilitarianism doesn't justify too much. One pictures it as an engine of justification which, if consistently adopted, could be used to justify cruel and arbitrary institutions. Retributionists may be supposed to concede that utilitarians *intend* to reform the law and to make it more humane; that utilitarians do not *wish* to justify any such thing as punishment of the innocent; and that utilitarians may appeal to the fact that punishment presupposes guilt in the sense that by punishment one understands an institution attaching penalties to the infraction of legal rules, and therefore that it is logically absurd to suppose that utilitarians in justifying *punishment* might also have justified punishment (if we may call it that) of the innocent. The real question, however, is whether the utilitarian, in justifying punishment, hasn't used arguments which commit him to accepting the infliction of suffering on innocent persons if it is for the good of society (whether or not one calls this punishment). More generally, isn't the utilitarian committed in principle to accepting many practices which he, as a morally sensitive person, wouldn't want to accept? Retributionists are inclined to hold that there is no way to stop the utilitarian principle from justifying too much except by adding to it a principle which distributes certain rights to individuals. Then the amended criterion is not the greatest benefit of society *simpliciter,* but the greatest benefit of society subject to the constraint that no one's rights may be violated. Now while I think that the classical utilitarians proposed a criterion of this more complicated sort, I do not want to argue that point here.[1] What I want to show is that there is *another* way of preventing the utilitarian principle from justifying too much, or at least of making it much less likely to do so: namely, by stating utilitarianism in a way which accounts for the distinction between the justification of an institution and the justification of a particular action falling under it.

I begin by defining the institution of punishment as follows: a person is said to suffer punishment whenever he is legally deprived of some of the normal rights of a citizen on the ground that he has violated a rule of law, the violation having been established by trial according to the due process of law, provided that the deprivation is carried out by the recognized legal authorities of the state, that the rule of law clearly specifies both the offence and the attached penalty, that the courts construe statutes strictly, and that the statute was on the books prior to the time of the offence. This definition specifies what I shall understand by punishment. The question is whether utilitarian arguments may be found to justify institutions widely different from this and such as one would find cruel and arbitrary.

This question is best answered, I think, by taking up a particular accusation. Consider the following from Carritt:

> . . . the utilitarian must hold that we are justified
> in inflicting pain always and only to prevent
> worse pain or bring about greater happiness.
> This, then, is all we need to consider in so-called
> punishment, which must be purely preventive.
> But if some kind of very cruel crime becomes
> common, and none of the criminals can be
> caught, it might be highly expedient, as an example, to hang an innocent man, if a charge against
> him could be so framed that he were universally
> thought guilty; indeed this would only fail to be
> an ideal instance of utilitarian 'punishment'
> because the victim himself would not have been
> so likely as a real felon to commit such a crime
> in the future; in all other respects it would be
> perfectly deterrent and therefore felicific.[2]

Carritt is trying to show that there are occasions when a utilitarian argument would justify taking an action which would be generally condemned; and thus that utilitarianism justifies too much. But the failure of Carritt's argument lies in the fact that he makes no distinction between the justification of the general system of rules which constitutes penal institutions and the justification of particular applications of these rules to particular cases by the various officials whose job it is to administer them. This becomes perfectly clear when one asks who the 'we' are of whom Carritt speaks. Who is this who has a sort of absolute authority on particular occasions to decide that an innocent man shall be 'punished' if everyone can be convinced that he is guilty? Is this person the legislator, or the judge, or the body of private citizens, or what? It is utterly crucial to know who is to decide such matters, and by what authority, for all of this must be written into the rules of the institution. Until one knows these things one doesn't know what the institution is whose justification is being challenged; and as the utilitarian principle applies to the institution one doesn't know whether it is justifiable on utilitarian grounds or not.

Once this is understood it is clear what the countermove to Carritt's argument is. One must describe more carefully what the *institution* is which his example suggests, and then ask oneself whether or not it is likely that having this institution would be for the benefit of society in the long run. One must not content oneself with the vague thought that, when it's a question of *this* case, it would be a good thing if *somebody* did something even if an innocent person were to suffer.

Try to imagine, then, an institution (which we may call 'telishment') which is such that the officials set up by it have authority to arrange a trial for the condemnation of an innocent man whenever they are of the opinion that doing so would be in the best interests of society. The discretion of officials is limited, however, by the rule that they may not condemn an innocent man to undergo such an ordeal unless there is, at the time, a wave of offences similar to that with which they charge him and telish him for. We may imagine that the officials having the discretionary authority are the judges of the higher courts in consultation with the chief of police, the minister of justice, and a committee of the legislature.

Once one realizes that one is involved in setting up an *institution,* one sees that the hazards are very great. For example, what check is there on the officials? How is one to tell whether or not their actions are authorized? How is one to limit the risks involved in allowing such systematic deception? How is one to avoid giving anything short of complete discretion to the authorities to telish anyone they like? In addition to these considerations, it is obvious that people will come to have a very different attitude towards their penal system when telishment is adjoined to it. They will be uncertain as to whether a convicted man has been punished or telished. They will wonder whether or not they should feel sorry for him. They, will wonder whether the same fate won't at any time fall on them. If one pictures how such an institution would actually work, and the enormous risks involved in it, it seems clear that it would serve no useful purpose. A utilitarian justification for this institution is most unlikely.

It happens in general that as one drops off the defining features of punishment one ends up with an institution whose utilitarian justification is highly doubtful. One reason for this is that punishment works like a kind of price system: by altering the prices one has to pay for the performance of actions it supplies a motive for avoiding some actions and doing others. The defining features are essential if punishment is to work in this way; so that an institution which lacks these features, e.g., an institution which is set up to 'punish' the innocent, is likely to have about as much point as a price system (if one may call it that) where the prices of things change at random from day to day and one learns the price of something after one has agreed to buy it.

If one is careful to apply the utilitarian principle to the institution which is to authorize particular actions, then there is *less* danger of its justifying too much. Carritt's example gains plausibility by its indefiniteness and by its concentration on the particular case. His argument will only hold if it can be shown that there are utilitarian arguments which justify an institution whose publicly ascertainable offices and powers are such as to permit officials to exercise that kind of discretion in particular cases. But the requirement of having to build the arbitrary features of the particular decision into the institutional practice makes the justification much less likely to go through.

II

I shall now consider the question of promises. The objection to utilitarianism in connexion with promises seems to be this: it is believed that on the utilitarian view when a person makes a promise the only ground upon which he should keep it, if he should keep it, is that by keeping it he will realize the most

good on the whole. So that if one asks the question 'Why should I keep *my* promise?' the utilitarian answer is understood to be that doing so in *this* case will have the best consequences. And this answer is said, quite rightly, to conflict with the way in which the obligation to keep promises is regarded.

Now of course critics of utilitarianism are not unaware that one defence sometimes attributed to utilitarians is the consideration involving the practice of promise-keeping. In this connexion they are supposed to argue something like this: it must be admitted that we feel strictly about keeping promises, more strictly than it might seem our view can account for. But when we consider the matter carefully it is always necessary to take into account the effect which our action will have on the practice of making promises. The promisor must weigh, not only the effects of breaking his promise on the particular case, but also the effect which his breaking his promise will have on the practice itself. Since the practice is of great utilitarian value, and since breaking one's promise always seriously damages it, one will seldom be justified in breaking one's promise. If we view our individual promises in the wider context of the practice of promising itself we can account for the strictness of the obligation to keep promises. There is always one very strong utilitarian consideration in favour of keeping them, and this will ensure that when the question arises as to whether or not to keep a promise it will usually turn out that one should, even where the facts of the particular case taken by itself would seem to justify one's breaking it. In this way the strictness with which we view the obligation to keep promises is accounted for.

Ross has criticized this defence as follows:[3] however great the value of the practice of promising, on utilitarian grounds, there must be some value which is greater, and one can imagine it to be obtainable by breaking a promise. Therefore there might be a case where the promisor could argue that breaking his promise was justified as leading to a better state of affairs on the whole. And the promisor could argue in this way no matter how slight the advantage won by breaking the promise. If one were to challenge the promisor his defence would be that what he did was best on the whole in view of all the utilitarian considerations, which in this case *include* the importance of the practice. Ross feels that such a defence would be unacceptable. I think he is right insofar as he is protesting against the appeal to consequences in general and without further explanation. Yet it is extremely difficult to weigh the force of Ross's argument. The kind of case imagined seems unrealistic and one feels that it needs to be described. One is inclined to think it would either turn out that such a case came under an exception defined by the practice itself, in which case there would not be an appeal to consequences in general on the particular case, or it would happen that the circumstances were so peculiar that the conditions which the practice presupposes no longer obtained. But certainly Ross is right in thinking that it strikes us as wrong for a person to defend breaking a promise by a general appeal to consequences. For a general utilitarian defence is not open to the promisor: it is not one of the defences allowed by the practice of making promises.

Ross gives two further counterarguments: First, he holds that it overestimates the damage done to the practice of promising by a failure to keep a promise. One who breaks a promise harms his own name certainly, but it isn't clear that a broken promise always damages the practice itself sufficiently to account for the strictness of the obligation. Second, and more important, I think, he raises the question of what one is to say of a promise which isn't known to have been made except to the promisor and the promisee, as in the case of a promise a son makes to his dying father concerning the handling of the estate. In this sort of case the consideration relating to the practice doesn't weigh on the promisor at all, and yet one feels that this sort of promise is as binding as other promises. The question of the effect which breaking it has on the practice seems irrelevant. The only consequence seems to be that one can break the promise without running any risk of being censured; but the obligation itself seems not the least weakened. Hence it is doubtful whether the effect on the practice ever weighs in the particular case; certainly it cannot account for the strictness of the obligation where it fails to obtain. It seems to follow that a utilitarian account of the obligation to keep promises cannot be successfully carried out.

From what I have said in connexion with punishment, one can foresee what I am going to say

about these arguments and counterarguments. They fail to make the distinction between the justification of a practice and the justification of a particular action falling under it, and therefore they fall into the mistake of taking it for granted that the promisor, like Carritt's official, is entitled without restriction to bring utilitarian considerations to bear in deciding whether to keep *his* promise. But if one considers what the practice of promising is one will see, I think, that it is such as not to allow this sort of general discretion to the promisor. Indeed, the point of the practice is to abdicate one's title to act in accordance with utilitarian and prudential considerations in order that the future may be tied down and plans coordinated in advance. There are obvious utilitarian advantages in having a practice which denies to the promisor, as a defence, any general appeal to the utilitarian principle in accordance with which the practice itself may be justified. There is nothing contradictory, or surprising, in this: utilitarian (or aesthetic) reasons might properly be given in arguing that the game of chess, or baseball, is satisfactory just as it is, or in arguing that it should be changed in various respects, but a player in a game cannot properly appeal to such considerations as reasons for his making one move rather than another. It is a mistake to think that if the practice is justified on utilitarian grounds then the promisor must have complete liberty to use utilitarian arguments to decide whether or not to keep his promise. The practice forbids this general defence; and it is a purpose of the practice to do this. Therefore what the above arguments presuppose—the idea that if the utilitarian view is accepted then the promisor is bound if, and only if, the application of the utilitarian principle to his own case shows that keeping it is best on the whole—is false. The promisor is bound because he promised: weighing the case on its merits is not open to him.

Is this to say that in particular cases one cannot deliberate whether or not to keep one's promise? Of course not. But to do so is to deliberate whether the various excuses, exceptions and defences, which are understood by, and which constitute an important part of, the practice, apply to one's own case. Various defences for not keeping one's promise are allowed, but among them there isn't the one that, on general utilitarian grounds, the promisor (truly) thought his action best on the whole, even though there may be the defence that the consequences of keeping one's promise would have been *extremely* severe. While there are too many complexities here to consider all the necessary details, one can see that the general defence isn't allowed if one asks the following question: what would one say of someone who, when asked why he broke his promise, replied simply that breaking it was best on the whole? Assuming that his reply is sincere, and that his belief was reasonable (i.e., one need not consider the possibility that he was mistaken), I think that one would question whether or not he knows what it means to say 'I promise' (in the appropriate circumstances). It would be said of someone who used this excuse without further explanation that he didn't understand what defences the practice, which defines a promise, allows to him. If a child were to use this excuse one would correct him; for it is part of the way one is taught the concept of a promise to be corrected if one uses this excuse. The point of having the practice would be lost if the practice did allow this excuse.

It is no doubt part of the utilitarian view that every practice should admit the defence that the consequences of abiding by it would have been extremely severe; and utilitarians would be inclined to hold that some reliance on people's good sense and some concession to hard cases is necessary. They would hold that a practice is justified by serving the interests of those who take part in it; and as with any set of rules there is understood a background of circumstances under which it is expected to be applied and which need not—indeed which cannot—be fully stated. Should these circumstances change, then even if there is no rule which provides for the case, it may still be in accordance with the practice that one be released from one's obligation. But this sort of defence allowed by a practice must not be confused with the general option to weigh each particular case on utilitarian grounds which critics of utilitarianism have thought it necessarily to involve.

The concern which utilitarianism raises by its justification of punishment is that it may justify too much. The question in connexion with promises is different: it is how utilitarianism can account for the obligation to keep promises at all. One feels that

the recognized obligation to keep one's promise and utilitarianism are incompatible. And to be sure, they are incompatible if one interprets the utilitarian view as necessarily holding that each person has complete liberty to weigh every particular action on general utilitarian grounds. But must one interpret utilitarianism in this way? I hope to show that, in the sorts of cases I have discussed, one cannot interpret it in this way.

III

So far I have tried to show the importance of the distinction between the justification of a practice and the justification of a particular action falling under it by indicating how this distinction might be used to defend utilitarianism against two long-standing objections. One might be tempted to close the discussion at this point by saying that utilitarian considerations should be understood as applying to practices in the first instance and not to particular actions falling under them except insofar as the practices admit of it. One might say that in this modified form it is a better account of our considered moral opinions and let it go at that. But to stop here would be to neglect the interesting question as to how one can fail to appreciate the significance of this rather obvious distinction and can take it for granted that utilitarianism has the consequence that particular cases may always be decided on general utilitarian grounds. I want to argue that this mistake may be connected with misconceiving the logical status of the rules of practices; and to show this I am going to examine two conceptions of rules, two ways of placing them within the utilitarian theory.

The conception which conceals from us the significance of the distinction I am going to call the summary view. It regards rules in the following way: one supposes that each person decides what he shall do in particular cases by applying the utilitarian principle; one supposes further that different people will decide the same particular case in the same way and that there will be recurrences of cases similar to those previously decided. Thus it will happen that in cases of certain kinds the same decision will be made either by the same person at different times or by different persons at the same time. If a case occurs frequently enough one supposes that a rule is formulated to cover that sort of case. I have called this conception the summary view because rules are pictured as summaries of past decisions arrived at by the *direct* application of the utilitarian principle to particular cases. Rules are regarded as reports that cases of a certain sort have been found on *other* grounds to be properly decided in a certain way (although, of course, they do not *say* this).

There are several things to notice about this way of placing rules within the utilitarian theory.

1. The point of having rules derives from the fact that similar cases tend to recur and that one can decide cases more quickly if one records past decisions in the form of rules. If similar cases didn't recur, one would be required to apply the utilitarian principle directly, case by case, and rules reporting past decisions would be of no use.

2. The decisions made on particular cases are logically prior to rules. Since rules gain their point from the need to apply the utilitarian principle to many similar cases, it follows that a particular case (or several cases similar to it) may exist whether or not there is a rule covering that case. We are pictured as recognizing particular cases prior to there being a rule which covers them, for it is only if we meet with a number of cases of a certain sort that we formulate a rule. Thus we are able to describe a particular case as a particular case of the requisite sort whether there is a rule regarding *that* sort of case or not. Put another way: what the *A*'s and the *B*'s refer to in rules of the form 'Whenever *A* do *B*' may be described as *A*'s and *B*'s whether or not there is the rule 'Whenever *A* do *B*,' or whether or not there is any body of rules which makes up a practice of which that rule is a part.

To illustrate this consider a rule, or maxim, which could arise in this way: suppose that a person is trying to decide whether to tell someone who is fatally ill what his illness is when he has been asked to do so. Suppose the person to reflect and then decide, on utilitarian grounds, that he should not answer truthfully; and suppose that on the basis of this and other like occasions he formulates a rule to the effect that when asked by someone fatally ill what his illness is, one should not tell him. The point to notice is that someone's being fatally ill and asking what his illness is, and someone's telling him, are things that can be described as such whether or not there is this rule. The performance of the action to which the rule refers doesn't require the stage-setting of a practice of which this rule is a part. This is what is meant by saying that on the summary view particular cases are logically prior to rules.

3. Each person is in principle always entitled to reconsider the correctness of a rule and to question whether or not it is proper to follow it in a particular case. As rules are guides and aids, one may ask whether in past decisions there might not have been a mistake in applying the utilitarian principle to get the rule in question, and wonder whether or not it is best in this case. The reason for rules is that people are not able to apply the utilitarian principle effortlessly and flawlessly; there is need to save time and to post a guide. On this view a society of rational utilitarians would be a society without rules in which each person applied the utilitarian principle directly and smoothly, and without error, case by case. On the other hand, ours is a society in which rules are formulated to serve as aids in reaching these ideally rational decisons on particular cases, guides which have been built up and tested by the experience of generations. If one applies this view to rules, one is interpreting them as maxims, as 'rules of thumb'; and it is doubtful that anything to which the summary conception did apply would be called a *rule*. Arguing as if one regarded rules in this way is a mistake one makes while doing philosophy.

4. The concept of a *general* rule takes the following form. One is pictured as estimating on what percentage of the cases likely to arise a given rule may be relied upon to express the correct decision, that is, the decision that would be arrived at if one were to correctly apply the utilitarian principle case by case. If one estimates that by and large the rule will give the correct decision, or if one estimates that the likelihood of making a mistake by applying the utilitarian principle directly on one's own is greater than the likelihood of making a mistake by following the rule, and if these considerations held of persons generally, then one would be justified in urging its adoption as a general rule. In this way *general* rules might be accounted for on the summary view. It will still make sense, however, to speak of applying the utilitarian principle case by case, for it was by trying to foresee

the results of doing this that one got the initial esti-mates upon which acceptance of the rule depends. That one is taking a rule in accordance with the sum-mary conception will show itself in the naturalness with which one speaks of the rule as a guide, or as a maxim, or as a generalization from experience, and as something to be laid aside in extraordinary cases where there is no assurance that the generalization will hold and the case must therefore be treated on its merits. Thus there goes with this conception the notion of a particular exception which renders a rule suspect on a particular occasion.

The other conception of rules I will call the prac-tice conception. On this view rules are pictured as defining a practice. Practices are set up for various reasons, but one of them is that in many areas of con-duct each person's deciding what to do on utilitar-ian grounds case by case leads to confusion, and that the attempt to coordinate behaviour by trying to foresee how others will act is bound to fail. As an al-ternative one realizes that what is required is the es-tablishment of a practice, the specification of a new form of activity; and from this one sees that a prac-tice necessarily involves the abdication of full liberty to act on utilitarian and prudential grounds. It is the mark of a practice that being taught how to engage in it involves being instructed in the rules which de-fine it, and that appeal is made to those rules to cor-rect the behaviour of those engaged in it. Those engaged in a practice recognize the rules as defining it. The rules cannot be taken as simply describing how those engaged in the practice in fact behave: it is not simply that they act as if they were obeying the rules. Thus it is essential to the notion of a practice that the rules are publicly known and understood as definitive; and it is essential also that the rules of a practice can be taught and can be acted upon to yield a coherent practice. On this conception, then, rules are not generalizations from the decisions of indi-viduals applying the utilitarian principle directly and independently to recurrent particular cases. On the contrary, rules define a practice and are themselves the subject of the utilitarian principle.

To show the important differences between this way of fitting rules into the utilitarian theory and the previous way, I shall consider the differences between the two conceptions on the points previ-ously discussed.

1. In contrast with the summary view, the rules of practices are logically prior to particular cases. This is so because there cannot be a particular case of an action falling under a rule of a practice unless there is the practice. This can be made clearer as fol-lows: in a practice there are rules setting up offices, specifying certain forms of action appropriate to various offices, establishing penalties for the breach of rules, and so on. We may think of the rules of a practice as defining offices, moves, and offences. Now what is meant by saying that the practice is logically prior to particular cases is this: given any rule which specifies a form of action (a move), a par-ticular action which would be taken as falling under this rule given that there is the practice would not be *described as* that sort of action unless there was the practice. In the case of actions specified by prac-tices it is logically impossible to perform them out-side the stage-setting provided by those practices, for unless there is the practice, and unless the req-uisite proprieties are fulfilled, whatever one does, whatever movements one makes, will fail to count as a form of action which the practice specifies. What one does will be described in some *other* way.

One may illustrate this point from the game of baseball. Many of the actions one performs in a game of baseball one can do by oneself or with others whether there is the game or not. For ex-ample, one can throw a ball, run, or swing a pecu-liarly shaped piece of wood. But one cannot steal base, or strike out, or draw a walk, or make an error, or balk; although one can do certain things which appear to resemble these actions such as sliding into a bag, missing a grounder and so on. Striking out, stealing a base, balking, etc., are all actions which can only happen in a game. No matter what a per-son did, what he did would not be described as stealing a base or striking out or drawing a walk un-less he could also be described as playing baseball, and for him to be doing this presupposes the rule-like practice which constitutes the game. The prac-tice is logically prior to particular cases: unless there is the practice the terms referring to actions speci-fied by it lack a sense.

2. The practice view leads to an entirely differ-ent conception of the authority which each person has to decide on the propriety of following a rule in particular cases. To engage in a practice, to perform

those actions specified by a practice, means to follow the appropriate rules. If one wants to do an action which a certain practice specifies then there is no way to do it except to follow the rules which define it. Therefore, it doesn't make sense for a person to raise the question whether or not a rule of a practice correctly applies to *his* case where the action he contemplates is a form of action defined by a practice. If someone were to raise such a question, he would simply show that he didn't understand the situation in which he was acting. If one wants to perform an action specified by a practice, the only legitimate question concerns the nature of the practice itself ('How do I go about making a will?').

This point is illustrated by the behaviour expected of a player in games. If one wants to play a game, one doesn't treat the rules of the game as guides as to what is best in particular cases. In a game of baseball if a batter were to ask 'Can I have four strikes?' it would be assumed that he was asking what the rule was; and if, when told what the rule was, he were to say that he meant that on this occasion he thought it would be best on the whole for him to have four strikes rather than three, this would be most kindly taken as a joke. One might contend that baseball would be a better game if four strikes were allowed instead of three; but one cannot picture the rules as guides to what is best on the whole in particular cases, and question their applicability to particular cases as particular cases.

3 and 4. To complete the four points of comparison with the summary conception, it is clear from what has been said that rules of practices are not guides to help one decide particular cases correctly as judged by some higher ethical principle. And neither the quasi-statistical notion of generality, nor the notion of a particular exception, can apply to the rules of practices. A more or less general rule of a practice must be a rule which according to the structure of the practice applies to more or fewer of the kinds of cases arising under it; or it must be a rule which is more or less basic to the understanding of the practice. Again, a particular case cannot be an exception to a rule of a practice. An exception is rather a qualification or a further specification of the rule.

It follows from what we have said about the practice conception of rules that if a person is engaged in a practice, and if he is asked why *he* does what *he* does, or if he is asked to defend what he does, then his explanation, or defence, lies in referring the questioner to the practice. He cannot say of *his* action, if it is an action specified by a practice, that he does it rather than some other because he thinks it is best on the whole. When a man engaged in a practice is queried about his action he must assume that the questioner either doesn't know that he is engaged in it ('Why are you in a hurry to pay him?' 'I promised to pay him today') or doesn't know what the practice is. One doesn't so much justify one's particular action as explain, or show, that it is in accordance with the practice. The reason for this is that it is only against the stage-setting of the practice that one's particular action is described as it is. Only by reference to the practice can one *say* what one is doing. To explain or to defend one's own action, as a particular action, one fits it into the practice which defines it. If this is not accepted it's a sign that a different question is being raised as to whether one is justified in accepting the practice, or in tolerating it. When the challenge is to the practice, citing the rules (saying what the practice is) is naturally to no avail. But when the challenge is to the particular action defined by the practice, there is nothing one can do but refer to the rules. Concerning particular actions there is only a question for one who isn't clear as to what the practice is, or who doesn't know that it is being engaged in. This is to be contrasted with the case of a maxim which may be taken as pointing to the correct decision on the case as decided on *other* grounds, and so giving a challenge on the case a sense by having it question whether these other grounds really support the decision on this case.

If one compares the two conceptions of rules I have discussed, one can see how the summary conception misses the significance of the distinction between justifying a practice and justifying actions falling under it. On this view rules are regarded as guides whose purpose it is to indicate the ideally rational decision on the given particular case which the flawless application of the utilitarian principle would yield. One has, in principle, full option to use the guides or to discard them as the situation warrants without one's moral office being altered in any way: whether one discards the rules or not, one always holds the office of a rational person seeking case by case to realize the best on the whole. But on the practice conception, if one holds an office defined by a practice then questions regarding one's actions in this office are settled by reference to the rules which define the practice. If one seeks to question these rules, then one's office undergoes a fundamental change: one then assumes the office of one empowered to change and criticize the rules, or the office of a reformer, and so on. The summary conception does away with the distinction of offices and the various forms of argument appropriate to each. On that conception there is one office and so no offices at all. It therefore obscures the fact that the utilitarian principle must, in the case of actions and offices defined by a practice, apply to the practice, so that general utilitarian arguments are not available to those who act in offices so defined.

Some qualifications are necessary in what I have said. First, I may have talked of the summary and the practice conceptions of rules as if only one of them could be true of rules, and if true of any rules, then necessarily true of *all* rules. I do not, of course, mean this. (It is the critics of utilitarianism who make this mistake insofar as their arguments against utilitarianism presuppose a summary conception of the rules of practices.) Some rules will fit one conception, some rules the other; and so there are rules of practices (rules in the strict sense), and maxims and 'rules of thumb'.

Secondly, there are further distinctions that can be made in classifying rules, distinctions which should be made if one were considering other questions. The distinctions which I have drawn are those most relevant for the rather special matter I have discussed, and are not intended to be exhaustive.

Finally, there will be many border-line cases about which it will be difficult, if not impossible, to decide which conception of rules is applicable. One expects border-line cases with any concept, and they are especially likely in connexion with such involved concepts as those of a practice, institution, game, rule, and so on. Wittgenstein has shown how fluid these notions are.[4] What I have done is to emphasize and sharpen two conceptions for the limited purpose of this paper.

IV

What I have tried to show by distinguishing between two conceptions of rules is that there is a way of regarding rules which allows the option to consider particular cases on general utilitarian grounds; whereas there is another conception which does not admit of such discretion except insofar as the rules themselves authorize it. I want to suggest that the tendency while doing philosophy to picture rules in accordance with the summary conception is what may have blinded moral philosophers to the significance of the distinction between justifying a practice and justifying a particular action falling under it; and it does so by misrepresenting the logical force of the reference to the rules in the case of a challenge to a particular action falling under a practice, and by obscuring the fact that where there is a practice, it is the practice itself that must be the subject of the utilitarian principle.

It is surely no accident that two of the traditional test cases of utilitarianism, punishment and promises, are clear cases of practices. Under the influence of the summary conception it is natural to suppose that the officials of a penal system, and one who has made a promise, may decide what to do in particular cases on utilitarian grounds. One fails to see that a general discretion to decide particular cases on utilitarian grounds is incompatible with the concept of a practice; and that what discretion one does have is itself defined by the practice (e.g., a judge may have discretion to determine the penalty within certain limits). The traditional objections to utilitarianism which I have discussed presuppose the attribution to judges, and to those who have made promises, of a plenitude of moral authority to decide particular cases on utilitarian grounds. But once one fits utilitarianism together with the notion of a practice, and notes that punishment and promising are practices, then one sees that this attribution is logically precluded.

That punishment and promising are practices is beyond question. In the case of promising this is shown by the fact that the form of words 'I promise' is a performative utterance which presupposes the stage-setting of the practice and the proprieties defined by it. Saying the words 'I promise' will only be promising given the existence of the practice. It would be absurd to interpret the rules about promising in accordance with the summary conception. It is absurd to say, for example, that the rule that promises should be kept could have arisen from its being found in past cases to be best on the whole to keep one's promise; for unless there were already the understanding that one keeps one's promises as part of the practice itself there couldn't have been any cases of promising.

It must, of course, be granted that the rules defining promising are not codified, and that one's conception of what they are necessarily depends on one's moral training. Therefore it is likely that there is considerable variation in the way people understand the practice, and room for argument as to how it is best set up. For example, differences as to how strictly various defences are to be taken, or just what defences are available, are likely to arise amongst persons with different backgrounds. But irrespective of these variations it belongs to the concept of the practice of promising that the general utilitarian defence is not available to the promisor. That this is so accounts for the force of the traditional objection which I have discussed. And the point I wish to make is that when one fits the utilitarian view together with the practice conception of rules, as one must in the appropriate cases, then there is nothing in that view which entails that there must be such a defence, either in the practice of promising, or in any other practice.

Punishment is also a clear case. There are many actions in the sequence of events which constitute someone's being punished which presuppose a practice. One can see this by considering the definition of punishment which I gave when discussing Carritt's criticism of utilitarianism. The definition there stated refers to such things as the normal rights of a citizen, rules of law, due process of law, trials and courts of law, statutes, etc., none of which can exist outside the elaborate stage-setting of a legal system. It is also the case that many of the actions for which people are punished presuppose

practices. For example, one is punished for stealing, for trespassing and the like, which presuppose the institution of property. It is impossible to say what punishment is, or to describe a particular instance of it, without referring to offices, actions, and offences specified by practices. Punishment is a move in an elaborate legal game and presupposes the complex of practices which make up the legal order. The same thing is true of the less formal sorts of punishment: a parent or guardian or someone in proper authority may punish a child, but no one else can.

There is one mistaken interpretation of what I have been saying which it is worthwhile to warn against. One might think that the use I am making of the distinction between justifying a practice and justifying the particular actions falling under it involves one in a definite social and political attitude in that it leads to a kind of conservatism. It might seem that I am saying that for each person the social practices of his society provide the standard of justification for his actions; therefore let each person abide by them and his conduct will be justified.

This interpretation is entirely wrong. The point I have been making is rather a logical point. To be sure, it has consequences in matters of ethical theory; but in itself it leads to no particular social or political attitude. It is simply that where a form of action is specified by a practice there is no justification possible of the particular action of a particular person save by reference to the practice. In such cases then action is what it is in virtue of the practice and to explain it is to refer to the practice. There is no inference whatsoever to be drawn with respect to whether or not one should accept the practices of one's society. One can be as radical as one likes but in the case of actions specified by practices the objects of one's radicalism must be the social practices and people's acceptance of them.

I have tried to show that when we fit the utilitarian view together with the practice conception of rules, where this conception is appropriate, we can formulate it in a way which saves it from several traditional objections. I have further tried to show how the logical force of the distinction between justifying a practice and justifying an action falling under it is connected with the practice conception of rules and cannot be understood as long as one regards the rules of practices in accordance with the summary view. Why, when doing philosophy, one may be inclined to so regard them, I have not discussed. The reasons for this are evidently very deep and would require another paper.

NOTES

1. By the classical utilitarians I understand Hobbes, Hume, Bentham, J. S. Mill, and Sidgwick.
2. *Ethical and Political Thinking* (Oxford, 1947), p. 65.
3. Ross, *The Right and the Good*, pp. 38–39.
4. *Philosophical Investigations* (Oxford, 1953), i, pars. 65–71, for example.

Extreme and Restricted Utilitarianism   30

J. J. C. SMART

I

UTILITARIANISM[1] is the doctrine that the rightness of actions is to be judged by their consequences. What do we mean by 'actions' here? Do we mean particular actions or do we mean classes of actions? According to which way we interpret the word 'actions' we get two different theories, both of which merit the appellation 'utilitarian'.

(1) If by 'actions' we mean particular individual actions we get the sort of doctrine held by Bentham, Sidgwick, and Moore. According to this doctrine we test individual actions by their consequences, and general rules, like 'keep promises', are mere rules of thumb which we use only to avoid the necessity of estimating the probable consequences of our actions at every step. The rightness or wrongness of keeping a promise on a particular occasion depends only on the goodness or badness of the consequences of keeping or of breaking the promise on that particular occasion. Of course part of the consequences of breaking the promise, and a part to which we will normally ascribe decisive importance, will be the weakening of faith in the institution of promising. However, if the goodness of 'the consequences of breaking the rule is *in toto* greater than the good-

ness of the consequences of keeping it, then we must break the rule, irrespective of whether the goodness of the consequences of *everybody's* obeying the rule is or is not greater than the consequences of *everybody's* breaking it. To put it shortly, rules do not matter, save *per accidens* as rules of thumb and as *de facto* social institutions with which the utilitarian has to reckon when estimating consequences. I shall call this doctrine 'extreme utilitarianism'.

(2) A more modest form of utilitarianism has recently become fashionable. The doctrine is to be found in Toulmin's book *The Place of Reason in Ethics*, in Nowell-Smith's *Ethics* (though I think Nowell-Smith has qualms), in John Austin's *Lectures on Jurisprudence* (Lecture II), and even in J. S. Mill, if Urmson's interpretation of him is correct (*Philosophical Quarterly*, Vol. 3, pp. 33–39, 1953). Part of its charm is that it appears to resolve the dispute in moral philosophy between intuitionists and utilitarians in a way which is very neat. The above philosophers hold, or seem to hold, that moral rules are more than rules of thumb. In general the rightness of an action is *not* to be tested by evaluating its consequences but only by considering whether or not it falls under a certain rule. Whether the rule is to be considered an acceptable moral rule, is, however, to

Philosophical Quarterly 6 (1956): 344–54. Reprinted by permission of Blackwell Publishing

be decided by considering the consequences of adopting the rule. Broadly, then, actions are to be tested by rules and rules by consequences. The only cases in which we must test an individual action directly by its consequences are (a) when the action comes under two different rules, one of which enjoins it and one of which forbids it, and (b) when there is no rule whatever that governs the given case. I shall call this doctrine 'restricted utilitarianism'.

It should be noticed that the distinction I am making cuts across, and is quite different from, the distinction commonly made between hedonistic and ideal utilitarianism. Bentham was an extreme hedonistic utilitarian and Moore an extreme ideal utilitarian, and Toulmin (perhaps) could be classified as a restricted ideal utilitarian. A hedonistic utilitarian holds that the goodness of the consequences of an action is a function only of their pleasurableness and an ideal utilitarian, like Moore, holds that pleasurableness is not even a necessary condition of goodness. Mill seems, if we are to take his remarks about higher and lower pleasures seriously, to be neither a pure hedonistic nor a pure ideal utilitarian. He seems to hold that pleasurableness is a necessary condition for goodness, but that goodness is a function of other qualities of mind as well. Perhaps we can call him a quasi-ideal utilitarian. When we say that a state of mind is good I take it that we are expressing some sort of *rational preference*. When we say that it is pleasurable I take it that we are saying that it is enjoyable, and when we say that something is a higher pleasure I take it that we are saying that it is more truly, or more deeply, enjoyable. I am doubtful whether 'more deeply enjoyable' does not just mean 'more enjoyable, even though not more enjoyable on a first look', and so I am doubtful whether quasi-ideal utilitarianism, and possibly ideal utilitarianism too, would not collapse into hedonistic utilitarianism on a closer scrutiny of the logic of words like 'preference', 'pleasure', 'enjoy', 'deeply enjoy', and so on. However, it is beside the point of the present paper to go into these questions. I am here concerned only with the issue between extreme and restricted utilitarianism and am ready to concede that both forms of utilitarianism can be either hedonistic or non-hedonistic.

The issue between extreme and restricted utilitarianism can be illustrated by considering the remark

'But suppose everyone did the same'. (Cf. A. K. Stout's article in *The Australian Journal of Philosophy,* Vol. 32, pp. 1–29) Stout distinguishes two forms of the universalization principle, the causal forms and the hypothetical form. To say that you ought not to do an action A because it would have bad results if everyone (or many people) did action A may be merely to point out that while the action A would otherwise be the optimific one, nevertheless when you take into account that doing A will probably cause other people to do A too, you can see that A is not, on a broad view, really optimific. If this causal influence could be avoided (as may happen in the case of a secret desert island promise) then we would disregard the universalization principle. This is the causal form of the principle. A person who accepted the universalization principle in its hypothetical form would be one who was concerned only with what would happen *if* everyone did the action A: he would be totally unconcerned with the question of whether in fact everyone would do the action A. That is, he might say that it would be wrong not to vote because it would have bad results if everyone took this attitude, and he would be totally unmoved by arguments purporting to show that my refusing to vote has no effect whatever on other people's propensity to vote. Making use of Stout's distinction, we can say that an extreme utilitarian would apply the universalization principle in the causal form, while a restricted utilitarian would apply it in the hypothetical form.

How are we to decide the issue between extreme and restricted utilitarianism? I wish to repudiate at the outset that milk and water approach which describes itself sometimes as 'investigating what is implicit in the common moral consciousness' and sometimes as 'investigating how people ordinarily talk about morality'. We have only to read the newspaper correspondence about capital punishment or about what should be done with Formosa to realize that the common moral consciousness is in part made up of superstitious elements, of morally bad elements, and of logically confused elements. I address myself to good hearted and benevolent people and so I hope that if we rid ourselves of the logical confusion the superstitious and morally bad elements will largely fall away. For even among good hearted and benevolent people it is possible to find superstitious and morally bad reasons for moral beliefs. These superstitious and morally bad reasons hide behind the protective screen of logical confusion. With people who are not logically confused but who are openly superstitious or morally bad I can of course do nothing. That is, our ultimate pro-attitudes may be different. Nevertheless I propose to rely on *my own* moral consciousness and to appeal to *your* moral consciousness and to forget about what people ordinarily say. 'The obligation to obey a rule', says Nowell-Smith (*Ethics*, p. 239), 'does not, *in the opinion of ordinary men*', (my italics), 'rest on the beneficial consequences of obeying it in a particular case'. What does this prove? Surely it is more than likely that ordinary men are confused here. Philosophers should be able to examine the question more rationally.

II

For an extreme utilitarian moral rules are rules of thumb. In practice the extreme utilitarian will mostly guide his conduct by appealing to the rules ('do not lie', 'do not break promises', etc.) of common sense morality. This is not because there is anything sacrosanct in the rules themselves but because he can argue that probably he will most often act in an extreme utilitarian way if he does not think as a utilitarian. For one thing, actions have frequently to be done in a hurry. Imagine a man seeing a person drowning. He jumps in and rescues him. There is no time to reason the matter out, but usually this will be the course of action which an extreme utilitarian would recommend if he did reason the matter out. If, however, the man drowning had been drowning in a river near Berchtesgaden in 1938, and if he had had the well known black forelock and moustache of Adolf Hitler, an extreme utilitarian would, if he had time, work out the probability of the man's being the villainous dictator, and if the probability were high enough he would, on extreme utilitarian grounds, leave him to drown. The rescuer, however, has not time. He trusts to his instincts and dives in and rescues the man. And this trusting to instincts and to moral rules can be justified on extreme utilitarian grounds. Furthermore, an extreme utilitarian who knew that the drowning

man was Hitler would nevertheless praise the rescuer, not condemn him. For by praising the man he is strengthening a courageous and benevolent disposition of mind, and in general this disposition has great positive utility. (Next time, perhaps, it will be Winston Churchill that the man saves!) We must never forget that an extreme utilitarian may praise actions which he knows to be wrong. Saving Hitler was wrong, but it was a member of a class of actions which are generally right, and the motive to do actions of this class is in general an optimific one. In considering questions of praise and blame it is not the expediency of the praised or blamed action that is at issue, but the expediency of the praise. It can be expedient to praise an inexpedient action and inexpedient to praise an expedient one.

Lack of time is not the only reason why an extreme utilitarian may, on extreme utilitarian principles, trust to rules of common sense morality. He knows that in particular cases where his own interests are involved his calculations are likely to be biased in his own favour. Suppose that he is unhappily married and is deciding whether to get divorced. He will in all probability greatly exaggerate his own unhappiness (and possibly his wife's) and greatly underestimate the harm done to his children by the break up of the family. He will probably also underestimate the likely harm done by the weakening of the general faith in marriage vows. So probably he will come to the correct extreme utilitarian conclusion if he does not in this instance think as an extreme utilitarian but trusts to common sense morality.

There are many more and subtle points that could be made in connexion with the relation between extreme utilitarianism and the morality of common sense. All those that I have just made and many more will be found in Book IV Chapters 3–5 of Sidgwick's *Methods of Ethics*. I think that this book is the best book ever written on ethics, and that these chapters are the best chapters of the book. As they occur so near the end of a very long book they are unduly neglected. I refer the reader, then, to Sidgwick for the classical exposition of the relation between (extreme) utilitarianism and the morality of common sense. One further point raised by Sidgwick in this connexion is whether an (extreme) utilitarian ought on (extreme) utilitarian principles to propagate (extreme) utilitarianism among the public. As most people are not very philosophical and not good at empirical calculations, it is probable that they will most often act in an extreme utilitarian way if they do not try to think as extreme utilitarians. We have seen how easy it would be to misapply the extreme utilitarian criterion in the case of divorce. Sidgwick seems to think it quite probable that an extreme utilitarian should not propagate his doctrine too widely. However, the great danger to humanity comes nowadays on the plane of public morality—not private morality. There is a greater danger to humanity from the hydrogen bomb than from an increase of the divorce rate, regrettable though that might be, and there seems no doubt that extreme utilitarianism makes for good sense in international relations. When France walked out of the United Nations because she did not wish Morocco discussed, she said that she was within her rights because Morocco and Algiers are part of her metropolitan territory and nothing to do with U. N. This was clearly a legalistic if not superstitious argument. We should not be concerned with the so-called 'rights' of France or any other country but with whether the cause of humanity would best be served by discussing Morocco in U.N. (I am not saying that the answer to this is 'Yes'. There are good grounds for supposing that more harm than good would come by such a discussion.) I myself have no hesitation in saying that on extreme utilitarian principles we ought to propagate extreme utilitarianism as widely as possible. But Sidgwick had respectable reasons for suspecting the opposite.

The extreme utilitarian, then, regards moral rules as rules of thumb and as sociological facts that have to be taken into account when deciding what to do, just as facts of any other sort have to be taken into account. But in themselves they do not justify any action.

III

The restricted utilitarian regards moral rules as more than rules of thumb for short-circuiting calculations of consequences. Generally, he argues, consequences are not relevant at all when we are deciding what to do in a particular case. In general, they are relevant only to deciding what rules are good rea-

sons for acting in a certain way in particular cases. This doctrine is possibly a good account of how the modern unreflective twentieth century Englishman often thinks about morality, but surely it is monstrous as an account of how it is most rational to think about morality. Suppose that there is a rule R and that in 99% of cases the best possible results are obtained by acting in accordance with R. Then clearly R is a useful rule of thumb; if we have not time or are not impartial enough to assess the consequences of an action it is an extremely good bet that the thing to do is to act in accordance with R. But is it not monstrous to suppose that if we *have* worked out the consequences and if we have perfect faith in the impartiality of our calculations, and if we *know* that in this instance to break R will have better results than to keep it, we should nevertheless obey the rule? Is it not to erect R into a sort of idol if we keep it when breaking it will prevent, say, some avoidable misery? Is not this a form of superstitious rule-worship (easily explicable psychologically) and not the rational thought of a philosopher?

The point may be made more clearly if we consider Mill's comparison of moral rules to the tables in the nautical almanack. (*Utilitarianism*, Everyman Edition, pp. 22–23). This comparison of Mill's is adduced by Urmson as evidence that Mill was a restricted utilitarian, but I do not think that it will bear this interpretation at all. (Though I quite agree with Urmson that many other things said by Mill are in harmony with restricted rather than extreme utilitarianism. Probably Mill had never thought very much about the distinction and was arguing for utilitarianism, restricted or extreme, against other and quite non-utilitarian forms of moral argument.) Mill says: 'Nobody argues that the art of navigation is not founded on astronomy, because sailors cannot wait to calculate the Nautical Almanack. Being rational creatures, they go out upon the sea of life with their minds made up on the common questions of right and wrong, as well as on many of the far more difficult questions of wise and foolish. . . . Whatever we adopt as the fundamental principle of morality, we require subordinate principles to apply it by'. Notice that this is, as it stands, only an argument for subordinate principles as rules of thumb. The example of the nautical almanack is misleading because the information given in the almanack is in all cases the same as the information one would get if one made a long and laborious calculation from the original astronomical data on which the almanack is founded. Suppose, however, that astronomy were different. Suppose that the behaviour of the sun, moon and planets was very nearly as it is now, but that on rare occasions there were peculiar irregularities and discontinuities, so that the almanack gave us rules of the form 'in 99% of cases,where the observations are such and such you can deduce that your position is so and so'. Furthermore, let us suppose that there were methods which enabled us, by direct and laborious calculation from the original astronomical data, not using the rough and ready tables of the almanack, to get our correct position in 100% of cases. Seafarers might use the almanack because they never had time for the long calculations and they were content with a 99% chance of success in calculating their positions. Would it not be absurd, however, if they *did* make the direct calculation, and finding that it disagreed with the almanack calculation, nevertheless they ignored it and stuck to the almanack conclusion? Of course the case would be altered if there were a high enough probability of making slips in the direct calculation: then we might stick to the almanack result, liable to error though we knew it to be, simply because the direct calculation would be open to error for a different reason, the fallibility of the computer. This would be analogous to the case of the extreme utilitarian who abides by the conventional rule against the dictates of his utilitarian calculations simply because he thinks that his calculations are probably affected by personal bias. But if the navigator were sure of his direct calculations would he not be foolish to abide by his almanack? I conclude, then, that if we change our suppositions about astronomy and the almanack (to which there are no exceptions) to bring the case into line with that of morality (to whose rules there are exceptions), Mill's example loses its appearance of supporting the restricted form of utilitarianism. Let me say once more that I am not here concerned with how ordinary men think about morality but with how they ought to think. We could quite well imagine a race of sailors who acquired a superstitious reverence for their almanack, even though it was only right in 99% of cases, and

who indignantly threw overboard any man who mentioned the possibility of a direct calculation. But would this behaviour of the sailors be rational?

Let us consider a much discussed sort of case in which the extreme utilitarian might go against the conventional moral rule. I have promised to a friend, dying on a desert island from which I am subsequently rescued, that I will see that his fortune (over which I have control) is given to a jockey club. However, when I am rescued I decide that it would be better to give the money to a hospital, which can do more good with it. It may be argued that I am wrong to give the money to the hospital. But why? (*a*) The hospital can do more good with the money than the jockey club can. (*b*) The present case is unlike most cases of promising in that no one except me knows about the promise. In breaking the promise I am doing so with complete secrecy and am doing nothing to weaken the general faith in promises. That is, a factor, which would normally keep the extreme utilitarian from promise breaking even in otherwise unoptimific cases, does not at present operate. (*c*) There is no doubt a slight weakening in my own character as an habitual promise keeper, and moreover psychological tensions will be set up in me every time I am asked what the man made me promise him to do. For clearly I shall have to say that he made me promise to give the money to the hospital, and, since I am an habitual truth teller, this will go very much against the grain with me. Indeed I am pretty sure that in practice I myself would keep the promise. But we are not discussing what my moral habits would probably make me do; we are discussing what I ought to do. Moreover, we must not forget that even if it would be most rational of me to give the money to the hospital it would also be most rational of you to punish or condemn me if you did, most improbably, find out the truth (e.g., by finding a note washed ashore in a bottle). Furthermore, I would agree that though it was most rational of me to give the money to the hospital it would be most rational of you to condemn me for it. We revert again to Sidgwick's distinction between the utility of the action and the utility of the praise of it.

Many such issues are discussed by A. K. Stout in the article to which I have already referred. I do not wish to go over the same ground again, especially as I think that Stout's arguments support my own point of view. It will be useful, however, to consider one other example that he gives. Suppose that during hot weather there is an edict that no water must be used for watering gardens. I have a garden and I reason that most people are sure to obey the edict, and that as the amount of water that I use will be by itself negligible no harm will be done if I use the water secretly. So I do use the water, thus producing some lovely flowers which give happiness to various people. Still, you may say, though the action was perhaps optimific, it was unfair and wrong.

There are several matters to consider. Certainly my action should be condemned. We revert once more to Sidgwick's distinction. A right action may be rationally condemned. Furthermore, this sort of offence is normally found out. If I have a wonderful garden when everybody else's is dry and brown there is only one explanation. So if I water my garden I am weakening my respect for law and order, and as this leads to bad results an extreme utilitarian would agree that I was wrong to water the garden. Suppose now that the case is altered and that I can keep the thing secret: there is a secluded part of the garden where I grow flowers which I give away anonymously to a home for old ladies. Are you still so sure that I did the wrong thing by watering my garden? However, this is still a weaker case than that of the hospital and the jockey club. There will be tensions set up within myself: my secret knowledge that I have broken the rule will make it hard for me to exhort others to keep the rule. These psychological ill effects in myself may be not inconsiderable: directly and indirectly they may lead to harm which is at least of the same order as the happiness that the old ladies get from the flowers. You can see that on an extreme utilitarian view there are two sides to the question.

So far I have been considering the duty of an extreme utilitarian in a predominantly non-utilitarian society. The case is altered if we consider the extreme utilitarian who lives in a society every member, or most members, of which can be expected to reason as he does. Should he water his flowers now? (Granting, what is doubtful, that in the case already considered he would have been right to water his flowers.) As a first approximation, the answer is that he should not do so. For since the situation is a completely symmetrical one, what is rational for him is

rational for others. Hence, by a *reductio ad absurdum* argument, it would seem that watering his garden would be rational for none. Nevertheless, a more refined analysis shows that the above argument is not quite correct, though it is correct enough for practical purposes. The argument considers each person as confronted with the choice either of watering his garden or of not watering it. However there is a third possibility, which is that each person should, with the aid of a suitable randomizing device, such as throwing dice, give himself a certain probability of watering his garden. This would be to adopt what in the theory of games is called 'a mixed strategy'. If we could give numerical values to the private benefit of garden watering and to the public harm done by 1, 2, 3, etc., persons using the water in this way, we could work out a value of the probability of watering his garden that each extreme utilitarian should give himself. Let a be the value which each extreme utilitarian gets from watering his garden, and let $f(1), f(2), f(3)$, etc., be the public harm done by exactly 1, 2, 3, etc., persons respectively watering their gardens. Suppose that p is the probability that, each person gives himself of watering his garden. Then we can easily calculate, as functions of p, the probabilities that exactly 1, 2, 3, etc., persons will water their gardens. Let these probabilities be $p_1, p_2, \ldots p_n$. Then the total net probable benefit can be expressed as

$$V = p_1(a - f(i)) + p_2(2a - f(2))$$
$$+ \ldots . p_n(na - f(n))$$

Then if we know the function $f(x)$ we can calculate the value of p for which $(dV/dp) = 0$. This gives the value of p which it would be rational for each extreme utilitarian to adopt. The present argument does not of course depend on a perhaps unjustified assumption that the values in question are measurable, and in a practical case such as that of the garden watering we can doubtless assume that p will be so small that we can take it near enough as equal to zero. However the argument is of interest for the theoretical underpinning of extreme utilitarianism, since the possibility of a mixed strategy is usually neglected by critics of utilitarianism, who wrongly assume that the only relevant and symmetrical alternatives are of the form 'everybody does X' and nobody does X'.[2]

I now pass on to a type of case which may be thought to be the trump card of restricted utilitarianism. Consider the rule of the road. It may be said that since all that matters is that everyone should do the same it is indifferent which rule we have, 'go on the left hand side' or 'go on the right hand side'. Hence the only *reason* for going on the left hand side in British countries is that this is the rule. Here the rule does seem to be a reason, in itself, for acting in a certain way. I wish to argue against this. The rule in itself is not a reason for our actions. We would be perfectly justified in going on the right hand side if (*a*) we knew that the rule was to go on the left hand side, and (*b*) we were in a country peopled by super-anarchists who always on principle did the opposite of what they were told. This shows that the rule does not give us a reason for acting so much as an indication of the probable actions of others, which helps us to find out what would be our own most rational course of action. If we are in a country not peopled by anarchists, but by non-anarchist extreme Utilitarians, we expect, other things being equal, that they will keep rules laid down for them. Knowledge of the rule enables us to predict their behaviour and to harmonize our own actions with theirs. The rule 'keep to the left hand side', then, is not a logical *reason* for action but an anthropological *datum* for planning actions.

I conclude that in every case if there is a rule R the keeping of which is in general optimific, but such that in a special sort of circumstances the optimific behaviour is to break R, then in these circumstances we should break R. Of course we must consider all the less obvious effects of breaking R, such as reducing people's faith in the moral order, before coming to the conclusion that to break R is right: in fact we shall rarely come to such a conclusion. Moral rules, on the extreme utilitarian view, are rules of thumb only, but they are not bad rules of thumb. But if we *do* come to the conclusion that we should break the rule and if we have weighed in the balance our own fallibility and liability to personal bias, what good reason remains for keeping the rule? I can understand 'it is optimific' as a reason for action, but why should 'it is a member of a class of actions which are usually optimific' or 'it is a member of a class of actions which as a class are more optimific than any alternative general class' be a good reason? You

might as well say that a person ought to be picked to play for Australia just because all of his brothers have been, or that the Australian team should be composed entirely of the Harvey family because this would be better than composing it entirely of any other family. The extreme utilitarian does not appeal to artificial feelings, but only to our feelings of benevolence, and what better feelings can there be to appeal to? Admittedly we can have a pro-attitude to anything, even to rules, but such artificially begotten pro-attitudes smack of superstition. Let us get down to realities, human happiness and misery, and make these the objects of our pro-attitudes and anti-attitudes.

The restricted utilitarian might say that he is talking only of *morality*, not of such things as rules of the road. I am not sure how far this objection, if valid, would affect my argument, but in any case I would reply that as a philosopher I conceive of ethics as the study of how it would be *most rational* to act. If my opponent wishes to restrict the word 'morality' to a narrower use he can have the word. The fundamental question is the question of rationality of action *in general*. Similarly if the restricted utilitarian were to appeal to ordinary usage and say 'it might be most rational to leave Hitler to drown but it would surely not be *wrong* to rescue him', I should again let him have the words 'right' and 'wrong' and should stick to 'rational' and 'irrational'. We already saw that it would be rational to praise Hitler's rescuer, even though it would have been most rational not to have rescued Hitler. In ordinary language, no doubt, 'right' and 'wrong' have not only the meaning 'most rational to do' and 'not most rational to do' but also have the meaning 'praiseworthy' and 'not praiseworthy'. Usually to the utility of an action corresponds utility of praise of it, but as we saw, this is not always so. Moral language could thus do with tidying up, for example by reserving 'right' for 'most rational' and 'good' as an epithet of praise for the motive from which the action sprang. It would be more becoming in a philosopher to try to iron out illogicalities in moral language and to make suggestions for its reform than to use it as a court of appeal whereby to perpetuate confusions.

One last defence of restricted utilitarianism might be as follows. 'Act optimifically' might be regarded as itself one of the rules of our system (though it would be odd to say that this rule was justified by its optimificality). According to Toulmin (*The Place of Reason in Ethics,* pp. 146–8) if 'keep promises', say, conflicts with another rule we are allowed to argue the case on its merits, as if we were extreme utilitarians. If 'act optimifically' is itself one of our rules then there will always be a conflict of rules whenever to keep a rule is not itself optimific. If this is so, restricted utilitarianism collapses into extreme utilitarianism. And no one could read Toulmin's book or Urmson's article on Mill without thinking that Toulmin and Urmson are of the opinion that they have thought of a doctrine which does *not* collapse into extreme utilitarianism, but which is, on the contrary, an improvement on it.

NOTES

1. Based on a paper read to the Victorian Branch of the Australian Association of Psychology and Philosophy, October 1955. [The article is discussed in H. J. McCloskey, 'An Examination of Restricted Utilitarianism' *Philosophical Review* (1957); also by D. Lyons, *Forms and Limits of Utilitarianism* (Clarendon Press, Oxford, 1965). Ed.]

2. [This paragraph has been substantially emended by the author.—Ed.]